Management Accounting

MANAGEMENT ACCOUNTING

(For B.Com., B.B.A., B.B.M., M.Com. and M.B.A., of all Universities of India and for C.A., ICWAI., CAIIB)

Dr. M. WILSON
M.Com., M.B.A., D.B.A., M.Phil., Ph.D.,
Reader in Commerce,
Scott Christian College (Autonomous), Nagercoil.

Himalaya Publishing House
ISO 9001:2015 CERTIFIED

First Edition : 2008
Second Edition : 2010
Reprint : 2012, 2013, 2014, 2015
Reprint : 2017, 2021
Reprint : 2023

Published by : Mrs. Meena Pandey
for **HIMALAYA PUBLISHING HOUSE PVT. LTD.,**
"Ramdoot", Dr. Bhalerao Marg, Girgaon, Mumbai - 400 004.
Phone: 022-23860170, 23863863; **Fax:** 022-23877178
E-mail: himpub@bharatmail.co.in; **Website:** www.himpub.com

Branch Offices :

New Delhi : "Pooja Apartments", 4-B, Murari Lal Street, Ansari Road, Darya Ganj, New Delhi - 110 002. Phone: 011-23270392, 23278631; Fax: 011-23256286

Nagpur : Kundanlal Chandak Industrial Estate, Ghat Road, Nagpur - 440 018. Phone: 0712-2721215, 2721216

Bengaluru : Plot No. 91-33, 2nd Main Road, Seshadripuram, Behind Nataraja Theatre, Bengaluru - 560 020. Phone: 080-41138821; Mobile: 09379847017, 09379847005

Hyderabad : No. 3-4-184, Lingampally, Besides Raghavendra Swamy Matham, Kachiguda, Hyderabad - 500 027. Phone: 040-27560041, 27550139

Chennai : No. 34/44, Motilal Street, T. Nagar, Chennai - 600 017. Mobile: 09380460419

Pune : "Laksha" Apartment, First Floor, No. 527, Mehunpura, Shaniwarpeth (Near Prabhat Theatre), Pune - 411 030. Phone: 020-24496323, 24496333; Mobile: 09370579333

Cuttack : Plot No. 5F-755/4, Sector-9, CDA Markat Nagar, Cuttack - 753 014, Odisha. Mobile: 09338746007

Kolkata : 3, S.M. Bose Road, Near Gate No. 5, Agarpara Railway Station, North 24 Parganas, West Bengal - 700 109. Mobile: 09674536325

Printed by : M/s. Giriraj Printers, Hyderabad. On behalf of HPH.

PREFACE

The subject Management Accounting is of recent origin which was introduced during 1950 only. It got a gradual development and got a good shape only after 1970s. The subject provides various tools and techniques for managerial planning, decision making and control of the cost. The reason for the development and its wide recognition at present is the enormous growth of Business i.e., Manufacturing and Trading activities. More people are involved in these activities which influenced the growth of small scale and large scale industrial units in all the countries. Hence, the factor of competition plays a crucial role in the success of the industrial units. Provision of quality products at low prices is the only factor which helps facing the competition. It depends upon how the affairs of the individual units are managed for providing quality products at low prices. Management Accounting provides various tools and strategies for efficient management with respect to cost. It provides techniques for managerial decision-making, planning and control of the cost. Hence, the subject Management Accounting assumes very great significance. This system of accounting is based on the information of Financial Accounting.

This book written by me is an additional contribution to the existing vast number of books of this kind. The book explains the concepts and theories in a systematic and organised manner through fourteen chapters. This book contains a lot of illustrations to explain the concepts and theories in all chapters. It also contains multiple choice questions, theory questions and problems with answers in sufficient number. Hence, it will satisfy the academic community concerned with Commerce and Management to the maximum extent. This book is the most suitable for the students of B.Com., B.B.A., B.B.M., M.Com. and M.B.A., of all Universities of India and also for C.A., ICWAI and CAIIB.

I express my thanks to God Almighty for giving me strength and vision to write this textbook. I express my thanks to the Management, Principal, Dr. E. James Reynold Daniel and all the members of the staff of Scott Christian College (Autonomous) for their encouragement and moral support.

My sincere thanks are due to Mr. Niraj Pandey and Mr. Vijay Pandey, Partners of Himalaya Publishing House for publishing the textbook. I also thank the representatives of Himalaya Publishing House. My thanks are also due to my parents **Mr. K. Muthiah (Rtd. D.F.O.) and Mrs. G. Rosamma,** relatives and to my wife Joyce and son W. Doyle for their encouragement in writing this textbook.

DR. M. WILSON

CONTENTS

1

INTRODUCTION

Accounting is considered as a process of recording the financial activities of a businessman. The concept of accounting existed in the very olden days itself when the activities of trading started in the history of human beings. It is believed that the accounting system existed during **4500 B.C.** itself, in the ancient civilization of **Babylonia** and **Assyria**. The businessmen need to know the profit or loss in his business and hence, he recorded the financial transactions. The accounting system adopted in the early periods got a good shape due to the introduction of double entry system in the place **Genova of Italy** during **1340**. This system was properly developed by **Fra Luco Pacioli** an Italian in the year **1340**. In the initial period, the accounting system is meant for recording the historical financial data for the calculation of profit. Later on, due to the economical and social developments brought by industrial revolution, the scope of the accounting increased to a very great extent. This is due to enormous growth of business units leading to high competition. Hence, companies are compelled to reduce the cost to face competition. In this respect, there is a need for analysis of the financial information so that more information can be generated for planning, decision making and cost control. This in turn developed new branches of accounting apart from financial accounting of the earlier period. The new branches of accounting are called Cost Accounting and Management Accounting. Hence, it is not proper to give a clear introduction about the Management Accounting without briefly explaining the important aspects of Financial Accounting and Cost Accounting.

I. Financial Accounting

The accounting that developed first and still exists is known as Financial Accounting. But the terminology used at that time is accounting only. Hence, the definition of accounting implied to mean Financial Accounting. The best and suitable definition is given by the **Committee on Terminology of American Institute of Certified Public Accountants**. According to the committee, "Accounting is the art of recording, classifying and summarising in a significant manner and in terms of money, transactions and events, which are in part at least, of a financial character, and interpreting the results thereo.". Hence, accounting is the art of recording financial transactions in order to ascertain the net result thereof. The net result of the business is ascertained through financial statements namely, **Profit and Loss Account and Balance Sheet**. The Profit & Loss exhibits the profit or loss and Balance Sheet exhibits the assets and liabilities in a financial year. The meaning of financial accounting is further known through its functions and principles.

Functions of Financial Accounting

The functions of Financial Accounting are stated as follows :

1. Recording the Financial Transactions: The primary function of financial accounting is recording the transactions. The transactions are first recorded in a book called **Journal** and from Journal it is transferred to other books which are called subsidiary books (**Ledger**).

2. Classification: The recorded transactions in the journal are classified according to the nature of transactions. The classified transactions are properly recorded in the name of different accounts. This process of recording in different accounts is done in a book named as ledger.

3. Summarising: The classified transactions which are recorded in ledger are represented in the form of many accounts. This should be brought into a summarised account form. The summarisation process is carried out through a statement called **Trial Balance**. From the Trial Balance, the summarised accounts are prepared as (i) Profit and Loss Account and (ii) Balance Sheet.

4. Concerned only with Financial Transactions: Financial account is concerned only with the financial transactions. The non-financial transactions like motivational factors, communications etc will not be recorded in the Financial Accounting.

5. Interpretation: The financial data recorded in the books are properly interpreted so that it can be used by the Owners, Financial Institutions, Creditors, Government and Public. The parties interested should have an idea about the company through proper interpretation.

Principles of Financial Accounting

Principles are concerned with the rules and regulations for the proper recording and maintenance of accounts. Principles of accounting are classified as :

(A) Accounting Concepts and (B) Accounting Conventions.

A. Accounting Concepts

The important concepts of accounting are stated as follows.

1. Business Entity Concept: This concept is based on the principle that Business is entirely different from Businessman for the accounting purpose. The capital contributed by the businessman is considered as the liability to be repaid to the businessman. Like that, the businessman expects fair returns for his capital from the business.

2. Going Concern Concept: This concept states that the business will exist for a indefinite period or at least for a fixed period in future.

3. Cost Concept: The assets of the company is valued on the basis of cost only. Like that, all the liabilities are considered. All transactions are recorded on the basis of objectivity and not on individual opinion.

4. Concept of Dual Aspect: All the transactions are classified into two aspects as debit and credit and recorded in two accounts. This is called dual aspect.

5. Money Measurement Concept: This concept states that all the transactions which can be measured in terms of monetary value only should be recorded in the account books. Non-monetary transactions should not be recorded in this system of accounts.

6. Accounting Period Concept: According to this concept, the expenses or revenue meant for a financial year should be considered in the preparation of Profit & Loss Account and Balance Sheet. The expenses whether paid or not, income whether received or not should be recorded if they are meant for the financial year.

7. Realisation Concept: This concept states that revenue is realised through sales and the sales value may be realised immediately as cash or through debtors and then cash from them.

8. Matching of Cost and Revenue Concept: According to this concept the cost and revenue are matched in the Profit and Loss account and balance is transferred to Balance Sheet so that the Assets and Liabilities aspects are matched.

B. Accounting Conventions

Convention means customs and traditions which are universally followed. The important conventions of accounting are stated as follows.

1. Convention of Disclosure: The important convention is disclosure of all the relevant accounting information so that it may be properly used by the parties interested in the company.

2. Convention of Consistency: It means that the principles adopted for preparing the accounting statements should be same for all the periods. Moreover, it shall be universally accepted.

3. Convention of Conservation: Conservation means safety measures with respect to the loss in future. Proper reserves should be maintained for meeting the losses in future.

4. Convention of Materiality: This convention states that only events of significant importance should be recorded. Insignificant information should be ignored and not recorded in the accounts.

Limitations of Financial Accounting

Financial Accounting is providing information to Owners, Creditors, Financial Institutions, Public and Government. Inspite of its many advantages, it has few limitations and the important limitations are stated as follows.

1. Provides only historical data: It provides only past data in the form of Profit & Loss account and Balance Sheet. There is no analysis carried on in Financial Accounting for planning and cost control for future.

2. Provides only limited information: The information provided are only related to financial operation. The data related to cost at different stages of production or the rate of growth in various activities are not provided by Financial Accounting.

3. Provides only quantitative information: It provides only quantitative information. The transactions which can be represented in monetary terms only are recorded in Financial Accounting. The information like performance of individuals are not recorded in this accounting system.

4. It will not help for price fixation: Fixation of price is a crucial factor for a concern. The information provided by Financial Accounting will not be useful for fixing the prices.

5. It will not provide tools for cost control: Since Financial Accounting is not concerned with the cost of production and cost of different activities carried on in a concern, there is no tool for cost control, in this system of accounting.

6. It is not possible to measure the comparative performance: The comparative performance related to operating and financial activities for different periods and for different activities could not be measured in Financial Accounting.

7. It will not provide information to management for planning and decision making: Financial accounting is not providing any information related to planning, control and decision making. It is only providing the profit or loss information and financial status of a company.

8. It is possible to manipulate accounts: In financial accounting there is possibility of manipulating accounts to show a good picture about the company. The fixed assets may be overvalued, low rate of depreciation may be charged to fixed assets etc.

II. Cost Accounting

Cost accounting emerged as an accounting system to face high competition in the business. In order to withstand competition the concerns have to supply goods at low prices. Companies could be able to supply goods at low prices only by reducing the cost of production. Cost Accounting as a subject is designed to provide many methods and techniques to reduce the cost of production through various stags of production.

Definitions of Costing, Cost Accounting and Cost Accountancy

1. Costing: The Institute of Cost and Management Accountants (ICMA) London defined, Costing as the ascertainment of costs. It includes the technique and process of ascertainment of costs. The technique means the principles and rules required for ascertainment of cost of production of products and services. This process refers to the procedures for the ascertainment of cost.

2. Cost Accounting: ICMA London defined Cost Accounting as "the process of accounting for cost from the point at which expenditure is incurred or committed to the establishment of its ultimate relationship with cost centres and cost units. In its widest usage, it embraces the preparation of statistical data, the application of cost control methods and the ascertainment of the profitability of activities carried out or planned". Hence, the Cost Accounting is the process of determining cost of activities of a concern and the ascertainment of the profitability from the activities.

3. Cost Accountancy: ICMA London defined Cost Accountancy as "the application of costing and cost accounting principles, methods and techniques to the science, art and practice of cost control and ascertainment of profitability as well as presentation of information for the purpose of managerial decision - making". Hence, it is clear that Cost Accountancy includes costing, cost accounting, budgetary control, cost control and cost audit.

Classification of Costs

Costs may be classified on the following basis

1. Element-wise Classification.
2. Functional-wise Classification.
3. On the basis of Identifiability.
4. Behaviour-wise Classification.
5. On the basis of Controllability.
6. On the basis of Time.
7. On the basis of Relevancy.

1. Element-wise Classification

On the basis of element-wise, costs may be classified into

(a) Material Cost (b) Labour Cost and (c) Expenses.

(a) Material Cost: The cost incurred for the purchase and storage of material is called material cost. Material Cost is classified into (i) Direct material cost and (ii) Indirect material cost. Direct Material costs are those material cost which can be easily identified in a product. It can be easily allocated to the process of production. Indirect material costs are those material costs which cannot be easily identified in the product. It cannot be allocated but apportioned, to the process of production.

(b) Labour Cost: The cost incurred in the form of wages and salaries to the employees of a concern is called labour cost. Labour cost may be classified into (i) Direct Labour cost and (ii) Indirect Labour cost. Direct labour costs are those labour costs which can be easily identified in a product. It can be easily allocated to the process of production. Indirect Labour costs are those labour costs which cannot be easily identified in the product. It cannot be allocated, but apportioned, to the process of production.

(c) Expenses: The costs other than the material cost and labour cost are called expenses. Expenses are also classified into Direct Expenses and Indirect Expenses. Direct expenses are those expenses which can be easily identified in a product and can easily be allocated to,the process of production. Indirect expenses are those expenses which cannot be easily identified but apportioned, to the process of production.

2. Functional-wise Classification

Classification of costs on the basis of the functions of an organisation is called functional-wise classification. It may be classified into (a) Production Cost (b) Administration Cost and (c) Selling and Distribution Cost.

(a) Production Cost: The cost incurred in the factory or work place of a concern is called production cost. It includes the cost of direct material, direct labour, direct expenses and factory indirect expenses (factory overhead). The total of direct material, direct labour and direct expenses is called "Prime Cost". When factory overhead is added with Prime cost, it is called Production Cost or Factory Cost.

(b) Administration Cost: The cost of administration of an organisation is called Administration cost. It includes indirect material, indirect labour and indirect expenses. (E.g.,) Stationery,salary,travelling expenses, refreshment expenses etc., incurred for the administration department.

(c) Selling and Distribution Cost: The costs incurred for selling and distribution of a product are called Selling and Distribution costs. It includes indirect material, indirect labour and indirect expenses. (E.g.,) Stationery,salary,travelling,refreshment expenses etc., incurred for the selling and distribution department.

3. On the basis of Identifiability

On the basis of Identifiability costs are classified into (a) Direct Costs, and (b) Indirect Costs.

(a) Direct Costs: Direct Costs are those costs which can easily be identified in a product. It can easily be allocated to the cost centre. It includes Direct Material, Direct Labour and Direct Expenses.

(b) Indirect Costs: Indirect costs are those costs which cannot easily be identified in a product. It cannot be allocated to the cost centre and it should be apportioned. It includes Indirect Material, Indirect Labour and Indirect Expenses.

4. Behaviour-wise Classification of Costs

On the basis of behaviour, cost may be classified into

(a) Fixed Cost, (b) Variable cost and (c) Semi Variable Cost.

(a) Fixed Cost: The cost which remains constant upto a certain level of activity is called fixed cost. It may also be stated that the cost which would not change due to the changes in the volume of production. This cost should be incurred irrespective of the number of units manufactured. This cost should be incurred eventhough the company do not produce any units. Fixed cost per unit is variable. (E.g.,) Salary to staff, Rent, Insurance etc.

(b) Variable Cost: The cost which changes according to the changes in the volume of production is called variable cost. It varies in direct proportion to the volume of production. Variable cost per unit remains fixed. (E.g.,) Direct material, Direct labour, Direct expenses.

(c) Semi-variable Cost: The cost which is partly fixed and partly variable is called semi-variable cost. (E.g.,) Salary to salesman based on monthly salary plus commission, Telephone charges etc.

5. On the basis of Controllability

On the basis of controllability cost may be classified into

(a) Controllable cost and (b) Uncontrollable cost.

(a) Controllable Costs: The costs which can be influenced by the action of the management of a concern are called controllable costs.

(E.g.,) Wages, Electricity, Telephone charges etc.

(b) Uncontrollable Costs: The costs which cannot be influenced by the action of the management of a concern are called uncontrollable costs.

(E.g.,) Price of raw material, Freight charges etc.

6. On the basis of Time

On the basis of time costs are classified into (a) Historical cost and (b) Pre-determined cost.

(a) Historical Costs: Costs which have already been incurred are called Historical costs. It is otherwise called as Actual Cost incurred for the production.

(b) Pre-determined Costs: Costs which are estimated in advance before the commencement of production are called Pre-determined Costs. It is also known as Estimated Cost or Standard Cost.

7. On the basis of Relevancy

On the basis of Relevancy costs are classified into (a) Relevant Costs and (b) Irrelevant Costs.

(a) Relevant Costs: Relevant Costs are those costs which are reliable for taking managerial decision. These costs are not subject to immediate changes. But relevant costs are subject to change in future due to the changes in the decision of management.

(b) Irrelevant Costs: Irrelevant costs are those costs which are not relevant for taking managerial decision. These costs may change often and also it is difficult to estimate these costs.

III. Management Accounting

Management Accounting is concerned with the accounting to management. Financial Accounting and Cost Accounting are not able to provide the relevant information to management for managerial planning and decision-making. Financial Accounting is providing the historical data in account form as Profit & Loss Account and Balance Sheet. Cost Accounting analyses the different elements related to the cost of production. But these information are not sufficient for managerial planning and control. Hence, a new accounting system, called **Management Accounting** emerged as an accounting system purely for providing the accounting information for planning, decision making and control of cost.

The term Management Accounting was first used by a team of accountants who attended the **Anglo-American Council on Productivity** during **1950**. Hence, the subject is of recent origin when compared to the other accounting system.

Meaning and Definitions of Management Accounting

Management Accounting generally means accounting for management. The meaning of Management Accounting is well known through the analysis of few important definitions given by organisations and accountants. The important definitions are stated as follows.

1. According to **Anglo-American Council on productivity**, "Management Accounting is the presentation of accounting information in such a way as to assist management in the creation of policy and the day-to-day operation of an undertaking".
2. The **Chartered Institute of Management Accountants, London**, defined Management Accounting as "The application of professional knowledge and skill in the preparation of accounting information in such a way as to assist management in the formation of policies and in the planning and control of the operations of the undertaking".
3. **American Accounting Association** defines, "Management Accounting is the application of appropriate techniques and concepts in processing historical and projected economic data of an entity to assist management in establishing plans for reasonable economic objectives in the making of rational decision with a view towards achieving these objectives.
4. **Institute of Chartered Accountants of England and Wales** defines, "Any form of accounting which enables a business to be conducted more efficiently can be regarded as Management Accounting".
5. The **Institute of Cost and Works Accountants of India** defines Management Accounting as "a system of collection and presentation of relevant economic information relating to an enterprise for planning, controlling and decision making".
6. **Batty** defines, "Management Accounting is the term used to describe the accounting methods, systems and techniques which, coupled with special knowledge and ability, assist management in its task of maximising profit or minimising losses.
7. **Brown and Howard** defines, "The essential aim of Management Accounting should be to assist management in decision making and control".

It is clear from the above definitions that Management Accounting is a system of accounting which provides information to management for efficient functioning and management through effective planning, control and decision making.

Functions of Management Accounting

The important functions of Management Accounting are stated as follows :

1. Provision of Data: The important function of Management Accounting is the provision of relevant data to the management for decision making purpose. It helps the management for proper planning and control of the cost.

2. Modification of Data: Management Accounting is concerned with the modification of the financial data provided by the financial accounting in a form suitable for management for decision making. It modifies the data like working capital, capital employed, debt and equity etc.

3. Analysis and interpretation of Data: The function of Management Accounting is to analyse the data in relation to the previous periods. It helps to find out whether there is growth in the operating and financial activities of a concern. In addition to this, the analysed data are properly interpreted for easy identification for the management.

4. Communicating Function: Management Accounting performs the function of communication at various levels of management. The interpreted data are provided to top level management. On the basis of the data decisions may be taken by the management which are communicated to various employees in the lower level of management.

5. Fix Standards at all Level: Management Accounting helps to fix standard of cost for various activities in an organisation. The standard related to material, labour and overheads are fixed on the basis of the past data and experiences.

6. Function of Control: Management Accounting helps to identify whether the actual performances are deviated from the standard performance. If there is any deviation on the negative side, it suggests some control measures to achieve efficiency at all levels.

7. Provides Qualitative Information: It provides qualitative information to the management related to the performance, training and motivational factors adopted or to be adopted in an organisation.

Scope of Management Accounting

The scope of Management Accounting is not only in the provision of accounting information to the management for planning and control of cost. It has many more scopes and the details of it are stated as follows:

1. Financial Accounting: Management Accounting is based on the data of Financial Accounting. It analysis the Profit & Loss Account and Balance Sheet at various periods and give more meaning for the information in the Financial Accounting.

2. Cost Accounting: Cost Accounting is concerned with the ascertainment of cost at various level of activities. Hence, the cost data are more required for the Management Accounting for further analysis so that relevant information can be provided to management.

3. Statistical Methods: In Management Accounting the statistical techniques like tabulations, diagrams and graphs are mostly applied for anlaysing the financial data.

4. Revaluation Accounting: Revaluation Accounting is concerned with the effective representation of capital in fixed assets. The fixed assets should be revalued to represent the real worth in order to ascertain the correct measurement of the return on capital employed. Management accounting informations are useful in Revaluation Accounting.

5. Budgetary Control: Management Accounting helps to prepare the budget for various activities in an organisation. It also suggests various methods for controlling deviations in the actual values with the budgetary values for different activities.

6. Inventory Control: Inventory is a most important factor for a concern. High inventory or low inventory are not good for a concern. High inventory means blocking of more capital in inventory and low inventory means interruption in production. The optimum inventory which is most required is determined through the Management Accounting techniques.

7. Interim Reporting: The net result of the activities of a business is known only at the end of a financial year through Final Accounting. But Management Accounting provides interim reports to the owners and management often so that they can know the progress of their business.

8. Internal Audit: Internal audit is an audit conducted within an organisation. For internal audit relevant records are required which are provided by the Management Accounting, so that the internal audit can be performed in an effective manner.

9. Taxation: Taxation is done through proper adjustment of depreciation (through proper valuation of fixed assets), correct valuation of inventory etc. Correct valuation of fixed assets and inventory are done through the Management Accounting principles.

10. Financial Management: Financial Management is concerned with the management of the finance in a company. It deals with the effective utilisation of the finance so that the fair rate of return on investment is achieved. It became a separate discipline to provide various tools for proper management of finance. The tools in financial management are developed through the data from the Management Accounting also.

Utility of Management Accounting

The important utilities of Management Accounting are stated as follows:

1. Planning: Planning is an important factor for efficient functioning of a management. Management Accounting helps for planning the cost at different levels, quantity to be produced, sales to be executed, inventory to be maintained etc.

2. Organising: Management Accounting properly defines the authority and responsibility for different people in the organisation. Hence, each one knows their responsibility in the organisation. It helps for determining the standard performance in the organisation.

3. Co-ordinating: It helps for co-ordinating all the activities in an organisation in order to attain the common objectives of the business. Linking of authority and responsibility of all individuals helps for co-ordination of various activities.

4. Motivating: The important tool of standard costing in Management Accounting is to make the employees more responsible. The employees are motivated to perform more than the standard fixed for them.

5. Communicating: It helps for effective communication at all levels of management. The information provided to top level management for decision making is one way of communication and the assignment of work and responsibilities by the top level management on the basis of the Management Accounting information is another way of communication.

6. Controlling: Management Accounting helps for taking effective control at all levels of management and for all activities. The cost of production can be reduced through the cost control measures taken at various stages of production.

Tools and Techniques of Management Accounting

Management Accounting functions with different tools and techniques in order to provide correct information to management. The important tools and techniques of Management Accounting are stated as follows.

1. Financial Statement Analysis: Financial statement analysis is concerned with the analysis of Profit and Loss Account and Balance Sheet of different periods. It helps to ascertain the rate of growth of a concern. This analysis is done through comparative financial statements, common size statements and ratio analysis.

2. Fund Flow Analysis: Fund flow analysis is an analysis to find out the movement of fund from one period to another. It helps to find out whether the fund is properly utilised or not in a year when compared to the previous year. It studies the Fund from Operation and the movement of Working Capital.

3. Cash Flow Analysis: It is an analysis about the movement of cash from one period to another. It helps to find out the reason for the change of cash balance between two periods. It studies the Cash from Operation and the movement of cash in a period.

4. Marginal Costing: Marginal costing is a technique adopted to fix the selling price and for other managerial decisions like acceptance or rejection of bulk orders, to produce or to purchase etc. It is an analysis based on the fixed cost, variable cost and contribution.

5. Standard Costing: Standard costing is one of the tools of Management Accounting. It facilitates for fixing the standard for all activities in a concern and to measure the variances of the actual from the standard. Hence, the unfavourable variances can be controlled through this technique.

6. Budgetary Control: Budgetary control is an important technique in Management Accounting. It is concerned with the preparation of different types of budgets like, Cash budget, Sales budget, Production budget, Maintenance budget etc. It is possible to compare the actual figure with budgetary figures and to take necessary action for correction.

7. Revaluation Accounting: Revaluation accounting is a method adopted to revalue the assets of the company so that the capital is properly represented with the assets. It helps to find out the fair return on capital employed. This is an important technique adopted in Management Accounting.

8. Management Information System: It is an information system adopted by the management to provide information to management in a meaningful manner. The information is prepared by applying the computer skill so that the management can early understand the information. The information is required for taking management decision making. The management can access the information anytime.

9. Management Reporting: Reporting to management is an important technique in Management Accounting. Management Accounting analyses the Profit and Loss Account and Balance Sheet by adopting different methods and explores the strength and weakness in different areas of operating activities and financial activities. These identification are properly reported to the management for management planning, control and decision-making.

Installation of Management Accounting System

The different stages of installation of Management Accounting system are stated as follows:

1. Preparation of Organisational Manual: The first step in the installation process is the preparation of organisational manual. Organisational manual is concerned with the division of work for effective execution of the functions of Management Accounting. It defines the authority and responsibility of all the individuals also.

2. Appointment and Training of Employees: The next step is the appointment of suitable candidates for the different work defined for the organisation. The candidates shall be given suitable off the job and on the job training so that they can prepare themselves as per the requirement.

3. Preparation of Forms and Returns: The form and returns required for the execution of the Management Accounting system should be prepared. The form and returns are not the same for all the concerns. Hence, according to the requirement and nature of work the form and returns should be prepared.

4. Classification and Codification of Accounts: The Financial Accounts are subject for analysis in Management Accounting. Hence, it should be well classified as per the nature of the account and the requirements. Since there are many accounts, there is a need for the classification and after that codification also. Codification is the process of assigning serial numbers or symbols for accounts. It helps for easy identification of accounts.

5. Formulating a suitable system for integration of cost and financial data: Since Management Accounting uses the data from Financial Accounting and Cost Accounting, there should be a suitable system for integration of the data from these accounts. It avoids duplication of data. The integration system should be accurate and reliable.

6. Setting up of suitable Budgetary Control System: Budgeting is an important tool in the Management Accounting. Hence, a suitable budgetary control system should be established. The system should be a flexible one to accumulate the changes in future.

7. Formulating suitable techniques for Standard Costing: The fixation of standard for all activities related to cost and revenue is a must to measure the deviations of actual performance from the standard performance. Hence, a suitable technique should be devised for Standard Costing to fix standard at all levels. The standard should be one which can be adopted by a normal employee.

8. Formulating suitable Operational Research techniques: Operational Research techniques are providing various tools for managerial decision making. The suitable tools for the purpose of Management Accounting should be identified on the basis of the nature of the business and managerial information requirement.

Limitations of Management Accounting

Management Accounting is providing information to management. Inspite of its many advantages, it has few limitations and the important limitations are stated as follows:

1. Management Accounting is based on Financial Accounting: All the analysis carried in the Management Accounting is based on the Financial Accounting information (i.e., Profit & Loss Account and Balance Sheet).Any manipulation and error committed in these statements will affect the results of the analysis of the Management Accounting.

2. It is considered only as a tool: Management Accounting is only a tool and it will not prepare any statutory documents except Cash Flow statement. Cash Flow statement is required only for the listed companies. It provides many techniques only for managerial decision making.

3. It can be adopted only by big concerns: The adoption of Management Accounting needs more expenditure towards maintaining additional staff for this purpose. Hence, it is possible only for big concerns and small concerns are not able to adopt this system.

4. Personal Judgements: Management Accounting information are mostly based on personal judgements about projection of costs and revenues about future. If the Management Accountant is not efficient the judgment may not be correct and accurate.

5. Personal Bias: There is possibility of showing personal bias in Management Accounting. This is possible in the area of allotment of work and responsibility accounting.

6. Evolutionary Stage: Management Accounting was a recently originated. The companies are adopting the system only from 1950 onwards. Hence, it has not developed much to meet the complete requirements of the management.

7. Opposition to Change: There is possibility of opposition from the employees of the company for the introduction of Management Accounting system. This is because Management Accounting may expose the performance of inefficient workers.

Management Accounting and Financial Accounting

The following are the differences between Management Accounting and Financial Accounting:

1. Management Accounting is concerned with the preparation of various statements meant for managerial planning, control and decision making. Hence, it is future oriented. But Financial Accounting is concerned with the recording of past events only.
2. Management Accounting aims at providing information for the management. Financial Accounting aims at providing information external to the management, like shareholders, debenture holders, creditors, Government etc.
3. There is no time limit in the preparation of accounts and statements in Management Accounting. It may be prepared for 15 days or 1 month, 2 months, 3 months, etc., as per the requirements of the management. But, Financial Accounting is prepared only for one year. The Profit and Loss account and the Balance Sheet are prepared at the end of the financial year.
4. Management Accounting is concerned with quantitative and qualitative information. But Financial Accounting is concerned only with quantitative information.

5. There is no compulsion for the preparation of Management Accounting. Financial Accounting is compulsory according to the Companies Act 1956.
6. Reports of the Management Accounting are not circulated to external parties. It is only provided for the management to take managerial decisions. But the reports of the Financial Accounting including the Profit & Loss Account and Balance Sheet are circulated to the external parties also.

Management Accounting and Cost Accounting

The important differences between Cost Accounting and Management Accounting are as follows:

1. The purpose of Management Accounting is to provide information to the management for decision making. The purpose of Cost Accounting is ascertainment of cost at each stages of production.
2. Management Accounting purely aims at the future on the basis of past information. Cost Accounting is prepared mainly on the basis of past and less emphasis is given for the future.
3. Management Accounting is prepared without adopting any specific and rigid rules. It may be prepared according to the will of the managerial personnel. But Cost Accounting is prepared on the basis of some rules and regulations prescribed by the ICWAI.
4. The reports of the Management Accounting are not subject to statutory audit. But the report of the Cost Accounting are subject to statutory audit.
5. The reports of the Management Accounting are useful only for the internal parties. But the reports of the Cost Accounting are useful both to the internal and external parties.

Management Accountant

The person responsible for providing information to management is called Management Accountant. There are different names for different companies for Management Accountant like, Chief Accountant, Financial Advisor, Financial Controller, Comptroller etc.

Management Accountant is responsible for the preparation of Management Accounting. He works with few subordinates. He has to assign work to them for effective preparation of accounts related to management. His work is not only to look after the activities of his subordinates, but also all the employees of the organisation. On the basis of the information provided by him the management fixes the standard and responsibility of all the employees of the organisation. The information provided by Management Accountant is also based on the efficiency, and performance of the employees and the infrastructure available for the company. Hence, he is more connected with the employees of a company. His main work is preparation of Budgets, Standard Costing, Marginal Costing and Financial Statement Analysis. On the basis of Financial Statement Analysis, he has to prepare the Fund Flow statement and Cash Flow statement. These statements help to ascertain whether the fund of the company is effectively utilised or not. Moreover, accounting ratios are also calculated based on the financial statements. This informations help to fixing good standards and effective responsibilities. Hence, the Management Accountant plays an important role in an organisation is the planning, co-ordinating, directing and controlling of all the activities, through the various information he provides to the management.

Functions of Management Accountant

The important functions of the Management Accountant are stated as follows:

1. Planning: Planning is an important function of Management Accountant. Planning is done through budgeting and standard costing. Proper planning based on Management Accounting helps in the efficient functioning of an organisation.

2. Coordinating: The objectives of a concern can be achieved through proper co-ordination. It is the duty of the Management Accountant to co-ordinate all the activities of an organisation.

3. Motivating: The employees of an organisation are properly motivated by fixing the standard of performance. The curiosity to perform more than the standard automatically motivated the employees to produce more goods. Management Accountant should take necessary steps in this respect.

4. Directing: Management Accountant takes steps to direct the employees to do different works efficiently through Standard Costing, Marginal Costing and Budgetary Control techniques. Each employee is directed to accomplish his responsibilities.

5. Controlling: Controlling is concerned with the control of cost for various activities. If the actual cost is greater than the standard cost, it requires some controlling mechanism. Management Accountant takes various steps for controlling costs at different stages.

Controller and Treasurer

Controller and Treasurer are the terms associated with Management Accounting. They are in charge of all the financial transactions. They provide crucial information to management. Due to the role played by these personnels, controller (or Comptroller) is a term used in USA for the top Management Accountant Executive in a firm. Hence, these terms are more associated with U.S.A. Controller is more concerned with the establishment, delegation and execution of the activities of an organisation. His duty is also to report to the management about the result of the activities in order to help the management for planning, controlling and decision-making. His duties are defined by Controllers Institute of America. These duties are the duties which are to be executed as a Management Accountant.

The Treasurer is responsible for the management of the funds of a concern. He has to ascertain the financial needs of a company, the ways in which the needs are to be met, utilisation of the funds and ascertainment of the fair return on the investment. He has to see that the funds are effectively utilised to give a fair return.

The role and status of Controller and Treasurer can be known through the organisational chart stated as follows:

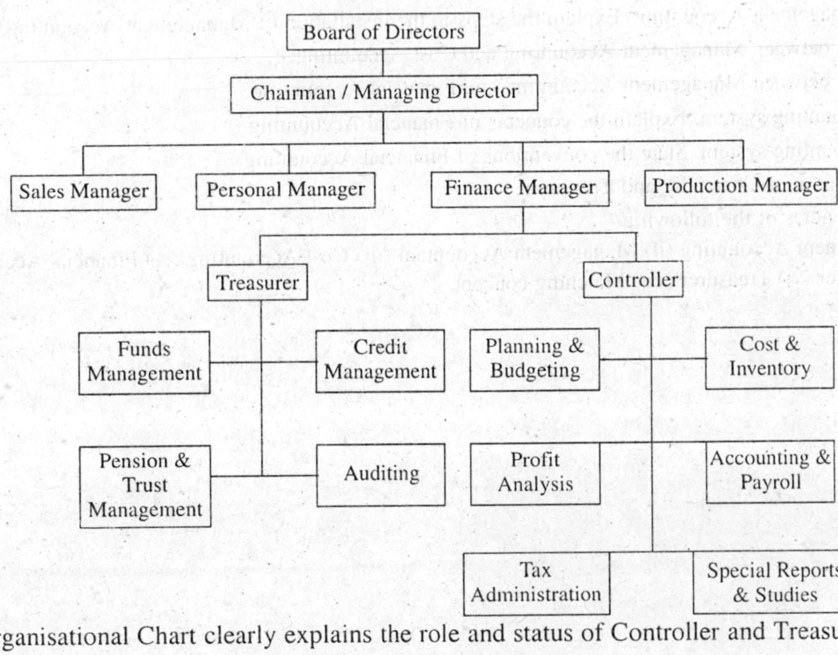

The Organisational Chart clearly explains the role and status of Controller and Treasurer.

EXERCISE

THEORY

I. Choose the correct answer for the following.

1. Accounting to management is known as:
   (i) Cost Accounting (ii) Financial Accounting (iii) Management Accounting (iv) Revenue Accounting
2. The nature of Financial Accounting is —
   (i) Historical (ii) Present (iii) Future (iv) Present and Future
3. The term used for Management Accountant, by U.S.A. is —
   (i) Auditor (ii) Cost Auditor (iii) Treasurer (iv) Controller
4. Double entry system was first introduced during 1340 by —
   (i) India (ii) Italy (iii) Indonesia (iv) Iran
5. The term Management Accounting is first used in the Anglo-American Council on Productivity during —
   (i) 1650 (ii) 1850 (iii) 1950 (iv) 1750
6. Audit conducted within an organisation is —
   (i) Internal audit (ii) External audit (iii) Statutory audit (iv) Balance Sheet audit
7. The process of recording the different elements of cost in an organisation is called —
   (i) Management Accounting (ii) Cost Accounting (iii) Financial Accounting (iv) Inflation Accounting

[**Ans:** 1. (iii) 2. (i) 3. (iv) 4. (ii) 5. (iii) 6. (i) 7. (ii)]

II. Answer the following questions.

1. Define Management Accounting.
2. What is Management Accounting? Explain the scope of Management Accounting.
3. Define Management Accounting. What are the utilities of Management Accounting?
4. Define Management Accountant. State the functions of Management Accountant.
5. What is Management Accounting? State the limitations of Management Accounting.
6. Explain the merits and demerits of Management Accounting.
7. Critically evaluate how the limitations of Financial Accounting are eradicated in Management Accounting.
8. Give a brief account of the tools and techniques of Management Accounting.
9. Define Management Accounting. Explain the steps in the installation of Management Accounting system.
10. Distinguish between Management Accounting and Cost Accounting.
11. Distinguish between Management Accounting and Financial Accounting.
12. Define accounting system. Explain the concepts of Financial Accounting.
13. Define accounting system. State the conventions of Financial Accounting.
14. Give an account of Controller and Treasurer.
15. Write short notes of the following:
    (i) Management Accounting (ii) Management Accountant (iii) Cost Accounting (iv) Financial Accounting (v) Controller (vi) Treasurer (vii) Matching concept.

❑ ❑ ❑

2

FINANCIAL STATEMENT ANALYSIS

The preparation Financial Statements (i)e., Trading and Profit & Loss Account and Balance Sheet is mandatory for a concern. It is compulsory to prepare the Financial Statements according to the Companies Act 1956. For the assessment of tax also, it is a must for preparing these statements. These statements exhibit the profit position and the financial strength of a company. It merely states the affairs of the company for a period. It is useful for the Owners, Creditors and General Public to find out the condition and status of the company. But it wont explain whether there is any improvement or not in the performance of the company. It wont be sufficient for the financial planning and decision making. Hence, there is a need for analysing the Financial Statements with the data provided by these statements for financial planning and decision making.

Meaning and Definitions of Financial Statement Analysis

Financial Statement Analysis is the process of determining the financial strength and weaknesses of a concern. It also establishes the strategic relationship between various accounts in the financial statements.

Metcalf and Titard defined as, "Financial Statement Analysis is a process of evaluating the relationship between component parts of a financial statement to obtain a better understanding of a firms position and performance".

According to Myers, "Financial Statement Analysis is largely a study of relationship among the various financial factors in a business as disclosed by a single set of statements and a study of the trend of these factors as shown in a series of statements".

These two definitions clearly explain that Final Statement Analysis is concerned with the establishment of relationship between various items in the Profit & Loss Account and Balance Sheet. The study about the relationship of various items of financial statements for various periods will help for the financial planning and to find out the trend of various items in future.

Objectives of Financial Statement Analysis

The objectives of Financial Statement Analysis are stated as follows:

(i) To find out the operating performance of a company.

(ii) To find out the financial performance of a company.

(iii) To compare the performance of a company for different periods.

(iv) To find out the long-term solvency and liquidity of a concern.

(v) To compare the performance of the company with other companies in the industry.

Advantages or Uses of Financial Statement Analysis

The following are the advantages of Final Statement Analysis.

1. Advantages to the owners of the Company: The proprietors, partners or shareholders are much interested in the Financial Statement Analysis. They are able to know the financial strength and weakness, profit conditions etc. It helps them to direct the management in an appropriate manner.

2. Advantages to the Investors: The investors are much interested in the good performance of the company so that their investment will be safely returned within proper time. The Financial Statement Analysis helps them to know it through the solvency analysis of the business.

3. Advantage to the Management: The management gets a lot of information through Financial Statement Analysis. They can know about the movement and utilisation of funds, solvency, profitability etc. It helps them to take managerial decisions and for various policy making.

4. Advantages to the Suppliers: Financial Statement Analysis provides information about the credit standing of a concern to the suppliers. It helps them to decide the quantum of credit and credit period for the credit sales.

Types of Financial Statement Analysis

Financial statement analysis is conducted according to the requirement of the parties interested in a concern. Accordingly, the Financial Statement Analysis is classified as follows.

1. Classification according to Material Used and
2. Classification according to Modus Operand(i)

1. Classification according to Material used

According to material used, Financial Statement Analysis is classified as

(i) Internal Analysis and

(ii) External Analysis.

(i) Internal Analysis: The analysis of financial statement by the Owners, Management or Employees of a company is known as Internal Analysis. This analysis is carried on to identify the strength and weakness of the Company to take necessary actions for the future. This analysis helps them to identify the rate of growth of the company.

(ii) External analysis: The analysis of Financial Statements by the external parties like Private Investors, Financial Institutions, Banks and General Public is called external analysis. The purpose of the analysis is to know the financial and operating performance and the credit worthiness of a concern. They want to know about the safety of their investment.

2. Classification according to Modus Operandi

According to Modus Operandi Financial Statement Analysis is classified as

(i) Horizontal Analysis and

(ii) Vertical Analysis

(i) Horizontal Analysis: Horizontal Analysis is concerned with the Financial Statement Analysis of different periods. It explains whether there is a growth of a concern over a period of years, related to Profit and Financial utilisation. This analysis may be conducted for two years or any number of years.

(ii) Vertical Analysis: Vertical Analysis is concerned with the Financial Statement Analysis of one period only (one year). It analysis the relationship of various items in the Profit and Loss Account and

Balance Sheet. The example of this type of analysis is about Current Assets and Current Liabilities, Working Capital, Return on Capital employed, Debt-Equity relationship etc.

This analysis can also be conducted through comparing the performance of the company with that of other companies in the industry.

Procedures for Financial Statement Analysis

The following are the procedures in the Financial Statement Analysis.

(i) The purpose for which the analysis is conducted should be determined well in advance.

(ii) On the basis of the purpose the items in the Financial Statements should be identified.

(iii) If the analysis to be carried on about the Income Statement, the items should be clearly arranged on the basis of Sales, Cost of goods sold, Gross Profit, Operating expenses, Operating Profit and Net Profit. This is to establish a relationship between various items of the income statement.

(iv) If the analysis is to be carried on about the Balance Sheet, then the items should be classified as Fixed Assets and Current Assets for Asset side and Current Liabilities, Debt and Equity for the Liability side.

(v) After the classification of the items in the Income Statement and Balance Sheet increase or decrease of each items from one period to another should be calculated. Also percentage of increase or decrease should be calculated. The comparison may be done for each item on the basis of percentage on sales for Income Statement and on total assets and total liabilities for Balance Sheet.

(vi) Interpretation about the analysis should be very clearly explained after the analysis in order to provide valuable information for managerial decision making.

Methods or Devices of Financial Statement Analysis

The following are the important methods of analysing the Financial Statements (Profit & Loss Account and Balance Sheets.)

1. Comparative Statements
2. Trend Analysis
3. Common-size Statements
4. Fund Flow Analysis
5. Cash Flow Analysis
6. Ratio Analysis
7. Cost-Volume – Profit Analysis.

In this chapter only the first three methods are discussed. The remaining four methods are discussed in the subsequent chapters.

1. Comparative Statements

Comparative Statements deal with the comparison of different items of the Profit & Loss Account and Balance Sheets of two or more periods. In the process of comparison, the good or poor performance of each items for a period can be known in order to take corrective action for the future. The comparative statements can be prepared separately for the Income Statement (Profit and Loss Account) and for Balance Sheet or for these two statements at a time.

Comparative Income Statement

Income statement gives detail about the Profit of a company. This statement explains the Profit in three different stages namely, Gross Profit, Operating Profit and Net Profit. The comparative income statement shows whether there is any improvement in the profitability of a concern over a period of time. If the profitability is low compared to the previous year, the management can able to identify the reasons for it so that corrective action can be taken.

Procedures in the preparation of Comparative Income Statement

The following are the procedure in the preparation of comparative income statement.

1. The statement should contain five columns, first one is for the particulars, next two are for the amounts in two periods and the last two columns are meant for increase and decrease of individual items. The increase or decrease may be mentioned in percentage also.
2. First of all, analysis about Gross Profit should be done. The reason for increase in Gross Profit should be identified. It may be due to increase in sales or decrease in cost of production. Like that, reasons for decrease in Gross Profit should be identified, if there is decrease in Gross Profit.
3. Next the increase or decrease of the Operating Profit should be analysed. Operating profit is the difference between Gross Profit and Operating expenses. The Operating expenses are Administrative expenses and Selling and Distribution expenses. The increase of Operating Profit from one period to another is due to increase in sales, increase in Gross Profit or decrease in Operating expenses. Like that, the decrease in Operating Profit may be due to these reasons. The correct reasons should be identified for managerial decision making.
4. After the analysis of Operating Profit, Net Profit for the two periods should be analysed. Net profit is calculated by adjusting the non-operating expenses and non-operating income with Operating Profit. Non-operating expenses like interest, loss on sale of fixed assets, writting off of fictitious assets (goodwill, preliminary expenses etc.), payment of tax etc should be deducted with Operating Profit. The non-operating income like dividend received, interest received, profit on sale of fixed assets etc., should be added with the Operating Profit to ascertain the Net Profit. Increase in Net Profit from one period to another is either due to increase in operating profit or increase in non-operating income or decrease in non-operating expenses. Like that, the decrease in Net Profit may be due to these reasons. The real cause for the increase or decrease should be identified for managerial decision making.
5. After preparing a statement of analysis, the interpretation about the analysis should be stated clearly for further action of the management.

Illustration: 1

Prepare a Comparative Income Statement of K Ltd. for the following Profit and Loss Account for the year ended 31st March 2006 and 2007.

Profit & Loss Account for the year ended 31st March 2006 and 2007

Particulars	*2006 Rs.*	*2007 Rs.*	*Particulars*	*2006 Rs.*	*2007 Rs.*
To Cost of goods sold	7,00,000	8,90,000	By Sales	10,00,000	12,00,000
To Operating expenses					
Administrative exp.	90,000	1,40,000			
Selling expenses	60,000	40,000			
To Net Profit	1,50,000	1,30,000			
	10,00,000	12,00,000		10,00,000	12,00,000

Solution:

Comparative Income Statement

Particulars	*2006 Rs.*	*2007 Rs.*	*Change Rs.*	*Percentage*
Sales	10,00,000	12,00,000	2,00,000	20
Less : Cost of Good Sold	7,00,000	8,90,000	1,90,000	27.14
Gross Profit	3,00,000	3,10,000	10,000	3.33
Operating Expenses:				
Administrative Expenses	90,000	1,40,000	50,000	55.55
Selling Expenses	60,000	40,000	-20,000	-33.33
Total Operating Expenses	1,50,000	1,80,000	30,000	20
Net profit	**1,50,000**	**1,30,000**	**-20,000**	**-13.33**

Interpretation:

1. Gross Profit of the company increased by 3.33%. But the Net Profit reduced by 13.33%.
2. The reasons for the reduced net profit is due to increase in administrative expenses and cost of goods sold.

Illustration: 2

Prepare a Comparative Income Statement from the following.

Particulars	*31 March 2006 Rs.*	*31st March 2007 Rs.*
Sales	21,50,000	25,00,000
Cost of Good Sold	13,00,000	14,50,000
Operating Expenses:		
Administrative Expenses	2,10,000	1,80,000
Selling Expenses	1,90,000	2,50,000
Non-operating Expenses:		
Interest	1,40,000	1,20,000
Income Tax	1,70,000	2,30,000

Solution:

Comparative Income Statement

Particulars	*2006 Rs.*	*2007 Rs.*	*Change Rs.*	*Percentage*
Sales	21,50,000	25,00,000	3,50,000	16.28
Less : Cost of Goods sold	13,00,000	14,50,000	1,50,000	11.54
Gross Profit	8,50,000	10,50,000	2,00,000	23.53
Operating Expenses				
Administrative Expenses	2,10,000	1,80,000	-30,000	-14.29
Selling Expenses	1,90,000	2,50,000	60,000	31.58

Total Operating Expenses	4,00,000	4,30,000	30,000	7.50
Operating Profit	4,50,000	6,20,000	1,70,000	37.78
Less : Non-operating Expenses Interest	1,40,000	1,20,000	-20,000	-14.29
Net Profit before Tax	3,10,000	5,00,000	1,90,000	61.29
Less : Tax	1,70,000	2,30,000	60,000	35.29
Net Profit after Tax	**1,40,000**	**2,70,000**	**1,30,000**	**92.85**

Interpretation:

(i) The Gross Profit increased only by 23.53%. But the Net Profit increased remarkably by 92.85%. This is due to reduction in Operating expenses.

(ii) The Administrative expenses reduced by 14.29% though there is an increase in sales by 16.28%.

(iii) Cost of goods sold increased only by 11.54% though there is an increase in sales by 16.28%.

Comparative Balance Sheet

This statement gives detail about the financial conditions of a concern. The various items of Balance Sheets of two different periods are normally compared through Comparative Balance Sheet. In this statement Assets are separately analysed as Current Assets and Fixed Assets. The Liabilities are analysed by classifying it into Current Liabilities, Debts (Long-term loans and advances) and Equity (Share Capital, Reserves and Surplus and all kinds of Reserves and Funds).

Procedures in the preparation of Comparative Balance Sheets

The following are the procedures in the preparation of Comparative Balance Sheets.

1. This statement should be prepared with five columns. The first column is for particulars, second and third columns are for periods (years), fourth column is for increase or decrease of various items and the last column is for percentage of increase or decrease.
2. The Assets side or Liabilities side can be taken first for analysis. If assets side is taken for analysis first, the assets should be separately classified as Current Assets and Current Liabilities. The values should be recorded in the second and third columns and the increase or decrease and the percentage of it should be recorded in the respective columns.
3. Then the Liability side should be analysed. The Liabilities should be classified as Current Liabilities, Debts and Equity separately. The values should be recorded in the respective columns.
4. After the preparation of the Comparative Balance Sheets, interpretation should be given. It should highlight the strength and weakness areas so that the management can take appropriate steps for the improvement in the performance of the Company for the future.

Illustration: 3

AB Ltd. provided the Balance Sheets for the year ended 31st March 2006 and 2007 as follows.

Balance Sheets

Particulars	*2006 Rs.*	*2007 Rs.*	*Particulars*	*2006 Rs.*	*2007 Rs.*
Share Capital	11,00,000	14,00,000	Fixed Assets	12,80,000	15,20,000
Profit & Loss A/c	1,45,000	1,75,000	Current Assets	2,40,000	3,00,000

Loan	2,00,000	1,50,000		
Current Liabilities	75,000	95,000		
	15,20,000	**18,20,000**	**15,20,000**	**18,20,000**

Prepare a Comparative Balance Sheet.

Solution:

Comparative Balance Sheet

Particulars	*2006 Rs.*	*2007 Rs.*	*Change Rs.*	*Percentage*
Assets				
Current Assets	2,40,000	3,00,000	60,000	25.00
Fixed Assets	12,80,000	15,20,000	2,40,000	18.75
Total Assets	**15,20,000**	**18,20,000**	**3,00,000**	**19.74**
Liabilities				
Current Liabilities:	75,000	95,000	20,000	26.67
Debt - Loan	2,00,000	1,50,000	-50,000	-25.00
Equity:				
Share Capital	11,00,000	14,00,000	3,00,000	27.27
Profit & Loss Account	1,45,000	1,75,000	30,000	20.69
Total Equity	12,45,000	15,75,000	3,30,000	26.51
Total Liabilities	**15,20,000**	**18,20,000**	**3,00,000**	**19.74**

Interpretation:

(i) There is an increase in the total Assets and liabilities by 19.74%.

(ii) The growth of Fixed Assets is low when compared to the growth of Current Assets.

(iii) There is an increase in the value of Equity to the extent of 26.51%. But the Debt reduced by 25%.

(iv) The Net Profit also increased by 20.69%.

(v) Increase in Current Assets when compared to Current Liabilities showed the increase in Working Capital.

Illustration: 4

Prepare a Comparative Balance Sheet as on 31st March 2006 and 2007 for the following Balance Sheets.

Particulars	*2006 Rs.*	*2007 Rs.*
Share Capital	4,00,000	5,00,000
Reserve and Surplus	1,15,000	80,000
Loan	2,50,000	2,00,000
Fixed Assets (Excluding Investments)	4,50,000	5,10,000
Investments	2,00,000	1,20,000
Current Assets	1,70,000	2,20,000
Current Liabilities	55,000	70,000

Solution:

Comparative Balance Sheets as on 31st March 2006 and 2007

Particulars	*2006 Rs.*	*2007 Rs.*	*Change Rs.*	*Percentage*
Assets				
Current Assets	1,70,000	2,20,000	50,000	29.41
Fixed Assets - (Excluding investments)	4,50,000	5,10,000	60,000	13.33
Investments	2,00,000	1,20,000	-80,000	-40.00
Total Fixed Assets	6,50,000	6,30,000	-20,000	-3.08
Total Assets	**8,20,000**	**8,50,000**	**30,000**	**3.66**
Liabilities				
Current liabilities	55,000	70,000	15,000	27.27
Debt - Loan	2,50,000	2,00,000	-50,000	-20.00
Equity Share capital	4,00,000	5,00,000	1,00,000	25.00
Reserves and Surplus	1,15,000	80,000	-35,000	-30.43
Total Equity	5,15,000	5,80,000	65,000	12.62
Total Liabilities	**8,20,000**	**8,50,000**	**30,000**	**3.66**

Interpretation:

(i) The Fixed Assets of the company reduced by 3.08% though there is an increase of Total Assets by 3.66%. This is due to high growth of Current Assets to the extent of 29.41%.

(ii) The reduction in Fixed Assets is due to the sale of Investments.

(iii) The decrease in Reserves and Surplus showed that there is an increase in the Net Profit for the current year.

(iv) The Share Capital increased by 25% and the Debt reduced by 20% which showed the improvement in the financial condition of the Company.

Illustration: 5

G Ltd. provided the Balance Sheets as on 31st March 2006 and 2007 as follows.

Balance Sheets

Particulars	*2006 Rs.*	*2007 Rs.*	*Particulars*	*2006 Rs.*	*2007 Rs.*
Equity Share Capital	7,00,000	9,00,000	Land & Building	5,00,000	7,50,000
Preference Sh. Cap.	2,00,000	1,00,000	Plant & Machinery	5,50,000	5,70,000
Profit & Loss A/c	-	1,20,000	Furniture & Fitting	1,50,000	1,90,000
General Reserve	60,000	80,000	Stock	50,000	23,000
Debentures	2,50,000	3,00,000	Debtors	43,000	54,000
Loan	1,40,000	50,000	Cash	35,000	24,000
Sundry Creditors	34,000	52,000	Salary paid in ad	12,000	19,000
Outstanding rent	13,000	9,000	Preliminary Exp.	30,000	10,000
Bank overdraft	23,000	29,000	Profit & Loss A/c	50,000	–
	14,20,000	16,40,000		14,20,000	16,40,000

Prepare a Comparative Balance Sheet.

Solution:

Comparative Balance Sheets as on 31st March 2006 and 2007

Particulars	*2006 Rs.*	*2007 Rs.*	*Change Rs.*	*Percentage*
Current Assets				
Stock	50,000	23,000	-27,000	-54.00
Debtors	43,000	54,000	11,000	25.58
Cash	35,000	24,000	-11,000	-31.43
Salary paid in advance	12,000	19,000	7,000	58.33
	1,40,000	1,20,000	-20,000	-14.29
Fixed Assets				
Land & Building	5,00,000	7,50,000	2,50,000	50
Plant & Machinery	5,50,000	5,70,000	20,000	3.64
Furniture & Fitting	1,50,000	1,90,000	40,000	26.67
	12,00,000	15,10,000	3,10,000	25.83
Total Assets	**13,40,000**	**16,30,000**	**2,90,000**	**21.64**
Liabilities				
(i) Current liabilities				
Sundry Creditors	34,000	52,000	18,000	52.94
Outstanding Rent	13,000	9,000	-4,000	-30.77
Bank Overdraft	23,000	29,000	6000	26.09
Total Current Liabilities	70,000	90,000	20,000	28.57
(ii) Debts				
Debentures	2,50,000	3,00,000	50,000	20.00
Loan	1,40,000	50,000	-90,000	-64.29
Total Debts	3,90,000	3,50,000	-40,000	-10.26
(iii) Equity				
Equity Share Capital	7,00,000	9,00,000	2,00,000	28.57
Preference Share Capital	2,00,000	1,00,000	-1,00,000	-50.00
Profit & Loss A/c	(50,000)	1,20,000	1,70,000	340.00
General Reserve	60,000	80,000	20,000	33.33
Less : Fictitious assets -				
Preliminary expenses	(30,000)	(10,000)	20,000	66.67
Total Equity	8,80.000	11,90,000	3,10,000	35.23
Total Liabilities (i)+(ii)+(iii)	**13,40,000**	**16,30,000**	**2,90,000**	**21.64**

Interpretation:

(i) The Assets and Liabilities of the Company increased by 21.64%.

(ii) The reduction in the Current Assets by 14.29 is adjusted by the increase in Fixed Assets by 25.83%. The increase in Current Assets is not good, though there is an increase in the growth of total Assets by 21.64%. Also the increase in Current Liabilities by 28.57% considerably reduce the Working Capital.

(iii) The reduction of Debt by 10.26% and improvement in the Equity by 35.23% is good work which shows the improvement in the financial strength of the Company.

(iv) The good performance is seen in the improvement of Profit by 340%.

Illustration: 6

K Ltd. provided the Profit & Loss Account and Balance Sheet as on 31st March 2006 and 2007 as follows.

Profit & Loss Account

Particulars	*2006 Rs.*	*2007 Rs.*	*Particulars*	*2006 Rs.*	*2007 Rs.*
To Cost of Good sold	6,90,000	8,10,000	By Sales	12,00,000	14,00,000
To Operating expenses					
Administrative exp.	1,50,000	1,20,000			
Selling exp.	1,80,000	2,30,000			
To Net Profit	1,80,000	2,40,000			
	12,00,000	14,00,000		12,00,000	14,00,000

Balance Sheets

Particulars	*2006 Rs.*	*2007 Rs.*	*Particulars*	*2006 Rs.*	*2007 Rs.*
Equity Share Capital	4,00,000	4,00,000	Land	4,00,000	3,00,000
Preference Share Capital	1,00,000	2,00,000	Building	3,00,000	3,50,000
Reserve & Surplus	1,25,000	1,90,000	Plant	3,20,000	2,70,000
Debentures	2,50,000	50,000	Stock	31,000	20,000
Loan	2,00,000	1,30,000	Debtors	42,000	53,000
Sundry Creditors	40,000	50,000	Cash	35,000	22,000
Bills Payable	25,000	10,000	Outstanding Interest	12,000	15,000
	11,40,000	10,30,000		11,40,000	10,30,000

Prepare a Comparative Profit & Loss Account and a Comparative Balance Sheet.

Solution:

Comparative Profit & Loss Account as on 31st March 2006 and 2007

Particulars	*2006 Rs.*	*2007 Rs.*	*Change Rs.*	*Percentage*
Sales	12,00,000	14,00,000	2,00,000	16.67
Less: Cost of good sold	6,90,000	8.10,000	1,20,000	17.39
Gross Profit	5,10,000	5,90,000	80,000	15.69
Less : Operating Expenses				
Administrative Expenses	1.50.000	1,20,000	-30,000	-20
Selling Expenses	1,80,000	2.30,000	50,000	27.78
Total Operating Expenses	3,30,000	3,50,000	20,000	6.06
Net Profit	1,80,000	2,40,000	60,000	33.33

Comparative Balance Sheet as on 31st March 2006 and 2007

Particulars	*2006 Rs.*	*2007 Rs.*	*Change Rs.*	*Percentage*
Assets:				
Current Assets:				
Stock	31,000	20,000	-11,000	-35.48
Debtors	42,000	53,000	11,000	26.19
Cash	35,000	22,000	-13,000	-37.14
Outstanding Interest	12,000	15,000	3,000	2.50
Total Current Assets	1,20,000	1,10,000	-10,000	-8.33
Fixed Assets				
Land	4,00,000	3,00,000	-1,00,000	-25
Building	3,00,000	3,50,000	50,000	16.67
Plant	3,20,000	2,70,000	-50,000	-15.63
Total Fixed Assets	10,20,000	9,20,000	-1,00,000	-9.80
Total Assets	**11,40,000**	**10,30,000**	**-1,10,000**	**-9.65**
Liabilities				
(i) Current Liabilities				
Sundry Creditors	40,000	50,000	10,000	25
Bills Payable	25,000	10,000	-15,000	-60
Total Current Liabilities	65,000	60,000	-5,000	-7.69
(ii) Debts (Long-term Liab.)				
Debentures	2,50,000	50,000	-2,00,000	-80
Loan	2,00,000	1,30,000	-70,000	-35
Total Debts	4,50,000	1,80,000	-2,70,000	-60
(iii) Equity (Proprietors Fund)				
Equity Share Capital	4,00,000	4,00,000	-	-
Preference Share Capital	1,00,000	2,00,000	1,00,000	100
Reserves and Surplus	1,25,000	1,90,000	65,000	52
Total Equity	6,25,000	7,90,000	1,65,000	26.40
Total Liabilities (i) + (ii) + (iii)	**11,40,000**	**10,30,000**	**-1,10,000**	**-9.65**

Interpretation:

(i) Gross Profit of the company improved by 15.69% and the Net Profit improved by 33.33%. This is due to low growth of Operating expenses.

(ii) The Assets and Liabilities decreased by 8.33% which shows poor financial performance of the Company.

(iii) Total Current Assets decreased by 8.33% whereas the Current Liabilities decreased by 7.69% only. It shows the decrease in Working Capital.

(iv) Total Debt has been reduced considerably by 60% and the Equity improved by 26.4%.

(v) Improvement in Profit recorded in the Balance Sheet is not considerable when compared to the current year Profit of Rs.2,40,000. This may be due to excess provision.

2. Trend Analysis

Trend analysis is one of the important devices in measuring the financial performance of a Company. In this analysis, the important items of the financial statements (both Profit & Loss Account and Balance Sheet) for a long period can be taken for Trend analysis. The period of comparison may be 5 years or more than that. Trend percentage should be calculated by taking one year as base. Normally, the first year of comparison is taken as base year. The index of base year should be 100 and from that trend percentages for the subsequent years should be calculated. From this analysis, it is possible to know whether there is any improvement in the items of financial statement. The improvement or not can be known through percentages. Hence, it is easy for the management to identify the weaknesses for corrective actions for the future.

Procedures for calculating Trend Percentages

The following are the procedures for calculating the Trend Percentage

(i) The base year should be identified. Normally the first year is considered as base year.

(ii) The items to be compared should also be identified.

(iii) The values of base year should be considered as 100.

(iv) Compare the values of the subsequent years with the base year and convert it into Trend values (by dividing the value of current year with the value of base year. This value should be multiplied by 100).

For example, the Profit for the year 2001 (Base year) is Rs.2,00,000 and in 2006 and 2007 are Rs.3,00,000 and Rs.5,00,000 respectively. Then the trend value for 2001 is 100, 2006 is

$$\frac{3,00,000}{2,00,000} \times 100 = 150; \text{ and 2007 is } \frac{5,00,000}{2,00,000} \times = 250$$

Illustration: 7

The following are the information related to Sales and Profit of G Ltd. Calculate the Trend Percentages by taking 2003 as base. Also interpret the result.

(Rs. in 000's)

Year	*Sales*	*Stock*	*Profit Before Tax*
2003	4,500	340	420
2004	5,300	450	370
2005	6,000	700	510
2006	6,500	550	300
2007	7,000	400	750

Solution:

Statement of Trend Percentage *(Rs. in 000's)*

Year	*Sales*		*Stock*		*Profit Before Tax*	
	Amount Rs.	*Trend Percentage*	*Amount Rs.*	*Trend Percentage*	*Amount Rs.*	*Trend Percentage*
2003	4,500	100	340	100	420	100
2004	5,300	117.78	450	132.35	370	88
2005	6,000	133.33	700	205.88	510	121.43
2006	6,500	144.44	550	161.76	300	71.42
2007	7,000	155.55	400	117.64	750	178.57

Interpretation:

(i) Sales improved by 155.55% in the year 2007 compared to the year 2003. The improvement is gradual and steady.

(ii). Stock position is very high during 2005 when compared to other periods. More or less same level of stock is maintained in 2007 also (i)e., 117.64% when compared to 2003.

(iii) There is a wide fluctuation in the improvement of Profit before tax. It reduced to 88% in 2004 and immediately raised to 121.43%. Then it reduced to 71.42% level in 2006 and improved to 178.57%. The overall improvement to 178.57% compared to 2003 is good.

3. Common Size Statement

Common size statement is concerned with the analysis of the financial statements (Income statement and Balance Sheet) on percentage basis. It explains each item of the financial statements in terms of the percentage to the total. Hence, the share of each items of Expenses or Income, Assets or Liabilities to total can be known through this analysis. The importance of each item in a statement can also be known through this analysis.

For Example, if the Land and Building is Rs.2,00,000 and the Total Asset is Rs.10,00,000. Then, the percentage of Land and Building is 20%.

Common size statements are prepared on the following basis.

(i) Common-size Income Statement

(ii) Common-size Balance Sheet

(i) Common Size Income Statement: In this statement, the value of each item of expenses are analysed as a percentage to the total sales. For example, if the sales is Rs.4,00,000 and the administrative expenses is Rs.50,000 then the administrative expense is expressed as 12.5% on Sales $\left[\frac{50{,}000 \times 100}{4{,}00{,}000}\right]$

Illustration: 8

The Income Statement of a manufacturing Company for 31st March 2006 and 2007 are stated as follows.

Particulars	*2006 Rs.*	*2007 Rs.*
Sales	29,00,000	34,00,000
Non-operating income (Dividend received)	1,50,000	1,00,000
	30,50,000	35,00,000
Expenses		
Cost of production	16,40,000	18,85,000
Administrative Expenses	5,40,000	6,20,000
Selling Expenses	2,10,000	2,75,000
Interest	3,70,000	3,90,000
Total Expenses	27,60,000	31,70,000
Net Profit	**2,90,000**	**3,30,000**

Also interpret the results.

Solution:

Particulars	*2006*		*2007*	
	Rs.	*%*	*Rs.*	*%*
Sales	29,00,000	100.00	34,00,000	100.00
Less : Cost of production	16,40,000	56.55	18,85,000	55.44
Gross profit	12,60,000	43.45	15,15,000	44.56
Operating Expenses				
Administrative Expenses	5,40,000	18.62	6,20,000	18.24
Selling Expenses	2,10,000	7.24	2,75,000	8.08
Total Operating Expenses	7,50,000	25.86	8,95,000	26.32
Operating Profit	5,10,000	17.59	6,20,000	18.23
Non-operating income (Dividend)	1,50,000	5.17	1,00,000	2.94
Total Income	6,60,000	22.76	7,20,000	21.17
Less : Non-operating Expenses	3,70,000	12.76	3,90,000	11.47
Interest				
Net profit	**2,90,000**	**10.00**	**3,30,000**	**9.70**

Interpretation

(i) The operating efficiency of the company is more or less same. This is seen from the percentage of Operating Expenses, Operating Profit and Net Profit on Sales.

(ii) The Gross Profit for 2006 and 2007 on Sale are almost same as 43.45% and 44.56% respectively.

(iii) The Net Profit on Sales for 2006 and 2007 are same as 10% and 9.7%.

Illustration: 9

Prepare a Common-size Income Statement for the following income statements of GT Ltd. for the year ended 31st March 2006 and 2007.

Income Statements as on 31st March 2006 and 2007

Particulars	*2006* *Rs.*	*2007* *Rs.*
Gross Sales	31,00,000	39,00,000
Less : Sales Return	1,00,000	2,00,000
Net Sales	30,00,000	37,00,000
Cost of Goods Sold	19,00,000	20,00,000
Gross Profit	11,00,000	17,00,000
Operating Expenses		
Administrative Expenses	3,75,000	5,30,000
Selling and Distribution Expenses	2,35,000	2,50,000
Total Expenses	6,10,000	7,80,000
Operating Income	4,90,000	9,20,000
Non-operating Income	1,35,000	2,15,000

Total Income	6,25,000	11,35,000
Non-operating expenses : Interest	1,95,000	2,15,000
Profit before tax	4,30,000	9,20,000
Less Tax	2,00,000	4,00,000
Net profit after tax	**2,30,000**	**5,20,000**

Solution:

Common-size Income Statement as on 31st March 2006-2007

Particulars	*2006*		*2007*	
	Rs.	*%*	*Rs.*	*%*
Net sales	30,00,000	100.00	37,00,000	100.00
Less : Cost of Goods Sold	19,00,000	63.33	20,00,000	54.05
Gross Profit	11,00,000	36.67	17,00,000	45.95
Operating Expenses				
Administrative Expenses	3,75,000	12.50	5,30,000	14.32
Selling & Distribution Exp.	2,35,000	7.83	2,50,000	6.76
Total Expenses	6,10,000	20.33	7,80,000	21.08
Operating Profit	4,90,000	16.33	9,20,000	24.87
Non-operating income	1,35,000	4.50	2,15,000	5.81
Total Income	6,25,000	20.83	11,35,000	30.68
Less : Non-operating Exp.	1,95,000	6.50	2,15,000	5.81
Profit before tax	4,30,000	14.33	9,20,000	24.87
Less : Tax	2,00,000	6.67	4,00,000	10.81
Net profit after tax	**2,30,000**	**7.66**	**5,20,000**	**14.06**

Interpretation:

(i) The efficiency of the Company improved in 2007 compared to 2006. This is because the Gross Profit on Sales increased from 36.67% in 2006 to 45.95% in 2007.

(ii) The Net Profit on Sales also increased from 7.66% in 2006 to 14.05% on Sales in 2007.

(iii) Only the Administrative expenses on Sales increased in 2007 as 14.32% when compared to 2006 as 12.50%.

(ii) Common-size Balance Sheet

Common size Balance Sheet is prepared by analysing each item of the Balance Sheet as on percentage of the Total Assets or Total Liabilities. It helps to identify the importance of each item of the Balance Sheet. For Example (i) if the Total Liabilities is Rs.20,00,000 and the Debenture is Rs.4,00,000, (4,00,000 × 100 / 20,00,000) then the Debenture is expressed as 20% of the Total Liabilities (ii) If the Total Assets is Rs.20,00,000 and the Debtors is Rs.10,000 then, the Debtors is expressed as 0.5% of the Total Assets (10,000 × 100 / 20,00,000).

Illustration: 10

The Balance Sheets of N Ltd. and H Ltd. as on 31st March 2007 are stated as follows.

Particulars	*N Ltd. Rs.*	*H Ltd. Rs.*
Assets		
Cash	75,000	95,000
Sundry Debtors	70,000	77,000
Stock	79,000	85,000
Outstanding Income	26,000	23,000
Prepaid Expenses	20,000	10,000
Fixed Assets	10,20,000	12,10,000
Total Assets	12,90,000	15,00,000
Liabilities		
Sundry Creditors	45,000	32,000
Bills Payable	25,000	13,000
Long-term Loan	4,00,000	5,55,000
Capital	8,20,000	9,00,000
Total Liabilities	12,90,000	15,00,000

Prepare a common size Balance Sheet and interpret the result.

Solution :

Common Size Balance Sheet

Particulars	*N Ltd. Rs.*		*H Ltd. Rs.*	
	Amount	*%*	*Amount*	*%*
Current Assets				
Cash	75,000	5.81	95,000	6.33
Sundry debtors	70,000	5.43	77,000	5.13
Stock	79,000	6.12	85,000	5.67
Outstanding Income	26,000	2.02	23,000	1.53
Prepaid expenses	20,000	1.55	10,000	0.67
Total Current Assets	2,70,000	20.93	2,90,000	19.33
Fixed Assets	10,20,000	79.07	12,10,000	80.67
Total Asset	**12,90,000**	100.00	**15,00,000**	**100.00**
Current Liabilities				
Sundry Creditors	45,000	3.49	32,000	2.13
Bills Payable	25,000	1.94	13,000	0.87
Total Current Liabilities	70,000	5.43	45,000	3.00
Long term Loan	4,00,000	31.00	5,55,000	37.00
Capital	8,20,000	63.57	9,00,000	60.00
Total Liabilities	**12,90,000**	100.00	**15,00,000**	**100.00**

Interpretation:

(i) H Ltd. has more Total Assets compared to N Ltd.

(ii) The Current Assets to Total Assets for H Ltd. is slightly low than N Ltd. But it is compensated by low amount of Current Liabilities for H Ltd. compared to N Ltd. Hence, the Working Capital of H Ltd. is comparatively better.

(iii) The Debt-Equity of H Ltd. is not good compared to N Ltd. since N Ltd. has more percentage of equity compared to H Ltd.

Illustration: 11

Prepare a Common size Balance Sheet of K Ltd. and M Ltd. from the Balance Sheets as on 31st March 2007.

Balance Sheets as on 31st March 2007

Particulars	*K Ltd. Rs.*	*M Ltd. Rs.*	*Particulars*	*K Ltd. Rs.*	*M Ltd. Rs.*
Equity Share Capital	9,00,000	5,00,000	Land & Building	7,00,000	5,00,000
Preference S.Capital	2,50,000	2,00,000	Plant & Machinery	6,00,000	4,00,000
Reserve & Surplus	1,40,000	70,000	Furniture & Fittings	3,00,000	1,00,000
Debenture	2,00,000	1,00,000	Stock	61,000	30,000
Loan	2,20,000	2,00,000	Debtors	35,000	25,000
Sundry Creditors	30,000	25,000	Cash	54,000	50,000
Bills Payable	17,000	15,000	Prepaid Expenses	20,000	15,000
Outstanding Expenses	13,000	10,000			
	17,70,000	11,20,000		17,70,000	11,20,000

Solution :

Common Size Balance Sheet of K Ltd. and M Ltd.

Particulars	*K Ltd.*		*M Ltd.*	
	Amount	*%*	*Amount*	*%*
Fixed Assets				
Land & Building	7,00,000	39.54	5,00,000	44.65
Plant & Machinery	6,00,000	33.90	4,00,000	35.71
Furniture & Fittings	3,00,000	16.95	1,00,000	8.93
Total Fixed Assets	16,00,000	90.39	10,00,000	89.29
Current Assets				
Stock	61,000	3.45	30,000	2.68
Debtors	35,000	1.98	25,000	2.23
Cash	54,000	3.05	50,000	4.46
Prepaid Expenses	20,000	1.13	15,000	1.34
Total Current Assets	1,70,000	9.61	1,20,000	10.71
Total Assets	17,70,000	100	11,20,000	100
Share Capital and Reserves				

Equity Share Capital	9,00,000	50.85	5,00,000	44.64
Preference Share Capital	2,50,000	14.12	2,00,000	17.86
Reserves & Surplus	1,40,000	7.91	70,000	6.25
Total Capital and Reserves	12,90,000	72.88	7,70,000	68.75
Long-term liabilities				
Debentures	2,00,000	11.30	1,00,000	8.93
Loan	2,20,000	12.43	2,00,000	17.86
Total long-term Liabilities	4,20,000	23.73	3,00,000	26.79
Current Liabilities				
Sundry creditors	30,000	1.70	25,000	2.23
Bills payable	17,000	0.96	15,000	1.34
Outstanding expenses	13,000	0.73	10,000	0.89
Total Current Liabilities	60,000	3.39	50,000	4.46
Total Liabilities	**17,70,000**	**100**	**11,20,000**	**100**

EXERCISE

THEORY

(i) Choose the correct answer for the following.

1. A study about the relationship of various items of the financial statement is known as the analysis of —
(i) Standard time (ii) Cost-Volume-Profit (iii) Budgeting (iv) Financial Statement.
2. Internal Analysis is an analysis conducted by —
(i) Management (ii) Creditors (iii) Government (iv) Public.
3. External Analysis is an analysis conducted by —
(i) Employees (ii) Financial institutions (iii) Management (iv) Proprietor.
4. Analysis of financial statement for different periods is called —
(i) Vertical Analysis (ii) Balance Sheet (iii) Horizontal Analysis (iv) Income Statement.
5. Analysis of financial statement for one year is known as —
(i) Horizontal Analysis (ii) Vertical Analysis (iii) Income Statement (iv) Balance Sheet.
6. Base year is a concept for —
(i) Comparative Income Statement (ii) Comparative Balance Sheet (iii) Trend Analysis (iv) Common-size Statement.
7. Increase or decrease of each items of Balance Sheet is compared by 2 periods in —
(i) Comparative Balance Sheet (ii) Comparative Income Statement (iii) Common-size Balance Sheet (iv) Trend Analysis.
8. Percentages of each items of expenses on sales is analysed in —
(i) Common-size Balance Sheet (ii) Common-size Income Statement (iii) Comparative Balance Sheet (iv) Comparative Income Statement.
9. Percentage of each items of Assets and Liabilities on Total Assets and Liabilities are analysed in —
(i) Comparative Balance Sheet (ii) Comparative - income Statement (iii) Common-size Income Statement (iv) Common-size. Balance Sheet.
10. Increase or decrease of important items of financial statements of many years on index basis by taking one year as base is studied in —
(i) Comparative Income Statement (ii) Comparative Balance Sheet (iii) Trend Analysis (iv) Common-size Financial Statements.

[Ans : 1. (iv) 2. (i) 3. (ii) 4. (iii) 5. (ii) 6. (iii) 7. (i) 8. (ii)9. (iv) 10. (iii)]

(ii) Answer the following questions.

1. Define Financial Statement Analysis. State the objectives of Financial Statement Analysis.
2. What do you mean by Financial Statement Analysis? Explain the advantages of Financial Statement Analysis.
3. Explain the different types of Financial Statement Analysis.
4. Define Financial Statement Analysis. State the procedures in the preparation of Financial Statement Analysis.
5. What is Comparative Statements? State the procedures of preparing the Comparative Income Statement.
6. What is Comparative Statements? State the procedures of preparing the Comparative Balance Sheet.
7. Define Trend Analysis. Explain the procedures in the calculation of Trend Percentages.
8. What is Financial Statement Analysis? Explain about the Common-size Financial Statements.
9. Distinguish between Comparative Statement and Common-size Statement.
10. Write short notes on the following :
    (i) Financial Statement Analysis (ii) Internal Analysis
    (iii) External Analysis (iv) Horizontal Analysis
    (v) Vertical Analysis (vi) Comparative Statement
    (vii) Common-size Statement (viii) Trend Percentages
    (ix) Comparative Income Statement (x) Comparative Balance Sheet.

(iii) Solve the following problems.

1. Prepare a Comparative Income Statement of G Ltd. for the following Profit and Loss Account for the year ended 31st March 2006 and 2007.

Profit & Loss Account for the year ended 31st March 2006 and 2007

Particulars	*2006 Rs.*	*2007 Rs.*	*Particulars*	*2006 Rs.*	*2007 Rs.*
To Cost of Goods sold	13,30,000	16,70,000	By Sales	20,00,000	25,00,000
To Operating expenses:					
Administrative exp.	2,70,000	3,10,000			
Selling expenses	1,50,000	1,90,000			
To Net Profit	2,50,000	3,30,000			
	20,00,000	25,00,000		20,00,000	25,00,000

2. Prepare a Comparative Income Statement from the following.

Particulars	*31 March 2006 Rs.*	*31st March 2007 Rs.*
Sales	17,50,000	21,00,000
Cost of Good Sold	10,00,000	13,50,000
Operating Expenses:		
Administrative Expenses	2,67,000	3,15,000
Non-operating Expenses:		
Interest	1,10,000	90,000
Income Tax	1,00,000	1,90,000

3. AB Ltd. provided to Balance Sheets for the year ended 31st March 2006 and 2007 as follows.

Balance Sheets

Particulars	*2006 Rs.*	*2007 Rs.*	*Particulars*	*2006 Rs.*	*2007 Rs.*
Share Capital	14,00,000	19,00,000	Fixed Assets	12,80,000	15,20,000
Profit & Loss A/c	1,75,000	2,00,000	Current Assets	2,40,000	3,00,000
Loan	4,00,000	2,50,000			
Current Liabilities	95,000	1,25,000			
	20,70,000	24,75,000		20,70,000	24,75,000

Prepare a Comparative Balance Sheet.

4. Prepare a Comparative Balance Sheet as on 31st March 2006 and 2007 for the following Balance Sheets.

Particulars	*2006 Rs.*	*2007 Rs.*
Share Capital	7,00,000	9,00,000
Reserve and Surplus	1,75,000	90,000
Loan	3,50,000	2,00,000
Fixed Assets (Excluding Investments)	7,50,000	6,30,000
Investments	3,50,000	2,70,000
Current Assets	2,05,000	3,50,000
Current Liabilities	80,000	60,000

5. K Ltd. provided the balance sheets as on 31st March 2006 and 2007 as follows.

Balance Sheets

Particulars	*2006 Rs.*	*2007 Rs.*	*Particulars*	*2006 Rs.*	*2007 Rs.*
Equity Share Capital	17,00,000	19,00,000	Land & Building	12,40,000	11,00,000
Preference Sh. Cap.	5,00,000	3,00,000	Plant & Machinery	11,50,000	15,30,000
Profit & Loss A/c	-	2,20,000	Furniture & Fitting	2,55,000	3,40,000
General Reserve	90,000	1,20,000	Stock	70,000	93,000
Debentures	3,50,000	5,00,000	Debtors	63,000	24,000
Loan	2,30,000	70,000	Cash	55,000	74,000
Sundry Creditors	84,000	92,000	Salary paid in ad	17,000	39,000
Outstanding rent	11,000	5,000	Preliminary Exp.	50,000	40,000
Bank Overdraft	25,000	33,000	Profit & Loss A/c	90,000	–
	29,90,000	32,40,000		29,90,000	32,40,000

Prepare a Comparative Balance Sheet.

6. H Ltd. provided the Profit & Loss Account and Balance Sheet as on 31st March 2006 and 2007 as follows.

Profit & Loss Account

Particulars	*2006 Rs.*	*2007 Rs.*	*Particulars*	*2006 Rs.*	*2007 Rs.*
To Cost of Goods sold	15,60,000	17,10,000	By Sales	25,00,000	30,00,000
To Operating expenses:					
Administrative exp.	3,40,000	4,20,000			
Selling exp.	2,90,000	4,30,000			
To Net Profit	3,10,000	4,40,000			
	25,00,000	30,00,000		25,00,000	30,00,000

Balance Sheet

Particulars	*2006 Rs.*	*2007 Rs.*	*Particulars*	*2006 Rs.*	*2007 Rs.*
Equity Share Capital	7,00,000	7,00,000	Land	9,00,000	4,60,000
Preference Share Cap.	4,00,000	3,00,000	Building	5,00,000	6,50,000
Reserve & Surplus	4,25,000	5,90,000	Plant	7,85,000	9,70,000
Debentures	4,50,000	1,50,000	Stock	51,000	70,000
Loan	3,00,000	4,50,000	Debtors	47,000	73,000
Sundry Creditors	47,000	59,000	Cash	35,000	22,000
Bills Payable	15,000	21,000	Outstanding Int.	19,000	25,000
	23,37,000	22,70,000		23,37,000	22,70,000

Prepare a Comparative Profit & Loss Account and a Comparative Balance Sheet.

7. The following are the information related to Sales and Profit of N Ltd. Calculate the Trend Percentages by taking 2003 as base. Also interpret the result. *(Rs. in 000's)*

Year	*Sales*	*Stock*	*Profit Before Tax*
2003	7,300	700	720
2004	9,300	600	970
2005	10,000	900	1210
2006	9,500	1000	950
2007	12,000	400	1000

8. The Income Statement of Joyce Ltd. for 31st March 2006 and 2007 are stated as follows.

Particulars	*2006 Rs.*	*2007 Rs.*
Sales	50,00,000	40,00,000
Non-operating income (Dividend received)	2,00,000	1,70,000
	52,00,000	41,70,000
Expenses		
Cost of production	29,60,000	23,20,000

Administrative Expenses	9,50,000	7,90,000
Selling Expenses	4,00,000	3,70,000
Interest	3,90,000	2,50,000
Total Expenses	47,00,000	37,30,000
Net Profit	**5,00,000**	**4,40,000**

Also interpret the results.

9. Prepare a Common-size Income Statement for the following income statements of KT Ltd. for the year ended 31st March 2006 and 2007.

Income Statements as on 31st March 2006 and 2007

Particulars	*2006 Rs.*	*2007 Rs.*
Gross Sales	24,00,000	20,00,000
Less : Sales Return	90,000	50,000
Net Sales	23,10,000	19,50,000
Cost of Goods Sold	16,10,000	14,50,000
Gross Profit	7,00,000	5,00,000
Operating Expenses		
Administrative Expenses	1,90,000	1,10,000
Selling and Distribution Expenses	1,20,000	90,000
Total Expenses	3,10,000	2,00,000
Operating Income	3,90,000	3,00,000
Non-operating Income	60,000	50,000
Total Income	4,50,000	3,50,000
Non-operating expenses : Interest	1,50,000	1,30,000
Profit before tax	3,00,000	2,20,000
Less Tax	1,50,000	1,10,000
Net profit after tax	**1,50,000**	**1,10,000**

10. The Balance Sheet of H Ltd. and N Ltd. as on 31st March 2007 are stated as follows.

Particulars	*H Ltd. Rs.*	*N Ltd. Rs.*
Assets		
Cash	100,000	125,000
Sundry Creditors	47,000	73,000
Stock	57,000	97,000
Outstanding Income	35,000	29,000
Prepaid Expenses	31,000	26,000
Fixed Assets	12,00,000	14,00,000
Total Assets	14,70,000	17,50,000
Liabilities		
Sundry Creditors	65,000	45,000

Bill Payable	35,000	25,000
Long-term Loan	4,00,000	6,80,000
Capital	9,70,000	10,00,000
Total Liabilities	14,70,000	17,50,000

Prepare a common size Balance Sheet and interpret the result.

11. Prepare a Common size Balance Sheet of M Ltd. and W Ltd. from the Balance Sheets as on 31st March 2007.

Balance Sheets as on 31st March 2007

Particulars	*M Ltd. Rs.*	*W Ltd. Rs.*	*Particulars*	*M Ltd. Rs.*	*W Ltd. Rs.*
Equity Share Capital	13,00,000	15,00,000	Land & Building	11,00,000	10,00,000
Preference S.Capital	4,50,000	3,00,000	Plant & Machinery	9,00,000	11,00,000
Reserve & Surplus	2,70,000	3,14,000	Furniture & Fittings	5,00,000	6,40,000
Debenture	4,00,000	3,00,000	Stock	32,000	55,000
Loan	1,70,000	4,00,000	Debtors	56,000	35,000
Sundry Creditors	50,000	34,000	Cash	72,000	59,000
Bills Payable	27,000	20,000	Prepaid Exp.	40,000	21,000
Outstanding Salary	33,000	42,000			
	27,00,000	29,10,000		27,00,000	29,10,000

12. G Ltd. provided the balance sheets as on 31st March 2006 and 2007 as follows.

Balance Sheets

Particulars	*2006 Rs.*	*2007 Rs.*	*Particulars*	*2006 Rs.*	*2007 Rs.*
Equity Share Capital	20,00,000	22,00,000	Land & Building	10,50,000	12,00,000
Preference Sh. Cap.	4,00,000	2,00,000	Plant & Machinery	12,50,000	14,00,000
Profit & Loss A/c	–	1,00,000	Furniture & Fitting	3,45,000	3,50,000
General Reserve	70,000	1,40,000	Stock	90,000	73,000
Debentures	2,70,000	4,00,000	Debtors	43,000	50,000
Loan	1,30,000	90,000	Cash	60,000	70,000
Sundry Creditors	80,000	72,000	Salary paid in ad	12,000	46,000
Outstanding rent	15,000	9,000	Preliminary Exp.	40,000	51,000
Bank Overdraft	25,000	29,000	Profit & Loss A/c	1,00,000	–
	29,90,000	32,40,000		29,90,000	32,40,000

Prepare a Comparative Balance Sheet.

❑ ❑ ❑

3

RATIO ANALYSIS

The financial conditions and financial performance of companies are measured by companies through financial analysis. There are various methods for financial analysis. Ratio analysis is one of the important methods for financial analysis. It helps to find out whether the company is utilising the finance effectively. The financial strength of the company to meet the obligation of long term loan and the composition of the capital structure are also known through ratio analysis.

Meaning of Ratio

Ratio is the arithmetical expression of the relationship of two numbers. The two numbers may be related to the financial information of a company. There are so many financial information in a company which are interconnected. Hence, the value of one information is related to another financial information can be measured through ratio analysis. For example, the Net Profit and Capital Employed which are two financial information and from this, the rate of profit on capital employed can be measured. It may be measured in terms of percentage. In some cases it should be expressed in number of times. The relationship of stock and sales can be measured through the number of times the stock is converted into sales. Hence, the ratios may either be based on percentage basis or number of times basis.

Objectives of Ratio Analysis

The following are the important objectives of the Ratio Analysis:

1. Ratio analysis helps to measure the actual financial performance of a company. Hence, it is possible to compare it with the standard performance and to take corrective measures wherever needed.
2. It helps to find out the return on capital employed in order to compare the return of the industry.
3. The capital structure i.e., the ratio between Debt to Equity of a company is measured through Ratio Analysis.
4. It helps to find out the extent of utilisation of the long-term loans.
5. It helps for correcting the imbalance in the Debt to Equity in order to give a fair return on investment to the owners.

Advantages of Ratio Analysis

The advantages of Ratio Analysis are stated as follows:

1. Ratio analysis helps for financial planning and control.
2. It provides information to the owners and directors to take various managerial decisions.
3. It helps for measuring the financial performance of the company over a period of time.
4. The ratio of return on capital employed for different periods can be compared.
5. It is possible to make a comparison of the performance of various departments in the organisation, through ratio analysis.
6. The performance of the firm with other firms of the industry can be compared.
7. The overall efficiency and performance of the company can be improved through corrective actions with the help of different ratios.

Limitations of Ratio Analysis

The limitations of Ratio Analysis are stated as follows:

1. Ratios are based on financial statements.If the financial statements are not exhibiting the true and fair value, the ratio analysis will give false information.
2. The standard differs due to different environment.There may not be a commonly accepted standard to measure the performance.
3. Window dressing of Balance Sheet items may affect the very purpose of the Ratio Analysis.
4. The changes in price level may affect the perfection of ratios.
5. If the ratios are calculated through manipulation, then the comparison of it with that of the other firm of the industry may give wrong information to the management.

Classification of Ratios

The ratios are classified into many ways. It may be classified on the basis of the financial statements or on the basis of different activities (Common Classification).

I. Classification of ratios on the basis of Financial Statements

On the basis of financial statements, ratios may be classified as follows:

1. Profit and Loss Account Ratios: The following are the important Profit and Loss Account ratios:

(i) Gross Profit ratio
(ii) Net Profit ratio
(iii) Operating ratio
(iv) Operating Profit ratio
(v) Expenses ratio
  (a) Direct material cost to sales ratio
  (b) Direct labour cost to sales ratio
  (c) Factory overhead to sales ratio.

2. Balance Sheet Ratios: The following are the important Balance Sheet ratios:

(i) Current ratio
(ii) Quick ratio
(iii) Fixed Assets ratio
(iv) Capital Gearing ratio
(v) Debt to Equity ratio.

3. Profit and Loss Account and Balance Sheet Ratios: The following are the important Profit and Loss Account and Balance Sheet ratios:

(i) Return on Capital Employed
(ii) Return on Shareholder's Equity
(iii) Return on Equity Fund
(iv) Return on Total Assets
(v) Earnings per Share
(vi) Dividend per Share
(vii) Earnings Yield
(viii) Dividend Yield
(ix) Interest Coverage Ratio
(x) Dividend Coverage Ratio.

II. Common Classification of Ratios

Normally, the ratios are classified on the following basis:

1. Profitability Ratios
2. Turnover Ratios (Activity Ratios or Efficiency Ratios)
3. Liquidity Ratios
4. Leverage Ratios.

1. Profitability Ratios

Profitability ratios explain the strength of a company with respect to the effective utilisation of finance. It also explains the rate of return on the basis of sales. Hence, these ratios are classified as:

(a) Profitability ratios based on investments and
(b) Profitability ratios based on sales.

a. Profitability Ratios Based on Investments:

These ratios explain the return on different types of capital employed. The following are the different types of these ratios:

1. Return on Capital Employed Ratio: The ratio between the Total profit less tax and the Total capital employed is called return on capital employed ratio. Capital employed is the total of Debt and Equity

$$\text{Return on Capital Employed} = \frac{\text{EAT + Interest}}{\text{Total Capital Employed}}$$

(EAT = Earnings after tax)

2. Return on Shareholders Equity: It is a ratio between the Earnings after tax and Equity Shareholders Fund. Equity Shareholder Fund is otherwise called as Equity. It is the total of Equity Share Capital, Preference Share Capital and Reserves and Surplus. Fictitious Assets should be deducted from this total amount.

$$\text{Return on Shareholders Equity} = \frac{\text{EAT}}{\text{Equity}}$$

3. Return on Equity Fund: The ratio between earnings meant for Equity Shareholders and the Equity Shareholders Fund is called Return on Equity Fund. Equity Shareholders Fund is the difference between the Equity and the Preference Share Capital.

$$\text{Return on Equity Fund} = \frac{\text{EAT} \quad \text{Preference Dividend}}{\text{Equity Shareholders fund}}$$

4. Return on Total Assets: The ratio between the Profit, to the Total Assets is called Return on Total Assets ratio. The Profit excludes the tax and the Total Assets excludes the Fictitious Assets.

$$\text{Return on Total Assets} = \frac{\text{EAT + Interest}}{\text{Total Assets}}$$

5. Earnings per Share (EPS): Earnings per share is calculated by dividing the Earnings for the Equity Shareholders with the number of Equity Shares.

$$\text{Earnings per Share} = \frac{\text{EAT} \quad \text{Preference Dividend}}{\text{Number of Equity Shares}}$$

6. Dividend per Share (DPS): Dividend per Share is calculated by dividing the Dividend for Equity Shareholders with the number of Equity Shares.

$$\text{Dividend per Share} = \frac{\text{Dividend for Equity Shareholders}}{\text{Number of Equity Shares}}$$

7. Earnings Yield: Earnings yield is the ratio between Earnings per Share (EPS) and market price per Share.

$$\text{Earnings Yield} = \frac{\text{EPS}}{\text{Market Price per Share}}$$

8. Dividend Yield: The ratio between the Dividend per Share and the Market Price per Share is called Dividend Yield.

$$\text{Dividend Yield} = \frac{\text{DPS}}{\text{Market Price per Share}}$$

9. Price Earnings Ratio (P/E Ratio): It is the ratio between Market Price per Share and Earnings per Share.

$$\text{Price Earnings Ratio} = \frac{\text{Market Price per Share}}{\text{EPS}}$$

10. Dividend Payout Ratio (D/P Ratio): The ratio between the Dividend per Share and Earnings per Share is called Dividend Payout ratio.

$$\text{Dividend Payout Ratio} = \frac{\text{DPS}}{\text{EPS}}$$

11. Book Value per Share: Book value of a Share is calculated by dividing the Equity Shareholders Fund with the number of Equity Shares.

$$\text{Book value per Share} = \frac{\text{Equity Shareholders Fund}}{\text{Number of Equity Shares}}$$

b. Profitability Ratios Based on Sales

These ratios explain the rate of profit as well as different kinds of expenses to the sales. For calculating total sales, sales return should be deducted from it.The following are the different type of Profitability ratios based on Sales.

1. Gross Profit Ratio: This ratio is otherwise called as G..P. ratio. It is the ratio between the Gross Profit to Total Sales.

$$\text{Gross Profit Ratio} = \frac{\text{Gross Profit}}{\text{Sales}}$$

2. Net Profit Ratio: This ratio is otherwise called as N.P. ratio. Net profit ratios is the ratio between Net Profit and the Total Sales.

$$\text{Net profit ratio} = \frac{\text{Net Profit}}{\text{Sales}}$$

3. Operating Profit Ratio: The ratio between the Earnings before Interest and Tax (EBIT) and the Total Sales is called Operating Profit Ratio. Operating Profit is otherwise called as EBIT. It may be calculated by adding the interest and tax with the Net Profit.

$$\text{Operating Profit Ratio} = \frac{\text{EBIT (Operating Profit)}}{\text{Sales}}$$

4. Expense Ratio: Expense otherwise known as cost, is an important factor in the amount of Profit earned. Reduction in cost will improve the profit of a company. The expenses are classified as Cost of production and Operating expenses. Operating expenses include Administration expense and Selling expense. The expense ratios are based on sales. The different types of expenses are related with sales, to calculate the different expenses ratios. The different types of expenses ratios are stated as follows:

(i) **Cost of Goods Sold Ratio** $= \frac{\text{Cost of Goods Sold}}{\text{Sales}}$

Cost of goods sold = Opening stock + Purchases + Direct expenses - Closing stock

(or)

= Sales – Gross Profit or Sales + Gross Loss

(ii) **Administrative expenses ratio** $= \frac{\text{Administrative expenses}}{\text{Sales}}$

(iii) **Selling expenses ratio** $= \frac{\text{Selling Expenses}}{\text{Sales}}$

(iv) **Operating expenses ratio** $= \frac{\text{Operating expenses}}{\text{Sales}}$

Operating expenses = Administrative expenses + Selling expenses

(v) **Operating ratio** $= \frac{\text{Cost of Good sold + Operating expenses}}{\text{Sales}}$

2. Turnover Ratios

Turnover ratios are otherwise called as Activity ratios or Efficiency ratios. This ratios explain the efficiency of the company to utilise the resources for production and sales. These ratios are related with different types of investors, debtors, creditors and Working Capital. The important turnover ratio are explained as follows.

1. Stock Turnover Ratio: The ratios between the Cost of Goods sold and Average Stock is called Turnover Ratio. Cost of goods sold may also be used instead of sales to calculate this ratio. It explains the number of times the stock is converted into sales.

$$\text{Stock Turnover Ratio} = \frac{\text{Cost of Goods sold}}{\text{Average Stock}}$$

This ratio may also be calculated in three different types, since there are three different types of inventories (stock) i.e., Raw material, Work-in-progress and Stock of Finished Goods. It is calculated by substituting Average Stock of Raw material or Work-in-progress or Finished goods, in the place of Average Stock. The different types of Turnover Ratios are as follows.

(i) **Raw material turnover ratio** $= \dfrac{\text{Cost of Goods sold}}{\text{Average Stock of Raw Material}}$

(ii) **Work-in-progress turnover ratio** $= \dfrac{\text{Cost of Goods sold}}{\text{Average Stock of finished goods}}$

(iii) **Finished goods stock turnover ratio** $= \dfrac{\text{Cost of Goods sold}}{\text{Average Stock of finished goods}}$

Average Stock $= \dfrac{\text{Opening Stock + Closing Stock}}{2}$

2. Debtors Turnover Ratio: The ratio between credit sales and the average debtors is called Debtors Turnover ratio. The debtors should include Bills Receivable.

$$\text{Debtors Turnover ratio} = \frac{\text{Credit Sales}}{\text{Average Debtors}}$$

$$\text{Average Debtors} = \text{Operating Debtors + Closing Debtors}$$

3. Debt Collection Period: On the basis of the Debtors Turnover ratio average collection period can be calculated as follows:

$$\text{Debt collection period} = \frac{365}{\text{Debtors Turnover Ratio}}$$

$$\text{or} = \frac{12}{\text{Debtors Turnover Ratio}}$$

The first equation gives the collection period in number of days and the second one will give in number of months. If the period is leap year 366 should be used instead of 365.

4. Creditors Turnover Ratio: The ratio between credit purchase and the Average credit is called Creditors Turnover ratio. The creditor should includes the Bills Payable.

$$\text{Creditors Turnover Ratio} = \frac{\text{Credit purchase}}{\text{Average Creditors}}$$

$$\text{Average Creditors} = \frac{\text{Opening Creditors + Closing Creditors}}{2}$$

5. Credit Payment Period: On the basis of the Creditors Turnover ratio the average payment period for the creditors can be calculated as follows:

$$\text{Credit payment period} = \frac{365}{\text{Creditors Turnover Ratio}}$$

$$\text{or} = \frac{12}{\text{Creditors Turnover Ratio}}$$

The first equation gives the payment period in number of days and the second one gives in number of months. If the period is leap year 366 should be used instead of 365.

6. Assets Turnover Ratio: The ratio between sales and the average assets is called Assets Turnover ratio. Since the assets may be classified as Current Assets, Fixed Assets and Total Assets this ratio may be calculated in three different types. The ratio are calculated as follows:

(a) Current Assets Turnover ratio $= \dfrac{\text{Sales}}{\text{Average Current Assets}}$

(b) Fixed Assets Turnover ratio $= \dfrac{\text{Sales}}{\text{Average Fixed Assets}}$

(c) Total Assets Turnover ratio $= \dfrac{\text{Sales}}{\text{Average Total Assets}}$

Average assets $= \dfrac{\text{Opening balance of Assets + Closing balance of Assets}}{2}$

7. Working Capital Turnover Ratio: The ratio between sales and average Working Capital is called Working Capital Turnover Ratio. Working capital is the difference between Current Assets and Current Liabilities.

Working Capital Turnover ratio $= \dfrac{\text{Sales}}{\text{Average Working Capital}}$

3. Liquidity Ratios

The ability of a company to meet the short-term obligations is measured through liquidity ratios. These ratios are related to Current Assets and Current Liabilities. The liquidity ratios are calculated as follows:

1. Current Ratio: The ratio between the current assets and current liabilities is called current ratio.

Current ratio $= \dfrac{\text{Current Assets}}{\text{Current Liabilities}}$

2. Quick ratio (Acid Test ratio): The ratio between the Quick (liquid) Assets and Current Liabilities is called Quick ratio.

Quick ratio $= \dfrac{\text{Quick Assets}}{\text{Current Liabilities}}$

Quick assets = Current assets – stock – Outstanding income prepaid expenses

or = Cash + Bills receivable + Debtors

4. Leverage Ratios

This ratio is otherwise called as Capital Structure ratio. The long-term solvency of a company is measured through this ratios. This ratio measures the composition of capital with respect to the Own Capital and Borrowed Capital. It also helps to measure the ability of the company to repay the long-term loan and interest from the earnings. This ratio is classified as:

(a) Debt - Equity ratio

(b) Coverage ratios

(a) Debt - equity ratios

This ratio is based on liability. It measure the relationship of the Debt with different types of Capital employed. The important Debt - Equity ratios are stated as follows.

(i) **Debt - Equity ratio** $= \dfrac{\text{Debt}}{\text{Equity}}$

Debt = Debenture + Long - term loans

Equity = Equity Share Capital + Preference Share Capital + Reserves and Surpluses - Fictitious Assets

(ii) **Debt to Total Capital ratio** $= \dfrac{\text{Debt}}{\text{Capital employed}}$

Capital employed = Debt + Equity

(iii) **Debt to Total Assets ratio** $= \dfrac{\text{Debt}}{\text{Total Assets}}$

(iv) **Proprietory ratio** $= \dfrac{\text{Equity}}{\text{Total Assets}}$

(v) **Capital Gearing ratio** $= \dfrac{\text{Preference Share Capital + Debt}}{\text{Equity}}$

(b) Coverage Ratios

This ratios are based on income. It helps to find out the ability of a company to meet the interest on the Long-term loan, and the Preference dividend. It also explains the capacity of the company to repay the instalment of the loans in addition to the interest and Preference dividend. The following are the important Coverage ratios.

(i) **Interest Coverage ratio** $= \dfrac{\text{EBIT}}{\text{Interest}}$

(EBIT = Earnings before Interest and Tax)

(ii) **Dividend Coverage ratio** $= \dfrac{\text{Earnings after Tax (EAT)}}{\text{Preference Dividend}}$

(EAT excludes the interest also)

(iii) **Debt Service Coverage ratio** $= \dfrac{\text{EBIT}}{\text{Interest} + \dfrac{\text{Principal Payment Instalment}}{1 \quad \text{Tax Rate}}}$

Illustration: 1

Calculate Current ratio and Acid Test ratio from the following.

	Rs.		*Rs.*
Stock	42,000	Outstanding expenses	14,000
Debtors	39,000	Expenses paid in advance	11,000
Cash	27,000	Interest received in advance	9,000
Bills Receivable	17,000	Outstanding interest Receivables	7,000
Sundry Creditors	30,000		
Bills Payable	15,000		

Solution:

Current Assets = Stock + Debtors + Cash + Bills Receivable + Expenses paid in advance + Outstanding interest

= 42,000 + 39,000 + 27,000 + 17,000 + 11,000 + 7,000 = Rs. 1,43,000

Liquid Assets = Debtors + Cash + Bills Receivable

= 39,000 + 27,000 + 17,000 = Rs. 83,000

$$\text{Current Liabilities} = \text{Creditors} + \text{Bills Payable} + \text{Outstanding expenses} + \text{Interest received in advance}$$

$$= 30{,}000 + 15{,}000 + 14{,}000 + 9{,}000$$

$$= \text{Rs.}68{,}000$$

$$\text{Current Ratio} = \frac{\text{Current Assets}}{\text{Current Liabilities}} = \frac{1{,}43{,}000}{68{,}000} = 1 : 2.1$$

$$\text{Acid Test Ratio} = \frac{\text{Liquid Assets}}{\text{Current Liabilities}} = \frac{83{,}000}{68{,}000} = 1 : 1.2$$

Illustration: 2

Calculate (i) Gross Profit ratio (ii) Net Profit ratio (iii) Operating Profit ratio (iv) Cost of goods sold ratio from the following:

Sales Rs. 5,00,000, Cost of goods sold Rs. 2,80,000, Operating Expenses Rs.50,000, Interest Rs.30,000, Tax Rs. 40,000

Solution:

$$\text{Gross Profit} = \text{Sales} - \text{Cost of goods sold}$$

$$= 5{,}00{,}000 - 2{,}80{,}000 = \text{Rs. } 2{,}20{,}000$$

$$\text{Operating Profit} = \text{Gross Profit} - \text{Operating Expenses}$$

$$= 2{,}20{,}000 - 50{,}000 = \text{Rs.}1{,}70{,}000$$

$$\text{Net Profit} = \text{Operating Profit} - \text{Interest} - \text{Tax}$$

$$= 1{,}70{,}000 - 30{,}000 - 40{,}000 = \text{Rs.}1{,}00{,}000$$

$$\text{Gross Profit ratio} = \frac{\text{Gross Profit}}{\text{Sales}} \times 100 = \frac{2{,}20{,}000}{5{,}00{,}000} \times 100 = 44\%$$

$$\text{Operating Profit ratio} = \frac{\text{Operating Profit}}{\text{Sales}} \times 100 = \frac{1{,}70{,}000}{5{,}00{,}000} \times 100 = 34\%$$

$$\text{Net Profit ratio} = \frac{\text{Net Profit}}{\text{Sales}} \times 100 = \frac{1{,}00{,}000}{5{,}00{,}000} \times 100 = 20\%$$

$$\text{Cost of Good Sold ratio} = \frac{\text{Cost of Goods sold}}{\text{Sales}} \times 100 = \frac{2{,}80{,}000}{5{,}00{,}000} \times 100 = 56\%$$

Illustration: 3

K Ltd., is providing the following information as on 31st March 2007.

Sales Rs.7,00,00, Wages Rs.80,000, Other direct expenses Rs.20,000, Purchases Rs.2,00,000, Administration expenses Rs.50,000, Selling and distribution expenses Rs.40,000, Interest Rs.60,000, Tax @ 40%.

Calculate (i) Gross Profit Ratio (ii) Net Profit Ratio (iii) Operating Profit Ratio (iv) Cost of Sales of Goods Sold Ratio (v) Administration Expenses Ratio (vi) Selling Expenses Ratio (vii) Operating Expenses Ratio.

Solution:

Statement of Profit

Particulars	*Rs.*	*Rs.*
Sales		7,00,000
Cost of Good Sold		
Purchases	2,00,000	
Wages	80,000	
Other Direct Expenses	20,000	3,00,000
Gross Profit		4,00,000
Operating Expenses		
Administration Expenses	50,000	
Selling & Distribution Expenses	40,000	90,000
Profit before Interest and Tax (EBIT)		
(Operating Profit)		3,10,000
Less : Interest		60,000
Profit before Tax		2,50,000
Less : Tax @ 40%		1,00,000
Net Profit		1,50,000

(i) Gross Profit ratio $= \dfrac{\text{Gross Profit}}{\text{Sales}} \times 100 = \dfrac{4,00,000}{7,00,000} \times 100 = 57\%$

(ii) Net Profit ratio $= \dfrac{\text{Net Profit}}{\text{Sales}} \times 100 = \dfrac{1,50,000}{7,00,000} \times 100 = 21\%$

(iii) Operation ratio $= \dfrac{\text{Operating Profit}}{\text{Sales}} \times 100 = \dfrac{3,10,000}{7,00,000} \times 100 = 44\%$

(iv) Cost of Good Sold Ratio $= \dfrac{\text{Cost of Goods Sold}}{\text{Sales}} \times 100 = \dfrac{3,00,000}{7,00,000} \times 100 = 43\%$

(v) Admn. Expenses Ratio $= \dfrac{\text{Administration Expenses}}{\text{Sales}} \times 100 = \dfrac{50,000}{7,00,000} \times 100 = 7\%$

(vi) Selling Expenses Ratio $= \dfrac{\text{Selling Expenses}}{\text{Sales}} \times 100 = \dfrac{40,000}{7,00,000} \times 100 = 6\%$

(vii) Operating Expenses Ratio $= \dfrac{\text{Operating Expenses}}{\text{Sales}} \times 100 = \dfrac{3,90,000}{7,00,000} \times 100 = 56\%$

Illustration: 4

Calculate (i) Return on Capital Employed (ii) Return on Shareholders Equity and (iii) Return on Equity Fund from the following.

	Rs.
Net Profit before Interest and Tax	2,10,000
Interest	50,000
Capital Employed	12,00,000

Debt	3,00,000
10% Preference Share Capital	2,00,000
Tax 50%	

Solution:

Calculations:

	Rs.
Net Profit before Interest and Tax	2,10,000
Less : Interest	50,000
	1,60,000
Less : Tax @ 50%	80,000
Profit after Tax	80,000
Capital Employed	12,00,000
Less : Debt	3,00,000
Equity (Shareholders Fund)	9,00,000
Less : Preference Share Capital	2,00,000
Equity Fund (Equity Shareholders Fund)	7,00,000

Calculation of ratios

(i) Return on Capital Employed $= \frac{\text{EAT + Interest}}{\text{Capital Employed}} = \frac{80,000 + 50,000}{12,00,000} \times 100 = 11\%$

(ii) Return on Shareholders Equity $= \frac{\text{EAT}}{\text{Equity}} = \frac{80,000}{9,00,000} \times 100 = 9\%$

(iii) Return on Equity Fund $= \frac{\text{EAT} \quad \text{Preference dividend}}{\text{Equity Fund}} = \frac{80,000 \quad 20,000}{7,00,000} \times 100 = 10\%$

Illustration: 5

D Ltd., is providing the following information as on 31st March 2007.

	Rs.
Capital Employed	25,00,000
Equity Share Capital (of nominal value @ Rs.10)	12,00,000
10% Preference Share Capital	4,00,000
16% Debentures	3,00,000
Long-term Loan	2,00,000
Earning after Tax	2,40,000
Interest on Long-term Loan 15%	
Market price of the Equity Share is @ Rs.40	
Corporate Tax @ 40%	

Calculate the following ratios:

(i) Return on Capital Employed (ii) Return on Equity (iii) Return on Equity Shareholders Fund (iv) Earnings per Share (v) Earnings Yield (vi) Price Earning ratio. Also calculate EBIT

Solution:

		Rs.
a. Capital employed		25,00,000
Less : Debt - Debenture	3,00,000	
Long term Loan	2,00,000	5,00,000
Equity		20,00,000
Less : Preference Share Capital		4,00,000
Equity Shareholders Fund		**16,00,000**
b. Earnings after Tax (EAT)		2,40,000
Add : Tax		1,60,000
Earnings before Tax (EBT)		4,00,000
Add : Interest Debenture	48,000	
Loan	30,000	78,000
Earnings before Interest and Tax (EBIT)		4,78,000

Calculation of Ratios

(i) Return on Capital Employed

$$\frac{\text{EAT + Interest}}{\text{Capital Employed}} \times 100 = \frac{2{,}40{,}000 + 78{,}000}{25{,}00{,}000} \times 100 = 13\%$$

(ii) Return on Equity

$$\frac{\text{EAT}}{\text{Equity}} \times 100 = \frac{2{,}40{,}000}{20{,}00{,}000} \times 100 = 12\%$$

(iii) Return on Equity Shareholders Fund

$$\frac{\text{EAT} \quad \text{Preference Dividend}}{\text{Equity Shareholders Fund}} \times 100 = \frac{2{,}40{,}000 \quad 40{,}000}{16{,}00{,}000} \times 100 = 12.5\%$$

(iv) Earnings per Share (EPS)

$$\frac{\text{EAT} \quad \text{Preference Dividend}}{\text{Number of Equity Shares}} \times 100 = \frac{2{,}40{,}000 \quad 40{,}000}{1{,}20{,}000} = \text{Rs. } 1.67$$

(v) Earnings Yield

$$\frac{\text{EAT}}{\text{Market Price per Share}} \times 100 = \frac{1.67}{40} = 0.042$$

(vi) Price earning ratio (P/E/ ratio)

$$\frac{\text{Market Price per Share}}{\text{EPS}} = \frac{40}{1.67} = \text{Rs.}23.95$$

Illustration: 6

Calculate (i) Return on Equity (ii) Return on Equity Shareholders Fund (iii) EPS (iv) DPS (v) Earnings Yield (vi) Dividend Yield (vii) Dividend Payout ratio (viii) P/E ratio (ix) Book value per Share from the following.

Equity Rs.20,00,000, Equity Share Capital Rs.15,00,000, 10% Preference Share Capital Rs.3,00,000, PAT Rs.3,00,000. Nominal value of Equity Share Rs.10, Dividend for Equity Shareholders @ 8%, Market price per Equity Share Rs.50.

Solution:

Calculation of ratios

(i) Return on Equity $= \frac{\text{EAT}}{\text{Equity}} = \frac{3{,}00{,}000}{20{,}00{,}000} \times 100 = 15\%$

(ii) Return on Equity Shareholders Fund

$$\frac{\text{EAT} \quad \text{Preference Dividend}}{\text{Equity Shareholder Fund}} = \frac{3{,}00{,}000 \quad 30{,}000}{20{,}00{,}000 \quad 3{,}00{,}000} \times 100 = \frac{2{,}70{,}000}{17{,}00{,}000} \times 100 = 15.88\%$$

(iii) Earnings per Share (EPS) =

$$\frac{\text{EAT} \quad \text{Preference Dividend}}{\text{Number of Equity Shares}} = \frac{3{,}00{,}000 \quad 30{,}000}{1{,}50{,}000} = \text{Rs. } 1.80$$

(iv) Dividend per Share (DPS) =

$$\frac{\text{Dividend for Equity Shareholders}}{\text{Number of Equity Shares}} = \frac{15{,}00{,}000}{1{,}50{,}000} \times 8\% = \frac{1{,}20{,}000}{1{,}50{,}000} = \text{Rs. } 0.80$$

(v) Earnings Yield $= \frac{\text{EPS}}{\text{Market Price per Shares}} = \frac{1.80}{50} = 0.036$

(vi) Dividend Yield $= \frac{\text{DPS}}{\text{Market Price per Shares}} = \frac{0.80}{50} = 0.016$

(vii) Dividend Payout ratio (D/P ratio) $= \frac{\text{DPS}}{\text{EPS}} = \frac{0.80}{1.80} = 0.44$

(viii) Price Earning ratio (P/E ratio) $= \frac{\text{Market Price per Share}}{\text{EPS}} = \frac{50}{1.80} = 27.78$

(ix) Book value per share $= \frac{\text{Equity Shareholders Funds}}{\text{Number of Equity Shares}} = \frac{17{,}00{,}000}{1{,}50{,}000} = \text{Rs. } 11.33$

Illustration: 7

Calculate (i) Stock Turnover ratio (ii) Debtors Turnover ratio (iii) Average Collection period (iv) Creditors Turnover ratio (v) Average Payment period from the following information

	As on 31st March 2006 (Rs.)	*As on 31st March 2007 (Rs.)*
Stock	1,20,000	1,50,000
Debtors	80,000	60,000
Creditors	40,000	50,000

Sales for the year Rs.10,00,000, Purchase for the year Rs. 5,00,000, Cost of goods sold Rs. 6,00,000. Assume the Sales and Purchase as for credit.

Solution:

$$\text{Average Stock} = \frac{\text{Opening Stock + Closing Stock}}{2} = \frac{1,20,000 + 1,50,000}{2} = \text{Rs. } 1,35,000$$

$$\text{Average Debtors} = \frac{\text{Opening Debtor + Closing Debtors}}{2} = \frac{80,000 + 60,000}{2} = \text{Rs. } 70,000$$

$$\text{Average Creditors} = \frac{\text{Opening Creditors + Closing Creditors}}{2} = \frac{40,000 + 50,000}{2} = \text{Rs. } 45,000$$

$$\text{(i) Stock Turnover ratio} = \frac{\text{Cost of Goods Sold}}{\text{Average Stock}} = \frac{6,00,000}{1,35,000} = 4.44 \text{ times}$$

$$\text{(ii) Debtor's Turnover ratio} = \frac{\text{Credit Sales}}{\text{Average Debtors}} = \frac{10,00,000}{70,000} = 14.29 \text{ times}$$

$$\text{(iii) Average Collection period} = \frac{365}{\text{Debtors Turnover Ratio}} = \frac{365}{14.29} = 26 \text{ days}$$

$$\text{(iv) Creditors Turnover ratio} = \frac{\text{Credit Purchase}}{\text{Average Creditors}} = \frac{5,00,000}{45,000} = 11.11 \text{ times}$$

$$\text{(v) Average Payment Period} = \frac{365}{\text{Creditors Turnover ratio}} = \frac{365}{11.11} = 33 \text{ days}$$

Illustration: 8

M. Ltd is providing the following information as on 31st March 2007.

Fixed Assets Rs. 12,00,000, Stock Rs.1,50,000 Debtors Rs. 60,000, Creditors Rs.80,000, Cash Rs.1,10,00, Sales Rs. 8,00,000. (Rs. 6,00,000 for credit) Purchase Rs. 5,00,000 (80% on credit) Cost of goods sold Rs. 7,00,000.

Calculate

(i) Stock Turnover ratio (ii) Debtors Turnover ratio (iii) Creditors Turnover ratio (iv) Fixed Assets Turnover ratio (v) Current Assets Turnover ratio (vi) Working Capital Turnover ratio (vii) Average Collection period (viii) Average Payment period (ix) Total Assets Turnover ratio.

Solution:

$$\text{Current Assets} = \text{Stock + Debtors + Cash}$$
$$= 1,50,000 + 60,000 + 1,10,000 = \text{Rs. } 3,20,000$$

$$\text{Current Liabilities} = \text{Creditor} = \text{Rs. } 80,000$$

$$\text{Working Capital} = \text{Current Assets} - \text{Current Liabilities}$$
$$= 3,20,000 - 80,000 = \text{Rs.}2,40,000$$

$$\text{Total assets} = \text{Fixed Assets + Current Assets}$$
$$= 12,00,000 + 3,20,000 = \text{Rs.}15,20,000$$

$$\text{(i) Stock Turnover ratio} = \frac{\text{Cost of Goods Sold}}{\text{Average Stock}} = \frac{7,00,000}{1,50,000} = 4.67 \text{ times}$$

$$\text{(ii) Debtors Turnover ratio} = \frac{\text{Credit Sales}}{\text{Average Debtors}} = \frac{6,00,000}{60,000} = 10 \text{ times}$$

(iii) Creditors Turnover ratio $= \dfrac{\text{Credit Purchase}}{\text{Average Creditors}} = \dfrac{4,00,000}{80,000} = 5$ times

(iv) Fixed Assets Turnover ratio $= \dfrac{\text{Sales}}{\text{Fixed Assets}} = \dfrac{8,00,000}{12,00,000} = 0.67$ times

(v) Current Assets Turnover ratio $= \dfrac{\text{Sales}}{\text{Current Assets}} = \dfrac{8,00,000}{3,20,000} = 2.5$ times

(vi) Working Capital Turnover ratio $= \dfrac{\text{Sales}}{\text{Working Capital}} = \dfrac{8,00,000}{2,40,000} = 3.3$ times

(vii) Average Collection Period $= \dfrac{365}{\text{Debtors Turnover ratio}} = \dfrac{365}{10} = 37$ days

(viii) Average Payment Period $= \dfrac{365}{\text{Creditors Turnover ratio}} = \dfrac{365}{5} = 73$ days

(ix) Total Assets Turnover ratio $= \dfrac{\text{Sales}}{\text{Total Assets}} = \dfrac{8,00,000}{15,20,000} = 0.53$ times

[*Note:* Since opening balances of Stock, Debtors and Creditors are not given the average values are not calculated. The calculation may also be done by taking the values of opening balances as zero].

Illustration: 9

G Ltd., provides the following information as on 31st March 2007.

Equity Share Capital Rs.20,00,000, Preference Share Capital Rs. 4,00,000, Profit and Loss Account Rs. 3,00,000, General Reserve Rs. 40,000, Debentures Rs.2,00,000, Long term Loan Rs. 1,00,000, Sundry Creditors Rs.60,000, Total Assets Rs.31,00,000.

Calculate

(i) Debt to Equity ratio (ii) Debt to Total Capital ratio (iii) Debt to Total Assets ratio (iv) Proprietory ratio and (v) Capital Gearing ratio.

Solution:

Equity = Equity Share Capital + Preference Share Capital + Profit & Loss Account + General Reserve

= 20,00,000 + 4,00,000 + 3,00,000 + 40.000

= Rs. 27,40,000

Debt = Debentures + Long term Loan

= 2,00,000 + 1,00,000 = Rs. 3,00,000

Capital Employed = Debt + Equity = 27,40,000 + 3,00,000

= Rs.30,40,000

(i) Debt to Equity ratio $= \dfrac{\text{Debt}}{\text{Equity}} = \dfrac{3,00,000}{27,40,000} = 0.109$

(ii) Debt to Total Capital ratio $= \dfrac{\text{Debt}}{\text{Total Capital employed}} = \dfrac{3,00,000}{30,40,000} = 0.099$

(iii) Debt to Total Assets ratio $= \dfrac{\text{Debt}}{\text{Total Assets}} = \dfrac{3,00,000}{31,00,000} = 0.097$

(iv) Proprietory ratio $= \dfrac{\text{Equity}}{\text{Total Assets}} = \dfrac{27,40,000}{31,00,000} = 0.88$

(v) Capital Gearing ratio $= \frac{\text{Preference Share Capital} + \text{Debt}}{\text{Equity}} = \frac{4,00,000 + 3,00,000}{27,40,000} = 0.26$

Illustration: 10

Calculate

(i) Debt - Equity ratio

(ii) Debt to Total Capital ratio from the following.

Equity Rs. 5,00,000; Debt Rs. 2,00,000

Solution:

(i) Debt to Equity ratio $= \frac{\text{Debt}}{\text{Equity}} = \frac{2,00,000}{5,00,000} = 0.4$

(ii) Debt to Total Capital Ratio $= \frac{\text{Debt}}{\text{Debt} + \text{Equity}} = \frac{2,00,000}{2,00,000 + 5,00,000} = 0.29$

Illustration: 11

Calculate (i) Debt to Equity ratio (ii) Debt to Total Capital Ratio (iii) Proprietory ratio (iv) Capital gearing ratio from the following.

Total Equity excluding Preference Share Capital Rs.22,00,000; Preference Share Capital Rs.3,00,000, Debenture Rs.5,00,000; Long Term Loan Rs.2,00,000 Sundry Creditors Rs.50,000.

Solution:

Equity = 22,00,000 + 3,00,000 = Rs.25,00,000

Debt = Debenture + Loan = 5,00,000 + 2,00,000

= Rs.7,00,000

Capital employed = Debt + Equity = 25,00,000 + 7,00,000

= Rs.32,00,000

Total assets = 32,00,000 + 50,000 = Rs.32,50,000

(i) Debt to Equity ratio $= \frac{\text{Debt}}{\text{Equity}} = \frac{7,00,000}{25,00,000} = 0.28$

(ii) Debt to Total Capital ratio $= \frac{\text{Debt}}{\text{Capital Employed}} = \frac{7,00,000}{32,00,000} = 0.22$

(iii) Proprietory ratio $= \frac{\text{Equity}}{\text{Total Assets}} = \frac{25,00,000}{32,50,000} = 0.77$

(iv) Capital Gearing ratio =

$\frac{\text{Preference Share Capital} + \text{Debt}}{\text{Equity}} = \frac{3,00,000 + 7,00,000}{25,00,000} = \frac{10,00,000}{25,00,000} = 0.4$

Illustration: 12

The Balance Sheet of KY Ltd., for the year ended 31st March 2007 is stated as follows

Balance Sheet

Liabilities	*Rs.*	*Assets*	*Rs.*
Equity. Share Capital	7,00,000	Goodwill	1,70,000
Profit & Loss A/c	2,10,000	Land	4,50,000

General Reserve	1,20,000	Premises	3,50,000
10% Debentures	2,00,000	Plant	2,00,000
12% Loan	1,00,000	Furniture & Fittings	50,000
Tax		Stock	80,000
Last year	30,000	Debtors	65,000
Current year	20,000	Cash	85,000
Sundry Creditors	70,000	Preliminary Expenses	30,000
Outstanding Expenses	30,000		
	14,80,000		14,80,000

The interest for Debentures and Loan for the current year are paid. Calculate ratios for (i) Testing Liquidity and (ii) Testing Solvency.

Solution:

Current Assets = Stock + Debtors + Cash

= 80,000 + 65,000 + 85,000 = Rs.2,30,000

Liquid Assets = Debtors + Cash

= 65,000 + 85,000 = Rs. 1,50,000

Current Liabilities = Sundry creditors + Outstanding expenses

= 70,000 + 30,000 = Rs.1,00,000

Fixed Assets = Land + Premises + Plant + Furniture & Fittings

= 4,50,000 + 3,50,000 + 2,00,000 + 50,000

= Rs. 10,50,000

Shareholders Fund (Equity) = Equity Share Capital + Profit & Loss A/c + General Reserve - Goodwill - Preliminary Expenses

= 7,00,000 + 2,10,000 + 1,20,000 – 1,70,000 – 30,000

= Rs. 8,30,000

Debt = Debentures + Loan + Provision for Taxation for next year

= 2,00,000 + 1,00,000 + 20,000

= Rs.3,20,000

Capital Employed = Shareholders Fund + Debt

= 8,30,000 + 3,20,000

= Rs.11,50,000

(i) Calculation of Liquidity Ratios

$$\text{(a) Current ratio} = \frac{\text{Current Assets}}{\text{Current Liabilities}} = \frac{2,30,000}{1,00,000} = 2.3$$

$$\text{(b) Quick ratio} = \frac{\text{Liquid Assets}}{\text{Current Liabilities}} = \frac{1,50,000}{1,00,000} = 1.5$$

(ii) Calculation of Solvency ratios

$$\text{(a) Debt to Equity ratio} = \frac{\text{Debt}}{\text{Equity}} = \frac{3,20,000}{8,30,000} = 0.39$$

(b) Fixed Assets ratio $= \dfrac{\text{Fixed Assets}}{\text{Capital employed}} = \dfrac{10{,}50{,}000}{11{,}50{,}000} = 0.91$

(c) Interest cover $= \dfrac{\text{Net profit before Interest and Tax}}{\text{Interest}} =$

$$\frac{2{,}10{,}000 + 20{,}000 + 12{,}000 + 20{,}000}{20{,}000 + 12{,}000} = 8.19$$

Illustration: 13

Calculate equity ratio and interest cover from the following.

Equity Share Capital Rs. 21,00,000; Preference share capital Rs. 4,00,000; General Reserve Rs.2,40,000; Preliminary expenses Rs. 40,000; Net Profit before Interest and Tax Rs. 3,00,000. Interest Rs.60,000; Debenture Rs. 5,00,000; Loan Rs. 4,00,000; Tax Rs. 1,00,000.

Solution :

(i) Debt to Equity ratio $= \dfrac{\text{Debt}}{\text{Equity}} = \dfrac{10{,}00{,}000}{28{,}40{,}000} = 0.35$

(ii) Interest Cover $= \dfrac{\text{Net Profit before Interest and Tax}}{\text{Interest}}$

$$= \frac{3{,}00{,}000}{60{,}000} = 5$$

Equity = Equity Share Capital + General Reserve + N.P after tax – Preliminary expenses

= 21,00,000 + 4,00,000 + 2,40,000 + (3,00,000 – 1,00,000 – 60,000) – 40,000 = Rs. 28,40,000

Illustration: 14

Prepare a comparative statement of the Liquidity, Profitability, Activity and Financial position (Solvency) ratios of K Ltd. and M Ltd., for the year ended 31st March 2007 from the following.

Particulars	*K Ltd. (Rs.)*	*M Ltd. (Rs.)*
Fixed Assets	7,50,000	10,00,000
Stock	1,20,000	1,00,000
Debtors	80,000	75,000
Cash	50,000	65,000
Sales	12,00,000	15,00,000
Net Profit after tax	2,50,000	2,70,000
Equity Share Capital	5,00,000	7,00,000
General Reserve	70,000	50,000
Debenture	2,00,000	3,00,000
Long-term loan	1,00,000	1,40,000
Bank overdraft	50,000	30,000
Creditors	80,000	20,000
Cost of Sales	10,00,000	13,00,000

Solution:

Statement of Comparative Ratios

Ratios	*K. Ltd.*	*M. Ltd.*
1. Liquidity Ratios		
(i) Current ratio (CA/CL)	$\frac{2,50,000}{1,30,000} = 1.92$	$\frac{2,40,000}{50,000} = 4.8$
(ii) Quick ratio (LA/CL)	$\frac{1,30,000}{1,30,000} = 1$	$\frac{1,40,000}{50,000} = 2.8$
2. Profitability ratios		
(i) Net Profit ratio (N.P / Sales)	$\frac{2,50,000}{12,00,000} \times 100 = 20.83\%$	$\frac{2,70,000}{15,00,000} \times 100 = 18\%$
(ii) Return on Total Assets (N.P / Total Assets)	$\frac{2,50,000}{10,00,000} \times 100 = 25\%$	$\frac{2,70,000}{12,40,000} \times 100 = 21.77\%$
(iii) Return on Equity (N.P/Equity)	$\frac{2,50,000}{5,70,000} \times 100 = 43.86\%$	$\frac{2,70,000}{7,50,000} \times 100 = 36\%$
(iv) EPS (NP No. of Equity Shares)	$\frac{2,50,000}{50,000} =$ Rs. 5	$\frac{2,70,000}{70,000} =$ Rs. 3.86
3. Activity Ratios		
(i) Stock Turnover ratio (Cost of Sales / Average stock)	$\frac{10,00,000}{1,20,000} = 8.3$ times	$\frac{13,00,000}{1,00,000} = 13$ times
(ii) Fixed Assets Turnover ratio (Sales / Fixed Assets)	$\frac{12,00,000}{7,50,000} = 1.6$ times	$\frac{15,00,000}{10,00,000} = 1.5$ times
(iii) Current Assets Turnover ratio (Sales / Current Assets)	$\frac{12,00,000}{2,50,000} = 4.8$ times	$\frac{15,00,000}{2,40,000} = 6.25$ times
(iv) Total Assets Turnover ratio (Sale / Total Assets)	$\frac{12,00,000}{10,00,000} = 1.2$ times	$\frac{15,00,000}{12,40,000} = 1.21$ times
4. Solvency Ratios		
(i) Debt-Equity ratio (Debt / Equity)	$\frac{3,00,000}{5,70,000} = 0.53$ times	$\frac{4,40,000}{7,50,000} = 0.59$ times
(ii) Debt to Total Capital ratio (Debt /Capital Emp.)	$\frac{3,00,000}{8,70,000} = 0.34$ times	$\frac{4,40,000}{11,90,000} = 0.37$ times

Illustration: 15

The financial statements of KM Ltd for three years are stated as follows.

Balance Sheets

Particulars	*2005 Rs.*	*2006 Rs.*	*2007 Rs.*
Land & Building	5,50,000	6,10,000	5,90,000
Plant & Machinery	4,20,000	4,00,000	3,50,000
Stock	1,40,000	1,00,000	1,10,000
Debtors	75,000	85,000	65,000

Cash	55,000	65,000	45,000
Prepaid expenses	10,000	20,000	10,000
Preliminary expenses	50,000	40,000	30,000
Total Assets	**13,00,000**	**13,20,000**	**12,00,000**
Equity Share Capital	5,00,000	5,00,000	6,00,000
Preference Share Capital	1,00,000	1,00,000	1,00,000
Profit & Loss a/c	1,70,000	1,50,000	1,60,000
General Reserve	60,000	50,000	50,000
Debentures	2,00,000	1,50,000	1,50,000
Long term Loan	1,50,000	2,60,000	50,000
Provision for Tax	40,000	30,000	30,000
Creditors	60,000	70,000	50,000
Outstanding expenses	20,000	10,000	10,000
Total Liabilities	**13,00,000**	**13,20,000**	**12,00,000**

Operating Statement

Particulars	*2005 Rs.*	*2006 Rs.*	*2007 Rs.*
Sales	4,10,000	3,80,000	5,40,000
Cost of sales	2,90,000	2,70,000	3,10,000
Gross Profit	1,20,000	1,10,000	2,30,000
Operating expenses (General expenses and selling expenses)	50,000	35,000	1,50,000
Net Profit	70,000	75,000	80,000

The following additional information are also provided.

(i) Credit sales is considered to be 50% of total sales.

(ii) The closing stock, closing debtors and closing creditors as on 31st March 2004 are Rs.90,000, Rs.60,000 and Rs.40,000 respectively.

(iii) Credit purchase is 80% of cost of sales.

Calculate

(i) Stock Turnover ratio (ii) Debtors Turnover ratio (iii) Average Collection period, (iv) Creditors Turnover ratio (v) Average Payment period (vi) Current ratio (vii) Acid Test ratio (viii) Gross Profit ratio (ix) Net Profit ratio (x) Fixed Assets to Shareholders Equity ratio (xi) Debt-Equity ratio (xii) Return on Capital Employed ratio.

Solution:

Calculation of Ratios as on 31st March

Ratios	*2005*	*2006*	*2007*
(i) Stock Turnover ratio (Cost of Sales / Average Stock)	$\frac{2,90,000}{1,15,000}$ = 2.52 times	$\frac{2,70,000}{1,20,000}$ = 2.25 times	$\frac{3,10,000}{1,05,000}$ = 2.95 times

(ii) Debtors Turnover ratio (Credit Sales / Avg. Debtors)	$\frac{2,05,000}{67,500}$ = 3.04 times	$\frac{1,90,000}{80,000}$ = 2.38 times	$\frac{2,70,000}{75,000}$ = 3.6 times
(iii) Average Collection period (365/Debtors turnover)	$\frac{365}{3.04}$ = 120 days	$\frac{365}{2.38}$ = 153 days	$\frac{365}{3.6}$ = 101 days
(iv) Creditors Turnover ratio (Credit Purchase / Creditors)	$\frac{2,32,000}{50,000}$ = 4.64 times	$\frac{2,16,000}{65,000}$ = 3.32 times	$\frac{2,48,000}{60,000}$ = 4.13 times
(v) Average Payment period (365/Creditors turnover period)	$\frac{365}{4.64}$ = 79 days	$\frac{365}{3.32}$ = 110 days	$\frac{365}{4.13}$ = 88 days
(vi) Current Ratio Current Assets / Current Liabilities	$\frac{2,80,000}{80,000}$ = 3.5	$\frac{2,70,000}{80,000}$ = 3.38	$\frac{2,30,000}{60,000}$ = 3.83
(vii) Acid Test Ratio (Quick Assets / Current Liabilities)	$\frac{1,30,000}{80,000}$ = 1.63	$\frac{1,50,000}{80,000}$ = 1.88	$\frac{1,10,000}{60,000}$ = 1.833
(viii) Gross Profit Ratio (Gross Profit / Sales) × 100	$\frac{1,20,000}{41,000}$ × 100 = 29%	$\frac{1,10,000}{3,80,000}$ × 100 = 29%	$\frac{2,30,000}{5,40,000}$ × 100 = 43%
(ix) Gross Profit Ratio (Gross Profit / Sales) × 100	$\frac{70,000}{4,10,000}$ × 100 = 17.07%	$\frac{75,000}{3,80,000}$ × 100 = 19.74%	$\frac{80,000}{5,40,000}$ × 100 = 14.81%
(x) Fixed Assets to Shareholders Equity ratio (Fixed Assets / Shareholders Funds)	$\frac{9,70,000}{7,80,000}$ = 1.24	$\frac{10,10,000}{7,60,000}$ = 1.33	$\frac{9,40,000}{8,80,000}$ = 1.07
(xi) Debt to Equity ratio (Debt / Equity)	$\frac{3,50,000}{7,80,000}$ = 0.45	$\frac{4,10,000}{7,60,000}$ = 0.54	$\frac{2,00,000}{8,80,000}$ = 0.23
(xii) Return on Capital employed (N.P / Capital employed) × 100	$\frac{70,000}{11,30,000}$ × 100 = 6.19%	$\frac{75,000}{11,70,000}$ × 100 = 6.41%	$\frac{80,000}{10,80,000}$ × 100 = 7.4%

Illustration: 16

KMW Ltd., provided the Profit & Loss Account and Balance Sheet for the year ended 31st March 2007 as follows.

Profit and Loss Account

Particulars	*Rs.*	*Particulars*	*Rs.*
To Op. Stock of Raw material	40,000	By Sales	11,91,000
To Op. Stock of Finished goods	70,000	By Cl.Stock of Raw materials	80,000
To Purchase of Raw materials	6,00,000	By Cl.Stock of Finished goods	90,000
To Direct Wages	1,40,000	By Profit on sale of Shares	65,000
To Manufacturing expenses	90,000		
To Administration Expenses	80,000		
To Selling and Distribution exp.	60,000		

To Loss on sale of Plant	45,000		
To Int. on Debentures and Loan	51,000		
To Net Profit	2,50,000		
	14,26,000		14,26,000

Balance Sheet

Liabilities	*Rs.*	*Assets*	*Rs.*
Equity Share Capital	5,00,000	Fixed Assets	12,40,000
Preference Share Capital	1,00,000	Stock of Raw materials	80,000
Profit & Loss Account	1,25,000	Stock of Finished goods	90,000
General Reserve	1,80,000	Sundry Debtors	75,000
Debentures (12%)	3,00,000	Bills Receivable	20,000
Loan (15%)	1,00,000	Cash	45,000
Sundry Creditors	80,000		
Bills Payable	40,000		
Provision for Tax	1,25,000		
	15,50,000		15,50,000

Calculate (i) Gross Profit ratio (ii) Net Profit ratio (iii) Operating Profit ratio (iv) Overall Profitability ratio (v) Current ratio (vi) Debt to Equity ratio (vii) Stock Turnover ratio (viii) Liquid ratio.

Solution:

(a) Gross Profit = Sales - Cost of Goods Sold

Cost of goods sold = Op.Stock + Purchase + Wages + Manufacturing expenses - Closing Stock

= (40,000+70,000) + 6,00,000 + 1,40,000 + 90,000 – (80,000 + 90,000) = Rs.7,70,000

Gross Profit = 11,91,000 – 7,70,000 = Rs.4,21,000

(b) Operating Profit = Gross Profit – Operating expenses

= 4,21,000 - (80,000 + 60,000) = Rs.2,81,000

(c) Net Profit after Tax = Net Profit before Tax - Tax

= 2,50,000 – 1,25,000 = Rs.1,25,000

(d) Current Assets = Stock + Debtors + Bills Receivable + Cash

= 80,000 + 90,000 + 75,000 + 20,000 + 45,000

= Rs.3,10,000

(e) Liquid Assets = Debtors + Bills Receivable + Cash

= 75,000 + 20,000 + 45,000 = Rs.1,40,000

(f) Current Liabilities = Sundry Creditors + Bills Payable + Provision for Tax

= 80,000 + 40,000 + 1,25,000 = Rs.2,45,000

(g) Average Stock $= \frac{\text{Op.Stock + Cl.Stock}}{2}$

$= \frac{(40{,}000 + 70{,}000) + (80{,}000 + 90{,}000)}{2} = \text{Rs. } 1{,}40{,}000$

Average Raw material $= \frac{40{,}000 + 80{,}000}{2} = \text{Rs. } 60{,}000$

Average Finished goods $= \frac{70{,}000 + 90{,}000}{2} = \text{Rs. } 80{,}000$

(h) Debt $= 3{,}00{,}000 + 1{,}00{,}000 = \text{Rs.}4{,}00{,}000$

Equity $= 5{,}00{,}000 + 1{,}00{,}00 + 1{,}25{,}000 + 1{,}80{,}000$

$= \text{Rs. } 9{,}05{,}000$

Capital Employed $= \text{Debt + Equity}$

$= 4{,}00{,}000 + 9{,}05{,}000 = \text{Rs.}13{,}05{,}000$

Calculation of ratios:

(i) Gross Profit ratio $= \frac{\text{Gross Profit}}{\text{Sales}} \times 100 = \frac{4{,}21{,}000}{11{,}91{,}000} \times 100 = 35.35\%$

(ii) Net Profit ratio $= \frac{\text{Net Profit}}{\text{Sales}} \times 100 = \frac{1{,}25{,}000}{11{,}91{,}000} \times 100 = 10.5\%$

(iii) Operating Profit ratio $= \frac{\text{Operating Profit}}{\text{Sales}} \times 100 = \frac{2{,}81{,}000}{11{,}91{,}000} \times 100 = 23.6\%$

(iv) Overall Profitability ratio $= \frac{\text{N.P after tax + Interest}}{\text{Capital employed}} \times 100 = \frac{1{,}76{,}000}{13{,}05{,}000} \times 100 = 13.48\%$

(v) Current ratio $= \frac{\text{Current Assets}}{\text{Current Liabilities}} \times 100 = \frac{3{,}10{,}000}{2{,}45{,}000} = 1.27$

(vi) Debt Equity ratio $= \frac{\text{Debt}}{\text{Equity}} = \frac{4{,}00{,}000}{9{,}05{,}000} = 0.44$

(vii) Stock Turnover ratio $= \frac{\text{Cost of Sales}}{\text{Average Stock}} = \frac{7{,}70{,}000}{1{,}40{,}000} = 5.5 \text{ times}$

(a) Raw Material Turnover ratio

$\frac{\text{Cost of Sales}}{\text{Average Stock of Raw Material}} = \frac{7{,}70{,}000}{60{,}000} = 12.83 \text{ times}$

(b) Finished Goods Stock Turnover ratio

$\frac{\text{Cost of Sales}}{\text{Average stock of finished goods}} = \frac{7{,}70{,}000}{80{,}000} = 9.63 \text{ times}$

(viii) Liquid ratio $= \frac{\text{Liquid Assets}}{\text{Current Liabilities}} = \frac{1{,}40{,}000}{2{,}45{,}000} = 0.57$

Illustration: 17

The Trading and Profit and Loss Account and Balance Sheet of GT Ltd. as on 31st March 2007 are stated as follows.

Trading and Profit & Loss Account

Particulars	*Rs.*	*Particulars*	*Rs.*
To Opening Stock	50,000	By Sales	18,00,000
To Purchase	12,40,000	By Closing Stock	1,00,000
To Wages	1,10,000		
To Gross Profit	5,00,000		
	19,00,000		**19,00,000**
To Administration expenses	70,000	**By Gross Profit**	5,00,000
To Selling Expenses	73,000	By Non-operating income	40,000
To Depreciation	55,000		
To Interest	42,000		
To Income Tax	1,50,000		
To Net Profit	1,50,000		
	5,40,000		**5,40,000**

Balance Sheet as on 31st March 2007

Liabilities	*Rs.*	*Assets*		*Rs.*
Equity Share Capital	5,00,000	Land & Building	6,00,000	
10% Preference Share Capital	2,00,000	**Less :** Depreciation	30,000	5,70,000
Reserves and Surplus	1,90,000	Plant & Machinery	4,50,000	
15% Debentures	2,00,000	**Less :** Depreciation	25,000	4,25,000
12% Long-term loan	1,00,000	Goodwill		80,000
Creditors	35,000	Stock		1,00,000
Outstanding expenses	15,000	Debtors		60,000
Bills Payable	20,000	Prepaid expenses		10,000
Provision for Tax	1,50,000	Marketable securities		85,000
		Cash		80,000
	14,10,000			**14,10,000**

The following further details are also given.

(i) Reserves and Surplus in the beginning is Rs.1,20,000. The dividend for Preference Shareholders is Rs.20,000 and for the Equity Shareholders is Rs.60,000.

(ii) The market price of the share as on 31st March 2007 is Rs.120.

(iii) 50% of Sales and 40% of Purchases are on credit basis.

(iv) Debtors and Creditors as on 31st March 2006 are Rs. 1,20,000 and Rs. 45,000 respectively.

Calculate (i) Current ratio (ii) Quick ratio (iii) Debt Equity ratio (iv) Stock Turnover ratio (v) Interest Coverage (vi) Fixed Charge Coverage (vii) Debtors Turnover ratio (viii) Average Collection period (ix) Creditors Turnover ratio (x) Average Payment period (xi) Gross Profit margin (xii) Net Profit margin (xiii) Operating ratio (xiv) Operating Profit ratio (xv) Return on Capital Employed (xvi) Return Shareholders Equity (xvii) Earnings per Share (xviii) Price Earning (P/E) ratio (xix) Earnings Yield.

Solution:

(i) Current ratio $= \dfrac{\text{Current Assets}}{\text{Current Liabilities}} = \dfrac{3,35,000}{2,20,000} = 1.52$

(ii) Quick ratio $= \dfrac{\text{Liquid Assets}}{\text{Current Liabilities}} = \dfrac{2,25,000}{2,20,000} = 1.02$

(iii) Debt-Equity ratio $= \dfrac{\text{Debt}}{\text{Equity}} = \dfrac{3,00,000}{8,10,000} = 0.37$

(iv) Stock Turnover ratio $= \dfrac{\text{Cost of goods sold}}{\text{Average Stock}} = \dfrac{13,00,000}{75,000} = 17.33$

(v) Interest Coverage $= \dfrac{\text{Net profit before Interest \& Tax}}{\text{Interest}}$

$$= \frac{1,50,000 + 1,50,000 + 42,000}{42,000} = \frac{3,42,000}{42,000} = 8.14$$

(vi) Fixed Charge Coverage $= \dfrac{\text{Net profit before Interest \& Tax}}{\text{Interest + Preference Dividend}}$

$$= \frac{3,42,000}{42,000 + 20,000} = 5.5 \text{ times}$$

(vii) Debtors Turnover ratio $= \dfrac{\text{Credit Sales}}{\text{Debtors}} = \dfrac{9,00,000}{90,000} = 10 \text{ times}$

(viii) Average Collection period $= \dfrac{365}{\text{Debtors Turnover}} = \dfrac{365}{10} = 37 \text{ days}$

(ix) Creditors Turnover ratio $= \dfrac{\text{Credit Purchase}}{\text{Creditors}} = \dfrac{4,96,000}{40,000} = 12.4 \text{ times}$

(x) Average Payment period $= \dfrac{365}{\text{Creditors Turnover ratio}} = \dfrac{365}{12.4} \times 100 = 29 \text{ days}$

(xi) Gross Profit margin $= \dfrac{\text{Gross Profit}}{\text{Sales}} \times 100 = \dfrac{5,00,000}{18,00,000} \times 100 = 27.78\%$

(xii) Net Profit margin $= \dfrac{\text{Net Profit}}{\text{Sales}} \times 100 = \dfrac{1,50,000}{18,00,000} \times 100 = 8.33\%$

(xiii) Operating ratio $= \dfrac{\text{Operating Cost}}{\text{Sales}} \times 100 = \dfrac{14,98,000}{18,00,000} \times 100 = 83.22\%$

(xiv) Operating Profit ratio $= \dfrac{\text{Operating Profit}}{\text{Sales}} \times 100 = \dfrac{3,02,000}{18,00,000} \times 100 = 16.78\%$

(xv) Return on Capital Employed $= \dfrac{\text{Net Profit after Tax + Interest}}{\text{Capital employed}} \times 100 = \dfrac{1,92,000}{11,10,000} \times 100 = 17.3\%$

(xvi) Return on Shareholders Equity $= \dfrac{\text{Net Profit after Tax}}{\text{Equity}} \times 100$

$$= \frac{1,50,000}{8,10,000} \times 100 = 18.52\%$$

(xvii) Earnings per Share

$$= \frac{\text{Profit for Equity Shareholders}}{\text{No. of Equity Share}} \times 100 = \frac{1,50,000 \quad \text{Pref.Dividend}}{50,000}$$

$$= \frac{1,50,000 \quad 20,000}{50,000} = \frac{1,30,000}{50,000} = \text{Rs. } 2.60$$

(xviii) Price Earning ratio $= \dfrac{\text{Market price of a Share}}{\text{Earnings per Share}} = \dfrac{120}{2.60} = 46.15$

(xix) Earnings yield $= \dfrac{\text{Earnings per Share}}{\text{Market price per Share}} = \dfrac{2.60}{120} = 0.02$

Workings:

(a) Current Assets = 1,00,000 + 60,000 + 10,000 + 85,000 + 80,000
= Rs.3,35,000

(b) Liquid Assets = 60,000 + 85,000 + 80,000 = Rs.2,25,000

(c) Equity = 5,00,000 + 2,00,000 + 1,90,000-80,000 = Rs.8,10,000

(d) Debt = 2,00,000 + 1,00,000 = Rs.3,00,000

(e) Capital Employed = Debt + Equity = 3,00,000 + 8,10,000 = Rs.11,10,000

(f) Cost of Goods sold = Sales – G.P = 18,00,000 – 5,00,000 = Rs. 13,00,000

(g) Credit Sales = 50% of 18,00,000 = Rs.9,00,000

(h) Credit Purchases = 40% of 12,40,000 = Rs.4,96,000

(i) Current Liabilities = 35,000 + 15,000 + 20,000 + 1,50,000 = Rs.2,20,000

Preparation of Trading and Profit & Loss Account and Balance Sheet from Accounting Ratios

Accounting ratios are used to prepare the Trading and Profit & Loss Account and Balance Sheet. Gross Profit ratio, Net Profit ratio, Operating Profit ratios and Stock Turnover ratios etc. are the ratios which help for the preparation of Trading and Profit and Loss Account. Current ratio, Debtors Turnover ratio, Creditors Turnover ratio, Debt to Equity ratio, Return on Capital Employed etc., are some of the ratios which help for the preparation of Balance Sheet.

Illustration: 18

Calculate (i) Sales (ii) Closing Stock (iii) Sundry Debtors and (iv) Sundry Creditors from the following ratios.

Gross Profit ratio - 20%, Stock Velocity - 5 times, Debtors Velocity - 3 months, Creditors Velocity - 2 months, Gross profit as on 31st March 2007 is Rs.1,40,000 and Opening Stock is Rs.80,000.

Solution:

(i) Calculation of Sales

Gross Profit ratio $= \dfrac{\text{Gross Profit}}{\text{Sales}} \times 100$

$20 = \dfrac{1,40,000}{\text{Sales}} \times 100$

Sales $= \dfrac{1,40,000}{20} = \text{Rs. } 7,00,000$

(ii) Calculation of Closing Stock

Cost of Goods sold = Sales – G.P.
= 7,00,000 – 1,40,000 = Rs.5,60,000

$$\text{Stock Velocity} = \frac{\text{Cost of Goods Sold}}{\text{Average Stock}} = \frac{5,60,000}{\text{Average Stock}}$$

$$\text{Average Stock} = \frac{5,60,000}{5} = \text{Rs. } 1,12,000$$

$$\text{Average Stock} = \frac{\text{Op.Stock} + \text{Cl.Stock}}{2}$$

$$1,12,000 = \frac{80,000 + \text{Cl.Stock}}{2}$$

$$80,000 + \text{Closing Stock} = 1,12,000 \times 2$$

$$\text{Closing Stock} = 2,24,000 - 80,000 = \text{Rs.}1,44,000$$

(iii) Calculation of Sundry Debtors

$$\text{Debtors Velocity} = \frac{\text{Debtors} \times 12}{\text{Credit Sales}}$$

$$3 = \frac{\text{Debtors} \times 12}{7,00,000}$$

$$\text{Debtors} = \frac{3 \times 7,00,000}{12} = \text{Rs. } 1,75,000$$

(iv) Calculation of Sundry Creditors

$$\text{Cost of Goods sold} = \text{Op. Stock} + \text{Purchases} - \text{Cl.Stock}$$

$$5,60,000 = 80,000 + \text{Purchases} - 1,44,000$$

$$\text{Purchases} = 5,60,000 + 1,44,000 - 80,000 = \text{Rs.}6,24,000$$

$$\text{Creditors Velocity} = \frac{\text{Creditors} \times 12}{\text{Credit Purchase}}$$

$$2 = \frac{\text{Creditors} \times 12}{6,24,000}$$

$$\text{Creditors} = \frac{2 \times 6,24,000}{12} = \text{Rs. } 1,04,000$$

[(i) All the Sales and Purchases are assumed as Credit Sales and Credit Purchases (ii) It is assumed that there is no Direct expenses.]

Illustration: 19

Prepare Trading and Profit & Loss Account from the following.

Gross Profit ratio 25%, Net Profit ratio 12% Operating Profit ratio 15%, Tax @ 40%, Opening Stock Rs.1,10,000, Direct cost Rs.70,000, Stock Turnover ratio 6 times, Gross Profit Rs.2,50,000, Depreciation Rs.30,000.

Solution:

$$\text{Gross Profit ratio} = \frac{\text{Gross Profit}}{\text{Sales}} \times 100$$

$$25 = \frac{2,50,000}{\text{Sales}} \times 100$$

$$\text{Sales} = \frac{2,50,000}{25} = \text{Rs. } 10,00,000$$

Cost of goods sold = Sales – Gross Profit = 10,00,000 – 2,50,000

= Rs.7,50,000

$$\text{Stock Turnover ratio} = \frac{\text{Cost of Goods sold}}{\text{Average Stock}}$$

$$6 = \frac{7,50,000}{\text{Average Stock}}$$

$$\text{Average Stock} = \frac{7,50,000}{6} = \text{Rs. } 1,25,000$$

$$\text{Average Stock} = \frac{\text{Op.Stock} + \text{Cl.Stock}}{2}$$

$$1,25,000 = \frac{1,10,000 + \text{Cl.Stock}}{2}$$

Closing Stock = 2,50,000 – 1,10,000 = Rs.1,40,000

Cost of Goods sold = Op.Stock + Purchases + Direct Cost - Cl.Stock

7,50,000 = 1,10,000 + Purchase + 70,000 – 1,40,000

Purchase = 7,50,000 + 1,40,000 – 1,10,000 – 70,000

= Rs. 7,10,000

$$\text{Operating Profit ratio} = \frac{\text{Operating Profit}}{\text{Sales}} \times 100$$

$$15 = \frac{\text{Operating Profit}}{10,00,000} \times 100$$

$$\text{Operating Profit} = \frac{15 \times 10,00,000}{100} = \text{Rs. } 1,50,000$$

Operating Profit = Gross Profit – Operating Expenses

1,50,000 = 2,50,000 – Operating Expenses

Operating Expenses = 2,50,000 – 1,50,000 = Rs.1,00,000

$$\text{Net Profit} = \frac{\text{Net Profit}}{\text{Sales}} \times 100$$

$$12 = \frac{\text{Net Profit}}{10,00,000} \times 100$$

$$\text{Net Profit} = \frac{12 \times 10,00,000}{100} = \text{Rs. } 1,20,000$$

Trading and Profit & Loss Account

Particulars	*Rs.*	*Particulars*	*Rs.*
To Opening Stock	1,10,000	By Sales	10,00,000
To Purchase	7,10,000	By Closing Stock	1,40,000
To Direct cost	70,000		
To Gross Profit	2,50,000		
	11,40,000		11,40,000
To Operating expenses	1,00,000	**By Gross Profit**	2,50,000
To Depreciation	30,000		

To Net Profit	1,20,000		
	2,50,000		2,50,000

Illustration: 20

G Ltd., provided the following information for the year ended 31st March 2007.

Gross Profit ratio 30%; Operating Profit ratio 20%; Tax @ 50%; 12% Debentures Rs.2,00,000; 10% Loan Rs.3,00,000; Gross Profit Rs.3,90,000. Stock Turnover ratio 8; Closing stock is Rs.41,500 more than the Opening stock; Wages Rs.1,50,000; Profit on sale of Plant Rs.40,000; Loss on sale of Furniture Rs.20,000, Ratio of Administration and Selling expenses is 3:2.

Prepare Trading and Profit and Loss Account.

Solution:

$$\text{Gross Profit ratio} = \frac{\text{Gross Profit}}{\text{Sales}} \times 100$$

$$30 = \frac{3,90,000}{\text{Sales}} \times 100$$

$$\text{Sales} = \frac{3,90,00,000}{30} = \text{Rs. } 13,00,000$$

$$\text{Cost of Goods sold} = \text{Sales} - \text{G.P}$$

$$= 13,00,000 - 3,90,000 = \text{Rs. } 9,10,000$$

$$\text{Stock Turnover ratio} = \frac{\text{Cost of Goods Sold}}{\text{Average Stock}}$$

$$8 = \frac{9,10,000}{\text{Average Stock}}$$

$$\text{Average Stock} = \frac{9,10,000}{8} = \text{Rs. } 1,13,750$$

$$\text{Average Stock} = \frac{\text{Op.Stock} + \text{Cl.Stock}}{2}$$

$$1,13,750 = \frac{\text{Op.Stock} + (\text{Op.Stock} + 41,500)}{2}$$

$$(2 \times \text{Op. Stock}) + 41,500 = 2,27,500$$

$$\text{Op. Stock} = \frac{2,27,500 \quad 41,500}{2} = \frac{1,86,000}{2} = \text{Rs. } 93,000$$

$$\text{Cl. Stock} = 93,000 + 41,500 = \text{Rs.}1,34,500$$

$$\text{Cost of Goods sold} = \text{Op. Stock} + \text{Purchase} + \text{Wages} - \text{Cl. Stock}$$

$$9,10,000 = 93,000 + \text{Purchase} + 1,50,000 - 1,34,500$$

$$\text{Purchase} = 9,10,000 + 1,34,500 - 93,000 - 1,50,000$$

$$= \text{Rs. } 8,01,500$$

$$\text{Operating profit ratio} = \frac{\text{Operating Profit}}{\text{Sales}}$$

$$20 = \frac{\text{Operating Profit}}{13,00,000} \times 100$$

$$\text{Operating Profit} = \frac{13,00,000}{100} \times 20 = \text{Rs. } 2,60,000$$

$$\text{Operating Profit} = \text{Gross Profit} - \text{Operating expenses}$$

$$2,60,000 = 3,90,000 - \text{Operating expenses}$$

$$\text{Operating expenses} = 3,90,000 - 2,60,000 = \text{Rs.}1,30,000$$

Administration expenses and selling expenses ratio = 3:2

$$\text{Administration expenses} = \frac{3}{5} \times 1,30,000 = \text{Rs. } 78,000$$

$$\text{Selling expenses} = \frac{2}{5} \times 1,30,000 = \text{Rs. } 52,000$$

$$\text{Net Profit ratio} = \frac{\text{N.P}}{\text{Sales}} \times 100$$

$$15 = \frac{\text{N.P}}{13,00,000} \times 100$$

$$\text{Net Profit} = \frac{15 \times 13,00,000}{100} = \text{Rs. } 1,95,000$$

Interest = Interest for Debentures + Interest for Loan

= 12% of 2,00,000 + 10% of 3,00,000

= 24,000 + 30,000 = Rs.54,000

Profit before Interest and Tax = Operating Profit + Profit on sale of Plant – Loss on sale of Furniture

= 2,60,000 + 40,000 – 20,000 = Rs.2,80,000

Profit after Interest = 2,80,000 – 54,000 = Rs.2,26,000

Tax @ 40% = Rs.90,400

Net Profit after Tax = 2,26,000 – 90,400 = Rs.1,35,600

Trading and Profit & Loss Account

Particulars	*Rs.*	*Particulars*	*Rs.*
To Opening Stock	93,000	By Sales	13,00,000
To Purchases	8,01,500	**By Closing Stock**	1,34,500
To Wages	1,50,000		
To Gross Profit	3,90,000		
	14,34,500		14,34,500
To Administration expenses	78,000	**By Gross Profit**	3,90,000
To Selling expenses	52,000	By Profit on sale of Plant	40,000
To Loss on sale of Furniture	20,000		
To Interest	54,000		
To Tax	90,400		
To Net Profit	1,35,600		
	4,30,000		4,30,000

Illustration: 21

Prepare the Balance Sheet of W.D. Ltd. from the following.

Gross Profit ratio 25%; Capital Turnover ratio 1.5; Stock Velocity 5; Fixed Assets Turnover ratio 2.5; Debtors collection period 50 days; Creditors payment period 60 days; Gross Profit is Rs.1,50,000; Closing stock is Rs.30,000 more than the Opening stock and Direct cost is Rs.80,000, Cash Rs.38,561.

Solution:

$$\text{Gross Profit ratio} = \frac{\text{Gross Profit}}{\text{Sales}}$$

$$25 = \frac{1,50,000}{\text{Sales}} \times 100$$

$$\text{Sales} = \frac{1,50,000}{25} = \text{Rs. } 6,00,000$$

$$\text{Cost of Goods sold} = \text{Sales} - \text{Gross Profit} = 6,00,000 - 1,50,000$$

$$= \text{Rs.}4,50,000$$

$$\text{Stock Velocity} = \frac{\text{Cost of goods sold}}{\text{Average Stock}}$$

$$5 = \frac{4,50,000}{\text{Average stock}}$$

$$\text{Average Stock} = \frac{4,50,000}{5} = 90,000$$

Let Opening Stock be 'x'

$$\text{Average Stock} = \frac{\text{Op.stock} + \text{Cl.stock}}{2} = [x + (x + 30,000)]/2$$

$$90,000 = x + 15,000$$

$$x \text{ (Opening Stock)} = 90,000 - 15,000 = \text{Rs.}75,000$$

$$\text{Closing stock} = 75,000 + 30,000 = \text{Rs.}1,05,000$$

$$\text{Capital Turnover ratio} = \frac{\text{Sales}}{\text{Capital}}$$

$$1.5 = \frac{6,00,000}{\text{Capital}}$$

$$\text{Capital} = \frac{6,00,000}{1.5} = \text{Rs.}4,00,000$$

$$\text{Fixed Assets Turnover ratio} = \frac{\text{Sales}}{\text{Fixed Assets}}$$

$$2.5 = \frac{6,00,000}{\text{Fixed Assets}}$$

$$\text{Fixed Assets} = \frac{6,00,000}{2.5} = \text{Rs. } 2,40,000$$

$$\text{Debt collection period} = \frac{\text{Debtors} \times 365}{6,00,000}$$

$$50 = \frac{\text{Debtors} \times 365}{6,00,000}$$

$$\text{Debtors} = \frac{50 \times 6,00,000}{365} = \text{Rs. } 82,192$$

Cost of Goods sold = Op.Stock + Purchase + Direct cost - Cl. Stock

4,50,000 = 75,000 + Purchase + 80,000 – 1,05,000

Purchase = 4,50,000 + 1,05,000 – 75,000 – 80,000 = Rs.4,00,000

$$\text{Creditors payment period} = \frac{\text{Creditors} \times 365}{\text{Credit purchase}}$$

$$60 = \frac{\text{Creditors} \times 365}{4,00,000}$$

$$\text{Creditors} = \frac{60 \times 4,00,000}{365} = \text{Rs. } 65,753.$$

Balance Sheet

Liabilities	*Rs.*	*Assets*	*Rs.*
Capital	4,00,000	Fixed Assets	2,40,000
Sundry Creditors	65,753	Stock	1,05,000
		Debtors	82,192
		Cash	38,561
	4,65,753		4,65,753

Illustration: 22

Prepare the Balance Sheet of GR Ltd., as on 31st March 2007 from the following.

Return on Capital employed 20%, Debt Equity ratio is 0.5, Interest Coverage is 5 times, Profit after Tax is Rs.2,00,000, Tax 50%, Interest on Debenture is Rs.30,000 (@ 10% p.a), Preference Share Capital is Rs.3,00,000, General Reserve Rs.50,000, Current ratio is 5:2, Sundry Creditors Rs.1,00,000, Ratio of Stock, Debtors and Cash is 2:2:1

Solution:

Profit after Tax = Rs.2,00,000

Profit before Tax = 2,00,000 + 2,00,000 = Rs.4,00,000
(Tax 50 %)

$$\text{Interest Coverage ratio} = \frac{\text{Profit before Tax and Interest}}{\text{Interest}}$$

$$5 = \frac{4,00,000 + x}{x}$$

5x = 4,00,000 + x

5x – x = 4,00,000; 4x = 4,00,000; x = Rs.1,00,000

$$\text{Return on Capital employed} = \frac{\text{Profit after tax + Interest}}{\text{Capital employed}}$$

$$20 = \frac{2,00,000 + 1,00,000}{\text{Capital employed}} \times 100$$

$$\text{Capital employed} = \frac{3,00,000}{20} = \text{Rs. } 15,00,000$$

$$\text{Debt Equity ratio} = \frac{\text{Debt}}{\text{Equity}} = \frac{\text{Capital} \quad \text{Equity}}{\text{Equity}}$$

$$0.5 = \frac{15,00,000 \quad x}{x}$$

$$0.5x = 15,00,000 - x;\ 1.5x = 15,00,000$$

$$\text{Equity, } x = \frac{15,00,000}{1.5} = \text{Rs. } 10,00,000$$

$$\text{Debt} = \text{Capital} - \text{Equity} = 15,00,000 - 10,00,000 = \text{Rs.}5,00,000$$

$$\text{Debenture interest} = 10\% = \frac{10}{\text{Debenture} \times 100}$$

$$\text{Debenture} = \frac{30,000 \times 100}{10} = \text{Rs. } 3,00,000$$

$$\text{Loan} = \text{Debt} - \text{Debentures} = 5,00,000 - 3,00,000 = \text{Rs.}2,00,000$$

Current ratio = Current Assets : Current Liabilities

3 : 2 = C.A. : 3,00,000

C.A. x 2 = 3,00,000 × 3

$$\text{C.A.} = \frac{9,00,000}{2} = \text{Rs. } 4,50,000$$

Ratio of Stock, Debtors and Cash = 2 : 2 : 1

$$\text{Stock} = \frac{2}{5} \times 4,50,000 = \text{Rs. } 1,80,000$$

$$\text{Debtors} = \frac{2}{5} \times 1,80,000 = \text{Rs. } 1,80,000$$

$$\text{Cash} = \frac{1}{5} \times 4,50,000 = \text{Rs. } 90,000$$

Equity = Eq.Share Capital + Pref.Share Capital + P&L a/c + General Reserve

10,00,000 = Eq.Sh.Capital + 3,00,000 + 2,00,000 + 50,000

Eq. Sh. Capital = 10,00,000 – 5,50,000 = Rs.4,50,000

Fixed Assets = Capital + Creditors + Tax – Current Assets
= 15,00,000 + 1,00,000 + 2,00,000 – 4,50,000
= Rs.13,50,000

$$\text{Land \& Building} = \frac{3}{5} \times 13,50,000 = \text{Rs. } 8,10,000$$

$$\text{Plant \& Machinery} = \frac{2}{5} \times 13,50,000 = \text{Rs. } 5,40,000.$$

Balance Sheet of GR Ltd. as on 31st March 2007

Liabilities	*Rs.*	*Assets*	*Rs.*
Equity Share Capital	4,50,000	Land Building	8,10,000
Preference Share Capital	3,00,000	Plant & Machinery	5,40,000
Profit & Loss Account	2,00,000	Stock	1,80,000
General Reserve	50,000	Debtors	1,80,000
Debentures	3,00,000	Cash	90,000
Loan	2,00,000		
Sundry Creditors	1,00,000		
Provision for Tax	2,00,000		
	18,00,000		18,00,000

Illustration: 23

W. Doyle Ltd. is providing the following information related to the year ending 31st March 2007.

Stock Turnover ratio 6 times; Debtors Turnover ratio is 5 times, Creditors Turnover ratio 3 times; Gross Profit ratio 25%, Working Capital Turnover ratio 4 times; Capital Turnover ratio 0.8; Debt to Equity ratio 0.4; Equity Share Capital Rs.4,50,000; Preference Share Capital Rs.2,00,000; Debentures and Loan are in the ratio 2:3; Gross Profit Rs.2,40,000; 50% of Purchase and 60% of Sales are on credit basis. Direct expense Rs.1,40,000; Opening Stock Rs.80,000; Opening Debtors Rs.95,400; Opening Creditors Rs.1,25,000; Ratio of Land & Building, Plant & Machinery and Furniture & Fittings is 4:3:1.

Prepare the Balance Sheet as on 31st March 2007.

Solution:

$$\text{Gross Profit ratio} = \frac{\text{Gross Profit}}{\text{Sales}} \times 100$$

$$25 = \frac{2,40,00,000}{\text{Sales}} \times 100$$

$$\text{Sales} = \frac{2,40,000}{25} = \text{Rs. } 9,60,000$$

$$\text{Cost of Goods sold} = \text{Sales} - \text{Gross Profit}$$

$$= 9,60,000 - 2,40,000 = \text{Rs.}7,20,000$$

$$\text{Stock Turnover ratio} = \frac{\text{Cost of Goods sold}}{\text{Average stock}}$$

$$6 = \frac{7,20,000}{\text{Average Stock}}$$

$$\text{Average Stock} = \frac{7,20,000}{6} = \text{Rs. } 1,20,000$$

$$= \frac{\text{Op.Stock} + \text{Cl.Stock}}{2}$$

$$1,20,000 = \frac{80,000 + \text{Cl.Stock}}{2}$$

$$\text{Closing Stock} = 2,40,000 - 80,000 = \text{Rs.}1,60,000$$

$$\text{Cost of Goods sold} = \text{Op. Stock} + \text{Purchases} + \text{Direct Expenses} - \text{Closing Stock}$$

$$7{,}20{,}000 = 80{,}000 + \text{Purchase} + 1{,}40{,}000 - 1{,}60{,}000$$

$$\text{Purchase} = 7{,}20{,}000 + 1{,}60{,}000 - 80{,}000 - 1{,}40{,}000$$

$$= \text{Rs.}6{,}60{,}000$$

$$\text{Credit Purchase} = 50\% \text{ of } 6{,}60{,}000 = \text{Rs.}3{,}30{,}000$$

$$\text{Credit Sales} = 60\% \text{ of } 9{,}60{,}000 = \text{Rs.}5{,}76{,}000$$

$$\text{Debtors Turnover ratio} = \frac{\text{Credit Sales}}{\text{Average Debtors}}$$

$$5 = \frac{5{,}76{,}000}{\text{Average Debtors}}$$

$$\text{Average Debtors} = \frac{5{,}76{,}000}{5} = \text{Rs. } 1{,}15{,}200$$

$$\text{Average Debtors} = \frac{\text{Op.Debtors} + \text{Cl.Debtors}}{2}$$

$$1{,}15{,}200 = \frac{95{,}400 + \text{Cl.Debtors}}{2}$$

$$\text{Closing Debtors} = 2{,}30{,}400 - 95{,}400 = \text{Rs.}1{,}35{,}000$$

$$\text{Creditors Turnover ratio} = \frac{\text{Credit Purchase}}{\text{Average Creditors}}$$

$$3 = \frac{3{,}30{,}000}{\text{Average Creditors}}$$

$$\text{Average Creditors} = \frac{3{,}30{,}000}{3} = \text{Rs. } 1{,}10{,}000$$

$$\text{Average Creditors} = \frac{\text{Op. Creditors} + \text{Cl.Creditors}}{2}$$

$$1{,}10{,}000 = \frac{1{,}25{,}000 + \text{Cl. Creditors}}{2}$$

$$\text{Closing Creditors} = 2{,}20{,}000 - 1{,}25{,}000 = \text{Rs.}95{,}000$$

$$\text{Working capital turnover ratio} = \frac{\text{Sales}}{\text{Working Capital}}$$

$$4 = \frac{9{,}60{,}000}{\text{Working Capital}}$$

$$\text{Working Capital} = \frac{9{,}60{,}000}{4} = \text{Rs. } 2{,}40{,}000$$

$$\text{Working Capital} = \text{Current Assets} - \text{Current Liabilities}$$

$$2{,}40{,}000 = \text{Current Assets} - 95{,}000$$

$$\text{Current Assets} = 2{,}40{,}000 + 95{,}000 = \text{Rs.}3{,}35{,}000$$

$$\text{Current Assets} = \text{Stock} + \text{Debtors} + \text{Cash}$$

$$3{,}35{,}000 = 1{,}60{,}000 + 1{,}35{,}000 + \text{Cash}$$

$$\text{Cash} = 3{,}35{,}000 - 1{,}60{,}000 - 1{,}35{,}000 = \text{Rs.}40{,}000$$

$$\text{Capital Turnover ratio} = \frac{\text{Sales}}{\text{Capital}}$$

$$0.8 = \frac{9,60,000}{\text{Capital}}$$

$$\text{Capital} = \frac{9,60,000}{0.8} = \text{Rs. } 12,00,000$$

$$\text{Debt to Equity ratio} = \frac{\text{Debt}}{\text{Equity}}$$

$$0.5 = \frac{\text{Debt}}{\text{Capital} \quad \text{Debt}}$$

$$0.5 = \frac{\text{Debt}}{12,00,000 \quad \text{Debt}}$$

$$\text{Debt} = 0.5\ (12,00,000 - \text{Debt})$$

$$\text{Debt} = 6,00,000 - 0.5\ \text{Debt}$$

$$1.5\ \text{Debt} = 6,00,000; \text{Debt} = \frac{60,000}{1.5} = \text{Rs. } 4,00,000$$

$$\text{Equity} = \text{Capital - Debt} = 12,00,000 - 4,00,000 = \text{Rs.}8,00,000$$

$$\text{Ratio of Debentures to Loan} = 2:3$$

$$\text{Debentures} = \frac{2}{5} \times 4,00,000 = \text{Rs. } 1,60,000$$

$$\text{Loan} = \frac{3}{5} \times 4,00,000 = \text{Rs. } 2,40,000$$

$$\text{Equity} = \text{Equity Share Capital + Preference Share Capital + Reserves and Surplus}$$

$$8,00,000 = 4,50,000 + 2,00,000 + \text{Reserves and Surplus}$$

$$\text{Reserves and Surplus} = 8,00,000 - 4,50,000 - 2,00,000 = \text{Rs.}1,50,000$$

$$\text{Total Liability side} = \text{Capital + Creditors} = 12,00,000 + 95,000 = \text{Rs. } 12,95,000$$

$$\text{Fixed Assets} = \text{Total of Liabilities - Current Assets} = 12,95,000 - 3,35,000 = \text{Rs.}9,60,000$$

Ratio of Land & Building, Plant and Machinery and Furniture & Fittings

$$= 4 : 3 : 1$$

$$\text{Land \& Building} = \frac{4}{8} \times 9,60,000 = \text{Rs. } 4,80,000$$

$$\text{Plant \& Machinery} = \frac{3}{8} \times 9,60,000 = \text{Rs. } 3,60,000$$

$$\text{Furniture \& Fittings} = \frac{1}{8} \times 9,60,000 = \text{Rs. } 1,20,000.$$

Balance Sheet as on 31st March 2007

Liabilities	*Rs.*	*Assets*	*Rs.*
Equity Share Capital	4,50,000	Land Building	4,80,000
Preference Share Capital	2,00,000	Plant & Machinery	3,60,000
Reserves & Surplus	1,50,000	Furniture & Fittings	1,20,000

Debentures	1,60,000	Stock	1,60,000
Loan	2,40,000	Debtors	1,35,000
Sundry Creditors	95,000	Cash	40,000
	12,95,000		12,95,000

Illustration: 24

Prepare the Balance Sheet of KT Ltd., as on 31st March 2007 from the following.

Gross Profit ratio 25%; Current ratio 2.3; Liquidity ratio 1.2; Stock Turnover ratio 4.5 times; Fixed Assets Turnover ratio 2 times; Debt collection period 1.5 months, Fixed Assets to Shareholders Net worth 1.2; Reserves and Surplus to Equity 0.3; and Net Working Capital is Rs.2,60,000.

Solution:

Current ratio = Current Assets : Current Liabilities

= 2.3 : 1

Working Capital = Current Assets – Current Liabilities

= 2.3 – 1 = 1.3 = 2,60,000

$$\text{Current Assets} = \frac{2,60,000}{1.3} \times 2.3 = \text{Rs.}4,60,000$$

$$\text{Current Liabilities} = \frac{2,60,000}{1.3} \times 1 = \text{Rs.}2,00,000$$

$$\text{Liquid Ratio} = \frac{\text{Liquid Assets}}{\text{Current Liabilities}}$$

$$1.2 = \frac{\text{Liquid Assets}}{2,00,000}$$

Liquid Assets = 2,00,000 × 1.2 = Rs.2,40,000

Liquid Assets = Current Assets – Stock

2,40,000 = 4,60,000 – Stock

Stock = 4,60,000 – 2,40,000 = Rs.2,20,000

$$\text{Stock Turnover ratio} = \frac{\text{Cost of Goods sold}}{\text{Stock}}$$

$$4.5 = \frac{\text{Cost of Goods sold}}{2,20,000}$$

Cost of Goods sold = 2,20,000 × 4.5 = Rs.9,90,000

Sales = Cost of Goods sold + G.P.

= 9,90,000 + (9,90,000 × 25/75) = 9,90,000 + 3,30,000

= Rs.13,20,000

$$\text{Fixed Assets Turnover ratio} = \frac{\text{Sales}}{\text{Fixed Assets}}$$

$$2 = \frac{13,20,000}{\text{Fixed Assets}}$$

$$\text{Fixed Assets} = \frac{13,20,000}{2} = \text{Rs.}6,60,000$$

$$\text{Fixed Assets to Shareholders Fund} = \frac{\text{Fixed Assets}}{\text{Shareholder'sFund}}$$

$$1.2 = \frac{6{,}60{,}000}{\text{Shareholder's Fund}}$$

$$\text{Shareholders Fund (Equity)} = \frac{6{,}60{,}000}{1.2} = \text{Rs. } 5{,}50{,}000$$

$$\text{Reserves and Surplus to Equity} = \frac{\text{Reserve and Surplus}}{\text{Equity}}$$

$$0.3 = \frac{\text{Reserve and Surplus}}{5{,}50{,}000}$$

$$\text{Reserves and Surplus} = 5{,}50{,}000 \times 0.3 = \text{Rs.}1{,}65{,}000$$

$$\text{Share Capital} = \text{Equity} - \text{Reserves and Surplus}$$
$$= 5{,}50{,}000 - 1{,}65{,}000 = \text{Rs.}3{,}85{,}000$$

$$\text{Debt Collection period} = \frac{12 \times \text{Debtors}}{\text{Credit Sales}}$$

$$1.5 = \frac{12 \times \text{Debtors}}{13{,}20{,}000}$$

$$\text{Debtors} = \frac{13{,}20{,}000 \times 1.5}{12} = \text{Rs. } 1{,}65{,}000$$

$$\text{Liquid Assets} = \text{Debtors} + \text{Cash}$$

$$2{,}40{,}000 = 1{,}65{,}000 + \text{Cash}$$

$$\text{Cash} = 2{,}40{,}000 - 1{,}65{,}000 = \text{Rs.}75{,}000$$

$$\text{Total Assets} = \text{Fixed Assets} + \text{Current Assets}$$
$$= 6{,}60{,}000 + 4{,}60{,}000 = \text{Rs.}11{,}20{,}000$$

$$\text{Long-term Loan} = \text{Total Assets} - \text{Equity} - \text{Current Liabilities}$$

$$\text{Long-term Loan} = 11{,}20{,}000 - 5{,}50{,}000 - 2{,}00{,}000 = \text{Rs.}3{,}70{,}000.$$

Balance Sheet as on 31st March 2007

Liabilities	*Rs.*	*Assets*	*Rs.*
Share Capital	3,85,000	Fixed Assets	6,60,000
Reserves and Surplus	1,65,000	Stock	2,20,000
Long-term Loan	3,70,000	Debtors	1,65,000
Current Liabilities	2,00,000	Cash	75,000
	11,20,000		11,20,000

Illustration: 25

Prepare the Trading and Profit & Loss Account and Balance Sheet as on 31st March 2007 from the following information.

(a) Gross Profit ratio 20%

(b) Net Profit ratio 16%

(c) Stock Turnover ratio 5

(d) Net Profit to Capital 1/8

(e) Fixed Assets to Capital 6/5

(f) Fixed Assets to Current Assets 4

(g) Capital to Total Liabilities 2/3

(h) Closing Stock Rs.1,40,000

(i) Fixed Assets Rs.12,00,000

(j) Sundry Debtors Rs. 70,000

(k) Current ratio is 3:1

(l) Long term Loan Rs. 2,75,000

(m) Operating Expenses Rs.20,000 and Non-operating Expenses Rs.11,250.

Solution:

(i) Fixed Assets to Capital $= \frac{\text{Fixed Assets}}{\text{Capital}}$

$$6/5 = \frac{12,00,000}{\text{Capital}}$$

$$\text{Capital} = \frac{12,00,000 \times 5}{6} = \text{Rs. } 10,00,000$$

(ii) Capital to Total Liabilities $= \frac{\text{Capital}}{\text{Total Liabilities}}$

$$2/3 = \frac{10,00,000}{\text{Total Liabilities}}$$

$$\text{Total Liabilities} = \frac{10,00,000 \times 3}{2} = \text{Rs. } 15,00,000$$

(iii) Net Profit to Capital $= \frac{\text{Net profit}}{\text{Capital}}$

$$1/8 = \frac{\text{Net profit}}{10,00,000}$$

$$\text{Net Profit} = \frac{10,00,000}{8} = \text{Rs. } 1,25,000$$

(iv) Net Profit ratio $= \frac{\text{Net profit}}{\text{Sales}} \times 100$

$$16 = \frac{1,25,000 \times 100}{\text{Sales}}$$

$$\text{Sales} = \frac{1,25,000 \times 100}{16} = \text{Rs. } 7,81,250$$

(v) Gross Profit ratio $= \frac{\text{Gross Profit} \times 100}{\text{Sales}}$

$$20 = \frac{\text{Gross Profit} \times 100}{7,81,250}$$

$$\text{Gross Profit} = \frac{7,81,250 \times 20}{100} = \text{Rs. } 1,56,250$$

$$\text{Cost of Goods sold} = \text{Sales} - \text{Gross Profit}$$

$$7{,}81{,}250 - 1{,}56{,}250 = \text{Rs.}6{,}25{,}000$$

$$\text{(vi) Stock Turnover ratio} = \frac{\text{Cost of Goods sold}}{\text{Average stock}}$$

$$5 = \frac{6{,}25{,}000}{\text{Average Stock}}$$

$$\text{Average Stock} = \frac{6{,}25{,}000}{5} = \text{Rs. } 1{,}25{,}000$$

$$\text{Average Stock} = \frac{\text{Op.Stock} + \text{Cl.Stock}}{2}$$

$$1{,}25{,}000 = \frac{\text{Op.Stock} + 1{,}40{,}000}{2}$$

$$\text{Opening Stock} = 2{,}50{,}000 - 1{,}40{,}000 = \text{Rs.}1{,}10{,}000$$

$$\text{(vii) Fixed Assets to Current Assets} = \frac{\text{Fixed Assets}}{\text{Current Assets}}$$

$$4 = \frac{12{,}00{,}000}{\text{Current Assets}}$$

$$\text{Current Assets} = \frac{12{,}00{,}000}{4} = \text{Rs. } 3{,}00{,}000$$

$$\text{Cash} = \text{Current Assets} - \text{Stock} - \text{Sundry Debtors}$$

$$= 3{,}00{,}000 - 1{,}40{,}000 - 70{,}000 = \text{Rs.}90{,}000$$

$$\text{(viii) Current ratio} = \text{Current Assets} : \text{Current Liabilities}$$

$$3 : 1 = 3{,}00{,}000 : \text{C.L}$$

$$\text{Current Liabilities} = 3{,}00{,}000/3 = \text{Rs. } 1{,}00{,}000.$$

Trading and Profit & Loss Account as on 31st March 2007

Particulars	*Rs.*	*Particulars*	*Rs.*
To Opening Stock	1,10,000	By Sales	7,81,250
To Purchases	6,55,000	By closing Stock	1,40,000
To Gross Profit	1,56,250		
	9,21,250		**9,21,250**
To Operating expenses	20,000	By Gross Profit	1,56,250
To Non Operating expenses	11,250		
To Net Profit	1,25,000		
	1,56,250		**1,56,250**

Balance Sheet as on 31st March 2007

Particulars	*Rs.*	*Particulars*	*Rs.*
Capital	10,00,000	Fixed Assets	12,00,000
Profit and Loss Account	1,25,000	Closing Stock	1,40,000
Loan	2,75,000	Sundry Debtors	70,000
Current Liabilities	1,00,000	Cash	90,000
	15,00,000		15,00,000

Illustration: 26

KMW Ltd., provided the following ratios and other information as on 31st March 2007.

Current Liabilities	Rs.1,50,000	Cost of Goods sold	Rs.5,60,000
Stock Velocity	8 times	Current ratio	2:1
Opening Stock	40,000	Net Profit after Tax	Rs.1,80,000
Return on Capital Employed 10%		Preference Share Capital	Rs.5,00,000
General Reserve (31.3.06)	Rs.50,000	Pre. expenses (31.3.06)	Rs.70,000
Operating Profit ratio	30%	Cash	Rs.50,000
Wages	Rs.1,20,000	Tax	40%
Interest (10%)	Rs.60,000	Profit on sale of Plant	Rs.60,000
Debtors Turnover ratio	6	Debtors (31.3.06)	Rs.30,000
Commission received	Rs.50,000		

Provision for General Reserve during the year is Rs.30,000 and Preliminary expenses written off is Rs.20,000. Ratio of Administrative expenses and Selling expenses is 4:1; Ratio of Land & Building and Plant & Machinery is 3:2 ; Cash Sales is 40% of the Total Sales.

Prepare Trading and Profit & Loss Account and Balance Sheet as on 31st March 2007.

Solution:

$$\text{Current ratio} = \text{Current Assets : Current Liabilities}$$

$$2:1 = \text{Current Assets} : 1,50,000$$

$$\text{Current Assets} = 2 \times 1,50,000 = \text{Rs.}3,00,000$$

$$\text{Stock Velocity} = \frac{\text{Cost of Goods sold}}{\text{Average stock}}$$

$$8 = \frac{5,60,000}{\text{Average Stock}} = \text{Rs. } 70,000$$

$$\text{Average Stock} = \frac{5,60,000}{8} = \text{Rs. } 70,000$$

$$\text{Average Stock} = \frac{\text{Op.Stock} + \text{Cl.Stock}}{2}$$

$$70,000 = \frac{40,000 + \text{Cl.Stock}}{2}$$

$$\text{Closing Stock} = 1,40,000 - 40,000 = \text{Rs.}1,00,000$$

$$\text{Closing Debtors} = \text{Current Assets} - \text{Stock} - \text{Cash}$$

$$= 3,00,000 - 1,00,000 - 50,000 = \text{Rs.}1,50,000$$

$$\text{Debtors Turnover ratio} = \frac{\text{Credit Sales}}{\text{Average Debtors}}$$

$$6 = \frac{\text{Credit Sales}}{(30,000 + 1,50,000)\ 2}$$

$$\text{Credit Sales} = 6 \times 90,000 = \text{Rs.}5,40,000$$

$$\text{Credit Sales} = 100 - 40 = 60\%$$

$$\text{Total Sales} = \frac{5,40,000}{60} \times 100 = \text{Rs. } 9,00,000$$

$$\text{Gross Profit} = \text{Sales} - \text{Cost of Goods sold}$$

$$= 9,00,000 - 5,60,000 = \text{Rs.}3,40,000$$

$$\text{Cost of Goods sold} = \text{Op. Stock} + \text{Purchase} + \text{Wages} - \text{Cl.Stock}$$

$$5,60,000 = 40,000 + \text{Purchase} + 1,20,000 - 1,00,000$$

$$\text{Purchase} = 5,60,000 - 60,000 = \text{Rs.}5,00,000$$

$$\text{Net Profit after Tax} = \text{Rs.}1,80,000;\ \text{Tax @ } 40\%$$

$$\text{Net Profit before Tax} = \frac{1,80,000}{60} \times 100 = \text{Rs.}3,00,000$$

$$\text{Operating Profit ratio} = \frac{\text{Operating Profit}}{\text{Sales}} \times 100$$

$$30 = \frac{\text{Operating Profit}}{9,00,000} \times 100$$

$$\text{Operating Profit} = \frac{9,00,000 \times 30}{100} = \text{Rs. } 2,70,000$$

$$\text{Operating expenses} = \text{G.P.} - \text{Operating Profit} = 3,40,000 - 2,70,000$$

$$= \text{Rs.}70,000$$

Ratio of Administrative expenses and Selling expenses = 4:1

$$\text{Administrative expenses} = \frac{4}{5} \times 70,000 = \text{Rs. } 56,000$$

$$\text{Selling expenses} = \frac{1}{5} \times 70,000 = \text{Rs. } 14,000$$

$$\text{Return on Capital employed} = \frac{\text{Profit after Tax} + \text{Interest}}{\text{Capital employed}}$$

$$10 = \frac{1,80,000 + 60,000}{\text{Capital employed}} \times 100$$

$$\text{Capital employed} = \frac{2,40,00,000}{10} = \text{Rs. } 24,00,000$$

$$\text{Interest on Long term Loan (10\%)} = \text{Rs.}60,000$$

$$\text{Long term Loan} = \frac{100}{10} \times 60,000 = \text{Rs. } 6,00,000$$

$$\text{Capital employed} = \text{Equity Share Capital} + \text{Preference Share Capital} + \text{Profit \& Loss Account} + \text{General Reserve} + \text{Long term Loan} - \text{Preliminary expenses}$$

$$24,00,000 = \text{Eq.Share Capital} + 5,00,000 + (1,80,000-30,000) + (50,000 + 30,000) + 6,00,000 - (70,000-20,000)$$

$$\text{Equity Share Capital} = 24,00,000 - 12,80,000 = \text{Rs.}11,20,000$$

$$\text{Total of Liability side} = (\text{Capital Employed} + \text{Preliminary Expenses}) + \text{Current Liabilities}$$

$$= (24,00,000 + 50,000) + 1,50,000 = \text{Rs.}26,00,000$$

Fixed Assets = Total of Asset side – Current Assets – Preliminary expenses
= 26,00,000 – 3,00,000 – 50,000 = Rs.22,50,000

Land & Building and Plant & Machinery = 3: 2

Land and Building $= \frac{3}{5} \times 22{,}50{,}000 =$ Rs. 13,50,000

Plant & Machinery $= \frac{2}{5} \times 22{,}50{,}000 =$ Rs. 9,00,000

Sundry Creditors = Current Liabilities – Provision for Tax
= 1,50,000 – 1,20,000 = Rs.30,000.

[*Note:* General Reserve provided for the current year is Rs.30,000 and is deducted in the Net Profit after Tax].

Trading and Profit and Loss Account as on 31st March 2007

Particulars	*Rs.*	*Particulars*	*Rs.*
To Opening Stock	40,000	By Sales	9,00,000
To Purchases	5,00,000	By Closing Stock	1,00,000
To Wages	1,20,000		
To Gross Profit	3,40,000		
	10,00,000		10,00,000
To Administrative expenses	56,000	By Gross Profit	3,40,000
To Selling expenses	14,000	By Profit on sale of Plant	60,000
To Preliminary exp. written off	20,000	By Commission received	50,000
To Interest	60,000		
To Tax	1,20,000		
To Net Profit after Tax	1,80,000		
	4,50,000		4,50,000

Profit and Loss Appropriation Account

Particulars	*Rs.*	*Particulars*	*Rs.*
To General Reserve	30,000	By Net Profit	1,80,000
To Net Profit transferred to Balance Sheet	1,50,000		
	1,80,000		1,80,000

Balance Sheet as on 31st March 2007

Liabilities	*Rs.*	*Assets*	*Rs.*
Equity Share Capital	1120,000	Land & Building	13,50,000
Preference Share Capital	5,00,000	Plant & Machinery	9,00,000
Profit & Loss Account	1,50,000	Stock	1,00,000

General Reserve (50,000 + 30,000)	80,000	Debtors	1,50,000
Long-term Loan	6,00,000	Cash	50,000
Provision for Tax	1,20,000	Preliminary Expenses	
Sundry Creditors	30,000	(70,000-2000)	50,000
	26,00,000		26,00,000

DU PONT CONTROL CHART

Du-pont Control Chart is a technique developed by an American Company named Du-pont Company. This is a system for management control. It is based on accounting ratios. The standard ratios are determined in advance and the actual ratios are compared with the standard ratios to measure the performance of the company. The performance, according to the Du-pont Control Chart is on the basis of Net Profit on Capital employed. Hence, the Du-pont chart has two components (i) Net Profit and (ii) Capital employed.

Net profit is measured by deducting Cost of sales with Sales. Cost of sales includes cost of goods sold, administration expenses and selling and distribution expenses.

Net Profit	=	Sales - Cost of Sales
Cost of Sales	=	Cost of Goods sold + Administration expenses + Selling and Distribution expenses.

Capital employed is calculated by adding the Debt with Equity. Debt means Long term Loan and Debentures. Equity includes Equity Share Capital, Preference Share Capital and all Reserves and Surpluses. From this, fictitious assets should be deducted. It may also be calculated by adding the Fixed Assets and Current Assets and deducting from it the Current Liabilities. Depreciation for Fixed Assets should be deducted from Fixed Assets account.

Capital employed	=	Debt + Equity
Debt	=	Debenture + Long-term Loans
Equity	=	Equity Share Capital + Preference Share Capital + Reserves and surplus - Fictitious Assets
		(or)
Capital employed	=	Fixed Assets + Current Assets - Current Liabilities.

Then the Net Profit on Capital employed will be calculated as:

$$\frac{\text{Net Profit}}{\text{Capital Employed}} \times 100.$$

A model of Du-pont Chart is presented as follows.

DU-PONT CHART

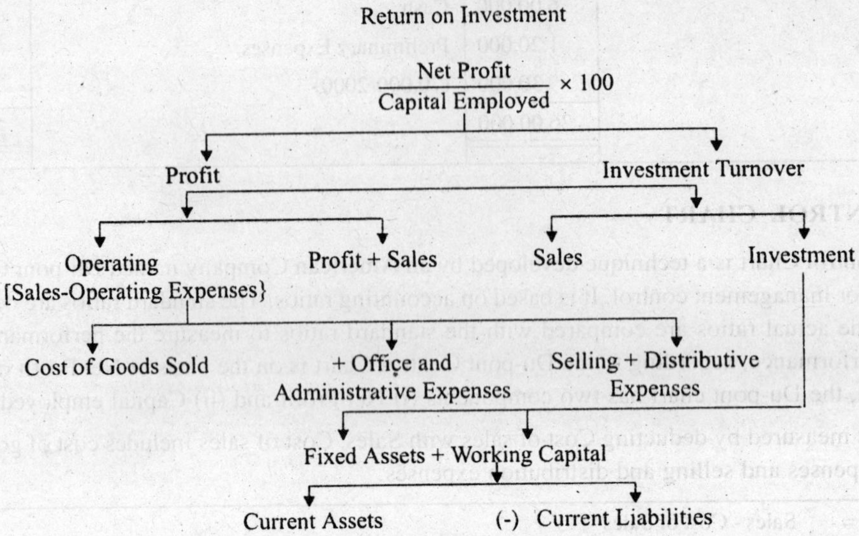

The Chart clearly shows the different components in Net Profit and Capital employed. Data related to these components should be mentioned in the Chart. The performance is measured by comparing the standard value with actual value for various periods. It helps the management to identify the area where special attention is required to improve the Profit. It may be in Sales, Cost of goods sold, Administrative cost or Selling and Distribution cost. Apart from the comparison of standard with actual ratios, inter-firm comparison can also be done.The ratios like Return on Capital, Net Profit ratio and Stock Turnover ratios of similar companies should be identified and compared with that of the company to know the comparative performance.

EXERCISE

I. Choose the correct answer for the following.

1. The difference between Current Assets and Current Liabilities is called —
   (i) Working Capital (ii) Debt (iii) Capital employed (iv) Fixed Assets
2. Turnover ratio is based on —
   (i) Purchase (ii) Capital (iii) Working Capital (iv) Sales
3. Long term loan is called —
   (i) Equity (ii) Debt (iii) Equity Share Capital (iv) Current Liability
4. Share Capital and reserves are called —
   (i) Debt (ii) Current Liability (iii) Equity (iv) Preference Share Capital
5. Current Assets excluding stock and adjustments is called —
   (i) Quick Assets (ii) Fixed Assets (iii) Total Assets (iv) Reserves
6. The Equity and Debt is called —
   (i) Fixed Assets (ii) Reserves and Surplus (iii) Owner's Fund (iv) Capital employed
7. The ratio between Current Assets and Current Liabilities is called —
   (i) Current ratio (ii) Fixed ratio (iii) Debt Equity ratio (iv) Turnover ratio
8. Debtors Turnover ratio helps to know the —
   (i) Payment period (ii) Collection period (iii) Period of Stock turnover (iv) Fixed Assets turnover
9. Creditor Turnover ratio helps to know the —
   (i) Payment period (ii) N.P ratio (iii) G.P. ratio (iv) Collection period

10. The ratio between Gross Profit and Sales is called —
(i) N.P ratio (ii) G.P ratio (iii) Debt-Equity ratio (iv) Return on Capital employed
11. The ratio between Net Profit and Sales is called —
(i) G.P. ratio (ii) Current ratio (iii) Quick ratio (iv) N.P ratio
12. Stock Turnover ratio is the ratio between Sales and —
(i) Opening Stock (ii) Closing Stock (iii) Average Stock (iv) Purchase
13. The ratio between Debt and Equity is called —
(i) Debt-Equity ratio (ii) Return on Equity ratio (iii) Current ratio (iv) Capital employed ratio
14. The different between Capital employed and Debt is called —
(i) Outsiders Fund (ii) Owner's Fund (iii) Current Assets (iv) Goodwill
15. The ratio between Net Profit after tax and the own fund is known as —
(i) Return on Capital employed (ii) Return on Debt (iii) Return on Investment (iv) Return on Equity

[**Ans:** 1. (i) 2. (iv) 3. (ii) 4. (iii) 5. (i) 6. (iv) 7. (i) 8. (ii) 9. (i) 10. (ii) 11. (iv) 12. (iii) 13. (i) 14. (ii) 15. (iv)]

II. Answer the following questions.

1. Define ratio. State the merits and limitations of ratios.
2. What is ratio? Explain the objectives of ratios.
3. Define ratio. Explain about the liquidity ratios.
4. What is ratio? State the concepts in Solvency ratios.
5. Define ratio. What is Turnover ratios?
6. What is Ratio Analysis? Explain how the Ratio Analysis helps in decision making.
7. Enumerate the different ways in which the long term creditors assess the performance of the company through different ratios.
8. Explain the different ways in which the financial performance of a company is assessed through Ratio Analysis.
9. Define Ratios and Ratio Analysis. State the concepts of Coverage ratios.
10. Distinguish between Return on Equity and Return on Capital employed.
11. What is Ratio Analysis? Distinguish between collection period and payment period.
12. Define ratio. Explain the method of calculating the Stock Turnover ratio.
13. Define ratio. State the procedures of calculating the Capital employed for a company.
14. Explain the method of calculating the Current ratio and Quick ratio.
15. Write short notes on the following :
(i) Debt (ii) Equity (iii) Capital employed (iv) Fictitious Assets (v) Solvency ratio (vi) Coverage ratio (vii) Liquidity ratio (viii) Turnover ratio (ix) Liquid Assets (x) Collection period (xi) Payment period.

III. Solve the following problems.

1. Calculate Current ratio and Acid Test ratio from the following.

	Rs.		*Rs.*
Stock	76,000	Outstanding expenses	10,000
Debtors	54,000	Expenses paid in advance	9,000
Cash	63,000	Interest received in advance	7,000
Bills Receivable	14,000	Outstanding interest	
Sundry Creditors	45,000	Receivable	5,000
Bills Payable	13,000		

(**Ans:** 3; 1.74)

2. Calculate (1) Gross Profit ratio (ii) Net Profit ratio (iii) Operating Profit ratio (iv) Cost of goods sold ratio from the following:

Sales Rs. 9,00,000, Cost of goods sold Rs. 6,80,000, Operating Expenses Rs.90,000, Interest paid Rs.41,000, Tax Rs. 50,000

(**Ans:** 24.4; 4.3; 14.4; 85.56)

3. G. Ltd., is providing the following information as on 31st March 2007.

Sales Rs.11,00,00, Wages Rs.2,40,000, Other direct expenses Rs.50,000, Purchases Rs.4,00,000, Administration expenses Rs.97,000, Selling and distribution expenses Rs.66,000, Interest paid Rs.47,000, Tax @ 40%.

Calculate (i) Gross Profit Ratio (ii) Net Profit Ratio (iii) Operating Profit Ratio (iv) Cost of Sales of Goods Sold Ratio (v) Administration Expenses Ratio (vi) Selling Expenses Ratio (vii) Operating Expenses Ratio.

(**Ans:** 37.27; 10.91; 22.45; 62.73; 8.82; 6; 77.54)

4. Calculate (i) Return on Capital Employed (ii) Return on Shareholders Equity and (iii) Return on Equity Shareholders Fund from the following:

	Rs.
Net Profit before interest and tax	3,44,000
Interest	62,500
Capital Employed	15,00,000
Debt	4,00,000
10% Preference Share Capital	3,00,000

(**Ans:** 8.76; 15.35; 17.36)

5. K Ltd., is providing the following information as on 31st March 2007

	Rs.
Capital Employed	29,00,000
Equity Share Capital (of nominal value @ Rs.10)	17,00,000
10% Preference Share Capital	5,00,000
12% Debentures	3,00,000
Long-term Loan	3,00,000
Earning after tax	2,50,000
Interest on Long-term Loan 15%	
Market price of the Equity Share is @ Rs.50	
Corporate Tax @ 50%	

Calculate the following ratios.

(i) Return on Capital Employed (ii). Return on Equity (iii). Return on Equity Shareholder Fund (iv) Earnings per Share (v) Earnings Yield (vi) Price Earning ratio. Also calculate EBIT.

(**Ans:** 11.41; 10.86; 11.11; Rs.1.18; 0.024; 42.37; Rs.5,81,000)

6. Calculate (i) Return on Equity (ii) Return on Equity Shareholders Fund (iii) EPS (iv) DPS (v) Earnings Yield (vi) Dividend Yield (vii) Dividend Payout ratio (viii) P/E ratio (ix) Book value per Share from the following.

Equity Rs.30,00,000, Equity Share Capital Rs.25,00,000, 10% Preference Share capital Rs.3,00,000, PAT Rs.4,00,000. Nominal value of Equity Share Rs.10, Dividend for Equity Shareholders @ 7%, Market price per Equity Share Rs.1.48.

(**Ans:** 13.33; 13.7; 1.48; Rs.0.70; 0.02; 0.008; 0.47; 60.81; Rs.10.80)

7. Calculate (i) Stock Turnover ratio (ii) Debtors Turnover ratio (iii) Average Collection period (iv) Creditors Turnover ratio (v) Average Payment period from the following information

Particulars	*As on 31st March 2006 (Rs.)*	*As on 31st March 2007 (Rs.)*
Stock	1,50,000	1,95,000
Debtors	75,000	61,000
Creditors	47,000	59,000

Sales for the year Rs.12,00,000; Purchase Rs.7,00,000.

(**Ans:** 6.96; 17.64; 21 days; 12.96; 28 days)

8. T. Ltd is providing the following information as an 31st March 2007.
Fixed Assets Rs. 17,50,000, Stock Rs.1,14,000 Debtors Rs. 71,500, Creditors Rs.55,500, Cash Rs.1,20,000, Sales Rs. 10,00,000, Cost of goods sold Rs. 7,50,000, Purchase Rs. 5,00,000.
Calculate
(i) Stock Turnover ratio (ii) Debtors Turnover ratio (iii) Creditors Turnover ratio (iv) Fixed Assets Turnover ratio (v) Current Assets Turnover ratio (vi) Working Capital Turnover ratio (vii) Average Collection period (viii) Average Payment period (ix) Total Assets Turnover ratio.
(**Ans:** 6.57; 13.99; 9; 0.57; 3.27; 0.4; 26 days; 41 days; 0.49)

9. K Ltd., provides the following information as on 31st March 2007.
Equity Share Capital Rs.22,00,000, Preference Share Capital Rs. 3,00,000, Profit and Loss Account Rs. 3,75,000, General Reserve Rs. 70,000, Debentures Rs.3,00,000, Long term Loan Rs. 2,00,000, Sundry Creditors Rs.49,500, Total Assets Rs.36,00,000.
Calculate
(i) Debt to Equity ratio (ii) Debt to total capital ratio (iii) Debt to Total Assets ratio (iv) Proprietory ratio and (v) Capital Gearing ratio.
(**Ans:** 0.17; 0.16; 0.14; 0.82; 0.23)

10. Calculate
(i) Debt - Equity ratio
(ii) Debt to Total Capital ratio from the following.
Equity Rs. 14,00,000; Debt Rs. 5,00.000
(**Ans:** 0.36; 0.26)

11. Calculate (i) Debt to Equity ratio (ii) Debt to Total Capital Ratio (iii) Proprietory ratio (iv) Capital gearing ratio from the following.
Total equity excluding Preference Share Capital Rs.10,00,000; Preference Share Capital Rs.2,00,000, Debenture Rs.3,00,000; Long Term Loan Rs.4,00,000 Sundry Creditors Rs.30,000.
(**Ans:** 0.58; 0.37; 0.62; 0.75)

12. The Balance Sheet of Doyle Ltd., for the year ended 31st March 2007 is stated as follows:

Balance Sheet

Liabilities	*Rs.*	*Assets*	*Rs.*
Equity. Share Capital	10,00,000	Goodwill	1,90,000
Profit & Loss A/c	2,50,000	Land	5,50,000
General Reserve	1,40,000	Premises	4,50,000
10% Debentures	3,50,000	Plant	5,60,000
12% Loan	2,50,000	Furniture & Fittings	90,000
Tax		Stock	99,000
Last year	40,000	Debtors	65,500

Current year	30,000	Cash	75,500
Sundry Creditors	47,000	Preliminary Expenses	50,000
Outstanding Expenses	23,000		
	21,30,000		21,30,000

The interest for Debentures and Loan for the current year are paid. Calculate ratios for (i) Testing Liquidity and (ii) Testing Solvency

(**Ans:** (i) 3.43; 2.01 (ii) 0.52; D.C 0.34; F.A. to capital 0.94)

13. Prepare a comparative statement of the Liquidity, Profitability, Activity and Financial position (Solvency) ratios of G Ltd. and T Ltd., for the year ended 31st March 2007 from the following.

Particulars	*G Ltd (Rs.)*	*T Ltd (Rs.)*
Fixed Assets	17,00,000	15,00,000
Stock	1,70,000	1,50,000
Debtors	60,000	55,000
Cash	75,000	45,000
Sales	14,00,00	12,00,000
Net profit after tax	3,00,000	2,00,000
Equity capital	10,00,000	9,00,000
General Reserve	90,000	70,000
Debenture	3,00,000	2,00,000
Long-term loan	1,80,000	2,70,000
Bank overdraft	44,000	33,000
Creditors	91,000	77,000

14. The financial statements of KT Ltd for three years are stated as follows.

Balance Sheets

Particulars	*2005 Rs.*	*2006 Rs.*	*2007 Rs.*
Land & Building	7,25,000	4,45,000	9,74,000
Plant & Machinery	5,45,000	3,15,000	6,50,000
Stock	1,25,000	1,12,000	1,70,000
Debtors	65,000	54,000	95,000
Cash	47,000	64,000	75,000
Prepaid expenses	9,000	10,000	15,000
Preliminary expenses	44,000	30,000	51,000
Total Assets	**15,60,000**	**10,30,000**	**20,30,000**
Equity Share Capital	7,00,000	5,00,000	10,00,000
Profit & Loss a/c	1,95,000	1,25,000	2,90,000
General Reserve	65,500	53,500	90,000
Debentures	3,00,000	1,50,000	2,50,000

Long term Loan	1,80,000	1,10,000	2,40,000
Provision for Tax	45,000	34,000	70,000
Creditors	54,500	44,500	75,000
Outstanding expenses	20,000	13,000	15,000
Total Liabilities	**15,60,000**	**10,30,000**	**20,30,000**

Operating Statements

Particulars	*2005 Rs.*	*2006 Rs.*	*2007 Rs.*
Sales	5,50,000	4,00,000	7,90,000
Cost of sales	3,40,000	3,50,000	4,60,000
Gross Profit	2,10,000	1,50,000	3,30,000
Operating expenses (General expenses and selling expenses)	90,000	45,000	1,10,000
Net Profit	1,20,000	1,05,000	2,20,000

The following additional information are also provided.

(i) Credit sales is considered to be 40% of total sales.

(ii) The closing stock as on 31st March 2004 is Rs.50,000.

(iii) Credit purchase is 70% of cost of sales.

Calculate

(i) Stock Turnover ratio (ii) Debtors Turnover ratio (iii) Average Collection period, (iv) Creditors Turnover ratio (v) Average Payment period (vi) Current ratio (vii) Acid Test ratio (viii) Gross Profit ratio (ix) Net Profit ratio (x) Fixed Assets to Shareholders Equity ratio (xi) Debt-Equity ratio (xii) Return on Capital Employed ratio.

15. GTR Ltd., provided the profit and loss account and balance sheet for the year ended 31st March 2007 as follows.

Profit and Loss Account

Particulars	*Rs.*	*Particulars*	*Rs.*
To Opening Stock of Raw material	50,000	By Sales	15,00,000
To Op. Stock of Finished goods	60,000	By Cl.Stock of Raw materials	75,000
To Purchase of Raw materials	6,10,000	By Cl.Stock of Finished goods	1,00,000
To Direct Wages	1,90,000	By Profit on sale of Shares	55,000
To Manufacturing expenses	1,05,000		
To Administration Expenses	94,000		
To Selling and Distribution exp.	71,000		
To Loss on sale of Plant	25,000		
To Int. on Debentures and Loan	78,000		
Net Profit	4,47,000		
	17,30,000		17,30,000

Balance Sheet

Assets	*Rs.*	*Assets*	*Rs.*
Equity Share Capital	9,00,000	Fixed Assets	21,20,000
Preference Share Capital	3,00,000	Stock of Raw materials	75,000
Profit & Loss Account	3,25,000	Stock of Finished goods	1,00,000
General Reserve	1,50,000	Sundry Debtors	96,000
Debentures (12%)	4,00,000	Bills Receivable	30,000
Loan (15%)	2,00,000	Cash	1,44,000
Sundry Creditors	57,000		
Bills Payable	33,000		
Provision for Tax	2,00,000		
	25,65,000		25,65,000

Calculate (i) Gross Profit ratio (ii) Net Profit ratio (iii) Operating Profit ratio (iv) Overall Profitability ratio (v) Current ratio (vi) Debt to Equity ratio (vii) Stock Turnover ratio (viii) Liquid ratio.

(Ans: 51; 29.8; 56.63; 19.4; 1.53; 2.79; 10.53)

16. The Trading and Profit and Loss Account and Balance Sheet of KM Ltd. as on 31st March 2007 are stated as follows.

Trading and Profit & Loss Account

Particulars	*Rs.*	*Particulars*	*Rs.*
To Opening Stock	77,000	By Sales	21,00,000
To Purchase	14,50,000	By Closing Stock	1,20,000
To Wages	2,93,000		
To Gross Profit	4,00,000		
	22,20,000		**22,20,000**
To Administration expenses	40,500	By Gross Profit	4,00,000
To Selling Expenses	45,500	By Non-operating income	70,000
To Depreciation	70,000		
To Interest	44,000		
To Income Tax	1,35,000		
To Net profit	1,35,000		
	4,70,000		**4,70,000**

Balance Sheet as on 31st March 2007

Liabilities	*Rs.*	*Assets*		*Rs.*
Equity Share Capital	7,00,000	Land & Building	7,90,000	
10% Pre. Share Capital	3,00,000	Less : Depreciation	40,000	7,50,000
Reserves and Surplus	2,90,000	Plant & Machinery	5,90,000	
10% Debentures	2,00,000	Less : Depreci.	30,000	5,60,000
12% Long-term loan	2,00,000	Goodwill		1,70,000
Creditors	40,000	Stock		1,20,000

Outstanding expenses	10,000	Debtors	75,000
Bills Payable	20,000	Prepaid expenses	23,000
Provision for Tax	1,35,000	Marketable securities	1,05,000
		Cash	92,000
	18,95,000		18,95,000

The following further details are also given.

(i) Reserves and Surplus in the beginning is Rs.2,35,000. The dividend for Preference Shareholders is Rs.30,000 and for the Equity Shareholders is Rs.50,000.

(ii) The market price of the share as on 31st March 2007 is Rs.90

(iii) 40% of Sales and 50% of Purchases are on credit basis.

Calculate (i) Current ratio (ii) Quick ratio (iii) Debt Equity ratio (iv) Stock Turnover ratio (v) Interest Coverage (vi) Fixed Charge Coverage (vii) Debtors Turnover ratio (viii) Average Collection period (ix)Creditors Turnover ratio (x) Average Payment period (xi), Gross Profit margin (xii) Net Profit margin (xiii) Operating ratio (xiv) Operating Profit ratio (xv) Return on Capital Employed (xvi) Return Shareholders Equity (xvii) Earnings per Share (xviii) Price Earning (P/E) ratio (xix) Earnings Yield.

(**Ans:** 2.02; 1.33; 0.36; 17.25; 7.14; 4.24; 11.2; 33 days 18.13; 20 days; 19; 6.43; 5.5; 14.95; 11.05; 12.05; 12.8; 1.5; 60; 0.02)

17. Calculate (i) Sales (ii) Closing Stock (iii) Sundry Debtors and (iv) Sundry Creditors for the following ratios.
Gross Profit ratio - 30%, Stock Velocity - 4 times, Debtors Velocity - 2 months, Creditors Velocity - 3 months, Gross profit as on 31st March 2007 is Rs.3,00,000 and Opening Stock is Rs.50,000
(**Ans:** Rs.10,00,000; Rs.4,50,000; Rs.1,66,667; Rs.75,000)

18. Prepare Trading and Profit & Loss Account from the following.
Gross Profit ratio 20%, Net Profit ratio 10% Operating Profit ratio 12%, Tax @ 40%, Opening stock Rs.90,000, Direct cost Rs.70,000, Stock Turnover ratio 5 times, Gross Profit Rs.4,00,000.
(**Ans:** N.P Rs.2,00,000; O.P. Rs.2,40,000)

19. K Ltd., provided the following information for the year ended 31st March 2007.
Gross Profit ratio 25%; Operating Profit ratio 20%; Tax @ 40%; 12% Debentures Rs.3,00,000; 10% Loan Rs.2,00,000; Gross Profit Rs.5,00,000. Stock Turnover ratio 5; Closing stock is Rs.40,000 more than the Opening stock; Wages Rs.1,70,000; Profit on sale of Plant Rs.30,000; Loss on sale of Furniture Rs.25,000, Ratio of Administration and Selling expenses is 7 : 3.
Prepare Trading and Profit and Loss Account
(**Ans:** N.P. Rs.3,49,000; PAT Rs.2,09,400)

20. Prepare the Balance Sheet of a Company from the following.
Gross Profit ratio 30%; Capital Turnover ratio 1.2; Stock Velocity 6; Fixed Assets Turnover ratio 3; Debtors collection period 60 days; Creditors payment period 45 days; Gross Profit is Rs.3,00,000; Closing stock is Rs.50,000 more than the Opening stock and Direct cost is Rs.1,00,000.
(**Ans:** B/S Total Rs.9,01,141)

21. Prepare the Balance Sheet of GR Ltd., as on 31st March 2007 from the following.
Return on Capital employed 25%, Debt Equity ratio is 0.4, Interest Coverage is 4 times, Profit after Tax is Rs.4,00,000, Tax 50%, Interest on Debenture is Rs.20,000 (@ 10% p.a), Preference Share Capital is Rs.2,00,000, General Reserve Rs.1,20,000, Current ratio is 4:1, Sundry Creditors Rs.90,000, Ratio of Stock, Debtors and Cash is 5:2:3
(**Ans:** B/S. Total Rs.31,56,668)

22. A manufacturing company is providing the following information related to the year ending 31st March 2007.
Stock Turnover ratio 5 times; Debtors Turnover ratio is 4 times, Creditors Turnover ratio 3 times; Gross Profit

ratio 30%, Working Capital Turnover ratio 5 times; Capital Turnover ratio 0.7; Debt to Equity ratio 0.5; Equity Share Capital Rs.7,00,000; Preference Share Capital Rs.3,00,000; Debentures and Loan are in the ratio 3:2; Gross Profit Rs.3,60,000; 60% of Purchase and 50% of Sales are on credit basis. Direct expense Rs.1,75,000; Opening Stock Rs.1,50,000; Opening Debtors Rs.40,000; Opening Creditors Rs.75,000; Ratio of Land & Building, Plant & Machinery and Furniture & Fittings is 5:3:2.

Prepare the Balance Sheet as on 31st March 2007.

(**Ans:** B/S Total Rs.19,77,286)

23. Prepare the Balance Sheet of KT Ltd as on 31st March 2007 from the following.

Gross Profit ratio 20%; Current ratio 2.5; Liquidity ratio 1.5; Stock Turnover ratio 5 times; Fixed Assets Turnover ratio 1.5 times; Debt collection period 1 month,Fixed Assets to Shareholders Net worth 1.7; Reserves and Surplus to Equity 0.4; and Net Working Capital is Rs.4,50,000.

(**Ans:** B/S Total 17,50,000; F.A. Rs.10,00,000; C.A.; Rs.7,50,000)

24. Prepare the Trading and Profit & Loss Account and Balance Sheet as on 31st March 2007 from the following information.

(a) Gross Profit ratio 30%
(b) Net Profit ratio 20%
(c) Stock Turnover ratio 6
(d) Net Profit to Capital 61/275
(e) Fixed Assets to Capital 12/11
(f) Fixed Assets to Current Assets 5
(g) Capital to Total Liabilities 4/5
(h) Closing Stock Rs.1,90,000
(i) Fixed Assets Rs.15,00,000
(j) Sundry Debtors Rs. 90,000
(k) Current ratio is 5:2
(l) Long term Loan Rs. 3,50,000.

(**Ans:** G.P. Rs.4,57,500; N.P. Rs.3,05,000; Sales Rs.15,25,000; B/S/ Total Rs.18,00,000).

25. KMW Ltd., provided to following ratios and other information as on 31st March 2007.

Current Liabilities	2,00,000	Cost of Goods sold	Rs.6,40,000
Stock Velocity	8 times	Current ratio	2:1
Opening Stock	Rs.60,000	Net Profit after Tax	Rs.1,20,000
Return on Capital Employed	12%	Preference Share Capital	Rs.7,00,000
General Reserve (31.3.06)	Rs.70,000	Preliminary exp. (31.3.06)	Rs.50,000
Operating Profit ratio	20%	Cash	Rs.1,60,000
Wages	Rs.1,50,000	Tax	40%
Interest (10%)	Rs.50,000	Profit on sale of Plant	Rs.40,000
Debtors Turnover ratio	5	Debtors (31.3.06)	Rs.60,000
Commission received	Rs.70,000		

Provision for General Reserve during the year is Rs.45,000 and Preliminary expenses written off is Rs.30,000. Ratio of Administrative expenses and Selling expenses is 3 : 2; Ratio of Land & Building and Plant & Machinery is 5 : 4; Cash sales is 50% of the total sales.

Prepare Trading and Profit & Loss Account and Balance Sheet as on 31st March 2007.

26. The Balance Sheet of W.D Ltd., for the year ended 31st March 2007 is stated as follows:

Balance Sheet

Liabilities	*Rs.*	*Assets*	*Rs.*
Equity Share Capital	12,00,000	Goodwill	1,00,000
Profit & Loss A/c	3,00,000	Land	7,00,000
General Reserve	1,50,000	Premises	7,50,000
10% Debentures	4,00,000	Plant	6,00,000
12% Loan	3,00,000	Furniture & Fitings	1,00,000
Tax		Stock	1,10,000
Last year	50,000	Debtors	60,000
Current year	70,000	Cash	70,000
Sundry Creditors	40,000	Preliminary Expenses	50,000
Outstanding Expenses	30,000		
	25,40,000		25,40,000

The interest for Debentures and Loan for the current year are paid. Calculate ratios for (i) Testing Liquidity and (ii) Testing Solvency

(Ans: (i) 3.43; 1.86 (ii) 0.51; 0.34; 5.87)

❑ ❑ ❑

4

FUND FLOW ANALYSIS

Fund Flow analysis is an analysis about the change of financial position of a company from one period to another period. The Profit and Loss Account and Balance Sheet explain the profitable and financial conditions of the company for a particular year. The Profit and Loss Account deals with the revenue and expenses and exhibits the profit after tax and all appropriations done during the year. There is no analysis or comparison about the profit with another year in this statement. Like that, the Balance Sheet deals with the assets and liabilities. The asset side explains the utilisation of the financial resources and the liability side explains the types of financial resources of the company. Therefore, these statements explain the static information for a period. The improvement of profit and the financial position may not be known through these statements. It is not possible to measure the change of fund invested in a company over a period of time through these statements. Hence, there is a need for preparing a statement to measure the movement of fund over a period of time. The analysis carried on in these financial statements, particularly Balance Sheet, about the movement of fund is called Fund Flow analysis.

Meaning of Fund

Fund generally means investments in long-term assets as well as the receipts concerned with a long period of time. According to the International Accounting Standard, fund refers to cash or cash and cash equivalents; or to working capital. Hence, the fund may be defined in two concepts. They are cash concept, and working capital concept. The cash concept define fund in a narrow sense and working capital concept defines it in a broad sense.

Concepts of Fund

1. Cash concept or narrow sense of fund: In this concept, fund means only cash. It is concerned with the inflow and outflow of cash only. According to this concept, the movement of fund means movement of cash only over a period of time. Hence, the statement prepared according to this concept, to measure the movement of fund is called statement of Cash Flow.

2. Working capital concept or broad sense of fund: According to working capital concept, fund means cash and cash equivalents. Cash equivalents are stock, debtors, bills receivable, outstanding income, and expenses paid in advance. This concept states that fund means working capital. Working capital is related with current assets and current liabilities. Working capital may be classified into (i) Gross Working Capital and (ii) Net Working Capital

(i) Gross working capital means investment of funds in current assets.

(ii) Net working capital is the difference between the current assets and current liabilities.

Working capital generally means the difference between the current assets and current liabilities (i.e., net working capital)

Meaning of Fund Flow

Fund flow means the movement of fund from one period to another. Movement of fund may either be inflow of fund or outflow of fund. Inflow of fund, increases the fund and outflow of fund decreases the fund of a company. Inflow of fund will be due to the sale of fixed assets or raising of fixed capital. Raising of fixed capital may be due to the issue of shares or debenture and long-term borrowing from banks or other sources. Outflow of fund will be due to purchase of fixed assets or decreasing of fixed capital. Decreasing fixed capital may be due to redemption of shares and debentures, and repayment of long-term loan. Inflow and outflow of funds will have a direct impact on the current assets and current liabilities i.e., on working capital. Inflow of funds will increase the cash balance or indirectly increase the position of other current assets like stock and debtors or it may decrease the current liabilities like sundry creditors indirectly. Hence, the inflow of fund will increase the working capital position. Outflow of funds will decrease the cash balance or indirectly decrease the position of other current assets like stock and debtors or it may increase the current liabilities like sundry creditor's indirectly. Hence, the outflow of fund will decrease the working capital position. It states that the movement of fund means the movement of working capital.

The movement or change or flow of fund between a fixed (non-current) item, or between a current item wont effect the real change in the fund position. It wont affect the working capital position. Example: (i) Purchase of a machinery by paying in the form of equity shares (ii) Redemption of debentures by paying equity shares of the company. (iii) Receipt of cash from sundry debtors. It reduces the debtors and increases the cash position. (iv) Payment to sundry creditors. It reduces the cash and the sundry creditors simultaneously. Hence, for the flow of funds, the following types of transactions should be taken place.

a. Transactions between current assets and fixed assets.
b. Transactions between current liabilities and fixed liabilities.
c. Transactions between current assets and fixed liabilities.
d. Transactions between current liabilities and fixed assets.

The concept of flow of fund is stated in diagrammatical form as follows:

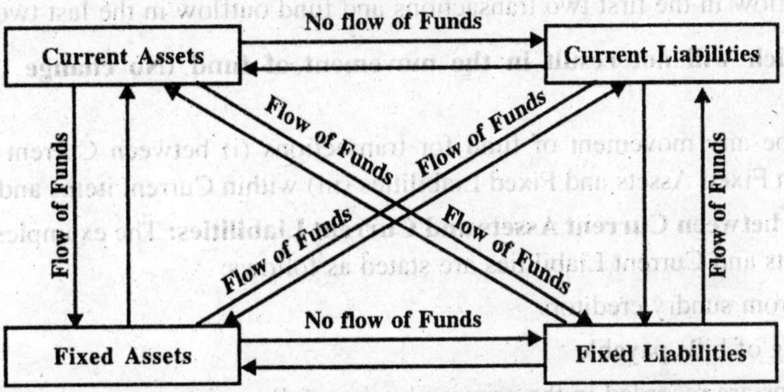

The diagram clearly explains the transactions which result is flow of fund and non-flow of funds.

I. Transactions which result in movement of fund (Change in working capital)

The flow of funds are mostly resulted from the transactions between (i) Current assets and fixed assets (ii) Current assets and fixed liabilities. The flow of funds are very rarely and indirectly resulted for the transactions between (i) Current liabilities and fixed asset (ii) Current liabilities and fixed liabilities.

1. Transaction between Current Assets and Fixed Assets: The examples for the transactions between current assets and fixed assets are as follows:

(i) Sale of Machinery

(ii) Purchase of Furniture

These transactions may be recorded in the primary book as follows.

(i)	Cash a/c	Dr
	To Machinery a/c	
(ii)	Furniture a/c	Dr
	To Cash a/c	

There is fund inflow in the first transaction and fund outflow in the second transaction.

2. Transactions between Current Assets and Fixed Liabilities: The examples for the transactions between current assets and fixed liabilities are as follows:

(i) Issue of Equity Share Capital

(ii) Borrowing Loans from Bank

(iii) Redemption of Debentures

(iv) Repayment of Loans

These transactions may be recorded in the primary book as follows:

(i)	Cash a/c	Dr
	To Equity Share Capital a/c	
(ii)	Cash a/c	Dr
	To Loan a/c	
(iii)	Debentures a/c	Dr
	To Cash a/c	
(iv)	Loan a/c	Dr
	To Cash a/c	

There is fund inflow in the first two transactions and fund outflow in the last two transactions.

II. Transactions which will not result in the movement of fund (No change in working capital)

There will not be any movement of fund for transactions (i) between Current Assets and Current Liabilities (ii) between Fixed Assets and Fixed Liabilities (iii) within Current items and within Fixed items.

1. Transactions between Current Assets and Current Liabilities: The examples for the transactions between Current Assets and Current Liabilities are stated as follows:

(i) Receipt from sundry creditors

(ii) Honouring of bills payable

These transactions are recorded in the primary book as follows:

(i)	Sundry Creditors a/c	Dr
	To Cash a/c	
(ii)	Bills payable a/c	Dr
	To Cash a/c	

In these transactions Current Assets and Current Liabilities are decreased equally at a time which results in no flow of fund.

2. Transactions between Fixed Assets and Fixed Liabilities: The examples for the transactions between Fixed Assets and Fixed Liabilities are as follows:

(i) Purchase of a machinery by paying equity shares.

(ii) Redemption of debentures through a machinery to debenture holders.

The transactions may be recorded in the primary book as follows.

(i) Machinery a/c Dr
To Equity Share Capital a/c

(ii) Debenture a/c Dr
To Machinery a/c

In the first transaction the Fixed Liability and Fixed Asset are reduced equally and in the second transaction the Fixed Liability and Fixed Asset are reduced equally.

3. Transactions within current items and within fixed items: The examples for the transactions within current item and within fixed item are as follows:

(i) Receipt from debtors

(ii) Bills accepted for sundry creditors

(iii) Exchange of a machine with furniture for other company

(iv) Redemption of debentures through equity shares

These transactions are recorded in the primary book as follows

(i) Cash a/c Dr
To Debtors a/c

(ii) Sundry creditors a/c Dr
To Bills payable a/c

(iii) Furniture a/c Dr
To Machinery a/c

(iv) Debenture a/c Dr
To Equity Share Capital a/c

In all these transactions, increase of one account resulted in the decrease of another account equally at a time. It may be in Current items as well as in Fixed items.

Current Item and Fixed Item affecting the Fund or Working Capital

Working Capital is the difference between Current Assets and Current Liabilities. Increase of decrease of working capital shows that the extent of fund utilised (movement of funds) between the two periods under comparison. The utilisation or movement of funds is due to the effect of changes in the Fixed items (Fixed Assets and Fixed Liabilities). Hence, both Current items and Fixed (non-current items) are considered as important in the Fund Flow Analysis.

1. Current items are classified as current assets and current liabilities. The important current items are stated as follows:

	Current Liabilities		Current Assets
i.	Sundry creditors	i.	Stock
ii.	Bank overdraft	ii.	Sundry debtors
iii.	Bills payable	iii.	Cash
iv.	Outstanding expenses	iv.	Bank balance
v.	Income received in advance	v.	Bills receivable
vi.	Provision for tax	vi.	Outstanding income
vii.	Proposed dividend	vii.	Expenses paid in advance

2. Fixed items are classified as follows:

	Fixed Liabilities		Fixed Assets
i.	Equity share capital	i.	Land & building
ii.	Preference share capital	ii.	Plant & machinery
iii.	Debenture	iii.	Furniture and fittings
iv.	Long-term loan	iv.	Investments

3. Other non-current item classified as follows

	Liability side		Asset side
i.	Profit & Loss a/c	i.	Goodwill
ii.	General Reserve	ii.	Preliminary expenses
iii.	Capital Redemption Reserve	iii.	Discount on issue of shares

Sources and Application of Funds

Sources of Fund

The important sources of funds are stated as follows:

1. Fund from Operations: The fund generated for the operating activities is called Fund from Operation. It is due to the sales deducted with operating expenses. It may be calculated through the net profit of the company. But there is a need to adjust the amortisation of fictitious assets (like, Discount on issue of Shares or Debentures, Preliminary expenses, Goodwill etc.) and appropriation on profits (provision for general reserve, and other reserves, dividend, tax etc.) in the current year profit. In the amortisation and appropriation, there will not be any actual fund flow. In addition to this other non-operating expenses like loss on sale of fixed assets, depreciation etc., and non-operating income like profit on sale of fixed assets would be adjusted in the current year profit. The profit after all such adjustments is called Fund from Operation which is considered as an important source of fund.

2. Issue of Share Capital: Issue of either Equity share capital or Preference share capital is considered as another important source of fund. If shares are issued for premium, the share premium is an additional source of fund. Like that, discount on issue of shares should be deducted from the nominal value of shares issued, if the shares are issued for discount.

3. Issue of Debentures: Debenture is a long term debt for the company. It is an important source of fund. The peculiar feature of debenture is that it should be repaid after certain period of time and there is no need for paying instalments every year. Interest for debentures account need to be paid every year.

4. Raising of Loan: Loan may be raised from banks or financial institutions. Interest and instalment of loan should be paid every year.

5. Sale of Fixed Assets: Fixed assets like machinery, plant, furniture etc., may be sold by the company for the purpose of replacement. The asset realised in the sale is considered as a source of fund for the company. Like that investment may also be sold by the company for profit or to meet the financial obligations.

Application of Funds

The important application of funds in a company are stated as follows:

1. Fund Lost in Operation: If there is no fund from operation due to heavy loss or high non-operating profit, the adjusted profit may show a negative balance. It is called Fund Lost in Operation. It means there is fund outflow due to operating activities.

2. Redemption of Preference Share Capital: The company may redeem the Preference Share Capital which results in the outflow of fund.

3. Redemption of Debentures: The debenture should be redeemed after certain period of issue of it. The redemption of debenture means outflow of funds.

4. Repayment of Loan: The company has to repay the loan in lumpsum or on instalment basis. The repayment of loan is called outflow of funds.

5. Purchase of Fixed Assets: The outflow of funds may take place due to purchase of fixed assets in a period. The company may purchase shares or invest in securities of other companies which is considered as outflow of fund.

6. Payment of Tax and Dividend: Funds will outflow due to the payment of tax and dividend.

Causes of Changes in Working Capital

Working capital is the difference between the current assets and current liabilities. Any change in the current assets or current liabilities will affect the working capital. Since Fund Flow analysis is concerned with the change of funds between two periods, the change in the individual current assets and current liabilities should be taken into consideration. The change in individual items of current assets and current liabilities are recorded in the statement of changes in working capital between two periods. The statement shows the increase or decrease in working capital. For example, working capital in 2006 is Rs.75,000 and in 2007 is Rs.1,00,000. It means increase in working capital of Rs.25,000. If it is Rs.70,000 in 2006 and Rs.50,000 in 2007, the decrease in working capital is Rs.20,000. This change is due to the change in individual current assets and current liabilities. The causes of changes in working capital are stated as follows:

1. Increase in Current Assets
2. Decrease in Current Assets
3. Increase in Current Liabilities
4. Decrease in Current Liabilities

1. Increase in Current Assets: Increase in current assets from one period to another will increase the working capital. It is due to the generation of funds from the operating activities.

2. Decrease in Current Assets: Decrease in current assets from one period to another will decrease the working capital. It is due to the utilisation of short-term fund for the operating activities.

3. Increase in Current Liabilities: Increase in current liabilities from one period to another will decrease the working capital. It is due to the outflow of short-term fund.

4. Decrease in Current Liabilities: Decrease in current liabilities from one period to another will decrease the working capital. It is due to the inflow of short term fund for the company.

Meaning of Fund Flow Statement

Fund flow statement is a statement of changes in fund. It may be called as a statement of sources and application of funds. It records the various sources of inflow of fund and various ways in which the fund is utilised or spend for a period. Fund flow statement contains the information about the flow of fund resulted in the fixed items (non-current items). The balance of this statement is the net change in the working capital. It may either increase in working capital or decrease in working capital. The result can be cross checked by calculating the increase or decrease of working capital through the current assets and current liabilities of two periods.

Objectives of Fund Flow Analysis

The objectives of fund flow analysis are as follows:

(i) To measure the movement of fund over a period of time.
(ii) To find out the financial performance of a company.
(iii) To take corrective action in case the performance is not upto the mark.
(iv) To measure the degree of increase of working capital for a period.
(v) To take various managerial decisions of a company.

Advantages of Fund Flow Analysis

The following are the advantages of fund flow analysis:

(i) It helps to find out the movement of fund over a period of time.
(ii) It facilities to decide the requirement of fund for a period.
(iii) The performance of a company when compared to the previous years can be ascertained.
(iv) It is one of the tools for the management for managerial decision making.
(v) It helps for allocating the fund for various requirement in a company.
(vi) It helps to determine actual working capital and the required working capital.

Limitations of Fund Flow Analysis

The limitations of fund flow analysis are stated as follows:

(i) It analyses only the historical facts. There is no projection of the fund in future in this method.
(ii) It wont be a substitute for the income statement.
(iii) Since the analysis is based on the Balance Sheet items, the manipulation of fixed assets done in the Balance Sheet will result in a wrong calculation of the movement of fund.
(iv) This analysis is meant only for two periods.

Parties Interested in Fund Flow Statement

Parties interested in Fund Flow statement are (i) Owner (ii) Financial institutions and (iii) Employees.

1. Owners: Owners may be individuals, partners or shareholders. Since large scale business units are preparing Fund Flow statement, the owners may be equity and preference shareholders. They are interested to know the effectiveness in which their funds are utilised. They are concerned with high profits, dividend, managerial efficiency, long-term survival, meeting the repayment obligations of long-term loan.

2. Financial Institutions: Financial institutions can know the credit worthiness of a company, availability of funds to meet their loan instalments for the present period and for the future. They want the security and safety for their investment and also the receipt of interest without any default.

3. Employees: Employees are also interested in the Fund Flow statement since the security of their job and high remuneration depend upon the effective utilisation of the fund.

Procedures in the Preparation of Fund Flow Statement

The following are the procedures in the preparation of Fund Flow statement:

1. Preparation of Statement of changes in Working Capital.
2. Preparation of Adjusted Profit and Loss Account.
3. Preparation of Fund Flow Statement.

1. Preparation of Statement of Changes in Working Capital: Statement of changes in working capital is prepared to find out the increase or decrease of working capital for current year compared to the previous year. Increase of working capital is considered as the excess of fund inflow over the fund outflow for a period. Working capital is the difference between current assets and current liabilities. The change in working capital is measured through the working capital of two periods. Hence, the statement should certain two columns for recording the amounts for two periods apart from the particular column to record the type of current assets and current liabilities. It may also contain two more columns to record the increase or decrease in working capital for individual current assets and current liabilities. It helps for cross checking the calculation and also to know to what extent individual current assets and current liabilities increase the working capital or decrease the working capital. A model of the Statement of changes in Working Capital is stated as follows:

Statement of Changes in Working Capital

Particulars	*Period I*	*Period II*	*Increase in Working Capital*	*Decrease in Working Capital*
Current Assets				
Stock				
Debtors				
Cash				
Bank				
Bills Receivable				
Outstanding income				
Expenses paid in advance				
Current Liabilities				
Sundry Creditors				
Bank Overdraft				
Bills Payable				
Outstanding expenses				
Income received in advance				
Working Capital (C.A-C.L.)				
Increase / Decrease of Working Capital				

In this statement working capital for two different periods can be calculated. From the two working capitals the difference should be calculated to find out the increase or decrease of working capital.

In the last two columns increase or decrease of working capital due to the individual current assets and current liabilities should be recorded.

Increase in current assets and decrease in current liabilities are called increase in working capital.

Decrease in current assets and increase in current liabilities are called decrease in working capital.

The total of the increase in working capital and decrease in working capital should be calculated. From this, the difference should be calculated. The difference is called net increase or decrease of working capital.

2. Preparation of Adjusted Profit and Loss Account: This account is prepared to calculate the Fund from Operation. The basic concept of Fund from Operation is to adjust the items in the Profit and Loss Account which increase (inflow), or decrease (outflow) the fund, but in fact there is no fund inflow or outflow. For example, provision for General Reserve, writing off of goodwill or preliminary expenses, loss on sale of fixed assets etc. In these transactions, actually there is no outflow of fund. Like that, in profit on sale of fixed assets, decrease in Workmen Compensation Fund etc., there is actually no fund inflow. But it may be treated as if there is fund inflow. These type of transactions should be adjusted in the current year profit to know the Fund from Operation.

As per the accounting concept, apart from the current items and fixed items in the Balance Sheet the items like Reserves and Surplus, Profit & Loss Account, other reserves and fictitious assets like goodwill, discount on issue of shares need to be treated. The current items are treated in statement of changes in working capital. Fixed items are treated in the Fund Flow statement. The remaining items like,Reserves and Surplus, Profit and Loss Account balance and fictitious assets accounts should be treated in the Adjusted Profit and Loss Account. The credit balance of this account is called Fund from Operation and the debit balance is called Fund lost in Operation.

A model of the Adjusted Profit and Loss account is stated as follows:

Adjusted Profit & Loss Account

Particulars	*Rs.*	*Particulars*	*Rs.*
To Depreciation	xxx	By Opening balance	xxx
To Provision for General Reserve	xxx	By Profit on sale of Fixed Assets	xxx
To Provision for Cap. Redemption Reserve	xxx	**By Fund from Operation**	xxx
To Other provisions	xxx		
To Provision for Taxation	xxx		
To Provision for Dividends	xxx		
To Preliminary expenses written off	xxx		
To Loss on sale of Fixed Assets	xxx		
To Closing balance	xxx		
	xxx		xxx

If there is debit balance, it is called Fund lost in Operation. If the opening balance is debit then it should be recorded on the debit side. If closing balance is debit, it should be recorded on the credit side. The provision for dividend and tax are not debited in the account if they are treated as current items.

Fund from Operation can also be calculated as follows:

Calculation of Fund from Operation

Particulars	*Rs.*	*Rs.*
Balance of Profit and Loss account or Retained Earnings at the end		
(After appropriation)		xxx
Add : Non-fund or non-operating items, already debited in the P & L A/c		
Depreciation of Fixed assets	xxx	
Amortisation of Fictitious assets	xxx	
(Goodwill, Preliminary expenses, Discount on issue of shares or debentures, Trade mark, etc.)		
Appreciation of Retained earnings	xxx	
(Provision for General reserve and other reserves)		
Loss on sale of Fixed Assets	xxx	
Interm dividend and provision for Final Dividend	xxx	
Provision for Taxation	xxx	xxx
Less : Non-fund or non-operating items credited in the Profit and Loss account :		
Profit on sale of Fixed Assets	xxx	
Appreciation in the value of Fixed Assets	xxx	
Dividend received	xxx	
Excess provision created in P & L A/c	xxx	
Balance of P & L a/c or Retained earnings in the beginning	xxx	xxx
Fund from Operation		xxx

3. Preparation of Fund Flow statement: The statement of inflow and outflow of fund is called Fund Flow statement. This statement may be prepared in account form also. The debit side is meant for Inflow (Sources) of fund and credit side is meant for Outflow (Application) of fund. All the inflow or outflow of funds related to fixed items of the Balance Sheet should be recorded in this statement. Increase in fixed liability and decrease in fixed assets mean inflow of fund. Decrease in fixed liability and increase in fixed assets mean outflow of fund. The real fund inflow and outflow related to operating activities should be determined after adjusting depreciation, profit or loss on sale of fixed assets etc. Fund from operation is debited and Fund lost in operation is credited in this statement. The balance of this account is due to the increase or decrease of working capital. The debit balance is due to excess of inflow of fund over outflow and is called increase in working capital. The credit balance is due to excess of outflow over inflow and is called decrease in working capital.

A model of Fund Flow statement is stated as follows:

Statement of Fund Flow

Particulars	*Rs.*
Sources of Funds	
Fund from Operation	xxx
Issue of Share Capital	xxx
Issue of Debentures	xxx
Raising of Long term Loans	xxx

Sale of Fixed Assets	xxx
Sale of Investments	xxx
Dividend received from investments	xxx
Decrease in Working Capital	xxx
Total	xxx
Application of Funds	
Fund Lost in Operation	xxx
Redemption of Preference Share Capital	xxx
Redemption of Debenture	xxx
Repayment of Long Term Loan	xxx
Purchase of Fixed Assets	xxx
Purchase of Investments	xxx
Payment of Dividend (if treated as non-current item)	xxx
Payment of Tax (if treated as non-current item)	xxx
Increase in Working Capital	xxx
Total	xxx

Statement of Fund Flow can be represented in T.form as follows:

Statement of Fund Flow

Sources	*Rs.*	*Applications*	*Rs.*
Fund from Operation	xxx	**Fund Lost in Operation**	xxx
Issue of Share Capital	xxx	Redemption of Pref. Share Capital	xxx
Issue of Debentures	xxx	Redemption of Debenture	xxx
Raising of Long term Loans	xxx	Repayment of Long term Loans	xxx
Sale of Fixed Assets	xxx	Purchase of Fixed Assets	xxx
Sale of Investments	xxx	Purchase of Investments	xxx
Div. received from Investments	xxx	Payment of Dividend *	xxx
Decrease in Working Capital	xxx	Payment of Tax *	xxx
		Increase in Working Capital	xxx
	xxx		xxx

* (If treated as non-current item)

Illustration: 1

Calculate the Working Capital from the following:

Stock	35,000	Cash	25,000
Debtors	50,000	Outstanding interest (debt)	6,000
Sundry Creditors	20,000	Outstanding wages	70,000
Bank Overdraft	10,000		

Solution :

Current Assets = Stock + Debtors + Cash + Interest outstanding

= 35,000 + 50,000 + 25,000 + 6,000 = Rs.1,16,000

Current Liabilities = Creditors + Bank overdraft + Outstanding wages

= 20,000 + 10,000 + 7,000 = Rs.37,000

Working Capital = Current Assets – Current Liabilities

= 1,16,000 – 37,000 = Rs. 79,000

Illustration: 2

Calculate the Working Capital from the following:

Particulars	*31st March 2006 Rs.*	*31st March 2007 Rs.*
Sundry Debtors	40,000	60,000
Sundry Creditors	30,000	35,000
Bank Overdraft	7,000	5,000
Outstanding Expenses	11,000	9,000
Outstanding Income	5,000	7,000
Expenses paid in advance	4,000	6,000
Income received in advance	8,000	3,000
Stock	10,000	12,000
Cash	14,000	20,000

Solution :

Calculation of Working Capital

Particulars	*31st March 2006 Rs.*	*31st March 2007 Rs.*
Current Assets		
Stock	10,000	12,000
Debtors	40,000	60,000
Cash	14,000	20,000
Outstanding Income	5,000	7,000
Expenses paid in advance	4,000	6,000
	73,000	1,05,000
Current Liabilities		
Creditors	10,000	12,000
Bank Overdraft	7,000	5,000
Outstanding expenses	11,000	9,000
Income received in advance	8,000	3,000
	36,000	29,000
Working Capital (C.A.-C.L)	37,000	76,000

Illustration: 3

Calculate Fund from Operation from the following

	Rs.
Profit and Loss account balance as on 31st March 2006	2,50,000
Profit and Loss account balance as on 31st March 2007	2,90,000
Depreciation for Fixed Assets	79,000
Profit on sale of Plant	20,000
Loss on sale of Furniture	10,000
Provision for General Reserve	25,000

(For B.Com., B.B.A., B.B.M)

Solution :

Calculation of Fund from Operation

Particulars	*Rs.*	*Rs.*
Balance of Profit & Loss a/c as on 31st March 2007		2,90,000
Add : Depreciation for Fixed Assets	79,000	
Loss on sale of Furniture	10,000	
Provision for General Reserve	25,000	1,14,000
		4,04,000
Less : Profit on sale of Plant	10,000	
Balance of P / L a/c as on 31st Mar. 2006	2,50,000	2,60,000
Fund from Operation		1,44,000

Illustration: 4

Calculate Fund from Operation from the following:

	Rs.
Balance of Profit & Loss a/c (debit) as on 31st March 2006	1,10,000
Balance of Profit & Loss a/c (debit) as on 31st March 2007	1,20,000
Depreciation for Land & Building	40,000
Depreciation for Plant & Machinery	30,000
Provision for Tax	45,000
Provision for Dividend	35,000
Income Tax refund	20,000
Loss on sale of Plant	15,000

(For B.Com., B.B.A., B.B.M)

Solution :

Calculation of Fund from Operation

Particulars		*Rs.*	*Rs.*
Balance of P & L a/c as on 31st March 2007 (Debit)			(1,20,000)
Add :	Depreciation for Land & Building	40,000	
	Depreciation for Plant & Machinery	30,000	
	Provision for Tax	45,000	
	Provision for Dividend	35,000	1,50,000
			30,000
Less :	Income Tax Refund	20,000	
	Loss on sale of Plant	15,000	
	Balance of P& L as on 31st March 2006 (Debit)	(110,000)	(75,000)
	Fund from Operation		1,05,000

Illustration: 5

Calculate Fund from Operation from the following

	Rs.
Profit and Loss account as on 31st March 2006	90,000
Profit & Loss account as on 31st March 2007	40,000
Provision for depreciation	20,000
Provision for General Reserve	10,000
Preliminary expenses written off	5,000
Loss on sale of Furniture	7,000
Profit on sale of Plant	31,000

(For B.Com., B.B.A., B.B.M)

Solution :

Calculation of Fund from Operation

Particulars		*Rs.*	*Rs.*
Profit and Loss a/c balance as on 31st March 2007			40,000
Add :	Provision for depreciation	20,000	
	Provision for General Reserve	10,000	
	Preliminary expenses written off	5,000	
	Loss on sale of Furniture	7,000	42,000
			82,000
Less : Profit on sale of Plant		31,000	
	Profit & Loss a/c balance as on 31st March 06	90,000	1,21,000
Fund lost in Operation			39,000

Illustration: 6

Calculate Fund from Operation for the following Trading and Profit & Loss account.

Trading and Profit and Loss Account

Particulars	*Rs.*	*Particulars*	*Rs.*
To Opening stock	30,000	By Sales	3,10,000
To Purchase	1,20,000	By Closing stock	45,000
To Wages	25,000		
To Gross Profit	1,80,000		
	3,55,000		3,55,000
To Salary	35,000	By Gross Profit	1,80,000
To Electricity	10,000	By Profit on sale of Land	20,000
To Rent	12,000		
To Depreciation	32,000		
To Loss on sale of Machinery	11,000		
To Provision for Tax	25,000		
To Net Profit	75,000		
	2,00,000		2,00,000

Solution :

Calculation of Fund from Operation

Particulars	*Rs.*
Net Profit for the year	75,000
Add : Depreciation	32,000
Loss on sale of Machinery	11,000
Provision for tax	25,000
	1,43,000
Less : Profit on sale of land	20,000
Fund from Operation	1,23,000

Illustration: 7

Prepare a Statement of Fund Flow and a Statement of changes in Working Capital from the following Balance Sheets:

Liabilities	*2006 Rs.*	*2007 Rs.*	*Assets*	*2006 Rs.*	*2007 Rs.*
Share Capital	5,00,000	5,50,000	Fixed Assets	4,95,000	5,50,000
Profit & Loss a/c	1,00,000	1,20,000	Stock	49,000	77,000
Sundry creditors	15,000	20,000	Debtors	30,000	10,000
			Cash	41,000	53,000
	6,15,000	6,90,000		6,15,000	6,90,000

(For B.Com., B.B.A., B.B.M)

Solution :

Statement of Changes in Working Capital

Particulars	*2006 Rs.*	*2007 Rs.*	*Increase Rs.*	*Decrease Rs.*
Current Assets				
Stocks	49,000	77,000	28,000	
Debtors	30,000	10,000		20,000
Cash	41,000	53,000	12,000	
	120,000	140,000		
Current Liabilities				
Sundry creditors	15,000	20,000		5,000
Working Capital (C.A - C.L)	1,05,000	1,20,000	40,000	25,000
Increase in Working Capital	15,000			15,000
	1,20,000	1,20,000	40,000	40,000

Statement of Fund Flow

Inflow	*Rs.*	*Outflow*	*Rs.*
Fund from Operation	20,000	Purchase of Fixed Assets	55,000
Issue of Share Capital	50,000	Increase in Working Capital	15,000
	70,000		70,000

Fund from Operation = Closing balance of Profit and Loss a/c – Opening balance of Profit & Loss a/c

= 1,20,000 – 1,00,000 = Rs.20,000

Illustration: 8

G Ltd., provided the Balance Sheet as on 31st March 2006 and 2007 as follows.

Liabilities	*2006 Rs.*	*2007 Rs.*		*2006 Rs.*	*2007 Rs.*
Share Capital	9,00,000	10,50,000	Land	4,00,000	3,40,000
Profit & Loss a/c	90,000	1,10,000	Premises	3,60,000	4,50,000
Mortgage Loan	1,70,000	85,000	Plant	3,50,000	4,20,000
Sundry Creditors	12,000	55,000	Stock	25,000	40,000
Bank overdraft	18,000	10,000	Debtors	20,000	16,000
			Cash	35,000	44,000
	11,90,000	13,10,000		11,90,000	13,10,000

Prepare a statement of Fund Flow. *(For B.Com., B.B.A., B.B.M)*

Solution :

Statement of Changes in Working Capital

Particulars	*2006 Rs.*	*2007 Rs.*	*Increase Rs.*	*Decrease*
Current Assets				
Stocks	25,000	40,000	15,000	
Debtors	20,000	16,000		4,000
Cash	35,000	44,000	9,000	
	80,000	100,000		
Current Liabilities				
Sundry creditors	12,000	55,000		43,000
Bank overdraft	18,000	10,000	8,000	
	30,000	65,000		
Working Capital (C.A - C.L)	50,000	35,000	32,000	47,000
Decrease in Working Capital		15,000	15,000	
	50,000	50,000	47,000	47,000

Statement of Fund Flow

Inflow	*Rs.*	*Outflow*	*Rs.*
Fund from Operation	20,000	Purchase of Premises	90,000
Issue of Share Capital	1,50,000	Purchase of Plant	70,000
Sale of Land	60,000	Repayment of mortgage loan	85,000
Decrease in Working Capital	15,000		
	2,45,000		2,45,000

Illustration: 9

Prepare a Statement of Fund Flow from the following Balance Sheet.

Liabilities	*2006 Rs.*	*2007 Rs.*		*2006 Rs.*	*2007 Rs.*
Share Capital	3,00,000	5,00,000	Land & Building	2,00,000	1,80,000
Profit & Loss a/c	1,50,000	1,00,000	Plant & Machinery	2,45,000	3,45,000
Loan	50,000	–	Stock	50,000	65,000
Sundry Creditors	30,000	40,000	Debtors	15,000	10,000
Bills Payable	10,000	5,000	Cash	30,000	45,000
	5,40,000	6,45,000		5,40,000	6,45,000

Consider decrease in Land & Building as depreciation. *(For B.Com., B.B.A., B.B.M)*

Solution :

Statement of Changes in Working Capital

Particulars	*2006 Rs.*	*2007 Rs.*	*Increase Rs.*	*Decrease Rs.*
Current Assets				
Stock	50,000	65,000	15,000	
Debtors	15,000	10,000		5,000
Cash	30,000	45,000	15,000	
	95,000	120,000		
Current Liabilities				
Sundry Creditors	30,000	40,000		10,000
Bills Payable	10,000	5,000	5,000	
	40,000	45,000		
Working Capital (C.A - C.L)	55,000	75,000	35,000	15,000
Increase in Working Capital	20,000	–	–	20,000
	75,000	75,000	35,000	35,000

Statement of Fund Flow

Inflow	*Rs.*	*Outflow*	*Rs.*
Issue of Share Capital	2,00,000	**Fund Lost in Operation**	30,000
		Purchase of Plant & Machinery	1,00,000
		Repayment of Loan	50,000
		Increase in Working Capital	20,000
	2,00,000		2,00,000

Calculation of Fund from Operation:	*Rs.*
Closing balance of Profit & Loss a/c	1,00,000
Add : Depreciation of Land & Building (2,00,000 – 1,80,000)	20,000
	1,20,000
Less : Opening balance of Profit & Loss a/c	1,50,000
Fund Lost in Operation	30,000

Note: Fund lost in operation in considered as an outflow of Fund.

Illustration: 10

Prepare a Statement of Fund Flow from the following:

Liabilities	*2006 Rs.*	*2007 Rs.*	*Assets*	*2006 Rs.*	*2007 Rs.*
Share Capital	7,00,000	9,00,000	Land & Building	4,10,000	4,30,000
Loan	2,00,000	50,000	Plant & Machinery	3,90,000	3,75,000
Sundry Creditors	40,000	59,000	Stock	40,000	65,000

Bank overdraft	20,000	11,000	Debtors	20,000	10,000
			Cash	30,000	50,000
			Profit & Loss A/c	70,000	90,000
	9,60,000	10,20,000		9,60,000	10,20,000

Depreciation for Land and Building is Rs.20,000 and Plant and Machinery is Rs.15,000.

(For B.Com., B.B.A., B.B.M)

Solution :

Statement of Changes in Working Capital

Particulars	*2006 Rs.*	*2007 Rs.*	*Increase Rs.*	*Decrease Rs.*
Current Assets				
Stock	40,000	65,000	25,000	
Debtors	20,000	10,000		10,000
Cash	30,000	50,000	20,000	
	90,000	125,000		
Current Liabilities				
Sundry creditors	40,000	59,000		19,000
Bank overdraft	20,000	11,000	9,000	
	60,000	70,000		
Working Capital (C.A - C.L)	30,000	55,000	54,000	29,000
Increase in Working Capital	25,000	–	–	25,000
	55,000	55,000	54,000	54,000

Statement of Fund Flow

Inflow	*Rs.*	*Outflow*	*Rs.*
Fund from Operation	15,000	Repayment of Loan	1,50,000
Issue of Share Capital	2,00,000	Purchase of Land & Building	40,000
		Increase in Working Capital	25,000
	2,15,000		2,15,000

Calculation of Fund from Operation:		
Closing balance of Profit & Loss a/c		(90,000)
Add : Depreciation for Land & Building	20,000	
Depreciation for Plant & Machinery	15,000	35,000
		(55,000)
Less : Opening balance of Profit & Loss a/c		70,000
Fund from Operation		15,000

Land & Building Account

Particulars	*Rs.*	*Particulars*	*Rs.*
To Balance c/d	4,10,000	By P & L a/c (Depreciation)	20,000
To Cash (Purchase)	40,000	By Balance c/d	4,30,000
	4,50,000		4,50,000

Plant & Machinery Account

Particulars	*Rs.*	*Particulars*	*Rs.*
To Balance c/d	3,90,000	By P&L a/c (Depreciation)	15,000
		By Balance c/d	3,75,000
	3,90,000		3,90,000

Illustration: 11

Prepare a statement of Fund Flow from the following Balance Sheets.

Liabilities	*2006 Rs.*	*2007 Rs.*	*Assets*	*2006 Rs.*	*2007 Rs.*
Capital	3,00,000	4,00,000	Land & Building	3,00,000	5,00,000
Profit & Loss a/c	1,15,000	1,40,000	Plant & Machinery	2,70,000	2,10,000
General Reserve	40,000	60,000	Stock	60,000	90,000
Debentures	2,00,000	2,50,000	Debtors	25,000	15,000
Loan	50,000	–	Cash	35,000	50,000
Sundry Creditors	30,000	43,000	Bills Receivable	20,000	15,000
Bills Payable	15,000	17,000	Preliminary Expenses	40,000	30,000
	7,50,000	9,10,000		7,50,000	9,10,000

Adjustments:

(i) Depreciation for Land & Building Rs. 35,000

(ii) Depreciation for Plant & Machinery Rs.20,000; Profit on sale of a Plant is Rs.10,000

(iii) Drawings of Capital for the year Rs.25,000. *(For M.Com., M.B.A., M.C.A)*

Solution :

Statement of Changes in Working Capital

Particulars	*2006 Rs.*	*2007 Rs.*	*Increase Rs.*	*Decrease Rs.*
Current Assets				
Stock	60,000	90,000	30,000	
Debtors	25,000	15,000		10,000
Cash	35,000	50,000	15,000	
Bills receivable	20,000	15,000		5,000
	140,000	170,000		

Current Liabilities				
Sundry creditors	30,000	43,000		13,000
Bills payable	15,000	17,000		2,000
	45,000	60,000		
Working Capital (C.A - C.L)	95,000	1,10,000	45,000	30,000
Increase in Working Capital	15,000	–	–	15,000
	1,10,000	1,10,000	45,000	45,000

Statement of Fund Flow

Inflow	*Rs.*	*Outflow*	*Rs.*
Fund from Operation	1,00,000	Drawings of Capital	25,000
Additional Capital	1,25,000	Repayment of Loan	50,000
Issue of Debentures	50,000	Purchase of Land & Building	2,35,000
Sale of Plant & Machinery	50,000	**Increase in Working Capital**	15,000
	3,25,000		3,25,000

Calculation of Fund from Operation

Particulars	*Rs.*	*Rs.*
Closing balance of Profit & Loss a/c		1,40,000
Add : Depreciation of Land & Building	35,000	
Depreciation for Plant & Machinery	20,000	
Provision for General Reserve	20,000	
Preliminary expenses written off	10,000	85,000
		2,25,000
Less : Profit on sale of Plant	10,000	
Opening balance of Profit & Loss a/c	1,15,000	1,25,000
Fund from Operation		1,00,000

Land & Building Account

Particulars	*Rs.*	*Particulars*	*Rs.*
To Balance c/d	3,00,000	By P&L a/c (Depreciation)	35,000
To Cash (Purchase)	2,35,000	By Balance c/d	5,00,000
	5,35,000		5,35,000

Plant & Machinery Account

Particulars	*Rs.*	*Particulars*	*Rs.*
To Balance c/d	2,70,000	By P&L a/c (Depreciation)	20,000
To Profit & Loss a/c	10,000	By Cash (sales)	50,000
		By Balance c/d	2,10,000
	2,80,000		2,80,000

Capital Account

Particulars	*Rs.*	*Particulars*	*Rs.*
To Cash (Drawings)	25,000	By Balance c/d	3,00,000
To Balance c/d	4,00,000	By Cash (Additional capital)	1,25,000
	4,25,000		4,25,000

Illustration: 12

Prepare a Statement of changes in Working Capital and Fund Flow Statement from the following.

Balance Sheet

Liabilities	*2006 Rs.*	*2007 Rs.*	*Assets*	*2006 Rs.*	*2007 Rs.*
Equity Share Capital	4,00,000	4,00,000	Land & Building	5,00,000	6,00,000
Profit & Loss a/c	90,000	1,30,000	Plant & Machinery	4,00,000	3,50,000
General Reserve	50,000	70,000	Stock	70,000	80,000
Debentures	2,90,000	3,60,000	Debtors	20,000	60,000
Loan	2,00,000	1,40,000	Cash	40,000	25,000
Sundry Creditors	29,000	34,000	Interest Outstanding	10,000	5,000
Salary outstanding	11,000	6,000	Preliminary Expenses	30,000	20,000
	10,70,000	11,40,000		10,70,000	11,40,000

Solution:

Statement of Changes in Working Capital

Particulars	*2006 Rs.*	*2007 Rs.*	*Increase Rs.*	*Decrease Rs.*
Current Assets				
Stock	70,000	80,000	10,000	
Debtors	20,000	60,000	40,000	
Cash	40,000	25,000		15,000
Outstanding Interest	10,000	5,000		5,000
	1,40,000	1,70,000		
Current Liabilities				
Creditors	29,000	34,000		5,000
Salary outstanding	11,000	6,000	5,000	
	40,000	40,000		
Working Capital (C.A-C.L)	1,00,000	1,30,000	55,000	25,000
Increase in Working Capital	30,000			30,000
	1,30,000	1,30,000	55,000	55,000

Calculation of Fund from Operation:

Adjusted Profit & Loss Account

Particulars	*Rs.*	*Particulars*	*Rs.*
To Increase in General reserve	20,000	By Balance	90,000
To Preliminary expenses written off	10,000	By Fund from Operation	70,000
To Balance at the end	1,30,000		
	1,60,000		1,60,000

Statement of Fund Flow

Inflow	*Rs.*	*Outflow*	*Rs.*
Fund from Operation	70,000	Purchase of	
Sale of Plant & Machinery	50,000	Land & Building	1,00,000
(4,00,000 – 3,50,000)		Repayment of Loan	60,000
Issue in Debenture	70,000	**Increase in W.C.**	30,000
	1,90,000		1,90,000

Illustration: 13

Prepare a statement of Fund Flow for the following Balance Sheets.

Balance Sheets

Liabilities	*2006 Rs.*	*2007 Rs.*	*Assets*	*2006 Rs.*	*2007 Rs.*
Equity Share Capital	3,00,000	3,00,000	Land & Building	4,00,000	4,95,000
Preference S.Capital	2,00,000	2,00,000	Plant & Machinery	3,00,000	2,50,000
Profit & Loss A/c	80,000	1,30,000	Stock	1,20,000	1,50,000
General Reserve	60,000	90,000	Debtors	90,000	80,000
Workmen			Cash	50,000	90,000
Compensation Fund	70,000	40,000	Outstanding interest	10,000	8,000
Debentures	1,40,000	2,50,000	Rent paid in advance	12,000	19,000
Loan	1,10,000	50,000	Preliminary expenses	40,000	20,000
Sundry Creditors	32,000	22,000			
Bank Overdraft	17,000	20,000			
Outstanding Salary	13,000	10,000			
	10,22,000	11,12,000		10,22,000	11,12,000

Adjustments:

Depreciation provided is @ 10% for all the Fixed Assets

During the year plant sold for Rs.30,000, on 30th March 2006.

Assume that the purchase of Building is at the end of the financial year.

Prepare the statement of changes in Working Capital and the statement of Fund Flow.

Solution :

Statement of Changes in Working Capital

Particulars	*2006 Rs.*	*2007 Rs.*	*Increase Rs.*	*Decrease Rs.*
Current Assets				
Stock	1,20,000	1,50,000	30,000	
Debtors	90,000	80,000		10,000
Cash	50,000	90,000	40,000	
Outstanding interest	10,000	8,000		2,000
Rent paid in advance	12,000	19,000	7,000	
	2,82,000	3,47,000		
Current Liabilities				
Sundry creditor	32,000	22,000	10,000	
Bank overdraft	17,000	20,000		3,000
Outstanding salary	13,000	10,000	3,000	
	62,000	52,000		
Working capital (C.A.-C.L)	2,20,000	2,95,000	90,000	15,000
Increase in Working Capital	75,000			75,000
	2,95,000	2,95,000	90,000	90,000

Land & Building Account

Particulars	*Rs.*	*Particulars*	*Rs.*
To Balance	4,00,000	By Profit & Loss A/c (Dep.)	40,000
To Cash (Purchase)	1,35,000	By Closing balance	4,95,000
	5,35,000		5,35,000

Plant & Machinery Account

Particulars	*Rs.*	*Particulars*	*Rs.*
To Balance	3,00,000	By Profit & Loss a/c (Depr.)	30,000
To Profit & Loss a/c (Profit)	10,000	By Cash	30,000
		By Closing balance	2,50,000
	3,10,000		3,10,000

Profit & Loss Adjustment Account

Particulars	*Rs.*	*Particulars*	*Rs.*
To Land Building a/c	40,000	By Balance b/d	80,000
To Plant & Machinery a/c	30,000	By Plant & Machinery a/c	10,000
To Preliminary Expenses a/c	20,000	By Workmen Comp. Fund	30,000
To General Reserve	30,000	By Fund from Operation	1,30,000
To Balance c/d	1,30,000		
	2,50,000		2,50,000

Statement of Fund Flow

Inflow	*Rs.*	*Outflow*	*Rs.*
Fund from Operation	1,30,000	Purchase of Land	1,35,000
Sale of Plant & Machinery	30,000	Repayment of Loan	60,000
Issue of Debentures	1,10,000	**Increase in Working Capital**	75,000
	2,70,000		2,70,000

Illustration: 14

Prepare a statement of Fund Flow and statement of changes in Working Capital from the following particulars.

Balance Sheets

Liabilities	*2006 Rs.*	*2007 Rs.*	*Assets*	*2006 Rs.*	*2007 Rs.*
Equity Share Capital	7,50,000	7,50,000	Land & Building	7,00,000	8,20,000
Profit & Loss a/c	80,000	1,50,000	Plant & Machinery	5,00,000	4,10,000
General Reserve	50,000	90,000	Stock	70,000	1,00,000
Workmen Comp. Fund	60,000	50,000	Debtors	40,000	80,000
Loan	2,00,000	2,20,000	Cash	60,000	40,000
Debentures	2,00,000	1,40,000	Preliminary expenses	50,000	30,000
Sundry Creditors	70,000	76,000			
Outstanding expenses	10,000	4,000			
	14,20,000	14,80,000		14,20,000	14,80,000

Depreciation for Fixed Assets is @ 10%. During the year Plant sold for Rs.60,000.

Assume that sale of Plant and purchase of land are at the end.

Solution :

Statement of Changes in Working Capital

Particulars	*2006 Rs.*	*2007 Rs.*	*Increase Rs.*	*Decrease Rs.*
Current Assets				
Stock	70,000	1,00,000	30,000	
Debtors	40,000	80,000	40,000	
Cash	60,000	40,000		20,000
	1,70,000	2,20,000		
Current Liabilities				
Sundry Creditors	70,000	76,000		6,000
Outstanding expenses	10,000	4,000	6,000	
	80,000	80,000		
Working Capital (C.A.-C.L)	90,000	1,40,000	76,000	26,000
Increase in Working Capital	50,000			50,000
	1,40,000	1,40,000	76,000	76,000

Land & Building Account

Particulars	*Rs.*	*Particulars*	*Rs.*
To Balance b/d	7,00,000	By Profit & Loss A/c (Dep.)	70,000
To Cash (Purchase)	1,90,000	By Balance c/d	8,20,000
	8,90,000		8,90,000

Plant & Machinery Account

Particulars	*Rs.*	*Particulars*	*Rs.*
To Balance b/d	5,00,000	By Profit & Loss a/c (Dep.)	50,000
To Adjusted P & L a/c (Profit)	20,000	By Cash (Sale)	60,000
		By Balance c/d	4,10,000
	5,20,000		5,20,000

Calculation of Fund from Operation:

Adjusted Profit & Loss A/c

Particulars	*Rs.*	*Particulars*	*Rs.*
To General Reserve	40,000	By Opening Balance	80,000
To Land & Building	70,000	By W.C.F.	10,000
To Plant & Machinery a/c	50,000	By Plant & Machinery a/c	20,000
To Preliminary Expenses	20,000	By Fund from Operation	2,20,000
To Closing Balance	1,50,000		
	3,30,000		3,30,000

Statement of Fund Flow

Inflow	*Rs.*	*Outflow*	*Rs.*
Fund from Operation	2,20,000	Purchase of L & B	1,90,000
Sale of Plant & Machinery	60,000	Redemption of Debentures	60,000
Increase in Loan	20,000	Increase in Working Capital	50,000
	3,00,000		3,00,000

Illustration: 15

GR Ltd. provided the Balance Sheets for the year ended 31st March 2006 and 31st March 2007 as follows.

Balance Sheets

Liabilities	*2006 Rs.*	*2007 Rs.*	*Assets*	*2006 Rs.*	*2007 Rs.*
Equity Share Capital	6,00,000	6,00,000	Land & Building	6,00,000	6,40,000
Profit & Loss a/c	1,60,000	1,00,000	Plant & Machinery	4,00,000	3,10,000
General Reserve	40,000	80,000	Stock	50,000	1,40,000

Debentures	1,00,000	2,20,000	Debtors	30,000	90,000
Loan	1,00,000	50,000	Cash	60,000	50,000
Provision for			Outstanding income	15,000	10,000
Tax liability	80,000	1,00,000	Expen. paid in adv.	5,000	7,000
Provision for Dividend	90,000	70,000	Preliminary expenses	60,000	30,000
Sundry Creditors	40,000	52,000			
Outstanding wages	10,000	5,000			
	12,20,000	12,77,000		12,20,000	12,77,000

Adjustments:

1. Depreciation for Land & Building is Rs.60,000
2. During the year Rs.50,000 worth of Plant is sold for Rs.35,000.

Solution :

Statement of Changes in Working Capital

Particulars	*2006 Rs.*	*2007 Rs.*	*Increase Rs.*	*Decrease Rs.*
Current Assets				
Stock	50,000	1,40,000	90,000	
Debtors	30,000	90,000	60,000	
Cash	60,000	50,000		10,000
Outstanding income	15,000	10,000		5,000
Exp. paid in advance	5,000	7,000	2,000	
	1,60,000	2,97,000		
Current Liabilities				
Sundry Creditors	40,000	52,000		12,000
Outstanding expenses	10,000	5,000	5,000	
Provision for tax	80,000	1,00,000		20,000
Provision for Dividend	90,000	70,000	20,000	
	2,20,000	2,27,000		
Working Capital (C.A.-C.L)	(60,000)	70,000	1,77,000	47,000
Increase in Working Capital	1,30,000			1,30,000
	70,000	70,000	1,77,000	1,77,000

Land & Building Account

Particulars	*Rs.*	*Particulars*	*Rs.*
To Balance b/d	6,00,000	By Adjusted P & L a/c (Dep.)	60,000
To Cash	1,00,000	By Balance c/d	6,40,000
	7,00,000		7,00,000

Plant & Machinery Account

Particulars	*Rs.*	*Particulars*	*Rs.*
To Balance b/d	4,00,000	By Cash (Purchase)	35,000
		By Adjust P & L a/c (Loss)	15,000
		By Adjust P & L a/c (Dep.)	40,000
		By Closing balance c/d	3,10,000
	4,00,000		4,00,000

Profit & Loss Adjustment A/c

Particulars	*Rs.*	*Particulars*	*Rs.*
To General Reserve	40,000	By Balance b/d	1,60,000
To Preliminary Expenses	30,000	**By Fund from Operation**	1,25,000
To Land & Building (Dep.)	60,000		
To Plant & Machinery (Dep.)	40,000		
To Plant & Machinery (Loss)	15,000		
To Closing balance c/d	1,00,000		
	2,85,000		2,85,000

Statement of Fund Flow

Inflow	*Rs.*	*Outflow*	*Rs.*
Fund from Operation	1,25,000	Purchase of L & B	1,00,000
Sale of Plant & Machinery	35,000	Repayment of loan	
Debentures	1,20,000	(1,00,000-50,000)	50,000
(2,20,000-1,00,000)		**Increase in Working Capital**	1,30,000
	2,80,000		2,80,000

Treatment of Provision for Taxation and Proposed Dividend

Provision for taxation and proposed dividend may be considered as current liabilities or fixed liabilities. If these are considered as current items, then it would be treated in the statement of changes in Working Capital. If they are treated as non-current items (fixed liabilities), then it would be treated in the Adjusted Profit and Loss Account and Statement of Fund Flow.

Treatment of Provision for Taxation and Proposed Dividend as current items

If Provision for Taxation and Proposed Dividend are considered as current items, then it would be treated in the Statement of changes in Working Capital. The increase in these items for the current year from the previous year should be considered as decrease in working capital, and the decrease in these items for the current year from the previous year in considered as increase in working capital. The dividend paid or tax paid if given in the adjustment will not be taken into account in any of the calculations.

Illustration: 16

GT Ltd. provided the Balance Sheets as on 31st March of 2006 and 2007 as follows:

Balance Sheets

Liabilities	*2006*	*2007*	*Assets*	*2006*	*2007*
Equity Share Capital	9,00,000	9,00,000	Land & Building	9,00,000	8,20,000
Preference Share Capital	6,00,000	7,00,000	Plant & Machinery	8,00,000	9,30,000
Profit & Loss A/c	1,10,000	1,80,000	Furniture & Fittings	2,60,000	2,10,000
General Reserve	70,000	90,000	Goodwill	50,000	40,000
Debentures	2,00,000	1,50,000	Stock	1,29,000	1,00,000
Long-term Loan	2,00,000	1,00,000	Debtors	86,000	97,000
Provision for Tax	70,000	80,000	Cash	65,000	1,13,000
Proposed Dividend	90,000	70,000			
Sundry Creditors	50,000	40,000			
	22,90,000	23,10,000		22,90,000	23,10,000

The following further information are also given.

1. Furniture worth Rs.35,000 (Accumulated depreciation Rs.10,000) was sold for Rs.30,000.
2. Depreciation for Plant & Machinery Rs.70,000.

Prepare a statement of Fund Flow and a statement of changes in Working Capital.

Solution :

Statement of Changes in Working Capital

Particulars	*2006 Rs.*	*2007 Rs.*	*Increase Rs.*	*Decrease Rs.*
Current Assets				
Stock	1,29,000	1,00,000		29,000
Debtors	86,000	97,000	11,000	
Cash	65,000	1,13,000	48,000	
Total	2,80,000	3,10,000		
Current Liabilities				
Sundry Creditors	50,000	40,000		10,000
Provision for Tax	70,000	80,000	10,000	
Provision for Dividend	90,000	70,000	20,000	
Total	2,10,000	1,90,000		
Working Capital (C.A.-C.L)	70,000	1,20,000	89,000	39,000
Increase in Working Capital	50,000			50,000
	1,20,000	1,20,000	89,000	89,000

Statement of Fund Flow

	Inflow	*Rs.*	*Outflow*
Fund from Operation	2,70,000	Redemption Debentures	50,000
Issue of Preference Share Capital	1,00,000	Repayment of Loan	1,00,000
Sale of Furniture	30,000	Purchase of P & M.	2,00,000
		Increase in Working Capital	50,000
	4,00,000		4,00,000

Profit & Loss Adjustment A/c

Particulars	*Rs.*	*Particulars*	*Rs.*
To Land & Building	80,000	By Balance b/d	1,10,000
To Plant & Machinery	70,000	By Furniture & Fittings	5,000
To Furniture & Fittings	25,000	(Profit on sale)	
To Goodwill	10,000	**By Fund from Operation**	2,70,000
To Increase in General Reserve	20,000		
To Balance c/d	1,80,000		
	3,85,000		3,85,000

Land & Building Account

Particulars	*Rs.*	*Particulars*	*Rs.*
To Balance b/d	9,00,000	By Adjusted P & L A/c (Dep.)	80,000
		By Balance c/d	8,20,000
	9,00,000		9,00,000

Plant & Machinery Account

Particulars	*Rs.*	*Particulars*	*Rs.*
To Balance	8,00,000	By Adjusted P&L a/c (Dep.)	70,000
To Cash (Purchase)	2,00,000	By Balance c/d	9,30,000
	10,00,000		10,00,000

Furniture and Fittings Account

Particulars	*Rs.*	*Particulars*	*Rs.*
To Balance b/d	2,60,000	By Adjusted P&L a/c (Dep.)	25,000
To Adjusted P&L a/c (Profit)	5,000	By Cash (Sales)	30,000
		By Balance c/d	2,10,000
	2,65,000		2,65,000

Goodwill Account

Particulars	*Rs.*	*Particulars*	*Rs.*
To Balance b/d	50,000	By Adjusted P&L a/c	10,000
		By Balance c/d	40,000
	50,000		50,000

Treatment of Provision for Taxation and Proposed Dividend as non-current items

If the provision for taxation and proposed dividends are considered as non current items, they would be treated in Adjusted Profit and Loss Account and Fund Flow statement. The appropriation of profits for the current year for these items should be debited in the Adjusted Profit and Loss account. Actual payment of tax and dividend for the year (which will be given in the adjustment) should be treated in the outflow of the statement of Fund Flow.

Illustration: 17

The Balance Sheets as on 31st March of 2006 & 2007 of KMH Ltd. are stated as follows:

Balance Sheets

Liabilities	*2006 Rs.*	*2007 Rs.*	*Assets*	*2006 Rs.*	*2007 Rs.*
Equity Share Capital	12,00,000	15,00,000	Land & Building	11,00,000	13,50,000
Preference Share Cap.	3,00,000	3,00,000	Plant & Machinery	8,50,000	11,00,000
Profit & Loss a/c	1,40,000	1,60,000	Furniture & Fittings	3,50,000	2,30,000
General Reserve	75,000	85,000	Goodwill	50,000	70,000
Workmen Comp.Fund	50,000	35,000	Stock	1,10,000	1,50,000
Debentures	3,00,000	2,00,000	Debtors	79,000	50,000
Long-term Loan	4,00,000	5,50,000	Cash	71,000	90,000
Provision for tax	1,20,000	1,10,000	Exp. paid in advance	15,000	10,000
Proposed Dividend	40,000	80,000	Preliminary expenses	70,000	50,000
Sundry Creditors	50,000	64,000			
Outstanding Salary	20,000	16,000			
	26,95,000	31,00,000		26,95,000	31,00,000

The following further information are also given

1. Depreciation for Land & Building is Rs.90,000
2. Depreciation of Plant & Machinery is Rs.80,000. During the year a Plant worth Rs.70,000 was sold for Rs.50,000
3. During the year Furniture worth Rs.60,000 was sold for Rs.70,000.

Prepare a statement of Fund Flow and a statement of changes in Working Capital by considering the Provision for tax and Proposed dividend as fixed items.

Solution :

Statement of Changes in Working Capital

Particulars	*2006 Rs.*	*2007 Rs.*	*Increase Rs.*	*Decrease Rs.*
Current Assets				
Stock	1,10,000	1,50,000	40,000	
Debtors	79,000	50,000		29,000
Cash	71,000	90,000	19,000	
Expenses paid in advance	15,000	10,000		5,000
Total	2,75,000	3,00,000		
Current Liabilities				
Sundry Creditors	50,000	64,000		14,000
Outstanding Salary	20,000	16,000	4,000	

Total	70,000	80,000		
Working Capital (C.A.-C.L)	2,05,000	2,20,000	63,000	48,000
Increase in Working Capital	15,000			15,000
	2,20,000	2,20,000	63,000	63,000

Statement of Fund Flow

Inflow	*Rs.*	*Outflow*	*Rs.*
Fund from Operation	4,45,000	Redemption of Debentures	1,00,000
Issue of Equity Shares	3,00,000	Purchase of Land & Building	3,40,000
Long-term loan borrowed	1,50,000	Purchase of Plant & Mach.	4,00,000
Sale of Plant & Machinery	50,000	Payment of Tax	1,20,000
Sale of Furniture	70,000	Payment of Dividend	40,000
		Increase in Working Capital	15,000
	10,15,000		10,15,000

Profit & Loss Adjustment A/c

Particulars	*Rs.*	*Particulars*	*Rs.*
To Land & Building (Depreciation)	90,000	By Balance b/d	1,40,000
To Plant & Machinery (Depreciation)	80,000	By Furniture & Fittings	10,000
To Plant & Machinery (Loss on Sale)	20,000	(Profit on sale)	
To Furniture & Fittings (Depreciation)	60,000	By Goodwill a/c	20,000
To Increase in General Reserve	10,000	By Decrease in Workmen	
To Preliminary expenses	20,000	Compensation Fund	15,000
To Provision for Tax	1,10,000	By Fund from Operation	4,45,000
To Proposed Dividend	80,000		
To Balance c/d	1,60,000		
	6,30,000		6,30,000

Land & Building Account

Particulars	*Rs.*	*Particulars*	*Rs.*
To Balance b/d	11,00,000	By Adjusted P & L A/c (Dep.)	90,000
To Cash (Purchase)	3,40,000	By Balance c/d	13,50,000
	14,40,000		14,40,000

Plant & Machinery Account

Particulars	*Rs.*	*Particulars*	*Rs.*
To Balance b/d	8,50,000	By Adjusted P & L (Dep.)	80,000
To Cash (Purchase)	4,00,000	By Cash (Sales)	50,000
		By Adjusted P & L a/c	20,000
		By Balance c/d	11,00,000
	12,50,000		12,50,000

Furniture and Fittings Account

Particulars	Rs.	Particulars	Rs.
To Balance b/d	3,50,000	By Adjusted P&L a/c (Dep.)	60,000
To Adjusted P&L a/c	10,000	By Cash (Sales)	70,000
		By Balance c/d	2,30,000
	3,60,000		3,60,000

Goodwill Account

Particulars	Rs.	Particulars	Rs.
To Balance b/d	50,000	By Balance c/d	70,000
To Adjusted P & L a/c	20,000		
	70,000		70,000

Note: Decrease in workmen compensation fund may also be considered as an outflow of cash.

Miscellaneous Illustrations

Illustration: 18

GC Ltd. provided the Balance Sheets as on 31st March of 2006 and 31st March 2007 as follows.

Balance Sheets

Liabilities	*2006 Rs.*	*2007 Rs.*	*Assets*	*2006 Rs.*	*2007 Rs.*
Equity Share Capital	15,00,000	15,00,000	Fixed Assets	26,00,000	27,50,000
Preference Share Cap.	5,00,000	7,00,000	Stock	1,15,000	1,50,000
Profit & Loss a/c	1,40,000	–	Debtors	80,000	95,000
General Reserve	1,20,000	1,50,000	Cash	90,000	70,000
Long-term Loan	4,00,000	3,00,000	Outstanding income	25,000	15,000
Provision for Tax	2,10,000	4,00,000	Profit & Loss a/c	–	75,000
Sundry Creditors	90,000	80,000	Discount on issue of		
Income received in adv.	50,000	65,000	Shares	1,00,000	40,000
	30,10,000	31,95,000		30,10,000	31,95,000

Prepare a Statement of Fund Flow and a Statement of changes in Working Capital.

Solution :

Statement of Changes in Working Capital

Particulars	*2006 Rs.*	*2007 Rs.*	*Increase Rs.*	*Decrease Rs.*
Current Assets				
Stock	1,15,000	1,50,000	35,000	
Debtors	80,000	95,000	15,000	
Cash	90,000	70,000		20,000

Outstanding income	25,000	15,000		10,000
Total	3,10,000	3,30,000		
Current Liabilities				
Sundry Creditors	90,000	80,000	10,000	
Income received in adv.	50,000	65,000		15,000
Total	1,40,000	1,45,000		
Working Capital (C.A.-C.L)	1,70,000	1,85,000	60,000	45,000
Increase in Working Capital	15,000			15,000
	1,85,000	1,85,000	60,000	60,000

Statement of Fund Flow

Inflow	*Rs.*	*Outflow*	*Rs.*
Fund from Operation	65,000	Repayment of Loan	1,00,000
Issue of Preference	2,00,000	Purchase of Fixed Assets	1,50,000
Share Capital		Increase in W.C.	15,000
	2,65,000		2,65,000

Profit & Loss Adjustment A/c

Particulars	*Rs.*	*Particulars*	*Rs.*
To Provision for depreciation	1,90,000	By Balance b/d	1,40,000
(4,00,000 – 2,10,000)		By Balance c/d (Debit balance)	75,000
To Increase in General Reserve	30,000	**By Fund from Operation**	65,000
To Decrease in Discount on issue of Shares	60,000		
	2,80,000		2,80,000

Illustration: 19

MN Ltd., provided the Balance Sheets as on 31st March of 2006 and 2007 as follows.

Balance Sheets

Liabilities	2006 *Rs.*	2007 *Rs.*	*Assets*	2006 *Rs.*	2007 *Rs.*
Equity S. Capital	10,00,000	10,00,000	Land & Building	8,00,000	9,50,000
Preference Share Cap.	4,00,000	6,00,000	Plant & Machinery	6,70,000	7,20,000
General Reserve	50,000	60,000	Furniture & Fittings	1,50,000	1,40,000
Debentures	3,00,000	4,50,000	Stock	90,000	1,10,000
Long-term loan	2,00,000	1,50,000	Debtors	47,000	60,000
Sundry creditors	70,000	25,000	Cash	78,000	66,000
Outstanding salary	30,000	35,000	Outstanding income	35,000	44,000
			Expenses paid in adv.	40,000	30,000
			Profit & Loss a/c	1,40,000	2,00,000
	20,50,000	23,20,000		20,50,000	23,20,000

The following further information are also given.

1. Purchase of Furniture during the year Rs.10,000.
2. Depreciation for Land & Building Rs.90,000 and Plant & Machinery Rs.60,000.

Prepare a statement of changes in Working Capital and a statement of Fund Flow.

Solution :

Statement of Changes in Working Capital

Particulars	*2006 Rs.*	*2007 Rs.*	*Increase Rs.*	*Decrease Rs.*
Current Assets				
Stock	90,000	1,10,000	20,000	
Debtors	47,000	60,000	13,000	
Cash	78,000	66,000		12,000
Outstanding income	35,000	44,000	9,000	
Expenses paid in advance	40,000	30,000		10,000
Total	2,90,000	3,10,000		
Current Liabilities				
Sundry Creditors	70,000	25,000	45,000	
Income received in advance	30,000	35,000		5,000
Total	1,00,000	60,000		
Working Capital (C.A.-C.L)	1,90,000	2,50,000	87,000	27,000
Increase in Working Capital	60,000			60,000
	2,50,000	2,50,000	87,000	87,000

Statement of Fund Flow

Inflow	*Rs.*	*Outflow*	*Rs.*
Fund from Operation	1,20,000	Purchase of L & B.	2,40,000
Issue of Preference Share Capital	2,00,000	Purchase of P & M.	1,10,000
Issue of Debenture	1,50,000	Purchase of Furniture	10,000
		Repayment of Loan	50,000
		Increase in Working Capital	60,000
	4,70,000		4,70,000

Profit & Loss Adjustment A/c

Particulars	*Rs.*	*Particulars*	*Rs.*
To Balance b/d	1,40,000	By Balance c/d	2,00,000
To Land & Building	90,000	By **Fund from Operation**	1,20,000
To Plant & Machinery	60,000		
To Furniture & Fittings	20,000		
To Increase in G.R.	10,000		
	3,20,000		3,20,000

Land & Building Account

Particulars	*Rs.*	*Particulars*	*Rs.*
To Balance b/d	8,00,000	By Adjusted P & L a/c (Dep.)	90,000
To Cash (Purchase)	2,40,000	By Balance c/d	9,50,000
	10,40,000		10,40,000

Plant & Machinery Account

Particulars	*Rs.*	*Particulars*	*Rs.*
To Balance b/d	6,70,000	By Adjusted P & L (Dep.)	60,000
To Cash (Purchase)	1,10,000	By Balance c/d	7,20,000
	7,80,000		7,80,000

Furniture & Fittings Account

Particulars	*Rs.*	*Particulars*	*Rs.*
To Balance b/d	1,50,000	By Adjusted P & L (Dep.)	20,000
To Cash (Purchase)	10,000	By Balance c/d	1,40,000
	1,60,000		1,60,000

Illustration: 20

Prepare Fund Flow statement and Statement of changes in Working Capital from the Balance Sheets provided by MWD Ltd. as on 31st March of 2006 and 2007 as follows.

Balance Sheet

Liabilities	*2006 Rs.*	*2007 Rs.*	*Assets*	*2006 Rs.*	*2007 Rs.*
Equity Share Capital	12,00,000	14,00,000	Land & Building	11,00,000	15,00,000
Preference Share Capital	4,00,000	5,00,000	Plant & Machinery	9,00,000	10,00,000
Profit Loss a/c	1,40,000	1,50,000	Investments	3,20,000	2,10,000
General Reserve	60,000	70,000	Inventory	95,000	40,000
Cap.Redemption Res.	50,000	75,000	Debtors	30,000	45,000
Workmen Comp.Fund	40,000	20,000	Cash	75,000	50,000
Debentures	3,00,000	4,00,000	Outstanding income	32,000	30,000
Long-term loan	2,50,000	1,00,000	Prepaid expenses	18,000	20,000
Provision for Tax	1,10,000	90,000	Discount on issue of	60,000	40,000
Sundry Creditors	40,000	65,000	Debenture		
Interest accrued	10,000	5,000			
Bank Overdraft	30,000	60,000			
	26,30,000	29,35,000		26,30,000	29,35,000

The following further information are also given.

1. Interim dividend paid @ 5% for Equity Shareholders on 1st November 2006.

2. Loss on sale of Investment is Rs.30,000.
3. Depreciation for Land & Building Rs.1,10,000 and Plant & Machinery Rs.90,000
4. Additional Equity Share Capital is raised on 1st January 2007.

Solution :

Statement of Changes in Working Capital

Particulars	*2006 Rs.*	*2007 Rs.*	*Increase Rs.*	*Decrease Rs.*
Current Assets				
Inventory	95,000	40,000		55,000
Debtors	30,000	45,000	15,000	
Cash	75,000	50,000		25,000
Outstanding income	32,000	30,000		2,000
Prepaid expenses	18,000	20,000	2,000	
Total	2,50,000	1,85,000		
Current Liabilities				
Sundry Creditors	40,000	65,000		25,000
Interest accrued	10,000	5,000	5,000	
Bank Overdraft	30,000	60,000		30,000
Provision for Tax	1,10,000	90,000	20,000	
Total	1,90,000	2,20,000		
Working Capital (C.A.-C.L)	60,000	(35,000)	42,000	1,37,000
Decrease in Working Capital	–	95,000	95,000	–
	60,000	60,000	1,37,000	1,37,000

Statement of Fund Flow

Inflow	*Rs.*	*Outflow*	*Rs.*
Fund from Operation	3,35,000	Purchase of Land & Buil.	5,10,000
Issue of Equity Share Capital	2,00,000	Purchase of Plant & Mach.	1,90,000
Issue of Pre.Sh.Capital	1,00,000	Repayment of Loan	1,50,000
Issue of Debentures	1,00,000	By Interim Dividend paid	60,000
Sale of Investment	80,000		
Decrease in Working Capital	95,000		
	9,10,000		9,10,000

Profit & Loss Adjustment A/c

Particulars	*Rs.*	*Particulars*	*Rs.*
To Land & Building	1,10,000	By Balance c/d	1,40,000
To Plant & Machinery	90,000	By Decrease in Workmen Compensation Fund	20,000
To Investment	30,000		
To Increase in General Reserve	10,000	**By Fund from Operation**	3,35,000

To Increase in Capital Redemption Reserve	25,000		
To Discount on Debentures written off	20,000		
To Interim Dividend	60,000		
To Balance c/d	1,50,000		
	4,95,000		4,95,000

Land & Building Account

Particulars	*Rs.*	*Particulars*	*Rs.*
To Balance b/d	11,00,000	By Adjusted P & L A/c	1,10,000
To Cash (Purchase)	5,10,000	(Depreciation)	
		By Balance c/d	15,00,000
	16,10,000		16,10,000

Plant & Machinery Account

Particulars	*Rs.*	*Particulars*	*Rs.*
To Balance b/d	9,00,000	By Adjusted P & L A/c	90,000
To Cash (Purchase)	1,90,000	(Depreciation)	
		By Balance c/d	10,00,000
	10,90,000		10,90,000

Investment Account

Particulars	*Rs.*	*Particulars*	*Rs.*
To Balance b/d	3,20,000	By Cash (Sales)	80,000
		By Adjusted P&L (Loss on sale)	30,000
		By Balance c/d	2,10,000
	3,20,000		3,20,000

Illustration: 21

Joyce& Co. Ltd. provided the Balance Sheets as on 31st March of 2006 and 2007 as follows.

Balance Sheets

Liabilities	*2006 Rs.*	*2007 Rs.*		*2006 Rs.*	*2007 Rs.*
Equity Share Capital	5,00,000	7,00,000	Land & Building	6,00,000	8,00,000
Preference Share Cap.	2,00,000	3,00,000	Plant & Machinery	3,00,000	5,30,000
Profit Loss a/c	1,20,000	1,45,000	Furniture	1,00,000	63,000
General Reserve	65,000	90,000	Investments	2,00,000	1,50,000
Capital Redemption			(Long term)		
Reserve	95,000	65,000	Stock	1,10,000	80,000
Secured Loan	3,00,000	1,00,000	Debtors	1,40,000	1,55,000
Secured Loan	2,50,000	3,00,000	Cash	1,30,000	60,000

Provision for Tax	90,000	1,10,000	Bills Receivable	35,000	12,000
Sundry Creditors	40,000	65,000	Preliminary Expenses	75,000	50,000
Bills Payable	30,000	25,000			
	16,90,000	19,00,000		16,90,000	19,00,000

Additional Information:

1. Depreciation was charged for Land and Building @ 6%, and Furniture @ 7%.
2. Land worth Rs.90,000 was sold for Rs.1,10,000 and a new Land was purchased on 1st April 2006.
3. A Machine worth Rs.70,000 was sold for Rs.50,000 and a new machine was purchased for Rs.3,50,000 during the year.
4. Furniture sold for Rs.40,000 on 31st March 2007.
5. Interim Dividend paid @ 5% for Equity Share Capital of Rs.5,00,000.
6. Income Tax paid during the year Rs.80,000.
7. Profit on sale of Investment Rs.10,000.

Prepare a statement of Fund Flow and statement of changes in Working Capital.

Solution :

Statement of Changes in Working Capital

Particulars	*2006 Rs.*	*2007 Rs.*	*Increase Rs.*	*Decrease Rs.*
Current Assets				
Stock	1,10,000	80,000		30,000
Debtors	1,40,000	1,55,000	15,000	
Cash	1,30,000	60,000		70,000
Bills Receivable	35,000	12,000		23,000
Total	4,15,000	3,07,000		
Current Liabilities				
Sundry Creditors	40,000	65,000		25,000
Bills Payable	30,000	25,000	5,000	
Total	70,000	90,000		
W. Capital (C.A.-C.L)	3,45,000	2,17,000	20,000	1,48,000
Decrease in Working Capital	–	1,28,000	1,28,000	
	3,45,000	3,45,000	1,48,000	1,48,000

Statement of Fund Flow

Inflow	*Rs.*	*Outflow*	*Rs.*
Fund from Operation	2,55,000	Purchase of Land & Buil.	3,38,000
Issue of Equity Share Cap.	2,00,000	Purchase of Machinery	3,50,000
Issue of Pref. Sh. Capital	1,00,000	Redemption of Debenture	2,00,000
Loan	50,000	Payment of Tax	80,000

Sale of Land & Building	1,10,000	Payment of Interim Dividend	25,000
Sale of Machinery	50,000		
Sale of Investment	60,000		
Sale of Furniture	40,000		
Decrease in Working Capital	1,28,000		
	9,93,000		9,93,000

Profit & Loss Adjustment A/c

Particulars	*Rs.*	*Particulars*	*Rs.*
To Land & Building	48,000	By Balance c/d	1,20,000
To Machinery	50,000	By Land & Building a/c	20,000
To Machinery a/c	20,000	By Furniture a/c	10,000
To Furniture a/c	7,000	By Investment a/c	10,000
To Provision for Taxation	1,00,000	By Capital Redemption Reserve a/c	30,000
To Increase in General Reserve	25,000		
To Preliminary expenses	25,000	By **Fund from Operation**	2,55,000
To Interim Dividend	25,000		
To Balance c/d	1,45,000		
	4,45,000		4,45,000

Land & Building Account

Particulars	*Rs.*	*Particulars*	*Rs.*
To Balance b/d	6,00,000	By P & L Adjust A/c(Dep.6%)	48,000
To P & L Ad. a/c (Profit on sale)	20,000	By Cash a/c (Sales)	1,10,000
To Cash (Purchase)	3,38,000	By Balance c/d	8,00,000
	9,58,000		9.58,000

Machinery Account

	Particulars	*Rs.*	*Particulars*
To Balance b/d	3,00,000	By P & L Adjust.A/c (Dep.)	50,000
To Cash (Purchase)	3,50,000	By Cash a/c (Sales)	50,000
		By P & L Adjust A/c (Loss on sale)	20,000
		By Balance c/d	5,30,000
	6,50,000		6,50,000

Furniture Account

Particulars	Rs.	Particulars	Rs.
To Balance b/d	1,00,000	By P & L Adjust. A/c (Dep.7%)	7,000
To P & L Adjustment A/c		By Cash (sales)	40,000
(Profit on sale)	10,000	By Balance c/d	63,000
	1,10,000		1,10,000

Investment Account

Particulars	Rs.	Particulars	Rs.
To Balance b/d	2,00,000	By P & L Adjusted A/c (Dep.)	60,000
To P & L Adjusted A/c	10,000	By Balance c/d	1,50,000
	2,10,000		2,10,000

Provision for Taxation Account

Particulars	Rs.	Particulars	Rs.
To Cash (Tax paid)	80,000	By Balance b/d	90,000
To Balance c/d	1,10,000	By P & L Adjust A/c (Provision)	1,00,000
	1,90,000		1,90,000

Illustration: 22

Prepare Fund Flow statement and Statement of changes in Working Capital from the Balance Sheets provided by KM Ltd., as on 31st March of 2006 and 2007 as follows.

Balance Sheets

Liabilities	2006 Rs.	2007 Rs.	Assets	2006 Rs.	2007 Rs.
Equity Share Capital	12,00,000	13,00,000	Land & Building	7,60,000	10,20,000
Retained Earnings	2,40,000	2,70,000	Plant & Machinery	7,00,000	6,50,000
General Reserve	79,000	86,000	(Accumulated Dep.)	(60,000)	(70,000)
Reserve for future loss on Investment	35,000	31,000	Patent	1,20,000	60,000
			Investment	2,80,000	3,40,000
Debentures	2,50,000	3,50,000	Stock	1,00,000	1,20,000
Long-term Loan	1,50,000	1,25,000	Debtors	60,000	45,000
Proposed Dividend	75,000	84,000	Cash	70,000	95,000
Sundry Creditors	31,000	39,000	Discount on Debentures	50,000	40,000
Outstanding salary	20,000	15,000			
	20,80,000	23,00,000		20,80,000	23,00,000

The following further information are also given

1. During the year a Plant with accumulated depreciation Rs.15,000 was sold for a loss of Rs.12,000

2. On 1st November 2006 an Investment worth Rs.30,000 was sold for a loss and the loss was adjusted with the reserve made for this purpose.
3. Depreciation for the Land & Building @ 10% on closing balance. Land sold during the year Rs.40,000 (Book value Rs.25,000).
4. Dividend paid during the year Rs.65,000.

Solution :

Statement of Changes in Working Capital

Particulars	*2006 Rs.*	*2007 Rs.*	*Increase Rs.*	*Decrease*
Current Assets				
Stock	1,00,000	1,20,000	20,000	
Debtors	60,000	45,000		15,000
Cash	70,000	95,000	25,000	
Total	2,30,000	2,60,000		
Current Liabilities				
Sundry Creditors	31,000	39,000		8,000
Outstanding salary	20,000	15,000	5,000	
Total	51,000	54,000		
Working Capital (C.A.-C.L)	1,79,000	2,06,000	50,000	23,000
Increase in Working Capital	27,000			27,000
	2,06,000	2,06,000	50,000	50,000

Statement of Fund Flow

Inflow	*Rs.*	*Outflow*	
Fund from Operation	2,45,000	Purchase of Land & Building	3,87,000
Sale of Land	40,000	Purchase of Investment	90,000
Sale of Plant	23,000	Payment of Dividend	65,000
Sale of Investment	26,000	Repayment of Loan	25,000
Sale of Patent	60,000	**Increase in Working Capital**	27,000
Issue of Share Capital	1,00,000		
Issue of Debenture	1,00,000		
	5,94,000		5,94,000

Retained Earnings Account (Adjusted Profit & Loss Account)

Particulars	*Rs.*	*Particulars*	*Rs.*
To Land & Building	1,02,000	By Balance b/d	2,40,000
To Plant & Machinery	12,000	By Land & Building a/c	15,000
To Accumulated Dep.	25,000	**By Fund from Operation**	2,45,000
To Proposed dividend	74,000		
To Increase in General Reserve	7,000		

To Redemption of Discount on issue of Debentures	10,000		
To Balance c/d	2,70,000		
	5,00,000		5,00,000

Land & Building Account

Particulars	Rs.	Particulars	Rs.
To Balance b/d	7,60,000	By Adjusted P & L A/c	1,02,000
To Adjusted P & L a/c (Profit on sale)	15,000	By Cash a/c (Sales)	40,000
To Cash (Purchase)	3,87,000	By Balance c/d	10,20,000
	11,62,000		11,62,000

Plant & Machinery Account

Particulars	Rs.	Particulars	Rs.
To Balance b/d	7,00,000	By Accumulated Dep. a/c	15,000
		By Cash a/c (Sales)	23,000
		By Adj.P & L a/c (Loss on sale)	12,000
		By Balance c/d	6,50,000
	7,00,000		7,00,000

Accumulated Depreciation Account

Particulars	Rs.	Particulars	Rs.
To Plant & Machinery a/c	15,000	By Balance b/d	60,000
To Balance c/d	70,000	By Adjusted P & L a/c	25,000
	85,000		85,000

Investment Account

Particulars	Rs.	Particulars	Rs.
To Balance b/d	2,80,000	By Cash - sales (30,000-4000)	26,000
To Cash - Purchase (Balancing figure)	90,000	By Reserve for future loss on Investment	4,000
		By Balance c/d	3,40,000
	3,70,000		3,70,000

Reserve for Future Loss on Investment Account

Particulars	Rs.	Particulars	Rs.
To Investment	4,000	By Balance b/d	35,000
To Balance c/d	31,000		
	35,000		35,000

Proposed Dividend Account

Particulars	*Rs.*	*Particulars*	*Rs.*
To Cash a/c	65,000	By Balance b/d	75,000
To Balance c/d	84,000	By Adjusted P & L a/c	74,000
	1,49,000		1,49,000

Share Capital Account

Particulars	*Rs.*	*Particulars*	*Rs.*
To Balance c/d	13,00,000	By Balance b/d	12,00,000
		By Cash a/c	1,00,000
	13,00,000		13,00,000

Debenture Account

Particulars	*Rs.*	*Particulars*	*Rs.*
To Balance c/d	3,50,000	By Balance b/d	2,50,000
		By Cash a/c	1,00,000
	3,50,000		3,50,000

Illustration: 23

Prepare Fund Flow statement and Statement of changes in Working Capital from the Balance Sheets provided by KM Ltd., as on 31st March of 2006 and 2007 as follows.

Balance Sheets

Liabilities	*2007 Rs.*	*2006 Rs.*	*Assets*	*2007 Rs.*	*2006 Rs.*
Equity Share Capital	24,00,000	20,00,000	Land & Building	18,00,000	15,00,000
Preference Sh.Cap.	5,00,000	2,00,000	Plant & Machinery	12,00,000	11,30,000
General Reserve	1,50,000	1,10,000	Furniture & Fittings	1,70,000	2,20,000
Debenture Redemption Reserve	90,000	1,40,000	Tools	1,50,000	1,25,000
			Inventories	1,20,000	92,000
Provision for Depre.	2,00,000	2,10,000	Debtors	60,000	75,000
Debentures	2,80,000	3,80,000	Cash	1,60,000	1,20,000
Long-term loan	3,00,000	1,70,000	Bills receivable	50,000	43,000
Provision for tax	1,45,000	1,30,000	Prepaid expenses	30,000	35,000
Provision for doubtful Debts	50,000	60,000	Investments-S.Term	1,10,000	90,000
Sundry Creditors	65,000	80,000	Discount on issue of shares	40,000	50,000
Bank Overdraft	40,000	25,000	Profit & Loss A/c	35,000	40,000
Bills payable	20,000	15,000			
	42,40,000	35,20,000		42,40,000	35,20,000

The following further information are also given.

1. Profit on sale of Furniture is Rs.12,000. Accumulated depreciation Rs.5,000.
2. A machinery costing Rs.80,000 was sold for Rs.60,000. Accumulated depreciation of the machinery is Rs.15,000.
3. Tools with cost Rs.40,000 was scrapped and written off. The accumulated depreciation of the tools is Rs.25,000.
4. Land sold during the year is Rs.2,00,000. The cost of the Land is Rs.1,20,000 and accumulated depreciation is Rs.20,000.
5. The Debenture redeemed for the year is Rs.100,000.Fifty percent of the Debentures redeemed are paid in the form of Equity Shares.

Prepare a Statement of Fund Flow and Statement of changes in Working Capital.

Solution :

Statement of Changes in Working Capital

Particulars	*2006 Rs.*	*2007 Rs.*	*Increase Rs.*	*Decrease Rs.*
Current Assets				
Inventories	92,000	1,20,000	28,000	
Debtors	75,000	60,000		15,000
Cash	1,20,000	1,60,000	40,000	
Bills receivable	43,000	50,000	7,000	
Prepaid expenses	35,000	30,000		5,000
Investments	90,000	1,10,000	20,000	
Total	4,55,000	5,30,000		
Current Liabilities				
Sundry Creditors	80,000	65,000	15,000	
Bank overdraft	25,000	40,000		15,000
Bills Payable	15,000	20,000		5,000
Prov. for doubtful debts	60,000	50,000	10,000	15,000
Provision for tax	1,30,000	1,45,000		
Total	3,10,000	3,20,000		
W. Capital (C.A.-C.L)	1,45,000	2,10,000	1,20,000	55,000
Increase in W.C	65,000			65,000
	2,10,000	2,10,000	1,20,000	1,20,000

Statement of Fund Flow

Inflow	*Rs.*	*Outflow*	*Rs.*
Sale of Land	2,00,000	**Fund Lost in Operation**	3,47,000
Sale of Plant & Mach.	60,000	Purchase of Land & Build.	4,20,000
Sale of Furniture	57,000	Purchase of Plant & Mach.	1,50,000

Issue of Equity Share Capital	3,50,000	Purchase of Tools	65.000
Issue of Preference Share Capital	3.00,000	Redemption of Debenture	50,000
Increase of Loan	1,30,000	**Increase in Working Capital**	65,000
	10,97,000		10,97,000

Adjusted Profit & Loss Account

Particulars	*Rs.*	*Particulars*	*Rs.*
To Balance b/d	40,000	By Land & Building a/c	1,00,000
To Plant & Machinery	5,000	By Furniture & Fittings a/c	12,000
To Tools	15,000	By Decrease in Debenture Redemption Reserve	50,000
To Provision for Depreciation	55,000	By Balance c/d	3,50,000
To Increase of General Reserve	40,000		
To Redemption of Discount on issue of shares	10,000		
To Fund Lost in Operation	3,47,000		
	5,12,000		5,12,000

Land & Building Account

Particulars	*Rs.*	*Particulars*	*Rs.*
To Balance b/d	15,00,000	By Provision for Depreciation	20,000
To Adj.P & L a/c (Profit on sale)	1,00,000	By Cash a/c (Sales)	2.00.000
To Cash (Purchase)	4,20,000	By Balance c/d	18,00,000
	20,20,000		20,20,000

Plant & Machinery Account

Particulars	*Rs.*	*Particulars*	*Rs.*
To Balance b/d	11,30,000	By Provision for Depreciation	15,000
To Cash (Purchase)	1,50,000	By Cash a/c (Sales)	60,000
		By Adj.P & L a/c (Loss on sale)	5,000
		By Balance c/d	12,00,000
	12,80,000		12,80,000

Furniture and Fittings Account

Particulars	*Rs.*	*Particulars*	*Rs.*
To Balance b/d	2,20,000	By Provision for Depreciation	5,000
To Adjusted P &L A/c (Profit on sale)	12,000	By Cash (Sales)	57,000
		By Balance c/d	1,70,000
	2,32,000		2,32,000

Tools Account

Particulars	Rs.	Particulars	Rs.
To Balance b/d	1,25,000	By Provision for Depreciation	25,000
To Cash-Purchase		By Adjusted P & L a/c	
(Balancing figure)	65,000	(Tools scrapped)	15,000
		By Balance c/d	1,50,000
	1,90,000		1,90,000

Provision for Depreciation Account

Particulars	Rs.	Particulars	Rs.
To Land & Building a/c	20,000	By Balance b/d	2,10,000
To Plant & Machinery a/c	15,000	By Adjusted P & L a/c	
To Furniture & Fittings a/c	5,000	(Balancing figure)	55,000
To Tools a/c	25,000		
To Balance c/d	2,00,000		
	2,65,000		2,65,000

Equity Share Capital Account

Particulars	Rs.	Particulars	Rs.
To Balance c/d	24,00,000	By Balance b/d	20,00,000
		By Debenture a/c	50,000
		By Cash (Balance)	3,50,000
	24,00,000		24,00,000

Debenture Account

Particulars	Rs.	Particulars	Rs.
To Equity Share Capital a/c	50,000	By Balance b/d	3,80,000
To Cash a/c	50,000		
To Balance c/d	2,80,000		
	3,80,000		3,80,000

Illustration: 24

GT Ltd. provided the Balance Sheet as on 31st March of 2006 and 2007 as follows.

Balance Sheets

Liabilities	2006 Rs.	2007 Rs.	Assets	2006 Rs.	2007 Rs.
Equity Share Capital	22,00,000	24,00,000	Land & Building	14,00,000	19,00,000
Preference Sh. Capital	2,00,000	4,00,000	Plant & Machinery	11,00,000	15,00,000
Profit & Loss	1,92,000	3,40,000	Furniture & Fittings	6,00,000	4,60,000

General Reserve	1,15,000	1,45,000	Investments	4,50,000	3,00,000
Cap. Redemption Res.	70,000	95,000	Inventories	1,06,000	1,63,000
Debenture	5,00,000	4,00,000	Debtors	64,000	50,000
Long-term Loan	3,60,000	4,91,000	Cash	97,000	1,30,000
Provision for Tax	1,63,000	1,74,000	Outstanding interest	15,000	22,000
Proposed Dividend	80,000	90,000	Expenses paid in adv.	43,000	30,000
Sundry Creditors	72,000	55,000	Preliminary expenses	95,000	65,000
Outstanding salary	18,000	30,000			
	39,70,000	46,20,000		39,70,000	46,20,000

The Profit and Loss Account for the year ended 31st March 2007 is stated as follows.

Profit & Loss Account

Particulars	*Rs.*	*Particulars*	*Rs.*
To Manufacturing expenses	60,000	By Sales	9,49,000
To Administration expenses	53,000	By Profit on sale of Plant	17,000
To Selling & Distribution expenses	26,000	By Profit on sale of Investment	22,000
To Interest on Debenture	45,000	By Interest received	24,000
To Interest on Loan	30,000		
To Dep.on Land & Building	1,45,000		
To Dep.on Plant & Machinery	1,15,000		
To Dep. of Furniture	50,000		
To Loss on sale of Furniture	11,000		
To Preliminary expenses written off	30,000		
To Provision for Tax	1,74,000		
To Net profit after Tax	2,73,000		
	10,12,000		10,12,000

The following further information are also given

1. Cost of plant sold is Rs.77,000.
2. Rs.70,000 worth of debenture was redeemed and is paid in the form of Preference Share Capital.
3. Dividend paid to Equity Shareholders is Rs.60,000.

Prepare a Statement of changes in Working Capital and a Statement of Fund Flow.

Solution :

Statement of Changes in Working Capital

Particulars	*2006 Rs.*	*2007 Rs.*	*Increase Rs.*	*Decrease Rs.*
Current Assets				
Inventories	1,06,000	1,63,000	57,000	
Debtors	64,000	50,000		14,000
Cash	97,000	1,30,000	33,000	

Outstanding Interest	15,000	22,000	7,000	
Expenses paid in advance	43,000	30,000		13,000
Total	3,25,000	3,95,000		
Current Liabilities				
Sundry creditors	72,000	55,000	17,000	
Outstanding Salary	18,000	30,000		12,000
Total	90,000	85,000		
Working Capital (C.A-C.L)	2,35,000	3,10,000	1,14,000	39,000
Increase in Working Capital	75,000	–	–	75,000
	3,10,000	3,10,000	1,14,000	1,14,000

Statement of Fund Flow

Inflow	*Rs.*	*Outflow*	*Rs.*
Fund from Operation	7,59,000	Purchase of Land & Building	6,45,000
Issue of Equity Share Capital	2,00,000	Purchase of Plant & Machinery	5,92,000
Issue of Pre. Share Capital	1,30,000	Redemption of Debenture	30,000
Sale of Plant & Machinery	94,000	Payment of Dividend	60,000
Sale of Furniture	79,000	Payment of Tax	1,63,000
Sale of Investments	1,72,000	**Increase in Working Capital**	75,000
Increase of Loan	1,31,000		
	15,65,000		15,65,000

Adjusted Profit & Loss Account

Particulars	*Rs.*	*Particulars*	*Rs.*
To Land & Building a/c (Dep.)	1,45,000	By Balance b/d	1,92,000
To Plant & Machinery a/c (Dep.)	1,15,000	By Profit on sale of Plant	17,000
To Furniture a/c (Dep.)	50,000	By Profit on sale of Investment	22,000
To Loss on sale of Furniture	11,000	**By Fund from Operation**	7,59,000
To Preliminary expenses written off	30,000		
To Provision for Tax	1,74,000		
To Proposed Dividend	70,000		
To Provision for General Reserve	30,000		
To Increase in Capital Redemption Reserve	25,000		
To Balance c/d	3,40,000		
	9,90,000		9,90,000

Land & Building Account

Particulars	*Rs.*	*Particulars*	*Rs.*
To Balance b/d	14,00,000	By Adjusted P & L (Dep.)	1,45,000
To Cash (Purchase)	6,45,000	By Balance c/d	19,00,000
	20,45,000		20,45,000

Plant & Machinery Account

Particulars	*Rs.*	*Particulars*	*Rs.*
To Balance b/d	11,00,000	By Adjusted P & L a/c (Dep.)	1,15,000
To Adjusted P & L a/c	17,000	By Cash a/c (Sales)	94,000
(Profit on sale)		By Balance c/d	15,00,000
To Cash a/c (Purchase)	5,92,000		
	17,09,000		17,09,000

Furniture and Fittings Account

Particulars	*Rs.*	*Particulars*	*Rs.*
To Balance b/d	6,00,000	By Adjusted P & L a/c (Dep.)	50,000
		By Cash (sales)	79,000
		By Adjusted P & L a/c (Loss on sale)	11,000
		By Balance c/d	4,60,000
	6,00,000		6,00,000

Investments Account

Particulars	*Rs.*	*Particulars*	*Rs.*
To Balance b/d	4,50,000	By Cash (Sales)	1,72,000
To Adjusted P & L a/c		(Balancing figure)	
(Profit on sale)	22,000	By Balance	3,00,000
	4,72,000		4,72,000

Proposed Dividend Account

Particulars	*Rs.*	*Particulars*	*Rs.*
To Cash	60,000	By Balance b/d	80,000
To Balance c/d	90,000	By Adjusted P & L a/c	70,000
	1,50,000		1,50,000

Preference Share Capital Account

Particulars	Rs.	Particulars	Rs.
To Balance c/d	4,00,000	By Balance b/d	2,00,000
		By Debenture a/c	70,000
		By Cash a/c	1,30,000
	4,00,000		4,00,000

Debenture Account

Particulars	Rs.	Particulars	Rs.
To Preference Share Capital	70,000	By Balance b/d	5,00,000
To Cash a/c	30,000		
To Balance c/d	4,00,000		
	5,00,000		5,00,000

Illustration: 25

The Balance Sheets of K. Ltd., as on 31st March of 2006 and 2007 are stated as follows.

Balance Sheets

Liabilities	2006 Rs.	2007 Rs.	Assets	2006 Rs.	2007 Rs.
Equity Share Capital	5,00,000	6,00,000	Fixed Assets	10,25,000	16,15,000
Profit & Loss A/c	1,00,000	1,82,000	Stock	1,70,000	40,000
General Reserve	64,000	80,000	Debtors	75,000	60,000
Capital Redem. Reserve	40,000	54,000	Cash	2,10,000	2,40,000
Provision for Depreciation	2,10,000	2,71,000	Discount on issue of		
Debentures	2,00,000	4,55,000	Debentures	65,000	45,000
Long-term Loan	2,00,000	72,000			
Provision for tax	1,30,000	1,40,000			
Proposed Dividend	66,000	87,000			
Sundry Creditors	20,000	46,000			
Outstanding expenses	15,000	13,000			
	15,45,000	20,00,000		15,45,000	20,00,000

The summarised Profit &Loss Account as on 31st March 2007 is stated as follows.

Particulars	Rs.	Rs.
Sales		7,70,000
Manufacturing expenses	1,45,000	
Administration expenses	1,10,000	
Selling expenses	90,000	
Provision for depreciation	75,000	

Loss on sale of Plant	17,000	
Discount on Debenture written off	20,000	4,57,000
		3,13,000
Less : Tax		1,20,000
Net Profit after Tax		1,93,000

Adjustments :

i. Cost of Plant sold is Rs.80,000 and accumulated depreciation of it is Rs.14,000.

ii. Dividend @ 10% is paid for the Equity Share Capital of Rs.6,00,000.

Prepare a statement of Fund Flow and Statement of changes in Working Capital.

Solution :

Statement of Changes in Working Capital

Particulars	*2006 Rs.*	*2007 Rs.*	*Increase Rs.*	*Decrease Rs.*
Current Assets				
Stock	1,70,000	40,000		1,30,000
Debtors	75,000	60,000		15,000
Cash	2,10,000	2,40,000	30,000	
Total	4,55,000	3,40,000		
Current Liabilities				
Sundry Creditors	20,000	46,000		26,000
Outstanding salary	15,000	13,000	2,000	
Total	35,000	59,000		
Working Capital (C.A-C.L)	4,20,000	2,81,000	32,000	1,71,000
Decrease in Working Capital	–	1,39,000	1,39,000	
	4,20,000	4,20,000	1,71,000	1,71,000

Statement of Fund Flow

Inflow	*Rs.*	*Outflow*	*Rs.*
Fund from Operation	4,25,000	By Purchase of Fixed Assets	6,70,000
Issue of Equity Share Capital	1,00,000	By Payment of Dividend	60,000
Issue of Debentures	2,55,000	By Payment of Tax	1,10,000
Sale of Fixed Assets	49,000	By Repayment of Loan	1,28,000
Decrease in Working Capital	1,39,000		
	9,68,000		9,68,000

Calculation of Fund from Operation

	Rs.	Rs.
Net Profit after Tax		1,93,000
Add : Tax	1,20,000	
Discount on Debenture written off	20,000	
Provision for Depreciation	75,000	
Loss on sale of Plant	17,000	2,32,000
Fund from Operation		4,25,000

Alternatively, Fund from Operation may be calculated as follows.

Adjusted Profit & Loss Account

Particulars	*Rs.*	*Particulars*	*Rs.*
To Provision for Tax	1,20,000	By Balance b/d	1,00,000
To Provision for Depreciation	75,000	**By Fund from Operation**	4,25,000
To Loss on Sale of Plant	17,000		
To Provision for General Reserve	16,000		
To Provision for Capital Redemption Reserve	14,000		
To Provision for Dividend	81,000		
To Discount on Debenture written off	20,000		
To Balance c/d	1,82,000		
	5,25,000		5,25,000

Fixed Assets Account

Particulars	*Rs.*	*Particulars*	*Rs.*
To Balance c/d	10,25,000	By Provision for Depreciation	14,000
To Cash (Purchase)	6,70,000	(Depreciation for plant sold)	
(80,000 – 14,000 – 17,000)		By Adjusted P & L a/c	
		(Loss on sale of Plant)	17,000
		By Cash (Sales)	49,000
		By Balance c/d	16,15,000
	16,95,000		16,95,000

Provision for Depreciation Account

Particulars	*Rs.*	*Particulars*	*Rs.*
To Fixed Assets a/c	14,000	By Balance b/d	2,10,000
(Depreciation for Plant sold)		By Adjusted P & L a/c	
To Balance c/d	2,71,000	(Dep. for current year)	75,000
	2,85,000		2,85,000

Provision for Taxation Account

Particulars	*Rs.*	*Particulars*	*Rs.*
To Cash a/c	1,10,000	By Balance b/d	1,30,000
(Balancing figure)		By Adjusted P & L a/c	1,20,000
To Balance c/d	1,40,000	(Provision for current year)	
	2,50,000		2,50,000

Proposed Dividend Account

Particulars	*Rs.*	*Particulars*	*Rs.*
To Cash a/c	60,000	By Balance b/d	66,000
(10% of Rs.6,00,000)		By Adjusted P & L a/c	81,000
To Balance c/d	87,000		
	1,47,000		1,47,000

EXERCISE

THEORY

I. Choose the correct answer for the following.

1. Fund in narrow sense means —
   (i) Bills (ii) Working Capital (iii) Cash and Cash equivalents (iv) Current Assets
2. Fund in broader sense means —
   (i) Working Capital (ii) Cash (iii) Current liabilities (iv) Bills of exchange
3. The balance of Fund Flow statement is the increase or decrease of —
   (i) Cash (ii) Cash from Operation (iii) Current Assets (iv) Working Capital
4. The difference between the Current Assets and Current Liabilities is known as :
   (i) Working Capital (ii) Cash from Operation (iii) Fund from Operation (iv) Investment
5. The credit balance of the Adjusted Profit & Loss Account is known as :
   (i) Fund from Operation (ii) Cash for Operation (iii) Working Capital (iv) Fund Lost in Operation
6. Fund Lost in Operation is the debit balance of the —
   (i) Balance Sheet (ii) Profit & Loss Account (iii) Cash Account (iv) Adjusted Profit & Loss Account
7. Depreciation is considered as a —
   (i) Source of Fund (ii) Application of Fund (iii) Income (iv) Fixed asset
8. Identify the Current Asset from the following :
   (i) Plant & Machinery (ii) Sundry Creditors (iii) Sundry Debtors (iv) Capital
9. Identify the Current Liability from the following :
   (i) Inventory (ii) Sundry Creditors (iii) Debentures (iv) General Reserve
10. Identify the non-current asset from the following :
    (i) Stock (ii) Debtors (iii) Cash (iv) Goodwill
11. Identify the non-current liability for the following :
    (i) Debenture (ii) Bills Payable (iii) Sundry Creditors (iv) Outstanding expenses
12. Increase in stock results in the —
    (i) Source of Fund (ii) Application of Fund (iii) Fictitious Assets (iv) Loss for the Company
13. Identify the source of fund from the following :
    (i) Purchase of Plant (ii) Redemption of Debenture (iii) Fund Lost in Operation (iv) Sale of Land
14. Identify the application of fund from the following :
    (i) Sale of Land (ii) Repayment of Loan (iii) Issue of Share Capital (iv) Fund from Operation

15. Fund from Operation is considered as —
(i) Source of Fund (ii) Application of Fund (iii) Loss of Fund (iv) Expenses
[Ans : 1. (iii) 2. (i) 3. (iv) 4. (i) 5. (iv) 6. (iv) 7. (i) 8 (iii) 9. (ii) 10. (iv) 11. (i) 12. (ii) , 13. (iv) 14. (ii) 15. (i)]

II. **Answer the following questions**

1. Explain the concept of Fund.
2. Define fund. What are the sources of Fund?
3. Analyse the concept that the balance of Fund Flow Statement is either increase or decrease of Working Capital.
4. What is Fund? State the different outflows of Fund.
5. What is Fund Flow statement?
6. Define Fund Flow statement. Explain the method of preparing the Fund Flow statement.
7. What is fund from operation? Explain procedures for ascertaining the Fund from Operation.
8. Distinguish between Fund from Operation and Fund Lost in Operation.
9. State the method of preparing the Adjusted Profit and Loss Account.
10. Explain the concept of Working Capital.
11. Explain the method of calculating the changes in Working Capital.
12. What are the merits and demerits of Fund Flow statement.
13. Define Fund. What are the objectives of Fund Flow statement?
14. Define Fund. Explain the parties interested and for what purpose they are interested in the Fund Flow statement.
15. Write short notes on the following.
(i) Fund (ii) Working Capital (iii) Fund from Operation (iv) Increase in Working Capital (v) Sources of Fund (vi) Application of Fund (viii) Amortization.

III. **Solve the following problems**

1. Calculate the Working Capital from the following.

	Rs.		Rs.
Stock	1,70,000	Cash	2,10,000
Debtors	1,20,000	Outstanding interest (Debit)	20,000
Sundry creditors	90,000	Outstanding wages	40,000
Bank overdraft	50,000		

(Ans : Working Capital Rs.3,40,000)

2. Calculate the Working Capital from the following.

Particulars	*31st March 2006 Rs.*	*31st March 2007 Rs.*
Sundry Debtors	70,000	90,000
Sundry Creditors	40,000	50,000
Bank Overdraft	14,000	10,000
Outstanding Expenses	12,000	15,000
Outstanding Income	12,000	16,000
Expenses paid in advance	7,000	5,000
Income received in advance	10,000	6,000
Stock	20,000	25,000
Cash	23,000	30,000

(Ans: W.C Rs.76,000; Rs.97,000; Increase Rs.21,000)

3. Calculate Fund from Operation from the following.

	Rs.
Profit and Loss account balance as on 31st March 2006	3,40,000
Profit and Loss account balance as on 31st March 2007	4,10,000
Depreciation for fixed assets	70,000
Profit on sale of plant	15,000
Loss on sale of furniture	10,000
Provision for General Reserve	30,000

(Ans: Rs.1,65,000) *(For B.Com., B.B.A., B.B.M)*

4. Calculate Fund from Operation from the following.

	Rs.
Balance of Profit & Loss A/c (debit) as on 31st March 2006	2,00,000
Balance of Profit & Loss A/c (debit) as on 31st March 2007	2,40,000
Depreciation for Land & Building	50,000
Depreciation for Plant & Machinery	40,000
Provision for tax	44,000
Provision for dividend	40,000
Income tax refund	15,000
Profit on sale of plant	10,000

(For B.G., B.B.A., B.B.M)

(Ans : Rs.109,000)

5. Calculate Fund from Operation from the following.

	Rs.
Profit and Loss account as on 31st March 2006	1,47,000
Profit & Loss account as on 31st March 2007	52,000
Provision for depreciation	24,000
Provision for General Reserve	30,000
Preliminary expenses written off	15,000
Loss on sale of Furniture	11,000
Profit on sale of Plant	29,000

(Ans : Fund Lost in operation Rs.44,000) *(For B.Com., B.B.A., B.B.M)*

6. Calculate Fund from Operation for the following Trading and Profit & Loss account.

Trading and Profit and Loss Account

Particulars	*Rs.*	*Particulars*	*Rs.*
To Opening stock	70,000	By Sales	4,20,000
To Purchase	1,90,000	By Closing stock	90,000
To Wages	40,000		

To Gross profit	2,10,000		
	5,10,000		5,10,000
To Salary	42,000	By Gross Profit	2,10,000
To Electricity	13,000	By Profit on sale of Land	19,000
To Rent	14,000		
To Depreciation	30,000		
To Loss on sale of Machinery	10,000		
To Provision for Tax	30,000		
To Net Profit	90,000		
	2,29,000		2,29,000

(**Ans :** Rs.1,41,000)

7. Prepare a Statement of Fund Flow and a Statement of changes in Working Capital from the following Balance Sheets.

Liabilities	*2006 Rs.*	*2007 Rs.*	*Assets*	*2006 Rs.*	*2007 Rs.*
Share Capital	7,00,000	8,00,000	Fixed Assets	6,70,000	7,20,000
Profit & Loss A/c	1,37,000	1,50,000	Stock	99,000	80,000
Sundry creditors	23,000	15,000	Debtors	41,000	75,000
			Cash	50,000	90,000
	8,60,000	9,65,000		8,60,000	9,65,000

(**Ans :** Increase in W.C. Rs.63,000; Fund from Operation Rs.13,000)

8. G. Ltd., provided the Balance Sheet as on 31st March 2006 and 2007 as follows.

Liabilities	*2006 Rs.*	*2007 Rs.*	*Assets*	*2006 Rs.*	*2007 Rs.*
Share Capital	12,00,000	14,00,000	Land	7,00,000	8,00,000
Profit & Loss A/c	1,27,000	1,97,000	Premises	3,20,000	4,40,000
Mortgage Loan	3,00,000	2,00,000	Plant	5,00,000	4,20,000
Sundry Creditors	33,000	53,000	Stock	65,000	35,000
Bank overdraft	20,000	10,000	Debenture	25,000	65,000
			Cash	70,000	1,00,000
	16,80,000	18,60,000		16,80,000	18,60,000

Prepare a statement of Fund Flow. *(For B.Com., B.B.A., B.B.M)*

(**Ans :** Increase in W.C. Rs.30,000; Fund from operation Rs.70,000; Total Rs.3,50,000)

9. Prepare a Statement of Fund Flow from the following Balance Sheet

Liabilities	*2006 Rs.*	*2007 Rs.*	*Assets*	*2006 Rs.*	*2007 Rs.*
Share Capital	4,00,000	7,00,000	Land & Building	1,30,000	3,00,000
Profit & Loss A/c	1,35,000	90,000	Plant & Machinery	4,00,000	3,85,000
Loan	70,000	–	Stock	85,000	95,000

Sundry Creditors	54,000	30,000	Debtors	23,000	11,000
Bills Payable	16,000	20,000	Cash	37,000	49,000
	6,75,000	8,40,000		6,75,000	8,40,000

Consider decrease in Plant & Machinery as depreciation. *(For B.Com., B.B.A., B.B.M)*

(**Ans :** Increase in W.C. Rs.30,000; Fund lost in operation Rs.30,000; Total Rs.3,00,000)

10. Prepare a Statement of Fund Flow from the following.

Liabilities	*2006 Rs.*	*2007 Rs.*	*Assets*	*2006 Rs.*	*2007 Rs.*
Share Capital	11,00,000	13,00,000	Land & Building	6,50,000	5,00,000
Loan	3,00,000	1,50,000	Plant & Machinery	7,00,000	8,70,000
Sundry Creditors	51,000	75,000	Stock	55,000	70,000
Bank overdraft	29,000	15,000	Debtors	31,000	23,000
			Cash	44,000	77,000
	14,80,000	15,40,000		14,80,000	15,40,000

Depreciation for Land and Building is Rs.35,000 and Plant and Machinery is Rs.30,000.

(For B.Com., B.B.A., B.B.M)

(**Ans :** Increase in W.C Rs.30,000; Fund from operation Rs.2,65,000; Total Rs.3,80,000

Note: Difference in the capital is considered as Net Profit.

11. Prepare a statement of Fund Flow for the following Balance Sheets.

Liabilities	*2006 Rs.*	*2007 Rs.*	*Assets*	*2006 Rs.*	*2007 Rs.*
Capital	7,00,000	9,00,000	Land & Building	5,20,000	9,30,000
Profit & Loss A/c	1,70,000	2,10,000	Plant & Machinery	6,00,000	5,00,000
General Reserve	60,000	90,000	Stock	56,000	70,000
Debentures	3,00,000	4,00,000	Debenture	37,000	28,000
Loan	90,000	–	Cash	45,000	70,000
Sundry creditors	17,000	49,000	Bills Receivable	32,000	22,000
Bills Payable	13,000	11,000	Preliminary Expenses	60,000	40,000
	13,50,000	16,60,000		13,50,000	16,60,000

Adjustments:

i. Depreciation for Land & Building Rs. 49,000

ii. Depreciation for Plant & Machinery Rs.40,000; Profit on sale of a plant is Rs.20,000

iii. Drawings of Capital for the year Rs.40,000 *(For M.Com., M.B.A., M.C.A)*

(**Ans :** Decrease in W.C. Rs.10,000;

Fund from operation Rs.1,59,000; Total Rs.5,89,000)

12. Prepare a Statement of changes in Working Capital and Fund Flow Statement from the following.

Balance Sheet

Liabilities	2006 Rs.	2007 Rs.	Assets	2006 Rs.	2007 Rs.
Equity Share Capital	10,00,000	10,00,000	Land & Building	9,00,000	11,00,000
Profit & Loss A/c	1,77,000	2,24,000	Plant & Machinery	8,00,000	7,70,000
General Reserve	90,000	1,30,000	Stock	60,000	40,000
Debentures	4,50,000	3,00,000	Debtors	51,000	75,000
Loan	2,00,000	4,00,000	Cash	79,000	1,10,000
Sundry Creditors	43,000	76,000	Interest Outstanding	15,000	10,000
Salary outstanding	20,000	10,000	Preliminary Expenses	75,000	35,000
	19,80,000	21,40,000		19,80,000	21,40,000

Decrease in Plant & Machinery is considered as depreciation. Depreciation for Land & Building Rs.3,30,000.

(**Ans :** Increase in W.C. Rs.7,000; Fund from Operation Rs.1,90,000; Total Rs.3,90,000)

13. Prepare a statement of Fund Flow for the following Balance Sheets.

Balance Sheet

Liabilities	2006 Rs.	2007 Rs.	Assets	2006 Rs.	2007 Rs.
Equity Share Capital	14,00,000	17,00,000	Land & Building	10,00,000	9,00,000
Preference S.Capital	3,00,000	4,00,000	Plant & Machinery	12,10,000	16,90,000
Profit & Loss A/c	1,05,000	1,40,000	Stock	1,00,000	1,20,000
General Reserve	70,000	1,00,000	Debtor	71,000	85,000
Workmen			Cash	95,000	70,000
Compensation Fund	50,000	70,000	Outstanding interest	15,000	10,000
Debentures	3,50,000	2,00,000	Rent paid in advance	19,000	25,000
Loan	2,20,000	2,50,000	Preliminary expenses	70,000	50,000
Sundry Creditors	43,000	50,000			
Bank Overdraft	30,000	21,000			
Outstanding salary	12,000	19,000			
	25,80,000	29,50,000		25,80,000	29,50,000

Adjustments:

Depreciation provided is @ 10% for all the fixed assets

Assume that the purchase of Plant is at the end of the financial year.

Prepare the statement of changes in Working Capital and the statement of Fund Flow.

(**Ans :** Increase in W.C. Rs.5,000; Fund from Operation Rs.4,26,000) Total Rs.7,56,000)

14. Prepare a statement of Fund Flow and statement of changes in Working Capital from the following particulars.

Balance Sheet

Liabilities	2006 Rs.	2007 Rs.	Assets	2006 Rs.	2007 Rs.
Equity Share Capital	9,00,000	9,00,000	Land & Building	4,00,000	6,80,000
Profit Loss a/c	91,000	1,31,000	Plant & Machinery	4,80,000	4,00,000
General Reserve	46,000	54,000	Stock	90,000	75,000
Workmen Comp. Fund	40,000	30,000	Debtors	41,000	63,000

Loan	–	1,50,000	Cash	54,000	77,000
Sundry Creditors	38,000	55,000	Preliminary expenses	65,000	35,000
Outstanding expenses	15,000	10,000			
	11,30,000	13,30,000		11,30,000	13,30,000

Depreciation for Fixed Assets is @ 10%. During the year plant sold for Rs.60,000.

Assume that sale of plant is at the end and purchase of land in the beginning.

(**Ans :** Increase in W.C Rs.18,000; Fund from Operation Rs.1,66,000; Total Rs.36,60,000)

15. GR Ltd., provided the Balance Sheets for the year ended 31st March 2006 and 31st March 2007 as follows.

Balance Sheet

Liabilities	*2006 Rs.*	*2007 Rs.*	*Assets*	*2006 Rs.*	*2007 Rs.*
Equity Share Capital	7,00,000	7,00,000	Land & Building	6,50,000	7,90,000
Profit Loss a/c	1,20,000	90,000	Plant & Machinery	6,40,000	5,00,000
General Reserve	50,000	90,000	Stock	47,000	84,000
Debentures	2,00,000	2,90,000	Debtors	31,000	44,000
Loan	2,50,000	1,50,000	Cash	71,000	65,000
Provision for			Outstanding income	17,000	12,000
Tax liability	70,000	90,000	Expen. paid in adv.	14,000	20,000
Provision for dividend	55,000	75,000	Preliminary expenses	30,000	25,000
Sundry Creditors	44,000	52,000			
Outstanding wages	11,000	3,000			
	15,00,000	15,40,000		15,00,000	15,40,000

Adjustments:

1. Depreciation for Land & Building is Rs.40,000
2. During the year Rs.90,000 worth of Plant is sold for Rs.1,00,000

Prepare a statement of Fund Flow.

(**Ans :** Increase in W.C Rs.5,000; Fund from Operation Rs.95,000 Total Rs.2,85,000; If provisions are treated as Fixed items - Rs.45,000; Rs.2,60,000 and Rs.4,50,000)

16. GT Ltd. provided the Balance Sheets as on 31st March of 2006 and 2007 as follows.

Balance Sheet

Liabilities	*2006 Rs.*	*2007 Rs.*	*Assets*	*2006 Rs.*	*2007 Rs.*
Equity Share Capital	14,00,000	14,00,000	Land & Building	8,50,000	10,00,000
Preference Share cap.	5,00,000	7,00,000	Plant & Machinery	9,70,000	8,70,000
Profit & Loss A/c	1,33,000	1,90,000	Furniture & Fittings	4,60,000	5,00,000
General Reserve	50,000	80,000	Goodwill	74,000	53,000
Debentures	2,00,000	1,00,000	Stock	1,32,000	1,10,000
Long-term loan	2,00,000	75,000	Debtors	74,000	93,000
Provision for Tax	90,000	1,15,000	Cash	1,10,000	1,34,000
Proposed Dividend	50,000	75,000			
Sundry Creditors	47,000	25,000			
	26,70,000	27,60,000		26,70,000	27,60,000

The following further information are also given:

1. Furniture worth Rs.60,000 was purchased during the year
2. Depreciation for Plant & Machinery Rs.50,000, Profit on sale of a plant is Rs.20,000.
3. Depreciation for Land & Building Rs.75,000.

Prepare a statement of Fund Flow and a statement of changes in Working Capital.

(**Ans :** Decrease in W.C. Rs.7,000; Fund from operation Rs.2,33,000; Total Rs.5,10,000; If provision are taken as fixed items; Increase in W.C. Rs.43,000; Fund from Operation Rs.4,23,000; Total Rs.6,93,000)

17. The Balance Sheets as on 31st March of 2006 & 2007 of KMH Ltd. are stated as follows:

Balance Sheet

Liabilities	*2006 Rs.*	*2007 Rs.*	*Assets*	*2006 Rs.*	*2007 Rs.*
Equity Share Capital	9,50,000	13,50,000	Land & Building	7,80,000	14,00,000
Preference Share Cap.	2,00,000	3,50,000	Plant & Machinery	7,20,000	6,00,000
Profit & Loss A/c	1,21,000	1,44,000	Furniture & Fittings	1,00,000	1,80,000
General Reserve	79,000	95,000	Goodwill	40,000	60,000
Workmen Comp.Fund	49,000	37,000	Stock	1,25,000	1,45,000
Debentures	2,00,000	3,00,000	Debtors	77,000	42,000
Long-term loan	3,00,000	1,90,000	Cash	93,000	1,14,000
Provision for tax	74,000	59,000	Exp. paid in advance	17,000	24,000
Proposed dividend	47,000	64,000	Preliminary exp.	60,000	40,000
Sundry Creditors	34,000	51,000	Goodwill	65,000	45,000
Outstanding salary	23,000	10,000			
	20,77,000	26,50,000		20,77,000	26,50,000

The following further information are also given

1. Depreciation for Land & Building is Rs.70,000
2. Depreciation of Plant & Machinery is Rs.50,000. Loss on sale of a plant is Rs.15,000
3. During the year Furniture worth Rs.50,000 was sold for Rs.60,000. Depreciation for Furniture is Rs.15,000.

Prepare a statement of Fund Flow and a statement of changes in Working Capital by considering the Provision for Tax and Proposed Dividend as fixed items.

(**Ans :** Increase in W.C. Rs.9,000; Fund from operation Rs.8,50,000)

18. GC Ltd., provided the Balance Sheets as on 31st March of 2006 and 31st March 2007 as follows.

Balance Sheet

Liabilities	*2006 Rs.*	*2007 Rs.*	*Assets*	*2006 Rs.*	*2007 Rs.*
Equity Share Capital	17,50,000	17,50,000	Fixed Assets	24,90,000	29,20,000
Preference Share Cap.	4,00,000	7,50,000	Stock	91,000	67,000
Profit & Loss A/c	–	95,000	Debtors	23,000	44,000
General Reserve	79,000	97,000	Cash	54,000	75,000
Long-term loan	3,00,000	2,10,000	Outstanding income	17,000	9,000
Provision for tax	1,12,000	1,20,000	Profit & Loss A/c	25,000	–
Sundry creditors	74,000	95,000	Discount on issue of		
Income received in adv.	25,000	13,000	Debentures	40,000	15,000
	27,40,000	31,30,000		27,40,000	31,30,000

Prepare a Statement of Fund Flow and a Statement of changes in Working Capital.

(**Ans :** Increase in W.C. Rs.1,000; Fund from Operation Rs.2,83,000; Total Rs.6,33,000)

19. KN Ltd., provided the Balance Sheets as on 31st March of 2006 and 2007 as follows.

Balance Sheet

Liabilities	*2006 Rs.*	*2007 Rs.*	*Assets*	*2006 Rs.*	*2007 Rs.*
Eqty Share Capital	9,00,000	9,00,000	Land & Building	7,00,000	7,40,000
Preference Share Capital	3,50,000	5,50,000	Plant & Machinery	6,10,000	6,95,000
General Reserve	71,000	92,000	Furniture & Fittings	2,70,000	2,55,000
Debentures	3,50,000	2,50,000	Stock	47,000	94,000
Long-term loan	1,50,000	2,75,000	Debtors	25,000	53,000
Sundry creditors	32,000	51,000	Cash	54,000	71,000
Outstanding salary	22,000	12,000	Outstanding income	32,000	21,000
			Expenses paid in adv.	27,000	11,000
			Profit & Loss A/c	1,10,000	1,90,000
	18,75,000	21,30,000		18,75,000	21,30,000

The following further information are also given.

1. Purchase of Furniture during the year Rs.15,000.
2. Depreciation for Land & Building Rs.50,000 and Plant & Machinery Rs.40,000.

Prepare a statement of changes in Working Capital and a statement of Fund Flow.

(**Ans :** Increase in W.C. Rs.56,000; Fund from Operation Rs.61,000; Total Rs.3,86,000)

20. Prepare Fund Flow statement and Statement of changes in Working Capital from the Balance Sheets provided by MWD Ltd., as on 31st March of 2006 and 2007 as follows.

Balance Sheet

Liabilities	*2006 Rs.*	*2007 Rs.*	*Assets*	*2006 Rs.*	*2007 Rs.*
Equity Share Capital	17,00,000	18,00,000	Land & Building	12,00,000	15,60,000
Preference share cap.	3,75,000	4,25,000	Plant & Machinery	8,30,000	7,50,000
Profit Loss a/c	91,000	74,000	Investments	5,00,000	4,50,000
General Reserve	50,000	75,000	Inventories	50,000	79,000
Cap.Redemption Res.	–	35,000	Debtors	52,000	40,000
Workmen Comp.Fund	30,000	40,000	Cash	91,000	77,000
Debentures	2,70,000	2,00,000	Outstanding income	27,000	39,000
Long-term loan	1,50,000	2,40,000	Prepaid expenses	15,000	11,000
Provision for tax	85,000	76,000	Discount on Debenture	55,000	34,000
Sundry creditors	32,000	43,000			
Interest accrued	14,000	19,000			
Bank overdraft	23,000	13,000			
	28,20,000	30,40,000		28,20,000	30,40,000

The following further information are also given.

1. Interim dividend paid @ 4% for Equity Shareholders on 1st November 2006.
2. Loss on sale of Investment is Rs.20,000.
3. Depreciation for Land & Building Rs.97,000 and Plant & Machinery Rs.60,000
4. Profit on sale of Plant & Machinery Rs.10,000.
5. Additional Equity Share Capital is raised on 1st February 2007.

(Ans : Increase in W.C. Rs.14,000; Fund from Operation Rs.3,09,000; Total Rs.6,09,000)

21. Joyce & Co.Ltd. provided the Balance Sheets as on 31st March of 2006 and 2007 as follows

Balance Sheet

Liabilities	*2006 Rs.*	*2007 Rs.*	*Assets*	*2006 Rs.*	*2007 Rs.*
Equity Share Capital	9,50,000	12,50,000	Land & Building	5,00,000	8,00,000
Preference Share Cap.	3,00,000	4,00,000	Plant & Machinery	4,45,000	8,40,000
Profit Loss a/c	1,14,000	1,32,000	Furniture	2,75,000	2,00,000
General Reserve	79,000	85,000	Investments	3,50,000	2,20,000
Capital Redemption			(Long term)		
Reserve	75,000	40,000	Stock	91,000	73,000
Debentures	2,00,000	1,00,000	Debtors	83,000	65,000
Secured Loan	1,75,000	2,50,000	Cash	1,39,000	1,00,000
Provision for Tax	70,000	90,000	Bills receivable	42,000	57,000
Sundry Creditors	37,000	62,000	Preliminary expen.	95,000	65,000
Bills Payable	20,000	11,000			
	20,20,000	24,20,000		20,20,000	24,20,000

Additional Information:

1. Depreciation was charged for Land and Building @ 5%, and Furniture @ 10%.
2. Land worth Rs.1,20,000 was sold for Rs.1,50,000 and a new Land was purchased on , 1st April 2006.
3. A machine worth Rs.90,000 was sold for Rs.70,000 and a new machine was purchased for Rs.4,30,000 during the year.
4. Furniture sold for Rs.70,000 on 31st March 2007.
5. Interim Dividend paid @ 4% for Equity Share Capital of Rs.9,50,000.
6. Income Tax paid during the year Rs.75,000.
7. Profit on sale of Investment Rs.25,000.

Prepare a statement of Fund Flow and statement of changes in Working Capital.

(Ans : Decrease in W.C. Rs.76,000; Fund from Operation Rs.2,07,000; Total Rs.12,03,000)

22. Prepare Fund Flow statement and Statement of changes in Working Capital from the Balance Sheets provided by KM Ltd., as on 31st March of 2006 and 2007 as follows.

Balance Sheet

Liabilities	*2006 Rs.*	*2007 Rs.*	*Assets*	*2006 Rs.*	*2007 Rs.*
Equity Share Capital	11,00,000	13,50,000	Land & Building	5,55,000	10,00,000
Retained Earnings	3,15,000	5,95,000	Plant & Machinery	10,25,000	9,95,000
General Reserve	71,000	91,000	(Accumulated Dep.)	(50,000)	(75,000)

Reserve for future loss on Investment	49,000	34,000	Patent	1,40,000	1,00,000
			Investment	2,10,000	3,57,000
Debentures	3,70,000	2,40,000	Stock	1,20,000	1,41,000
Long-term loan	1,89,000	2,55,000	Debtors	85,000	71,000
Proposed dividend	69,000	77,000	Cash	74,000	99,000
Sundry creditors	44,000	62,000	Discount on Debentures	71,000	32,000
Outstanding salary	23,000	16,000			
	22,30,000	27,20,000		22,30,000	27,20,000

The following further information are also given.

1. During the year a Plant with accumulated depreciation Rs.20,000 was sold for a profit of Rs.15,000
2. On 1st November 2006 an Investment worth Rs.60,000 was sold for a loss and the loss was adjusted with the reserve made for this purpose.
3. Depreciation for the Land & Building @ 10% on closing balance. Land sold during the year Rs.70,000 (Book value Rs.75,000).
4. Dividend paid during the year Rs.70,000.

(**Ans :** Increase in W.C. Rs.43,000; Fund from Operation Rs.5,89,000; Total Rs.10,70,000)

23. Prepare Fund Flow statement and Statement of changes in Working Capital from the Balance Sheets provided by KMH Ltd., as on 31st March of 2006 and 2007 as follows.

Balance Sheet

Liabilities	*2006 Rs.*	*2007 Rs.*	*Assets*	*2006 Rs.*	*2007 Rs.*
Equity Share Capital	5,00,000	7,00,000	Land & Building	7,00,000	11,30,000
Preference Share Capital	3,00,000	4,00,000	Plant & Machinery	5,53,000	8,00,000
General Reserve	1,21,000	1,52,000	Furniture & Fittings	1,50,000	2,00,000
Debenture Redemption Reserve	4,50,000	4,00,000	Tools	1,50,000	2,00,000
			Inventories	50,000	60,000
Provision for Depreciation	1,10,000	1,25,000	Debtors	30,000	50,000
Debentures	3,00,000	2,00,000	Cash	72,000	55,000
Long-term loan	2,00,000	6,00,000	Bills receivable	35,000	20,000
Provision for tax	95,000	80,000	Prepaid expenses	25,000	37,000
Prov. for doubtful debts	21,000	30,000	Investments-Short Term	2,00,000	1,50,000
Sundry creditors	70,000	90,000	Discount on issue of shares	32,000	50,000
Bank overdraft	23,000	30,000			
Bills payable	17,000	15,000	Profit & Loss A/c	2,10,000	70,000
	22,07,000	28,22,000		22,07,000	28,22,000

The following further information are also given.

1. Profit on sale of Furniture for the year is Rs.15,000. Accumulated depreciation Rs.10,000. Purchase of Furniture Rs.90,000.
2. A machinery costing Rs.70,000 was sold for Rs.50,000. Accumulated depreciation of the machinery is Rs.10,000.
3. Tools with cost Rs.30,000 was scrapped and written off. The accumulated depreciation of the tools is Rs.15,000.
4.

Land sold during the year is Rs.1,50,000. The cost of the Land is Rs.1,30,000 and accumulated depreciation is Rs.50,000.

5. The Debenture redeemed for the year is Rs.100,000.Fifty percent of the Debentures redeemed, are paid in the form of Equity Shares.

Prepare a Statement of Fund Flow and Statement of changes in Working Capital.

(Ans : Decrease in W.C. Rs.59,000; Fund from Operation Rs.1,93,000)

24. GT Ltd., provided the balance sheet as on 31st March of 2006 and 2007 as follows.

Balance Sheet

Liabilities	*2006 Rs.*	*2007 Rs.*	*Assets*	*2006 Rs.*	*2007 Rs.*
Equity Share Capital	25,00,000	27,00,000	Land & Building	17,00,000	20,00,000
Preference Sh. Cap.	4,00,000	5,00,000	Plant & Machinery	13,00,000	14,00,000
Profit & Loss A/c	1,50,000	2,40,000	Furniture & Fittings	5,50,000	6,60,000
General Reserve	2,10,000	2,90,000	Investments	4,70,000	4,00,000
Cap. Redemption Res.	90,000	1,25,000	Inventories	95,000	73,000
Debenture	4,00,000	3,00,000	Debtors	35,000	60,000
Long-term Loan	3,70,000	4,03,000	Cash	90,000	1,40,000
Provision for Tax	1,12,000	1,25,000	Outstanding interest	19,000	12,000
Proposed Dividend	73,000	80,000	Expenses paid in advance	31,000	39,000
Sundry Creditors	65,000	79,000	Preliminary expenses	1,10,000	80,000
Outstanding salary	30,000	22,000			
	44,00,000	48,64,000		44,00,000	48,64,000

The Profit and Loss Account for the year ended 31st March 2007 is stated as follows.

Profit & Loss Account

Particulars	*Rs.*	*Particulars*	*Rs.*
To Manufacturing expenses	1,45,000	By Sales	9,90,000
To Administration expenses	65,000	By Profit on sale of Plant	25,000
To Selling & Distribution expenses	45,000	By Profit on sale of Investment	23,000
To Interest on Debenture	50,000	By Interest received	32,000
To Interest on Loan	40,000		
To Dep.on Land & Building	1,00,000		
To Dep.on Plant & Machinery	1,23,000		
To Dep. of Furniture	40,000		
To Loss on sale of Furniture	20,000		
To Preliminary expenses written off	30,000		
To Provision for Tax	1,25,000		
To Net profit after Tax	2,87,000		
	10,70,000		10,70,000

The following further information are also given.

1. Cost of plant sold is Rs.95,000.

2. Rs.50,000 worth of debenture was redeemed is paid in the form of Preference Share Capital.
3. Dividend paid to Equity Shareholders is Rs.75,000.

Prepare a Statement of changes in Working Capital and a Statement of Fund Flow.

(**Ans :** Increase in Working Capital Rs.48,000; Fund from Operation Rs.6,57,000)

25. The Balance Sheets of K Ltd., as on 31st March of 2006 and 2007 are stated as follows.

Balance Sheet

Liabilities	*2006 Rs.*	*2007 Rs.*	*Assets*	*2006 Rs.*	*2007 Rs.*
Equity Share Capital	9,00,000	9,00,000	Fixed Assets	18,50,000	21,60,000
Profit & Loss A/c	2,19,000	1,37,000	Stock	28,000	54,000
General Reserve	77,000	99,000	Debtors	53,000	42,000
Capital Redem. Reserve	35,000	55,000	Cash	1,90,000	2,10,000
Provision for Dep.	1,90,000	2,40,000	Discount on issue of		
Debentures	4,00,000	4,50,000	Debentures	75,000	55,000
Long-term loan	1,50,000	3,70,000			
Provision for tax	1,15,000	1,25,000			
Proposed Dividend	59,000	79,000			
Sundry Creditors	31,000	49,000			
Outstanding expenses	20,000	17,000			
	21,96,000	25,21,000		21,96,000	25,21,000

The summarised Profit &Loss Account as on 31st March 2007 is stated as follows.

Particulars	*Rs.*	*Rs.*
Sales		14,22,000
Manufacturing expenses	6,10,000	
Administration expenses	3,90,000	
Selling expenses	1,30,000	
Provision for depreciation	70,000	
Loss on sale of Plant	20,000	
Discount on Debenture written off	20,000	12,40,000
		1,82,000
Less : Tax		1,25,000
Net Profit after Tax		57,000

Adjustments :

i. Cost of Plant sold is Rs.1,00,000 and accumulated depreciation of it is Rs.22,000.

ii. Dividend @ 7% is paid for the Equity Share Capital of Rs.11,00,000.

Prepare a statement of Fund Flow and Statement of changes in Working Capital.

(**Ans :** Increase in Working Capital Rs.20,000; Fund from Operation Rs.2,92,000; Total Rs.6,22,000)

❑ ❑ ❑

5

CASH FLOW ANALYSIS

Cash is considered as an important factor in a company as well as in all places. The efficient functioning of a concern depends upon the sufficient cash at all times. Cash is required right from the purchase of raw material till the final product is sold to the consumers. The requirement of cash is to pay for the raw material, wages and salary, administrative and selling and distribution expenses. In addition to this, cash is required for the procurement of fixed assets like Land and Building, Plant and Machinery etc. This requirement of cash is met with different sources of cash, like from sales, contribution of owners (capital) and borrowing from banks and financial institutions. Hence, there is a need for proper management of cash to avoid any shortage of cash. Cash Flow Statement is one of the important tools for managing the cash like Fund Flow Statement and Budgetary Control.

Meaning of Cash Flow Statement

A statement of sources and application of cash in a period is called Cash Flow Statement. Sources are otherwise called as inflow and application or otherwise called as outflow of cash. This statement explains the various sources from which cash inflow to the company and various ways in which cash outflow took place.

Cash Flow Statement otherwise means the increase or decrease of cash between two periods. It compares the inflows and outflows of various items and find out the reason for the net increase or decrease of cash in a period when compared to another period. Normally, the period of comparison is between the current year and the previous year or any two continuous periods. Hence, it helps to know the financial conditions and the area in which the management should take much care for correction and control.

The movement or changes of cash is known through the Balance Sheets of two periods. The increase or decrease of the value of Balance Sheet items shows the inflow or outflow of cash in the respective items. Normally, the increase in the individual assets from one period to the previous period means the outflow of cash and the decrease of it means the inflow of cash. Like that, the increase in the individual liabilities from one period to the previous period means the inflow of cash and the decrease of it means the outflow of cash.

Sources and Application of Cash (Inflow and Outflow of cash)

1. Sources of Cash

The important sources of cash are stated as follows:

1. Cash from Operation: Cash from Operation is otherwise called as the internal source of cash. It is calculated by adjusting the amortisations (like writing off of Preliminary expenses, Goodwill, Patent, Discount on issue of Shares or Debentures) and appropriations (like Provision for taxation, General Reserve, Dividend and other reserves). Also the other non-operating items like Depreciation, Loss on sale of Fixed Assets and Profit on sale of Fixed Assets should also be adjusted. In addition to this, increase or decrease of Current Assets and Current Liabilities should be adjusted.

2. Issue of Share Capital: The company might have issued Equity Share Capital or Preference Share Capital in a year which is considered to be a source of cash. It is known through the increase of share capital position from the previous year.

3. Issue of Debenture: Issue of debenture is an important long-term source of cash for the company. It is known through the increase of Debenture in the Balance Sheet when compared to the value of Debenture for the previous period.

4. Raising of long-term Loan: Loan may be raised from banks and other financial institutions. It is an important source of cash for a company.

5. Sale of Fixed Assets and Investments: Sale of Fixed Assets is a important sources of cash. Actual cash inflow from the sale is to be taken into account. Like that, sale of Investment should be considered as an important inflow of cash.

Application of Cash

The important applications or outflow of cash are stated as follows:

1. Cash lost in operation: In the adjustment of net profit with non-cash and non-operating items and the Current Assets and Current Liabilities, there may be debit balance instead of credit balance. The debit balance is called Cash Lost in Operation and it is due to the cash outflow compared to the previous period.

2. Redemption of Preference Share Capital: Redeemable Preference Share Capital can be redeemed. If this capital is decreased when compared to the previous period, it means outflow of cash.

3. Redemption of Debenture: Debenture is to be redeemed after certain period of time. If in the period of the analysis any decrease is the Debenture position when compared to the previous period, it is called redemption of Debenture. It means outflow of cash.

4. Purchase of Fixed Assets: The purchase of Fixed Assets and Investments will reduce the cash position. It is considered as an outflow of cash.

5. Payment of Tax: Payment of tax will decrease the cash and it is considered as a cash outflow.

6. Payment of Dividend: Payment of dividend decreases the cash and it is considered as a cash outflow.

Objectives of Cash Flow Statement

The objectives of Cash Flow Statement are as follows:

1. To measure the movement of cash over a period of time.
2. To find out whether the cash is utilised properly.
3. To take corrective action if there is any default in the utilisation of cash.
4. To assess the requirement of cash for the smoothful functioning of a concern.
5. To take various managerial decisions of a company.

Advantages of Cash Flow Statement

The following are the advantages of Cash Flow Statement:

(i) It helps to find out the movement of cash over a period of time.

(ii) It is possible to assess the requirement of cash for a period.

(iii) The cash performance of a company at present when compared to the previous periods can be ascertained.

(iv) It helps for allocating cash for various requirements in a Company.

(v) It is an important tool for the management for managerial decision making.

Limitations of Cash Flow Statement

The limitations of Cash Flow Statement are stated as follows:

(i) Cash flow statement analyses only the historical facts. There is no projection of cash in future in this method.

(ii) The manipulation done in Balance Sheets will affect the accuracy of the movement of cash for a period.

(iii) It analyses the movement of cash only for two periods.

(iv) It won't be a substitute for the Income Statement.

Procedures in the preparation of Cash Flow Statement

There are two methods in the preparation of Cash Flow Statement. They are,

I. Traditional Method

II. Revised Method

I. Traditional method of preparation of Cash Flow Statement

The following are the procedures in the preparation of Cash Flow Statement under Traditional Method.

1. Calculation of Cash from Operating activities
2. Preparation of Cash Flow Statement.

1. Calculation of Cash from Operating Activities: Cash from Operating activities means the cash received through production and sale of goods. The net cash received after meeting all the production expenses is called Cash from Operation. Since there are many items of expenses with outstanding and advance payments, there is a need for adopting a method for the calculation. There are two methods of calculating of Cash from Operation. They are called (i) Direct method and (ii) Indirect method. Direct method is based on the Sales revenue and the adjustments like expenses; and Indirect method is based on the Net Profit and the adjustments. The most common method adopted for the calculation of Cash from Operation is indirect method.

i. Direct method of calculating Cash from Operation

The following is the procedure for calculating Cash from Operation in Direct method.

Calculation of Cash from Operating Activities

Particulars	Rs.
Cash receipt from customers	xxxxx
Less : Cash paid to suppliers and employees	xxxxx
Cash generated from operation	xxxxx
Less : Income Tax Paid	xxxxx
Cash from Operating Activities	xxxxx

The cash receipt from customers includes cash sales and receipt from debtors. The cash paid to suppliers and employees include cash purchase, payment to sundry creditors and payment of operating expenses.

ii. Indirect method of calculating Cash from Operation

Net Profit is the basis for calculating Cash from Operation in this method. The following is the procedure for calculating Cash from Operation.

Statement of Cash from Operation

Particulars	*Rs.*	*Rs.*
Net Profit before tax		
Add : Non-cash and non-trading items		XXXXX
(Debited in Profit & Loss Account)		
i. Depreciation on Fixed Assets	XXXXX	
ii. Goodwill, Patent or Trade mark written of (Intangible assets)	XXXXX	
iii. Preliminary expenses, Underwriting commission, Discount on issue of Shares or Debentures written off (Fictitious assets)	XXXXX	
iv. Provision for Bad and Doubtful Debts	XXXXX	
v. Loss on sale of Fixed Assets and Investment	XXXXX	
vi. Provision for Taxation	XXXXX	
vii. Provision for General Reserve	XXXXX	
viii. Proposed Dividend	XXXXX	XXXXX
Less : Non-cash and non-trading items		XXXXX
(Credited in Profit & Loss Account)		
i. Profit on sale of Fixed Assets	XXXXX	
ii. Interest, Commission, Dividend received	XXXXX	
iii. Income Tax refund	XXXXX	XXXXX
Net Cash flow before adjusting		
Working Capital items		XXXXX
Add : Increase in Current Liabilities	XXXXX	
Decrease in Current Assets	XXXXX	XXXXX
		XXXXX
Less : Increase in Current Assets	XXXXX	
Decrease in Current Liabilities	XXXXX	XXXXX
Net cash flow from Operating Activities		XXXXX

In the above statement if Net Profit is not given the difference in the Opening and Closing balance of Profit & Loss Account should be adjusted instead of Net Profit.

Cash from Operating Activities can also be calculated through indirect method by Adjusted Profit and Loss Account as follows.

Adjusted Profit & Loss Account

Particulars	*Rs.*	*Particulars*	*Rs.*
To Depreciation on Fixed Assets		By Balance b/d	
To Loss on sale of Fixed Assets		(Opening Credit balance)	
To Goodwill or Patent		By Profit on sales of Fixed Assets	

To Trademark written off		By Dividend received	
To Preliminary expenses		By Commission received	
To Dis. on issue of Shares written off.		By Interest received	
To Provision for Bad and Doubtful Debts		By Income Tax refund	
To Provision for Taxation		By Cash from Operating Activities before adjustment of Working Capital items **(Fund from Operation)**	
To Provision General Reserve or any other Reserve			
To Provision for Dividend			
To Balance c/d			
	xxxxx		**xxxxx**

Statement of Cash from Operation

Particulars	*Rs.*	*Rs.*
Fund from Operation		xxx
Add : Increase in Current Liabilities	xxx	
Decrease in Current Assets	xxx	xxx
		xxx
Less : Increase in Current Assets	xxx	
Decrease in Current Liabilities	xxx	xxx
Cash from Operating Activities		**xxx**

Illustration: 1

Calculate Cash from Operation from the following.

Trading and Profit & Loss Account

Particulars	*Rs.*	*Particulars*	*Rs.*
To Opening Stock	74,000	By Sales	12,33,000
To Purchase	9,14,000	By Closing stock	87,000
To Manufacturing expenses	82,000		
To Gross Profit	2,50,000		
	13,20,000		13,20,000
To Depreciation	40,000	**By Gross Profit**	2,50,000
To Administrative Expenses	70,000		
To Provision for Taxation	50,000		
To Net Profit	90,000		
	2,50,000		2,50,000

Additional Information:

i.	Net Profit	Rs.90,000
	Dividend	Rs.35,000
	Profit transferred to Balance Sheet	Rs.55,000

ii. Opening and Closing balances of Debtors are Rs.54,000 and Rs.74,000 respectively.

iii. Opening and Closing balances of Sundry Creditors are Rs.32,000 and Rs.17,000 respectively.

iv. Opening and Closing balances of Provision for Tax are Rs.47,000 and Rs.52,000 respectively.

(For B.Com., B.B.A. B.B.M., M.Com.)

Solution :

Calculation of Cash from Operating Activities

Particulars	*Rs.*
Cash receipts from customers	12,53,000
Cash paid to suppliers and employees	10,81,000
Cash generated from Operation	1,72,000
Income tax paid	45,000
Cash from Operating Activities	**1,27,000**

Workings i. **Cash receipts from customers**

	Rs.
Sales	12,33,000
Add : Closing Debtors	74,000
	13,07,000
Less : Opening Debtors	54,000
	12,53,000

ii. **Cash paid to suppliers and employees**

Purchase	9,14,000
Add : Opening Sundry Creditors	32,000
	9,46,000
Less : Closing Sundry Creditors	17,000
	9,29,000
Add : Manufacturing expenses	82,000
Administration expenses	70,000
	10,81,000

iii. **Tax paid**

Opening balance of Provision for Tax	47,000
Add : Provision for the year	50,000
	97,000
Less : Closing balance of Provision for Tax	52.000
	45,000

Note : Payment of Dividend should be treated as the cash flow from Financing Activities.

Illustration: 2

Calculate Cash from Operation from the following

Statement of Profit

Particulars	*Rs.*	*Rs.*
Sales		42,00,000
Opening Stock	1,60,000	
Add : Purchase	19,00,000	
	20,60,000	
Less : Closing Stock	80,000	
	19,80,000	
Manufacturing expenses	1,70,000	20, 50,000
Gross Profit		21,50,000
Depreciation	1,10,000	
Administration expenses	2,40,000	
Selling expenses	1,90,000	
Provision for Taxation	3,00,000	8,40,000
		13,10,000
Add : Profit on sale of Fixed Assets		40,000
Net Profit		13,50,000
Payment of Dividend		2,50,000
Net Profit to be transferred to Balance Sheet		11,00,000

Balances of Current items for 31st March 2006 and 2007 are stated as follows.

	31st March 2006	*31st March 2007*
Debtors	1,15,000	1,45,000
Cash	2,20,000	2,00,000
Sundry Creditors	1,00,000	1,20,000
Outstanding Administrative expenses	30,000	20,000
Provision for Taxation	2,40,000	2,90,000

(For M.Com., M.B.A.)

Solution :

Note: Cash from Operating Activities can be calculated by deducting cash payment to suppliers, payment to the creditors on account of credit purchase and operating expenses from the Cash received on account of cash sales and credit sales. In addition to this, payment of tax should also be deducted.

Calculation of Cash from Operation

Particulars		*Rs.*	*Rs.*
i. Cash receipts from customers			
Sales			42,00,000
Add : Debtors at the end			1,45,000
			43,45,000
Less : Debtors in the beginning			1,15,000
			42,30,000
ii. Cash paid to suppliers and employees			
Purchases		19,00,000	
Add : Sundry Creditors in the beginning		1,00,000	
		20,00,000	
Less : Sundry Creditors at the end		1,20,000	
		18,80,000	
Administrative expenses	2,40,000		
Add : Outstanding in the beginning	20,000		
	2,60,000		
Less : Outstanding at the end	30,000	2,30,000	
Selling expenses		1,90,000	23,20,000
Cash generated from Operation			**19,10,000**
iii. Income Tax paid			
Opening balance of Provision for Tax		2,40,000	
Add : Provision for the year		3,00,000	
		5,40,000	
Less : Closing balance of Provision for Tax		2,90,000	2,50,000
Net Cash flow from Operating Activities			**16,60,000**

Illustration: 3

Calculate Cash from Operation by direct method and indirect method from the following.

Trading & Profit and Loss Account

Particulars	*Rs.*	*Particulars*	*Rs.*
To Cost of goods sold	1,90,000	By Sales	4,00,000
To Gross Profit	2,10,000		
	4,00,000		4,00,000
To Salaries	35,000	**By Gross Profit**	**2,10,000**
To Rent paid	20,000		
To Telephone expenses	10,000		
To Insurance	14,000		
To Depreciation	17,000		
To Net Profit	1,14,000		
	2,10,000		2,10,000

The following additional information are also given.

	31st March 2006 Rs.	31st March 2007 Rs.
Stock	50,000	75,000
Debtors	32,000	27,000
Cash	40,000	60,000
Prepaid rent	5,000	3,000
Sundry Creditors	24,000	17,000
Salary outstanding	12,000	15,000

(For B.Com., B.B.A., B.B.M., M.Com.)

Solution :

(i) Calculation of Cash from Operating Activities (Direct Method)

Particulars	Rs.	Rs.
1. Cash inflow from sales (cash received from customers)		
Sales - Opening Debtors + Closing Debtors		
(4,00,000 – 32,000 + 27,000)		3,95,000
2. Cash outflow on cost of sales (cash paid to suppliers and employees)		
Cost of goods sold - Opening Stock +		
Closing stock + Opening Creditors - Closing Creditors		
(1,90,000 – 50,000 + 75,000 + 24,000 – 17,000)	2,22,000	
3. Cash outflow on expenses		
i. Salaries + Outstanding in the beginning -		
Outstanding at the end (35,000 + 12,000 – 15,000)	32,000	
ii. Rent – prepaid in the beginning + prepaid at the end		
(20,000 – 5,000 + 3,000)	18,000	
iii. Insurance premium	14,000	
Cash outflow in Operating Activities		2,86,000
Cash from operating activities		**1,09,000**

(ii) Calculation of Cash from Operating Activities (Indirect Method)

Particulars	Rs.	Rs.
Net Profit for the year		1,14,000
Add : Non cash expenses:		
Depreciation		17,000
Fund from Operation		1,31,000
Add : Increase in Current Liabilities:		
Salary outstanding (15,000 – 12,000)	3,000	
Decrease in Current Assets:		
Debentures (32,000 – 27,000)	5,000	
Prepaid rent (5,000 – 3,000)	2,000	10,000

		1,41,000
Less : Increase in Current Assets:		
Stock (75,000 – 50,000)	25,000	
Decrease in Current Liabilities:		
Sundry Creditors (24,000 – 17,000)	7,000	32,000
Cash from Operating Activities		**1,09,000**

Illustration: 4

Calculate Cash from Operating Activities from the following

Particulars	*Rs.*	*Particulars*	*Rs.*
To Operating Stock	53,000	By Sales	5,50,000
To Purchase	1,80,000	By Closing Stock	70,000
To Wages	20,000		
To Gross Profit	3,67,000		
	6,20,000		6,20,000
To Salary	59,000	**By Gross Profit**	**3,67,000**
To Telephone	14,000	By Profit on sale of Plant	13,000
To Electricity	19,000	By Refund of Income Tax	15,000
To Rent	24,000		
To Depreciation	30,000		
To Loss on sale of Furniture	7,000		
To Goodwill written off	14,000		
To Provision for Taxation	90,000		
To Net profit	1,38,000		
	3,95,000		3,95,000

(For B.Com., B.B.A., B.B.M.)

Solution :

Calculation of Cash from Operating Activities

Particulars	*Rs.*	*Rs.*
Net Profit after tax		1,38,000
Add : Appropriation and non cash expenses		
Provision for Taxation	90,000	
Goodwill written off	14,000	
Depreciation	30,000	
Loss on sale of Furniture	7,000	1,41,000
		2,79,000
Less : Non cash income & adjustments		
Profit on Sale of Plant	13,000	
Refund of Income Tax	15,000	
Increase in Stock	17,000	45,000
Cash from Operating Activities		**2,34,000**

Illustration: 5

Calculate Cash from Operating Activities from the following:

Profit and Loss Account as on 31st March 2007

Particulars	*Rs.*	*Particulars*	*Rs.*
To Salary	40,000	**By Gross Profit**	**2,75,000**
To Electricity	10,000	By Profit on sale of Investment	25,000
To Telephone	12,000		
To Selling expenses	19,000		
To Dep. on Land & Building	21,000		
To Dep. on Plant & Machinery	27,000		
To Dep. on Furniture	10,000		
To Loss on sale of Machinery	9,000		
To Provision for Taxation	60,000		
To Net Profit	92,000		
	3,00,000		3,00,000

Adjustments:

	31st March 2006 *Rs.*	*31st March 2007* *Rs.*
Inventories	30,000	45,000
Debtors	29,000	20,000
Cash	50,000	70,000
Outstanding salary	10,000	12,000
Sundry creditors	19,000	11,000
Bank overdraft	12,000	17,000

(For B.B.A., M.Com., M.B.A.)

Solution :

Calculation of Cash from Operating Activities

Particulars	*Rs.*	*Rs.*
Net Profit after Tax		92,000
Add : Provision for Taxation	60,000	
Depreciation for Land & Building	21,000	
Depreciation for Plant & Machinery	27,000	
Depreciation for Furniture	10,000	
Loss on sale of Machinery	9,000	1,27,000
		2,19,000
Less : Profit on sale of Investment		25,000
Fund from Operation		1,94,000
Add : Increase in Current Liabilities		

Outstanding salary (12,000 – 10,000)	2,000	
Bank overdraft (17,000-12,000)	5,000	
Decrease in Current Assets		
Debtors (29,000-20,000)	9,000	16,000
		2,10,000
Less : Increase in Current Assets		
Inventories (45,000 – 30,000)	15,000	
Decrease in Current Liabilities		
Sundry Creditors (19,000 – 11,000)	8,000	23,000
Cash from Operating Activities		**1,87,000**

Illustration: 6

Calculate Cash from Operating Activities from the following

	Rs.
Net Profit transferred to Balance Sheet	3,50,000
Depreciation for Fixed Assets	55,000
Provision for Taxation	79,000
Goodwill written off	20,000
Preliminary expenses written off	15,000
Profit on sale of Fixed Assets	19,000
Refund of Income Tax	10,000
Provision for General Reserve	30,000
Proposed Dividend	40,000

The details of current items are as follows.

	Opening Balance Rs.	*Closing Balance Rs.*
Stock	35,000	50,000
Debtors	20,000	15,000
Sundry creditors	10,000	17,000

(For B.Com., B.B.A., B.B.M.)

Solution :

Calculation of Cash from Operating Activities

Particulars	*Rs.*	*Rs.*
Net Profit		3,50,000
Add : Depreciation	55,000	
Provision for Taxation	79,000	
Goodwill written off	20,000	
Preliminary expenses written off	15,000	

Provision for General Reserve	30,000	
Proposed Dividend	40,000	2,39,000
		5,89,000
Less : Profit on sale of Fixed Assets	19,000	
Refund of Income Tax	10,000	29,000
		5,60,000
Add : Increase in Current Liabilities		
Sundry creditors	7,000	
Decrease in Current Assets: Debtors	5,000	12,000
		5,72,000
Less : Increase in Current Assets: Stock		15,000
Cash from Operating Activities		5,57,000

Illustration: 7

Calculate Cash from Operating Activities from the following:

	Rs.
Net Loss transferred to Balance Sheet	1,70,000
Depreciation for Fixed Assets	30,000
Loss on sale of Plant	7,000
Profit on sale of Furniture	5,000

The balances of current items are as follows:

	31st March 2006 *Rs.*	*31st March 2007* *Rs.*
Stock	32,000	24,000
Debtors	17,000	27,000
Bills Receivable	12,000	17,000
Sundry Creditors	29,000	23,000
Bills Payable	10,000	14,000

(For B.Com., B.B.A., B.B.M., M.Com.)

Solution :

Calculation of Cash from Operating Activities

Particulars	*Rs.*	*Rs.*
Net Loss		(1,70,000)
Add : Depreciation	30,000	
Loss on sale of Plant	7,000	37,000
		(1,33,000)
Less : Profit on sale of Furniture		7,000
Fund Lost in Operation		(1,40,000)

Add : Increase in Current Liabilities:		
Bills Payable	4,000	
Decrease in Current Assets:		
Stock	8,000	12,000
		(1,28,000)
Less : Increase in Current Assets:		
Debtors	10,000	
Bills Receivable	5,000	
Decrease in Current Liabilities:		
Sundry Creditors	6,000	21,000
Cash Lost in Operating Activities		**1,49,000**

Illustration: 8

Calculate Cash from Operating Activities from the following

	Rs.
Net Loss after adjustment	70,000
Depreciation	1,20,000
Goodwill written off	20,000
Outstanding salary	10,000
Rent accrued	17,000
Dividend received	30,000
Preliminary expenses written off	5,000

Solution :

Calculation of Cash from Operating Activities

Particulars	*Rs.*	*Rs.*
Net Loss		(70,000)
Add : Depreciation	1,20,000	
Goodwill written off	20,000	
Preliminary expenses written off	5,000	
Outstanding salary	10,000	1,55,000
		85,000
Less : Dividend received	30,000	
Rent accrued	17,000	47,000
Cash from Operation		**38,000**

Illustration: 9

Calculate Cash from Operating Activities from the following.

	Rs.
Net Loss after adjustment	1,00,000
Depreciation	30,000
Preliminary expenses written off	7,000
Goodwill written off	10,000
Provision for Doubtful Debts	5,000
Commission accrued	14,000
Dividend received	24,000
Outstanding wages	9,000

(For B.Com., B.B.A., B.B.M)

Solution :

Calculation of Cash from Operating Activities

Particulars	*Rs.*	*Rs.*
Net Loss		(1,00,000)
Add : Depreciation	30,000	
Provision for Doubtful Debtors	5,000	
Preliminary expenses written off	7,000	
Goodwill written off	10,000	
Outstanding wages	9,000	61,000
		(39,000)
Less : Dividend received	24,000	
Commission accrued	14,000	38,000
Fund Lost in Operation		**74,000**

Illustration: 10

The Net Profit of K Ltd., as on 31st March 2007, after the following adjustments is Rs.2,30,000.

	Rs.
Depreciation on Fixed Assets	40,000
Profit on sale of Plant	20,000
Loss on sale of Furniture	7,000
Goodwill written off	12,000
Provision for Doubtful Debts	5,000
Provision for Taxation	70,000
Transfer to General Reserve	15,000
Preliminary expenses written off	9,000

The following additional information are also given.

	31st March 2006 Rs.	31st March 2007 Rs.
Stock	27,000	32,000
Debtors	40,000	31,000
Cash	50,000	60,000
Bills receivable	17,000	22,000
Bills payable	20,000	25,000
Outstanding wages	10,000	14,000
Prepaid expenses	7,000	-
Sundry Creditors	27,000	20,000

Calculate cash from operating activities. *(For B.Com., B.B.A., B.B.M, M.Com.)*

Solution :

Calculation of Cash from Operating Activities

Particulars	*Rs.*	*Rs.*
Net Profit		2,30,000
Add : Depreciation		40,000
Loss on sale of Furniture		7,000
Goodwill written off		12,000
Preliminary expenses written off		9,000
Provision for Doubtful Debtors		5,000
Provision for General Reserve		15,000
Provision for Tax		70,000
		3,88,000
Less: Profit on sale of Plant		20,000
Fund from Operation		3,68,000
Add : Increase in Bills Payable	5,000	
Increase in Outstanding wages	4,000	
Decrease in Debtors	9,000	
Decrease in Prepaid expenses	7,000	25,000
		3,93,000
Less : Increase in Stock	5,000	
Increase in Bills Receivable	5,000	
Decrease in Sundry creditors	7,000	17,000
Cash from Operation		**3,76,000**

Illustration: 11

Calculate Cash from Operating Activities from the following.

	31st March 2006 Rs.	31st March 2007 Rs.
Profit & Loss Account	1,45,000	2,99,000
General Reserve	70,000	1,00,000
Workmen Compensation Fund	50,000	30,000
Goodwill	1,40,000	1,25,000
Discount on issue of Debentures	40,000	30,000
Stock	50,000	64,000
Debtors	42,000	30,000
Outstanding salary	11,000	7,000
Sundry creditors	24,000	33,000
Bills Payable	12,000	15,000

(For B.Com., B.B.A., B.B.M, M.Com.)

Solution :

Calculation of Cash from Operating Activities

Particulars	*Rs.*	*Rs.*
Closing Balance of Profit & Loss Account		2,99,000
Opening Balance of Profit & Loss Account		1,45,000
Net Profit for the year		1,54,000
Add : Provision for General Reserve (1,00,000 – 70,000)	30,000	
Goodwill written off (1,40,000 – 1,25,000)	15,000	
Discount on issue of Debentures written off (40,000 – 30,000)	10,000	55,000
		2,09,000
Less : Reduction in Workmen Compensation Fund (50,000 – 30,000)		20,000
Fund from Operation		1,89,000
Add : Increase in Current Liabilities		
Sundry Creditors (33,000 – 24,000)	9,000	
Bills Payable (15,000 – 12,000)	3,000	
Decrease in Current Assets		
Debtors (42,000 – 30,000)	12,000	24,000
		2,13,000
Less : Increase in Current Assets		
Stock (64,000 – 50,000)	14,000	
Decrease in Current Liabilities:		
Outstanding salary (11,000 – 7,000)	4,000	18,000
Cash from Operation		**1,95,000**

2. Calculation of Cash flow from Investing Activities

Investing activities are concerned with the purchase and sale of Fixed Assets and Investments. Sale of Fixed Assets and Investment are inflow of cash and purchase of it are outflow of cash. The difference between the total sale and purchase is called either net cash from Investing Activities (if sales is more than purchase) or net cash used for Investing Activities (if purchase is more than sales). For Example, if the total sale of Fixed Assets during a year is Rs.1,50,000 and total purchase of Fixed Assets is Rs.1,00,000, then the Net Cash Inflow from Investing Activities is Rs.50,000. On the other hand, if the total sale of Fixed Assets during a year is Rs.1,50,000 and total purchase of Fixed Assets is Rs.2,20,000, then the Net Cash Outflow from Investing Activities is Rs.70,000.

Illustration: 12

Calculate Cash flow from Investing Activities from the following.

	Rs.
Fixed Assets in the beginning	7,50,000
Fixed Assets at the end	7,00,000
Accumulated depreciation of the Fixed Asset sold	15,000
Loss on sale of Fixed Asset	12,000

(For B.Com., B.B.A., B.B.M)

Solution :

Fixed Assets Account

Particulars	*Rs.*	*Particulars*	*Rs.*
To Balance b/d	7,50,000	By Depreciation	15,000
		By Loss on sale	12,000
		By Cash-Sales (Balancing figure)	23,000
		By Balance c/d	7,00,000
	7,50,000		7,50,000

Hence, **Cash from Investing Activity is Rs.23,000.** It may also be calculated as follows.

Particulars	*Rs.*	*Rs.*
Balance of Fixed Asset in the beginning		7,50,000
Balance of Fixed Asset at the end		7,00,000
Difference		50,000
Less : Loss on sale	12,000	
Accumulated Depreciation	15,000	27,000
Net Cash from Investing Activities		**23,000**

Illustration: 13

Calculate Cash flow from Investing Activities from the following.

	31st March 2006 Rs.	31st March 2007 Rs.
Plant & Machinery account	5,00,000	5,40,000
Accumulated Depreciation account	70,000	95,000
Investment account	3,00,000	2,60,000

During the year a machine worth Rs.50,000 was sold for Rs.65,000. Accumulated depreciation of the machine is Rs.10,000. Loss on sale of investment is Rs.7,000. *(For B.Com., B.B.A., B.B.M.)*

Solution :

Calculation of Cash from Investing Activities

Particulars	*Rs.*
Cash flow for Plant & Machinery	
Sale of Machinery	65,000
Purchase of Machinery (5,40,000 – 50,000)	90,000
Net Cash Outflow	15,000
Cash inflow from sale of Investment (3,00,000 – 2,60,000 – 7,000)	33,000
Net cash inflow from Investing Activities	**18,000**

The treatment of Plant & Machinery Account is stated as follows.

Plant & Machinery Account

Particulars	*Rs.*	*Particulars*	*Rs.*
To Balance	5,00,000	By Accumulated Depreciation a/c	10,000
To Adjusted P & L a/c (Profit on sale)	25,000	By Cash a/c (Sales)	65,000
To Cash (Purchase) - Balancing figure	90,000	By Balance c/d	5,40,000
	6,15,000		6,15,000

Accumulated Depreciation Account

Particulars	*Rs.*	*Particulars*	*Rs.*
To Plant & Machinery a/c	10,000	By Balance b/d	70,000
To Balance c/d	95,000	By Profit & Loss a/c	35,000
	1,05,000		1,05,000

3. Cash Flow from Financing Activities

Cash flow from Financing Activities is related to the Capital and Long-term Loan. The issue of Share Capital, issue of Debentures and raising of Loan are called Cash inflow from Financing

Activities.Redemption of Debentures and Repayment of Loan are called Cash outflow due to Financing Activities. The difference of the total inflow and outflow is called Cash Flow from Financing Activities (if inflow is greater than outflow) or Cash utilised for Financing Activities (if outflow is greater than inflow).

Illustration: 14

Calculate Cash Flow from Financing Activities from the following.

	31st March 2006 *Rs.*	*31st March 2007* *Rs.*
Preference Share Capital	5,00,000	7,00,000
Debentures	3,00,000	2,00,000
Loan	2,50,000	3,25,000

Solution :

Calculation of Cash Flow from Financing Activities

Particulars	*Rs.*
Inflow:	
Issue of Preference Share Capital (7,00,000 – 5,00,000)	2,00,000
Raising of Loan (3,25,000 – 2,50,000)	75,000
	2,75,000
Outflow:	
Redemption of Debentures (3,00,000 – 2,00,000)	1,00,000
Cash flow from Financing Activities	**1,75,000**

Preparation of Cash Flow Statement

There are two methods for preparing Cash Flow Statement. They are,

I. Traditional method, and

II. Revised Method

I. Traditional Method of preparing Cash Flow Statement

In this method, first of all, Cash from Operation should be calculated. It may be calculated either through statement form or 'T' form. After that Statement of Cash Flow should be prepared. The Cash Flow Statement contains details about inflow and outflow of cash related to non-current assets and non-current liabilities. The Cash from Operation should be treated as inflow. (Cash lost in Operation should be treated as outflow). The difference in the inflow and outflow of cash is called the increase or decrease of the cash balance. Cash flow statement can be prepared either in

(a) Statement form or (b) 'T' form

a. Statement Form of preparing Cash Flow Statement

A model of the Cash Flow Statement in statement form is stated as follows:

Statement of Cash Flow

	Rs.	Rs.
Cash balance in the beginning		xxxxx
Add : Sources		
Cash from Operation	xxxxx	
Issue of Share Capital	xxxxx	
Issue of Debentures	xxxxx	
Raising of Loan	xxxxx	
Sale of Fixed Assets	xxxxx	
Sale of Investments	xxxxx	xxxxx
Less : Applications		**xxxxx**
Purchase of Fixed Assets	xxxxx	
Purchase of Investments	xxxxx	
Redemption of Share Capital	xxxxx	
Redemption of Debenture	xxxxx	
Repayment of Loan	xxxxx	
Payment of Tax	xxxxx	
Payment of Dividend	xxxxx	
Payment of Tax	xxxxx	xxxxx
Cash balance at the end		**xxxxx**

(b) T-form of preparation of Cash Flow statement

A model of the Statement of Cash Flow in T-form is stated as follows.

Statement of Cash Flow

Particulars	*Rs.*	*Particulars*	*Rs.*
Opening balance of Cash	xxxx	Purchase of Fixed Assets	xxxx
Cash from Operation	xxxx	Redemption of Share Capital	xxxx
Issue of Share Capital	xxxx	Redemption of Debenture	xxxx
Issue of Debentures	xxxx	Redemption of Loan	xxxx
Sale of Fixed Assets	xxxx	Payment of Dividend	xxxx
Sale of Investments	xxxx	Payment of Tax	xxxx
		Closing balance of Cash	xxxx
	xxxx		xxxx

Illustration: 15

Prepare a Cash Flow Statement from the following Balance Sheets.

Balance Sheets

Liabilities	*2006 Rs.*	*2007 Rs.*	*Assets*	*2006 Rs.*	*2007 Rs.*
Share Capital	4,00,000	5,50,000	Fixed Assets	4,00,000	5,70,000
Profit & Loss a/c	1,20,000	1,50,000	Stock	45,000	60,000

Sundry Creditors	40,000	55,000	Debtors	25,000	15,000
			Cash	90,000	1,10,000
	5,60,000	7,55,000		5,60,000	7,55,000

(For B.Com., B.B.A., B.B.M)

Solution :

Statement of Cash Flow

Inflow	*Rs.*	*Outflow*	*Rs.*
Opening Balance of cash	90,000	Purchase of Fixed Assets	1,70,000
Cash from Operation	40,000	Closing Balance of Cash	1,10,000
Issue of Share Capital	1,50,000		
	2,80,000		2,80,000

Calculation of Cash from Operation

Particulars	*Rs.*	*Rs.*
Closing Balance of Profit & Loss Account		1,50,000
Add : Increase in Sundry Creditors		15,000
Decrease in Debtors		10,000
		1,75,000
Less : Increase in Stock	15,000	
Opening Balance of P&L a/c	1,20,000	1,35,000
Cash from Operation		**40,000**

Note:

i. Purchase of Fixed Assets = 5,70,000 – 4,00,000 = Rs.1,70,000

ii. Issue of Share Capital = 5,50,000 – 4,00,000 = Rs.1,50,000

iii. Changes in current assets and current liabilities are adjusted in the calculation of cash from Operation.

Illustration: 16

The Balance Sheets of WD Ltd., as on 31st March 2006 and 2007 are stated as follows.

Balance Sheets

Liabilities	*2006 Rs.*	*2007 Rs.*	*Assets*	*2006 Rs.*	*2007 Rs.*
Share Capital	7,00,000	9,00,000	Land	3,00,000	4,00,000
Profit & Loss a/c	87,000	75,000	Premises	2,50,000	3,70,000
Mortgage Loan	2,00,000	1,20,000	Plant	3,60,000	2,70,000
Sundry Creditors	34,000	53,000	Stock	38,000	24,000
Bank Overdraft	29,000	12,000	Debtors	27,000	41,000
			Cash	75,000	55,000
	10,50,000	11,60,000		10,50,000	11,60,000

Prepare a Statement of Cash Flow. *(For B.Com., B.B.A., B.B.M)*

Solution :

Statement of Cash Flow

Inflow	*Rs.*	*Outflow*	*Rs.*
Cash Balance in the beginning	75,000	Cash Lost in Operation	10,000
Issue of Share Capital	2,00,000	Purchase of Land	1,00,000
Sale of Plant	90,000	Purchase of Premises	1,20,000
		Repayment of Loan	80,000
		Cash Balance at the end	55,000
	3,65,000		3,65,000

Calculation of Cash from Operation

Particulars	*Rs.*	*Rs.*
Closing Balance of Profit & Loss Account		75,000
Add : Increase in Sundry Creditors		19,000
Decrease in Stock		14,000
		1,08,000
Less : Increase in Debtors	14,000	
Decrease in Bank Overdraft	17,000	
Opening Balance of Profit & Loss Account	87,000	1,18,000
Cash Lost in Operation		**10,000**

Illustration: 17

Prepare a Cash Flow Statement from the following Balance Sheets.

Balance Sheets

Liabilities	2006 *Rs.*	2007 *Rs.*	*Assets*	2006 *Rs.*	2007 *Rs.*
Share Capital	5,00,000	6,00,000	Land & Building	4,50,000	3,80,000
Loan Account	3,00,000	2,50,000	Plant & Machinery	2,40,000	3,50,000
Sundry Creditors	40,000	60,000	Stock	37,000	28,000
Bills Payable	20,000	10,000	Debtors	43,000	52,000
			Cash	40,000	30,000
			Profit & Loss A/c	50,000	80,000
	8,60,000	9,20,000		8,60,000	9,20,000

(*For B.Com., B.B.A., B.B.M*)

Solution :

Statement of Cash Flow

Inflow	*Rs.*	*Outflow*	*Rs.*
Cash Balance in the beginning	40,000	**Cash Lost in Operation**	20,000
Issue of Share Capital	1,00,000	Purchase of Plant & Machinery	1,10,000

	Rs.		Rs.
Sale of Land & Building	70,000	Repayment of Loan	50,000
		Cash Balance at the end	30,000
	2,10,000		2,10,000

Calculation of Cash from Operation

Particulars	*Rs.*	*Rs.*
Closing Balance of Profit & Loss Account		(80,000)
Add : Increase in Sundry Creditors	20,000	
Decrease in Stock	9,000	29,000
		(51,000)
Less : Increase in Debtors	9,000	
Decrease in Bills Payable	10,000	
Opening Balance of Profit & Loss a/c	(50,000)	(31,000)
Cash Lost in Operation		**20,000**

Illustration: 18

Prepare a Statement of Cash Flow for the following Balance Sheets

Balance Sheets

Liabilities	*2006 Rs.*	*2007 Rs.*	*Assets*	*2006 Rs.*	*2007 Rs.*
Share Capital	4,00,000	5,00,000	Land & Building	3,00,000	2,70,000
Profit & Loss a/c	50,000	–	Plant & Machinery	2,70,000	1,40,000
Loan	2,00,000	90,000	Stock	27,000	38,000
Sundry Creditors	32,000	25,000	Debtors	26,000	19,000
Outstanding Wages	18,000	15,000	Cash	45,000	57,000
			Bank	32,000	27,000
			Profit & Loss a/c	-	79,000
	7,00,000	6,30,000		7,00,000	6,30,000

(For B.Com., B.B.A., B.B.M)

Solution :

Statement of Cash Flow

Inflow	*Rs.*	*Outflow*	*Rs.*
Cash Balance in the beginning	77,000	**Cash Lost in Operation**	1,43,000
Issue of Share Capital	1,00,000	Repayment of Loan	1,10,000
Sale of Land & Building	30,000	Cash and cash equi. at the end	84,000
Sale of Plant & Machinery	1,30,000		
	3,37,000		3,37,000

Calculation of Cash from Operation

Particulars	Rs.	Rs.
Closing Balance of Profit & Loss Account		(79,000)
Add : Decrease in Debtors		7,000
		(72,000)
Less : Increase in Stock	11,000	
Decrease in Sundry Creditors	7,000	
Decrease in Outstanding wages	3,000	
Opening Balance of Profit & Loss a/c	50,000	71,000
Cash Lost in Operation		**1,43,000**

Illustration: 19

GC Ltd., provided the Balance Sheets of 31st March 2006 and 2007 as follows.

Balance Sheets

Liabilities	*2006 Rs.*	*2007 Rs.*	*Assets*	*2006 Rs.*	*2007 Rs.*
Share Capital	5,00,000	5,00,000	Land & Building	5,70,000	4,90,000
Profit & Loss a/c	92,000	99,000	Plant & Machinery	3,00,000	3,80,000
General Reserve	30,000	40,000	Stock	21,000	35,000
Debenture a/c	2,00,000	2,50,000	Debtors	29,000	13,000
Loan a/c	1,00,000	–	Cash	30,000	17,000
Sundry Creditors	28,000	45,000	Bank	10,000	15,000
Rent received in adv.	10,000	16,000			
	9,60,000	9,50,000		9,60,000	9,50,000

Prepare a statement of cash flow. *(For B.Com., B.B.A., B.B.M)*

Solution :

Statement of Cash Flow

Inflow	*Rs.*	*Outflow*	*Rs.*
Op.Balance of Cash & Bank	40,000	Purchase of Plant & Machinery	80,000
Cash from Operation	42,000	Repayment of Loan	1,00,000
Issue of Debenture	50,000	Closing balance of Cash & Bank	32,000
Sale of Land & Building	80,000		
	2,12,000		2,12,000

Calculation of Cash from Operation

Particulars		*Rs.*
Closing Balance of Profit & Loss Account		99,000
Add : Increase in General Reserve		10,000
Increase in Sundry creditors		17,000

Increase in Rent received in advance		6,000
Decrease in Debtors		16,000
		1,48,000
Less : Increase in Stock	14,000	
Opening Balance of Profit & Loss Account	92,000	1,06,000
Cash from Operation		**42,000**

Illustration: 20

Prepare a Statement of Cash Flow for the following Balance Sheets.

Balance Sheets

Liabilities	*2006 Rs.*	*2007 Rs.*	*Assets*	*2006 Rs.*	*2007 Rs.*
Share Capital	7,00,000	6,10,000	Fixed Assets	6,50,000	5,47,000
Sundry Creditors	50,000	39,000	Stock	42,000	34,000
Bank Overdraft	22,000	25,000	Debtors	27,000	32,000
			Cash	53,000	61,000
	7,72,000	6,74,000		7,72,000	6,74,000

Assume that there is no drawings and no purchase or sale of Fixed Assets. *(For B.Com., B.B.A., B.B.M)*

Solution :

Statement of Cash Flow

Inflow	*Rs.*	*Outflow*	*Rs.*
Opening Balance of Cash	53,000	Closing Balance of Cash	61,000
Cash from Operation	8,000		
	61,000		61,000

Calculation of Cash from Operation

Particulars	*Rs.*	*Rs.*
Net Loss for current year (7,00,000 – 6,10,000)		(90,000)
Add : Depreciation on Fixed Assets	1,03,000	
Increase in Bank overdraft	3,000	
Decrease in Stock	8,000	1,14,000
		24,000
Less : Increase in Debtors	5,000	
Decrease in Sundry creditors	11,000	16,000
Cash from Operation		**8,000**

Note :

(i) The difference in Capital Rs.90,000 is considered as loss since there is no Drawings during the year.

(ii) Decrease in Fixed Assets is considered as depreciation since there is no sale of fixed assets.

Illustration: 21

Calculate a Statement of Cash Flow from the following Balance Sheets.

Balance Sheets

Liabilities	2006 Rs.	2007 Rs.	*Assets*	2006 Rs.	2007 Rs.
Share Capital	9,00,000	10,00,000	Fixed Assets	13,50,000	15,10,000
Profit & Loss a/c	77,000	1,12,000	Stock	33,000	49,000
General Reserve	42,000	54,000	Debtors	37,000	30,000
Debenture	2,50,000	2,00,000	Cash	44,000	59,000
Loan	1,75,000	2,40,000			
Account Payable	20,000	42,000			
	14,64,000	16,48,000		14,64,000	16,48,000

Adjustments:

i. Depreciation for Fixed Assets Rs.75,000.

ii. Provision for General Reserve during the year Rs.12,000. *(For B.Com., B.B.A. B.B.M)*

Solution :

Statement of Cash Flow

Inflow	*Rs.*	*Outflow*	*Rs.*
Opening Balance of Cash	44,000	Purchase of Fixed Assets	2,35,000
Cash from Operation	1,35,000	Redemption of Debentures	50,000
Issue of Share Capital	1,00,000	Closing Balance of Cash	59,000
Raising of Loan	65,000		
	3,44,000		3,44,000

Calculation of Cash from Operation

Particulars	*Rs.*	*Rs.*
Closing Balance of Profit & Loss Account		1,12,000
Add : Provision for General Reserve		12,000
Depreciation for Fixed Assets		75,000
Increase in Account Payable		22,000
Decrease in Debtors		7,000
		2,28,000
Less : Increase in Stock	16,000	
Opening Balance of Profit & Loss Account	77,000	93,000
Cash from Operation		**1,35,000**

Fixed Assets Account

Particulars	*Rs.*	*Particulars*	*Rs.*
To Balance b/d	13,50,000	By Profit & Loss Account	
To Cash (Purchase)	2,35,000	(Depreciation)	75,000
		By Balance c/d	15,10,000
	15,85,000		15,85,000

Illustration: 22

Joyce & Co. Ltd. provided the Balance Sheets for the year ended 31st March 2006 and 2007 as follows:

Balance Sheets

Liabilities	*2006 Rs.*	*2007 Rs.*	*Assets*	*2006 Rs.*	*2007 Rs.*
Equity Share Capital	11,00,000	12,00,000	Fixed Assets	16,30,000	17,30,000
Profit & Loss A/c	1,70,000	1,50,000	Stock	67,000	71,000
General Reserve	35,000	67,000	Debtors	51,000	57,000
Debentures	3,50,000	4,00,000	Cash	37,000	49,000
Loan	1,50,000	1,00,000	Preliminary expenses	50,000	35,000
Sundry Creditors	30,000	25,000			
	18,35,000	19,42,000		18,35,000	19,42,000

Adjustments:

Depreciation for Fixed Assets Rs.1,10,000; Fixed Assets with cost Rs.40,000 was sold for Rs.33,000. Prepare a Statement of Cash Flow. *(For B.Com., B.B.A., B.B.M)*

Solution :

Statement of Cash Flow

Inflow	*Rs.*	*Outflow*	*Rs.*
Opening Balance of Cash	37,000	Purchase of Fixed Assets	2,50,000
Cash from Operation	1,29,000	Repayment of Loan	50,000
Issue of Equity Shares	1,00,000	Closing balance of Cash	49,000
Issue of Debentures	50,000		
Sale of Fixed Assets	33,000		
	3,49,000		3,49,000

Calculation of Cash from Operation

Particulars	*Rs*	*Rs.*
Closing Balance of Profit & Loss Account		1,50,000
Add : Provision for General Reserve		32,000
Preliminary expenses written off		15,000
Provision for depreciation of Fixed Assets		1,10,000

Loss on sale of Fixed Assets		7,000
		3,14,000
Less : Increase in Stock	4,000	
Increase in Debtors	6,000	
Decrease in Sundry Creditors	5,000	
Opening Balance of Profit & Loss Account	1,70,000	1,85,000
Cash from Operation		**1,29,000**

Fixed Assets Account

Particulars	*Rs.*	*Particulars*	*Rs.*
To Balance b/d	16,30,000	By Profit & Loss Account (Dep.)	1,10,000
To Cash (Purchase)	2,50,000	By Cash (Sales)	33,000
		By Profit & Loss a/c (Loss on sale)	7,000
		By Balance c/d	17,30,000
	18,80,000		18,80,000

Illustration: 23

The Balance Sheets of KC for the year ending 31st March 2006 and 2007 are stated as follows.

Balance Sheets

Liabilities	*2006 Rs.*	*2007 Rs.*	*Assets*	*2006 Rs.*	*2007 Rs.*
Share Capital	5,00,000	5,00,000	Land & Building	3,50,000	4,00,000
General Reserve	30,000	40,000	Plant & Machinery	2,50,000	2,10,000
Loan	1,70,000	2,00,000	Stock	27,000	43,000
Sundry Creditors	35,000	52,000	Debtors	17,000	22,000
Outstanding rent	15,000	8,000	Cash	32,000	40,000
			Profit & Loss a/c	74,000	85,000
	7,50,000	8,00,000		7,50,000	8,00,000

Adjustments:

(i) Depreciation for Land & Building Rs.35,000. Profit on sale of Land Rs.20,000. Purchase of Land for the year Rs.1,00,000.

(ii) Depreciation for Plant and Machinery @ 10% on Rs.2,00,000. Plant sold in 2007 is Rs.15,000.

Prepare a Statement of Cash Flow. *(For B.B.A., B.B.M,M.Com.)*

Solution:

Statement of Cash Flow

Inflow	*Rs.*	*Outflow*	*Rs.*
Opening Balance of Cash	32,000	Purchase of Land & Building	1,00,000
Cash from Operation	28,000	Closing Balance of Cash	40,000
Sale of Land	35,000		

Sale of Plant	15,000		
Increase of Loan	30,000		
	1,40,000		1,40,000

Adjusted Profit & Loss Account

Particulars	Rs.	Particulars	Rs.
To Balance b/d	74,000	By Profit on sale of Land	20,000
To Land & Building (Dep.)	35,000	By Balance c/d	85,000
To Plant & Machinery (Dep.)	20,000	By Fund from Operation	39,000
To Loss on sale of Plant	5,000		
To Provision for G.Reserve	10,000		
	1,44,000		1,44,000

Calculation of Cash from Operation

Particulars	Rs.	Rs.
Fund from Operation		39,000
Add : Increase in Sundry Creditors		17,000
		56,000
Less : Increase in Stock	16,000	
Increase in Debtors	5,000	
Decrease in Outstanding rent	7,000	28,000
Cash from Operation		**28,000**

Land & Building Account

Particulars	Rs.	Particulars	Rs.
To Balance b/d	3,50,000	By Adjusted P & L A/c (Dep.)	35,000
To Adjusted P & L A/c (Profit)	20,000	By Cash (Sale)	35,000
To Cash (Purchase)	1,00,000	By Balance c/d	4,00,000
	4,70,000		4,70,000

Plant & Machinery Account

Particulars	Rs.	Particulars	Rs.
To Balance b/d	2,50,000	By Adjusted P & L a/c (Dep.)	20,000
		By Cash	15,000
		By Adjusted P&L a/c (Loss on sale)	5,000
		By Balance b/d	2,10,000
	2,50,000		2,50,000

Illustration: 24

The Balance Sheets of Z Ltd. for the year ending 31st March 2006 and 2007 are stated as follows.

Balance Sheets

Liabilities	*2006 Rs.*	*2007 Rs.*	*Assets*	*2006 Rs.*	*2007 Rs.*
Share Capital	15,00,000	17,00,000	Fixed Assets	18,10,000	19,90,000
Profit & Loss a/c	1,50,000	1,75,000	Stock	23,000	55,000
General Reserve	50,000	70,000	Debtors	40,000	33,000
Workmen	30,000	25,000	Cash	39,000	47,000
Compensation Fund			Outstanding rent	14,000	20,000
Loan	2,00,000	1,50,000	Salary paid in advance	19,000	15,000
Sundry creditors	32,000	44,000	Preliminary expenses	45,000	30,000
Bank overdraft	15,000	17,000			
Outstanding wages	13,000	9,000			
	19,90,000	21,90,000		19,90,000	21,90,000

Adjustments:

i. Depreciation for Fixed Assets during the year is Rs.90,000. A Plant worth Rs.50,000 was sold for a loss of Rs.15,000.

ii. Compensation paid for a worker is Rs.9,000.

iii. Provision for General Reserve is Rs.20,000.

iv. Preliminary expenses written off during the year is Rs.15,000.

Prepare a Statement of Cash Flow. *(For M.Com., M.B.A.)*

Solution :

Statement of Cash Flow

Particulars	*Rs.*	*Particulars*	*Rs.*
Opening Balance of Cash	39,000	Purchase of Fixed Assets	3,20,000
Cash from Operation	1,52,000	Repayment of Loan	50,000
Issue of Equity Share Capital	2,00,000	Compensation paid for workers	9,000
Sale of Plant	35,000	Closing Balance of Cash	47,000
	4,26,000		4,26,000

Adjusted Profit & Loss Account

Inflow	*Rs.*	*Outflow*	*Rs.*
To Fixed Assets a/c (Dep.)	90,000	By Balance b/d	1,50,000
To Fixed Assets a/c (Loss)	15,000	By **Fund from Operation**	1,69,000
To Provision for G.Reserve	20,000		
To Pro.for Workmen C.Fund	4,000		
To Preli. exp. written off	15,000		
To Balance c/d	1,75,000		
	3,19,000		3,19,000

Calculation of Cash from Operation

Particulars	*Rs.*	*Rs.*
Fund from Operation		1,69,000
Add : Increase in Sundry Creditors		12,000
Increase in Bank Overdraft		2,000
Decrease in Debtors		7,000
Decrease in Salary paid in advance		4,000
		1,94,000
Less : Increase in Stock	32,000	
Increase in Outstanding rent	6,000	
Decrease in Outstanding wages	4,000	42,000
Cash from Operation		**1,52,000**

Fixed Assets Account

Particulars	*Rs.*	*Particulars*	*Rs.*
To Balance b/d	18,10,000	By Adjusted P & L a/c (Dep.)	90,000
To Cash (Sales)	3,20,000	By Cash (Sale)	35,000
		By Adj. P & L a/c (Loss on sale)	15,000
		By Balance c/d	
	21,30,000		21,30,000

Workmen Compensation Fund

Particulars	*Rs.*	*Particulars*	*Rs.*
To Cash	9,000	By Balance b/d	30,000
To Balance c/d	25,000	By Adjusted P & L a/c	4,000
	34,000		34,000

Illustration: 25

Prepare a Statement of Cash Flow from the following Balance Sheets.

Balance Sheets

Liabilities	*2006 Rs.*	*2007 Rs.*	*Assets*	*2006 Rs.*	*2007 Rs.*
Capital	5,00,000	6,10,000	Fixed Assets	6,00,000	7,10,000
Profit & Loss a/c	79,000	82,000	Stock	61,000	40,000
General Reserve	34,000	49,000	Debtors	33,000	54,000
Loan	1,00,000	75,000	Cash	37,000	41,000
Sundry Creditors	17,000	30,000	Outstanding Rent	19,000	15,000
Bank Overdraft	20,000	14,000			
	7,50,000	8,60,000		7,50,000	8,60,000

Adjustments:

i. Drawings by owners for the year is Rs.40,000.

ii. Provision for depreciation on 31st March 2006 is Rs.55,000 and as on 31st March 2007 is Rs.85,000.

Prepare a Statement of Cash Flow *(For B.Com., B.B.A., B.B.M, M.Com.)*

Solution :

Statement of Cash Flow

Inflow	*Rs.*	*Outflow*	*Rs.*
Opening Balance of Cash	37,000	Purchase of Fixed Assets	1,40,000
Cash from Operation	59,000	Repayment of Loan	25,000
Additional Capital	1,50,000	Drawings	40,000
		Closing Balance of Cash	41,000
	2,46,000		2,46,000

Adjusted Profit & Loss Account

Particulars	*Rs.*	*Particulars*	*Rs.*
To Provision for depreciation	30,000	By Balance b/d	79,000
To Provision for General Reserve	15,000	**By Fund from Operation**	48,000
To Balance c/d	82,000		
	1,27,000		1,27,000

Calculation of Cash from Operation

Particulars	*Rs.*	*Rs.*
Fund from Operation		48,000
Add : Increase in Sundry creditors		13,000
Decrease in Stock		21,000
Decrease in Outstanding rent		4,000
		86,000
Less: Increase in Debtors	21,000	
Decrease in Bank overdraft	6,000	27,000
Cash from Operation		**59,000**

Fixed Assets Account

Particulars	*Rs.*	*Particulars*	*Rs.*
To Balance b/d (6,00,000 + 55,000)	6,55,000	By Balance c/d (7,10,000 + 85,000)	7,95,000
To Cash (Purchase)	1,40,000		
	7,95,000		7,95,000

Provision for Depreciation A/c

Particulars	*Rs.*	*Particulars*	*Rs.*
To Balance c/d	85,000	By Balance b/d	55,000
		By Adjusted P & L a/c	30,000
	85,000		85,000

Capital Account

Particulars	*Rs.*	*Particulars*	*Rs.*
To Cash (Drawings)	40,000	By Balance b/d	5,00,000
To Balance c/d	6,10,000	By Cash a/c	1,50,000
	6,50,000		6,50,000

Illustration: 26

N Ltd. provided the Balance Sheets as on 31st March 2006 and 2007 as follows.

Balance Sheets

Liabilities	*2006 Rs.*	*2007 Rs.*	*Assets*	*2006 Rs.*	*2007 Rs.*
Share Capital	5,00,000	5,00,000	Land & Building	3,50,000	4,00,000
Profit & Loss a/c	40,000	1,00,000	Plant & Machinery	2,70,000	2,50,000
Loan	1,70,000	1,20,000	Goodwill	50,000	35,000
Sundry Creditors	25,000	33,000	Stock	35,000	65,000
Provision for Taxation	40,000	50,000	Debtors	30,000	20,000
Unclaimed Dividend	-	7,000	Accrued Interest	10,000	-
			Cash	30,000	40,000
	7,75,000	8,10,000		7,75,000	8,10,000

Adjustments:

i. Net Profit after providing Rs.80,000 for depreciation is Rs.1,10,000.

ii. Dividend declared during the year is @ 10%.

iii. Income Tax paid for the year is Rs.35,000.

iv. Depreciation for Land & Building is Rs.60,000 and Plant & Machinery is Rs.20,000,

(For M.Com., M.B.A.)

Solution :

Statement of Cash Flow

Particulars	*Rs.*	*Particulars*	*Rs.*
Opening Balance of Cash	30,000	Purchase of Land & Building	1,10,000
Cash from Operation	2,48,000	Repayment of Loan	50,000
		Payment of Dividend (50,000-7000)	43,000
		Payment of Tax	35,000
		Closing Balance of Cash	40,000
	2,78,000		2,78,000

Calculation of Cash from Operation

Particulars	Rs.	Rs.
Difference in the balances of Profit & Loss Account		60,000
Add : Proposed Dividend		50,000
Net profit before Depreciation		1,10,000
Add : Depreciation		80,000
Goodwill written off		15,000
Provision for Taxation		45,000
Fund from Operation		2,50,000
Add : Increase in Sundry Creditors	8,000	
Decrease in Debtors	10,000	
Decrease in Accrued interest	10,000	28,000
		2,78,000
Less : Increase in Stock		30,000
Cash from Operation		**2,48,000**

Land & Building Account

Particulars	Rs.	Particulars	Rs.
To Balance b/d	3,50,000	By Profit & Loss a/c (Dep.)	60,000
To Cash (Purchase)	1,10,000	By Balance c/d	4,00,000
	4,60,000		4,60,000

Plant & Machinery Account

Particulars	Rs.	Particulars	Rs.
To Balance c/d	2,70,000	By Profit & Loss a/c (Dep.)	20,000
		By Balance c/d	2,50,000
	2,70,000		2,70,000

Provision for Taxation

Particulars	Rs.	Particulars	Rs.
To Cash	35,000	By Balance b/d	40,000
To Balance c/d	50,000	By Profit & Loss a/c (Provision for the year)	45,000
	85,000		85,000

Illustration: 27

WD Ltd., provided the Balance Sheets for the year ended 31st March 2006 and 31st March 2007 as follows.

Balance Sheets

Liabilities	*2006 Rs.*	*2007 Rs.*	*Assets*	*2006 Rs.*	*2007 Rs.*
Share Capital	4,00,000	5,00,000	Fixed Assets	4,10,000	6,40,000
Profit & Loss a/c	–	90,000	Stock	37,000	25,000
General Reserve	30,000	50,000	Debtors	23,000	30,000
Loan	50,000	–	Cash	25,000	45,000
Provision for Tax	40,000	50,000	Outstanding Rent	15,000	10,000
Provision for Doubtful Debtors	20,000	37,000	Preliminary expenses	30,000	20,000
Sundry Creditors	29,000	36,000	Profit & Loss a/c	40,000	–
Outstanding expenses	11,000	7,000			
	5,80,000	7,70,000		5,80,000	7,70,000

Adjustments:

i. Provision for Taxation for the year is Rs.45,000.

ii. Depreciation for Fixed Assets is Rs.45,000. An old Plant was sold for Rs.30,000 (cost of the Plant is Rs.25,000)

iii. Debtors of Rs.10,000 was considered as bad debtors and was written off against the Provision for Doubtful Debts.

iv. Interim Dividend of Rs.30,000 was paid during the year.

Prepare a Statement of Cash Flow. *(For M.Com., M.B.A., M.C.A.)*

Solution :

Statement of Cash Flow

Inflow	*Rs.*	*Outflow*	*Rs.*
Opening Balance of Cash	25,000	Purchase of Fixed Assets	3,00,000
Cash from Operation	3,05,000	Repayment of Loan	50,000
Issue of Share Capital	1,00,000	Payment of Tax	35,000
Sale of Plant	30,000	Payment of Interim Dividend	30,000
		Closing Balance of Cash	45,000
	4,60,000		4,60,000

Adjusted Profit & Loss Account

Particulars	*Rs.*	*Particulars*	*Rs.*
To Balance b/d	40,000	By Profit on sale of Plant	5,000
To Fixed Assets (Dep.)	45,000	By **Fund from Operation**	3,02,000
To Provision for Debtors	27,000		

Particulars	Rs.	Particulars	Rs.
To Preliminary expenses written off	10,000		
To Provision for Taxation	45,000		
To Provision for Interim Dividend	30,000		
To Provision for General Reserve	20,000		
To Balance c/d	90,000		
	3,07,000		3,07,000

Note: The treatments about provision for taxation, depreciation, provision for doubtful debtors are calculated seperately in different respective accounts.

Calculation of Cash from Operation

Particulars	*Rs.*	*Rs.*
Fund for Operation		3,02,000
Add : Increase in Sundry Creditors		7,000
Decrease in Stock		12,000
Decrease in Outstanding rent		5,000
		3,26,000
Less : Increase in Debtors	17,000	
Decrease in Outstanding expenses	4,000	21,000
Cash from Operation		**3,05,000**

Fixed Assets Account

Particulars	*Rs.*	*Particulars*	*Rs.*
To Balance b/d	4,10,000	By Adjusted P & L a/c (Dep.)	45,000
To Adjusted P & L a/c (Profit)	5,000	By Balance (Sales)	30,000
To Cash (Purchase)	3,00,000	By Balance c/d	6,40,000
	7,15,000		7,15,000

Provision for Taxation Account

Particulars	*Rs.*	*Particulars*	*Rs.*
To Cash	35,000	By Balance b/d	40,000
To Balance c/d	50,000	By Adjusted Profit & Loss a/c	45,000
	85,000		85,000

Sundry Debtors Account

Particulars	*Rs.*	*Particulars*	*Rs.*
To Balance b/d	23,000	By Provision for Doubtful Debtors	10,000
To Increase in Debtors	17,000	By Balance c/d	30,000
	40,000		40,000

Provision for Doubtful Debtors Account

Particulars	*Rs.*	*Particulars*	*Rs.*
To Sundry Debtors a/c	10,000	By Balance b/d	20,000
To Balance c/d	37,000	By Adjusted P & L a/c	27,000
	47,000		47,000

II. Revised method of preparing Cash Flow Statement

There is no specific format provided by **AS-3** (Accounting Standard - 3) for the preparation of Cash Flow Statement. Traditionally some methods are adopted in the preparation of Cash Flow Statement. The revised method of preparing the Cash Flow Statement is suggested by **SEBI** (Security and Exchange Board of India). SEBI amended in 1995 the Clause 32 of the Listing Agreement, requiring all the Listed companies in Stock Exchanges to give a Cash Flow Statement in their Annual Report. The Cash Flow Statement according to the SEBI should be in the following format.

Cash Flow Statement

(for the year ended . . . .)

	Rs.
A. Cash Flow From Operating Activities	
Net Profit / Loss before tax and extraordinary items	
Adjustments for :	
Depreciation	
Gain / Loss on sale of fixed assets	
Foreign Exchange	
Miscellaneous expenditure written off	
Investment income	
Interest	
Dividend	
Operating profit before working capital changes	
Adjustments for :	
Trade and other receivables	
Inventories	
Trade Payables	
Cash generated from operations	
Interest paid	
Direct taxes paid	
Cash flow before items	
Extraordinary items	
Net Cash from Operating Activities	
B. Cash Flow from Investing Activities	
Purchase of fixed assets	
Sales of fixed assets	
Purchase of investments	
Sale of investments	
Interest received	

Dividend received
Net cash from / used in Investing Activities
C. Cash Flow From Financing Activities
Proceeds from issue of share capital
Proceeds from long-term borrowings / banks
Payment of long-term borrowings
Dividend paid
Net Cash from / used in Financing Activities
Net Increase / Decrease in Cash and Cash Equivalents
Cash and Cash Equivalents as at .... (Opening Balance)
Cash and Cash Equivalents as at .... (Closing Balance)

Illustration: 28

KMW Ltd., provided the Balance Sheets for two years as follows.

Balance Sheets

Liabilities	*2006 Rs.*	*2007 Rs.*	*Assets*	*2006 Rs.*	*2007 Rs.*
Capital	7,10,000	9,20,000	Fixed Assets	8,88,000	10,83,000
Loan from Bank	2,50,000	2,90,000	Stock	45,000	59,000
Loan from K	70,000	20,000	Debtors	33,000	13,000
Creditor	21,000	25,000	Cash	85,000	1,00,000
	10,51,000	12,55,000		10,51,000	12,55,000

Adjustments:

A Plant costing Rs.70,000 was sold for Rs.55,000. The accumulated depreciation of the Plant is Rs.7,000. Provision for depreciation as on 31st March 2006 is Rs.80,000 and as on 31st March 2007 is Rs.1,05,000. Prepare a Cash Flow Statement. *(For C.A., ICWAI, M.C.A.)*

Solution:

Cash Flow Statement

Particulars	*Rs.*	*Rs.*
Cash Balance in the beginning		85,000
Add : Sources		
Cash from Operation	2,60,000	
Loan from Bank	40,000	
Sale of Plant	55,000	3,55,000
		4,40,000
Less: Applications		
Purchase of Fixed Assets	2,90,000	
Repayment of Loan to K	50,000	3,40,000
Cash Balance at the end		1,00,000

Workings:

Calculation of Cash from Operation

Particulars	*Rs.*	*Rs.*
Profit for the year (9,20,000 – 7,10,000)		2,10,000
Add : Depreciation for Fixed Assets	32,000	
Loss on sale of Fixed Assets	8000	
Increase in Creditors	4,000	
Decrease in Debtors	20,000	64,000
		2,74,000
Less : Increase in Stock		14,000
Cash from Operation		**2,60,000**

Fixed Assets Account

Particulars	*Rs.*	*Particulars*	*Rs.*
To Balance b/d	9,68,000	By Cash a/c (Sale)	55,000
(8,88,000 + 80,000)		By Provision for Depreciation	7,000
To Cash (Purchase)	2,90,000	By Loss on sale	8,000
		By Balance c/d (10,83,000+1,05,000)	11,88,000
	12,58,000		12,58,000

Provision for Depreciation Account

Particulars	*Rs.*	*Particulars*	*Rs.*
To Fixed Assets a/c	7,000	By Balance b/d	80,000
To Balance c/d	1,05,000	By Profit & Loss a/c	32,000
	1,12,000		1,12,000

Note: The balance of Fixed Assets in the Balance sheet is given after deducting the provision for depreciation. Since the provision for depreciation is treated separately, the balance of provision for depreciation are added with the opening and closing balances of Fixed Assets.

Cash Flow Statement (Revised method)

Particulars	*Rs.*	*Rs.*
i. Cash from Operating Activities		
Net Profit (9,20,000 – 7,10,000)	2,10,000	
Add : Depreciation for Fixed Assets	32,000	
Loss on sale of Fixed Assets	8,000	
Operating Profit before Working Capital	2,50,000	
Adjustments for Working Capital		
Increase in Creditors	4,000	
Decrease in Debtors	20,000	
Increase in Stock	(14,000)	
Net Cash flow from Operating Activities		2,60,000

ii. Cash flow from Investing Activities		
Sale of Plant	55,000	
Purchase of Fixed Assets	(2,90,000)	(2,35,000)
iii. Cash flow from Financing Activities		
Loan from bank	40,000	
Repayment of loan of K	(50,000)	
Net cash flow from Financing Activities		(10,000)
Net increase in Cash and Cash equivalent		15,000
Cash and Cash equivalent in the beginning		85,000
Cash and Cash equivalent at the end		1,00,000

Illustration: 29

KMWD Ltd. provided the Balance Sheets as on 31st March of 2006 and 2007 as follows.

Balance Sheets

Liabilities	*2006 Rs.*	*2007 Rs.*	*Assets*	*2006 Rs.*	*2007 Rs.*
Equity Share Capital	5,00,000	7,50,000	Land & Building	4,80,000	9,00,000
Profit & Loss a/c	1,71,000	2,94,000	Plant & Machinery	4,20,000	3,90,000
General Reserve	72,000	89,000	Furniture & Fittings	1,60,000	1,70,000
Debentures	2,40,000	3,10,000	Stock	51,000	72,000
Long-term Loan	1,80,000	1,50,000	Debtors	75,000	64,000
Provision for Tax	93,000	87,000	Cash	84,000	1,14,000
Sundry Creditors	44,000	55,000	Bank	30,000	25,000
	13,00,000	17,35,000		13,00,000	17,35,000

The following further information are also given.

1. Land worth Rs.1,00,000, was purchased in exchange of Equity Shares of the company. Depreciation for Land & Building Rs.50,000.
2. Purchase of Furniture during the year is Rs.50,000. Loss on sale of Furniture is Rs.11,000. Depreciation provided for Furniture is Rs.13,000.
3. Tax provided for the year is Rs.60,000.

Prepare a Statement of Cash Flow. *(For ICWAI, CA, MCA)*

Solution:

Statement of Cash Flow

Particulars	*Rs.*	*Rs.*
i. Cash flows from Operating Activities		
Difference in the balance of Profit & Loss a/c	1,23,000	
Adjustments of non-cash and non-operating items		
Depreciation for Land & Building	50,000	
Depreciation for Plant & Machinery	30,000	
Depreciation for Furniture & Fittings	13,000	

Loss on sale of Furniture	11,000	
Provision for General Reserve	17,000	
Provision for Tax	60,000	
Operating Profit before Working Capital Changes		3,04,000
Adjustments for Current Assets and Liabilities		
Increase in Stock	(21,000)	
Decrease in Debtors	11,000	
Increase in Sundry Creditors	11,000	1,000
Cash generated from Operation		3,05,000
Less : Income Tax paid		66,000
Net Cash from Operating Activities		2,39,000
ii. Cash flows from Investing Activities		
Sale of Furniture	46,000	
Purchase of Furniture	(80,000)	
Purchase of Land & Building	(3,70,000)	
Net Cash used in Investing Activities		(4,04,000)
iii. Cash flows from Financing Activities		
Issue of Equity Share Capital	1,50,000	
Issue of Debentures	70,000	
Repayment of Loan	(30,000)	
Net Cash flow from Financing Activities		1,90,000
Net increase in Cash and Cash equivalents		**25,000**
Cash and Cash equivalent in the beginning of the period		1,14,000
Cash and Cash equivalent at the end of the period		1,39,000

Land & Building Account

Particulars	*Rs.*	*Particulars*	*Rs.*
To Balance b/d	4,80,000	By Profit & Loss a/c (Dep.)	50,000
To Equity Share Capital a/c	1,00,000	By Balance c/d	9,00,000
To Cash (Purchase)	3,70,000		
	9,50,000		9,50,000

Plant & Machinery Account

Particulars	*Rs.*	*Particulars*	*Rs.*
To Balance b/d	4,20,000	By Profit & Loss a/c (Dep.)	30,000
		By Balance c/d	3,90,000
	4,20,000		4,20,000

Furniture & Fittings Account

Particulars	Rs.	Particulars	Rs.
To Balance b/d	1,60,000	By Profit & Loss a/c (Dep.)	13,000
To Cash (Purchase)	80,000	By Profit & Loss a/c (Loss on sale)	11,000
		By Cash a/c - Sales (Balancing fig.)	46,000
		By Balance c/d	1,70,000
	2,40,000		2,40,000

Equity Share Capital Account

Particulars	Rs.	Particulars	Rs.
To Balance c/d	7,50,000	By Balance b/d	5,00,000
		By Land & Building a/c	1,00,000
		By Cash a/c	1,50,000
	7,50,000		7,50,000

Provision for Taxation Account

Particulars	Rs.	Particulars	Rs.
To Cash (Tax paid)	66,000	By Balance b/d	93,000
To Balance c/d	87,000	By Profit & Loss a/c (Provision for the year)	60,000
	1,53,000		1,53,000

Debenture Account

Particulars	Rs.	Particulars	Rs.
To Balance c/d	3,10,000	By Balance b/d	2,40,000
		By Cash a/c	70,000
	3,10,000		3,10,000

Illustration: 30

KR Ltd. provided the Balance Sheets as on 31st March of 2006 and 2007 as follows.

Balance Sheets

Liabilities	2006 Rs.	2007 Rs.	Assets	2006 Rs.	2007 Rs.
Equity Share Capital	10,00,000	11,00,000	Land & Building	10,20,000	10,95,000
Pref. Share Cap.	3,00,000	2,00,000	Plant & Machinery	9,85,000	7,50,000
Profit & Loss a/c	2,40,000	1,50,000	Furniture & Fittings	55,000	65,000
General Reserve	47,000	59,000	Stock	42,000	37,000
Debentures	2,00,000	1,00,000	Debtors	33,000	43,000
Long-term Loan	3,00,000	3,40,000	Cash	84,000	1,10,000

Provision for Tax	70,000	85,000	Outstanding income	17,000	15,000
Proposed Dividend	49,000	53,000	Rent paid in advance	14,000	20,000
Sundry Creditors	32,000	25,000	Discount on issue of Shares	20,000	15,000
Bills Payable	12,000	15,000			
Bank Overdraft	20,000	23,000			
	22,70,000	21,50,000		22,70,000	21,50,000

The following further information are also given.

1. Provision for depreciation on Land & Building is @ 4% on Rs.10,00,000.
2. An old Plant was sold and a new one was purchased for Rs.70,000. Profit on sale of Plant , was Rs.15,000. Depreciation on Plant & Machinery is provided @ 5% on Rs.7,00,000.
3. Depreciation for Furniture was provided as Rs.7,000.
4. Furniture worth Rs.15,000 (accumulated depreciation Rs.5000) was sold for Rs.8,000. The loss on sale is adjusted with the General Reserve.
5. Dividend paid for the year is Rs.50,000.
6. Provision for Tax during the year is Rs.40,000.

Prepare a Statement of Cash Flow. *(For ICWAI, CA, MCA)*

Solution:

Statement of Cash Flow

Particulars	*Rs.*	*Rs.*
i. Cash flows from Operating Activities		
Difference in the Profit & Loss a/c		(90,000)
Adjustments of non-cash and non-operating items		
Depreciation on Land & Building	45,000	
Depreciation on Plant & Machinery	35,000	
Depreciation on Furniture & Fittings	7,000	
Profit on sale of Plant	(15,000)	
Discount on issue of Shares written off	5,000	
Provision for Tax	40,000	
Provision for Dividend	54,000	
Provision for General Reserve	14,000	1,85,000
Operating profit before Working Capital changes		95,000
Assets and Liabilities:		
Decrease in Stock	5,000	
Increase in Debtors	(10,000)	
Decrease in Outstanding income	2,000	
Increase in Rent paid in advance	(6,000)	
Decrease in Sundry Creditors	(7,000)	
Increase in Bills payable	3,000	
Increase in Bank overdraft	3,000	(10,000)
Cash generated from Operation		85,000

Less : Income Tax paid		25,000
Net Cash from Operation Activities		60,000
ii. Cash flows from Investing Activities		
Purchase of Land & Building	(1,20,000)	
Purchase Plant	(70,000)	
Sale of Plant	2,85,000	
Purchase of Furniture	(27,000)	
Sale of Furniture	8,000	
Net Cash used in Investing Activities		76,000
iii. Cash flows from Financing Activities		
Issue of Equity Share Capital	1,00,000	
Redemption of Preference Share Capital	(1,00,000)	
Redemption of Debentures	(1,00,000)	
Increase of Loan	40,000	
Dividend paid	(50,000)	
Net Cash flow from Investing Activities		(1,10,000)
Net increase in Cash and Cash equivalent		26,000
Cash and Cash equivalent in the beginning of the period		84,000
Cash and Cash equivalent at the end of the period		1,10,000

Land & Building Account

Particulars	*Rs.*	*Particulars*	*Rs.*
To Balance b/d	10,20,000	By Profit & Loss a/c (Dep.)	45,000
To Cash (Purchase)	1,20,000	By Balance c/d	10,95,000
	11,40,000		11,40,000

Plant & Machinery Account

Particulars	*Rs.*	*Particulars*	*Rs.*
To Balance b/d	9,85,000	By Profit & Loss a/c (Dep.)	35,000
To Profit & Loss a/c	15,000	By Cash (Sale)	2,85,000
(Profit on sale)	70,000	By Balance c/d	7,50,000
	10,70,000		10,70,000

Furniture & Fittings Account

Particulars	*Rs.*	*Particulars*	*Rs.*
To Balance b/d	55,000	By Profit & Loss a/c (Dep.)	7,000
To Cash (Purchase)	27,000	By Cash (Sale)	8,000
		By General Reserve (Loss on sale)	2,000
		By Balance c/d	65,000
	82,000		82,000

Provision for Taxation Account

Particulars	*Rs.*	*Particulars*	*Rs.*
To Cash	25,000	By Balance b/d	70,000
To Balance c/d	85,000	By Profit & Loss a/c	40,000
	1,10,000		1,10,000

Proposed Dividend Account

Particulars	*Rs.*	*Particulars*	*Rs.*
To Cash	50,000	By Balance b/d	49,000
To Balance c/d	53,000	By P & L a/c (Prov. for the year)	54,000
	1,03,000		1,03,000

General Reserve Account

Particulars	*Rs.*	*Particular*	*Rs.*
To Furniture a/c	2,000	By Balance b/d	47,000
To Balance c/d	59,000	By Profit & Loss a/c	14,000
	61,000		61,000

Traditional method of preparing Cash Flow Statement

Statement of Cash Flow

Inflow	*Rs.*	*Outflow*	*Rs.*
Cash and cash equivalent in the beginning	84,000	Purchase of Land & Building	1,20,000
Cash from Operation	85,000	Purchase of Plant	70,000
Issue of Eq.Share Capital	1,00,000	Purchase of Furniture	27,000
Increase of Loan	40,000	Redemption of Pre.Share Capital	1,00,000
Sale of Plant	2,85,000	Redemption of Debentures	1,00,000
Sale of Furniture	8,000	Payment of Tax	25,000
		Payment of Dividend	50,000
		Cash and Cash equi. at the end	1,10,000
	6,02,000		6,02,000

Illustration: 31

N Ltd. provided the Balance Sheets as on 31st March of 2006 and 2007 as follows:

Balance Sheets

Liabilities	*2006 Rs.*	*2007 Rs.*	*Assets*	*2006 Rs.*	*2007 Rs.*
Equity Share Capital	10,70,000	12,60,000	Land & Building	6,70,000	7,70,000
Pref. Share Cap.	2,00,000	–	Plant & Machinery	6,00,000	4,50,000
General Reserve	43,000	32,000	Furniture & Fittings	2,00,000	1,50,000,

Debentures	1,50,000	2,50,000	Stock	62,000	50,000
Mortgage Loan	2,40,000	80,000	Debtors	47,000	30,000
Sundry Creditors	31,000	29,000	Cash	35,000	52,000
Outstanding salary	17,000	24,000	Bank	14,000	8,000
Rent received in adv.	19,000	15,000	Preliminary exp.	30,000	40,000
			Profit & Loss a/c	1,12,000	1,40,000
	17,70,000	16,90,000		17,70,000	16,90,000

The following further information are also given.

1. The purchase of Land is settled by Rs.40,000 of Equity Shares and balance in cash. Depreciation for Land and Building is provided @ 5% for a cost of Rs.7,00,000.
2. Loss on sale of Furniture of Rs.5,000 is written off to General Reserve. Depreciation provided for Furniture is Rs.10,000.
3. Plant sold for the year Rs.1,45,000. Depreciation for Plant & Machinery is Rs.30,000.

Prepare a Statement of Cash Flow *(For M.Com., M.B.A., M.C.A. ICWAI)*

Solution :

Statement of Cash Flow

Particulars	*Rs.*	*Rs.*
i. Cash flows from Operating Activities		
Difference in the Profit & Loss a/c [(-1,40,00 – (-1,12,000)]		(28,000)
Adjustments of non-cash and non-operating items		
Depreciation on Land & Building	35,000	
Depreciation on Plant & Machinery	30,000	
Depreciation on Furniture & Fittings	10,000	
Profit on sale of Plant	(25,000)	
Increase in Preliminary expenses	(10,000)	
Decrease in General Reserve	(6,000)	34,000
Operating Profit before Working Capital changes		6,000
Adjustments for changes in Current operating Assets and Liabilities		
Decrease in Stock	12,000	
Increase in Debtors	17,000	
Decrease in Sundry Creditors	(2,000)	
Increase in Outstanding salary	7,000	
Decrease in Rent received in advance	(4,000)	30,000
Net cash generated from Operation		36,000
ii. Cash flows from Investing Activities		
Purchase of Land & Building	(95,000)	
Sale of Plant	1,45,000	
Sale of Furniture	35,000	

Net Cash used in Investing Activities		85,000
iii. Cash flows from Financing Activities		
Issue of Equity Share Capital	1,50,000	
Redemption of Preference Share Capital	(2,00,000)	
Issue of Debentures	1,00,000	
Repayment of Mortgage Loan	(1,60,000)	
Net Cash used for financing activities		(1,10,000)
Net increase in cash and cash equivalent		**11,000**
Cash and Cash equivalent in the beginning of the period		49,000
Cash and Cash equivalent at the end of the period		60,000

Land & Building Account

Particulars	*Rs.*	*Particulars*	*Rs.*
To Balance b/d	6,70,000	By Profit & Loss a/c (Dep.)	35,000
To Share Capital	40,000	By Balance c/d	7,70,000
To Cash	95,000		
	8,05,000		8,05,000

Plant & Machinery Account

Particulars	*Rs.*	*Particulars*	*Rs.*
To Balance b/d	6,00,000	By Profit & Loss a/c (Dep.)	30,000
To Profit & Loss a/c (Profit on sale)	25,000	By Cash (Sale)	1,45,000
		By Balance c/d	4,50,000
	6,25,000		6,25,000

Furniture & Fittings Account

Particulars	*Rs.*	*Particulars*	*Rs.*
To Balance b/d	2,00,000	By Profit & Loss a/c (Dep.)	10,000
		By Cash (Sale)	35,000
		By General Reserve (Loss on sale)	5,000
		By Balance c/d	1,50,000
	2,00,000		2,00,000

Share Capital Account

Particulars	*Rs.*	*Particulars*	*Rs.*
To Cash	12,60,000	By Balance b/d	10,70,000
		By Land & Building	40,000
		By Cash	1,50,000
	12,60,000		12,60,000

General Reserve Account

Particulars	Rs.	Particulars	Rs.
To Furniture a/c	5,000	By Balance b/d	43,000
(Loss on sale)			
To Profit & Loss a/c	6,000		
To Balance c/d	32,000		
	43,000		43,000

Traditional method of preparing Cash Flow Statement

Statement of Cash Flow

Inflow	Rs.	Outflow	Rs.
Cash and cash equivalent in the beginning	49,000	Purchase of Land & Building	95,000
Cash from Operation	36,000	Redemption of Preference Share Capital	2,00,000
Issue of Share Capital	1,50,000	Repayment of Mortgage Loan	1,60,000
Issue of Debentures	1,00,000	Cash and cash equivalent at the end	60,000
Sale of Plant & Machinery	1,45,000		
Sale of Furniture	35,000		
	5,15,000		5,15,000

Illustration: 32

GR Ltd., has provided the Balance Sheets as on 31st March 2006 and 31st March 2007 as follows.

Balance Sheets

Liabilities	2006 Rs.	2007 Rs.	Assets	2006 Rs.	2007 Rs.
Equity Share Cap.	3,00,000	4,00,000	Fixed assets	6,00,000	7,50,000
Profit & Loss a/c	1,15,000	1,90,000	Additions	1,20,000	90,000
General Reserve	50,000	65,000		7,20,000	8,40,000
Mortgage Loan	3,00,000	20,000	Depreciation	2,30,000	2,90,000
Prov. for Taxation	1,07,000	1,29,000		4,90,000	5,50,000
Proposed Dividend	85,000	99,000	Investments	1,50,000	–
Sundry Creditors	27,000	33,000	Goodwill	70,000	50,000
Bank Overdraft	31,000	24,000	Stock	90,000	1,00,000
Bills Payable	15,000	20,000	Debtors	55,000	40,000
			Cash	1,75,000	2,40,000
	10,30,000	9,80,000		10,30,000	9,80,000

The Company earned a Profit of Rs.3,00,000 after tax during the year. The Profit was further adjusted as follows.

		Rs.
Profit & Loss account balance as on 31st March 2006		1,15,000
Profit for the current year		3,00,000
		4,15,000
Provision for Tax	1,10,000	
Provision for Dividend	1,00,000	
Provision for General Reserve	15,000	
Balance of Profit transferred to Balance Sheet		1,90,000

Adjustments:

1. Profit on sale of Investment is Rs.30,000.
2. A Plant costs Rs.74,000 (Accumulated depreciation Rs.11,000) was sold for a loss of Rs.10,000.

Prepare a Cash Flow Statement by Traditional method and Revised method. *(For M.C.A., C.A. ICWAI)*

Solution:

(i) Preparation of Cash Flow statement by Traditional Method.

Statement of Cash Flow

Inflow	*Rs.*	*Outflow*	*Rs.*
Opening Balance of Cash	1,75,000	Purchase of Fixed Assets	1,94,000
Cash from Operation	3,80,000	Repayment of Loan	2,80,000
Sale of Fixed Assets	53,000	Payment of Tax	88,000
Issue of Equity Share Capital	1,00,000	Payment of Dividend	86,000
Sale of Investments	1,80,000	Closing Balance of Cash	2,40,000
	8,88,000		8,88,000

Adjusted Profit & Loss Account

Particulars	*Rs.*	*Particulars*	*Rs.*
To Fixed Assets (Depreciation)	71,000	By Balance b/d	1,15,000
To Fixed Assets (Loss on sale)	10,000	By Investment a/c (Profit on sale)	30,000
To Proposed Dividend	1,00,000	**By Fund from Operation**	3,71,000
To Provision for Tax	1,10,000		
To Provision for General Reserve	15,000		
To Goodwill written off	20,000		
To Balance c/d	1,90,000		
	5,16,000		5,16,000
To Fund from Operation	**3,71,000**	By Increase in Stock	10,000
To Decrease in Debtors	15,000	By Decrease in Bank Overdraft	7,000

To Increase in Creditors	6,000	**By Cash from operation**	**3,80,000**
To Increase in Bills Payable	5,000		
	3,97,000		3,97,000

Fixed Assets Account

Particulars	*Rs.*	*Particulars*	
To Balance b/d	7,20,000	By Cash a/c (Sales)	53,000
To Cash (Purchase)	1,94,000	By Depreciation a/c (For sale)	11,000
		By Fixed Assets (Loss on sale)	10,000
		By Balance c/d	8,40,000
	9,14,000		9,14,000

Depreciation Account

Particulars	*Rs.*	*Particulars*	*Rs.*
To Fixed Assets a/c		By Balance b/d	2,30,000
(Dep. for plant sold)	11,000	By Adjusted P & L a/c	71,000
To Balance c/d	2,90,000		
	3,01,000		3,01,000

Investment Account

Particulars	*Rs.*	*Particulars*	*Rs.*
To Balance b/d	1,50,000	By Cash	1,80,000
To Adjusted P & L a/c	30,000		
	1,80,000		1,80,000

Provision for Dividend Account

Particulars	*Rs.*	*Particulars*	*Rs.*
To Cash	86,000	By Balance b/d	85,000
To Balance c/d	99,000	By Adjusted P & L a/c	1,00,000
	1,85,000		1,85,000

Provision for Taxation Account

Particulars	*Rs.*	*Particulars*	*Rs.*
To Cash	88,000	By Balance b/d	1,07,000
To Balance c/d	1,29,000	By Adjusted P & L a/c	1,10,000
	2,17,000		2,17,000

Equity Share Capital Account

Particulars	*Rs.*	*Particulars*	*Rs.*
To Balance c/d	4,00,000	By Balance b/d	3,00,000
		By Cash a/c	100,000
	4,00,000		4,00,000

Mortgage Loan Account

Particulars	*Rs.*	*Particulars*	*Rs.*
To Balance c/d	20,000	By Balance b/d	3,00,000
To Cash a/c	2,80,000		
	3,00,000		3,00,000

(ii) Preparation of Cash Flow Statement by Revised method

Statement of Cash Flow

Particulars	*Rs.*	*Rs.*
(i) Cash flows from Operating Activities		
Difference in the Profit & Loss a/c		75,000
Adjustments of non-cash and non-operating items		
Provision for Depreciation	71,000	
Loss on sale of Fixed Assets	10,000	
Profit on sale of Investment	(30,000)	
Goodwill written off	20,000	
Provision for Tax	1,10,000	
Provision for Dividend	1,00,000	
Provision for General Reserve	15,000	2,96,000
Operating Profit before Working Capital changes		3,71,000
Adjustments for Current Operating Assets & Liabilities		
Increase in Stock	(10,000)	
Decrease in Debtors	15,000	
Increase in Creditors	6,000	
Increase in Bills payable	5,000	
Decrease in Bank overdraft	(7,000)	9,000
Cash generated from operation		3,80,000
Income tax paid		88,000
Net Cash generated from Operation		2,92,000
(ii) Cash flows from Investing Activities		
Purchase of Fixed Assets	(1,94,000)	
Sale of Fixed Assets	53,000	
Sale of Investments	1,80,000	
Net Cash Flow from Investing Activities		39,000

(iii) Cash flow for Financing Activities		
Issue of Equity Share Capital	1,00,000	
Repayment of Loan	(2,80,000)	
Payment of Dividend	(86,000)	
Net Cash used for Financing Activities		(2,66,000)
Net increase in Cash and Cash equivalent		**65,000**
Cash and Cash equivalent in the beginning of the period		1,75,000
Cash and Cash equivalent at the end of the period		2,40,000

Difference between Fund Flow Statement and Cash Flow Statement

Fund Flow and Cash Flow statements are prepared to ascertain the change of Fund between two periods. It helps to find out whether there is increase or decrease of fund for the current period when compared to the previous period. Since fund may be defined as Working Capital in broad sense and Cash and cash equivalents in narrow sense, there are two types of measurement about the change of fund. Measurement of changes of fund in the broader sense is done through Fund Flow Statement. Measurement of change of fund in the narrow sense is done through Cash Flow Statement.

Even though these statements are focusing about the concept of fund, there are slight differences in the procedures in the preparation of these two statements. The differences are stated as follows.

(i) Fund Flow statement is prepared on the basis of broad concept (Working Capital) of fund and Cash Flow statement is prepared on the basis of narrow concept (Cash and Cash equivalent) of fund.

(ii) In Fund Flow statement, Fund from Operation is calculated but in Cash Flow statement Cash from Operation is calculated. Cash from Operation is calculated after adjusting the changes in Current Assets and Current Liabilities, in the Fund from Operation.

(iii) Statement of changes is Working Capital is prepared to find out the net increase or decrease of Working Capital in the Fund Flow Analysis. But the statement of changes in Working Capital is not prepared in the Cash Flow Analysis.

(iv) The balance of Fund Flow statement shows the increase or decrease of Working Capital between two periods. But the balance in Cash Flow statement shows the increase or decrease of Cash and Cash equivalent between two periods.

(v) The reasons for the change in Working Capital is known through Fund Flow statement and the reasons for the change in Cash is known through Cash Flow statement

(vi) Fund Flow statement helps for medium and long term financial planning of a Company. Cash Flow statement helps the management for short term financial planning.

Illustration: 33

The Balance Sheets of G Ltd., as on 31st March 2006 and 2007 are stated as follows.

Balance Sheets

Liabilities	*2006 Rs.*	*2007 Rs.*	*Assets*	*2006 Rs.*	*2007 Rs.*
Share Capital	5,00,000	6,00,000	Fixed Assets	6,30,000	7,30,000
Profit & Loss a/c.	1,15,000	1,50,000	Stock	52,000	44,000
General Reserve	30,000	59,000	Debtors	48,000	92,000

Loan	1,50,000	1,00,000	Cash	85,000	79,000
Sundry Creditors	30,000	21,000	Discount on issue of Shares	25,000	5,000
Outstanding rent	15,000	20,000			
	8,40,000	9,50,000		8,40,000	9,50,000

Adjustments:

1. Dividend paid @ 5% on Rs.6,00,000
2. Income tax paid Rs.40,000
3. Depreciation for Fixed Assets is Rs.50,000. A Plant was sold for Rs.40,000 (cost of the Plant is Rs.27,000).

Prepare a Statement of Fund Flow and a Statement of Cash Flow.

Solution:

(i) Preparation of Statement of Fund Flow

(a) Statement of changes in Working Capital

Particulars	*2006 Rs.*	*2007 Rs.*	*Increase Rs.*	*Decrease Rs.*
Current Assets				
Stock	52,000	44,000		8,000
Debtors	48,000	92,000	44,000	
Cash	85,000	79,000		6,000
Total	1,85,000	2,15,000		
Current Liabilities				
Sundry creditors	30,000	21,000	9,000	
Outstanding rent	15,000	20,000		5,000
Total	45,000	41,000		
Working Capital (C.A.-C.L)	1,40,000	1,74,000	53,000	19,000
Increase in Working Capital	34,000	-	-	34,000
	1,74,000	1,74,000	53,000	53,000

(b) Statement of Fund Flow

Inflow	*Rs.*	*Outflow*	*Rs.*
Fund from Operation	1,91,000	Purchase of Fixed asset	1,77,000
Issue of Equity Share Cap.	1,00,000	Repayment of Loan	50,000
Sale of Plant	40,000	Payment of Dividend	30,000
		Payment of Tax	40,000
		Increase in Working Capital	34,000
	3,31,000		3,31,000

(ii) Preparation of Cash Flow Statement

Statement of Cash Flow

Inflow	*Rs.*	*Outflow*	*Rs.*
Cash and cash equivalent in the beginning	85,000	Purchase of Fixed Asset	1,77,000
		Repayment of Loan	50,000
Cash from Operation	1,51,000	Payment of Dividend	30,000
Issue of Eq.Share Capital	1,00,000	Payment of Tax	40,000
Sale of Plant	40,000	Cash and cash equi. at the end	79,000
	3,76,000		3,76,000

Adjusted Profit & Loss Account

Particulars	*Rs.*	*Particulars*	*Rs.*
To Fixed Assets (Depreciation)	50,000	By Balance b/d	1,15,000
To Discount on issue of Shares written off	20,000	By Fixed Asset (Profit on sale)	13,000
To Provision for Taxation	40,000	**By Fund from Operation**	**1,91,000**
To Provision for General Reserve	29,000		
To Provision for Dividend	30,000		
To Balance c/d	1,50,000		
	3,19,000		3,19,000

Calculation of Cash from Operation

Particulars	*Rs.*	*Rs.*
Fund from Operation		1,91,000
Add : Increase in Outstanding rent		5,000
Decrease in Stock		8,000
		2,04,000
Less : Increase in Debtors	44,000	
Decrease in Sundry Creditors	9,000	53,000
Cash from Operation		**1,51,000**

Fixed Assets Account

Particulars	*Rs.*	*Particulars*	*Rs.*
To Balance b/d	6,30,000	By Adjusted P & L a/c	50,000
To Adj.P&L a/c (Profit on sale)	13,000	By Cash (Sale)	40,000
To Cash (Purchase)	1,77,000	By Balance c/d	7,30,000
	8,20,000		8,20,000

EXERCISE

THEORY

I. Choose the correct answer for the following.

1. Cash and cash equivalent mean in the narrow sense as —
(i) Fund (ii) Current Assets (iii) Fixed Assets (iv) Total Assets
2. The balance of Cash Flow statement is the increase or decrease of —
(i) Working Capital (ii) Current Assets (iii) Cash and Bank balances (iv) Total Assets
3. The statement of changes in cash is known as —
(i) Fund Flow Statement (ii) Cash Flow Statement (iii) Adjusted Profit & Loss Account (iv) Balance Sheet
4. Fund from operation after adjustment with current items of balance sheet is called —
(i) Fund Lost in Operation (ii) Working Capital (iii) Capital (iv) Cash from Operation
5. Cash from Investing activities is related to the purchase and sale of —
(i) Fixed Assets (ii) Current Assets (iii) All Assets (iv) Fictitious Assets
6. Cash from Financing activities is related to the increase or decrease of —
(i) All assets (ii) Fixed Assets (iii) Non Current Liabilities (iv) Current Liabilities
7. Sale of Plant means —
(i) Inflow of Cash (ii) Outflow of Cash (iii) Increase of Capital (iv) Decrease of Current Asset
8. Cash from operating activities —
(i) Outflow of cash (ii) Loss (iii) Inflow of cash (iv) Expenses
9. Cash Lost in Operating activities is considered as —
(i) Inflow of Cash (ii) Profit (iii) Current Asset (iv) Outflow of Cash
10. Increase in Current Assets is —
(i) Application of Cash (ii) Source of Cash (iii) Decrease in Working Capital (iv) Loss
11. Decrease in current assets means —
(i) Loss (ii) Increase in Working Capital (iii) Application of Cash (iv) Source of Cash
12. Increase in Current Liabilities is —
(i) Working Capital (ii) Source of Cash (iii) Application of Cash (iv) Expenses
13. Decrease is Current Liability is —
(i) Application of cash (ii) Source of Cash (iii) Income (iv) Loss
14. Identify the inflow of Cash from the following :
(i) Issue of Equity Share Capital (ii) Redemption of Debentures (iii) Cash Lost in Operation (iv) Purchase of Building
15. Identify the outflow of Cash from the following :
(i) Sale of Machinery (ii) Issue of Debentures (iii) Purchase of Land (iv) Sale of Investment

[**Ans :** 1. (i) 2. (iii) 3. (ii) 4. (iv) 5. (i) 6. (iii) 7. (i) 8. (iii) 9. (iv) 10. (i) 11 (iv) 12. (ii) 13. (i), 14. (i) 15. (iii)]

II. Answer the following

1. Define Cash Flow statement. State the objectives of Cash Flow statement.
2. Explain the merits and demerits of Cash Flow statement.
3. State the procedures for preparing the Cash Flow statement.
4. Enumerate the concept of Cash from Operating activities.
5. Distinguish between Cash from Operation and Fund from Operation.
6. Distinguish between Cash from Investing activities and Cash from Financing activities.
7. Explain the traditional method of preparing Cash Flow statement.
8. State the revised method of preparing Cash Flow statement.
9. Explain the procedures of calculating Cash from Operating activities.
10. Distinguish between Fund Flow statement and Cash Flow statement.

11. Analyse the concept that the balance of Cash Flow statement is either increase or decrease of Cash.
12. What is Cash Flow statement? Explain the sources of cash in Cash Flow statement.
13. Define Cash Flow statement. What are the outflows of cash in Cash Flow statement?
14. Define Cash Flow statement. Explain the treatment of current items of balance sheet in Cash Flow statement.
15. Write short notes on the following :
    (i) Cash from Operating activities
    (ii) Cash Lost in Operating activities
    (iii) Cash from Investing activities
    (iv) Cash from Financing activities
    (v) Cash Flow statement.

III. Solve the following problems:

1. Calculate Cash from Operation from the following.

Trading and Profit & Loss Account

Particulars	*Rs.*	*Particulars*	*Rs.*
To Opening Stock	54,500	By Sales	13,33,500
To Purchase	7,15,000	By Closing stock	75,500
To Manufacturing expenses	79,500		
To Gross Profit	5,60,000		
	14,09,000		14,09,000
To Depreciation	71,400	**By Gross Profit**	5,60,000
To Administrative Expenses	1,17,600		
To Provision for Taxation	1,60,000		
To Net Profit	2,11,000		
	5,60,000		5,60,000

Additional Information:

(i)	Net Profit	Rs.2,11,000
	Dividend	Rs. 96,000
	Profit transferred to Balance Sheet	Rs.1,15,000

(ii) Opening and closing balances of Debtors are Rs.47,000 and Rs.59,000 respectively.

(iii) Opening and closing balances of Sundry Creditors are Rs.37,500 and Rs.42,500 respectively.

(iv) Opening and closing balances of Provision for tax are Rs.87,000 and Rs.90,000 respectively.

(Ans: Rs.4,38,400)

2. Calculate Cash from Operation from the following

Statement of Profit

Particulars	*Rs.*	*Rs.*
Sales		30,00,000
Opening Stock	1,23,000	
Add : Purchase	14,00,000	
	15,23,000	

Less : Closing Stock	1,00,000	
	14,23,000	
Manufacturing expenses	1,50,000	15,73,000
Gross profit		14,27,000
Depreciation	50,000	
Administration expenses	2,10,000	
Selling expenses	1,60,000	
Provision for Taxation	2,90,000	7,10,000
		7,17,000
Add : Profit on sale of Fixed Assets		30,000
Net Profit		7,47,000
Payment of Dividend		2,70,000
Net Profit to be transferred to Balance Sheet		4,77,000

Balances of Current items for 31st March 2006 and 2007 are stated as follows.

	31st March 2006	*31st March 2007*
Debtors	1,17,400	1,32,400
Cash	1,20,000	1,30,000
Sundry Creditors	71,000	93,000
Outstanding Administrative expenses	22,000	11,000
Provision for Taxation	2,53,000	2,74,000

(**Ans:** Rs.10,87,000)

3. Calculate Cash from Operation by direct method and indirect method from the following.

Trading & Profit and Loss Account

Particulars	*Rs.*	*Particulars*	*Rs.*
To Cost of goods sold	2,99,000	By Sales	5,39,000
To **Gross Profit**	2,40,000		
	5,39,000		5,39,000
To Salary	44,000	By **Gross Profit**	2,40,000
To Rent paid	23,000		
To Telephone expenses	21,000		
To Insurance	19,000		
To Depreciation	24,000		
To **Net Profit**	1,14,000		
	2,45,000		2,40,000

The following additional information are also given.

	31st March 2006 Rs.	31st March 2007 Rs.
Stock	61,000	79,000
Debtors	33,700	47,500
Cash	47,000	71,000
Prepaid rent	7,000	5,000
Sundry Creditors	29,100	37,200
Salary outstanding	14,000	17,000

(**Ans:** Rs.95,300)

4. Calculate Cash from Operating Activities from the following

Particulars	Rs.	Particulars	Rs.
To Operating Stock	77,700	By Sales	7,37,000
To Purchase	2,64,000	By Closing Stock	71,700
To Wages	70,000		
To **Gross Profit**	3,97,000		
	8,08,700		8,08,700
To Salary	99,000	By **Gross Profit**	3,97,000
To Telephone	32,000	By Profit on sale of Plant	19,000
To Electricity	29,000	By Refund of Income Tax	17,000
To Rent	27,000		
To Depreciation	40,000		
To Loss on sale of Furniture	12,000		
To Goodwill written off	20,000		
To Provision for Taxation	75,000		
To **Net profit**	99,000		
	4,33,000		4,33,000

(**Ans:** Rs.2,16,000)

5. Calculate Cash from Operating Activities from the following.

Profit and Loss Account as on 31st March 2007

Particulars	Rs.	Particulars	Rs.
To Salary	76,000	By **Gross Profit**	3,20,000
To Electricity	32,300	By Profit on sale of Investment	19,000
To Telephone	17,500		
To Selling expenses	42,700		
To Dep. on Land & Building	27,500		
To Dep. on Plant & Machinery	29,000		
To Dep. on Furniture	13,000		
To Loss on sale of Machinery	10,000		

To Provision for Taxation	71,000		
To **Net Profit**	1,20,000		
	3,39,000		3,39,000

Adjustments:

	31st March 2006 Rs.	31st March 2007 Rs.
Inventories	42,000	47,400
Debtors	24,500	29,600
Cash	32,000	44,000
Outstanding salary	12,300	13,700
Sundry creditors	22,200	19,300
Bank overdraft	14,000	20,000

(**Ans:** Rs.2,52,500)

6. Calculate Cash from Operating Activities from the following

	Rs.
Net Profit transferred to Balance Sheet	2,55,000
Depreciation for Fixed Assets	51,000
Provision for Taxation	72,000
Goodwill written off	30,000
Preliminary expenses written off	25,000
Profit on sale of Fixed Assets	23,000
Refund of Income Tax	23,000
Provision for General Reserve	50,000
Proposed Dividend	60,000

The details of current items are as follows.

	Opening Balance Rs.	Closing Balance Rs.
Stock	65,000	76,000
Debtors	35,000	25,000
Sundry Creditors	27,000	14,000

(**Ans:** Rs.4,83,000)

7. Calculate Cash from Operating Activities from the following

	Rs.
Net Profit transferred to Balance Sheet	2,30,000
Depreciation for Fixed Assets	43,000
Profit on sale of Plant	17,000
Loss on sale of Furniture	15,000

The balances of Current items are as follows

	31st March 2006 Rs.	31st March 2007 Rs.
Stock	42,700	34,600
Debtors	27,500	34,400
Bills Receivable	15,000	19,000
Sundry Creditors	36,900	47,700
Bills Payable	17,500	14,200

(**Ans:** Rs.2,77,700)

8. Calculate Cash from Operating Activities from the following

	Rs.
Net Loss after adjustment	90,000
Depreciation	72,000
Goodwill written off	31,000
Outstanding salary	15,700
Rent recently accrued	14,700
Dividend received	25,000
Preliminary expenses written off	17,000

(**Ans:** Rs.6,000)

9. Calculate Cash from Operating Activities from the following.

	Rs.
Net Loss after adjustment	1,40,000
Depreciation	45,000
Preliminary expenses written off	22,000
Goodwill written off	34,000
Provision for Doubtful Debts	12,000
Commission accrued	15,000
Dividend received	49,000
Outstanding wages	11,700

(For B.Com., B.B.A., D.B.M)

(**Ans :** Rs.79,300)

10. The Net Profit of K Ltd., as on 31st March 2007, after the following adjustments is Rs.2,30,000

		Rs.
(i)	Depreciation on Fixed Assets	74,000
(ii)	Profit on sale of Plant	23,200
(iii)	Loss on sale of Furniture	14,000
(iv)	Goodwill written off	24,000

(v)	Provision for Doubtful Debts	15,000
(vi)	Provision for Taxation	93,000
(vii)	Transfer to General Reserve	35,000
(viii)	Preliminary expenses written off	19,000

The following additional information are also given.

	31st March 2006 *Rs.*	*31st March 2007* *Rs.*
Stock	37,000	45,500
Debtors	42,000	32,400
Cash	60,000	90,000
Bills receivable	19,000	24,000
Bills payable	15,000	23,000
Outstanding wages	11,000	16,700
Prepaid expenses	12,000	-
Sundry creditors	21,000	17,700

(For B.Com., B.B.A., D.B.M, M.Com.)

Calculate cash from operating activities

(Ans: Rs.4,75,900)

11. Calculate Cash from Operating Activities from the following.

	31st March 2006 *Rs.*	*31st March 2007* *Rs.*
Profit & Loss Account	1,12,000	2,77,000
General Reserve	60,000	1,10,000
Workmen Compensation Fund	40,000	24,000
Goodwill	1,50,000	1,15,000
Discount on issue of Debentures	50,000	40,000
Stock	63,000	72,300
Debtors	32,000	25,000
Outstanding salary	17,100	10,300
Sundry creditors	27,000	35,000
Bills Payable	14,000	17,200

(Ans : Rs.1,46,100)

12. Calculate Cash flow from Investing Activities from the following.

	Rs.
Fixed Assets in the beginning	10,50,000
Fixed Assets at the end	9,00,000
Accumulated depreciation of the Fixed Asset sold	20,000
Loss on sale of Fixed Asset	32,000

(Ans : Rs.98,000)

13. Calculate Cash flow from Investing Activities from the following.

	31st March 2006 Rs.	31st March 2007 Rs.
Plant & Machinery account	7,70,000	9,00,000
Accumulated Depreciation account	54,000	75,000
Investment account	5,00,000	4,10,000

During the year a machine worth Rs.70,000 was sold for Rs.95,000. Accumulated depreciation of the machine is Rs.15,000. Loss on sale of investment is Rs.10,000.

(**Ans :** Cash Outflow Rs.40,000)

14. Calculate Cash Flow from Financing Activities from the following.

	31st March 2006 Rs.	31st March 2007 Rs.
Preference Share Capital	7,30,000	9,00,000
Debentures	4,00,000	2,70,000
Loan	2,40,000	3,50,000

(**Ans :** Cash Inflow Rs.1,50,000)

15. Prepare a Cash Flow Statement from the following Balance Sheets.

Balance Sheets

Liabilities	*2006 Rs.*	*2007 Rs.*	*Assets*	*2006 Rs.*	*2007 Rs.*
Share Capital	5,00,000	7,50,000	Fixed Assets	4,90,000	7,87,000
Profit & Loss a/c	1,50,000	2,10,000	Stock	43,400	64,300
Sundry Creditors	39,000	57,000	Debtors	45,600	25,700
			Cash	1,10,000	1,40,000
	6,89,000	10,17,000		6,89,000	10,17,000

(For B.Com., B.B.A., B.B.M.)

(**Ans :** Cash from Operation Rs. 2,17,000; Total Rs.5,77,000)

16. The Balance Sheets of WD Ltd., as on 31st March 2006 and 2007 are stated as follows.

Balance Sheets

Liabilities	*2006 Rs.*	*2007 Rs.*	*Assets*	*2006 Rs.*	*2007 Rs.*
Share Capital	10,00,000	12,00,000	Land	4,50,000	5,10,000
Profit & Loss a/c	75,000	55,000	Premises	3,50,000	5,79,000
Mortgage Loan	3,00,000	2,30,000	Plant	4,91,000	3,50,000
Sundry Creditors	44,000	59,000	Stock	47,300	33,000
Bank Overdraft	21,000	10,000	Debtors	22,000	36,700
			Cash	79,700	45,300
	14,40,000	15,54,000		14,40,000	15,54,000

Prepare a Statement of Cash Flow. *(For B.Com., B.B.A., B.B.M.)*

(**Ans :** Fund Lost in Operation Rs.16,400; Total Rs.4,20,700)

17. Prepare a Cash Flow Statement from the following Balance Sheets.

Balance Sheets

Liabilities	*2006 Rs.*	*2007 Rs.*	*Assets*	*2006 Rs.*	*2007 Rs.*
Share Capital	3,50,000	5,00,000	Land & Building	2,50,000	2,10,000
Loan Account	2,00,000	1,10,000	Plant & Machinery	1,70,000	2,60,000
Sundry Creditors	47,900	62,400	Stock	39,400	25,000
Bills Payable	22,100	12,600	Debtors	63,000	50,000
			Cash	54,600	65,000
			Profit & Loss A/c	43,000	75,000
	6,20,000	6,85,000		6,20,000	6,85,000

(For B.Com., B.B.A., B.B.M.)

(**Ans :** Cash from Operation Rs.400; Total Rs.2,45,000)

18. Prepare a Statement of Cash Flow for the following Balance Sheets.

Balance Sheets

Liabilities	*2006 Rs.*	*2007 Rs.*	*Assets*	*2006 Rs.*	*2007 Rs.*
Share Capital	9,00,000	11,00,000	Land & Building	7,35,000	4,90,000
Profit & Loss a/c	70,000	–	Plant & Machinery	4,16,000	5,39,000
Loan	2,95,000	1,15,000	Stock	37,500	59,700
Sundry Creditors	37,500	21,000	Debtors	32,500	22,300
Outstanding Wages	14,500	19,000	Cash	35,000	51,000
			Bank	61,000	34,000
			Profit & Loss a/c	–	59,000
	13,17,000	12,55,000		13,17,000	12,55,000

(For B.Com., B.B.A., B.B.M.)

(**Ans :** Cash lost in Operation Rs.1,53,000; Total Rs.5,41,000)

19. KC Ltd., provided the Balance Sheets of 31st March 2006 and 2007 as follows.

Balance Sheets

Liabilities	*2006 Rs.*	*2007 Rs.*	*Assets*	*2006 Rs.*	*2007 Rs.*
Share Capital	10,00,000	10,00,000	Land & Building	5,50,000	7,00,000
Profit & Loss a/c	1,21,000	1,31,000	Plant & Machinery	9,50,000	8,80,000
General Reserve	43,000	59,000	Stock	44,000	31,000
Debenture a/c	2,00,000	4,50,000	Debtors	49,000	33,000
Loan a/c	1,50,000	–	Cash	40,000	37,000
Sundry Creditors	42,000	55,500	Bank	13,000	19,000
Rent received in adv.	9,000	4,500			
	16,46,000	17,00,000		16,46,000	17,00,000

(For B.Com., B.B.A., B.B.M.)

Prepare a statement of cash flow.

(**Ans :** Cash lost in operation Rs.17,000; Total Rs.3,73,000)

20. Prepare a Statement of Cash Flow for the following Balance Sheets.

Balance Sheets

Liabilities	*2006 Rs.*	*2007 Rs.*	*Assets*	*2006 Rs.*	*2007 Rs.*
Share Capital	9,00,000	7,10,000	Fixed Assets	8,50,000	6,55,000
Sundry Creditors	70,000	59,000	Stock	40,000	23,000
Bank Overdraft	35,000	56,000	Debtors	36,000	52,000
			Cash	79,000	95,000
	10,05,000	8,25,000		10,05,000	8,25,000

Assume that there is no drawings and no purchase or sale of Fixed Assets. *(For B.Com., B.B.A., B.B.M.)*

(**Ans :** Cash from Operation Rs.16,000; total Rs.79,000)

21. Calculate a Statement of Cash Flow from the following Balance Sheets.

Balance Sheets

Liabilities	*2006 Rs.*	*2007 Rs.*	*Assets*	*2006 Rs.*	*2007 Rs.*
Share Capital	14,00,000	17,00,000	Fixed Assets	20,45,000	25,39,000
Profit & Loss a/c	97,000	1,42,000	Stock	53,000	79,000
General Reserve	57,000	84,000	Debtors	47,000	23,000
Debenture	3,50,000	3,00,000	Cash	64,000	79,000
Loan	2,75,000	4,40,000			
Account payable	30,000	54,000			
	22,09,000	27,20,000		22,09,000	27,20,000

Adjustments:

(i) Depreciation for Fixed Assets Rs.1,25,000.

(ii) Provision for General Reserve during the year Rs.27,000 *(For B.Com., B.B.A., B.B.M.)*

(**Ans :** Cash from Operation Rs.2,19,000; Total Rs.7,48,000)

22. JW Ltd., provided the Balance Sheets for the year ended 31st March 2006 and 2007 as follows.

Balance Sheets

Liabilities	*2006 Rs.*	*2007 Rs.*	*Assets*	*2006 Rs.*	*2007 Rs.*
Equity Share Capital	20,00,000	22,00,000	Fixed Assets	27,50,000	29,90,000
Profit & Loss a/c	2,70,000	3,50,000	Stock	70,000	96,000
General Reserve	1,05,000	1,35,000	Debtors	37,000	20,000
Debentures	2,50,000	4,00,000	Cash	47,000	69,000
Loan	3,00,000	1,00,000	Preliminary expenses	63,000	35,000
Sundry Creditors	42,000	55,000			
	29,67,000	32,40,000		29,67,000	32,40,000

(**Ans :** Cash from Operation Rs.3,12,000; Total Rs.7,69,000)

23. The Balance Sheets of XYZ for the year ending 31st March 2006 and 2007 are stated as follows.

Balance Sheets

Liabilities	*2006 Rs.*	*2007 Rs.*	*Assets*	*2006 Rs.*	*2007 Rs.*
Equity Share Capital	30,00,000	35,00,000	Land & Building	19,70,000	21,00,000
Pre. Share Capital	7,00,000	7,00,000	Plant & Machinery	15,50,000	19,00,000
General Reserve	1,90,000	2,40,000	Furniture & Fittings	4,50,000	3,10,000
Loan	3,70,000	1,00,000	Stock	87,000	1,00,000
Sundry Creditors	85,000	93,000	Debtors	77,000	62,000
Outstanding rent	35,000	17,000	Cash	71,000	93,000
			Profit & Loss a/c	1,75,000	85,000
	43,80,000	46,50,000		43,80,000	46,50,000

Adjustments:

(i) Depreciation for Land & Building Rs.95,000. Profit on sale of Land Rs.30,000. Purchase of Land for the year Rs.3,00,000.

(ii) Depreciation for Plant and Machinery @ 10% on Rs.19,00,000. Plant sold in 2007 is Rs.1,15,000 for a loss of Rs.20,000.

Prepare a Statement of Cash Flow. *(For B.B.A., B.B.M., M.Com.)*

(**Ans :** Cash from Operation Rs.4,07,000; Total Rs.13,38,000)

24. The Balance Sheets of K Ltd., for the year ending 31st March 2006 and 2007 are stated as follows.

Balance Sheets

Liabilities	*2006 Rs.*	*2007 Rs.*	*Assets*	*2006 Rs.*	*2007 Rs.*
Share Capital	25,00,000	27,00,000	Fixed Assets	32,90,000	34,90,000
Profit & Loss a/c	3,50,000	4,75,000	Stock	21,000	65,000
General Reserve	1,50,000	2,00,000	Debtors	50,000	30,000
Workmen	50,000	20,000	Cash	79,000	97,000
Compensation Fund Loan	4,00,000	2,50,000	Outstanding rent	19,000	12,000
Sundry Creditors	72,000	94,000	Salary paid in advance	27,000	45,000
Bank overdraft	19,000	11,000	Preliminary expenses	65,000	25,000
Outstanding wages	10,000	14,000			
	35,51,000	37,64,000		35,51,000	37,64,000

Adjustments:

(i) Depreciation for Fixed Assets during the year Rs.2,10,000. A Plant worth Rs.1,50,000 was sold for a loss of Rs.32,000.

(ii) Compensation paid for a worker is Rs.30,000.

(iii) Provision for General Reserve is Rs.50,000.

(iv) Preliminary expenses written off during the year is Rs.40,000.

Prepare a Statement of Cash Flow. *(For M.Com., M.B.A.)*

(**Ans :** Cash from Operation Rs.2,40,000; Total Rs.6,37,000)

25. Prepare a Statement of Cash Flow from the following Balance Sheets.

Balance Sheets

Liabilities	2006 Rs.	2007 Rs.	Assets	2006 Rs.	2007 Rs.
Capital	7,50,000	9,00,000	Fixed Assets	9,60,000	10,17,000
Profit & Loss a/c	59,000	89,500	Stock	53,000	39,300
General Reserve	24,000	47,500	Debtors	37,900	57,300
Loan	2,40,000	1,00,000	Cash	47,100	61,400
Sundry Creditors	32,600	41,700	Outstanding Interest	21,000	14,000
Bank Overdraft	13,400	10,300			
	11,19,000	11,89,000		11,19,000	11,89,000

Adjustments:

(i) Drawings by owners for the year is Rs.70,000.

(ii) Provision for depreciation on 31st March 2006 is Rs.45,000 and as on 31st March 2007 is Rs.95,000.

Prepare a Statement of Cash Flow. *(For B.Com., B.B.A., B.B.M., M.Com.)*

(Ans : Cash from Operation Rs.1,41,300; Total Rs.3,78,400)

26. G Ltd., provided the Balance Sheets as on 31st March 2006 and 2007 as follows.

Balance Sheets

Liabilities	2006 Rs.	2007 Rs.	Assets	2006 Rs.	2007 Rs.
Share Capital	11,00,000	11,00,000	Land & Building	7,50,000	3,60,000
Profit & Loss a/c	50,000	1,20,000	Plant & Machinery	5,54,000	2,55,000
Loan	2,70,000	1,90,000	Goodwill	65,000	45,000
Sundry Creditors	27,600	39,700	Stock	37,400	66,300
Provision for Taxation	51,400	76,000	Debtors	37,200	21,100
Unclaimed Dividend	–	27,300	Accrued Interest	14,000	–
			Cash	41,400	62,600
	14,99,000	8,10,000		14,99,000	8,10,000

Adjustments:

(i) Dividend declared during the year is @ 10%.

(ii) Income Tax paid for the year is Rs.50,000.

(iii) Depreciation for Land & Building is Rs.70,000 and Plant & Machinery is Rs.40,000. *(For M.Com., M.B.A.)*

(**Ans :** Cash lost in Operation Rs.3,17,800; Total Rs.6,20,400)

27. W.Doyle Ltd. provided the Balance Sheets for the year ended 31st March 2006 and 31st March 2007 as follows.

Balance Sheets

Liabilities	2006 Rs.	2007 Rs.	Assets	2006 Rs.	2007 Rs.
Share Capital	2,00,000	25,00,000	Fixed Assets	23,06,000	25,83,000
Profit & Loss a/c	–	1,70,000	Stock	1,27,000	1,20,000
General Reserve	70,000	1,00,000	Debtors	1,21,100	1,31,400

Loan	90,000	–	Cash	29,900	43,600
Provision for Tax	60,000	55,000	Outstanding Rent	13,000	7,000
Provision for Doubtful Debtors	22,700	39,400	Preliminary expenses	47,000	22,000
Sundry Creditors	39,100	32,900	Profit & Loss a/c	50,000	–
Outstanding expenses	12,200	9,700			
	26,94,000	29,07,000		26,94,000	29,07,000

Adjustments:

(i) Provision for Taxation for the year is Rs.75,000

(ii) Depreciation for Fixed Assets is Rs.1,50,000. An old Plant was sold for Rs.77,000 (Cost of the Plant is Rs.1,00,000)

(iii) Debtors of Rs.20,000 was considered as bad debtors and was written off against the Provision for Doubtful Debts.

(iv) Interim Dividend of Rs.50,000 was paid during the year.

Prepare a Statement of Cash Flow. *(For M.Com., M.B.A., M.C.A.)*

(Ans : Cash from Operation Rs.5,83,700)

28. MW Ltd., provided the Balance Sheets for two years as follows.

Balance Sheets

Liabilities	*2006 Rs.*	*2007 Rs.*	*Assets*	*2006 Rs.*	*2007 Rs.*
Capital	12,20,000	14,30,000	Fixed Assets	14,07,000	17,12,000
Loan from Bank	3,50,000	4,90,000	Stock	96,000	1,20,000
Loan from K	90,000	40,000	Debtors	63,000	43,000
Creditors	41,000	65,000	Cash	1,35,000	1,50,000
	17,01,000	20,25,000		17,01,000	20,25,000

Adjustments:

A Plant costing Rs.1,10,000 was sold for Rs.90,000. The accumulated depreciation of the Plant is Rs.10,000. Provision for depreciation as on 31st March 2006 is Rs.1,70,000 and as on 31st March 2007 is Rs.2,40,000.

Prepare a Cash Flow Statement. *(For C.A., ICWAI, M.C.A.)*

(Ans : Cash from Operation Rs.3,20,000)

29. KMWD Ltd., provided the Balance Sheets as on 31st March of 2006 and 2007 as follows.

Balance Sheets

Liabilities	*2006 Rs.*	*2007 Rs.*	*Assets*	*2006 Rs.*	*2007 Rs.*
Equity Share Capital	17,00,000	19,50,000	Land & Building	13,20,000	14,00,000
Profit & Loss a/c	3,71,000	3,56,000	Plant & Machinery	9,30,000	11,20,000
General Reserve	92,000	1,09,000	Furniture & Fittings	3,63,000	2,47,000
Debentures	3,50,000	4,90,000	Stock	63,500	79,300
Long-term Loan	2,70,000	1,20,000	Debtors	71,500	64,700
Provision for Tax	90,000	60,000	Cash	92,000	1,34,000
Sundry Creditors	37,000	65,000	Bank	70,000	1,05,000
	29,10,000	31,50,000		29,10,000	31,50,000

The following further information are also given:

1. Land worth Rs.1,50,000 was purchased in exchange of Equity Shares of the company.
2. Purchase of Furniture during the year is Rs.60,000. Loss on sale of Furniture is Rs.17,000. Depreciation provided for Furniture is Rs.30,000.
3. Depreciation provided for Plant & Machinery is Rs.64,000.
4. Tax provided for the year is Rs.76,000.

Prepare a Statement of Cash Flow. *(For ICWAI, C.A., M.C.A.)*

(**Ans :** Cash from Operation Rs.5,83,500; Total s.7,90,600)

30. KC Ltd., provided the Balance Sheets as on 31st March of 2006 and 2007 as follows.

Balance Sheets

Liabilities	*2006 Rs.*	*2007 Rs.*	*Assets*	*2006 Rs.*	*2007 Rs.*
Equity Share Capital	14,00,000	15,00,000	Land & Building	13,20,000	14,50,000
Pref. Share Cap.	4,00,000	3,00,000	Plant & Machinery	11,55,000	10,60,000
Profit & Loss a/c	2,75,000	3,10,000	Furniture & Fittings	2,50,000	3,46,000
General Reserve	77,000	1,10,000	Stock	72,000	57,000
Debentures	3,00,000	4,40,000	Debtors	53,000	73,000
Long-term Loan	3,00,000	2,10,000	Cash	72,000	1,19,000
Provision for Tax	90,000	1,05,000	Outstanding income	21,000	12,000
Proposed Dividend	69,000	93,000	Rent paid in advance	19,000	27,000
Sundry Creditors	52,000	35,000	Discount on issue of Debentures	50,000	25,000
Bills Payable	22,000	32,000			
Bank overdraft	27,000	34,000			
	30,12,000	31,69,000		30,12,000	31,69,000

The following further information are also given.

1. Provision for depreciation on Land & Building is @ 5% on Rs.14,00,000.
2. An old Plant was sold and a new one was purchased for Rs.90,000.Loss on sale of Plant , was Rs.20,000. Depreciation on Plant & Machinery is provided @ 5% on Rs.10,00,000.
3. Depreciation for Furniture was provided as Rs.25,000.
4. Furniture worth Rs.35,000 (accumulated depreciation Rs.7000) was sold for Rs.19,000. The loss on sale is adjusted with the General Reserve.
5. Dividend paid for the year is Rs.70,000.
6. Provision for Tax during the year is Rs.77,000.

Prepare a Statement of Cash Flow. *(For ICWAI, C.A., M.C.A.)*

(**Ans :** Cash from Operation Rs.4,91,000; Total Rs.7,97,000)

31. H Ltd., provided the Balance Sheets as on 31st March of 2006 and 2007 as follows:

Balance Sheets

Liabilities	*2006 Rs.*	*2007 Rs.*	*Assets*	*2006 Rs.*	*2007 Rs.*
Equity Share Capital	30,00,000	33,90,000	Land & Building	17,50,000	24,50,000
Pref. Share Cap.	2,00,000	–	Plant & Machinery	15,00,000	14,10,000
General Reserve	2,10,000	2,70,000	Furniture & Fittings	5,00,000	3,50,000

Debentures	4,50,000	2,50,000	Stock	91,000	40,000
Mortgage Loan	3,50,000	5,70,000	Debtors	55,000	90,000
Sundry creditors	73,000	99,000	Cash	55,000	72,000
Outstanding salary	37,000	20,000	Bank	74,000	93,000
Rent received in adv.	20,000	36,000	Preliminary exp.	70,000	30,000
			Profit & Loss a/c	2,45,000	1,00,000
	43,40,000	46,35,000		43,40,000	46,35,000

The following further information are also given.

1. The purchase of Land is settled by Rs.1,00,000 of Equity Shares and balance in cash. Depreciation for Land and Building is provided @ 4% for a cost of Rs.20,00,000.
2. Loss on sale of Furniture of Rs.25,000 is written off to General Reserve. Depreciation provided for Furniture is Rs.30,000.
3. Plant sold for the year Rs.60,000. Depreciation for Plant & Machinery is Rs.50,000.

Prepare a Statement of Cash Flow *(For M.Com., M.B.A., M.C.A. ICWAI)*

(**Ans :** Cash from Operation Rs.3,66,000; Total Rs.8,45,000)

32. MWD Ltd., has provided the Balance Sheets as on 31st March 2006 and 31st March 2007 as follows.

Balance Sheets

Liabilities	*2006 Rs.*	*2007 Rs.*	*Assets*	*2006 Rs.*	*2007 Rs.*
Equity Share Cap.	25,00,000	27,00,000	Fixed assets	28,14,000	30,70,000
Profit & Loss a/c	2,15,000	1,50,000	Additions	3,50,000	2,90,000
General Reserve	79,000	1,05,000		31,64,000	3,60,000
Mortgage Loan	4,00,000	2,50,000	Depreciation	3,00,000	3,90,000
Prov. for Taxation	1,00,000	1,25,000		28,64,000	29,70,000
Proposed Dividend	75,000	93,000	Investments	2,50,000	1,97,000
Sundry Creditors	47,000	70,000	Goodwill	90,000	70,000
Bank Overdraft	37,000	15,000	Stock	92,000	1,10,000
Bills Payable	17,000	23,000	Debtors	59,000	41,000
			Cash	1,15,000	1,43,000
	34,70,000	35,31,000		34,70,000	35,31,000

The Company earned a profit of Rs.1,79,000 after tax during the year. The profit was further adjusted as follows.

		Rs.
Profit & Loss account balance as a 31st March 2006		2,15,000
Profit for the current year		1,79,000
		3,94,000
Provision for Tax	1,25,000	
Provision for Dividend	93,000	
Provision for General Reserve	26,000	2,44,000
Balance of Profit transferred to Balance Sheet		1,50,000

Adjustments:

1. Profit on sale of Investment is Rs.50,000.
2. A Plant at cost Rs.1,50,000 (Accumulated depreciation Rs.20,000) was sold for a loss of Rs.34,000.

Prepare a Cash Flow Statement by Traditional method and Revised method. *(For M.C.A., C.A. ICWAI)*

(**Ans :** Cash from Operation Rs.40,000; Total Rs.5,74,000)

33. The Balance Sheets of G Ltd., as a 31st March 2006 and 2007 are stated as follows.

Balance Sheets

Liabilities	*2006 Rs.*	*2007 Rs.*	*Assets*	*2006 Rs.*	*2007 Rs.*
Share Capital	12,00,000	15,00,000	Fixed Assets	16,90,000	19,60,000
Profit & Loss a/c.	1,20,000	1,90,000	Stock	37,000	24,000
General Reserve	1,01,000	1,31,000	Debtors	22,000	43,000
Loan	3,50,000	2,00,000	Cash	47,500	61,500
Sundry Creditors	50,000	90,000	Discount on issue	43,500	21,500
Outstanding rent	19,000	9,000	of Shares		
	18,40,000	21,20,000		18,40,000	21,20,000

Adjustments:

1. Dividend paid @ 4% on Rs.15,00,000
2. Income tax paid Rs.70,000
3. Depreciation for Fixed Assets is Rs.95,000. A Plant was sold for Rs.120,000 (cost of the Plant , is Rs.105,000).

Prepare a Statement of Fund Flow and a Statement of Cash Flow.

(**Ans :** Decrease in W.C. Rs.8,000; Fund from Operation Rs.1,87,000; Total Rs.6,15,000; Cash from Operation Rs.2,09,000; Total Rs.6,76,500)

❑ ❑ ❑

6

MANAGEMENT OF WORKING CAPITAL

Capital is the life blood of a business. Capital is required for a business for its establishment and functioning. Establishment means acquisition of assets like Land, Building, Plant and Machinery, Furniture and Fittings. These assets are called Fixed or permanent assets. Functioning means carrying the activities like trading, service or manufacturing. Trading means buying and selling without any manufacturing activities. Service means intangible one like, electricity, telephone etc. Manufacturing means conversion of raw material into finished products and then to sale. The capital required for the establishment of the business is called Fixed Capital. It is otherwise called as the capital invested mostly in Fixed Assets. It may also be called as Long term or Permanent Capital. But the capital required for meeting the day-to-day activities is called Working Capital. It is also called Short term Capital. Since the purpose of the capital is to make conversion of material or conduct of some services, it may also be called as Circulating Capital or Revolving Capital.

Meaning and Definitions of Working Capital

Working Capital means the capital invested in Current Assets. It may also be defined as the difference between Current Assets and Current Liabilities. The following definitions give more meaning to the Working Capital.

(i) According to **Shubin** "Working Capital is the amount of funds necessary to cover the cost of operating the enterprise."

(ii) **Genestenberg** defined Working Capital as, "Circulating Capital means Current Assets of a company that are changed in the ordinary course of business from one form to another, as for example, from cash to inventories, inventories to receivables, receivables to cash."

According to the definitions, Working Capital is the capital meant for meeting the operating activities of an enterprise. It may be called as Circulating Capital since cash outflow through purchase and conversion process is recovered through sales. In case of credit sales, cash is recovered through debtors after sometime.

Classification of Working Capital (or Types or Kinds of Working Capital)

Working capital can be classified on the following basis.

A. On the basis of concept. B. On the basis of Time.

The classification of Working Capital is diagrammatically represented as follows.

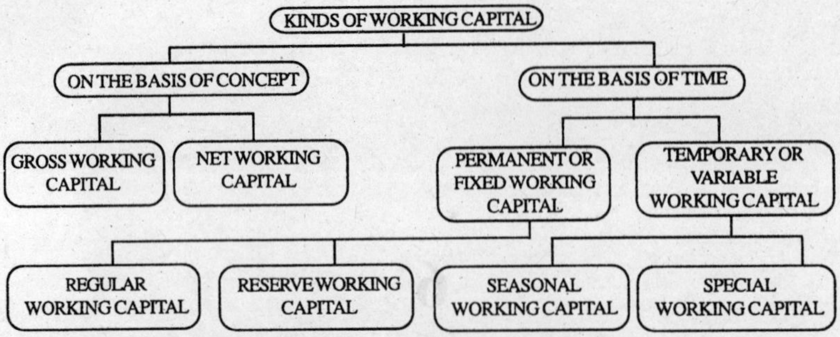

A. Classification of Working Capital on the basis of Concept

[CONCEPT OF WORKING CAPITAL]

The Working Capital is classified on the basis of concept as follows.

1. Balance Sheet concept of Working Capital.
2. Operating Cycle Concept of Working Capital.

1. Balance Sheet concept of Working Capital

According to Balance Sheet concept Working Capital is classified as:

(a) Gross Working Capital (b) Net Working Capital.

(a) Gross Working Capital: The fund invested in Current Assets is called Gross Working Capital. Gross Working Capital defines the Working Capital in broad sense. The investment in Current Assets includes, stock, debtors, cash, etc. The details of Gross Working Capital is stated as follows.

Gross Working Capital (Current Assets) :–

(i) Cash and Bank balances (ii) Debtors (iii) Temporary investments (iv) Bills receivables (v) Accrued (or outstanding) income (vi) Prepaid expenses (vii) Stock (Raw material, Work-in-progress, Finished goods)

(b) Net Working Capital: Net Working Capital is the difference between Current Assets and Current Liabilities.

Net Working Capital = Current Assets - Current Liabilities.

Net Working Capital is the definition of working capital in narrow sense. The details of calculation of Net Working Capital is stated as follows.

Net Working Capital

Particulars	*Rs.*	*Rs.*
Current Assets:		
Stock		x x x
Debtors		x x x
Cash		x x x
Bills Receivable		x x x
Temporary Investments		x x x
Outstanding Income		x x x
Prepaid Expenses		x x x
		x x x
Less : Current Liabilities:		
Sundry Creditors (Account payable)	x x x	

Outstanding (Accrued) expenses	x x x	
Income received in advance	x x x	
Bank Overdraft	x x x	
Short-term loan advances	x x x	
Dividend payable	x x x	x x x
Net Working Capital		x x x

2. Operating Cycle Concept of Working Capital (Circular Flow Concept)

According to operating cycle concept of Working Capital there will be continuous inflow and outflow of cash through operating activities. Outflow of cash is for purchase of raw material, cost of conversion into finished goods. Inflow of cash is through sales. The cycle will be purchase of raw-material, payment to creditors (for credit purchase) payment of wages and operating expenses, sale of finished goods for cash, collection from debtors (for credit sales) **[Cash - Raw Material - Work-in-progress - Finished goods - Sales - Debtors - Cash]**. This is known as one cycle of the rotation of Working Capital. The cash is circulated in this process [Operating Expenses - Cash - Sales]. The speed (time) in which the cycle is completed determines the size of the Working Capital. If the period for completing one cycle is large, then the requirement of Working Capital is high and if the period is short, then the requirement is low. The Operating Cycle is represented by a chart as follows.

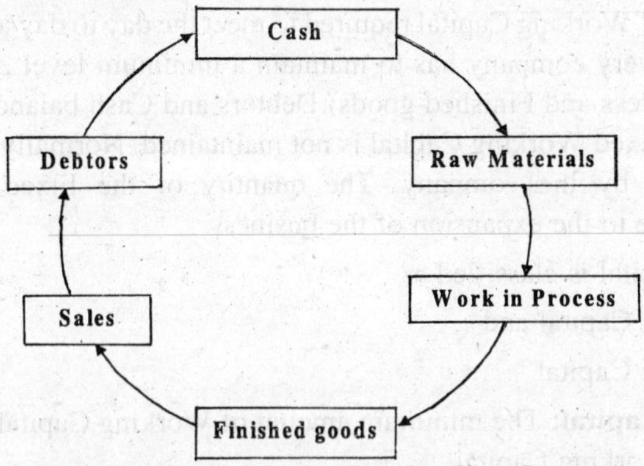

(Working Capital Cycle: Circular Flow Concept)

The Operating Cycle is classified as

(i) Gross Operating Cycle and

(ii) Net Operating Cycle.

(i) Gross Operating cycle

Gross Operating Cycle is the sum of Raw Material Conversion Period (RCP), Work-in-progress Conversion Period (WIPCP), Finished Goods Conversion Period (F&CP) and Receivables Conversion Period (RCP).

Gross operating cycle = RCP + WIPCP + F&CP + RCP

(ii) Net Operating, Cycle

Net Operating Cycle is the difference between Gross Operating Cycle and Payable deferral period.

Net Operating Cycle = Gross Operating Cycle period - Payable deferral period

= (GOCP – PDP)

The conversion periods can be determined through the following formulae.

(i) Raw material Conversion Period $= \dfrac{\text{Average Stock of Raw Material}}{\text{Per day Consumption of Raw Material}}$

(ii) Work-in-progress Conversion Period $= \dfrac{\text{Average Stock of Work in progress}}{\text{Cost of Production per day}}$

(iii) Finished goods Conversion Period $= \dfrac{\text{Average Stock of Finished Goods}}{\text{Cost of Sales per day}}$

(iv) Receivable Conversion Period $= \dfrac{\text{Average Debtors (Account receivable)}}{\text{Credit Sales per day}}$

(v) Payable Deferral Period $= \dfrac{\text{Average Creditors}}{\text{Credit Purchase per day}}$

B. Classification of Working Capital on the basis of time

The Working Capital is classified on the basis of time as follows:

1. Permanent or Fixed Working Capital
2. Temporary or Variable Working Capital.

1. Permanent or Fixed Working Capital

The minimum amount of Working Capital required to meet the day to day activities is called Permanent or Fixed Working Capital. Every company has to maintain a minimum level of Current Assets like Stock (Raw material, Work-in-progress and Finished goods) Debtors and Cash balance. The production activities will be affected much if the Fixed Working Capital is not maintained. Normally, the Fixed Working Capital will always be experienced by the company. The quantity of the Fixed Working Capital will be proportionately increasing due to the expansion of the business.

The Fixed Working Capital is classified as

(a) Regular Working Capital and

(b) Reserve Working Capital

(a) Regular Working Capital: The minimum amount of Working Capital to be maintained in normal condition is called Regular Working Capital.

(b) Reserve Working Capital: The excess amount of Working Capital maintained by the company over the Regular Working Capital is called Reserve Working Capital. Reserve Working Capital is maintained to meet contingencies like, rise in prices, strike, scarcity of materials etc.

Permanent Working Capital is diagrammatically represented as follows.

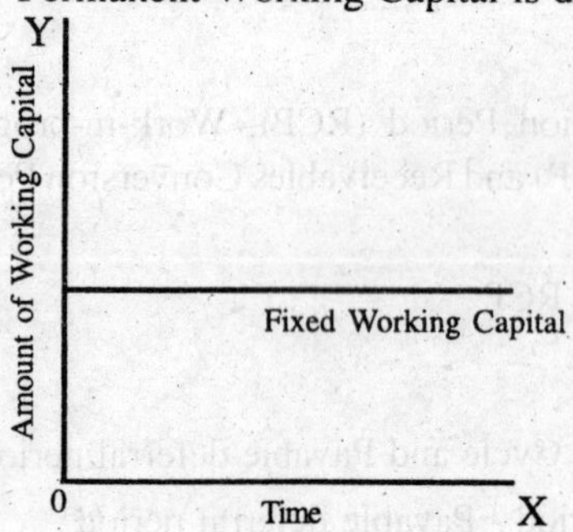

Diagram No. 1

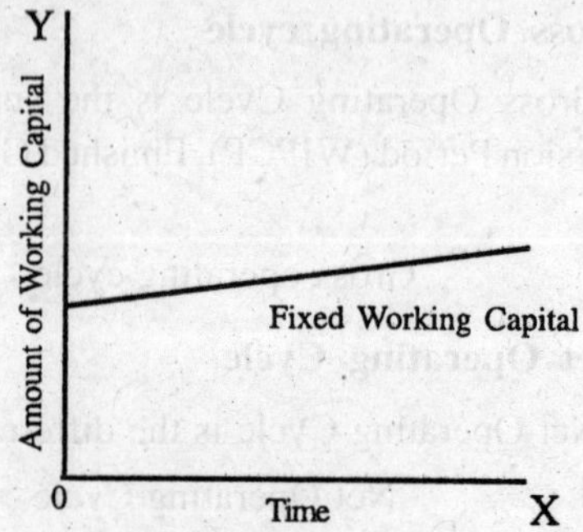

Diagram No. 2

It is clear from Diagram No.1 that Fixed Working Capital remains same for all the periods. Diagram No.2 states that the Fixed Working Capital increases consistently due to the passage of time. This is due to the expansion of the business.

2. Temporary or Variable Working Capital

The amount of Working Capital required to meet the seasonal demand or special needs is called Temporary or Variable Working Capital. This Working Capital is over and above the Permanent Working Capital. Permanent Working Capital should always be maintained. But Temporary Working Capital will fluctuate for different periods. Temporary Working Capital is classified as,

(a) Seasonal Working Capital and (b) Special Working Capital

(a) Seasonal Working Capital: Seasonal Working Capital is the amount of Working Capital required to meet the seasonal demand of the product. The seasonal demand arises due to festival, economical conditions like income of the people, demand, price etc.

(b) Special Working Capital: The amount of Working Capital required to meet the special need of the company is called Special Working Capital. The special need may be like, advertisement and sales promotion measures, research, launching of new products, expansion of markets etc.

The Temporary or Variable Working Capital is diagrammatically represented as follows.

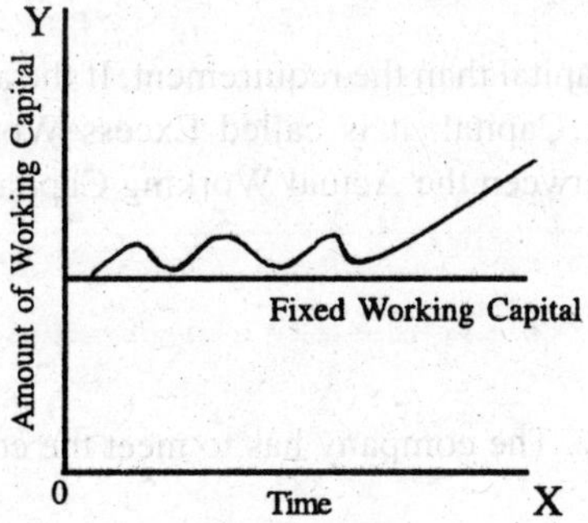

Diagram No. 1

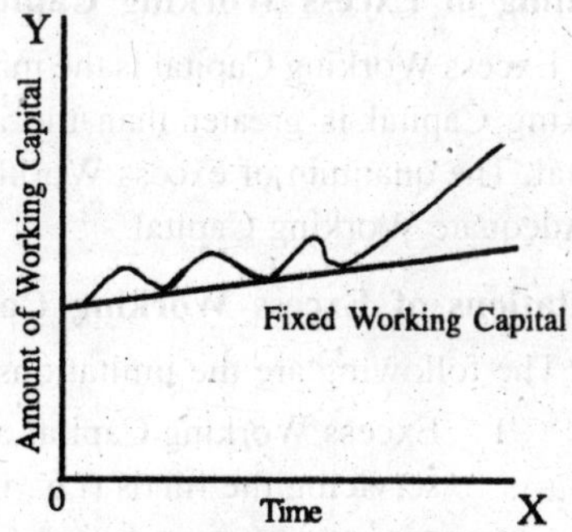

Diagram No. 2

It is clear from Diagram No.1 that the Temporary Working Capital is the difference between the Total Working Capital and Fixed Working Capital. It is also known that the amount of the Variable Working Capital is fluctuating for different periods. Diagram No.2 shows that the Permanent Working Capital fluctuates in direct proportion of the increase in the quantity of Fixed Working Capital. This is due to the expansion of business from one period to another.

Concept of Optimum Working Capital

Optimum Working Capital means sufficient or adequate Working Capital to meet the day to day operational activities of an enterprise. It is in between high Working Capital and low Working Capital. There are many drawbacks in high (excess) and low (inadequate) Working Capital. Optimum Working Capital eliminates to drawbacks in the excess and inadequate Working Capital. The drawbacks of excess and inadequate Working Capital will define the concept of Optimum Working Capital.

Advantages of Optimum (Adequate) Working Capital

The following are the advantages of Optimum Working Capital:

1. Adequate Working Capital provides funds for day-to-day activities without interruption. Hence, the operating activities will be carried on smoothly.

2. The inventory level will be maintained sufficiently.
3. The employees will be working with high job satisfaction and contribute more for the company. This is because they will be getting reasonable wages and salary in time.
4. The creditors can be paid within the allowed credit period. Hence, they will provide more credit sales.
5. The banking institutions which provide short-term credit will have a good reputation about the company.
6. The customers will be getting the product of the company without any interruption. It brings goodwill for the company from the pubic.
7. Adequate Working Capital will induce the management for expansion of the business.
8. It helps for improving the performance of management of the Company.
9. The company can be able to get cash discount due to reasonable quantity of purchase from the supplier.
10. The company can be able to get a reasonable return on investment.
11. The influence of economical conditions like prosperity and depression can easily be solved through adequate Working Capital.

Meaning of Excess Working Capital

Excess Working Capital is the maintenance of more Working Capital than the requirement. If the actual Working Capital is greater than the adequate (Optimum) Working Capital, it is called Excess Working Capital. The quantum of excess Working Capital is the difference between the Actual Working Capital and the Adequate Working Capital.

Limitations of Excess Working Capital

The following are the limitations of excess Working Capital.

1. Excess Working Capital creates idle funds in a company. The company has to meet the cost of servicing the funds (i.e., interest for the loan).
2. It induces to maintain large quantity of stock of raw materials. Hence, there may be loss in the inventory due to theft or deterioration of quality of materials.
3. Excess Working Capital may motivate the management for speculative activities which in turn may create more losses for the company.
4. Excess Working Capital means more borrowings and thereby, there is a need for paying more interest.
5. The rate of return on investment will proportionately reduce due to excess Working Capital.
6. The reputation of the company will be affected because it shows the inefficiency of the management.

Meaning of Inadequate Working Capital

Inadequate Working Capital means shortage of Working Capital to meet all the day-to-day operating activities.If the actual Working Capital is less than the adequate (optimum) Working Capital, there will be inadequacy of Working Capital. The quantum of inadequate Working Capital is measured as the difference between the Optimum Working Capital and the Actual Working Capital.

Limitations of Inadequate Working Capital

The following are the limitations of inadequate Working Capital.

1. It is difficult to meet the day-to-day activities if there is shortage in Working Capital.
2. It affects the reputation of the company.
3. The short-term liabilities could not be met in time.
4. The company could not get the advantage of cash discount through bulk purchase.
5. The Fixed Assets like Plant & Machinery could not be fully utilised.
6. It will not be possible to produce enough quantities of the product to meet the regular demands. Hence, the customers may switch over to some other products.
7. The profit of the company will decrease due to inadequate Working Capital.

Factors Determining the Working Capital Requirement

There are many factors which determine the requirement of Working Capital in a company. The important factors are stated as follows.

1. Nature of the Business: Nature of the business is one of the factors determining the amount of Working Capital. Manufacturing concerns require more Working Capital than other type of concerns like Public Utility, Trading and Finance companies. Among the Public Utility, Trading and Finance companies, Public Utility companies require very low amount of Working Capital since there is mostly no provision of services for credit. Example for Public Utility concerns are Electricity, Water service, Telephone etc.

2. Size of the Business: Size of the business has a direct proportion in the requirement of Working Capital. The requirement of Working Capital is more for big business and low for small business.

3. Production Policy of the Company: The policy of the company related to production may be to produce more quantity and keep it in store for future or to produce small quantity for present period only. The requirement of Working Capital is more if production is for future period also. Otherwise, the requirement is small.

4. Credit Policy of the Company: If the company allows longer period of credit for the debtors the company require more Working Capital. But the requirement is low when the credit period is short.

5. Credit Period Allowed by the Suppliers: If the company purchases goods for long credit, then the requirement of Working Capital is low. The requirement of Working Capital is more if the credit period allowed by the suppliers is short.

6. Process of Production: A product manufactured by a company may undergo one or two processes or may processes. If the number of process are more, the requirement of Working Capital is also more and low Working Capital is required when the number of processes are few.

7. Working Capital Cycle: Working Capital Cycle is the time required to purchase and convert the raw material into finished products and sales.Working Capital Cycle also determines the size of the Working Capital. If the duration of the cycle is long, the requirement of Working Capital is high. If the duration is short the requirement is low.

8. Business Cycle: Business Cycle means periods of Prosperity, Recession, Depression and Recovery. During the period of prosperity, the demand and prices of products increases. In this period there is more requirement of Working Capital. During the period of depression the demand and prices of products decreases. Hence, the company needs to produce low quantity and the requirement of Working Capital will be low.

9. Seasonal Variations: The demand of the product may be subject of seasonal variations (Example, products like cloth, cool drinks, air-conditioners etc.) or non-seasonal variations (tea, coffee, sugar, food products etc.) If the product has to face seasonal variations (fluctuation in demand), the company need more Working Capital to produce more to meet the season of high demand. If the product need not face seasonal variations (normal demand) the company need low Working Capital.

10. Status of Stock Turnover rate: Rate of stock turnover is one of the important factors to assess the size of the Working Capital requirement. The requirement of Working Capital is low, if the rate of stock turnover is high and the requirement is high if the rate of stock turnover in low. The reason is that high stock turnover facilitates inflow of cash in short period of time.

11. Growth of the Company: The requirement of Working Capital is high if the rate of growth of the company is high and the requirement is low if the rate of growth is low.

12. Changes in Price of the Product: If the price of the product manufactured by the company is fluctuating often, then the company need more Working Capital. If the price of the products is steady, then the requirement of Working Capital is low.

13. Profit of the Company: The profit of the company also determines the size of the Working Capital. If the profit of the company is high, then it has enough resources and the requirement Working Capital is low. If the profit is low then there is a need for more Working Capital.

14. Dividend policy of the Company: Declaration of high dividend means outflow of more cash and hence, there is greater need of Working Capital. If the company declared low dividend, then it may have enough resources for Working Capital and the need of Working Capital is low.

Procedures for the Estimation of Working Capital Requirement

The following are the procedures in the estimation of Working Capital requirement:

1. Estimation of total Current Assets.
2. Estimation of total Current Liabilities.
3. Ascertainment of Net Working Capital requirement.

1. Estimation of Total Current Assets

The different types of Current Assets to be estimated are stated as follows.

(i) Inventory (Stock): The quantity of stock to be maintained in the store determines the cost of the stock. Inventory is classified into Stock of raw material, Stock of work-in-process and Stock of finished goods. In the determination of the quantity and value, optimum stock level should be calculated.

(ii) Debtors: The quantum of credit sales and the credit period allowed to the customers should be clearly ascertained to find out the normal debtors of the company.

(iii) Outstanding Income: The lag in receipt of rent, interest etc (Accrued Interest) should be estimated properly.

(iv) Expenses Paid in Advance: Some expenses like salary, commission etc need to be paid in advance (salary paid in advance, commission paid in advance). The period and amount should be estimated correctly.

(v) Bills Receivable: Some companies receive Bills of exchange from debtors. Such comparison should estimate the amount of the total bills receivable and the period of the bill to calculate the estimated Bills receivables.

(vi) Cash and Bank Balance: Cash and bank balance to be maintained should also be known. It depends upon the payment for wages, salaries and other day-to-day operating activities.

2. Estimation of Total current liabilities

The different types of Current Liabilities to be estimated are stated as follows.

(i) Sundry Creditors: The total creditors for a period depends upon the credit purchase and the credit period allowed by the suppliers. On this basis, the amount of Sundry creditors should be estimated.

(ii) Bank Overdraft: The quantum of Bank overdraft required for a period should be estimated on the basis of period and amount.

(iii) Outstanding Expenses: The lag in payment of various operating expenses should be correctly estimated. The total expense in a year and the lag in payment of such expenses will show the estimated outstanding expenses.

(iv) Income Received in Advance: Income such as rent, commission etc., might have been received in advance. The lag in receipt of such income and the total income will show the estimated income received in advance.

(v) Bills Payable: Some companies have the practice of accepting Bills of exchange from their creditors. Such companies should estimate the total amount of Bills payable and the period of the bills to ascertain the exact amount of Bills payable.

3. Ascertainment of Net Working Capital requirement

The Net Working Capital requirement can be ascertained by deducting the total estimated Current Liabilities from the total estimated Current Assets. If the management feels to add some amount for contingencies, it should also be added with the difference in the estimated Current Assets and Current Liabilities.

Statement of Estimated Working Capital Requirement

The statement which explains the estimated Current Assets, Current Liabilities and the Working Capital is called the statement of estimated Working Capital requirement. A model of the Statement of Estimated Working Capital is stated as follows:

Statement of Estimated Working Capital Requirement

Particulars	*Rs.*	*Rs.*
Current Assets		
Stock - Raw material	x x x	
Work-in-progress	x x x	
Finished Goods	x x x	x x x
Debtors		x x x
Bills receivable		x x x
Outstanding Income		x x x
Expenses paid in advance		x x x
Short-term investments, if any		x x x
Cash Balance		x x x
Bank Balance		x x x
Total estimated Current Assets		x x x
Less : Current Liabilities		
Sundry creditors	x x x	
Bills Payable	x x x	

Bank Overdraft	x x x	
Outstanding expenses	x x x	
Income received in advance	x x x	
Short-term borrowings, if any	x x x	
Total estimated Current Liabilities		x x x
Working Capital (C.A – C.L)		x x x
Add : Contingencies		x x x
Net Working Capital requirement		x x x

Illustration: 1

Calculate the operating cycle in days, for a company from the following

	Rs.
Cost of average stock maintained	
Raw material	1,40,000
Work-in-progress	1,90,000
Finished Goods	2,50,000
Purchase of Raw material	20,00,000
Raw material consumption	21,00,000
Cost of production	40,00,000
Sales	50,00,000
Average total Debtors outstanding	2,00,000
Average total Creditors outstanding	1,20,000

The information stated above are meant for one year.

Solution:

Calculation of Operating Cycle

Particulars	*Number of Days*	
(i) Raw material conversion period		
$\frac{\text{Average Stock of Raw Material}}{\text{Raw material consumption per day}}$	$\frac{1,40,000}{21,00,000/365}$ =	24
(ii) Work-in-progress conversion period		
$\frac{\text{Average Stock of Work in progress}}{\text{Cost of production per day}}$	$\frac{1,90,000}{40,00,000/365}$ =	17
(iii) Finished goods conversion period		
$\frac{\text{Average Stock of Finished Goods}}{\text{Cost of Sales per day}}$	$\frac{2,50,000}{40,00,000/365}$ =	23
(iv) Debtors conversion period		
(Average period of credit allowed to debtors)		
$\frac{\text{Average Total Debtors}}{\text{Credit Sales per day}}$	$\frac{2,00,000}{50,00,000/365}$ =	15
Gross total period of Operating Cycle		**79**

Less : Creditors conversion period (Average period of credit allowed by suppliers) $\frac{\text{Average Total Creditors}}{\text{Credit Purchase per day}}$	$\frac{1,20,000}{20,00,000/365} =$	22
Period of Operating Cycle (Working Capital)		**57**

Note:

(i) All the purchase and sales are assumed as on credit.

(ii) If credit purchase is not available the material consumption is considered as credit purchase.

(iii) If cost of sales is not available sales is considered for calculation of finished goods conversion period.

Illustration: 2

Calculate the estimated Total Working Capital from the following.

	Rs.
Closing stock	50,000
Estimated Credit sales	6,00,000
Wages	1,80,000
Factory Overhead	1,40,000
Administrative Overhead	2,20,000
Selling and Distribution Overhead	1,20,000

Average credit period is 8 weeks; Lag in payment of wages is 2 weeks and Lag in payment of overheads is 4 weeks.

Solution:

Statement of Estimated Working Capital

Particulars		*Rs.*
Current Assets		
Stock		50,000
Debtors	$\frac{6,00,000}{52} \times 8 =$	92,308
		1,42,308
Current Liabilities		
Outstanding Wages	$\frac{1,80,000}{52} \times 2 =$	6,923
Outstanding Factory Overheads	$\frac{1,40,000}{52} \times 4 =$	10,769
Outstanding Administration Overheads	$\frac{2,20,000}{52} \times 4 =$	16,923
Outstanding Selling & Distribution Overheads	$\frac{1,20,000}{52} \times 4 =$	9,230
		43,845
Estimated requirement of Working Capital (C.A. - C.L.)		**98,463**

Illustration: 3

WD Ltd., provided the following estimated values

		Rs.
Average credit given for sales:	Inland 5 weeks	7,20,000
	Export 6 weeks	4,80,000
Lag in payment of expenses:	Wages 3 weeks	1,70,000
	Overheads 4 weeks	2,90,000
Closing stock		70,000

Prepare a statement of estimated Working Capital requirement. Add 10% for contingencies.

Solution:

Statement of Estimated Working Capital Requirement

Particulars			*Rs.*
Current Assets			
Stock			70,000
Debtors:	Inland	$\frac{7,20,000}{52} \times 5 =$	69,231
	Export	$\frac{4,80,000}{52} \times 6 =$	55,385
			1,94,616
Current Liabilities			
Wages		$\frac{1,70,000}{52} \times 3 =$	9,808
Overheads		$\frac{2,90,000}{52} \times 4 =$	22,308
			32,116
Working Capital (C.A. - C.L)			1,62,500
Add : Contingencies 10%			16,250
Requirement of Working Capital			**1,78,750**

Illustration: 4

Forecast the Working Capital requirement from the following.

Projected Sales	Rs. 15,00,000
Rate of Net Profit on Sales	10%
Average credit period allowed to Debtors	5 weeks
Average credit period allowed to Creditors	2 weeks
Average Stock carrying	4 weeks
Direct cost	Rs.50,000
Contingencies to be allowed	15%

Solution:

Estimated Working Capital Requirement

Particulars		*Rs.*
Current Assets		
Stock		1,03,846
Debtors	$\frac{15,00,000}{52} \times 5 =$	1,44,231
		2,48,077
Current Liabilities		
Sundry Creditors	$\frac{11,96,154}{52} \times 2 =$	46,006
Working Capital (C.A. - C.L)		**2,02,071**
Add : Contingencies 15%		30,311
Working Capital Requirement		**2,32,382**

Workings:

Sales			15,00,000
Net Profit	=	$\frac{10}{100} \times 15,00,000$	1,50,000
Cost of goods sold			13,50,000
Stock carrying	=	$\frac{13,50,000}{52} \times 4$	1,03,846

Cost of goods sold = Op. Stock + Purchases + Direct Cost – Closing Stock

13,50,000 = 0 + Purchases + 50,000 – 1,03,846

Purchase = 13,50,000 – 50,000 + 1,03,846

= Rs.11,96,154

Illustration: 5

G Ltd., provided the following information related to the requirement of Working Capital.

Particulars	*Average period of Credit*	*Estimated Values (Rs.)*
Purchase of materials	2 weeks	30,00,000
Wages	2 weeks	4,40,000
Salaries	1 month	5,40,000
Rent	2 months	1,20,000
Selling expenses	3 months	1,50,000
Cash Sales		25,00,000
Credit Sales	45 days	18,00,000
Stock		3,40,000

Estimate the Working Capital requirement.

Solution:

Statement of Working Capital Requirement

Particulars		*Rs.*	*Rs.*
Current Assets			
Stock			3,40,000
Debtors	$\frac{18,00,000}{12} \times 1.5 =$		2,25,000
			5,65,000
Current Liabilities			
Sundry Creditors	$\frac{30,00,000}{52} \times 2 =$	1,15,385	
Wages outstanding	$\frac{4,40,000}{52} \times 2 =$	16,923	
Salaries outstanding	$\frac{5,40,000}{12} \times 1 =$	45,000	
Rent outstanding	$\frac{1,20,000}{12} \times 2 =$	20,000	
Selling expenses outstanding	$\frac{1,50,000}{12} \times 3 =$	37,500	2,34,808
Working Capital requirement (C.A. - C.L)			**3,30,192**

Illustration: 6

Calculate the estimated Working Capital from the following

Sales (15 days credit)	Rs. 55,00,000
Rate for Gross Profit on cost of production	10%
Raw materials	Rs. 15,00,000
Wages (Lag in payment 2 weeks)	Rs. 6,00,000
Manufacturing expenses (Lag in payment 2 weeks)	Rs. 4,50,000
Administration expenses (Lag in payment 3 weeks)	Rs. 5,00,000
Selling expenses (Lag in payment 1 week)	Rs. 2,40,000
Rent to be received (Lag in payment one and half month)	Rs. 4,20,000
Credit from the suppliers of raw material	2 months
Stock of raw material maintained	2 months
Stock of Finished goods	1 month
Cash balance to be maintained	Rs. 2,00,000
Add for contingencies	10%

Solution:

Statement of Working Capital Requirement

Particulars		*Rs.*	*Rs.*
Current Assets			
Stock of Raw material	$\frac{15,00,000}{12} \times 2$		2,50,000
Stock of Finished goods	$\frac{50,00,000}{12} \times 1$		4,16,667
Debtors	$\frac{55,00,000}{12} \times 0.5$		2,29,167
Outstanding rent	$\frac{4,20,000}{12} \times 1.5$		52,500
Cash			2,00,000
			11,48,334
Current Liabilities			
Sundry Creditors	$\frac{46,16,667}{12} \times 1$	3,84,722	
Outstanding wages	$\frac{6,00,000}{52} \times 2$	23,077	
Outstanding manufacturing expenses	$\frac{4,50,000}{52} \times 2$	17,307	
Outstanding administration expenses	$\frac{5,00,000}{52} \times 3$	28,846	
Outstanding selling expenses	$\frac{2,40,000}{52} \times 1$	4,615	4,58,567
			6,89,767
Add : Contingencies 10%			68,977
Working Capital requirement			**7,58,744**

Workings:

(i) Cost of goods sold = $\frac{55,00,000}{110} \times 100$ = Rs. 50,00,000

(ii) Calculation of purchase

Trading Account

Particulars	*Rs.*	*Particulars*	*Rs.*
To Purchase	46,16,667	By Sales	55,00,000
To Wages	6,00,000	By Closing stock	
To Manufacturing expenses	4,50,000	Raw material	2,50,000
To Gross Profit $\frac{10}{110} \times 55,00,000$	5,00,000	Finished goods	4,16,667
	61,66,667		61,66,667

Note: All purchases are assumed as credit purchase.

Illustration: 7

GC Ltd., provided the following information related to the estimation of requirement of Working Capital.

	Rs.
Stock of raw material	55,000
Stock of finished goods	79,000
Sales : Inland (3 weeks credit)	9,50,000
Export (6 weeks credit)	12,50,000
Estimated expenses (Lag in payment)	
Wages and salary (1 1/2 months)	2,40,000
Purchase of material (4 weeks)	6,00,000
Rent and rates (2 months)	70,000
Miscellaneous expenses (2 months)	40,000
Directors remuneration (1 month)	60,000
Advance payments	
Transport expenses (2 months)	39,000
Average amount of undrawn profit	50,000

80% of inland sales and 70% of export sales are on credit basis. Out of the total purchase 90% are on credit basis. Allow 10% for contingencies.

Calculate the estimated Working Capital requirement.

Solution:

Statement of Working Capital Requirement

Particulars		Rs.	Rs.
Current Assets			
Stock of raw material		55,000	
Stock of Finished goods		79,000	1,34,000
Debtors: Inland	$\frac{9,50,000}{52} \times 3 \times \frac{80}{100}$	43,846	
Export	$\frac{12,50,000}{52} \times 6 \times \frac{70}{100}$	1,00,962	1,44,808
Advance payment of transport expenses	$\frac{39,000}{12} \times 2$		6,500
			2,85,308
Current Liabilities			
Sundry Creditors	$\frac{6,00,000}{52} \times 4 \times \frac{90}{100} \times 4$	41,538	
Outstanding wages and salary	$\frac{2,40,000}{12} \times 1.5$	30,000	
Outstanding rent & rates	$\frac{70,000}{12} \times 2$	11,667	

Outstanding miscellaneous expenses	$\frac{40,000}{12} \times 2$	6,667	
Outstanding Director's remuneration	$\frac{60,000}{12} \times 1$	5,000	94,872
Working Capital (C.A. – C.L)			1,90,436
Add : Contingencies – 10%			19,044
Working Capital requirement			**2,09,480**

Illustration: 8

The details of cost consumed by a product manufactured by G Ltd are Direct material 50%; Direct labour 30%; Overhead 10%.

The related information for Working Capital are as follows.

(i) The expected output is 60,000 units.

(ii) Raw material will remain in store for an average period of half month.

(iii) Material will be in process for an average period of one and half months.

(iv) Finished goods are expected to be in store for an average period of 2 months.

(v) The debtors are allowed a credit period of one and half months.

(vi) The suppliers allowed a credit period of 2 months.

(vii) Selling price is Rs.20 per unit.

Prepare a statement of Working Capital requirement.

Solution:

Statement of Working Capital Requirement

Particulars			*Rs.*	*Rs.*
Current Assets				
Stock of Raw material	$\frac{50}{100} \times \frac{12,00,000}{12} \times .5$		25,000	
Stock of Work-in-progress				
Material	$\frac{50}{100} \times \frac{12,00,000}{12} \times 1.5 =$	75,000		
Labour	$\frac{30}{100} \times \frac{12,00,000}{12} \times 1.5 =$	45,000		
Overhead	$\frac{10}{100} \times \frac{12,00,000}{12} \times 1.5 =$	15,000	1,35,000	
Stock of Finished goods				
Material	$\frac{50}{100} \times \frac{12,00,000}{12} \times 2 =$	1,00,000		
Labour	$\frac{30}{100} \times \frac{12,00,000}{12} \times 2 =$	60,000		
Overhead	$\frac{10}{100} \times \frac{12,00,000}{12} \times 2 =$	20,000	1,80,000	3,40,000
Debtors	$\frac{12,00,000}{12} \times 1.5$			1,50,000
				4,90,000

Less : Current Liabilities			
Sundry Creditors	$\frac{50}{100} \times \frac{12,00,000}{12} \times 2$		1,00,000
Net Working Capital required			**3,90,000**

Note:

Total element of cost = 50 + 30 + 10 = 90%

Hence, Stock of Work-in-progress may be calculated as $= \frac{90}{100} \times \frac{12,00,000}{12} \times 1.5 = 1,35,000$

and Stock of Finished goods as $\frac{90}{100} \times \frac{12,00,000}{12} \times 2 =$ Rs.1,80,000

Illustration: 9

Calculate the estimated Working Capital from the following.

(i) Elements of total cost of production-material 40%, labour 35% and overhead 25%.

(ii) Profit is 20% on sales.

(iii) Estimated sales 1,00,000 units @ Rs.6 per unit.

(iv) Suppliers allowed a credit period of one and half months and the debtors are allowed a credit period of 2 months.

(v) The stock position is raw material one and half months, work-in-progress half month and finished goods 1 month.

vi. Work-in-progress is considered, as 50% on cost of production.

vii. Add 10% for contingencies.

Solution:

Statement of Working Capital Requirement

Particulars		*Rs.*	*Rs.*
Current Assets			
Stock of Raw material	$\frac{40}{100} \times \frac{4,80,000}{12} \times 1.5 =$	24,000	
Stock of Work-in-progress	$\frac{50}{100} \times \frac{4,80,000}{12} \times .5 =$	10,000	
Stock of Finished goods	$\frac{4,80,000}{12} \times 1 =$	40,000	74,000
Debtors	$\frac{6,00,000}{12} \times 2 =$		1,00,000
			1,74,000
Current Liabilities			
Sundry Creditors	$\frac{40}{100} \times \frac{4,80,000}{12} \times 1.5 =$		24,000
			1,50,000
Add : Contingencies 10%			15,000
Net Working Capital requirement			**1,65,000**

Note:

Sales = 1,00,000 × 6 = Rs.6,00,000

Cost of production = $\frac{80}{100}$ × 6,00,000 = Rs.4,80,000.

Illustration: 10

Calculate the Working Capital requirement of a company from the following.

Element of cost per unit	*Rs.*
Direct material	300
Direct wages	200
Overheads	100
Profit	150
Selling price	750

Additional Information:

(i) Number of units to be produced is 78,000
(ii) Stock of Raw material average 2 weeks
(iii) Stock of Work-in-progress average 1 week
(iv) Stock of Finished goods average 2 weeks
(v) Credit period allowed by suppliers average 2 weeks
(vi) Credit period allowed to debtors average 1 week

Assume that the production is in all the weeks of the year and the Work-in-progress is in 60% stage of completion and with full material consumption.

Solution:

Statement of Working Capital Requirement

Particulars		*Rs.*	*Rs.*
Current Assets			
Stock of Raw material	$\frac{300 \times 78{,}000}{52} \times 2 =$	9,00,000	
Stock of Work-in-progress			
Material	$\frac{300 \times 78{,}000}{52} \times 1 =$	4,50,000	
Wages	$\frac{60}{100} \times \frac{200 \times 78{,}000}{52} \times 1 =$	1,80,000	
Overheads	$\frac{60}{100} \times \frac{100 \times 78{,}000}{52} \times 1 =$	90,000	
Stock of Finished goods	$\frac{600 \times 78{,}000}{52} \times 2 =$	1,80,000	18,00,000
Debtors	$\frac{750 \times 78{,}000}{52} \times 1 =$		11,25,000
			29,25,000

Current Liabilities			
Sundry Creditors	$\frac{300 \times 78{,}000}{52} \times 2 =$		9,00,000
Net Working Capital requirement			**20,25,000**

Illustration: 11

W.Doyle Ltd., provided the following estimated values as on 31st March 2007.

Element of Cost (per unit)	*Rs.*
Direct material	500
Direct wages	250
Direct expenses	100
Overhead	150
Cost of sales	1000
Profit	200
Selling price	1200

Additional Information:

(i) Output 15,600 units.

(ii) Stock of raw material 1 week on an average.

(iii) Work-in-progress (stages of completion 100% material, 60% labour, 50% overhead and 40% direct expenses) 2 weeks on an average.

(iv) Stock of Finished goods 1 week on an average.

(v) Credit allowed by Suppliers 3 weeks on an average.

(vi) Credit allowed to Debtors 2 weeks on an average.

(vii) Credit purchase is 60% of the total Purchase and Credit Sales is 80% of the total Sales.

(viii) Cash in hand and bank balance are expected to be Rs.2,50,000.

Prepare a statement of Working Capital requirement.

Solution:

Statement of Working Capital Requirement

Particulars		*Rs.*	*Rs.*
Current Assets			
Stock of Raw material	$\frac{500 \times 15{,}600}{52} \times 1 =$		1,50,000
Stock of Work-in-progress			
Direct Material	$\frac{500 \times 15{,}600}{52} \times 2 =$	3,00,000	
Direct Wages	$\frac{60}{100} \times \frac{250 \times 15{,}600}{52} \times 2 =$	90,000	
Direct Expenses	$\frac{40}{100} \times \frac{100 \times 15{,}600}{52} \times 2 =$	24,000	

Overhead	$\frac{50}{100} \times \frac{150 \times 15,600}{52} \times 2 =$	45,000	4,59,000
Stock of Finished goods	$\frac{1,000 \times 15,600}{52} \times 1 =$		3,00,000
Debtors	$\frac{80}{100} \times \frac{1,200 \times 15,600}{52} \times 2 =$		5,76,000
Cash and Bank Balances			2,50,000
			17,35,000
Current Liabilities			
Sundry Creditors	$\frac{60}{100} \times \frac{500 \times 15,600}{52} \times 3 =$		2,70,000
Net Working Capital requirement			14,65,000

Illustration: 12

Prepare a statement of Working Capital from the following.

Element of Cost Per Unit	*Rs.*
Direct material	150
Direct labour	100
Overheads	50
Total Cost	300

Additional Information:

(i) Output 26,000 units and expected profit is Rs.100 per unit.

(ii) Stock of raw material and finished goods are on an average of 3 weeks and 4 weeks respectively.

(iii) Stock of work-in-progress is on an average two and half weeks. The stages of completion of work-in-progress is full material, 70% labour and 80% overhead.

(iv) Lag in payment of wages is 2 weeks on an average.

(v) Lag in payment of overheads is one and half weeks on an average.

(vi) Rent to be received is Rs.1,30,000 and the lag in payment is two and half weeks on an average.

(vii) Creditors allowed a credit period of 5 weeks.

(viii) Debtors are allowed a credit period of four and half weeks.

(ix) Cash balance to be maintained is estimated as Rs.1,50,000.

(x) Credit purchase is 75% and credit sales is 70%.

Solution:

Statement of Working Capital Requirement

Particulars		*Rs.*	*Rs.*
Current Assets			
Stock of Raw material	$\frac{150 \times 26,000}{52} \times 3 =$		2,25,000
Stock of Work-in-progress			

Material	$\frac{150 \times 26,000}{52} \times 2.5 =$	1,87,500	
Labour	$\frac{70}{100} \times \frac{100 \times 26,000}{52} \times 2.5 =$	87,500	
Overheads	$\frac{80}{100} \times \frac{50 \times 26,000}{52} \times 2.5 =$	50,000	3,25,000
Stock of Finished goods	$\frac{300 \times 26,000}{52} \times 4 =$		6,00,000
Debtors	$\frac{70}{100} \times \frac{400 \times 26,000}{52} \times 4.5 =$		6,30,000
Cash			1,50,000
Rent outstanding	$\frac{1,30,000}{52} \times 2.5 =$		6,250
			19,36,250
Current Liabilities			
Sundry Creditors	$\frac{75}{100} \times \frac{150 \times 26,000}{52} \times 5 =$	2,81,250	
Wages outstanding	$\frac{100 \times 26,000}{52} \times 2 =$	1,00,000	
Overhead outstanding	$\frac{50 \times 26,000}{52} \times 1.5 =$	37,500	4,18,750
Net Working Capital requirement			**15,17,500**

Illustration: 13

K Ltd., provides the following information with respect to the estimation of Working Capital requirement for 31st March, 2007 as follows.

(a) Position of non-current assets and liabilities

	Rs.
Share Capital	20,00,000
General Reserve	78,750
Debentures	3,50,000
Loan	3,00,000
Fixed Assets	22,60,000

(b) Element of Cost

Material	50%
Labour	30%
Overheads	10%

(c) Additional Information:

(i) Estimated annual sales 3,00,000 units @ Rs.10 per unit.

(ii) Credit allowed by suppliers is one and half months.

(iii) Credit allowed to customers is one month.

(iv) Stock conversion periods are given as raw material half month. Work-in-progress three - fourth of a month. Finished goods one and half months.

(v) Administration overhead Rs.1,20,000, Selling overhead Rs.80,000.

(vi) Cash Balance Rs.1,50,000.

Prepare a statement of estimated Working Capital requirement and the projected Profit and Loss Account and Balance Sheet as on 31st March 2007.

Solution:

Statement of Estimated Working Capital Requirement

Particulars		*Rs.*	*Rs.*
Current Assets			
Stock of Raw material	$\frac{15,00,000}{12} \times 0.5 =$	62,500	
Stock of Work-in-progress	$\frac{25,00,000}{12} \times 0.75 =$	1,56,250	
Stock of Finished goods	$\frac{27,00,000}{12} \times 1.5 =$	3,37,500	5,56,250
Debtors	$\frac{30,00,000}{12} \times 1 =$		2,50,000
Cash			1,50,000
			9,56,250
Current Liabilities			
Sundry Creditors	$\frac{15,00,000}{12} \times 1.5 =$		1,87,500
Working Capital requirement			**7,68,750**

Projected Profit & Loss Account as on 31st March 2007

Particulars	*Rs.*	*Particulars*	*Rs.*
To Direct material	15,00,000	By Sales	30,00,000
To Direct wages	9,00,000		
To Manufacturing overhead	1,00,000		
To Gross Profit	5,00,000		
	30,00,000		30,00,000
To Administration overhead	1,20,000	**By Gross Profit**	5,00,000
To Selling overhead	80,000		
To Net Profit	3,00,000		
	5,00,000		5,00,000

Projected Balance Sheet as on 31st March 2007

Particulars	*Rs.*	*Particulars*	*Rs.*
Share Capital	20,00,000	Fixed Assets	22,60,000
Profit & Loss Account	3,00,000	Stock	5,56,250
General Reserve	78,750	Debtors	2,50,000
Debentures	3,50,000	Cash	1,50,000
Loan	3,00,000		
Sundry Creditors	1,87,500		
	32,16,250		32,16,250

Workings

Sales	$3,00,000 \times 10$	30,00,000
Material	$\frac{50}{100} \times 30,00,000 =$	15,00,000
Labour	$\frac{30}{100} \times 30,00,000 =$	9,00,000
Overhead	$\frac{10}{100} \times 30,00,000 =$	3,00,000
Cost of sales (90% of 30,00,000)		27,00,000
Less : Administration overhead	1,20,000	
Selling overhead	80,000	2,00,000
Manufacturing cost		25,00,000
Manufacturing overhead = 3,00,000 – 2,00,000 = Rs. 1,00,000		

Illustration: 14

Calculate the estimated Working Capital and Net Profit from the following.

(i) Estimated sales Rs.15,00,000 and the selling price is above 20% on cost.

(ii) The estimated Fixed cost is Rs.3,00,000 and Variable cost is 10% of the sales, for one year.

(iii) The expected stock turnover is 5 times a year.

(iv) 50% of sales and 70% purchase are on credit basis.

(v) Credit period allowed by suppliers are 2 months and the credit period allowed to customers are 1 month.

(vi) The requirement of Working Capital related to expenses are for one month.

(vii) Fixed and variable cost estimated are excluding the direct material cost.

Solution:

Statement of Estimated Working Capital Requirement

Particulars		*Rs.*	*Rs.*
Current Assets			
Stock	$\frac{12,50,000}{5}$	2,50,000	
Debtors	$\frac{7,50,000}{12} \times 1$	62,500	

Cash to meet expenses			
Fixed cost	$\frac{3,00,000}{12}$	25,000	
Variable cost	$\frac{1,50,000}{12}$	12,500	3,50,000
Current Liabilities			
Sundry Creditors	$\frac{5,60,000}{12}\times 2$		93,333
Working Capital requirement			**2,56,667**

Statement of Estimated Profit

Particulars	*Rs.*	*Rs.*
Sales		15,00,000
Less : Cost Sales		
Purchase	8,00,000	
Fixed cost	3,00,000	
Variable cost	1,50,000	12,50,000
Net Profit		**2,50,000**

Workings:

Cost of Sales $= \frac{100}{120}\times 15,00,000 =$ Rs.12,50,000

Purchase = Cost of sales – Fixed Cost – Variable Cost

= 12,50,000 – 3,00,000 – 1,50,000 = Rs.8,00,000

Credit Purchase $= \frac{8,00,000}{100}\times 70 =$ Rs.5,60,000

Credit Sales $= \frac{15,00,000}{100}\times 50 =$ Rs.7,50,000

Illustration: 15

KMWD Ltd., provided the following estimated values for April 2007 to September 2007.

(i) The cost per unit of the product manufactured by the company are Direct material Rs.20, , Direct labour Rs.15 and Variable overhead Rs.10. The Fixed overhead per month is Rs.60,000.

(ii) The expected number of units sold are

February	2000	June	2400
March	2200	July	1300
April	1400	August	1500
May	1600	September	2500

(iii) Selling price is Rs.90 per unit.

(iv) The lag in payment for Direct material is two months, Wages is one month and Variable overhead is one month.

(v) Forty percent of sale is on credit basis and the settlement is done on the following months.

(vi) All the purchase of material is considered as on credit.

Prepare a statement of Working Capital requirement on month by month basis for six months from the month of April 2007.

Solution:

Statement of Estimated Working Capital Requirement

Particulars	*April Rs.*	*May Rs.*	*June Rs.*	*July Rs.*	*Aug. Rs.*	*Sept. Rs.*
Receipts						
Cash Sales	75,600	86,400	1,29,600	70,200	81,000	1,35,000
Receipt from Debtors	79,200	50,400	57,600	86,400	46,800	54,000
	1,54,800	1,36,800	1,87,200	1,56,600	1,27,800	1,89,000
Payments						
Direct material	4.00.00	44,000	28,000	32,000	48,000	26,000
Direct wages	33,000	21,000	24,000	36,000	19,500	22,500
Variable overhead	22,000	14,000	16,000	24,000	13,000	15,000
Fixed overhead	55,000	60,000	60,000	60,000	60,000	60,000
	1,55,000	1,39,000	1,28,000	1,52,000	1,40,500	1,23,500
Surplus (Deficit) of Working Capital	(1,200)	(2,200)	59,200	4,600	(12,700)	65,500
Cumulative Working Capital	(1,200)	(3,400)	55,800	60,400	47,700	1,13,200

Illustration: 16

Calculate lag in payments of Creditors, Stock and credit period allowed to Debtors from the following.

	Rs.
Purchase of material	70,000
Credit Sales	1,20,000
Cash Sales	1,00,000
Wages	30,000
Overheads - Manufacturing	10,000
- Administration and Selling	39,000
Stock	13,750
Sundry Creditors	17,500
Debtors	20,000

Solution:

$$\text{Time lag for Stock} = \frac{12 \times \text{Stock}}{\text{Cost of Goods Sold}}$$

$$= \frac{12 \times 13{,}750}{1{,}10{,}000} = 1.5 \text{ months}$$

$$\text{Time lag for Debtors} = \frac{12 \times \text{Debtors}}{\text{Credit Sales}}$$

$$= \frac{12 \times 20{,}000}{1{,}20{,}000} = 2 \text{ months}$$

$$\text{Time lag for Creditors} = \frac{12 \times \text{Creditors}}{\text{Credit purchase}}$$

$$= \frac{12 \times 17{,}500}{70{,}000} = 3 \text{ months}$$

Note:

(i) Stock $= \dfrac{\text{Cost of Goods Sold} \times \text{Lag in time}}{12}$

Lag in time $= \dfrac{12 \times \text{Stock}}{\text{Cost of Goods Sold}}$

(ii) Cost of goods sold = 70,000 + 30,000 + 10,000 = Rs.1,10,000

(iii) Lag in time of stock may be calculated through Cost of Sales also (Rs.1,49,000)

Illustration: 17

The cost details of a manufacturing company at 50% capacity as on 31st March 2007 are stated as follows.

(i)	Number of units produced	60,000
(ii)	Elements of Cost and Sales per unit are	Rs.
	Material	15
	Wages	10
	Variable Overheads	7
	Fixed Overheads	12
	Profit	6
	Selling Price	50

(iii) The details of Current Assets and Current Liabilities are stated as follows:

	Rs.
Sundry Debtors	5,00,000
Sundry Creditors	75,000
Wages outstanding	25,000
Overheads outstanding	95,000
Stock - Raw material (10,000 units)	1,50,000
Work-in-progress (5000 units)	1,33,500
Finished goods (7500 units)	3,30,000

(iv) Stages of completion of Work-in-progress are material 100%, wages 60% and overheads 30%.

Estimate the Working Capital of the company at 80% capacity and also the additional Working Capital required.

Assume that there is no change in lag in periods due to increase in capacity.

Solution:

Statement of Working Capital Requirement

Particulars		*Rs.*
Current Assets		
Stock of Raw material	$\frac{15 \times 96,000}{12} \times 2$	2,40,000
Stock of Work-in-progress	$\frac{25.35 \times 96,000}{12} \times 1$	2,02,800
Stock Finished goods	$\frac{39.5 \times 96,000}{12} \times 1.5$	4,74,000
Sundry Debtors	$\frac{50 \times 96,000}{12} \times 2$	8,00,000
		17,16,800
Less : Current Liabilities		
Sundry Creditors	$\frac{15 \times 96,000}{12} \times 1$	1,20,000
Outstanding wages	$\frac{10 \times 96,000}{12} \times 0.5$	40,000
Outstanding overheads	$\frac{14.5 \times 96,000}{12} \times 1$	1,16,000
		2,76,000
Working Capital requirement (C.A.-C.L)		14,40,800
Working Capital at 50% capacity		9,18,500
Additional Working Capital for 80% capacity		5,22,300

Workings:

(a) Calculation of Working Capital at 50% capacity

Current Assets = 1,50,000 + 1,33,500 + 3,30,000 + 5,00,000 = Rs.11,13,500

Current Liabilities = 75,000 + 25,000 + 95,000 = Rs.1,95,000

Working Capital = C.A. – C.L = 11,13,500 – 1,95,000 = Rs.9,18,500.

(b) Calculation of lag in periods

Cost of sales for 60,000 units

Material	=	60,000 × 15	=	9,00,000
Wages	=	60,000 × 10	=	6,00,000
Variable overhead	=	60,000 × 7	=	4,20,000
Fixed overhead	=	60,00 × 12	=	7,20,000
Cost of sales				26,40,000
Sales = 60,000 × 50				30,00,000

(i) Lag in period of Raw material $= \dfrac{12 \times \text{Stock}}{\text{Total production}}$

Work-in-progress $= \dfrac{12 \times 10{,}000}{60{,}000} = 2$ months

(ii) Lag in period of Work-in-progress $= \dfrac{12 \times 5{,}000}{60{,}000} = 1$ month

(iii) Lag in period of Finished goods $= \dfrac{12 \times 7{,}500}{60{,}000} = 1.5$ months

(iv) Lag in period of Debtors $= \dfrac{12 \times \text{Debtors}}{\text{Credit sales}}$

$= \dfrac{12 \times 5{,}00{,}000}{30{,}00{,}000} = 2$ months

(v) Lag in period of Creditors $= \dfrac{12 \times \text{Creditors}}{\text{Credit Purchase}}$

$= \dfrac{12 \times 75{,}000}{9{,}00{,}000} = 1$ month

(vi) Lag in period of Outstanding wages $= \dfrac{12 \times \text{Wages outstanding}}{\text{Wages}}$

$= \dfrac{12 \times 25{,}000}{60{,}000} = 0.5$ month

(vii) Lag in period of Outstanding overhead $= \dfrac{12 \times \text{overhead outstanding}}{\text{Overheads}}$

$= \dfrac{12 \times 95{,}000}{4{,}20{,}000 + 7{,}20{,}000} = 1$ month

(c) Number of units at 80% capacity $= \dfrac{60{,}000}{50} \times 80{,}000 = 96{,}000$

(d) Calculation of cost per unit

Fixed overhead $= 60{,}000 \times 12 = \text{Rs.}7{,}20{,}000$

Fixed overhead per unit for 96,000 units $= \dfrac{7{,}20{,}000}{96{,}000} = \text{Rs. } 7.50$

Cost per unit-Material	=	15
Wages	=	10
Variable overhead	=	7
Fixed overhead	=	7.50
		39.50

Overhead per unit = 7 + 7.50 + = Rs.14.50

Cost per unit for work- in- progress		Rs.
Material 100%	=	15
Wages 60% of Rs.10	=	6
Overhead 30% of Rs.14.50	=	4.35
		25.35

EXERCISE

THEORY

I. Choose the correct answer for the following.

1. Capital invested in Current Asset is known as —
(i) Gross Working Capital (ii) Net Working Capital (iii) Debenture (iv) Preference Share Capital
2. The difference between the Current Assets and Current Liabilities is called —
(i) Gross Working Capital (ii) Net Worth (iii) Net Working Capital (iv) Capital Employed
3. The process of conversion of Cash into Raw material - Finished goods - Sales - Cash is called —
(i) Continuous Cycle (ii) Operating Cycle (iii) Performance Cycle (iv) Non-operating Cycle
4. The Working Capital maintained to meet the contingencies like strike, rise in prices etc., is called —
(i) Fixed Working Capital (ii) Regular Working Capital (iii) Variable Working Capital (iv) Reserve Working Capital
5. The amount of Working Capital required to meet the seasonal or special need is known as —
(i) Variable Working Capital (ii) Permanent Working Capital (iii) Reserve Working Capital (iv) Fixed Working Capital
6. Idle fund is created in a company due to —
(i) Shortage of Working Capital (ii) Optimum Working Capital (iii) Excess Working Capital (iv) Normal Working Capital
7. It is difficult to meet the day-to-day activities due to —
(i) Excess Working Capital (ii) Shortage of Working Capital (iii) Optimum Working Capital (iv) Normal Working Capital
8. The quantum of Working Capital depends upon —
(i) Standard costing (ii) Banks (iii) Government (iv) Size of the business
9. The requirement of Working Capital is more during the period of —
(i) Prosperity (ii) Depression (iii) Calamity (iv) Strike
10. The desirable Working Capital should be —
(i) Excess (ii) Shortage (iii) Optimum (iv) Abnormal

[**Ans:** 1. (i) 2 (iii) 3. (ii) 4 (iv) 5. (i) 6 (iii) 7. (ii) 8. (iv) 9. (i) 10. (iii)]

II. Answer the following questions

1. Define Working Capital. Explain the concept of Working Capital.
2. Explain the different types of Working Capital according to concept.
3. Explain the different types of Working Capital on the basis of time.
4. Define Working Capital. Distinguish between permanent Working Capital and temporary Working Capital.
5. What is Working Capital? State the Operating Cycle concept of Working Capital.
6. Illustrate with a model about the Gross Working Capital and Net Working Capital.
7. Define Working Capital. Explain the concept of Optimum Working Capital.
8. What is Working Capital? State the merits of Optimum Working Capital.
9. Explain the limitations of Excess Working Capital and Inadequate Working Capital.
10. "Optimum Working Capital eliminates the limitations of excess and inadequate Working Capital" - Comment.
11. Explain the factors determining the Working Capital requirement.
12. What are the procedures in the estimation of Working Capital requirement?
13. Define Working Capital. State a model of the Statement of Working Capital requirement.
14. What is Working Capital? Distinguish between Gross Operating Cycle and Net Operating Cycle.
15. Write short notes on the following:
(i) Gross Working Capital, (ii) Net Working capital (iii) Gross Working Capital (iv) Net Operating Cycle (v) Operating Cycle (vi) Optimum Working Capital (vii) Excess Working Capital (viii) Inadequate Working Capital

(ix) Statement of Working Capital requirement (x) Fixed Working Capital (xi) Variable Working Capital (xii) Working Capital.

1. Calculate the operating cycle in days, for a company from the following:

	Rs.
Cost of Average Stock maintained	
Raw Material	2,35,000
Work-in-progress	2,50,000
Finished Goods	3,70,000
Purchase of Raw material	19,00,000
Raw material consumption	20,00,000
Cost of Production	31,00,000
Sales	39,00,000
Average Total Debtors outstanding	1,00,000
Average Total Creditors outstanding	90,000
The information stated above are meant for one year.	

(**Ans :** 111 days)

2. Calculate the estimated Working Capital from the following.

	Rs.
Closing Stock	90,000
Estimated Credit Sales	9,30,000
Wages	2,12,000
Factory Overhead	1,79,000
Administrative Overhead	3,20,000
Selling and Distribution Overhead	75,000

Average credit period is 7 weeks; Lag in payment of wages 3 weeks and Lag in payment of overheads 5 weeks.
(**Ans :** Rs.1,68,653)

3. KM Ltd., provided the following estimated values:

		Rs.
Average credit given for sales:	Inland 4 weeks	15,70,000
	Export 8 weeks	20,50,000
Lag in payment of expenses:	Wages 3 weeks	2,74,000
	Overheads 4 weeks	1,94,000
Closing stock		1,20,000

Prepare a statement of estimated Working Capital requirement. Add 10% for contingencies.

(**Ans :** Rs.5,46,235)

4. Forecast the Working Capital requirement from the following.

Projected Sales	Rs. 50,00,000
Rate of Net Profit on Sales	15%
Average credit period allowed to Debtors	6 weeks
Average credit period allowed by Creditors	3 weeks
Average Stock carrying	5 weeks
Direct cost	Rs.2,50,000
Contingencies to be allowed	10%

(**Ans :** Rs.7,93,335)

5. K Ltd., provided the following information related to the requirement of Working Capital.

Particulars	*Average period of Credit*	*Estimated Values (Rs)*
Purchase of materials	3 weeks	70,00,000
Wages	3 weeks	9,40,000
Salaries	1 month	10,00,000
Rent	2 months	2,40,000
Selling expenses	2 months	3,50,000
Cash Sales		45,00,000
Credit Sales	60 days	64,00,000
Stock		2,76,000

Estimate the Working Capital requirement.

(**Ans :** Rs.2,29,846)

6. Calculate the estimated Working Capital from the following:

Sales (20 days credit)	Rs. 24,00,000
Rate for Gross Profit on cost of production	20%
Raw materials	Rs. 9,00,000
Wages (Lag in payment 3 weeks)	Rs. 3,00,000
Manufacturing expenses (Lag in payment 1 weeks)	Rs. 2,50,000
Administration expenses (Lag in payment 2 weeks)	Rs. 3,50,000
Selling expenses (Lag in payment 2 week)	Rs. 1,70,000
Rent to be received (Lag in payment one and half month)	Rs. 1,20,000
Credit from the suppliers of raw material	3 months
Stock of raw material maintained	One and half month
Stock of Finished goods	2 months
Cash balance to be maintained	Rs. 1,40,000
Add for contingencies	10%

(**Ans :** Rs.1,27,895)

7. KT Ltd., provided the following information related to the estimation of the requirement of Working Capital.

	Rs.
Stock of Raw material	1,25,000
Stock of Finished goods	1,99,000
Sales : Inland (4 weeks credit)	21,50,000
Export (10 weeks credit)	45,50,000
Estimated expenses (Lag in payment)	
Wages and salary (1 months)	19,00,000
Purchase of material (3 weeks)	22,00,000
Rent and rates (1 months)	1,00,000
Miscellaneous expenses (3 weeks)	1,10,000
Directors remuneration (1 month)	90,000
Advance payments	
Transport expenses (3 months)	50,000
Average amount of undrawn profit	70,000

70% of inland sales and 50% of export sales are on credit basis. Out of the total purchase 60% are on credit basis. Allow 10% for contingencies.

Calculate the estimated Working Capital requirement.

(**Ans :** Rs.6,92,183)

8. The details of cost consumed by a product manufactured by K Ltd., are Direct material 40%; Direct labour 30%; Overhead 15%.

The related information for Working Capital are as follows.

(i) The expected output is 50,000 units.

(ii) Raw material will remain in store for an average period of 1 month.

(iii) Material will be in process for an average period of one and half month.

(iv) Finished goods are expected to be in store for an average period of 1 month.

(v) The Debtors are allowed a credit period of two and half months.

(vi) The Suppliers allowed a credit period of 1 month.

(vii) Selling price is Rs.50 per unit.

Prepare a statement of Working Capital requirement.

(**Ans :** Rs.9,63,541)

9. Calculate the estimated Working Capital from the following:

(i) Elements of total cost of production-material 50%, labour 30% and overhead 20%.

(ii) Profit is 25% on sales.

(iii) Estimated Sales 2,00,000 units @ Rs.20 per unit.

(iv) Suppliers allowed a credit period of one month and the Debtors are allowed a credit period of one and half months.

(v) The stock position is, Raw material half months, Work-in-progress one and half months and Finished goods 1 month.

(vi) Work-in-progress is considered as 60% on cost of production.

(vii) Add 15% for contingencies.

(**Ans :** Rs.9,12,500)

10. Calculate the Working Capital requirement of W.Doyle Ltd., from the following.

Element of Cost Per Unit	Rs.
Direct material	900
Direct wages	600
Overheads	300
Profit	250
Selling price	2,050

Additional Information:

(i) Number of units to be produced is 1,00,000

(ii) Stock of Raw material average 3 weeks

(iii) Stock of Work-in-progress average 3 weeks

(iv) Stock of Finished goods average 2 weeks

(v) Credit period allowed by Suppliers average 3 weeks

(vi) Credit period allowed to Debtors average 2 weeks

Assume that the production is in all the weeks of the year and the Work-in-progress is in 50% stage of completion and with full material consumption.

(Ans : Rs.16,07,690)

11. KMWD Ltd., provided the following estimated values as on 31st March 2007.

Element of Cost (per unit)	*Rs.*
Direct material	1400
Direct wages	1100
Direct expenses	500
Overhead	900
Cost of sales	3900
Profit	300
Selling price	4200

Additional Information:

(i) Output 30,000 units.

(ii) Stock of raw material 2 weeks on an average.

(iii) Work-in-progress (Stages of completion: 100% Material, 70% Labour, 60% Overhead and 50%, Direct expenses) 2 weeks on an average.

(iv) Stock of Finished goods 2 weeks on an average.

(v) Credit allowed by Suppliers 4 weeks on an average.

(vi) Credit allowed to Debtors 3 weeks on an average.

(vii) Credit Purchase is 70% of the total Purchase and Credit Sales in 80% of the total Sales.

(viii) Cash in hand and bank balance is expected to be Rs.10,00,000.

Prepare a statement of Working Capital requirement.

(Ans : Rs.1,37,96,154)

12. Prepare a statement of Working Capital from the following.

Element of Cost Per Unit	*Rs.*
Direct material	550
Direct labour	450
Overheads	200
Total Cost	1200

Additional information:

(i) Output 50,000 units and expected profit is Rs.70 per unit.

(ii) Stock of Raw material and Finished goods are on an average of 4 weeks and 3 weeks respectively.

(iii) Stock of Work-in-progress is on an average two and half weeks. The stages of completion of Work-in-progress is full material, 60% labour and 70% overhead.

(iv) Lag in payment of wages is 3 weeks on an average.

(v) Lag in payment of overheads is two and half weeks on an average.

(vi) Rent to be received is Rs.2,00,000 and the lag in payment is three and half weeks on an average.

(vii) Creditors allowed a credit period of 4 weeks.

(viii) Debtors are allowed a credit period of three and half weeks.

(ix) Cash balance to be maintained is estimated as Rs.10,00,000.

(x) Credit Purchase is 70% and Credit Sales is 50%.

(**Ans :** Rs.1,13,33,171)

13. MW Ltd provides the following information with respect to the estimation of Working Capital requirement for 31st March, 2007 as follows.

(a) Position of non-current assets and liabilities.

	Rs.
Share Capital	30,00,000
General Reserve	4,50,000
Debentures	5,00,000
Loan	4,00,000
Fixed Assets	35,70,000

(b) Element of Cost

Material	50%
Labour	20%
Overheads	15%

(c) Additional Information

(i) Estimated annual sales 22,00,000 units @ Rs.10 per unit.

(ii) Credit allowed by suppliers is two and half months.

(iii) Credit allowed to customers is two months.

(iv) Stock conversion periods are given as, raw material one and half months. Work-in-progress three - fourth of a month. Finished goods one month.

(v) Administration overhead Rs.7,20,000, Selling overhead Rs.5,90,000.

(vi) Cash Balance Rs.1,50,000.

Prepare a statement of estimated Working Capital requirement and the projected Profit and Loss Account and Balance Sheet as on 31st March 2007.

(**Ans :** Rs.16,77,683)

14. Calculate the estimated Working Capital and Net Profit from the following.
    (i) Estimated Sales Rs.75,00,000 and the selling price is above 25% on cost.
    (ii) The estimated Fixed cost is Rs.20,00,000 and Variable cost is 20% of the sales.
    (iii) The expected Stock turnover is 4 times a year.
    (iv) 60% of sales and 50% Purchase are on credit basis.
    (v) Credit period allowed by suppliers are 1 month and the credit period allowed to customers are 2 months.
    (vi) The requirement of Working Capital related to expenses are for one month.
    (vii) Fixed and variable cost estimated are excluding the direct material cost.

    (**Ans :** Rs.24,50,000)

15. KMWD Ltd., provided the following estimated values for April 2007 to September 2007.
    (i) The cost per unit of the product manufactured by the company are Direct material Rs.20, Direct labour Rs.20 and Variable overhead Rs.10. The Fixed overhead per month is Rs.2,40,000.
    (ii) The expected number of units sold are:

January	5000	May	4400
February	4500	June	4000
March	5200	July	4400
April	4600	August	5200

    (iii) Selling price is Rs.120 per unit.
    (iv) The lag in payment for Direct material is 1 month, Wages is half a month and Variable overhead is one month.
    (v) Fifty percent of Sale is on credit basis and the settlement is done on the following months.
    (vi) Sixty percent of Purchase of material is considered as on credit.

    Prepare a statement of Working Capital requirement on month by month basis for six months from the month of March 2007.

    (**Ans :** Rs.1,30,000; Rs.1,24,000; Rs.88,000; Rs.96,000; Rs.92,000; Rs.48,000)

16. Calculate lag in payments of Creditors, Stock and time allowed to Debtors from the following.

	Rs.
Purchase of material	1,90,000
Credit sales	3,50,000
Cash sales	2,00,000
Wages	1,40,000
Overheads - Manufacturing	70,000
- Administration and Selling	55,000
Stock	47,500
Sundry Creditors	32,500
Debtors	50,000

(**Ans :** Rs.1.425; 1,714; 2.05)

17. The cost details of a manufacturing company at 60% capacity as on 31st March 2007 are stated as follows.

(i)	Number of units produced	1,20,000
(ii)	Elements of Cost and Sales per unit are	Rs.
	Material	66
	Wages	42
	Variable Overheads	24
	Fixed Overheads	48
	Profit	12
	Selling Price	192

(iii) The details of Current Assets and Current Liabilities are stated as follows:

	Rs.
Sundry Debtors	10,00,000
Sundry Creditors	5,00,000
Wages outstanding	2,50,000
Overheads outstanding	2,00,000
Stock - Raw material (2,000 units)	1,32,000
Work-in-progress (3000 units)	2,30,000
Finished goods (2500 units)	4,50,000

(iv) Stages of completion of Work-in-progress are material 100%, Wages 70% and Overheads 50%.

Estimate the Working Capital of the company at 90% capacity and also the additional Working Capital required.

Assume that there is no change in lag in periods due to increase in capacity.

(Ans : Rs.18,70,950)

❑ ❑ ❑

7

MARGINAL COSTING

The technique of analysing the changes of Cost due to the changes in Volume of Production is called Marginal Costing. Cost of production is classified into Fixed cost and Variable cost. The Fixed cost remains constant upto certain level of production. The variable cost changes due to the changes in volume of production. The variable cost is otherwise known as marginal cost. Hence, Marginal costing analyses the relationship of the changes of Variable cost due to changes in Volume of production.

Meaning of Marginal Cost

The Institute of Cost and Management Accountants, London defines marginal cost as "the amount of a given volume of output by which aggregate costs are changed if the volume of output is increased by one unit."

Blocker and Weltmere define, "Marginal cost is the increase or decrease in total cost which results from producing or selling additional or fewer units of a product or from a change in the method of production or distribution such as the one of improved machinery,addition or exclusion of a product or territary or selection of an additional sales channel."

According to these definitions marginal cost means additional or difference in cost due to the increase or decrease of producing one unit from the normal production.

Since Marginal cost means total variable cost, it includes the prime cost and variable overhead.

(Eg) Material cost per unit is Rs 10, Labour cost per unit is Rs 12, Variable overhead is Rs 7 per unit and number of units produced is 1000 units.

The marginal cost may be calculated as follows:

	Per unit Rs.	*Total Rs.*
Direct Material	10	10,000
Direct Labour	12	12,000
Prime cost	22	22,000
Variable overhead	7	7,000
Marginal cost or variable cost	29	29,000

Marginal costing

The Institute of Cost and Management Accountants, London defined Marginal costing as " The ascertainment of marginal cost and of the effect on profit of changes in volume or type of output by differentiating between fixed cost and variable cost".

It is clear from the definition that marginal costing is a technique of analysing the marginal (or variable) cost and profit in relation to the changes in volume of production.

Characteristics of Marginal Costing

The important characteristics of marginal costing are stated as follows.

1. The total cost of production is classified into fixed and variable cost. Hence, all the functional cost like production, administration and selling cost are grouped into fixed cost and variable cost.
2. Marginal costing technique helps the management to take various managerial decisions.
3. Marginal cost technique is adopted to value stock of finished goods and work-in-progress.
4. The technique of contribution is adopted to fix the price of the products.
5. Variable cost is considered as the important cost of the product.

Assumptions of Marginal Costing

The following are the important assumptions of marginal costing.

1. All the functional elements of cost like production, administration and selling and distribution costs should be classified into fixed and variable cost.
2. Variable cost per unit would remain constant. It varies according to the changes in volume of production.
3. Fixed cost remains constant for all the levels of production. Hence, fixed cost per unit varies.
4. The selling price per unit should remain constant at all levels of activity.
5. The volume of production should be the only factor of production which influences the cost.

Advantages of Marginal Costing

The following are the advantages of marginal costing.

1. It is simple to operate and easy to understand.
2. It helps the management to take various managerial decisions.
3. It facilitates to fix the prices.
4. Marginal costing technique can be applied for profit planning.
5. It facilitates for taking decision regarding the acceptance or rejection of a bulk order.
6. Marginal Costing helps the management to calculate the Break- even-point.
7. It facilitates the management to decide the optimum product mix, when the company is producing more than one product.

Limitations of Marginal Costing

The following are the important limitations of marginal costing.

1. Changes in the selling price affects the results of marginal costing.
2. The assumption that the fixed cost remains constant may not be always correct, since it may also vary due to various reasons.
3. Marginal costing technique excludes fixed cost for various managerial decisions.

4. The assumption that the variable cost per unit remains constant is practically not possible always. Increase in volume of production may reduce the variable cost per unit.
5. Marginal costing technique considers only the value of contribution for deciding the profitability of a product. It ignores the time factor. Product which gives maximum contribution the best product compared to other, irrespective of the duration of production.

Calculation of Costing Profit by Absorption Costing and Managerial Costing Methods

In the Absorption Costing method Costing Profit is calculated by sales minus all the cost. For this purpose total cost is classified according to the functions like manufacturing, administration and selling and distribution. Hence, it is possible to ascertain the cost in stage by stage in Absorption Costing method. But in Marginal Costing total cost is divided into Fixed cost and Variable cost.

Calculation of costing profit by absorption costing method and marginal costing method

(a) Calculation of costing profit by Absorption Costing Method:

Statement of Cost

Particulars	*Amount (Rs.)*
Direct material	x x x
Direct wages	x x x
Direct expenses	x x x
PRIME COST	x x x
Add : Factory overhead	x x x
WORKS COST	x x x
Add : Administration overhead	x x x
COST OF PRODUCTION	x x x
Add : Selling & distribution overhead	x x x
COST OF SALES	x x x
COSTING PROFIT	x x x
SALES	x x x

(b) Calculation of Costing profit by Marginal cost method.

A model of the Statement of cost under Marginal Costing Method is stated as follows.

Statement of Cost

Particulars		*Amount Rs.*
Sales		x x x
Less: Variable cost:		
Direct material	x x x	
Direct wages	x x x	
Direct expenses	x x x	
Variable Factory overhead	x x x	
Variable Administration overhead	x x x	
Variable selling overhead	x x x	x x x

Contribution		x x x
Less : Fixed cost:		
Fixed Factory overhead	x x x	
Fixed Administration overhead	x x x	
Fixed selling & distribution overhead	x x x	x x x
Costing Profit		x x x

Illustration: 1

Prepare a statement of cost by

(a) Absorption costing method and

(b) Marginal costing method

Particulars	*Period-1 Rs.*	*Period-2 Rs.*	*Period-3 Rs.*
Direct material consumed	90,000	70,000	85,000
Direct wages paid	44,000	37,000	30,000
Direct expenses	17,000	12,000	20,000
Sales	2,50,000	2,40,000	2,70,000
Factory overhead	24,000	31,000	32,000
Administration overhead	37,000	35,000	39,000
Selling & Distribution overhead	20,000	22,000	25,000

20% of the administration overhead and 30% of the selling overhead are variable in nature.

Solution:

(a) Statement of cost by Absorption Costing Method

Particulars	*Period-1 Rs.*	*Period-2 Rs.*	*Period-3 Rs.*
Direct material consumed	90,000	70,000	85,000
Direct wages	44,000	37,000	30,000
Direct expenses	17,000	12,000	20,000
Prime Cost	151,000	119,000	135,000
Add : Factory overhead	24,000	31,000	32,000
Factory Cost	175,000	150,000	167,000
Add : Administration overhead	37,000	35,000	39,000
Cost of Production	212,000	185,000	206,000
Add : Selling & Distribution overhead	20,000	22,000	25,000
Cost of Sales	232,000	207,000	231,000
Costing Profit	18,000	33,000	39,000
Sales	2,50,000	2,40,000	2,70,000

(b) Statement of cost by Marginal Costing Method

Particulars	*Period-1*	*Period-2*	*Period-3*
SALES	2,50,000	2,40,000	2,70,000
Less : Variable costs:			
Direct material consumed	90,000	70,000	85,000
Direct wages	44,000	37,000	30,000
Direct expenses	17,000	12,000	20,000
Factory overhead	24,000	31,000	32,000
Variable Administration OH	6,400	7,000	7,800
Variable Selling & Distribution OH	6,000	6,600	7,500
Total Variable Cost	188,400	163,600	182,300
Contribution (Sales - V.C)	61,600	76,400	87,700
Less : Fixed Cost			
Fixed Administration OH	29,600	28,000	31,200
Fixed Selling & distribution OH	14,000	15,400	17,500
Total Fixed Cost	43,600	43,400	48,700
Costing profit	18,000	33,000	39,000

Illustration: 2

A manufacturing company produces three products namely X,Y and Z. The information related to the production and sales of these products for 3 months ending 30th June 2007 are as follows.

		X (Rs.)	*Y (Rs.)*	*Z (Rs.)*
Direct material		24,000	14,000	29,000
Direct wages		15,000	17,500	24,500
Factory overhead -	Fixed	7,500	11,000	13,000
	Variable	6,000	5,000	8,000
Administration overhead -	Fixed	14,000	12,000	9,000
	Variable	9,000	8,000	7,000
Selling and Distribution overhead -	Fixed	10,000	9,000	5,000
	Variable	8,500	9,500	5,500
Sales 200,000		140,000	150,000	

Prepare a statement of cost by (a) Marginal Costing method and (b) Absorption Costing method.

(a) Statement of Cost
(Marginal Costing Method)

Particulars	*Products*			
	X Rs.	*Y Rs.*	*Z Rs.*	*Total Rs.*
Sales	200,000	140,000	150,000	490,000
Variable Costs:				
Direct material	24,000	14,000	29,000	

Direct Wages	15,000	17,500	24,500	
Variable Overhead:				
Factory	6,000	5,000	8,000	
Administration	9,000	8,000	7,000	
Selling and Distribution	8,500	9,500	5,500	
Marginal cost	62,500	54,000	74,000	190,500
Contribution	1,37,500	86,000	76,000	299,500
(Contribution = Sales – M.C)				
Less : Fixed overhead				
Factory	7,500	11,000	13,000	
Administration	14,000	12,000	9,000	
Selling and Distribution	10,000	9,000	5,000	
Total FOH	31,500	32,000	27,000	90,500
Profit: (Contribution – Fixed overhead)	106,000	54,000	49,000	209,000

(b) Statement of Cost
(Absorption Costing Method)

Particulars		*Products* X Rs.	Y Rs.	Z Rs.	*Total* Rs.
Direct material		24,000	14,000	29,000	
Direct wages		15,000	17,500	24,500	
Prime cost		39,000	31,500	53,500	124,000
Factory overhead:	Fixed	7,500	11,000	13,000	
	Variable	6,000	5,000	8,000	
Works cost		52,500	47,500	74,500	174,500
Administration overhead:	Fixed	14,000	12,000	9,000	
	Variable	9,000	8,000	7,000	
Cost of Production		75,500	67,500	90,500	233,500
Selling and Distribution overhead:					
	Fixed	10,000	9,000	5,000	
	Variable	8,500	9,500	5,500	
Cost of Sales		94,000	86,000	101,000	281,000
Costing Profit		1,06,000	54,000	49,000	209,000
Sales		200,000	140,000	150,000	490,000

Contribution:

The difference between sales and variable cost is known as Contribution. Contribution includes Fixed cost and Profit or loss. Hence, contribution can be calculated by adding the profit with the Fixed cost or deducting loss with the Fixed cost.

Contribution = Sales - Variable cost or
= Fixed cost + Profit or Loss.

Marginal Cost Equation

The equation Contribution = Sales - Variable cost is called Marginal Cost Equation. Fixed Cost or Variable Cost can be calculated through this equation.

Profit/Volume Ratio

The ratio between contribution and sales is called Profit/Volume Ratio. It is otherwise known as 'Contribution ratio' or 'Marginal ratio'.

$$\text{P/V Ratio} = \frac{\text{Contribution}}{\text{Sales}} \quad \text{or}$$

$$= \frac{\text{Sales} \quad \text{Variable Cost}}{\text{Sales}} \quad \text{or}$$

$$= \frac{\text{Fixed Cost + Profit}}{\text{Sales}} \quad \text{or}$$

$$\frac{\text{Change in Profit or Contribution}}{\text{Change in Sales}}$$

Sales for an expected profit can be calculated by P/V Ratio through the following formula

$$\text{Expected Sales} = \frac{\text{Fixed Cost + Expected Profit}}{\text{P/V Ratio}}$$

BREAK-EVEN ANALYSIS

The analysis about the relationship between Cost, Volume and Profit is called as Break-even analysis. In narrow sense, it is an analysis to know the level of production. In the broader sense, it is an analysis to find out the relationship between cost, volume and profit at different levels of sales or production.

Break-even Point:

The point of sales volume at which the total revenue is equal to the total cost is called Break-even Point. At break-even point there will be neither profit nor loss. The contribution is equal to fixed cost at this point. Break-even point is otherwise called as 'Critical Point', or 'Equilibrium Point' or 'Balancing Point'.

Break-even point can be calculated through the following formula.

$$\text{Break even Point (in units)} = \frac{\text{Fixed Cost}}{\text{Contribution per unit}}$$

$$\text{Break even Point (in value)} = \frac{\text{Fixed Cost} \times \text{Selling price per unit}}{\text{Contribution per unit}}$$

$$\text{Contribution} = \text{Sales} - \text{Variable Cost}$$

Through P/V Ratio, B.E.P can be calculated as,

$$\text{B.E.P.} = \frac{\text{Fixed Cost}}{\text{P/V Ratio}}$$

The expected sales to earn a given profit can be calculated through Break-even analysis.

$$\text{Expected Sales for an expected profit} = \frac{\text{Fixed Cost + Expected Profit}}{\text{Contribution per unit}}$$

B.E.P Chart

Break-even chart is a graphical representation of the Break-even point. Break-even point can be measured by a graph through the following procedures.

1. Number of units should be denoted in X axis and cost and revenue in Y axis.
2. Through a common scale number of units should be provided conveniently in the X axis and the amount should be marked uniformly in Y axis.
3. Mark the Fixed cost on the Y axis and draw a parallel line to X axis through the point.
4. Plot points in the graph for the total cost (Fixed cost + Variable cost) at various levels of production. Join all the points to get a straight line from the point of fixed cost at Y axis. This is called total cost line.
5. The sales value at different levels (units) of sales should be plotted in the graph. Join the points from O of the graph to get a straight line. This is called sales line.
6. The sales line cuts at a point in the Total Cost line. This point is called Break-even point.
7. A perpendicular line to X axis from this B.E.P.should be drawn. Measure the number of units in the X axis, where the perpendicular line cuts, to know the B.E.P. of sales in units.
8. A perpendicular line to Y axis from the B.E.P should be drawn to measure the value in the Y axis.This is called the B.E.P in Sales value.

The model B.E.P chart is shown as follows.

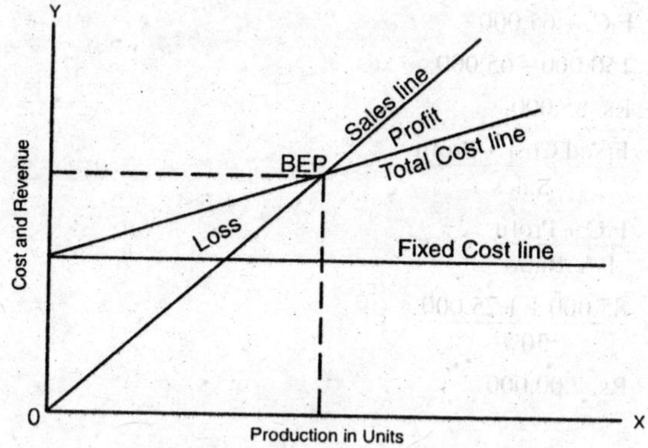

Illustration: 3

Find out the profit earned by a company during the year 2006 from the following.

Fixed Cost	Rs. 10,00,000
Variable Cost	Rs. 30 per unit
Selling Price	Rs. 75 per unit
Number of units produced	70,000.

Solution:

Sales	$= 70{,}000 \times 75$	= Rs. 52,50,000
Fixed Cost		= Rs. 10,00,000
Variable Cost	$= 70{,}000 \times 30$	= Rs. 21,00,000
S – V.C	= F.C. + Profit	
Profit	= S – V.C – F.C	
	= 52,50,000 – 21,00,000 – 10,00,000	
	= Rs. 21,50,000	

Illustration: 4

Calculate (a) P/V ratio (b) Fixed Cost (c) Sales volume to earn a profit of Rs. 125,000.

Sales, Rs. 5,00,000

Profit, Rs 65,000

Variable Cost is 70% of sales

Solution:

Sales = Rs 5,00,000

Variable Cost $= \frac{70}{100} \times 5{,}00{,}000 = \text{Rs } 350{,}000$

(a) P/V Ratio $= \frac{\text{Sales} - \text{Variable Cost}}{\text{Sales}} \times 100$

$= \frac{5{,}00{,}000 - 3{,}50{,}000}{5{,}00{,}000} \times 100 = 30\%$

(b) Contribution = Fixed Cost + Profit

Sales – Variable Cost = F.C. + Profit

5,00,000 – 350,000 = F.C. + 65,000

F.C. = 150,000 – 65,000

= Rs. 85,000

(c) P/V Ratio $= \frac{\text{Fixed Cost} + \text{Profit}}{\text{Sales}}$

Sales $= \frac{\text{F.C} + \text{Profit}}{\text{P/V Ratio}}$

$= \frac{85{,}000 + 1{,}25{,}000}{30\%}$

= Rs. 7,00,000

Illustration: 5

Calculate the P/V ratio if the fixed cost for manufacturing 1000 units of a product is Rs. 4500 per month variable cost is Rs.22.50 per unit and Selling price is Rs.30 per unit. If the selling price is reduced by 10%, find out the P/V ratio. Also calculate the number of units to be sold to earn the present total profit.

Solution:

(i) Calculation of present P/V Ratio:

Sales	=	1000 × 30	=	Rs 30,000
Variable cost	=	1000 × 22.50	=	Rs 22,500
Contribution	=	Sales - Variable Cost	=	30,000 – 22,500
			=	Rs 7,500
P/V Ratio	=	$\frac{\text{Contribution} \times 100}{\text{Sales}}$	=	$\frac{7{,}500 \times 100}{30{,}000} = 25\%$
Profit	=	Contribution – Fixed Cost		
	=	7,500 – 4,500	=	Rs. 3,000

(ii) Calculation of P/V Ratio when selling price is reduced by 10%

Selling price = 30 – 10% of 30 = 30 – 3

= Rs. 27 per unit

Sales = 27 × 1,000 = Rs. 27,000

Variable Cost = 1,000 × 22.50

= Rs. 22,500

Contribution = 27,000 – 22,500

= Rs. 4,500

Contribution per unit = $\frac{4,500}{1,000}$ = Rs.4.50

P/V Ratio = $\frac{4,500 \times 100}{27,000}$ = 16.67%

(iii) Expected Sales earn the present profit of Rs. 3000 = $\frac{\text{Fixed Cost + Expected Profit}}{\text{Contribution per unit}}$

= $\frac{4500 + 3000}{4.50}$

= $\frac{7,500}{4.50}$ = *1,667 units*

Expected Sales in value = 1,667 × 27

= Rs. 45,009

Illustration: 6

Calculate (i) P/V ratio (ii) sales required to earn a profit of Rs 155,000. (iii) the profit if sales is Rs. 10,00,000 from the following information.

Year	*Sales* *Rs.*	*Profit* *Rs.*
2006	300,000	50,000
2007	500,000	120,000

Solution:

(i) P/V Ratio = $\frac{\text{Changes in Profit}}{\text{Changes in Sales}}$

Changes in Sales = 5000,000 – 300,000 = Rs. 200,000

Changes in Profit = 120,000 – 50,000 = Rs 70,000

P/V Ratio = $\frac{70,000}{2,00,000}$ × 100 = 35%

(ii) Contribution = 5000,000 × 35% = $\frac{500,000 \times 35}{100}$ = Rs. 175,000

Contribution = Fixed Cost + Profit

175,000 = F.C + 120,000

Fixed Cost = 175,000 – 120,000 = Rs. 55,000

$$\text{Expected sales earn profit of Rs. 150,000} = \frac{\text{Fixed Cost + Expected Profit}}{\text{P/V Ratio}}$$

$$= \frac{55{,}000 + 155{,}000}{35\%}$$

$$= \frac{210{,}000 \times 100}{35}$$

$$= \text{Rs. } 600{,}000$$

(iii) Calculation of profit when sales is Rs 10,00,000:

Contribution = 10,00,000 × 35%

= Rs 350,000

Contribution = F.C + Profit

350,000 = 55,000 + Profit

Profit = 350,000 – 55,000 = Rs. 295,000

Illustration: 7

Calculate B.E.P in units and sales value from the following.

Production, 9,000 units

Total Fixed Cost	Rs 140,000
Variable Cost	Rs 42 per unit
Selling Price	Rs 70 per unit

Solution:

Sales = 9000 × 70 = Rs. 630,000

Variable Cost = 9000 × 42 = Rs. 378,000

Contribution per unit = Sales - V.C = 70 – 42 = Rs.28

$$\text{Break-even point} = \frac{\text{F.C}}{\text{Contribution per unit}}$$

$$= \frac{140{,}000}{28} = 5000 \text{ units}$$

B.E.P in Sales value = 5000 × 70 = Rs. 350,000

Illustration: 8

WD & Co. provided the following information

	Rs.
Fixed factory overheads	150,000
Fixed selling overheads	50,000
Variable manufacturing cost per unit	25
Variable selling cost per unit	15
Selling price per unit	90

Calculate B.E.P and Number of units to be sold to earn a profit of Rs.100,000

Solution:

Fixed Cost = 150,000 + 50,000 = Rs 200,000

Variable Cost per unit = 25 + 15 = Rs. 40

Sales = Rs. 90

Contribution = S – V.C = 90 – 40 = Rs. 50 per unit

B.E.P. = $\frac{\text{Fixed Cost}}{\text{Contribution per unit}} = \frac{2,00,000}{50}$

= 4000 units

B.E.P in value = 4000 × 90

= Rs. 3,60,000

Number of units be sold earn a profit of Rs. 100,000 = $\frac{\text{F.C + Expected Profit}}{\text{Contribution per unit}}$

= $\frac{200,000 + 100,000}{50}$

= $\frac{300,000}{50}$ = 6000 units

Illustration: 9

The following information are related to a manufacturing company.

Selling price per unit - Rs. 200

Fixed Cost - Rs. 6,30,000

Variable cost per unit:

Direct material - 50

Direct wages - 40

Variable overheads - 50% of direct wages.

Calculate (i) P/V ratio (ii) Sales required to earn a profit of Rs.2,70,000 (iii) Break-even sales with the help of P/V ratio.

Solution:

Sales = Rs 200 per unit

Variable cost per unit = 50 + 40 + (50% of Rs 40)

= 50 + 40 + 20

= Rs.110

Contribution = S – V.C

= 200 – 110

= Rs.90 per unit

(i) P/V Ratio = $\frac{\text{Contribution}}{\text{Sales}} \times 100$

= $\frac{90}{200} \times 100 = 45\%$

(ii) Sales required to earn a profit of Rs. 2,00,000

$$= \frac{\text{F.C + Expected Profit}}{\text{Contribution per unit}}$$

$$= \frac{630{,}000 + 270{,}000}{90}$$

$$= \frac{9{,}00{,}000}{90}$$

$$= 10{,}000 \text{ units}$$

i.e., $10{,}000 \times 200$ = Rs. 20,00,000 **in value**

(iii) $$\text{B.E.P} = \frac{\text{F.C}}{\text{P/V Ratio}} = \frac{6{,}30{,}000}{45\%}$$

$$= \frac{6{,}30{,}000}{45} \times 100 = \text{Rs.}14{,}00{,}000\ (14{,}00{,}000/200{=}7000 \text{ units})$$

Illustration: 10

The fixed cost for manufacturing a product is Rs 180,000. The variable cost is 55% of sales. If sales are Rs 7,00,000 at 100% capacity, calculate the break-even point and percentage capacity at B.E.P. Also calculate the profit at 70% capacity.

Solution:

Variable cost $= 55\% \text{ of Sales} = \frac{55}{100} \times 700{,}000$

$= \text{Rs. } 385{,}000$

Contribution = Sales – Variable Cost = 700,000 – 385,000 = Rs.315,000

Fixed Cost = Rs. 180,000

$$\text{B.E.P} = \frac{\text{Fixed Cost}}{\text{P/V Ratio}}$$

$$\text{P/V Ratio} = \frac{\text{Contribution}}{\text{Sales}} \times 100$$

$$= \frac{315{,}000}{700{,}000} \times 100 = 45\%$$

$$\text{B.E.P.} = \frac{180{,}000}{45\%} = \frac{180{,}000 \times 100}{45}$$

$$= \text{Rs. } 400{,}000$$

$$\text{Capacity} = \frac{100 \times 400{,}000}{700{,}000} = 57.14\%$$

$$\text{Sales at 70\% of Capacity} = 700{,}000 \times \frac{70}{100}$$

$$= \text{Rs. } 490{,}000$$

Fixed Cost = Rs. 180,000

Variable Cost = 55% × 490,000

= Rs. 269,500

Total cost = 180,000 + 269,500

= Rs.449,500

Profit = Sales – Total Cost

= 490,000 – 449,500 = Rs. 40,500

Illustration: 11

The sales of a company for 2 different periods are 4,000 units and 7,000 units, and the profits are Rs 80,000 and Rs 170,000. Calculate (i) Fixed cost (ii) Break-even point, (iii) Number of units to be sold to earn a profit of Rs 200,000. Assume selling price as Rs 100 per unit.

Solution:

$$\text{P/V Ratio} = \frac{\text{Difference in Profit of two periods}}{\text{Difference in Sales of two periods}}$$

$$= \frac{170{,}000 \quad 80{,}000}{(7{,}000 \times 100) \quad (4{,}000 \times 100)}$$

$$= \frac{90{,}000 \times 100}{300{,}000} = 30\%$$

Contribution = (4,000 × 100) × 30/100 = Rs. 120,000

Contribution = Fixed cost + Profit

120,000 = F.C + 80,000

(i) Fixed Cost = 120,000 - 80,000 = Rs. 40,000

(ii) BEP = F.C./P.V. ratio = 40,000/0.30 = Rs.1,33,333

(iii) Sales to earn

$$\text{a profit of Rs. 200,000} = \frac{\text{F.C + Expected Profit}}{\text{P/V Ratio}}$$

$$= \frac{40{,}000 + 200{,}000}{30\%}$$

$$= \frac{240{,}000 \times 100}{30}$$

= Rs. 800,000 i.e., **8,000 units**

Illustration: 12

A manufacturing company is providing the following information

Fixed expenses	Rs 120,000
Selling price per unit	Rs 60/-
Variable expenses - Material	Rs 21 per unit
Wages	Rs 15 per unit

Draw a break-even chart and verify the result through a schedule. Also calculate the new break-even point if the selling price is reduced by 20%.

Solution :

Fixed Cost = Rs.120,000

Variable cost per unit = Rs.36

Selling price per unit = Rs.60

Contribution = Selling price- Variable cost

= 60 – 36 = Rs.24

$$\text{B.E.P.} = \frac{\text{Fixed Cost}}{\text{Contribution per unit}}$$

$$= \frac{120{,}000}{24} = 5{,}000 \text{ units}$$

If selling price is reduced by 20%

Selling price per unit = 60 – (20% of 60)

= 60 - 12 = Rs. 48

Contribution = 48 – 36 = Rs. 12 per unit

$$\text{New B.E.P} = \frac{120{,}000}{12} = 10{,}000 \text{ units}$$

Calculation of Break-even Point

Units	*Fixed Cost*	*Variable Cost (Cost Rs. 36 per unit)*	*Total Cost*	*Sales at Rs. 60 per unit*	*Sales at Rs. 48 per unit*
	Rs.	*Rs.*	*Rs.*	*Rs.*	*Rs.*
500	120,000	18,000	138,000	30,000	24,000
1000	120,000	36,000	156,000	60,000	48,000
2500	120,000	90,000	210,000	150,000	120,000
5,000	120,000	180,000	300,000	300,000	240,000
7,500	120,000	270,000	390,000	450,000	360,000
10,000	120,000	360,000	480,000	600,000	480,000
12,500	120,000	450,000	570,000	750,000	600,000
14,000	120,000	504,000	624,000	840,000	672,000
15,000	120,000	540,000	660,000	900,000	720,000
20,000	1,20,000	7,20,000	8,40,000	12,00,000	9,60,000
25,000	1,20,000	9,00,000	10,20,000	15,00,000	12,00,000

It is clear from the above table that the B.E.P is 5,000 units when selling price is Rs 60/- per unit, since total cost is equal to total sales at this point. When selling price is Rs 48/- per unit B.E.P. is 10000 units.

Values of BEP are graphically represented as follows.

B.E.P. Chart

(i) B.E.P. Chart when Selling Price is Rs. 60.

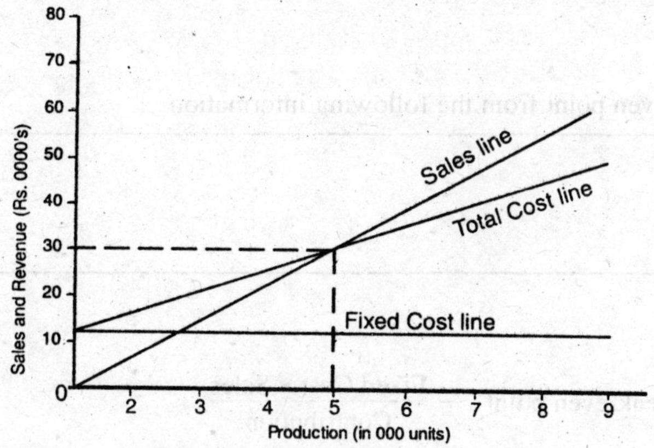

(ii) B.E.P. Chart when Selling Price is Rs. 48.

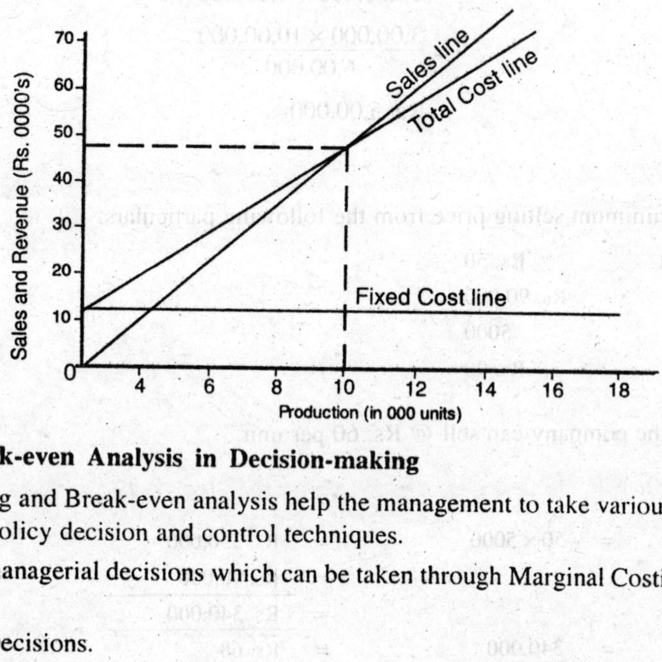

Application of Break-even Analysis in Decision-making

Marginal Costing and Break-even analysis help the management to take various managerial decisions, like profit planning, policy decision and control techniques.

The important managerial decisions which can be taken through Marginal Costing technique are stated as follows.

1. Pricing Decisions.
2. Decisions regarding the acceptance or rejection of foreign orders.
3. Profit Planning.
4. Problems of Key of Limiting Factor.
5. Make or Buy Decisions.
6. The effect of changes in selling price.
7. Selection of suitable sales mix.
8. Determination of optimum level of activity.
9. Measurement of performance.

1. Pricing Decisions

Marginal costing technique assists the management in fixing prices. It suggests the management to fix price at least above the marginal cost.

Illustration: 13

Calculate Break-even point from the following information

Sales	Rs.10,00,000
Fixed Cost	Rs. 3,00,000
Variable cost	Rs. 4,00,000

Solution:

$$\text{Break-even point} = \frac{\text{Fixed Cost} \times \text{Sales}}{\text{Contribution}}$$

$$= \frac{3,00,000 \times 10,00,000}{10,00,000 \quad 4,00,000}$$

$$= \frac{3,00,000 \times 10,00,000}{6,00,000}$$

$$= \text{Rs. } 5,00,000$$

Illustration: 14

Calculate the minimum selling price from the following particulars.

Marginal cost per unit	Rs. 50
Fixed Cost	Rs. 90,000
Number of units sold	5000
Present selling price	Rs. 90

State whether the company can sell @ Rs. 60 per unit.

Solution:

Marginal Cost	=	50×5000	=	Rs. 250,000
Fixed Cost			=	Rs. 90,000
Total cost			=	Rs. 340,000
Total cost per unit	=	$\frac{340,000}{5,000}$	=	Rs. 68
Hence, present profit	=	90 - 68	=	Rs. 22 per unit
	=	22×5000	=	Rs. 110,000

When the selling price is Rs. 60

Sales	=	60×5000 = 300,000
Total cost	=	Rs. 340,000
Loss	=	340,000 – 300,000
	=	Rs. 40,000

If there is no sales then the company is facing a loss of Rs. 90,000 in the form of Fixed Cost. It can be reduced to Rs. 40,000, if selling price is @ Rs. 60 per unit.The minimum selling price should be at least Rs 68 per unit to avoid the loss.

2. Decisions regarding the acceptance of Bulk orders, Special orders, Additional orders and Export orders.

The decision by the management about the acceptance or rejection of a foreign order or special order can be taken through marginal costing technique. If a company charged the fixed cost for the period to the cost of production and sold the products for profit, then the marginal cost for the additional sales would be the profit of the company (provided the company has not yet utilised the full capacity.)

Illustration: 15

Joyce & Co. Ltd manufactures and sells 10,000 units of product 'A' @ Rs.50 per unit. The details regarding the cost of production are stated below.

	Rs.
Direct material	150,000
Direct labour	100,000
Electricity	35,000
Other Variable expenses	15,000
Fixed Manufacturing expenses	77,000
Fixed Administration expenses	33,000

The normal production capacity is 20,000 units per month.The company received an order of 7,000 units @ Rs. 40 per month from a foreign market. Advise the management whether the order can be accepted or not.

Solution:

Statement of the cost

Particulars	*Unit Rate*	*Present Capacity 50% (10000 units)*	*Additional Capacity 35% (7,000 units)*	*Total Capacity 85% (17,000 units)*
Sales (units)		10,000	7,000	17,000
Sales - value (Rs.)		500,000	280,000	780,000
Less : Variable cost				
Material (Rs.)	15	150,000	105,000	255,000
Labour (Rs.)	10	100,000	70,000	170,000
Electricity (Rs.)	3.50		35,000	24,500
Other Variable expenses	1.50	15,000	10,500	25,500
Total Variable Cost	30.00	300,000	210,000	510,000
Contribution: (Rs.)				
(Sales - Variable Cost)	20.00	200,000	70,000	270,000
Fixed cost (Rs.)		110,000	-	110,000
Profit (Rs.)		90,000	70,000	160,000

The company should accept the order since it earns an additional amount of Rs.70,000 as profit. This is due to the fact that the additional order is within 100% capacity. If the order is from local market the order should not be accepted since it affects the local sales @ Rs 50 per unit.

3. Profit Planning

Marginal costing technique can be applied for Profit planning. Profit planning means planning for future production.It is concerned with determination of the number of units to be produced in future to get maximum profit. The expected sales to earn a desired profit can be calculated through the following formula

$$\text{Expected Sales} = \frac{\text{Fixed Cost + Expected Profit}}{\text{Contribution per unit}}$$

Illustration: 16

KM & Co.Ltd provided the details regarding the cost of manufacturing one unit of a product manufactured as follows.

	Rs.
Direct material	45
Direct labour	34
Variable overheads	26
	105
Fixed overheads	50
Profit	25
Selling price	180

The capacity of the company is 60,000 units per month. The company has to reduce the selling price due to competition.Calculate the number of units the company should manufacture to earn the present profit if the selling price is reduced by 10% and 20% respectively. Assume that the present sales is 30,000 units.

Solution:

Fixed overhead = 30,000 × 50 = Rs 15,00,000

Contribution = Sales – Variable Cost

= 180 – (45 + 34 + 26)

= Rs. 75 per unit

Present profit = 30,000 × 25 = Rs. 750,000

Calculation of expected sales when selling price is reduced by 10%

Selling price = 180 – 10% of 180 = Rs.162

Contribution = 162 – 105 = Rs. 57 per unit

$$\text{Expected sales} = \frac{\text{Fixed cost + Expected profit}}{\text{Contribution per unit}}$$

$$= \frac{15{,}00{,}000 + 750{,}000}{57} = \frac{22{,}50{,}000}{57} = 39{,}474 \text{ units}$$

Calculation of expected sales when selling price is reduced by 20%

Selling price = 180 - 20% of 180 = Rs.144

Contribution = 144 - 105 = Rs.39

$$\text{Expected sales} = \frac{15,00,000 + 750,000}{39}$$

$$= \frac{22,50,000}{39} = 57,692 \text{ units}$$

4. Problems of Key or Limiting Factor

A factor which restricts the company from earning profit is called limiting factor or key factor. The limiting factor may be raw material, labour, electricity, finance, capacity of plant and sales. When a company is facing any of the limiting factor, the contribution per unit of the limiting factor should be the criterion to assess the profitability. The product which gives the highest contribution per unit of the limiting factor should be preferred. If the limiting factors are more than one, then all of the factors should be analysed.

Illustration: 17

W.Doyle & Co. is manufacturing two different products namely A and B. The cost for manufacturing these products are as follows.

	Product A (Rs.)	*Product B (Rs.)*
Materials:		
10 Kg @ Rs. 12	120	88
8 Kg @ Rs. 11		
Labour:	50	42
Fixed cost:	80	60
	250	190
Selling price:	280	230
Profit	30	40

The total number of units produced in a month are A 2000 units and B 2400 units. The raw material is the key factor. Availability of raw material is 22,000 kgs each for Product A and B.

Find out the product which gives the maximum profit through marginal costing technique.

Solution:

		Product A (per unit) Rs.	*Product B (per unit)* Rs.
Selling price		280	230
Variable cost :	Material	120	88
	Labour	50	42
		170	130
Contribution per unit (Sales - variable cost)		110	100
Contribution per 1 kg of material		110/10 = 11	100/8 = 12.50

Though product A gives more contribution per unit, product B is more profitable as per the material as key factor.

Proof:

	Product A	Product B
Maximum capacity	22,000 kgs	22,000 kgs
Material required per unit	10 kgs	8 kgs
Maximum capacity in units	$\frac{22,000}{10}$ = 2,200 units	$\frac{22,000}{8}$ = 2,750 units
Sales (Rs.)	6,16,000	6,32,500
Material (Rs)	2,64,000	2,42,000
Labour (Rs)	1,10,000	1,15,500
Fixed cost (Rs)	1,60,000	1,44,000
Total cost	5,34,000	5,01,500
Profit	82,000	1,31,000

5. Make or Buy decisions

The decision regarding whether a product should be manufactured or bought from outside can be decided through marginal costing technique. The analysis of fixed cost and variable cost of manufacturing the product should be done in this regard. According to the marginal costing technique, it is advisable to produce the product if the marginal cost (variable cost) is lower than the purchase price. It is advisable to buy the product if the purchase price is lower than the marginal cost. It is based on the technique that the fixed cost should be incurred whether the company manufacture the product or not during a period.

Illustration: 18

Joyce & Co. is manufacturing a product @ Rs 200 per unit. The product is available in the market @ Rs. 190. Advise the management whether the product can be produced or bought from the market. Also suggest the management whether to make or buy if the purchasing price is reduced from Rs.190 to Rs 140.

The cost of manufacturing one unit of the product, material Rs.90; labour Rs. 40, variable overhead Rs.20 ;and fixed cost Rs.50.

Solution :

Marginal cost (variable cost) per unit	*Rs.*
Material	90
Wages	40
Variable overhead	20
Total	150

It is advisable to produce the product when the purchase price is @ Rs.190 per unit, since the purchase price is more than the marginal cost.

When the purchase price is reduced to Rs 140 per unit, it is advisable to buy the product since the purchase price is less than the marginal cost.

6. The effect of changes in selling price

The marginal costing technique analyses and measures the effect of changes in selling price. It helps to determine the new B.E.P. due to the changes in the selling price.

Illustration: 19

KM Ltd.provided the following information

Sales	Rs.11,00,000
Variable cost	Rs. 6,60,000
Fixed cost	Rs. 2,00,000

Calculate (i) P/V ratio, BEP and Margin of safety (ii) The effect of 20% increase in selling price and (iii) The effect of 25% decrease in selling price, from the following information.

Solution :

(i)

Sales = Rs. 11,00,000

Variable cost = Rs. 6,60,000

Fixed cost = Rs. 2,00,000

Contribution = Sales - Variable cost

= 11,00,000 – 6,60,0,000 = Rs. 4,40,000

$$\text{P/V Ratio} = \frac{\text{Contribution} \times 100}{\text{Sales}} = \frac{4,40,000 \times 100}{11,00,000}$$

= 40%

$$\text{B.E.P} = \frac{\text{Fixedcost}}{\text{P/V Ratio}} = \frac{2,00,000}{40\%}$$

= Rs. 5,00,000

Margin of safety = Present Sales - Sales at B.E.P

= 11,00,000 – 5,00,000 = Rs 6,00,000

(ii) The effect of 20% increase in selling price

Sales = 11,00,000 + 20% of 11,00,000

= 11,00,000 + 2,20,000 = Rs 13.20,000

Contribution = 13,20,000 – 6,60,000 = Rs 6,60,000

$$\text{P/V ratio} = \frac{\text{Contribution} \times 100}{\text{Sales}} = \frac{6,60,000 \times 100}{13,20,000}$$

= 50%

$$\text{B.E.P} = \frac{\text{Fixed cost}}{\text{Pv ratio}} = \frac{2,00,000 \times 100}{50} \times 100$$

= Rs. 4,00,000

Margin of safety = 13,20,000 – 4,00,000 = Rs. 9,20,000

(iii) The effect of 25% decrease in selling price

Sales = 11,00,000 – 25% of 11,00,000

= 11,00,000 – 2,75,000 = Rs. 8,25,000

Contribution = 8,25,000 – 6,60,000 = Rs. 1,65,000

$$\text{P/V ratio} = \frac{\text{Contribution} \times 100}{\text{Sales}} = \frac{1,65,000 \times 100}{8,25,000}$$

= 20%

$$\text{B.E.P} = \frac{\text{Fixed cost}}{\text{P V ratio}} = \frac{2,00,000}{20} \times 100$$

$$= \text{Rs. } 10,00,000$$

When selling price is reduced by 25% there will not be any margin of safety units since the present sales is below the B.E.P. sales. Margin of safety is the sales above the B.E.P. sales.

7. Selection of suitable Product / Sales mix :

It is very common that companies are manufacturing more than one product. The maximum profit of the company depends upon the number of units of each product produced. There may be different compositions of the products manufactured by the company. The composition of various products which gives the maximum contribution should be preferred. It is called the optimum product or sales mix which can be determined through marginal costing principle.

Illustration: 20

KMW Ltd. is providing the following information related to the month of December 2006.

	Product X (Per unit) Rs.	*Product Y (Per unit) Rs.*
Direct material	55	45
Direct wages	30	20
Selling price	150	145

Variable overhead is 50% of direct wages. Total fixed cost for manufacturing the two products is Rs. 50,000.

Different Sales Mixes:

(i) 1200 units of Product X and 1800 units of Product Y

(ii) 1800 units of Product X and 1200 units of Product Y

(iii) 1500 units of Product X and 1500 units of Product Y

Solution:

Statement of Cost

Particulars	*Product X (Per unit) Rs.*	*Product Y (Per unit) Rs.*
Selling Price	150	145
Variable Cost:		
Material	55	45
Wages	30	20
Variable Overhead (50% of wages)	15	10
	100	75
Contribution (S - VC)	50	70

Calculation of profit for different sales mixes

(i) 1200 units of product X and 1800 units of product Y

				Rs.
Contribution	X	=	1200 × 50	60,000
	Y	=	1800 × 70	1,26,000
Total				1,86,000
Fixed cost				50,000
Profit				1,36,000

(ii) 1800 units of product X and 1200 units of product Y

				Rs.
Contribution	X	=	1800 × 50	90,000
	Y	=	1200 × 70	84,000
Total				1,74,000
Fixed cost				50,000
Profit				1,24,000

(iii) 1500 units of product X and 1500 units of product Y

				Rs.
Contribution	X	=	1500 × 50	75,000
	Y	=	1500 × 70	1,05,000
Total				1,80,000
Fixed cost				50,000
Profit				1,30,000

It is clear from the calculations that sales mix (i), (i.e, 1200 units of X and 1800 units of Y) is more profitable.

8. Determination of Optimum Level of Activity

The optimum level of activity can be determined through marginal costing principle. The contribution at different levels of activity should be calculated. The level of activity which gives the highest contribution is called optimum level of activity.

Illustration: 21

G Ltd. provided the details regarding the cost of one unit of the product manufactured at 60% capacity as follows.

	Rs.
Material cost	37
Wages	33
Overhead	30 (60% fixed)

The number of units produced at 60% capacity is 24,000 units.The selling price is Rs. 125 per unit.

The company has a plan to increase the capacity from 60% to 80% and 90% capacity. At 80% capacity the selling price is to be reduced by 10%. At 90% capacity the selling price is reduced by Rs.20 per unit and the material cost is reduced by 10%.

Calculate the profit and break-even point at 80% and 90% capacities. Also state which one is the optimum capacity.

Solution :

Number of units produced at 60% capacity = 24,000

Number of units produced at 80% capacity $= \frac{24,000 \times 80}{60}$

= 32,000

Number of units produced at 90% capacity $= \frac{24,000}{60} \times 90$

= 36,000

Selling price at 60% capacity = Rs. 125

Selling price at 80% capacity = 125 - 10 % of 125

= 125 – 12.50

= Rs. 112.50

Selling price at 90% capacity = 125 – 20

= Rs. 105

Material cost at 90% capacity = 37 – 10% of 37

= Rs. 33.30

Statement of cost

Particulars	*60% capacity*		*75% capacity*		*90% capacity*	
	Per unit	*Total Rs.*	*Per unit*	*Total Rs.*	*Per unit*	*Total Rs.*
Sales	125	30,00,000	112.50	36,00,000	105	37,80,000
Material	37	8,88,000	37	11,84,000	33.30	11,98,800
Wages	33	7,92,000	33	10,56,000	33	11,88,000
Variable Over head	12	2,88,000	12	3,84,000	12	4,32,000
Total Variable Cost	82	19,68,000	82	26,24,000		78.30
Contribution (S - VC)	43	10,32,000	30.50	9,76,000	26.70	9,61,200
Fixed Overhead	18	4,32,000	13.50	4,32,000	12	4,32,000
Profit	25	6,00,000	17	5,44,000	14.70	5,29,200

Break-even point at 60% capacity $= \frac{\text{Fixed Cost}}{\text{Contribution per unit}}$

$= \frac{4,32,000}{43} = 10,047$ units

Break-even point at 75% capacity $= \frac{4,32,000}{30.5} = 14,164$ units

Break-even point at 90% capacity $= \frac{4,32,000}{26.7} = 16,180$ units

It is advisable to maintain 60% capacity, since the total profit and contribution per unit is greater when compared to 80% and 90 % capacity. If the selling price is not reduced then 90% capacity will give maximum profit.

9. Measurement of performance

Marginal costing technique helps to measure the performance of various department. It facilitates to identify the departments which are performing efficiently and also to identify the products which are giving more profit so that the management can take necessary steps to increase the efficiency and profit.

Illustration: 22

H Ltd provided the following information, regarding cost of manufacturing of three different products.

Particulars	*Product A Rs.*	*Product B Rs.*	*Product C Rs.*
Selling Price	200	160	120
Direct Material	90	60	40
Direct Labour:			
Dept X	35	28	20
Dept Y	15	12	10
Dept Z	10	7	5

The expenses towards overhead are stated below.

	Dept X	*Dept Y*	*Dept Z*
Variable overhead (% on Direct Labour)	40%	50%	60%

Give your suggestions regarding the performance of the three products.

Solution:

Statement of cost

Particulars	*Product A Rs.*	*Product B Rs.*	*Product C Rs.*
Selling price	200	160	120
Direct Material	90	60	40
Direct Labour	60	47	35
Variable overhead			
Dept X	14	11.20	8
Dept Y	7.50	6	5
Dept Z	6	4.20	3
Total Marginal cost	177.50	128.40	91.00
Contribution	22.50	31.60	29.00
P/V Ratio	11.25	19.75	24.17

$$\text{P/V Ratio} = \frac{\text{Contribution} \times 100}{\text{Sales}} \quad \frac{22.50 \times 100}{200}; \quad \frac{31.60 \times 100}{160}; \quad \frac{29 \times 100}{120}$$

Out of the three products C is considered as best since, it gives highest P/V Ratio though Product B gives highest contribution.

MISCELLANEOUS ILLUSTRATIONS

Illustration: 23

Calculate (i) P/V Ratio (ii) Profit when sales is Rs. 900,000 (iii) New BEP when selling price is increased by 20% (iv) New BEP when the selling price is reduced by 20% from the following information.

Fixed cost Rs. 273,000; Sales Rs. 390,000 at B.E.P

Solution:

Contribution = Sales - Variable cost or

Fixed cost + Profit

Since at BEP there is no profit or loss,

Contribution = Rs. 2,73,000

Contribution = Sales - Variable cost

273,000 = 390,000 – V.C

V.C = 390,000 – 2,73,000 = Rs. 117,000

$$\left(\text{i.e. } \frac{117{,}000 \times 100}{3{,}90{,}000} = 30\% \text{ on sales}\right)$$

(i) $$\text{P/V Ratio} = \frac{\text{Contribution}}{\text{Sales}} = \frac{117{,}000 \times 100}{390{,}000} \times 100 = 70\%$$

(ii) Contribution when sales is Rs. 9,00,000 = 900,000 × 70%

= Rs. 630,000

Profit when sales is Rs. 9,00,000 = Contribution – Fixed cost

= 630,000 – 273,000

= Rs. 357,000

(iii) Calculation of BEP when selling price is increased by 20%

Sales = Rs. 9,00,000 + 20% of 900,000

= Rs. 10,80,000

$$\text{Variable cost} = 30\% \text{ of sales} = \frac{9{,}00{,}000 \times 30}{100}$$

= Rs. 270,000

Contribution = 10,80,000 – 270,000 = Rs. 810,000

$$\text{P/V Ratio} = \frac{C}{S} = \frac{810{,}000 \times 100}{10{,}80{,}000} = 75\ \%$$

$$\text{New BEP} = \frac{\text{Fixed Cost}}{\text{P/V Ratio}} = \frac{273{,}000 \times 100}{75}$$

= Rs.364,000

(iv) Calculation of New BEP when selling price is decreased by 20%

Sales = 900,000 – 20% of 900,000

$$= \text{Rs. } 720{,}000$$

$$\text{Variable cost} = 30\% \text{ of Sales} = \frac{9{,}00{,}000 \times 30}{100}$$

$$= \text{Rs. } 270{,}000$$

$$\text{Contribution} = 7{,}20{,}000 - 270{,}000 = \text{Rs. } 4{,}50{,}000$$

$$\text{P/V Ratio} = \frac{C}{S} = \frac{450{,}000 \times 100}{720{,}000} = 62.5\%$$

$$\text{New BEP} = \frac{\text{F.C}}{\text{P/V Ratio}} = \frac{273{,}000 \times 100}{62.5}$$

$$= \text{Rs.}436{,}800$$

[It is assumed that variable cost is not changing due to the reduction or increase of selling price.]

Illustration : 24

GT Ltd provided the following data related to cost of manufacturing a product.

Fixed expenses Rs. 500,000 Profit Rs. 250,000 and Sales Rs. 12,00,000

Calculate (i) P/V Ratio (ii) sales if the company incurred a loss of Rs. 150,000 and (iii) the margin of safety when the profit is Rs. 4,00,000 and Rs. 5,00,000. *(Adapted ICWAI Inter)*

Solution:

(i) Contribution = Fixed Cost + Profit

$$= 500{,}000 + 250{,}000 = \text{Rs. } 750{,}000$$

$$\text{P/V Ratio} = \frac{C \times 100}{S} = \frac{750{,}000 \times 100}{12{,}00{,}000} = 62.5\%$$

(ii) Contribution when the company incurred a loss of Rs. 150,000 is

$$\text{Contribution} = \text{Fixed Cost} - \text{Loss}$$

$$= 500{,}000 - 150{,}000 = \text{Rs. } 350{,}000$$

$$\text{P/V Ratio} = \frac{C}{S}$$

$$62.5\% = \frac{350{,}000}{S}$$

$$S \times 62.5/100 = 350{,}000$$

$$S = \frac{350{,}000 \times 100}{62.5}$$

$$\text{i.e. Sales} = \text{Rs. } 560{,}000$$

(iii) $$\text{Margin of safety} = \frac{\text{Profit}}{\text{P/V Ratio}}$$

$$\text{When, profit is Rs.}400{,}000 \text{ Margin of safety} = \frac{400{,}000 \times 100}{62.5} = \text{Rs.}640{,}000$$

$$\text{When profit is Rs.}500{,}000 \text{ Margin of safety} = \frac{500{,}000 \times 100}{62.5} = \text{Rs.}800{,}000$$

Illustration: 25

KT Ltd., a manufacturing company provides the following information related to the cost of production of product A

Cost of production per unit: Consumption of material Rs.70, wages Rs. 30, variable overhead Rs. 20 and fixed overhead Rs.60. The selling price per unit is Rs. 210 and profit per unit is Rs.30.

The present production of the company is 15,000 units of product A.

It was decided to reduce the selling price due to competition. If the company wants to maintain the same profit how many units it should produce when the selling price is reduced by (i) 10% and (ii) 20%

Solution:

Profit per unit = Rs. 30

Profit for 15,000 units = 15,000 × 30

= Rs. 450,000

(i) When selling price is reduced by 10%

Selling price = 210 – 10% of 210

= 210 – 21 = Rs.189

$$\text{Expected sales} = \frac{\text{Fixed cost + Expected Profit}}{\text{Contribution per unit}}$$

Contribution = Sales – Variable cost

= 189 – (70 + 30 + 20)

= Rs. 69 per unit

Expected profit = Rs. 450,000

Fixed cost = 60 × 15,000 = Rs. 9,00,000

$$\text{Expected sales} = \frac{900{,}000 + 450{,}000}{69}$$

$$= \frac{13{,}50{,}000}{69} = 19{,}565 \text{ units}$$

(ii) When selling price is reduced by 20%,

Selling price = 210 – 20% of 210

= 210 – 42 = Rs. 168 per unit

Contribution = Sales – Variable cost

= 168 – (25 + 20 + 15)

= 168 – 120 = Rs.48 per unit

Expected profit = Rs. 450,000

Fixed cost = Rs. 900,000

$$\text{Expected sales} = \frac{\text{Fixed cost + Expected profit}}{\text{Contribution per unit}}$$

$$= \frac{900{,}000 + 450{,}000}{48}$$

$$= \frac{13{,}50{,}000}{48} = 28{,}125 \text{ units}$$

Illustration: 26

GC Ltd. provides the following data related to manufacturing a product.

	Rs.
Selling price	55 per unit
Variable manufacturing cost	20 per unit
Variable selling cost	10 per unit
Fixed factory overhead	300,000 per annum
Fixed administrative overhead	3,50,000 per annum
Fixed selling overhead	1,00,000 per annum

Calculate : (i) Break-even point, (ii) The profit if sales in units are 25% above break-even point, (iii) Sales required to earn a profit of Rs.250,000 (iv) Sales required to earn a profit of 20% of sales.

Solution:

(i) Break-even point:

Contribution = Sales – Variable cost

= 55 – (20 + 10)

= 55 – 30 = Rs. 25 per unit

Fixed cost = Fixed FOH + Fixed AOH + Fixed SOH

= 3,00,000 + 3,50,000 + 1,00,000 = Rs.7,50,000

$$\text{Break-even point} = \frac{\text{Fixed Cost}}{\text{Contribution per unit}}$$

$$= \frac{750{,}000}{25} = 30{,}000 \text{ units}$$

or, 30,000 × 55 = Rs. 16,50,000 in value

(ii) Calculation of profit when sales is 25% above BEP

BEP = 30,000 units

Sales above 25% of BEP = 30,000 + 25% of 30,000

= 37,500 units

Contribution per unit = Rs. 25

Total Contribution = 37,500 × 25 = Rs. 937,500

Profit = Contribution – Fixed Cost

= 937,500 – 750,000 = Rs. 187,500

(iii) Expected sales for a profit of Rs. 250,000

$$\text{Expected sales} = \frac{\text{Fixed Cost + Expected Profit}}{\text{Contribution per unit}}$$

$$= \frac{750{,}000 + 250{,}000}{25} = \frac{10{,}00{,}000}{25}$$

= 40,000 units

= 40,000 × 55 = Rs. 22,00,000

(iv) **Expected Sales to earn a profit of 20% on sales.**

Assume sales units as 'a'

$$\text{Sales value} = 55a$$
$$\text{Profit} = 55a \times 20\% = 11a$$
$$\text{Sales} = \text{Total Cost} + \text{Profit}$$
$$55a = (30a + 750{,}000) + 11a$$
$$55a - 30a - 11a = 750{,}000$$
$$14a = 750{,}000$$
$$a = \frac{750{,}000}{14} = 53{,}571 \text{ units}$$

Expected Sales is 53,571 units × 55

= Rs. 29,46,405 in value

Illustration: 27

KMW Ltd. provides the following information from its cost records.

		Rs.	*Rs.*
Budgeted Sales: 20,000 units @ Rs. 40 per unit			800,000
Budgeted Costs:			
Variable :	**Direct material**	110,000	
	Direct labour	97,000	
	Factory overhead	83,000	
	Administration overhead	92,000	
	Selling & distribution overhead	88,000	470,000
Fixed :	**Factory overhead**	90,000	
	Administration overhead	69,000	
	Selling & distribution overhead	41,000	200,000
Budgeted Profit			130,000

Calculate Break-even point when

(i) **Variable cost increased by 30%**

(ii) **Fixed cost increased by 30%**

(iii) **30% increase in selling price**

(iv) **30% increase in fixed overhead and 30% decrease in variable cost.**

(Adapted Company Secretary Course)

Solution:

$$\text{Sales} = \text{Rs. } 800{,}000$$
$$\text{Variable Cost} = \text{Material} + \text{Labour} + \text{VFOH} + \text{VAOH} + \text{VSDOH}$$
$$= 110{,}000 + 97{,}000 + 83{,}000 + 92{,}000 + 88{,}000$$
$$= \text{Rs. } 470{,}000$$
$$\text{Fixed Cost} = \text{FFOH} + \text{FAOH} + \text{FSDOH}$$
$$= 90{,}000 + 69{,}000 + 41{,}000 = \text{Rs. } 200{,}000$$

(i) B.E.P when variable cost increased by 30%

New variable cost = 4700,000 + 30% of 470,000

= 470,000 + 141,000 = Rs. 611,000

Contribution = Sales - Variable Cost

= 800,000 - 611,000 = Rs. 189,000

$= \frac{189,000}{20,000}$ = Rs. 9.45 per unit

B.E.P. $= \frac{\text{Fixed Cost Cost}}{\text{Contribution per unit}} = \frac{200,000}{9.45}$

= 21,164 units

(ii) B.E.P. when Fixed Cost increased by 30%

New Fixed Cost = 200,000 + 30% of 200,000

= 200,000 + 60,000 = Rs. 260,000

Contribution = Sales - V.C

= 800,000 - 470,000 = Rs. 330,000

$\frac{330,000}{20,000}$ = Rs. 16.50 per unit

B.E.P. $= \frac{F.C}{C} = \frac{260,000}{16.50}$

= 15,758 units

(iii) B.E.P. when selling price increased by 30%

Actual selling price = Rs. 40 per unit

New selling price = 40 + 30% of 40

= 40 + 12 = Rs.52 per unit

Variable cost per unit $= \frac{470,000}{20,000}$ = Rs. 23.50

Contribution per unit = Sales - V.C

= 52 - 23.50= Rs. 28.50

B.E.P. $= \frac{F.C.}{C} = \frac{200,000}{28.50}$ = 7018 units

(iv) BEP when Fixed cost increased by 30% and Variable cost decreased by 30%

New Fixed Cost = 200,000 + 30% of 200,000

= Rs. 260,000

New variable cost = 470,000 - 30% of 470,000

= Rs. 329,000

Contribution per unit $= \frac{S \quad V.C}{\text{No. of units}}$

$= \frac{800,000 \quad 329,000}{20,000}$

= Rs. 23.55 per unit

$$\text{B.E.P.} = \frac{\text{F.C}}{\text{C}} = \frac{260{,}000}{23.55}$$
$$= 11{,}040 \text{ units}$$

Illustration: 28

The profit earned by a company is 25% on sales during 2006 and it is 30% on sales during 2007. If the sales for 2006 is Rs. 200,000 and 2007 is Rs. 300,000; find out (i) P/V Ratio (ii) BEP (iii) Expected sales to earn a profit of Rs. 100,000 (iv) The profit for sales of Rs. 5,00,000.

Solution:

$$\text{Sales in 2006} = \text{Rs. } 2{,}00{,}000$$
$$\text{Profit} = 25\%$$
$$= \frac{200{,}000 \times 25}{100} = \text{Rs. } 50{,}000$$
$$\text{Sales in 2007} = \text{Rs. } 3{,}00{,}000$$
$$\text{Profit} = 30\%$$
$$= \frac{300{,}000 \times 30}{100} = \text{Rs. } 90{,}000$$

(i)
$$\text{P/V ratio} = \frac{\text{Difference in profit}}{\text{Difference in sales}} \times 100$$
$$= \frac{90{,}000 \quad 50{,}000}{3{,}00{,}000 \quad 2{,}00{,}000} \times 100$$
$$= 40\%$$

(ii) Calculation of BEP

$$\text{P/V ratio} = \frac{\text{Contribution}}{\text{Sales}} \text{ or } \frac{\text{F.C} + \text{P}}{\text{S}}$$
$$40\% = \frac{\text{Contribution}}{300{,}000}$$
$$\text{Contribution} = 300{,}000 \times 0.4 = 120{,}000$$
$$40\% = \frac{\text{F.C} + 90{,}000}{3{,}00{,}000}$$ (F.C = Contribution- Profit; 120,000- 90,000)
$$300{,}000 \times 0.4 = \text{FC} + 90{,}000$$
$$\text{FC} = 120{,}000 - 90{,}000 = \text{Rs.}30{,}000$$
$$\text{BEP} = \frac{\text{Fixed Cost}}{\text{P/V ratio}}$$
$$= \frac{30{,}000}{0.4} = \text{Rs. } 75{,}000$$

(iii)
$$\text{Expected sales} = \frac{\text{F.C} + \text{Expected Profit}}{\text{P/V Ratio}}$$
$$= \frac{30{,}000 + 100{,}000}{0.4}$$
$$= \text{Rs. } 3{,}25{,}000$$

(iv) Profit for Sales of Rs. 5,00,000

$$\text{P/V ratio} = \frac{\text{Contribution}}{\text{Sales}}$$

$$40\% = \text{Fixed cost} + \frac{\text{Profit}}{\text{Sales}}$$

$$40\% = \frac{30{,}000 + P}{5{,}00{,}000}$$

$$30{,}000 + P = 5{,}00{,}000 \times 0.4$$

$$\text{Profit} = 200{,}000 - 30{,}000$$

$$= \text{Rs.. } 1{,}70{,}000$$

Illustration: 29

GR Ltd has to spent Rs. 200,000 as fixed cost for a sales of Rs. 600,000. If the profit earned is 25% of the sales, and the sales per unit is Rs. 30, find out the (i) P/V ratio (ii) BEP (iii) No. of units of sales to earn a profit of Rs. 90,000 (iv) The profit for the sales of Rs. 7,00,000 (v) Estimated sales to earn a profit of 30% on sales.

Solution

Fixed cost = Rs. 200,000

Sales = Rs. 600,000

Profit = 25% of sales

= Rs. 150,000

Contribution = Fixed Cost + Profit

= 200,000 + 150,000

= Rs.350,000

or = S - V.C

350,000 = 600,000 – V.C.

V.C = 600,000 – 350,000 = Rs. 250,000

$$\text{No. of units sold} = \frac{\text{Sales}}{\text{Selling price per unit}}$$

$$= \frac{600{,}000}{30} = 20{,}000 \text{ units}$$

Variable cost = Rs.250,000

$$\text{Variable cost per unit} = \frac{250{,}000}{20{,}000} = \text{Rs. } 12.50$$

$$\text{Contribution per unit} = \frac{350{,}000}{20{,}000} = \text{Rs. } 17.50$$

(i)

$$\text{P/V ratio} = \frac{\text{Contribution} \times 100}{\text{Sales}} \times 100$$

$$= \frac{350{,}000 \times 100}{60{,}0000} = 58.33\%$$

(ii) $$\text{BEP} = \frac{\text{Fixed cost}}{\text{Contribution per unit}}$$

$$= \frac{200,000}{17.50} = 11,429 \text{ units}$$

$$\text{BEP in value} = 11,429 \times 30 = \text{Rs. } 342,870$$

(iii) Estimated sales to earn a profit of Rs. 90,000

$$= \frac{\text{Fixed cost + Estimated profit}}{\text{Contribution per unit}}$$

$$= \frac{200,000 + 90,000}{17.50} = 16,571 \text{ units}$$

(iv) $$\text{Estimated sales} = \frac{(\text{F.C + Estimated profit}) \times \text{Selling price per unit}}{\text{Contribution per unit}}$$

$$700,000 = \frac{(200,000 + \text{E.P.}) \times 30}{17.50}$$

$$\text{E.P.} = \frac{1,22,50,000 \quad 60,00,000}{30}$$

$$\text{Estimated profit} = \frac{62,50,000}{30} = \text{Rs. } 208,333$$

[or]

$$\text{P/V ratio} = \frac{\text{Fixed Cost + E.P}}{\text{Sales}}$$

$$58.33\% = \frac{200,000 + \text{E.P}}{700,000}$$

$$0.583333 \times 700,000 = 200,000 + \text{E.P}$$

$$408,333 = 200,000 + \text{E.P}$$

$$\text{E.P.} = 408,333 - 200,000$$

$$= \text{Rs.}208,333$$

(v) Calculation of sales for profit of 30% on sales.

Profit = 30% on sales (Assume 'x' as sales)

$$= \frac{30 \times x}{100} = 0.3\,x$$

$$\text{P/V ratio} = \frac{\text{F.C + EP}}{\text{Sales}} = \frac{200,000 \times .3x}{x}$$

$$58.33\% = (200,000 + .3x)/x$$

$$.5833\,x = 200,000 + .3x$$

$$.5833\,x - 3\,x = 200,000$$

$$.2833\,x = 200,000$$

$$x = \frac{200,000}{.2833} = \text{Rs. } 705,965$$

$$\text{Profit} = .3x$$

$$= .3 \times 705,965$$

$$= \text{Rs. } 211,790$$

Illustration: 30

GC Ltd., is earning 20% profit for a sales of Rs. 450,000 with fixed cost Rs. 170,000. Find out the (i) BEP units (ii) P/V ratio (iii) Estimated sales for a profit of Rs.1,30,000 (iv) Profit for sales of Rs. 750,000 (v) Estimated sales to earn a profit of 30% on sales.

Assume that the number of units sold at present is 10,000.

Solution :

$$\text{Sales} = \text{Rs. } 450{,}000$$

$$\text{Profit} = \frac{450{,}000 \times 20}{100} = \text{Rs. } 90{,}000$$

$$\text{Fixed cost} = \text{Rs. } 170{,}000$$

$$\text{Contribution} = \text{Fixed Cost} + \text{Profit} = S - V.C$$

$$170{,}000 + 90{,}000 = 450{,}000 - V.C$$

$$260{,}000 = 450{,}000 - V.C$$

$$\text{Variable cost} = 450{,}000 - 260{,}000 = \text{Rs. } 1{,}90{,}000$$

$$\text{No. of units sold} = 10{,}000$$

$$\text{Selling price per unit} = \frac{450{,}000}{10{,}000} = \text{Rs. } 45$$

$$\text{Variable cost per unit} = \frac{190{,}000}{10{,}000} = \text{Rs. } 19$$

$$\text{Contribution per unit} = \frac{260{,}000}{10{,}000} = \text{Rs. } 26$$

(i)
$$\text{BEP units} = \frac{\text{Fixed cost}}{\text{Contribution per unit}}$$

$$= \frac{170{,}000}{26} = 6{,}538 \text{ units}$$

(ii)
$$\text{P/V ratio} = \frac{\text{Contribution} \times 100}{\text{Sales}}$$

$$= \frac{260{,}000 \times 100}{450{,}000} = 57.78\%$$

(iii) Estimated sales to earn a profit of Rs. 1,30,000

$$= \frac{\text{Fixed Cost} + \text{Expected profit}}{\text{Contribution per unit}}$$

$$= \frac{170{,}000 + 130{,}000}{26} = 11{,}538 \text{ units}$$

$$\text{i.e., } 11{,}538 \times 45 = \text{Rs.}519{,}210$$

(iv) Profit for sales of Rs. 750,000

$$= \frac{(\text{Fixed cost} + \text{Estimated profit}) \times \text{Selling price per unit}}{\text{Contribution per unit}}$$

[or]

$$\text{P/V ratio} = \frac{\text{Contribution}}{\text{Sales}}$$

$$57.78\% = \frac{\text{F.C} + \text{Profit}}{\text{Sales}}$$

$$57.78\% = \frac{170{,}000 + P}{750{,}000}$$

$$170{,}000 + P = 750{,}000 \times 0.5778$$

$$170{,}000 + P = 433{,}350$$

$$P = 433{,}350 - 170{,}000$$

$$\text{Profit} = \text{Rs. } 263{,}350$$

(v) Estimated sales to earn a profit of 30% on sales.

$$\text{Profit is 30\% of Sales} = \frac{30 \times x}{100} = 0.3x \text{ (Assume x as Sales)}$$

$$\text{P/V ratio} = \frac{\text{Fixed Cost} + \text{E.P}}{\text{Sales}}$$

$$57.78\% = \frac{170{,}000 + 0.3x}{x}$$

$$0.5778x - 0.3x = 170{,}000$$

$$0.2778x = 170{,}000$$

$$x = \frac{170{,}000}{0.2778} = \text{Rs.}611{,}951$$

$$\text{No. of units to be sold} = \frac{\text{Sales}}{\text{Sales per unit}} = \frac{611{,}951}{45} = 13{,}599 \text{ units}$$

$$\text{Profit} = 0.3x$$

$$= 0.3 \times 611{,}951$$

$$= \text{Rs. } 183{,}585$$

EXERCISE

THEORY

I. Choose the correct answer for the following

1. The concept of marginal costing is based on —
   (i) Fixed cost (ii) Standard cost (iii) Variable cost (iv) Prime cost
2. The difference in cost due to the increase or decrease of one unit from the normal production is known as —
   (i) Marginal cost (ii) Budget (iii) Fixed cost (iv) Works cost
3. The difference between the selling price and the variable cost is called —
   (i) Marginal cost (ii) Fixed cost (iii) Prime cost (iv) Contribution
4. The condition of no profit - no loss is known as —
   (i) Mid point (ii) Break-even point (iii) Fixed point (iv) Starting point
5. The sales above Break-even point will give —
   (i) Loss (ii) Costing loss (iii) Profit (iv) Fixed cost
6. The ratio between contribution and sales is called —
   (i) Contribution ratio (ii) P/V ratio (iii) Sales ratio (iv) Profit ratio
7. The difference between actual sales and sales at break-even point is called —
   (i) Margin of safety (ii) Margin of loss (iii) Sales margin (iv) Margin of contribution
8. Margin of safety is the ratio between profit and —
   (i) B.E.P. (ii) P/V Ratio (iii) Sales ratio (iv) Current ratio

9. The factor which puts a limit on production and profit is known as —
(i) Sales factor (ii) Purchase factor (iii) Profit factor (iv) Key factor
10. A graphical representation of marginal costing is called —
(i) Break-even chart (ii) ABC chart (iii) VED chart (iv) LPP chart
[**Ans :** 1. (iii) 2 (i) 3 (iv) 4 (ii) 5 (iii) 6 (ii) 7 (i) 8 (ii) 9 (iv) 10 (i)]

II. Answer the following

11. Define marginal costing. State the advantages and disadvantages of marginal costing.
12. What is marginal costing? State the assumptions of marginal costing.
13. State the procedures of preparing the statement of cost by marginal costing method.
14. Define B.E.P. State the procedures of preparing Break-even chart.
15. State briefly the important managerial decisions which can be taken through marginal costing technique.
16. Write short notes of the following.
(i) BEP (ii) Marginal cost (iii) Marginal costing (iv) Break-even-point (v) P\V Ratio (vi) Marginal Costing Equation (vii) Contribution
17. Calculate BEP and P/V ratio from the following information

	Rs.		*Rs.*
Sales	275,000	Direct material	67,000
Direct wages	84,000	Variable overhead	19,000
Fixed cost	64,000		

(**Ans.** Rs. 1,67,627; 38.18%)

18. H Ltd., provided the following information related to the cost of production of a product.
Selling price Rs. 75 per unit; Variable cost Rs. 35 per unit; Fixed Cost Rs. 130,000.
Calculate : (1) BEP in units and value (ii) Profit when sales is Rs.4,40,000 and (iii) profit when sales is Rs.550,000
(**Ans:** (1) 32,500 Rs.2,43,750, (ii)Rs.1,04,667, (iii) Rs.1,63,333)
19. Calculate (i) P/V Ratio (ii) Profit when sales is Rs.690,000 and (iii) New Break-even point when the selling price is increased by 20% and (vi) New BEP when the selling price is reduced by 20%, from the following information
Fixed cost Rs. 190,000; BEP Rs.340,000
(**Ans:** (i) 55.88% (ii) Rs.1,95,572 (iii) Rs.2,50,395 (iv) Rs.5,29,542)
20. WD Ltd.,a manufacturing company is providing the following information for three months ending 31st December 2007.

Direct material consumed	Rs. 79,000
Direct wages	Rs. 44,000
Direct expenses	Rs. 33,000

Factory overhead absorbed is 70% of the direct material; Administration overhead absorbed is 50% of the works cost; Selling and distribution overhead absorbed is 15% of the cost of production. Costing profit is 25% on sales. Prepare the cost statement by Absorption costing method and Marginal costing method.
(**Ans:** Costing profit Rs. 1,21,498)

21. Calculate (i) BEP (ii) Sales to earn a profit of Rs. 170,000 (iii) Margin of safety (iv) BEP when the selling price is reduced by 10%, if the sales of a company is Rs.400,000, the profit is 20% on cost, fixed cost is Rs. 175,000 and the number of units sold is 40,000
(**Ans:** (i) 27,451 units, Rs. 274510 (ii) 54118 units (iii) Rs. 125490 (iv) 32,558 units, Rs.293022)

22. Joyce & Co.Ltd is providing the following information from its costing records. Fixed cost Rs. 150,000; Variable cost Rs. 200,000; Sales Rs. 420,000. Calculate (i) P/V Ratio (ii) The expected sales to earn a profit of Rs. 220,000 (iii) Profit when the sales is Rs. 900,000 (iv) BEP (v) New P/V Ratio and BEP when the selling price is increased by 15%.

    (Ans: (i) 52.38% (ii) Rs. 7,06,376 (iii) Rs. 3,21,420 (iv) Rs. 2,86,369 (v) 58.59%; Rs. 256,016)

23. KMW Ltd., is providing the profit and sales for two periods, as follows

	Period I (Rs.)	*Period II (Rs.)*
Sales	900,000	12,20,000
Profit	120,000	200,000

Find out the (i) P/V Ratio (ii) Sales to earn a profit of Rs.250,000 (iii) Profit when sales is Rs.15,00,000 (iv) BEP.
(Ans: (i) 25% (ii) Rs. 14,20,000 (iii) Rs. 2,70,000 (iv) Rs. 4,20,000)

24. T Ltd has to spend Rs 135,000 as fixed cost for a sales of Rs. 390,000. If the profit earned is 25% on sales and the sales per unit is Rs.30, find out (i) P/V Ratio (ii) BEP (iii) Number of units of sales to earn a profit of Rs. 170,000 (iv) Expected sales for a profit of 20% on sales.

    (Ans: (i) 59.62% (ii) 7548; Rs. 226,434 (iii) 17,052 units (iv) Rs.3,40,737)

25. C Ltd., is spending Fixed cost Rs.20 per unit, Direct material Rs.12 per unit, Direct wages Rs. 8 per unit and Direct expenses Rs.5 per unit at 100% capacity. At 80% capacity, the company is manufacturing and selling 10,000 units.

    If the selling price per unit is Rs.60, find out

    (i) How many units should be sold for break-even
    (ii) How many units should be sold for a profit of Rs.100,000
    (iii) How much sales to be done for 25% profit on sales.

    If the demand of the product is 12,000 units, find out

    (a) Selling price is to be charged per unit to break- even
    (b) Selling price to earn a profit of Rs.150,000
    (c) Selling price to earn a profit of 25% on sales

    (Ans: (i) 5,714 units (ii) 8,571 units (iii) 10,000 units)

26. Sales of a company is Rs. 750,000; Profit is Rs. 75,000; and Variable cost is 70% on sales.Calculate (a) P/V Ratio (b) Fixed cost (c) Sales to earn a profit of Rs. 145,000.

    (Ans: (a) 30% (b) Rs.1,50,000 (c) Rs.9,83.333)

27. The cost for manufacturing 2000 units of a product for KMWD & Co., is on the basis of fixed cost Rs. 30,000 and variable cost is Rs. 22 per unit. Selling price is Rs.50 per unit. Calculate the P/V Ratio. If the selling price is reduced by 25% find out the new P/V Ratio. Also calculate the number of units to be sold to earn the present total profit.

    (Ans: 56%; 41.33%; 3613 units)

28. Calculate (i) P/V Ratio (ii) Sales required to earn a profit of Rs. 150,000 (iii) Profit when sales are Rs. 500,000 from the following information

Year	*Sales (Rs.)*	*Profit (Rs.)*
2006	450,000	60,000
2007	600,000	1,20,000

(Ans: 40%: Rs.675,000; Rs.80,000)

29. Calculate BEP ; the percentage capacity at BEP and the profit at 75% capacity if the fixed cost for manufacturing a product is Rs.135,000; variable cost is 60% on sales and the sales is Rs.550,000 at 100% capacity.

    (**Ans:** Rs.337,500; 61.36%; Rs.30,000)

30. K Ltd is providing the following information.

    Fixed cost Rs. 350,000; Selling price per unit Rs.75; Variable expenses - Material Rs.25 per unit; Wages Rs.15 per unit. Draw a Break-even chart and verify the result through a table. Also calculate the new BEP if the selling price is reduced by 15%.

    (**Ans:** 10,000 units (Rs. 7,50,000); 14,737 units (Rs. 9,39,484))

31. KN Ltd is working in 60% capacity and produces and sells 120,000 units @ Rs.10 per unit. The expenses are as follows.

    Administration overhead (fixed) Rs.135,000; Selling & distribution overhead (fixed) Rs. 125,000; Direct material Rs.1.50 per unit; Direct wages Rs.1.00 per unit; Direct expenses Rs.0.50 per unit; Variable manufacturing overhead Rs.1.20 per unit. Calculate B.E.P.

    The company received an order for 4000 units @ Rs.6.50 per unit from a foreign country. Find out whether, it is advisable for the company to accept the order. In case, if it is advisable for the company calculate the total profit.

    (**Ans:** 44828 units, Advisable; Rs. 4,45,200)

32. KH Ltd is manufacturing and selling 10,000 units of a product per month @ Rs.70 per unit. The company has to spend the following expenses for the month.

    Direct material Rs 144,000; Direct wages Rs 111,000; Carriage inwards Rs. 15,000; Administration overhead Rs.133,000; Selling and distribution overhead Rs.126,000 (25% of the overheads are variable).

    Find out the number of units the company has to sell to earn the present profit after reducing the selling price by 15% and by 20%. Also prepare the statement of cost.

    (**Ans:** Present profit Rs. 1,71,000;Expected Sales - 14037 units; 16219 units)

33. GC Ltd is providing the following information in order to decide whether to manufacture or buy a product. Direct material Rs.19 per unit; Direct wages Rs.11 per unit; Direct expenses Rs.5 per unit; Variable overhead Rs.10 per unit; Selling price is Rs.74 per unit.Find out whether to manufacture or buy the product if the market price is (i) Rs.27.(ii) Rs.55

    (**Ans:** (i) Buy (ii) Make)

34. GT Ltd is manufacturing two products namely A and B and the details of the cost are as follows.

	A *Rs.*	*B* *Rs.*
Selling price per unit	67	89
Direct material	30	40
5 kgm @ Rs.6 for A		
8 kgm @ Rs.5 for B		
Direct wages per unit	13	19
Variable overhead per unit	7	11
Fixed cost	15,000	17,000

The company manufactures 2,000 units of product A and 3000 units of product B. Suggest the management about the type of product to be manufactured more, by taking into account direct material as the constant factor. Also prepare a statement of cost.

(**Ans:** Contribution for A Rs. 34,000; B Rs. 57,000; Contribution per unit of material consumed for A is Rs.3.40 and B is Rs.2.38.Hence, B is preferred)

35. GR & Co Ltd is manufacturing and selling two products namely, X and Y. The details of the cost are stated as follows.

		X Rs.
Selling price per unit	159	170
Direct material per unit	65	71
Direct wages per unit	15	20
Direct expenses per unit	10	12

The variable overhead is 40% of direct wages. The common fixed overhead is Rs.200,000. Advise the management, which of the following combination of production of products A and B will give maximum contribution and profit. (i) 2,000 units of X and 3,000 units of Y (ii) 3,000 units of X and 2,000 units of Y (iii) 2,500 units of X and 2,500 units of Y.

(**Ans:** (ii) is adviseable since total profit for (i), (ii) and (iii) are Rs. 1,03,000, Rs. 1,07,000 and Rs. 10,50,000 respectively)

36. JW Ltd., wants to decide the optimum capacity among the different capacities of production as 70%, 80% and 90%. In this regard, the expenses incurred at 70% capacity are as follows.

Direct material Rs.49,000; Direct wages Rs. 42,000; Direct expenses Rs.14,000; Variable overhead 50% of the direct wages; Fixed overhead Rs.63,000.

It is also given that the company is compelled to reduce the selling price by 5% at 80% capacity and by 10% at 90% capacity. It is also given that the company is manufacturing 14,000 units at 70% capacity, and the selling price is Rs.17 per unit at this capacity.

(**Ans:** Profits at 70%, 80% and 90% capacities are Rs.49,000,Rs. 51,400 and Rs. 50,400 respectively. 80% capacity is the optimum one)

37. Calculate the minimum selling price from the following.

Marginal cost per unit Rs.40. Fixed cost Rs.1000,000. Number of units sold is 5,000. Present selling price is Rs.77 per unit. State whether the company can sell the product @ Rs.59 per unit. What is the minimum selling price to prevent loss?

(**Ans:** No; Rs. 60)

38. G Ltd is manufacturing and selling 11,000 units of a product @ Rs.50 per unit. The details regarding the cost of production are as follows.

Direct material Rs. 131,000; Direct labour Rs.120,000 Electricity Rs.37,000; Miscellaneous expenses Rs. 31,000; Fixed manufacturing expenses Rs.75,000.Fixed Administration expenses Rs.50,000.

The normal production capacity is 17,000 units per month. The company received an order for 5,000 units @ Rs.32 per unit from a foreign market. Advise the management, whether the order can be accepted or not. Calculate the total profit if the order is accepted.

(**Ans:** Accepted Rs.96,000)

39. H Ltd., provided the following details regarding the cost of manufacturing one unit of a product

	Rs.
Direct material	77
Direct labour	43
Variable overhead	27
Fixed overhead	93
Profit	25
Selling price	265

The capacity of the company is 40,000 units per month. The company has to reduce the selling price due to competition. Calculate the number of units the company should manufacture to earn the present profit if the selling price is reduced by 5% and 10% respectively. Assume that the present sales is 30,000 units.

(**Ans:** 33,795 units; 38,689 units)

40. Doyle & Co Ltd.,is manufacturing two different products namely X and Y. The expenses connected with the manufacturing of the products are as follows.

	Product X Cost per unit (Rs.)	*Product Y Cost per unit (Rs.)*
Material		
7 kgm @ Rs.30	210	
9 kgm @ Rs.20		180
Labour	130	98
Fixed cost: Administration	150	115
Selling	90	80
Selling price	610	500
Profit	30	27

The total number of units produced in a month are X 4,000 units and Y 5,000 units. The raw material is the key factor and the availability of raw material is 60,000 kgm.Find out the product which gives the maximum profit, through marginal costing technique.

(**Ans:** Y gives maximum profit. But product X can be preferred as per the constraint factor i.e.. Rs. 38.57 and Rs.24.67)

41. N Ltd.,provided the details of the cost of producing one unit of product X at 60% capacity as follows.

	Rs.
Material Cost	90
Wages	40
Overhead	80 (70% Fixed)

The number of units produced at 60% capacity is 3000. The selling price is Rs. 230 per unit. The company has a plan to increase the capacity from 60% to 70% and 90%. At 70% capacity the selling price is to be reduced by 5%. At 90% capacity the selling price is reduced by Rs.20 per unit and the material cost is reduced by 10%. Calculate the profit and BEP at 60%, 70% and 90% capacities. Also state which one gives the optimum capacity.

(**Ans:** Rs. 53,630; Rs. 42,320; Rs. 53,280; BEP - 556; 727; 717)

42. KN Ltd is manufacturing two products namely X and Y and the details of the costs are as follows.

	X Rs.	*Y Rs.*
Selling price per unit	125	105
Direct material	50	45
10 kgm @ Rs. 5 for X		
9 kgm @ Rs. 5 for Y		
Direct wages per unit	25	15
Variable overhead per unit	15	5
Fixed cost	60,000	40,000

The company manufactures 3000 units of product X and 2000 units of product Y. Suggest the management about the type of product to be manufactured more, by taking into account direct material as the constraint factor. Also prepare a statement of cost.

(**Ans:** Contribution for × Rs. 105,000; Y Rs. 80,000; Contribution per unit of material consumed for Y is Rs.2.50 and B is Rs.4.44.Hence, Y is preferred)

43. KM Ltd is manufacturing and selling two products namely, A and B. The details of the cost are stated as follows.

		A *Rs.*
Selling price per unit	120	105
Direct material per unit	40	50
Direct wages per unit	20	30
Direct expenses per unit	10	15

The variable overhead is 100% of direct wages. The common fixed overhead is Rs.40,000. Advise the management, which of the following combination of production of products X and Y will give maximum contribution and profit, (i) 1000 units of A and 1000 units of B (ii) 1200 units of A and 800 units of B (iii) 800 units of A and 1200 units of B.

(**Ans:** (ii) is adviseable since total profit for (i),(ii) and (iii) are Rs. 15,000, Rs. 16,000 and Rs. 14,000 respectively)

44. Calculate the minimum selling price, from the following.

Marginal cost per unit Rs.200. Fixed cost Rs.12,00,000. Number of units sold is 10,000. Present selling price is Rs.350 per unit. State whether the company can sell the product @ Rs.290 per unit. What is the minimum selling price to prevent loss?

(**Ans:** Yes. Rs.320)

8

STANDARD COSTING

The method of determining the cost in advance is called Standard Costing. It is otherwise called as predetermined cost. It is a tool to control the cost so as to achieve maximum profit. Standard costing helps for managerial planning and decision making. This method helps to compare the actual performance with the expected standard performance. If the actual performance is below standard performance, necessary control measures can be taken by the management. Hence, it facilitates for the improvement in the organisation and the performance of employees.

Meaning and Definitions of Standard Cost and Standard Costing

Standard Cost

Standard cost means predetermined cost.

According to the **Chartered Institute of Management Accountants**, London, Standard cost means a predetermined cost which is computed in advance of production on the basis of specification of all the factors affecting cost and used in standard costing.

According to **Eric L.Kohler**, standard cost is a forecast or predetermination of what actual cost should be under projected conditions, serving as a cost control and as a measure of production efficiency or standard of comparison when ultimately aligned against actual cost.

According to **T.Lucy**, standard cost is a target cost which should be attained. The build up of a standard cost is based on sound technical and engineering studies.

It is clear from the definitions that the standard cost is a predetermined cost. The cost is determined in advance for every stage of cost on the basis of past experience and the rate of growth of technological development.

Standard costing

Standard costing is the process of preparing standard cost. It also involves the measurement and analysis of variance of actual cost and standard cost. In this way, it is possible to apply effective control measures to correct the deviations and to achieve maximum efficiency.

The **Chartered Institute of Management Accountants**, London defines Standard costing as the preparation and use of standard costs, their comparison with actual cost and analysis of variances to their causes and points of evidence.

It is clear from the definitions that Standard costing includes the following functions.

(i) Determination of standard cost

(ii) Measurement and recording of actual cost

(iii) Calculation of variations by comparing the actual cost with standard cost

(iv) Analysis of variances from standard cost in order to find out the reasons in the variations for the purpose of corrective action.

Historical Costing and Standard Costing

The differences between historical costing and standard costing are as follows:

(i) The costs which are already incurred are called Historical costs. It is a method of recording the cost after they are incurred. But standard cost is a predetermined cost. Standard costing is the method of calculating the standard cost.

(ii) It is not possible to measure the efficiency of operations in historical costing. But in standard costing the efficiency of operation can be measured by comparing the standard cost with actual cost.

(iii) There is no tool for cost control in historical costing. But standard costing provides information for cost control measures.

(iv) Historical cost data are used for standard cost. But standard cost data have no value for the historical costing.

Standard Costing and Budgetary Control

The purpose of Standard costing and Budgetary control are same. Both of them are important tools for managerial planning and decision making. Hence the ideas, approaches and techniques adopted in Standard costing and Budgetary control are more or less same. Inspite of their similarities there are some differences in Standard costing and Budgetary control. The important differences are stated as follows.

(i) The scope of budgeting is greater than the scope of standard costing. Budgeting is prepared for the operation of the business as a whole. But Standard costing is prepared only for the manufacturing section of the business.

(ii) Budgeting is concerned with the total activities of the organisation. Hence, there is no division of cost in budgeting. But in Standard costing each element of cost like material, labour and overhead are estimated and analysed.

(iii) Budgeting emphasises more on planning than control whereas standard costing emphasises more on control than on planning.

Advantages of Standard Costing

The advantages of standard costing are as follows.

(i) Standard costing improves the efficiency of the employees in an organisation. The motivation for the employees to perform above the standard increases the efficiency.

(ii) It is possible to identify the area where performance is below standard so as to take corrective control measures.

(iii) It helps to compare the performance of one period to another and of one division to another division.

(iv) Standard costing facilitates for the determination of wage structure and incentive schemes.

(v) Standard costing provides information for fixing prices of the products.

(vi) Standard costing helps for cost reduction in every stage of production.

(vii) It provides information for the preparation of budgeting and for budgetary control.

(viii) It facilitates for the inventory control. It helps for the correct valuation of inventory like raw materials, work-in- progress and finished goods.

Limitations of Standard Costing

The limitations of standard costing are stated as follows:

(i) Standard costing is expensive for companies to adopt. It is possible only for large scale enterprises to adopt standard costing system.

(ii) It is not possible to adopt standard costing method for all manufacturing companies. The companies which are producing non standard products could not adopt standard costing.

(iii) It is difficult to estimate the cost in future since future is uncertain.

(iv) The employees may oppose through trade unions for the adoption of standard costing.

(v) Standard costing focuses on cost per unit . But correct estimation of fixed cost per unit is not possible.

VARIANCE ANALYSIS

An analysis about the actual cost and standard cost is called variance analysis. Variance is the difference between the actual and standard cost. When the actual cost is less than the standard cost then the variance is called " Favourable variance' and when the actual cost is greater than standard cost then the variance is called unfavorable variance."

The variances may be classified as:

I Material Cost variance

II Labour Cost variance

III Overhead Variance.

IV Sales Variance

I. MATERIAL COST VARIANCE

Material cost variance is the difference between the actual cost of material and the standard cost of material.

Material cost variance can be classified as follows:

Material Cost Variance

Material Price Variance   Material Usage Variance

Material Mix Variance   Material Yield Variance

1. Material Cost Variance: Material cost variance is the difference between the standard cost of material and the actual cost of material. It may be calculated as follows:

Material Cost Variance = Standard Cost of Material-Actual Cost of Material

(or)

(Standard Qty. × Std.Price) – (Actual Qty. × Actual Price)

2. Material Price Variance:

Material Price Variance = (Std.Price - Actual Price) × Actual Quantity

3. Material Usage Variance: Material Usage Variance is otherwise called as Material Quantity Variance.

It may be calculated as follows:

Material Usage Variance = (Standard Quantity – Actual Quantity) × Standard Price.

4. Material Mix Variance:

Material Mix Variance = (Revised Standard Quantity – Actual Quantity) × Standard Price.

$$\text{Revised Std. Quantity} = \frac{\text{Std. Quantity of a Material} \times \text{Total Actual Qty.}}{\text{Total Std. Qty. of Material}}$$

5. Material Yield Variance

Material Yield Variance = (Actual Yield – Standard Yield) × Standard Material Price per unit.

Standard Yield = Standard output for actual mix

Actual Yield = Actual output

Standard Material Cost per unit = Total cost of Standard mix at standard price / Net Standard output.

Relations between the various Material Cost variances

1. Material Cost Variance = Material Price Variance + Material Quantity Variance
2. Material Quantity Variance = Material Mix Variance + Material Yield Variance.

Illustration: 1

Calculate Material Cost Variance, Material Quantity Variance and Material Price Variance from the following.

Material	*Standard*		*Actual*	
	Qty.	*Rate (Rs.)*	*Qty.*	*Rate (Rs.)*
A	2,000	5	1,800	6
B	1,000	8	1,100	7

Solution:

Material Cost Variance = Standard Cost - Actual Cost

Material A = $(2000 \times 5) - (1800 \times 6)$ = Rs. 800 (Adverse)

Material B = $(1000 \times 8) - (1100 \times 7)$ = Rs. 300 (Favourable)

Total Material Cost Variance = 800 – 300 = Rs. 500 (Adverse)

Material Price Variance = Actual Quantity (Std. Price - Actual Price)

Material A = 1800 (5 - 6) = Rs. 1800 (Adverse)

Material B = 1100 (8 - 7) = Rs. 1100 (Favourable)

Total MPV = 1800 – 1100 = Rs. 700 (Adverse)

Material Quantity Variance = Std. Price × (Std. Quantity - Actual Quantity)

Material A = 5 (2000 – 1800) = Rs. 1000 (Favourable)

Material B = 8 (1000 – 1100) = Rs. 800 (Adverse)

Total MQV = 1000 – 800 = Rs. 200 (Favourable)

Verification:

Material Cost Variance = MPV + MQV = - 700 + 200 = Rs. 500 (Adverse)

Illustration: 2

Doyle & Co Ltd. purchased 4000 units of a material for Rs. 12,000. The standard material required for producing 1 tonne of the final product is 50 units. The standard price of the material is Rs. 3.40 per unit. The stocks of material in the beginning and at the end are 1800 units and 500 units respectively. Actual production is 100 tonnes. Calculate material cost variance, material price variance and material usage variance.

Solution:

Actual production = 100 tonnes

Standard units for 1 tonne = 50

Standard units for 100 tonnes = $100 \times 50 = 5,000$

Standard price per unit = Rs. 3.40

Actual price per unit = $\frac{12,000}{4,000} = \text{Rs.}3$

Material Consumed:

Opening Stock of material = 1,800

Add : Purchase = 4,000

5,800

Less : Closing stock of material = 500

Actual Quantity = 5,300

Material Cost Variance = $(SQ \times SP) - (AQ \times AP)$

= $(5,000 \times 3.40) - (5,300 \times 3)$

= $17,000 - 15,900 = \text{Rs. } 1,100 \text{ (F)}$

Material Price Variance = $AQ\,(SP - AP)$

= $5,300\,(3.40 - 3)$

= $5,300 \times 0.40 = \text{Rs. } 2,120\text{(F)}$

Material Usage Variance = $SP\,(SQ - AQ)$

= $3.40\,(5,000 - 5,300)$

= $3.40 \times 300 = \text{Rs. } 1,020 \text{ (A)}$

Verification: MCV = MPV + MUV = $2,120 - 1,020 = \text{Rs.}1,100 \text{ (F)}$

Illustration: 3

K Ltd., provided the following information from its costing records for the month of December 2007. The details regarding the standard cost of manufacturing 10 units of product A are as follows:

Material	*Qty. (Kgm)*	*Unit Price (Rs.)*	*Value (Rs.)*
X	20	10	200
Y	15	8	120
Total	35		320

The actual cost for manufacturing 2000 units is as follows:

Material	*Qty. (Kgm)*	*Unit Price (Rs.)*	*Value (Rs.)*
X	4,550	12	54,600
Y	2,800	7	19,600
Total	7,350		74,200

Calculate material cost variance, material quantity variance, material price variance and material mix variance.

Solution:

	Standard Quantity of Material X	=	20/10 = 2 per unit
	Standard Quantity of Material Y	=	15/10 = 1.5 per unit
	Standard Quantity of Material X for 2000 units	=	$2 \times 2000 = 4000$ Kgm
	Standard Quantity of Material Y for 2000 units	=	$1.5 \times 2000 = 3000$ Kgm
	Revised standard Mix of Material X	=	$(4000/7000) \times 7350 = 4,200$ Kgm
	Revised standard Mix of Material Y	=	$(3000/7000) \times 7350 = 3,150$ Kgm
(i)	Material Cost Variance	=	(SQ × SP) – (AQ × AP)
	Material X	=	(4000 × 10) – (4550 × 12)
		=	40,000 – 54,600 = Rs.14,600 (A)
	Material Y	=	(3000 × 8) – (2800 × 7)
	=	=	24,000 - 19,600 = Rs.4,400 (F)
	Total MCV	=	–14,600 + 4,400 = Rs.10,200 (Adverse)
(ii)	Material Quantity Variance	=	SP (SQ – AQ)
	Material X	=	10 (4000 – 4550) = 10 × 550 = Rs.5,500 (A)
	Material Y	=	8 (3000 – 2800) = 8 × 200 = Rs.1,600 (F)
	Total MQV	=	–5,500 + 1,600 = Rs.3,900 (Adverse)
(iii)	Material Price Variance	=	AQ (SP – AP)
	Material X	=	4550 (10 – 12)
		=	4550 × 2 = Rs.9,100 (A)
	Material Y	=	2800 (8 – 7) = 2800 × 1 = Rs.2,800 (F)
	Total MPV	=	–9,100 + 2,800 = Rs.6,300 (Adverse)
(iv)	Material Mix Variance	=	Standard Price × (Revised Standard Mix – Actual Mix)
	Material X	=	10 × (4,200 – 4,550)
		=	10 × 350 = Rs.3500 (A)
	Material Y	=	8 × (3150 – 2800)
		=	8 × 350 = Rs.2800 (F)
	Total MMV	=	–3500 + 2800 = Rs.700 (Adverse)
	Verification: MCV	=	MQV + MPV = –3900 + 6300
		=	Rs.10,200 (A)

Illustration: 4

Find out Material Cost Variance, Material Quantity Variance, Material Price Variance, Material Mix Variance and Material Yield Variance from the following particulars.

Material	*Standard*			*Actual*		
	Qty.	*Rate (Rs.)*	*Amount (Rs.)*	*Qty.*	*Rate (Rs.)*	*Amount (Rs.)*
X	30,000	4.00	120,000	27,000	4.50	121,500
Y	20,000	3.00	60,000	28,000	2.00	56,000
Total	50,000		180,000	55,000		177,500

Actual production is 45,000 units. Standard loss is 10%.

Solution:

(i)	Material Cost Variance	=	Standard Cost – Actual Cost
		=	1,80,000 — 1,77,500 = Rs. 2500 (F)
(ii)	Material Quantity Variance	=	SP (SQ – AQ)
	Material X	=	4 (30,000 – 27,000)
		=	4 × 3,000 = Rs.12,000 (F)
	Material Y	=	3 (20,000 – 28,000)
		=	3 × 8,000 = Rs.24,000 (A)
	Total MQV	=	12,000 – 24,000 = Rs.12,000 (A)
(iii)	Material Price Variance	=	AQ (SP – AP)
	Material X	=	27,000 (4 – 4.50)
		=	27,000 × 0.50 = Rs.13,500 (A)
	Material Y	=	28,000 (3 – 2)
		=	28,000 × 1 = Rs.28,000 (F)
	Total MPV	=	–13,500 + 28,000 = Rs.14,500 (F)
(iv)	Material Mix Variance	=	SP (RSM – ASM)
	Material X	=	4 (33,000 – 27,000)
		=	4 × 6,000 = Rs.24,000 (F)
	Material Y	=	3 (22,000 – 28,000)
		=	3 × 6,000 = Rs.18,000 (A)
	Total MMV	=	24,000 – 18,000 = Rs.6,000 (F)
(v)	Material Yield Variance	=	Std. Rate for actual output × (AY – SY)
		=	4 (45,000 – 49,500)
		=	4 × 4500 = Rs.18,000 (A)
	Verification: MCV = MPV + MQV	=	–12,000 + 14,500 = Rs.2,500 (F)
	MQV = MMV + MYV	=	6,000 – 18,000 = Rs. 12,000 (A)

Workings:

Revised Std. Mix (RSM):	Material X	=	(30,000 / 50,000) × 55,000 = 33,000 units
	Material Y	=	(20,000 / 50,000) × 55,000 = 22,000 units
	Total	=	55,000 units
Standard output		=	Actual input – Std. Loss
		=	55,000 – (5 / 100) × 55,000
		=	55,000 – 5,500 = 49,500 units
Standard Rate for actual output		=	1,80,000 / 45,000 = Rs.4

Illustration: 5

A manufacturing company provides that the standard cost for manufacturing 10 units of the finished product as follows.

Material	*Qty.*	*Rate (Rs.)*	*Amount (Rs.)*
X	500	7	3,500
Y	300	5	1,500
Z	200	4	800
Total	100		5,800

Actual costs of manufacturing 100 units of finished products are as follows:

Material	*Qty.*	*Rate (Rs.)*
X	5,700	34,200
Y	2,900	20,300
Z	2,400	7,200
Total	11,000	61,700

Calculate (i) Material Cost Variance (ii) Material Quantity Variance (iii) Material Price Variance (iv) Material Mix Variance and (v) Material Yield Variance.

Solution:

Actual Price per unit of Material X = $34200 / 5700 = Rs.6$

Material Y = $20300 / 2900 = Rs.7$

Material Z = $7200 / 2400 = Rs.3$

Revised Standard Quantity of Material X = $(5000 / 10000) \times 11000 = 5500$ units

Material Y = $(3000 / 10000) \times 11000 = 3300$ units

Material Z = $(2000 / 10000) \times 11000 = 2200$ units

Revised Standard output = $(100 / 10000) \times 11000 = 110$ units

Standard Rate = $5800 / 10 = Rs.580$

(i) Material Cost Variance = Standard Cost – Actual Cost

= 58000 - 61700 = Rs.3700 (Adverse)

(ii) Material Quantity Variance = $(SQ - AQ) \times SR$

Material X = $(5000 - 5700) \times 7 = 700 \times 7$

= Rs.4900 (A)

Material Y = $(3000 - 2900) \times 5 = 100 \times 5$

= Rs.500 (F)

Material Z = $(2000 - 2400) \times 4 = 400 \times 4$

= Rs.1600 (A)

Total = $-4900 + 500 - 1600 =$ Rs.6000 (Adverse)

(iii) Material Price Variance = $(SP - AP) \times AQ$

Material X = $(7 - 6) \times 5700 = 1 \times 5700$

	=	Rs.5700 (F)
Material Y	=	$(5-7)\times 2900 = 2\times 2900$
	=	Rs.5800 (A)
Material Z	=	$(4-3)\times 2400 = 1\times 2400$
	=	Rs.2400 (F)
Total	=	$5700-5800+2400 =$ Rs.2300 (F)
(iv) Material Mix Variance	=	(Revised Standard Mix – Actual Mix) × Standard Rate
Material X	=	$(5500-5700)\times 7 = 200\times 7$
	=	Rs.1400 (A)
Material Y	=	$(3300-2900)\times 5 = 400\times 5$
	=	Rs.2000 (F)
Material Z	=	$(2200-2400)\times 4 = 200\times 4$
	=	Rs.800 (A)
Total	=	$-1400+2000-800 =$ Rs.200 (A)
Material Yield Variance	=	(Actual Yield – Revised Standard Yield) × Standard Rate of Actual Output
Rate for Actual output	=	$(100-110)\times 580$
	=	Rs. 5800 (Adverse)
Verification: MCV	=	MQV + MPV = – 6000 + 2300
	=	Rs.3700 (Adverse)
MQV	=	MMV + MYV = –200 – 5800 = Rs.6000 (A).

Illustration: 6

GR Ltd., provides the following information from its costing records.

Material	*Standard*			*Actual*		
	Qty.	*Rate Rs.*	*Amount Rs.*	*Qty.*	*Rate Rs.*	*Amount Rs.*
K	250	10	2,500	270	9	2,430
L	150	12	1,800	230	14	3,220
Total	400		4,300	500		5,650

The standard normal loss is estimated as 10%. Calculate all material cost variances.

Solution:

(i) Material Cost Variance	=	(Standard Qty. × S.P.) – (Actual Qty. × AP)
Material K	=	$(250\times 10)-(270\times 9)$
	=	$2500-2430 =$ Rs.70 (F)
Material L	=	$(150\times 12)-(230\times 14)$
	=	$1800-3220 =$ Rs.1420 (A)
Total MCV	=	$70-1420 =$ Rs.1350 (A)
(ii) Material Price Variance	=	(SP – AP) × AQ
Material K	=	$(10-9)\times 270 = 1\times 270$
	=	Rs.270 (F)

Material L	=	$(12-14)\times 230 = 2\times 230$
	=	Rs. 460 (A)
Total MPV	=	$270-460 =$ Rs.190 (A)
(iii) Material Quantity Variance	=	SP (SQ – AQ)
Material K	=	$10\,(250-270) = 10\times 20$
	=	Rs.200 (A)
Material L	=	$12\,(150-230) = 12\times 80$
	=	Rs. 960 (A)
Total MQV	=	$-200-960 =$ Rs.1160 (A)
(iv) Material Mix Variance	=	(Revised Standard Mix – Actual Mix) × SP
Revised Std. Mix of Actual Input	=	$\frac{\text{Std. Mix}}{\text{Total Standard Input}}\times$ Total Actual Input
Material K	=	$\frac{250}{400}\times 500 = 312.5$ units
Material L	=	$\frac{150}{400}\times 500 = 187.5$ units
MMV : Material K	=	$(312.5-270)\times 10 = 42.5\times 10$
	=	Rs. 425 (F)
Material L	=	$(187.5-230)\times 12 = 42.5\times 12$
	=	Rs. 510 (A)
Total MMV	=	$425-510 =$ Rs. 85 (A)
(v) Material Yield Variance	=	(Std. loss on Actual Input-Actual Loss) × Average Std. Cost per unit of output
	=	$(10\%\text{ of }500/140)\times\frac{4300}{(400\quad 40)}$
	=	$(50-140)\times 11.94 = 90\times 11.94$
	=	Rs. 1075 (A)
Verification: (i) MCV	=	MPV + MQV = – 190/1160
	=	Rs. 1350 (A)
(ii) MQV	=	MMV + MYV = – 85/1075
	=	Rs. 1160 (A)

II. LABOUR COST VARIANCE

Labour cost variance analyses the actual cost of labour with the standard cost of labour.

The different types of labour variances are as follows:

1. Labour Cost Variance
2. Labour Rate Variance
3. Labour Efficiency Variance
4. Labour Mix Variance
5. Labour Yield variance
6. Idle Time Variance

1. Labour Cost Variance

The difference between the standard cost of labour and actual cost of labour is called Labour Cost Variance. It may be calculated as follows.

Labour Cost Variance = Standard Cost of Labour – Actual Cost of Labour; (SC-AC)

(or) = (Std. Hours for actual output × Standard Rate) - (Actual Hours for Actual output × Actual Rate)

= [(SH × AQ) × SR] – [(AH × AQ) × AR]

= AQ [(SH × SR) – (AH × AR)]

2. Labour Rate Variance

It is also known as Labour Wage Variance.

Labour Rate Variance = Actual Hours (Standard Rate – Actual Rate); AH (SR – AR)

3. Labour Efficiency Variance

Labour Efficiency Variance is also known as Labour Time Variance.

Labour Efficiency Variance = Standard Rate (Standard Hours – Actual Hours); SR (SH – AH)

4. Labour Mix Variance

It is also known a Gang Composition Variance. It can be calculated when two or more types of labour cost are given. There are two different situations for the calculation of labour mix variance

(a) Labour mix variance when both the Total Standard hours and Total Actual hours are equal; and the ratio of standard mix is different from the ratio of actual mix.

Labour Mix Variance = Standard Rate (Standard Hours for Actual output – Actual Hours for Actual output)

(b) Labour Mix Variance when the Total Standard hours and Total Actual hours are not equal; and the ratio of standard mix is different from the ratio of actual mix.

Labour Mix Variance = Standard Rate (Revised Standard mix of actual hours – Actual mix of actual hours)

5. Labour Yield Variance

Labour Yield Variance = Standard Labour Cost per unit × (Standard Yield for Actual hours – Actual Yield)

6. Idle Time Variance

Idle time arises due to Machine break-down, Power failure, Strike, Shortage of raw material etc.

Idle time Variance = Abnormal Idle Time × Standard Rate

Illustration:7

Calculate Labour Cost Variance from the following.

Particulars	*Standard*	*Actual*
Wage Rage per hour (Rs.)	24	26
Labour hours per unit	5	4

The company produced 5000 units during the period

Solution:

Labour Cost Variance $= AQ [(SH \times SR) - (AH \times AR)]$

$= 5000 [(5 \times 24) - (4 \times 26)]$

$= 5000 (120 - 104)$

$= 5000 \times 18 =$ Rs.90,000 (Favourable)

Illustration: 8

Calculate labour rate variance for actual output of 4000 units.

Particulars	*Standard*	*Actual*
Number of labour hours per unit	5	5.5
Wage rate per hour (Rs.)	20	22

Solution:

Actual hours for one unit $= 5.5$

Actual hours for 4000 units $= 5.5 \times 4000 = 22{,}000$

Labour Rate Variance $= AH (SR - AR)$

$= 22{,}000 (20 - 22)$

$= 22{,}000 \times 2$

$=$ Rs.44,000 (Adverse)

Illustration: 9

Calculate Labour Efficiency Variance from the following.

Particular	*Standard*	*Actual*
Wage rate per hour (Rs.)	20	19
Labour hours per unit	11	11.5

Actual output 1000 units.

Solution:

Standard hours for 1000 units $= 11 \times 1000 = 11{,}000$

Actual hours for 1000 units $= 11.5 \times 1000 = 11{,}500$

Labour Efficiency Variance $= SR (SH - AH)$

$= 20 (11{,}000 - 11{,}500)$

$= 20 \times 500 =$ Rs. 10,000 (Adverse)

Illustration: 10

The standard labour cost per unit of a product manufactured by D Ltd., is stated as follows.

Workers	*Hours per unit of output*	*Hourly Rate Rs.*	*Amount Rs.*
X	7	27	189
Y	5	25	125
	12		314

The actual cost for producing 500 units is as follows.

Workers	*Hours*	*Hourly Rate Rs.*	*Amount Rs.*
X	3700	29	107,300
Y	2300	24	55,200
	6000		162,500

Calculate (i) Labour Cost Variance (ii) Labour Rate Variance (iii) Labour Efficiency Variance (iv) Labour Mix Variance.

Solution:

(i) LCV = AQ [(SH × SR) – (AH × AR)]

X = 500 [(7 × 27) – (7.4 × 29)] = 500 (189 – 214.6)

= 500 × 25.6 = Rs. 12,800 (Unfavourable)

Y = 500 [(5 × 25) – (4.6 × 24)] = 500 (125 - 110.4)

= 500 × 14.6 = Rs.7300 (Favourable)

LCV = –12,800 + 7300 = Rs.5500 (Unfavourable)

(ii) LRV = AH (SR – AR)

X = 3700 (27 – 29) = 3700 × 2 = Rs.7400 (Unfavourable)

Y = 2300 (25 – 24) = 2300 × 1 = Rs.2300 (Favourable)

LRV = –7400 + 2300 = Rs.5100 (Unfavourable)

(iii) LEV = SR (SH – AH)

X = 27 (3500 – 3700) = 27 × 200 = Rs.5400 (Unfavourable)

Y = 25 (2500 – 2300) = 25 × 200 = Rs.5000 (Favourable)

LEV = – 5400 + 5000 = Rs.400 (Unfavourable)

(iv) LMV = SR (RSH – AH)

X = 27 (3500 – 3700) = 27 × 200 = Rs.5400 (Unfavourable)

Y = 25 (2500 – 2300) = 25 × 200 = Rs.5000 (Favourable)

LMV = – 5400 + 5000 = Rs.400 (Unfavourable)

When total standard hours are equal to total actual hours, then the LMV is equal to LEV.

Verification: LCV = LRV + LEV = 5100 + 400 = Rs.5,500 (U)

Workings: (a) AH per unit : X = 3700 / 500 = 7.4

Y = 2300 / 500 = 4.6

(b) SH for 500 units: X = 7 × 500 = 3500

Y = 5 × 500 = 2500

Illustration: 11

XYZ Co. Ltd., provided the following information from the costing records.

Standard labour costs per unit are as follows.

Workers	*Hours per unit*	*Hourly Rate Rs.*	*Amount Rs.*
Male	3	30	90
Female	2	27	54
	5		144

Actual labour cost for 1000 units are as follows.

Workers	*Hours per unit*	*Hourly Rate Rs.*	*Amount Rs.*
Male	2900	32	92,800
Female	2500	26	65,000
	5400		157,800

Calculate (i) Labour Cost Variance (ii) Labour Rate Variance (iii) Labour Efficiency Variance (iv) Labour Mix Variance (v) Labour Yield Variance.

Solution:

Standard hours for 1000 units:

Male	=	3×1000	= 3000
Female	=	2×1000	= 2000
Total	=		5000

Revised Standard Hours:

Male	=	$(3000/5000) \times 5400$	=	3240
Female	=	$(2000/5000) \times 5400$	=	2160
Total	=			5400

Standard Labour Cost for 1000 units= 144×1000 = Rs.144,000

$$\text{Standard Rate} = \frac{1{,}44{,}000}{5{,}000}$$

$$= \text{Rs. } 28.80$$

(i) LCV = Standard Cost – Actual Cost

= 144,000 – 157,800 = Rs.13,800 (Adverse)

(ii) LRV = AH (SR – AR)

Male = 2900 (30 – 32) = 2900×2 = Rs. 5800 (Adverse)

Female = 2500 (27 – 26) = 2500×1 = Rs. 2500 (Favourable)

LRV = – 5800 + 2500 = Rs. 3300 (Adverse)

(iii) LEV = SR (SH – AH)

	Male	=	30 (3000 – 2900) = 30 × 100 = Rs.3000 (Favourable)
	Female	=	27 (2000 – 2500) = 27 × 500 = Rs.13,500 (Adverse)
	LEV	=	3000 – 13500 = Rs.10,500 (Adverse)
(iv)	LMV	=	SR (RSH – AH)
	Male	=	30 (3240 – 2900) = 30 × 340 = Rs. 10,200 (Favourable)
	Female	=	27 (2160 – 2500) = 27 × 340 = Rs. 9180 (Adverse)
	LMV	=	10200 – 9180 = Rs.1020 (Favourable)
(v)	LYV	=	SR (SY – AY)
		=	28.8 (5000 – 5400) = Rs. 11520 (Adverse)

Verification: LCV = LRV + LEV = –3300 – 10500
= Rs.13,800 (Adverse)

LEV = LMV + LYV = 1020 – 11520 = Rs. 10500 (Adverse)

Illustration: 12

Standard hours required for manufacturing 1 unit of a product is 5 hours @ Rs.30 per hour. If the company paid Rs.297,000 for manufacturing 2000 units @ Rs.27 per hour, find out LCV, LRV and LEV.

Solution:

Standard hours for 2000 units	=	5 × 2000 = 10000
Actual hours for 2000 units	=	2,97,000 / 27 = 11000
Actual hours for 1 unit	=	11,000 / 2,000 = 5.5
Standard Cost	=	10,000 × 30 = Rs.300,000
SR	=	Rs.30; AR = Rs.27
LCV	=	Standard Cost – Actual Cost
	=	3,00,000 – 2,97,000 = Rs. 3,000 (Favourable)
LRV	=	AH (SR – AR) = 11,000 (30 – 27) = 11,000 × 3
	=	33,000 (Favourable)
LEV	=	SR (SH – AH) = 30 (10,000 – 11,000)
	=	30 × 1,000 = Rs. 30,000 (Unfavourable)
LCV	=	LRV + LEV = 33,000 – 30,000
	=	Rs.3,000 (Favourable)

Illustration: 13

KT Ltd., provided the following information related to the payment of wages.

Particulars	*Skilled Workers*	*Semi-Skilled Workers*	*Unskilled Workers*
Standard number of workers in the gang	50	30	20
Standard rate per hour (Rs.)	27	24	20
Actual number of workers in the gang	55	27	18
Actual rate per hour (Rs.)	29	25	22

The Company worked for 50 hours in the week and produced 4500 standard hours of work.

Calculate (i) Labour Cost Variance (ii) Labour Rate Variance (iii) Labour Efficiency Variance (iv) Labour Mix Variance and (v) Labour Yield Variance.

Solution:

Calculation of Labour Variances

(i)	LCV	=	Standard Labour Cost – Actual Labour Cost
		=	(4500/5000) × 123,500 – 133,300 = Rs.22,150 (Adverse)
(ii)	LRV	=	AH (SR – AR)
	Skilled	=	2750 (27 – 29) = 2750 × 2 = Rs. 5,500 (Adverse)
	Semi-Skilled	=	1350 (24 – 25) = 1350 × 1 = Rs. 1,350 (Adverse)
	Unskilled	=	900 (20 – 22) = 900 × 2 = Rs.1,800 (Adverse)
	LRV	=	5500 + 1350 + 1800 = Rs.8,650 (Adverse)
(iii)	LEV	=	SR (RSH – AH)
	Skilled	=	27 (2250 – 2750) = 27 × 500 = Rs.13,500 (Adverse)
	Semi-Skilled	=	24 (1350 – 1350) = 24 × 0 = 0
	Unskilled	=	20 (900 – 900) = 20 × 0 = 0
	LEV	=	13,500 + 0 + 0 = Rs. 13,500 (Adverse)
(iv)	LMV	=	SR (SH – AH)
	Skilled	=	27 (2500 – 2750) = 27 × 250 = Rs. 6,750 (Adverse)
	Semi-Skilled	=	24 (1500 – 1350) = 24 × 150 = Rs. 3,600 (Favourable)
	Unskilled	=	20 (1000 – 900) = 20 × 100 = Rs. 2,000 (Favourable)
	LMV	=	– 6750 + 3600 + 2000 = Rs. 1,150 (Adverse)
(v)	LYV	=	SR (AY – SY)
		=	24.70 (4500 – 5000) = Rs. 12,350 (Adverse)
			(SR = 123,500 / 5000 = Rs.24.70)

Verification:

LCV	=	LRV + LEV = 8650 + 13500	= Rs.22,150 (Adverse)
LEV	=	LMV + LYV= 1,150 + 12,350	= Rs.13,500 (Adverse)

Workings:

(a) Calculation of Standard and Actual Labour Cost

Labour	*Standard*			*Actual*		
	Rate Rs.	*Hours*	*Amount Rs.*	*Rate Rs.*	*Hours*	*Amount Rs.*
Skilled	27	50×50 = 2500	67,500	29	55×50 = 2750	79,750
Semi-skilled	24	30×50 = 1500	36,000	25	27×50 = 1350	33,750
Unskilled	20	30×50 = 1000	20,000	22	18×50 = 900	19,800
Total		5000	1,23,500		5000	1,33,300

(b) Calculation of Revised Standard hours

$$\text{Skilled workers} = \frac{2500}{5000} \times 4500 = 2250 \text{ hours}$$

$$\text{Semi-skilled workers} = \frac{1500}{5000} \times 4500 = 1350 \text{ hours}$$

$$\text{Unskilled workers} = \frac{1000}{5000} \times 4500 = 900 \text{ hours.}$$

Note: Mix variance is related to total actual hours and total standard hours.

Illustration: 14

Calculate various Labour variances from the following information

Workers	*Standard*		*Actual*	
	Number	*Wage Rate per week (Rs.)*	*Number*	*Wage Rate per week (Rs.)*
X	60	2,000	65	2,200
Y	42	1,500	38	1,300
Z	18	1,000	17	900
	120		120	

The Standard time required is 10 weeks and Actual time taken for completing the work is 9 weeks.

Solution:

Calculation of Labour Variances

Workers	*Standard*			*Actual*		
	Hours (weeks)	*Weekly Rate Rs.*	*Total Wage Rs.*	*Hours (weeks)*	*Weekly Rate Rs.*	*Total Wage Rs.*
X	60 × 10 = 600	2,000	12,00,000	65 × 9 = 585	2,200	12,87,000
Y	42 × 10 = 420	1,500	6,30,000	38 × 9 = 342	1,300	4,44,600
Z	18 × 10 = 180	1,000	1,80,000	17 × 9 = 153	900	1,37,700
Total	1,200		20,10,000	1,080		18,69,300

Revised Standard hours:
X = (600 / 1200) × 1080 = 540
Y = (420 / 1200) × 1080 = 378
Z = (180 / 1200) × 1080 = 162
Total = 1080

(i) LCV = SLC – ALC
= 20,10,000 – 18,69,300 = Rs.1,40,700 (Favourable)

(ii) LRV = AH (SR – AR)
X = 585 (2000 – 2200) = 585 × 200 = Rs.1,17,000 (Unfavourable)
Y = 342 (1500 – 1300) = 342 × 200 = Rs.68,400 (Favourable)
Z = 153 (1000 – 900) = 153 × 100 = Rs.15,300 (Favourable)
LRV = – 1,17,000 + 68,400 + 15,300 = Rs. 33,300 (Unfavourable)

(iii)	LEV	=	SR (SH – AH)
	X	=	2000 (600 – 585) = 2000 (600 – 585) = 2000 × 15 = Rs. 30,000 (Favourable)
	Y	=	1500 (420 – 342) = 1500 (420 – 342) = 1500 × 78 = Rs. 1,17,000 (Favourable)
	Z	=	1000 (180 – 153) = 1000 (180 – 153) = 1000 × 27 = Rs. 27,000 (Favourable)
	LEV	=	30,000 + 1,17,000 + 27,000 = Rs.1,74,000 (Favourable)
(iv)	LMV	=	SR (RSH – AH)
	X	=	2000 (540 – 585) = 2000 × 45 = Rs.90,000 (Unfavourable)
	Y	=	1500 (378 – 342) = 1500 × 36 = Rs.54,000 (Favourable)
	Z	=	1000 (162 – 153) = 1000 × 9 = Rs.9,000 (Favourable)
	LMV	=	– 90000 + 54000 + 9000 = Rs.27,000 (Unfavourable)
(v)	LYV	=	SR (AY – SY)
		=	1675 (1200 – 1080) = 1675 × 120 = Rs.2,01,000 (Favourable)
	SR	=	20,10,000 / 1200 = Rs.1,675.

Verification:

LCV = LRV + LEV = –33,300 + 1,74,000 = Rs.1,40,700 (Favourable)

(or) = LRV + LMV + LYV

= – 33,300 – 27,000 + 2,01,000 = Rs.1,40,700 (Favourable)

LEV = LMV + LYV = – 27,000 + 2,01,000 = Rs.1,74,000 (Favourable).

Illustration: 15

GR Ltd., provided the following information from the costing records.

Workers	Standard		Actual	
	Labour	*Rate (Rs.)*	*Labour*	*Rate (Rs.)*
Male	200	22	170	24
Female	100	20	130	19

The company also provided that the Budgeted hours as 500, Actual hours as 480, Budgeted gross production 30,000 units, Standard loss 10%, Actual loss 2500 units. Calculate all the labour variances.

Solution:

Calculation of Standard and Actual Cost

Workers	*Standard*			*Actual*		
	Hour	*Rate Rs.*	*Amount Rs.*	*Hour*	*Rate Rs.*	*Amount Rs.*
Male	1,00,000	22	22,00,000	81,600	24	19,58,400
Female	50,000	20	10,00,000	62,400	19	11,85,600
Total	1,50,000		32,00,000	1,44,000		31,44,000

Labour Cost Variance = Std. Cost for Actual Production – Actual Cost

$$= \frac{32,00,000}{27,000} \times 27,500 - 31,44,000$$

= 32,59,259 - 31,44,000 = Rs.1,15,259 (F)

Labour Rate Variance = Actual Hours (Std. Rate – Actual Rate)

Male = 81,600 (22 – 24) = 81,600 × 2 = Rs. 1,63,200 (A)

Female = 62,400 (20 – 19) = 62,400 × 1 = Rs. 62,400 (F)

LRV = –1,63,200 + 62,400 = Rs. 1,00,800 (Adverse)

Labour Efficiency Variance = SR (Std. Hours for actual output – Actual hours)

Male $= 22\left[\frac{1,00,000}{27,000} \times 27,500 \quad 81,600\right]$

= 22 (1,01,852 – 81,600) = 22 × 20,252

Rs. 4,45,544 (F)

Female $= 20\left[\frac{50,000}{27,000} \times 27,500 \quad 62,400\right]$

= 20 (50,926 – 62,400) = 20 × 11,474

= Rs. 2,29,480 (A)

LEV = 4,45,544 – 2,29,480 = Rs. 2,16,064 (F)

Labour Mix Variance = SR (Revised Std. Hours – Actual Hours)

Male $= 22\left[\frac{1,00,000}{1,50,000} \times 1,44,000 \quad 81,600\right]$

= 22(96,000 – 81,600) = 22 × 1440)

= Rs.3,16,800 (F)

Female $= 20\left[\frac{50,000}{1,50,000} \times 1,44,000 \quad 62,400\right]$

= 20 (48,000 – 62,400) = 20 × 1,440

= Rs.2,88,000 (A)

LMV = 3,16,800 – 2,88,000 = Rs.28,800 (F)

LYV = SR (Actual Yield – Std.Yield)

= 118.52 (27,500 – 25,920) = 118.52 × 1,580 = Rs.1,87,262 (F)

[Std. Yield = (27,00,000/500) × 480 = 25,920; Std. Rate = 32,00,000/27,000 = Rs.118.52]

Verification:

LCV = LRV + LEV = –1,08,000 + 2,16,064 = 1,15,264 (F)

LEV = LMV + LYV = 28,800 + 1,87,262 = Rs.2,16,062 (F)

Illustration: 16

The normal standard hours in a week of a company is 50 and the standard production is 6000 units. The workers required for producing standard output are 30 skilled workers, 25 semi-skilled workers and 15 unskilled workers and they have to be paid @ Rs.30, Rs.25 and Rs.20 per hour respectively.

Actual production is 5500 units. Actual workers employed are 33 skilled workers, 24 semi-skilled workers and 13 unskilled workers and they are paid @ Rs.32, Rs.23 and Rs.19 per hour respectively. The abnormal idle time is 5 hours.

Calculate (i) Labour Cost Variance, (ii) Labour Rate Variance, (iii) Labour Efficiency Variance, (iv) Labour Mix Variance, (v) Labour Yield Variance and (vi) Idle Time Variance.

Solution:

Calculation of Standard and Actual Cost

Workers	*Standard*			*Actual*		
	Hours	*Rate Rs.*	*Amount Rs.*	*Hours*	*Rate Rs.*	*Amount Rs.*
Skilled	1500	30	45,000	1650	32	52,800
Sem-skilled	1250	25	31,250	1200	23	27,600
Unskilled	750	20	15,000	650	19	12,350
Total	3500		91,250	3500		92,750

Calculation of Labour Variances:

(i) Labour Cost Variance = Std. Cost for Actual output – Actual Cost

$= \frac{91,250}{6,000} \times 5,500 - 92,750 = \text{Rs.}9,105\ (A)$

(ii) Labour Rate Variance = Actual Hours (Std. Rate – Actual Rate)

Skilled $= 1650\ (30 - 32) = 1650 \times 2 = \text{Rs.}3300\ (A)$

Semi-skilled $= 1200\ (25 - 23) = 1200 \times 2 = \text{Rs. } 2400\ (F)$

Unskilled $= 650\ (20 - 19) = 650 \times 1 = \text{Rs. } 650\ (F)$

LRV $= -3300 + 2400 + 650 = \text{Rs. } 250\ (A)$

(iii) Labour Efficiency Variance = SR (Std. hour for actual output – Actual hours for wage paid)

Skilled $= 30\left[\frac{1500}{6,000} \times 5000 - 1650\right]$

$= 30\ (1375 - 1650) = 30 \times 275 = \text{Rs. } 8,250\ (A)$

Semi-skilled $= 25\left[\frac{1250}{6,000} \times 5500 - 1200\right]$

$= 25\ (1145 - 1200) = 25 \times 55 \quad = \text{Rs. } 1,375\ (A)$

Unskilled $= 20\left[\frac{750}{6,000} \times 5500 - 650\right]$

$= 20\ (688 - 650) = 20 \times 38 = \text{Rs. } 760\ (F)$

LEV $= -8250 - 1375 + 760 = \text{Rs. } 8,865\ (A)$

Labour Efficiency Variance can be calculated by adjusting the Idle time also as follows.

Labour Efficiency Variance = SR (Std. hours for actual output – Actual hours worked)

Skilled $= 30\ [1375 - (33 \times 45)] \quad = 30\ (1375 - 1485)$

$= 30 \times 110 \quad = \text{Rs. } 3,300\ (A)$

Semi-skilled $= 25\ [1145 - (24 \times 45)] \quad = 25\ (1145 - 1080)$

$= 25 \times 65 \quad = \text{Rs. } 1,625\ (F)$

Unskilled $= 20\ [687 - (13 \times 45)] \quad = 20\ (687 - 585)$

$= 20 \times 102 \quad = \text{Rs. } 2,040\ (F)$

LEV $= -3300 + 1625 + 2040 \quad = \text{Rs.}365\ (F)$

(iv) Labour Mix Variance = SR (Revised Std. Hour - Actual Hour Worked)

Skilled = $30\left[\frac{1500}{3500} \times 3150 \quad (33 \times 45)\right]$

= 30 (1350 – 1485) = 30 × 135 = Rs. 4,050 (A)

Semi-skilled = $25\left[\frac{1250}{3500} \times 3150 \quad (24 \times 45)\right]$

= 25 (1125 – 1080) = 25 × 45 = Rs. 1,125 (F)

Unskilled = $20\left[\frac{750}{3500} \times 3150 \quad (13 \times 45)\right]$

= 20 (675 – 585) = 20 × 90 = Rs. 1,800 (F)

LMV = –4050 + 1125 + 1800 = Rs. 1,125 (A)

(Actual hours without Idle time = 3500 – (70 × 5) = 3500 – 350 = 3150)

(v) Labour Yield Variance = Std. Rate per unit (Std. output for Actual Hours – Actual output)

= 15.20 (5400 – 5500) = 15.20 × 100 = Rs.1,520 (F)

(Std. Rate = 91,250 / 6000 = Rs. 15.20

Std. output for Actual Hour = $\frac{6000}{35,000} \times 31500 = 5400$ units)

(vi) Idle Time Variance = Idle hours × SR

Skilled = (33 × 5) × 30 = Rs. 4,950

Semi-skilled = (24 × 5) × 25 = Rs. 3,000

Unskilled = (13 × 5) × 20 = Rs. 1,300

ITV = 4900 + 3000 + 1300 = Rs.9,250 (A)

Verification:

(i) LCV = LRV + LEV = –250 – 8865 = Rs. 9,115 (A)

(ii) LEV = LEV + ITV = –365 – 9250 = Rs. 8,885 (A)

= LMV + LYV + ITV

= –1125 + 1520 – 9250 – 891 = Rs. 8,850 (A).

(*Note :* Slight variations are due to approximation of fractions)

III. OVERHEAD VARIANCE

Overhead means indirect cost. Indirect cost incurred in a concern may be classified on the basis of elementwise, functionwise and behaviour wise. Elementwise, overhead constitutes indirect material, indirect labour and indirect expenses. Function wise, overhead included production overhead, administration overhead and selling and distribution overhead. Behaviour wise, Overhead is classified as fixed and variable overheads.

Overhead Cost variance is the difference between the standard cost of overhead and the actual cost of overhead.

Overhead Cost Variance = Overhead recovered – Actual overhead incurred

Overhead Recovered = Standard hours for Actual output × Standard

Overhead rate per hour (Or) = Actual output × Standard overhead rate per unit

Overhead Cost variance is classified as follows:

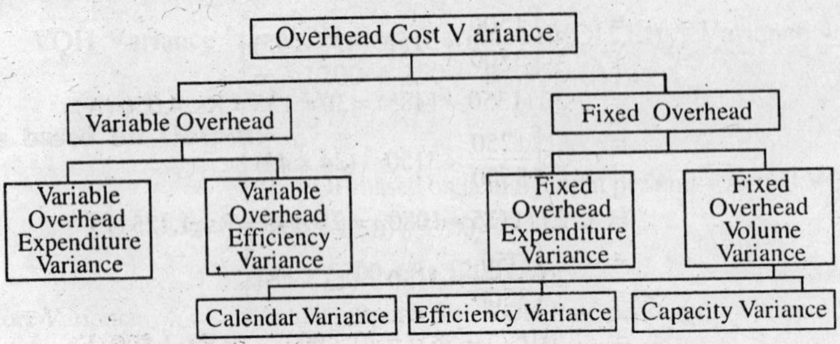

A. VARIABLE OVERHEAD VARIANCE

Variable Overhead Variance is the difference between the standard variable overhead for actual output and the actual variable overhead.

VOH Variance = (Actual Output × Std. VOH rate per unit) – Actual Overhead.

(or)

(Std. VOH for actual hours × Std. VOH rate per hour) - Actual Overhead.

Variable overhead variance is classified as follows:

1. Variable Overhead Expenditure Variance

It is otherwise called as Variable Overhead Spending Variance or Variable Overhead Budget Variance.

VOH Expenditure Variance = (Actual hours × Std. VOH rate per hour) – Actual VOH

(or)

(Actual Output × Std. VOH rate per unit) – Actual VOH

2. Variable Overhead Efficiency Variance

VOH Efficiency Variance = Std.Cost per hour × (Std. hours for actual output – Actual hours)

B. FIXED OVERHEAD VARIANCE

Fixed overhead variance is the difference between Standard Fixed Overhead and the Actual Fixed Overhead.

FOH Variance = Standard Fixed Overhead – Actual Fixed Overhead

(or)

(Std. hours for actual output × Std. FOH rate per hour) – Actual Fixed Overhead.

Fixed overhead variance is classified as follows.

1. Fixed Overhead Expenditure Variance

It is otherwise called as Fixed Overhead Spending Variance or Fixed Overhead Budget Variance.

FOH Expenditure Variance = (Actual hours × Std. FOH rate per hour) – Actual FOH

(or)

(Actual output × Std. FOH rate per unit) – Actual FOH.

2. Fixed Overhead Volume Variance

FOH Volume Variance = Std. FOH rate per unit × (Budgeted production – Actual production) (or)

Budgeted Fixed overhead based on Std. hours allowed by actual output - Budgeted Fixed overhead for actual output.

Fixed Overhead Volume Variance is classified as follows:

(a) Fixed Overhead Calendar Variance

FOH Calendar Variance = Std. FOH rate per hour × (Budgeted hours – Revised budgeted capacity hours)

(or) = Std. FOH rate per unit × (Budgeted Quantity – Revised Quantity in terms of actual no.of days worked).

(b) Fixed Overhead Efficiency Variance

FOH Efficiency Variance = Std. FOH rate per hour × (Std. hours for actual production – Actual hours)

(or) = Std. FOH rate per unit × (Std. production as per actual time available Actual production)

(c) Fixed Overhead Capacity Variance

FOH Capacity Variance = Std. FOH rate per hour × (Budgeted Capacity hours – Actual Capacity hours)

(or) = Std. FOH rate per unit × (Revised budgeted units – Actual Capacity units)

The VOH Variances and FOH Variances are calculated either on the basis of hours or on the basis of number of units of production.

Illustration: 17

Calculate Variable Overhead Cost variances from the following information.

Particulars	*Budget*	*Actual*
Labour hours	1,000	900
Output (units)	2,000	1,900
Variable Overhead (Rs.)	5,000	5,700

Solution:

Standard VOH rate per hour = 5000/1000 = Rs.5

Standard VOH rate per unit = 5000/2000 = Rs.2.50

Standard hours based on actual output = 1000/2000 × 1900 = 950 hours

Standard output based on actual hours = 2000/1000 × 900 = 1800 units

(a) VOH variances based on Hours:

(i) VOH Variance = Std.VOH based on Actual hours – Actual VOH

= (950 × 5) – 5700

= 4750 – 5700 = Rs. 950 (A)

(ii) VOH Expenditure Variance = Actual hours × Std.VOH Rate per hour – Actual VOH

= (900 × 5) — 5700 = 4500 – 5700

= Rs. 1200 (A)

(iii) VOH Efficiency Variance = Std. VOH Rate (Standard hours for actual production – Actual hours)

= 5 (950 – 900) = Rs.250 (F)

Verification:

VOH Variance = VOH Exp. Variance+VOH Effy. Variance

= – 1200 + 250 = Rs.950 (A)

(a) VOH variances based on Output:

(i) VOH Variance = Std. VOH based on actual output per unit – Actual VOH

VOH = $(1800 \times 2.50) - 5700$

= 4500 – 5700 = Rs.1200 (A)

(ii) VOH Expenditure Variance = (Actual output × Std. VOH Rate per output) – Actual VOH

= $(1900 \times 2.50) - 5700$

= 4750 – 5700 = Rs. 950 (A)

(iii) VOH Efficiency Variance = Std. VOH rate (Std. output for actual hours – Actual VOH)

= 2.50 (1800 – 1900)

= 2.50×100 = Rs. 250 (A)

Verification:

VOH Variance = VOH Expenditure Variance + VOH Efficiency Variance

= –950 – 250 = Rs. 1200 (A)

Illustration: 18

Calculate Variable Overhead variances from the following information.

	Budgeted	*Actual*
Production (in units)	12,000	15,000
Man hours to produce above units	36,000	42,000
Variable overheads (Rs.)	45,000	54,000

The standard time to produce one unit of the product is 3 hours.

Solution:

Standard VOH rate per hour = 45000/36000 = Rs. 1.25

Standard VOH rate per unit = 45000/12000 = Rs. 3.75

Standard VOH based on actual output = 15000×3.75 = Rs.56,250

Standard VOH based on actual hours = 42000×1.25 = Rs.52,500

Standard hours for actual output = 15000×3 = 45000 hours

Standard output for actual hours = $(12000/36000) \times 42000$ = 14000 units

(a) VOH variances based on Hours:

(i) VOH Variance = Standard VOH based on Actual output – Actual VOH

= 56,250 – 54,000 = Rs.2250 (F)

(ii) VOH Expenditure Variance = Std. VOH based on Actual hours – Actual VOH

= 52,500 – 54,000 = Rs.1500 (A)

(iii) VOH Efficiency Variance = Std. VOH Rate (Standard hours for Actualproduction – Actual Hours)

= 1.25 (45000 – 42000) = Rs.3750 (F)

Verification:

VOH Variance = VOH Expenditure Variance + VOH Efficiency Variance = – 1500 + 3750 = Rs.2250 (F)

(b) VOH variances based on Output:

(i)	VOH Variance	=	Standard VOH based on actual hours – Actual VOH
		=	52500 - 54,000 = Rs.1500 (A)
(ii)	VOH Expenditure Variance	=	Standard VOH based on actual output – Actual VOH
		=	56,250 – 54,000 = Rs.2250 (F)
(iii)	VOH Efficiency Variance	=	Std. VOH rate per unit (Std. output for actual hours – Actual output)
		=	3.75 (14000 – 15000) = 3.75 × 1000 = Rs.3750 (A)

Verification:

VOH Variance = VOH Expenditure Variance + VOH Efficiency Variance = 2250 – 3750 = Rs. 1,500 (A).

Illustration: 19

Calculate the Fixed overhead variances from the following:

Particulars	*Budget*	*Actual*
Fixed Overhead (Rs.)	50,000	40,000
Output (units)	20,000	23,000
Working Days	30	33

Solution:

	Standard FOH rate per unit	=	50000/20000 = Rs. 2.50
(i)	Fixed Overhead Variance	=	(Actual Output × Std. FOH rate) – Actual FOH
		=	(23000 × 2.50) – 40,000
		=	57500 – 40,000 = Rs. 17500 (F)
(ii)	FOH Expenditure Variance	=	Budgeted FOH – Actual FOH
		=	50000 - 40,000 = Rs. 10000 (F)
(iii)	FOH Volume Variance	=	(Actual Output × Std. FOH rate) – Budgeted FOH
		=	(23000 × 2.50) – 50000
		=	57500 – 50000 = Rs. 7,500 (F)
(iv)	FOH Capacity Variance	=	Std. FOH Rate (Budgeted Output – Actual Output)
		=	2.50 (20000 – 23000)
		=	2.50 × 3000 = Rs. 7,500 (F)
	[Revised Budgeted Output	=	(20000 /30) × 33 = 22000]
(v)	FOH Calendar Variance	=	Std. FOH Rate (Budgeted Output – Revised Budgeted Output)
		=	2.50 × (20000 – 22000) = 2.50 × 2000 = 5000 (A)
(vi)	FOH Efficiency Variance	=	Std. Rate × (Std. Output for Actual hours – Actual Output
		=	2.50 × (22000 – 23000) = Rs.2,500 (F)

Verification:

FOHV = FOHEV + FOHVV = 10000 + 7500 = 17500 (F)

FOH Eff. Variance = FOH Cap. V + FOH Cal. V

= 7500 – 5000 = Rs. 2500 (F)

B. SALES VARIANCE

Sales Variance is the difference between Actual Sales and Budgeted Sales. It helps the management for making decision in future with respect to sales. It is possible for the management to take necessary steps if there is unfavourable sales variance. There are two methods for calculating sales variance.

They are:

1. Profit Method or Sales Margin Method
2. Sales Value Method.

1. Profit Method or Sales Margin Method

The following are the different Sales Variances under Profit Method.

(a) Total Sales Margin Variance

(b) Sales Margin Variance due to Selling Price

(c) Sales Margin Variance due to Sales Volume

(d) Sales Margin Variance due to Sales Mixture

(e) Sales Margin Variance due to Sales Quantity

The formula for the variances are stated as follows:

(a) Total Sales Margin Variance = Actual Profit – Budgeted Profit

(or) = (AP × AQ) – (BP × BQ)

(b) Sales Margin Variance due to Selling Price = AQ (ASP – BSP)

(c) Sales Margin Variance due to Sales Volume = BP (AQ – BQ)

(d) Sales Margin Variance due to Sales Mixture = BP (AQ – RBQ)

(e) Sales Margin Variance due to Sales Quantity = BP (RBQ – BQ)

[Where AQ = Actual Quantity, BQ = Budgeted Quantity, AP = Actual Profit per unit, BP = Budgeted Profit per unit, ASP = Actual Selling Price per unit, BSP = Budgeted Selling Price per unit, RBQ= Revised Budgeted Quantity]

$$\text{RBQ} = \frac{\text{Individual Budgeted Quantity} \times \text{Total Actual Quantity}}{\text{Total Budgeted Quantity}}$$

2. Sales Value Method

The following are the different sales variances under Sales Value method:

(a) Total Sales Value Variance = Actual Sales – Budgeted Sales

(or) = (ASP × AQ) – (BSP × BQ)

(b) Sales Price Variance = AQ (ASP – BSP)

(c) Sales Volume Variance = BSP (AQ – BQ)

(d) Sales Mix Variance = BSP (AQ – RBQ)

(e) Sales Quantity Variance = BSP (RBQ – BQ)

[Where AQ = Actual Quantity, BQ = Budgeted Quantity, ASP = Actual Selling Price per unit, BSP = Budgeted Selling Price per unit, RBQ = Revised Budgeted Quantity.]

$$RBQ = \frac{\text{Individual Budgeted Quantity} \times \text{Total Actual Quantity}}{\text{Total Budgeted Quantity}}$$

Illustration: 20

N Ltd., provided the following information from the costing records for the month March 2006.

	Budgeted	*Actual*
Product: X Sales quantity	6000	5500
Selling price per unit (Rs.)	50	60
Product: Y Sales quantity	4000	5000
Selling price per unit (Rs.)	30	27

The cost of production for Product X and Y are Rs. 47 and Rs. 25 respectively.

Calculate (i) Sales Margin Variance, (ii) Sales Price Variance (iii) Sales Volume Variance (iv) Sales Mix Variance and (v) Sales Quantity Variance by Sales Margin Method.

Solution:

Budgeted Profit per unit for Product X = 50 – 47 = Rs. 3

Budgeted Profit per unit for Product Y = 30 – 25 = Rs. 5

Actual Profit per unit for Product X = 60 – 47 = Rs. 13

Actual Profit per unit for Product Y = 27 – 25 = Rs. 2

(i) Sales Margin Variance = (Actual Quantity × Actual Profit per unit) – (Budgeted Quantity × Budgeted Profit per unit)

Product X = (5500 × 13) – (6000 × 3)

= 71500 – 18000 = Rs. 53,500 (F)

Product Y = (5000 × 2) – (4000 × 5)

= (10000 – 20000) = Rs. 10,000 (A)

SMV = 53500 – 10000 = Rs. 43,500 (F)

(ii) Sales Price Variance = AQ (ASP – BSP)

X = 5500 (60 – 50)

= 5500 × 10 = Rs. 55,000 (F)

Y = 5000 (27 – 30)

= 5000 × 3 = Rs.15,000 (A)

SPV = 55000 – 15000 = Rs.40,000 (F)

(iii) Sales Volume Variance = Budgeted Profit per unit (AQ - BQ)

X = 3 (5500 – 6000) = 3 × 500 = 1,500 (A)

Y = 5 (5000 – 4000) = 5 × 1000 = 5,000 (F)

SVV = –1500 + 5000 = Rs. 3,500 (F)

(iv) Sales Mix Variance = Budgeted Profit per unit (AQ-RBQ)

$$\text{Revised Budgeted Quantity} = \frac{\text{Individual Budgeted Qty.} \times AQ}{\text{Total Budgeted Qty.}}$$

X = (6000/10000) × 10,500 = 6,300

Y	=	$(4000/10000) \times 10{,}500 = 4{,}200$
Sales Mix Variance: X	=	$3\,(5500 - 6300) = 3 \times 800 = 2400$ (A)
Y	=	$5\,(5000 - 4200) = 5 \times 800 = 4000$ (F)
SMV	=	$4000 - 2400 =$ Rs. 1,600 (F)
(v) Sales Quantity Variance	=	Budgeted Profit per unit (RBQ – BQ)
	=	$3\,(6300 - 6000) = 3 \times 300 = 900$ (F)
	=	$5\,(4200 - 4000) = 5 \times 200 = 1000$ (F)
SQV	=	$900 + 1000 =$ Rs. 1900 (F)

Verification:

SMV = SPV + SVV = Rs. 43,500 (F)
= 40000 + 3500 = Rs. 43,500 (F)

SVV = SMV + SQV = 1600 + 1900
= Rs. 3,500 (F)

SMV = SPV + SMV + SQV = 40000 + 1600 + 1900
= Rs. 43,500 (F)

Illustration: 21

G Ltd., provided the following information from the costing records for the month April 2006.

Budgeted Sales	:	A 3000 units @ Rs. 10 per unit
	:	B 2000 units @ Rs. 15 per unit
Actual Sales	:	A 3500 units @ Rs. 9 per unit
	:	B 1800 units @ Rs. 17 per unit

Calculate (i) Sales Value Variance (ii) Sales Price Variance (iii) Sales Volume Variance (iv) Sales Mix Variance and (v) Sales Quantity Variance by Sales Value Method.

Solution:

$$\text{Revised Budgeted Quantity (RBQ)} = \frac{\text{Individual BQ} \times \text{Total AQ}}{\text{Total BQ}}$$

Product	A = (3000 / 5000) × 5300	=	3180
Product	B = (2000 / 5000) × 5300	=	2120
			5300

(i) Sales Value Variance	=	(AQ × ASP) – (BQ × BSP)
A	=	(3500 × 9) – (3000 × 10)
	=	31500 – 30000 = Rs. 1500 (F)
B	=	(1800 × 17) – (2000 × 15)
	=	30600 – 30000 = Rs. 600 (F)
SVV	=	1500 + 600 = Rs. 2100 (F)
(ii) Sales Price Variance	=	AQ (ASP – BSP)
A	=	3500 (9 – 10) = 3500 × 1 = Rs. 3500 (A)
B	=	1800 (17 – 15) = 1800 × 2 = Rs. 3600 (F)
SPV	=	–3500 + 3600 = Rs. 100 (F)
(iii) Sales Volume Variance	=	BSP (AQ – BQ)

A	=	10 (3500 – 3000) = 10 × 500 = Rs. 5,000 (F)
B	=	15 (1800 - 2000) = 15 × 200 = Rs.3,000 (A)
SVV	=	5000 – 3000 = Rs. 2,000 (F)
(iv) Sales Mix Variance	=	BSP (AQ – RBQ)
A	=	10 (3500 – 3180) = 10 × 320 = Rs.3,200 (F)
B	=	15 (1800 – 2120) = 15 × 320 = Rs.4,800 (A)
SMV	=	3200 – 4800 = Rs. 1,600 (A)
(v) Sales Quantity Variance	=	BSP (RBQ – BQ)
A	=	10 (3180-3000) = 10 × 180 = Rs. 1,800 (F)
B	=	15 (2120-2000) = 15 × 120 = Rs. 1,800 (F)
SQV	=	1800 + 1800 = Rs. 3,600 (F)

Verification:

Sales Value Variance = SPV + SVV = 100 + 2000 = Rs.2100 (F)

= SPV + SMV + SQV = 100 – 1600 + 3600 = Rs. 2100 (F)

Sales Volume Variance = SMV + SQV = – 1600 + 3600 = Rs.2000 (F).

Illustration: 22

Find out the sales variances from the following information.

Budgeted sales for the month of December 2007 are stated as follows.

X 12000 units @ Rs. 25 per unit

Y 15000 units @ Rs. 20 per unit

Z 13000 units @ Rs. 30 per unit

Actual Sales are stated as follows

X 14000 units @ Rs. 29 per unit

Y 13000 units @ Rs. 22 per unit

Z 15000 units @ Rs. 24 per unit

Cost of production X Rs. 20, Y Rs. 17 and Z Rs. 23 per unit.

Solution:

I. Sales Margin Variances (Profit Method)

Standard Margin on Standard Mix

Products	*Units*	*Rates (Rs.)*	*Amount (Rs.)*
X	12000	5	60,000
Y	15000	3	45,000
Z	13000	7	91,000
	40000		1,96,000

(a) Standard Margin per unit of Standard Mix = 196000 /40000 = Rs.4.90

Standard Margin on Actual Mix

Products	Units	Rates (Rs.)	Amount (Rs.)
X	14,000	5	70,000
Y	13,000	3	39,000
Z	15,000	7	1,05,000
	42,000		2,14,000

(b) Standard margin per unit of Actual Mix = 214000/42000 = Rs. 5.095

Actual Margin on Actual Mix

Products	Units	Rates (Rs.)	Amount (Rs.)
X	14,000	9	1,26,000
Y	13,000	5	65,000
Z	15,000	1	15,000
	42,000		2,06,000

1. Sales Margin Variance:

= [Actual Qty. × Actual Profit per unit] – [Standard Qty. × Budgeted profit per unit]

X : [14000 × 9] – [12000 × 5] = Rs.66,000 [F]

Y : [13000 × 5] – [15000 × 3] = Rs.20,000 [F]

Z : [15000 × 1] – [13000 × 7] = Rs.76,000 [A]

Total = Rs. 10,000 [F]

2. Sales Margin Price Variance:

= Actual Qty. [Actual Price – Standard Price]

X : 14000 [29 - 25] = Rs. 5,6000 [F]

Y : 13000 [22 - 20] = Rs. 26,000 [F]

Z : 15000 [24 - 30] = Rs. 90,000 [A]

Total = Rs. 8000 [A]

3. Sales Margin Volume Variance:,

= Std. Margin per unit [Actual Sales - Budgeted Sales]

X : 5 [14000 – 12000] = Rs. 10,000 [F]

Y : 3 [13000 – 15000] = Rs. 6,000 [A]

Z : 7 [15000 – 13000] = Rs. 14,000 [F]

Total = Rs. 18,000 [F]

(i) Sales Margin Mix Variance:

= Budgeted Profit per unit [Actual Qty. – Revised Budgeted Qty.] Revised Budgeted Qty:

X : 42000/40000 × 12000 = 12600 units

Y : 42000/40000 × 15000 = 15750 units

Z : 42000/40000 × 13000 = 13650 units

Total = 42000 units

X	: 5 [14000 – 12600]	=	Rs. 7,000 [F]
Y	: 3 [13000 – 15750]	=	Rs. 8,250 [A]
Z	: 7 [15000 – 13650]	=	Rs. 9,450 [F]
	Total	=	Rs. 8,200 [F]

(ii) Sales Margin Qty. Variance:,

= Budgeted Profit per unit [Revised Budgeted Qty. – Budgeted Qty.]

X	: 5[12600 – 12000]	=	Rs. 3,000 [F]
Y	: 3[15750 – 15000]	=	Rs. 2,250 [F]
Z	: 7[13650 – 13000]	=	Rs. 4,550 [F]
	Total	=	Rs. 9,800 [F]

Verification:

SMV	=	SMPV + S.M.VO.V		
	=	8000 [A] + 18000 [F]	=	Rs. 10,000 [F]
S.M.VO.V	=	S.M.M.V + S.M.Q.V		
	=	8200[F] + 9800 [F]	=	Rs. 18,000 [F]

II. Sales Variances [Sales Value method]:

1. Sales Value Variance = [Actual Qty. × Actual selling price per unit] – [Budgeted Qty. × Budgeted selling price per unit]

X	: [14000 × 29] – [12000 × 25]	=	Rs.1,06,000 [F]
Y	: [13000 × 22] – [15000 × 20]	=	Rs.14,000 [A]
Z	: [15000 × 24] – [13000 × 30]	=	Rs.30,000 [A]
	Total	=	Rs. 62,000 [F]

2. Sales Price Variance =, Actual Qty. [Actual Rate – Std.Rate]

X	: 14000 [29 – 25]	=	Rs. 56,000 [F]
Y	: 13000 [22 – 20]	=	Rs. 26,000 [F]
Z	: 15000 [24 – 30]	=	Rs. 90,000 [A]
	Total	=	Rs. 8,000 [A]

3. Sales Volume Variance = Standard Rate [Actual Qty. – Budgeted Qty.]

X	: 25 [14000 – 12000]	=	Rs. 50,000 [F]
Y	: 20 [13000 – 15000]	=	Rs. 40,000 [A]
Z	: 30 [15000 – 13000]	=	Rs. 60,000 [F]
	Total	=	Rs. 70000 [F]

(i) Sales Mix Variance:
Std. Rate [Actual Qty. - Revised Std. Qty.]

$$\text{RSQ} = \frac{\text{Total Actual Mix of Sales} \times \text{Std. Qty}}{\text{Total Standard Mix of Sales}}$$

X	: 42000/40000 × 12000	=	12600 units
Y	: 42000/40000 × 15000	=	15750 units

	Z	: 42000/40000 × 13000	=	13650 units
		Total	=	42000 units
SMV:	X	: 25 [14000 - 12600]	=	Rs. 35,000 [F]
	Y	: 20 [13000 - 15750]	=	Rs. 55,000 [A]
	Z	: 30 [15000 - 13650]	=	Rs. 40,500 [F]
		Total	=	Rs. 20,500 [F]

(ii) Sales Qty. Variance: [Sub-volume variance]
= Std. Selling price [Revised Std. Sales Qty. - Budgeted Sales Qty.]

X	: 25 [12600 - 12000]	=	Rs. 15,000 [F]
Y	: 20 [15750 - 15000]	=	Rs. 15,000 [F]
Z	: 30 [13650 - 13000]	=	Rs. 19,500 [F]
	Total	=	Rs. 49,500 [F]

Verification:

Sales Variance	=	SPV + S.Q.V
	=	8000 [A] + 70000 [F] = Rs. 62,000 [F]
SQV	=	S.M.V. + S.Q.V
	=	20500 [F] + 49500 [F] = Rs. 70,000 [F]

Illustration: 23

Calculate sales variances from the following.

Budgeted Sales	K	60,000 units @ Rs. 44 per unit
	L	40,000 units @ Rs. 55 per unit
Actual Sales	K	57,000 units @ Rs. 46 per unit
	L	43,000 units @ Rs. 53 per unit

Solution:

Sales Value Variance		=	(AQ × ASP) – (BQ × BSP)
	K	=	(57,000 × 46) - (60,000 × 44)
		=	26,22,000 – 26,40,000 = Rs. 18,000 (A)
	L	=	(43,000 × 53) - (40,000 × 55)
		=	22,79,000 - 22,00,000 = Rs. 79,000 (F)
	Total	=	– 18,000 + 79,000 = Rs. 61,000 (F)
Sales Price Variance		=	AQ (ASP – BSP)
	K	=	57,000 (46 – 44)
		=	57,000 × 2 = Rs. 1,14,000 (F)
	L	=	43,000 (53 – 55)
		=	43,000 × 2 = Rs. 86,000 (A)
	Total	=	1,14,000 – 86,000 = Rs. 28,000 (F)
Sales Volume Variance		=	BSP (AQ - BQ)
	K	=	44 (57,000 – 60,000)

$= 44 \times 3000 = \text{Rs. } 132,000\ (A)$

$L = 55\ (43,000 - 40,000)$

$= 55 \times 3,000 = \text{Rs. } 165,000\ (F)$

$\text{Total} = -132,000 + 165,000 = \text{Rs. } 33,000\ (F)$

Verification:

Sales Value Variance = Sales Price Variance + Sales Volume Variance

= 28,000 + 33,000 = Rs. 61,000 (F)

(*Note:* Since the total actual quantity and total budged quantity are equal, sales mix variance and sales quantity variance could not be calculated.)

EXERCISE

THEORY

I. Choose the correct answer for the following.

1. Predetermined cost is called —
(i) Budget cost (ii) Actual cost (iii) Standard cost (iv) Historical cost
2. Analysis of the deviation from actual and standard cost is called —
(i) Variance analysis (ii) Cost analysis (iii) Budget analysis (iv) Inventory analysis
3. If the actual cost is greater than standard cost it is known as —
(i) Favourable variance (ii) Budget (iii) Marginal cost (iv) Unfavourable variance
4. If the actual cost is less than the standard cost, it is known as —
(i) Unfavourable variance (ii) Favourable variance (iii) Cost centre (iv) Cost unit
5. Material usage variance is otherwise called as —
(i) Material mix variance (ii) Material price variance (iii) Material quantity variance (iv) Material cost variance
6. The difference between the standard labour hours specified for the output achieved and the actual labour hours spent is called —
(i) Labour efficiency variance (ii) Labour mix variance (iii) Labour cost variance (iv) Labour rate variance
7. The difference between the standard cost of material and actual cost of material is called —
(i) Labour cost variance (ii) Material cost variance (iii) Sales variance (iv) Material quantity variance
8. Variance is the difference between actual cost and —
(i) Budget (ii) Fixed cost (iii) Variable cost (iv) Standard cost
9. The difference between the budgeted fixed overhead and actual fixed overhead is called —
(i) Expenditure variance (ii) Variable overhead variance (iii) Volume variance (iv) Fixed overhead variance
10. The ratio between standard overheads and standard output is called —
(i) Volume variance (ii) Actual rate (iii) Standard rate (iv) Budget rate

[**Ans :** 1. (iii) 2 (i) 3 (iv) 4 (ii) 5 (iii) 6 (i) 7 (ii) 8 (iv) 9 (iv) 10 (iii)]

II. Answer the following.

11. Define Standard Costing. Distinguish between Historical Costing and Standard Costing.
12. What is Standard Costing? Distinguish between Standard Costing and Budgetary Control.
13. Define Standard Costing .Explain the merits and demerits of standard costing.
14. Define Variance analysis. Explain the different types of Material Cost Variances.
15. Distinguish between Standard Costing and Variance Analysis. Explain the different types of Labour Cost Variances.
16. What is Variances analysis? Explain the different types of Labour Cost Variances.
17. Define Variance analysis. Explain the different types of Sales Variances.

18. Calculate Material Cost Variance, Material Price Variance and Material Quantity Variance from the following.

	Material X	*Material Y*
Actual Quantity	550	750
Standard Quantity	600	710
Actual Price per unit (Rs.)	22	30
Standard Price per unit (Rs.)	19	33

(**Ans:** Rs. 230 (F); Rs. 600 (F); Rs. 370 (A))

19. M.Ltd., spent on an average Rs.1,40,000 for purchase 7,000 units. The standard material required for producing 200 kgms is 400 units. The standard price of the material is Rs.22 per unit. The stock of material in the beginning and at the end are 1,200 units and 1,400 units respectively. Actual production is 3000 kgms. Calculate the material cost variance material price variance and material usage variance.

(**Ans:** Rs. 4,000 (A); Rs. 13,600 (A); Rs. 17,600 (A); AQ 6800; SQ 6000)

20. K Ltd., provided the following information from the costing records. The particulars about the standard production of 100 units of Product A are stated as follows:

Material	*Qty*	*Unit Price (Rs.)*	*Value (Rs.)*
C	120	5.50	660
D	100	3.50	350
Total	220		1,010

The actual cost of manufacturing 1000 units are as follows:

Material	*Qty. (Kgm)*	*Unit Price (Rs.)*	*Value (Rs.)*
C	1300	6.00	7,800
D	1010	3.00	3,030
Total	2310		10,830

Calculate material cost variance, material quantity variance, material price variance material mix variance and material yield variance.

(**Ans:** Rs. 730 (A); Rs. 585 (A); Rs. 145 (A); Rs. 100 (F); Rs. 685 (A))

21. Calculate material cost variance, material quantity variance, material price variance, material mix variance and material yield variance from the following.

Material	*Standard*			*Actual*		
	Qty.	*Rate (Rs.)*	*Amount (Rs.)*	*Qty.*	*Rate (Rs.)*	*Amount (Rs.)*
X	7,000	2.50	17,500	6,900	2.70	18,630
Y	4,000	3.20	12,800	3,000	3.10	9,300
Total	11,000	–	30,300	9,900	–	27,930

(**Ans:** Rs. 2370 (F); Rs. 1080 (A); Rs. 3450 (F); Rs. 420 (A); Rs. 3030 (F))

22. KT Ltd., provided the following information as on 31st March 2007. The standard cost of manufacturing 50 units and actual cost for 2000 units are stated as follows.

Material	Standard		Actual	
	Qty. (Kgm)	*Amt. (Rs.)*	*Qty. (Kgm)*	*Amt. (Rs.)*
K	400	4,000	16,500	1,48,500
L	600	3,000	23,000	1,26,500
M	500	2,000	19,000	66,500
Total	1500	9,000	58,500	3,41,500

Calculate all the possible material variances.

(**Ans:** Rs. 18,500 (F); Rs. 4000 (F); Rs. 14,500 (F); Rs. 5,000 (A); Rs. 9,500 (F))

23. N Ltd., provided the following information from its costing records with respect to the production of 400 units of product 'C'.

Material	Standard			Actual		
	Qty.	*Rate (Rs.)*	*Amount (Rs.)*	*Qty.*	*Rate (Rs.)*	*Amount (Rs.)*
H	540	6.40	3,456	650	5.50	3,575
N	360	4.60	1,656	340	5.00	1,700
Total	900	–	1,560	990		14,26

The standard normal loss is estimated as 10 %.Actual output is 702 units. Calculate all the material variances.

(**Ans:** Rs. 134 (A); Rs. 24 (F); Rs. 158 (A); Rs. 15 (A); Rs. 39 (A))

24. Calculate Labour Cost Variances from the following.

	Standard	*Actual*
Wage rate per hour (Rs.)	50	55
Labour hours per unit	5	4
Production of the company is 5000 units		

(**Ans:** Rs. 1,50,000 (F); Rs. 1,00,000 (A); Rs. 2,50,000 (F))

25. Calculate Labour Cost Variance, Labour Efficiency Variance and Labour Rate Variance from the following.

	Standard	*Actual*
Labour hours per 100 units	50	45
Labour rate per hour (Rs.)	10.50	10.00

(**Ans:** Rs. 75 (F); Rs. 22.5 (F); Rs. 52.5 (F))

26. The Standard Labour cost of a product manufactured by KT & Co. Ltd., is stated as follows:

Workers	*Hours per unit of output*	*Hourly Rate Rs.*	*Amount Rs.*
X	11	30	330
Y	6	40	240
Total	17	–	570

The actual cost for producing 300 units are as follows.

Workers	Hours	Hourly Rate Rs.	Amount Rs.
A	3,500	28	98,000
B	1,500	43	64,500
Total	5,000	–	1,62,500

Calculate (i) Labour Cost Variance (ii) Labour Rate Variance (iii) Labour Efficiency Variance and (iv) Labour Mix Variance (v) Labour Yield Variance.

(**Ans:** Rs. 8,500 (F); Rs. 2,500 (F); Rs. 6,000 (F); Rs. 2650 (F); Rs.3,350 (F))

27. The following information are extracted from the book of GC & Co.Ltd., Standard Labour Cost are as follows.

Workers	Hours per unit of output	Hourly Rate Rs.	Amount Rs.
Male	3	39	117
Female	4	33	132
Total	7	–	249

Actual labour cost for 1000 units are as follows.

Workers	Hours per unit of output	Hourly Rate Rs.	Amount Rs.
Male	2900	41	1,18,900
Female	4200	30	1,26,000
Total	7100	–	2,44,900

Calculate all the labour cost variances.

(**Ans:** 4,100 (F); Rs. 6,800 (F); Rs. 2,700 (A); Rs. 840 (A))

28. KM Ltd., provided the following information related to the payment of wage.

	Skilled worker	Semi-Skilled worker	Unskilled worker
Standard Number of workers in the gang	80	70	100
Standard Rate per hour	30	25	20
Actual Number of workers in the gang	82	63	95
Actual Rate per hour	32	23	17

The company worked for 40 hours in the week and produced 9,000 standard hours of work.

Calculate (i) Labour Cost Variance (ii)) Labour Rate Variance (iii) Labour Efficiency Variance (iv) Labour Mix Variance (v) Labour Yield Variance.

(**Ans:** (i) Rs. 18,480 (F), (ii) Rs. 9,880 (F), (iii) Rs. 8,600 (F), (iv) Rs. 1,240 (F), Rs. 7,360 (F))

29. Standard hours required for manufacturing 1 unit is 5 hours @ Rs. 50 per hour. If the company paid Rs. 1,05,750 for manufacturing 500 units @ Rs. 47 per hour find out LCV,LRV and LEV.

(**Ans:** Rs. 2000 (F); Rs. 17000 (F); Rs. 15000 (A))

30. Calculate all Labour Variances from the data provided by a manufacturing company.

The standard time required for completing a job is 20 weeks and Actual time taken for completing the job is 17 weeks.

Workers	*Standard*		*Actual*	
	Number	*Rate per week*	*Number*	*Rate per week*
Male	70	900	70	950
Female	50	700	55	650
Children	30	500	35	440
Total	150	–	155	–

(**Ans:** LCV-Rs. 2,59,950 (F); LRV-Rs. 22,950 (F), LEV-Rs. 2,37,000 (F); LMV Rs.26,000 (A), LYV-Rs. 2,63,000 (F))

31. A company provided the following information from the costing records for the month October 2007.

Budgeted Sales	:	Product C 7000 units @ Rs. 24 per unit
	:	Product T 5000 units @ Rs. 32 per unit
Actual Sales	:	Product C 7500 units @ Rs. 27 per unit
	:	Product T 4700 units @ Rs. 30 per unit

Calculate (i) Sales Value Variance (ii) Sales Price Variance (iii) Sales Quantity Variance by Sales Value method.
(**Ans:** (i) Rs. 15,500 (F); (ii) Rs. 13,100 (F); (iii) Rs. 2,400 (F))

32. Calculate Variable overhead cost variances for a manufacturing company from the following information.

Particulars	*Budget*	*Actual*
Labour hours	1,200	1,300
Output (units)	700	750
Variable Overhead (Rs.)	10,000	11,000

(**Ans:** (i) Rs. 1,350 (A); (Rs. 650 (A); (Rs. 700 (A);
(ii) Rs. 1,350 (A); Rs. 750 (A); Rs. 600 (A)]

33. Calculate the Fixed overhead variances from the following:

	Budget	*Actual*
Fixed Overhead Rs.	140,000	143,000
Output (units)	10,000	11,000
Working Days	27	25

(**Ans:** Rs. 3,000 (A); Rs. 14,000 (A); Rs. 11,000 (F))

34. X Ltd., provided the following information from the costing records for the month March 2006.

	Budgeted	*Actual*
Product: X Sales quantity	15000	14400
Selling price per unit (Rs.)	30	32
Product: Y Sales quantity	20,000	22,000
Selling price per unit (Rs.)	40	38

Calculate (i) Sales Margin Variance, (ii) Sales Price Variance (iii) Sales Volume Variance (iv) Sales Mix Variance and (v) Sales Quantity Variance by Sales Margin Method.
(**Ans:** Rs. 46,800 (F); Rs. 15,200 (A); Rs. 62,000 (F); Rs. 12,000 (F); Rs. 50,000 (F))

35. H Ltd., provided the following information from the costing records for the month April 2006.

Budgeted Sales : A 3500 units @ Rs. 17 per unit

: B 4000 units @ Rs. 21 per unit

Actual Sales : A 3800 units @ Rs. 15 per unit

: B 4300 units @ Rs. 19 per unit

The cost of production for Product A and B are Rs. 12 and Rs. 15 respectively.

Calculate (i) Sales Value Variance (ii) Sales Price Variance (iii) Sales Volume Variance (iv) Sales Mix Variance and (v) Sales Quantity Variance by Sales Value Method.

(**Ans:** Rs. 12,900 (A); Rs. 16,200 (A); Rs. 3,300 (F); Rs. 20 (A); Rs. 3320 (F))

36. Find out the sales variances from the following information. Budgeted sales for the month of November 2007 are stated as follows:

X 9000 units @ Rs. 115 per unit

Y 5000 units @ Rs. 95 per unit

Z 7000 units @ Rs. 70 per unit

Actual sales are stated as follows:

X 9500 units @ Rs. 105 per unit

Y 4400 units @ Rs. 100 per unit

Z 7500 units @ Rs. 64 per unit

Cost of production: X Rs. 80, Y Rs. 44, Z Rs. 40 per unit

(**Ans:** 1. Sales Margin Method: Rs. 15300 (F); Rs. 17,600 (F); Rs. 2,300 (A); Rs. 968 (A); Rs. 1332 (A); Rs. 1,332 (A); 2. Selling-Price Rs. 4,565 (A); Rs. 17600 (F); Rs. 12,500 (A); Rs. 4565 (A); Rs. 7935 (A))

37. The standard labour cost of a product manufactured by G.R & Co.Ltd., is stated as follows:

Workers	*Hours per unit of output*	*Hourly Rate Rs.*	*Amount Rs.*
A	5	45	225
B	3	55	165
Total	7	–	390

The actual cost for producing 500 units are as follows.

Workers	*Hours*	*Hourly Rate Rs.*	*Amount Rs.*
A	2,700	42	1,13,400
B	1,400	51	71,400
Total	4,100	–	1,84,800

Calculate (i) Labour Cost Variance (ii) Labour Rate Variance (iii) Labour Efficiency Variance and (iv) Labour Mix Variance.

(**Ans:** Rs. 10,200 (F); Rs. 13,700 (F); Rs.3,500 (A); Rs. 1,370 (F))

38. The following information are extracted from the book of C & Co.Ltd., Standard Labour Cost are as follows.

Workers	*Hours per unit*	*Hourly Rate Rs.*	*Amount Rs.*
Male	9	70	630
Female	6	60	360
Total	15	–	990

Actual labour cost for 1000 units are as follows.

Workers	*Hours per unit*	*Hourly Rate Rs.*	*Amount Rs.*
Male	9,500	74	703,00
Female	5,500	63	346,500
Total	15,000	–	10,49,500

Calculate all the labour cost variances.

(**Ans:** Rs.59,500 (A); Rs.54,500 (A); Rs.5,000 (A))

39. XY Ltd., provided the following information from its costing records with respect to the production of 1000 units of product 'C'.

Material	*Standard*			*Actual*		
	Qty.	*Rate (Rs.)*	*Amount (Rs.)*	*Qty.*	*Rate (Rs.)*	*Amount (Rs.)*
A	1800	4	7200	1900	4.50	8550
B	1200	3	3600	1300	2.20	2860
Total	3000	–	9,200	3200		11,410

The standard normal loss is estimated as 10 %. Actual output is 900 units. Calculate all the material variances.

(**Ans:** Rs. 610 (A); Rs.98 (F); Rs. 700 (A); Rs. 20 (F); Rs. 720 (A))

40. Calculate material cost variance, material quantity variance, material price variance and material mix variance from the following.

Material	*Standard*			*Actual*		
	Qty.	*Rate (Rs.)*	*Amount (Rs.)*	*Qty.*	*Rate (Rs.)*	*Amount (Rs.)*
A	33,000	17	5,61,000	30,000	17.40	5,22,000
B	22,000	14	3,08,000	21,000	13.20	2,77,200
Total	55,000		8,69,000	51,000	–	7,99,200

(**Ans:** Rs. 69,800 (F); Rs.4,800 (F); Rs. 65,000 (F); Rs. 1,800 (F))

❑ ❑ ❑

9

BUDGET AND BUDGETARY CONTROL

Budget is an important tool of planning and control of cost for the management. CIMA London defines budget as, "a financial and / or quantitative statement prepared and approved prior to a defined period of time, of the policy to be pursued during the period for the purpose of attaining a given objective." Budgeting means the process of preparing the budget.

Characteristics of a Good Budget

The following are the important characteristics of good budget:

1. Persons at different levels of management should be involved in the preparation of budgets.
2. The targets of the budgets should be realistic.
3. The authority and responsibility should be clearly defined.
4. A good system of accounting should be followed.
5. The employees should be given education with regard to budget.
6. The actual results should be properly recorded for the purpose of performance appraisal.

Budgetary Control

Budgetary control is the process of comparing the budgetary figures with the actual performance, for calculating variances, in order to control the variances.

Brown and Howard defined as "Budgetary control is a system of controlling costs which includes the preparation of budgets, co-ordinating the department and establishing responsibility, comparing actual performance with the budgeted and acting upon results to achieve maximum profitability.

J.Batty defines Budgetary control as "A system which uses budgets as a means of planning and controlling all aspects of producing and / or selling commodities and services".

According to **Welsch**, "Budgetary control involves the use of budget and budgetary reports throughout the period to co-ordinate, evaluate and control day-to-day operations in accordance with the goals specified by the budget".

It is clear from the definitions that budgetary control is a process of comparing the budget figures with actual figures. It helps to know the variances so that it can be controlled and also to plan for the future. Hence, the efficiency of the company can be improved through budgetary control.

Objectives of Budgetary Control

The following are the important objectives of budgetary control:

1. To provide a detailed plan of action for a business over a period of time.
2. To co-ordinate all activities of the organisation.
3. To increase profitability and to eliminate waste.
4. To operate various cost centres and departments efficiently and economically.
5. To control the variances.
6. To fix responsibilities of various individuals in the organisation.

Essentials of Budgetary Control

The important essential steps for budgetary control are stated as follows.

1. Organisation for Budgetary Control: A budget committee should be formed with heads of various departments as members. They should be entrusted to prepare the budgets. The Chief Executive should be in charge of overall budgetary system. A Budget Officer is the convener of the budget committee. He co-ordinates the different departments in the process of preparing budgets.

2. Budget Centres: A Budget centre is that part of the organisation for which the budget is prepared, (e.g.) departments. The establishment of various centres should be done as per the requirement of the organisation.

3. Budget Manuals: Budget manual is a written document which gives guidance to the functional managers about the procedures to be followed in the preparation of budgets. It contains the methods of preparation and execution of budgets. It defines the role of each individual in the preparation of budgets. It includes the details about the authority and responsibility of each functional heads. The budget manual should be very clear and there should not be any ambiguity in the expressions.

4. Budget Officer: The Budget Officer is appointed by the Chief Executive. He scrutinises all the budgets prepared by various functional heads. He can make necessary corrections in the budgets so prepared. He should compare the actual performance with budget. He should take necessary steps to rectify the variances. He also reports to the management about the various aspects related to budget.

5. Budget Committee: In business concerns, Budget Committee is formed to prepare the budget. The committee is responsible for the preparation and execution of budget with the Heads of various departments as its members.

6. Budget Period: There is no strict rule for the period of budget. The period depends upon the nature of the business and objectives of the company. It may be a very short period like one or two months, or a reasonably long period of one year. Normally, the period of budget is one year. Companies prepare short term budgets to have effective control. Companies engaged in manufacturing of seasonal products definitely have to prepare short-term budgets. Companies may prepare both short-term and long-term budgets at the same time. Short-term budgets may be a supplement to the long-term budget.

7. Key Factor or Limiting Factor: The factor which will limit the volume of production, at a particular point of time is called Key Factor or Limiting Factor. The factor may be demand for the product, availability of material, availability of technicians and other employees, capacity of plant and the availability of finance.Any of these factors may be a constraint for the smooth production. It may limit the quantity of production. It is the duty of the management to identify the key factor. The key factors must be considered for the preparation of budgets.

Advantages of Budgetary Control

The important advantages of budgetary control are stated as follows:

1. The budgetary control helps in co-ordinating activities of various departments.
2. It aims at maximisation of profits.
3. It helps in making suitable plans, policies and goals.
4. It helps in measuring the performance of managerial personnels, and thereby helps in improving their performance.
5. It measures the variances in all aspects and helps in identifying the reasons for the variances.
6. The planning of expenditure will be systematic and there will be economy in spending.
7. It creates budget consciousness among employees.

Limitations of Budgetary Control

The limitations of budgetary control are stated as follows:

1. The future uncertainties affect the performance of budgetary control system.
2. It discourages efficient persons to perform more than expected.
3. The lack of co-ordination of various departments affects the performance of the budgetary control.
4. It may lead to conflicts among the managers of various departments.
5. Lack of support from top management affects the budgetary control system.

Classification of Budgets

The budgets may be classified as follows:

I. Classification on the basis of Time

1. Long-term budgets
2. Short-term budgets
3. Current budgets.

II. Classification on the basis of Function

1. Master budget.
2. Functional or Subsidiary budget.

III. Classification on the basis of Flexibility

1. Fixed budget
2. Flexible budget.

I. Classification on the basis of Time

1. Long-term Budget: The period of long-term budget varies between five to ten years. It is based on long-term planning and prepared by top level management. Long-term budgets are prepared for the management. (E.g.,) Capital expenditure, research and development etc.

2. Short-term Budget: The period of short-term budget is one or two years. The consumer goods industries like textile, cotton, sugar, coffee, cosmetics etc., prepare short-term budget.

3. Current Budget: The period of current budget is generally of weeks or a month or few months.

II. Classification on the basis of Function

1. Master Budget
2. Functional Budgets.

The important functional budgets are as follows:

(i) Sales Budget
(ii) Production Budget
(iii) Cost of Production Budget
(iv) Purchase Budget
(v) Cash Budget
(vi) Capital Expenditure Budget.

1. Master Budget

The Chartered Institute of Management Accountants (CIMA) London defines the master budget as "the summary budget, incorporating its component functional budget, which is finally approved, adopted and employed". According to **ICWA London**, "The Master Budget is the summary budget incorporating its functional budgets".

It is clear from the definitions that master budget is a summary budget which includes all the functional budgets. This budget should be approved by the Budget committee of the company.

2. Functional Budget

(i) Sales Budget: Sales Budget is a budget for forecasting the sales in future in terms of quantity and value. It is prepared on the basis of past sales, production capacity, report of salesmen, pricing policy and competition.

(ii) Production Budget: Production budget is a budget for forecasting the quantity of production for different types of products and for different periods. It is based on Sales Budget.

(iii) Cost of Production Budget: This budget forecasts the cost of production for different types of products of a company. A company may prepare separate budget for different elements of cost.

They are,

(a) Direct Material Budget
(b) Direct Labour Budget
(c) Factory Overhead Budget
(d) Administration Overhead Budget.
(e) Selling and Distribution Overhead Budget.

(a) Direct Material Budget: It is otherwise called as Raw Material Budget. It is concerned with forecasting about the requirement of different types of raw materials and its value. This budget is based on the production budget, price of raw material, seasonal factors, inventory levels and storage facilities.

(b) Direct Labour Budget: This budget is concerned with the forecast of the requirement of different types of labourers in a company. It is also concerned with the cost of each type of labour. It explains the standard labour hours required for the estimated production and the estimated labour cost per hour for different types of labour.

(c) Factory Overhead Budget: This budget is prepared to forecast the indirect factory cost. It includes indirect material, indirect labour and indirect expenses to be incurred in the factory for certain level of production.

(d) Administration Overhead Budget: This budget is prepared to forecast the indirect administration cost. It includes indirect material, indirect labour and indirect expenses to be spent in the administration department in future.

(e) Selling and Distribution Overhead Budget: This budget is prepared to forecast the indirect selling and distribution cost. It includes indirect material, indirect labour and indirect expenses to be spent in the selling and distribution department in future.

(iv) Purchase Budget: Purchase Budget is prepared to find out the total cost of purchase in future. It involves the purchase of direct and indirect materials. Indirect materials are concerned with the materials used in Factory, Administration and Selling and Distribution departments.

(v) Cash Budget: Cash Budget is concerned with the inflow and outflow of cash in the budget period. This budget estimates the net cash flow in a concern. It facilitates the management to make necessary arrangements for the future cash requirements. This budget is prepared only after the preparation of all the functional budgets.

(vi) Capital Expenditure Budget: This budget is prepared to know the estimated expenditure on all fixed assets like Plant &Machinery, Land & Building and Furniture & Fittings during the budget period.

III. Classification on the basis of Flexibility

1. Fixed Budget: ICWA London defined "fixed budget is a budget which is designed to remain unchanged irrespective to the level of activity actually attained". It is related to a given level of activity and it is prepared before the budgeting of the financial year.

2. Flexible Budget: A Flexible Budget is a budget for different levels of activities. Example for flexible budget is the budget for various capacity utilisations like 50%, 60%, 70%,100% etc. This budget is useful when the levels of activity in a company changes from time to time.

Organisation of Budgetary Control

There should be an organisation for the budget control. The organisation is headed by a Budget Officer. The budget officer is otherwise called as 'Budget Controller' or 'Budget Director'. The budget officer is appointed by the Chief Executive of the organisation of the company. He got the authority to prepare budget and to execute control, from the chief executive. He will prepare different types of budgets, as per the requirement of the company, in coordination with all the functional heads like, Sales Manager, Production Manager, Purchase Manager, Personal Manager and Accountant. All the functional heads together with the General Manager and the Budget Officer prepare the budgets meant for all departments. The function of the Budget Committee is to approve the individual budgets prepared by various functional heads, after making necessary corrections.

Forecasts and Budget

According to **Chartered Institute of Management Accountants** (CIMA) London, forecast is 'a statement of probable events'. But budget has more meaning than forecast. Budget is a quantitative statement prepared for the future period. Forecast in the basic set up adopted in the preparation of budget. Hence, the meaning of budget includes forecasting. The important differences between forecast and budget are stated as follows:

(i) Forecast is only an estimate of the future. But budget is concerned with what should be done in future.

(ii) In forecast there is no control required whereas budget is based on the control of deviations from the budgeted estimates.

(iii) Forecast is a general term which can be applied to any situation. But budget is concerned only with the financial aspect of the future expenses and income.

(iv) The process of forecast is over with the statement of probable events whereas the process of budget starts with forecast.

Performance Budgeting or Responsibility Accounting

Budget, nowadays focus on the performance of the employees in an organisation also. Budget in the past focused only on money concept. Performance budgeting is the process of preparing budget by associating money concept with the performance of the employees. In this type of budget the expenditure and income of the concern are related with specific responsibility centre. The budgeted expenses like purchase of material, wages, and other expenses are all related with respective responsibility centres. In this way, the income like sales of different products and from different places are related with the respective responsibility centres. The centres should at least maintain the expected level of expenses and income specified in the budget. The reduction in cost or increase in income shows their good performance.

In order to measure the performance, the budget expenses and income should be compared with actual expenses and income with respect to each responsibility centres. This will help to create a competitive environment which will in fact improve the overall performance of the company.

Zero Base Budgeting

Zero Base Budgeting (ZBB) was first used by U.S Department of Agriculture during 1961. The logical framework of it was developed during 1970 by Peter A Pyher. Hence, he is called as the father of Zero Base Budgeting. The Zero Base Budgeting got popularity when Mr. Jimmy Carter, President of U.S.A issued order to all the Federal Governments to use ZBB instead of the conventional budgeting. The State Government of U.S.A also adopted the ZBB.

In the Conventional budgeting, budgets are prepared by taking into account of previous year values as base. Increment to the previous year values are considered as the values of budget for current year. But the economical, social and financial conditions are changing day by day. Hence, the basis of previous year will not provide accurate data to suit the current situation. The inefficiencies and all defects of previous year are carried forward in the conventional budgeting. The new system named Zero Based Budgeting, provides solution for avoiding the defects in the conventional budgeting.

Meaning of Zero Base Budgeting

Zero Base Budgeting is a budget prepared by taking zero as base. Previous year data are not considered in the preparation of budget under this method.

According to Peter A. Pyhrr, "An operating, planning and budgeting process which requires each manager to justify his entire budget requests in detail from scratch (hence, Zero-Basis). Each Manager state why he should spend any money at all. This approach requires that all activities be identified as decision packages which would be evaluated by systematic analysis."

It is clear from the statement of Peter A. Pyhrr that the process of Zero Base Budgeting is

(i) Identification of all activities of the organisation as decision packages

(ii) Evaluation of the decision packages.

According to David Lieninger and Rolland C.Wong, "Zero Base Budgeting is a management tool which provides a systematic method for evaluating all operations and programmes current or new, allow for budget reductions and expansions in a rational manner and allows reallocation of source from low to high priority programme" It is clear from the definition that ZBB is concerned with periodical and systematic evaluation of all programmes of a company in order to improve the efficiency.

Advantages of Zero Base Budgeting:

The advantages of Zero Base Budgeting are stated as follows:

1. It considers all activities of an organisation as important and hence, focuses on the efficiency in the performance of these activities.
2. It helps for the systematic evaluation of different activities, so that mistakes if any can be rectified immediately.
3. It suggests alternative ways of doing a job every time when budget is prepared since Zero is taken as base.
4. It prevents the unnecessary expenditure in different activities of the organisation.
5. It helps to prepare various budgets on the basis of cost benefit analysis.
6. It gives proper direction to all managers to perform the activities in economical and efficient manner.

1. Preparation of Sales Budget

Illustration: 1

Joyce & Co. manufactures 2 types of products namely A and B and sells them in Bangalore and Hyderabad markets. The following information are related to the year ending 31st March 2006.

Market	*Product*	*Budgeted sales*	*Actual sales*
Bangalore	A	15,000 @ Rs. 22	15,500 @ Rs. 20
	B	12,000 @ Rs. 45	11,500 @ Rs. 47
Hyderabad	A	10,000 @ Rs. 22	9,000 @ Rs. 20
	B	7,000 @ Rs. 45	8,000@ Rs. 47

Market studies reveal that product A is popular as it is under priced. It is observed if the price is reduced by Re.1 it will find a good market. On the other hand, product B is over priced and it will get good market if the selling price is reduced to Rs.43. The management has agreed for this. The impact of the change in price is reported as follows.

Product	*Increase in sales over current budget*	
	Bangalore	*Hyderabad*
A	+30%	+20%
B	+10%	+15%

In addition to this, the following additional sales above the estimated sales are possible with an intensive advertisement.

Product	*Bangalore*	*Hyderabad*
A	400 units	300 units
B	500 units	200 units

Prepare a budget for sales by incorporating the above estimates.

Solution:

SALES BUDGET

Area	*Product*	*Budget for the current year*			*Actual Sales*			*Budget for the future period*		
		Units	*Price Rs.*	*Value*	*Units*	*Price Rs.*	*Value*	*Units*	*Price Rs.*	*Value*
Bangalore	A	15,000	22	3,30,000	15,500	20	3,10,000	19,900	21	4,17,900
	B	12,000	45	5,40,000	11,500	47	5,40,500	13,700	43	5,89,100
	Total	27,000		8,70,000	27,000		8,50,500	33,600		10,07,000
Hyderabad	A	10,000	22	2,20,000	9,000	20	1,80,000	12,300	21	2,58,300
	B	7,000	45	3,15,000	8,000	47	3,76,000	8,250	43	3,54,750
	Total	17,000		5,35,000	17,000		5,56,000	20,550		5,13,050
Total	A	25,000	22	5,50,000	24,500	20	4.90,000	32,200	21	6,76,200
	B	19,000	45	8,55,000	19,500	47	9,16,500	21,950	43	9,43,850
	Total	44,000		14,05,000	44,000		14,06,500	20,550		16,20,050

Workings :

	A Units	*B Units*
Budgeted Sales of Bangalore:	15,000	12,000
Add : Increase	4500 (30%)	1200 (10%)
	19,500	13,200
Increase due to Advertisement	400	500
Total	19,900	13,700
Budgeted Sales of Hyderabad:	10,000	7,000
Add : Increase	2000 (20%)	1050 (15%)
	12,000	8.050
Increase due to Advertisement	300	200
Total	12,300	8,250

. Preparation of Production Budget

llustration: 2

The following information are related to a company for 6 months ending 31st December 2007.

The units to be sold for the different months are,

July	2007	15,000
August	2007	17,000
September	2007	19,000
October	2007	15.500
November	2007	20,000
December	2007	21,000
January	2008	22,000

Finished units equal to half the sales for the next month will be in stock at the end of each month including June 2007. Budgeted production for the year ending 31st December 2007 is 250,000 units. Budgeted material and labour cost per unit are Rs.20 and Rs.15 respectively. Total factory overhead absorbed for one year is Rs. 10,00,000.

Prepare production budget for each month and summarised production cost budget for six months ending 31st December 2007.

Solution:

Production budget for 6 months from July 2007 to 31st December 2007

Months	*Opening Stock (Units)*	*Sales (Units)*	*Closing Stock (Units)*	*Production (Units)*
July 2007	7,500	15,000	8,500	16,000
August 2007	8,500	17,000	9,500	18,000
September 2007	9,500	19,000	7,750	17,250
October 2007	7,750	15,500	10,000	17,750
November 2007	10,000	20,000	10,500	20,500
December 2007	10,500	21,000	11,000	21,500
			Total	**1,11,000**

Production = Sales + Closing stock - Opening stock

July 2007	=	15,000 + 8,500 – 7,500 = 16,000 units
August 2007	=	17,000 + 9,500 – 8,500 = 18,000 units
September 2007	=	19,000 + 7,750 – 9,500 = 17,250 units
October 2007	=	15,500 + 10,000 – 7,750 = 17,750 units
November 2007	=	20,000 + 10,500 – 10,000 = 20,500 units
December 2007	=	21,000 + 11,000 – 10,500 = 21,500 units

Production Cost Budget for 6 months ending 31st December 2007 (for 1,11,000 units)

Particulars	*Rate per unit Rs.*	*Amount Rs.*
Direct Material	20	22,20,000
Direct Wages	15	16,65,000
Factory Overheads (10,00,000/2,50,000)	4	4,44,000
Total		**43,29,000**

Illustration: 3

A manufacturing company provided the following information about the manufacturing of two products namely, Q and R as follows.

The budgeted sales in units are as follows:

Months	Product Q (Units)	Product R (Units)
January	500	1000
February	700	1200
March	900	900
April	720	1300
May	800	1100
June	640	1400
July – December	700 per month	1000 per month

The details of expense are as follows:

	Product Q Rs.	Product R Rs.
Direct Material per unit	25	17
Direct Wages per unit	20	12
Total Factory Overhead	1,50,000	2,80,000
Total Administration Overhead	2,00,000	3,00,000
Total Selling & Distribution Overhead	90,000	1,50,000
Selling price per unit	79	60

It is assumed that (i) there is no work-in-progress at the end of any months and (ii) finished units equal to quarter the sales for the following months will be kept in stock.

Prepare a Production Budget and Product Cost Budget for one year.

Solution :

Production Budget

Months	Product Q				Product R			
	Sales	Cl. Stock	Op. Stock	Production	Sales	Cl. Stock	Op. Stock	Production
January	500	175	125	550	1000	300	250	1050
February	700	225	175	750	1200	225	300	1125
March	900	180	225	855	900	325	225	1000
April	720	200	180	740	1300	275	325	1250
May	800	160	200	760	1100	350	275	1175
June	640	175	160	655	1400	250	350	1300
July	700	175	175	700	100	250	250	1000
August	700	175	175	700	100	250	250	1000
September	700	175	175	700	100	250	250	1000
October	700	175	175	700	100	250	250	1000
November	700	175	175	700	100	250	250	1000
December	700	175	175	700	100	250	250	1000
	8,460			8,510	12,900			12,900

Summarised Production Cost Budget

Particulars	Product Q		Product R		Total Rs.
	Cost / Unit	Amount Rs.	Cost / Unit	Amount Rs.	
Direct Material	25.00	212,750	17.00	219,300	432,050
Direct Wages	20.00	170,200	12.00	154,800	325,000
Factory Overhead	17.63	150,000	21.71	280,000	430,000
Works Cost	62.63	532,950	50.71	654,100	11,87,050
Administration Overhead	23.50	200,000	23.26	300,000	500,000
Cost of Production	86,13	732,950	73.97	954,100	16,87,050
Selling overhead	10.57	90,000	11.63	150,000	240,000
Cost of Sales	96.70	822,950	85.60	11,04,100	19,27,050

Note : (i) Production = Sales + Closing Stock – Opening Stock

(ii) Opening Stock is calculated by dividing by 4 from the respective sales units.

3. Preparation of Material Budget

Illustration: 4

Prepare raw materials purchase budget from the following figures.

	Materials (Units)					
Estimated Stock on 1st Dec. 2007	120,000	90,000	45,000	25,000	20,000	35,000
Estimated Stock on 31st Dec. 2007	180,000	70,000	30,000	40,000	32,000	50,000
Estimated Consumption	900,000	750,000	600,000	550,000	400,000	650,000
Standard Price per unit (Rs.)	5	7	3	10	12	9

Solution:

Raw Materials Purchase Budget for December 2007

Particulars	Cost of raw materials (Rs.)					
	I	J	K	L	M	N
Estimated Consumption (units)	900,000	750,000	600,000	550,000	400,000	650,000
Add : Estimated Stock on 31st Dec.	180,000	70,000	30,000	40,000	32,000	50,000
	10,80,000	820,000	630,000	590,000	432,000	700,000
Less : Estimated Stock on 1st Dec.	120,000	90,000	45,000	25,000	20,000	35,000
Estimated Purchase (Units)	960,000	730,000	585,000	565,000	412,000	665,000
Rate per Unit (Rs.)	5	7	3	10	12	9
Estimated Purchase (Rs.)	48,00,000	51,10,000	17,55,000	56,50,000	49,44,000	59,85,000

Note: Purchase of raw material is calculated by adding the estimated closing stock with estimated consumption of material and then deducting from it the estimated opening stock of material.

4. Preparation of Overhead Budget.

Illustration: 5

The details of overhead of a Company at 60% capacity are stated as follows:

Particulars	*Rs.*
Variable Overheads:	
Indirect Material	36,000
Indirect Wages	30,600
Indirect Expenses	12,000
Fixed Overheads:	
Salary	72,000
Insurance	24,000
Depreciation	15,000
Semi-Variable Overheads:	
Repairs & Maintenance	18,000
(80% Fixed and 20% Variable)	
Electricity	6,600
(60% Fixed and 20% Variable)	30,000
Total Overheads	2,44,200

Estimated direct labour hours are 120,000 at 60% capacity.

Prepare a Manufacturing Overhead Budget and find out the manufacturing overhead rates at 70% and 90% capacities.

Solution:

Manufacturing Overhead Budget

Particulars	*Capacity*		
	60% (Rs.)	70% (Rs.)	90% (Rs.)
Variable Overheads:			
Indirect Material	36,000	42,000	54,000
Indirect Wages	30,600	35,700	45,900
Indirect Expenses	12,000	14,000	18,000
Repairs & Maintenance	3,600	4,200	5,400
Electricity	2,640	3,080	3,960
Supervisor's Salary	6,000	7,000	9,000
Fixed Overheads:			
Salary	72,000	72,000	72,000
Insurance	24,000	24,000	24,000
Depreciation	15,000	15,000	15,000
Repairs & Maintenance	14,400	14,400	14,4000
Electricity	3,960	3,960	3,960
Supervisors Salary	24,000	24,000	24,000

Total Overheads	2,44,200	2,59,340	2,89,620
Est. Direct Labour Hrs.	1,20,000	1,40,000	1,80,000
Overhead Rates (Rs.)	2.04	1.85	1.61

5. Preparation of Cash Budget

Cash budget is prepared to know the net cash flow in future, by taking into consideration of cash inflow and cash outflow. There are three methods for preparing cash budgets. They are,

a. Receipts and Payment Method

b. Adjusted Profit and Loss Account Method, and

c. Balance Sheet Method.

(a) Receipts and Payments Method

In this method, cash receipts and cash payments of various sources should be estimated for future. The cash receipts should include all the receipts of revenue and capital nature. The cash payment should include all the payments of revenue and capital nature. The cash budget will show the estimated closing balance of cash. It may be a debit balance or a credit balance.

Illustration: 6

Prepare a Cash Budget for 4 months ending 31st December 2007 from the following information.

Months	*Sales Rs.*	*Purchase Rs.*	*Wages Rs.*	*Manuf. Expenses Rs.*	*Admin. Expenses Rs.*	*Selling Expenses Rs.*
July 2007	1,50,000	40,000	17,000	10,000	11,000	5,000
August 2007	1,70,000	44,000	19,000	12,000	13,000	6,000
September 2007	2,00,000	59,000	20,000	13,000	10,000	7,000
October 2007	1,80,000	51,000	21,000	15,000	14,000	4,000
November 2007	1,90,000	55,000	22,000	16,000	15,000	8,000
December 2007	2,20,000	60,000	24,000	18,000	17,000	9,000

Additional Information:

1. Balance of cash in hand on 1st September 2007 is Rs.55,000.
2. Land purchased Rs.140,000 in the month of November.
3. A dividend of Rs.65,000 payable in the month of December.
4. Furniture worth Rs.15,000 to be purchased in the month of October.
5. A Machinery worth Rs.100,000 purchased on June 2007 and the payment is to be done on installment basis @ Rs.10,000 per month.
6. The creditors are allowing a credit of 2 months.
7. Wages are paid on the 1st of next month.
8. Lag in payment of manufacturing and selling expense is ½ month.
9. The customers are allowed a credit period of 2 months.
10. Lag in payment of administration expense is one month.

Solution:

Cash Budget for 4 months ending 30th April 2006

Particulars	*Sep. Rs.*	*Oct. Rs.*	*Nov. Rs.*	*Dec. Rs.*
Receipts:				
Balance b/d	55,000	104,000	155,500	90,000
Cash received from Drs.	1,50,000	1,70,000	2,00,000	1,80,000
Total	**2,05,000**	**2,74,000**	**3,55,500**	**2,70,000**
Payments:				
Payment to Creditors	40,000	44,000	59,000	51,000
Wages payable	19,000	20,000	21,000	22,000
Manufacturing expenses	12,500	14,000	15,500	17,000
Administration expenses	13,000	10,000	14,000	15,000
Selling expenses	6,500	5,500	6,000	8,500
Purchase of Land	–	–	1,40,000	–
Dividend payable	–	–	–	65,000
Purchase of Furniture	–	15,000	–	–
Payment for purchase of Machinery	10,000	10,000	10,000	10,000
Total	**1,01,000**	**1,18,500**	**2,65,500**	**1,88,500**
Closing Balance	**1,04,500**	**1,55,500**	**90,000**	**81,500**

Illustration: 7

Prepare a Cash Budget from the following data for 3 months ending 31st March 2008

Months	*Sales Rs.*	*Purchase Rs.*	*Wages Rs.*	*Other Expenses Rs.*
November 2007	5,50,000	2,00,000	70,000	1,90,000
December 2007	6,00,000	2,40,000	90,000	2,20,000
January 2008	7,00,000	2,90,000	1,00,000	2,40,000
February 2008	5,00,000	3,20,000	85,000	2,30,000
March 2008	7,50,000	3,90,000	1,10,000	2,50,000

Additional information.

1. Corporate Tax due on 31st March Rs.120,000.
2. Interest to be received for investment Rs.25,000 monthly.
3. Cash in hand on 1st January 2006 Rs. 57,000.
4. Dividend of Rs.100,000 to be paid during March.
5. 40% of the sales amount received in the month of sales, discount allowed 5%.The balance amount is received equally in the following two months.
6. Lag in payment of purchase 2 months.
7. 30% of the wages remain arrears and will be paid in the following month.

8. Other expenses are paid in the following month.

Solution:

Cash Budget for the months from 1st January to 31st March 2008

Particulars	*January Rs.*	*February Rs.*	*March Rs.*
Receipts:			
Opening Balance	57,000	1,76,000	2,11,500
Receipts from Drs. and Cash Sales	6,11,000	5,80,000	6,45,000
Interest received	25,000	25,000	25,000
Total	**6,93,000**	**7,81,000**	**8,81,500**
Payments:			
Creditors	2,00,000	2,40,000	2,90,000
Wages	97,000	89,500	1,02,500
Other Expenses	2,20,000	2,40,000	2,30,000
Corporate Tax	–	–	1,20,000
Dividend	–	–	1,00,000
Total	5,17,000	**5,69,500**	**8,42,500**
Closing Balance	**1,76,000**	**2,11,500**	**39,000**

Workings:

(i) **Calculation of receipts from Drs and Sales**

		Rs.
January:	Cash Sales (40% of 7,00,000)	2,80,000
	Less: Discount @ 5%	14,000
		266,000
	Add : 30% of Rs. 6,00,000 (Sales of December 2007)	1,80,000
	30% of Rs. 550,000 (Sales of November 2005)	1,65,000
		6,11,000
February:	Cash Sales (40% of 5,00,000)	2,00,000
	Less : Discount @ 5%	10,000
		1,90,000
	Add : 30% of Rs. 7,00,000 (Sales of January)	2,10,000
	Add : 30% of Rs. 6,00,000 (Sales of December)	1,80,000
		5,80,000
March:	Cash Sales (40% of Rs. 7,50,000)	3,00,000
	Less: Discount @ 5%	15,000

		2,85,000
	Add : 30% of Rs. 5,00,000 (Sales of February)	1,50,000
	30% of Rs. 7,00,000 (Sales of January)	2,10,000
		6,45,000

(ii) Calculation of payment for wages

January:	Wages of January 70% of Rs.100,000	70,000
	Arrear wage of December- 30% of Rs. 90,000	27,000
		97,000
February:	Wages of February 70% of Rs.85,000	59,500
	Arrear wage of January- 30% of Rs.100,000	30,000
		89,500
March:	Wages of March 70% of Rs.110,000	77,000
	Arrear wage of February- 30% of Rs. 85,000	25,500
		102,500

(b) Adjusted Profit and Loss Account Method

In this method, cash budget is prepared by taking into account of the opening balances of cash and bank, projected Profit and Loss account and the balances of the assets and liabilities. The balance of Profit and Loss account should be adjusted with non-operating items like depreciation, profit or loss on sale of fixed assets, etc. The cash inflow and outflow related to the capital items should be known by taking their differences between the opening and closing balances.

Illustration: 8

Prepare Cash Budget by Adjusted Profit and Loss Account method from the following

Balance Sheet as on 31st March 2007

Liabilities	*Rs.*	*Assets*	*Rs.*
Share Capital	7,00,000	Land & Building	7,10,000
Profit & Loss A/c	1,40,000	Plant & Machinery	4,50,000
Reserve	45,000	Stock	85,000
Debenture	2,00,000	Debtors	34,000
Loan	2,50,000	Cash	120,000
Creditors	55,000	Interest prepaid	7,000
Bills payable	20,000	Bills receivable	14,000
Outstanding Salary	10,000		
	14,20,000		**14,20,000**

Projected Trading and Profit & Loss Account as on 31st March 2008

Particulars		Rs.	Particulars	Rs.
To Opening Stock		85,000	By Sales	5,25,000
To Purchase		1,20,000	By Closing Stock	100,000
To Wages		70,000		
To Gross Profit c/d		3,50,000		
		6,25,000		6,25,000
To Salary	50,000		By Gross Profit b/d	3,50,000
Less: Outst. Last year.	10,000		By Commission received	40,000
	40,000			
Add : Outstanding Current year	17,000	57,000		
To Telephone charges		13,000		
To Electricity		15,000		
To Interest	25,000			
Less: Prepaid Current year	10,000			
	15,000			
Add: Prepaid - Last year	7,000	22,000		
To Admission expenses		27,000		
To Depreciation Land & Building 5%		35,500		
Plant 10%		50,000		
To Net Profit c/d		1,70,500		
		3,90,000		**3,90,000**
To Provision for Dividend		90,000	By Balance of Profit last year	1,40,000
To General Reserve		70,000		
To Balance of Profit to be transferred to Balance Sheet		1,50,500	By Net Profit b/d	1,70,500
		3,10,500		**3,10,500**

Closing balances estimated:

	Rs.
Plant & Machinery	5,00,000
Debentures	2,20,000
Loan	2,80,000
Creditors	40,000
Debtors	50,000
Bills Receivable	10,000
Bills Payable	15,000
Share Capital	7,40,000

Solution:

Cash Budget

Particulars	*Rs.*	*Rs.*
Opening Balance as on 1st April, 2007		1,20,000
Add: Net Profit for the year	1,70,500	
Depreciation (35,500+50,000)	85,500	
Decrease in Bills Receivable	4,000	
Issue of Share Capital	40,000	
Issue of Debentures	20,000	
Increase in Salary Outstanding	7,000	
Increase of Loan	30,000	3,57,000
		4,77,000
Less : Purchase of Plant		
(5,00,000 – 4,50,000 + dep. 50,000)	1,00,000	
Increase in Stock (100,000 – 85,000)	15,000	
Increase in Debtors (50,000 – 34,000)	16,000	
Increase in Prepaid Interest	3,000	
Decrease in Creditors	15,000	
Decrease in Bills Payable (20,000 – 15,000)	5,000	1,54,000
Estimated Closing Balance of Cash		**3,23,000**

(c) Balance Sheet Method

In this method, a projected Balance Sheet should be prepared with estimated assets and liabilities. The cash balance should not be projected. It should be ascertained from the balance of estimated assets and liabilities.

Illustration: 9

Prepare a cash budget on the basis of Balance Sheet method from the following.

Balance Sheet as on 31st March 2005

Liabilities	*Rs.*	*Assets*	*Rs.*
Share Capital	10,00,000	Freehold property	7,40,000
Profit & Loss A/c	1,50,000	Plant & Machinery	5,20,000
General Reserve	70,000	Stock	50,000
Loan	2,50,000	Debtors	32,000
Creditors	30,000	Cash	1,44,000
Bills payable	10,000	Bills receivable	20,000
Salary outstanding	5,000	Prepaid interest	9,000
	15,15,000		**15,15,000**

Adjustments:

(1) Balance as on 31st March 2007 -Profit & Loss A/c Rs. 1,95,000, Loan Rs.1,70,000; Creditors Rs.45,000; Debtors Rs. 50,000; Salary Outstanding Rs. 12,000; Stock Rs.72,000; General Reserve Rs. 75,000

(2) Purchase of Furniture at the end of March 2007 Rs. 50,000.

(3) Depreciation for Fixed Assets @ 10% p.a.

(4) Plant to be purchased on 1st October 2007 for Rs. 70,000.

Solution:

Preparation of Cash Budget

Budgeted Balance Sheet as on 31st March, 2006

Liabilities	*Rs.*	*Assets*		*Rs.*
Share Capital	10,00,000	Freehold Property	7,40,000	
Profit & Loss A/c	1,95,000	**Less :** Depreciation	74,000	6,66,000
General Reserve	75,000	Plant & Machinery	5,20,000	
Loan	1,70,000	**Add :** Purchases	70,000	
Creditors	45,000		5,90,000	
Outstanding Salary	12,000	**Less :** Depreciation (52,000 + 3,500)	55,500	5,34,500
		Furniture		70,000
		Stock		72,000
		Debtors		50,000
		Cash (Balancing Figure)		1,04,500
	14,97,000			**14,97,000**

6. Preparation of Flexible Budget

Illustration: 10

The information regarding the expenses of a company at 50% capacity is as follows.

	Rs.
Fixed expenses:	
Salary	110,000
Rent	30,000
Administrative expenses	70,000
Depreciation	45,000
Variable expenses:	
Material	24,000
Labour	66,000
Others	36,000
Semi-Variable expenses:	
Indirect Labour	50,000
Repairs & Maintenance	40,000
Electricity	20,000

The estimated sales at various levels of capacity are,

Rs. 5,00,000 at 40% Capacity

Rs. 6,25,000 at 50% Capacity

Rs. 7,50,000 at 60% Capacity

Rs. 8,75,000 at 70% Capacity

The fixed expense will remain same till 100% Capacity. Semi-variable expenses remain constant till 50% of capacity. It will increase by 10% between 50% and 65% capacity and further increased by 5% above 65% capacity.

Prepare a flexible budget and calculate the profit at various levels of capacities (40%, 50%, 60% and 70%)

Solution:

Flexible Budget

Particulars	*Capacity*			
	40% *Rs.*	*50%* *Rs.*	*60%* *Rs.*	*70%* *Rs.*
Fixed Expenses:				
Salary	1,10,000	1,10,000	1,10,000	1,10,000
Rent	30,000	30,000	30,000	30,000
Administrative Expenses	70,000	70,000	70,000	70,000
Depreciation	45,000	45,000	45,000	
Variable Expenses:				
Material	19,200	24,000	28,800	33,600
Labour	52,800	66,000	79,200	92,400
Others	28,800	36,000	43,200	50,400
Semi Variables Expenses:				
Indirect Labour	50,000	50,000	50,000	
Repairs & Maintenance	40,000	40,000	40,000	
Electricity	20,000	20,000	20,000	
Total Cost	**4,65,800**	**4,86,000**	**5,27,200**	**5,57,900**
Profit	**34,200**	**1,39,000**	**2,22,800**	**3,17,100**
Estimated Sales	**5,00,000**	**6,25,000**	**7,50,000**	**8,75,000**

Illustration: 11

The following information are related to the budgeted production of 20,000 units of a product manufactured by K Ltd. The actual production during the period is 15000 units. Calculate the budgeted cost per unit.

	Rs.
Direct Materials	220,000
Direct Labour	110,000
Direct Expenses	80,000

Works Overhead (70% Fixed)	230,000
Administration Overhead (90% Fixed)	260,000
Selling Overhead (60% Fixed)	100,000

Solution:

Flexible Budget

Particulars	Production Cost for 20,000 Units		Production Cost for 15,000 Units	
	Per Unit Rs.	Total Rs.	Per Unit Rs.	Total Rs.
Direct Material	11.00	2,20,000	11.00	1,65,000
Direct Wages	5.50	1,10,000	5.50	82,500
Direct Expenses	4.00	80,000	4.00	60,000
Prime Cost	**20.50**	**4,10,000**	**20.50**	**3,07,500**
Works Overhead – Fixed	8.05	1,61,000	10.73	1,61,000
Variable	3.45	69,000	3.45	51,750
Work Cost	**32.00**	**6,40,000**	**34.68**	**520,250**
Administration Overhead – Fixed	11.70	2,34,000	15.60	2,34,000
Variable	1.30	26,000	1.30	19,500
Cost of Production	**45.00**	**9,00,000**	**51.58**	**7,73,750**
Selling overhead – Fixed	3.00	60,000	4.00	60,000
Variable	2.00	40,000	2.00	30,000
Cost of Sales	**50**	**10,00,000**	**57.58**	**8,63,750**

Workings:

Works Overhead: (For 20,000 units) Rs. 2,30,000

Fixed 70% Rs. 1,61,000

Variable 30% Rs. 69,000

Works Overhead: (For 15,000 units)

Fixed 70% = Rs. 1,61,000

Variable $\frac{69,000}{20,000} \times 15000$ = Rs. 51,750

Total = Rs. 212,750

7. Preparation of Master Budget

Illustration: 12

G Ltd. presents the following information as on 31st March 2007.

Sales	Rs. 9,00,000
Direct Material Cost - 25% of Sales	
Direct Wages	Rs. 80,000
Direct Expenses	Rs. 70,000
Factory Overheads:	

Supervisors Salary Rs. 9,000 per month Manager's Salary Rs. 12,000 per month Foreman's Salary Rs. 4,000 per month Light & Power Rs. 30,000 Depreciation on Plant & Machinery Rs. 35,000 Spares and Lubricating oil 2% of Sales Repairs & Maintenance 3% of Plant & Machinery Administration overhead Rs.30,000 per year Selling and distribution overhead Rs. 20,000 per year. Value of Plant & Machinery Rs. 7,00,000

Prepare a Master Budget

Solution :

Master Budget

Particulars			*Rs.*	*Rs.*
Sales				900,000
Less : Cost of Production				
	Direct Material		2,25,000	
	Direct Wages		80,000	
	Direct Expenses		70,000	
	Prime Cost		**3,75,000**	
Factory overhead:				
Fixed :	Manager's Salary	1,08,000		
	Supervisor's Salary	1,44,000		
	Foreman's Salary	48,000		
	Depreciation	35,000	3,35,000	
Variable :	Light & Power	30,000		
	Spares & Lubricating Oil	18,000		
	Repairs & Maintenances	21,000	69,000	
	Works Cost			**7,79,000**
	Gross Profit			**1,21,000**
Less : Administration Overhead			30,000	
	Selling & Distribution Overhead		20,000	50,000
	Net Profit			**71,000**

8. Preparation of Performance Budgeting

Illustration: 13

M Ltd. provided the following information for the month of November 2007.

The budgeted sales is 50,000 units @ Rs. 20 per unit. The Fixed Cost is estimated as Rs. 250,000 and the Variable Cost is estimated as Rs. 12 per unit. The company could able to produce only 40,000 units due to low demand in the market. Moreover the variable cost per unit increased by Re 2 per unit, and the selling price increased by Rs. 2.50 per unit. The company has to spend Rs. 30,000 for research and development, in addition to the usual increase in the cost of production.

Prepare a Performance Budget and a Summary Report. *(Adopted ICWA Inter)*

Solution:

Performance Budget

Particulars	*Original Plan Rs.*	*Adjusted Plan Rs.*	*Actual Rs.*
Sales	10,00,000	800,000	900,000
Variable Cost	6,00,000	4,80,000	5,60,000
Contribution	4,00,000	3,20,000	3,40,000
Fixed Cost	2,50,000	2,50,000	2,80,000
Profit	1,50,000	70,000	60,000

Summary Report

Particulars		*Rs.*
Budgeted Profit		150,000
Selling Price Variance		
[(40,000 × (22.50 – 20.00)]	= 100,000 (Favourable)	
Variable Cost Variance		
[(40,000 × (12 – 14)]	= 80,000 (Unfavourable)	
Fixed Cost Variance		
(280,000 – 250,000)	= 30,000 (Unfavorable)	
Profit Volume Variance		
[(10,000 × (20 – 12)]	= 80,000 (Unfavourable)	(90,000)
Actual Profit		**60,000**

EXERCISE

THEORY

I. Choose the correct answer for the following.

1. Budget is prepared for —
   (i) Future period (ii) Present period (iii) Past period (iv) Any period
2. The document which explains the responsibility of individuals, involved in the preparation of budget is called —
   (i) Cost statement (ii) Profit statement (iii) Budget manual(iv) Fund flow statement
3. The consolidated summary of the various functional budgets is called —
   (i) Budget committee (ii) Budget manual (iii) Master Budget (iv) Fixed Budget
4. The budget prepared for a given level of activity is known as —
   (i) Variable budget (ii) Fixed budget (iii) Market budget (iv) Budget manual
5. A budget designed to change in accordance with the level of activity is —
   (i) Flexible budget (ii) Master budget (iii) Fixed budget (iv) Budget manual
6. The budget which forecasts the total output of the organisation is called —
   (i) Master budget (ii) Functional budget (iii) Fixed budget (iv) Production budget

7. The budget which estimates the total amount of capital required for acquiring fixed assets is called —
(i) Fixed Budget (ii) Capital Expenditure Budget (iii) Sales Budget (iv) Cash Budget

8. The budget which estimates the receipt and payment of cash is called —
(i) Cash Budget (ii) Sales budget (iii) Production budget (iv) Master budget

9. Previous year data are not considered in —
(i) Master budget (ii) Fixed budget (iii) Zero-base budget (iv) Flexible budget

10. The process of preparing budget by associating money concept with the performance of employees is called —
(i) Performance Budgeting (ii) Zero-base Budgeting (iii) Master Budgeting (iv) Functional Budgeting

[**Ans :** 1.(i) 2. (iii) 3.(iii) 4. (ii) 5. (i) 6. (iv) 7. (ii) 8. (i) 9. (iii) 10.(i)]

II. Answer the following.

11. Define budget. State the characteristics of a good budget.
12. What is budgetary control? State the objectives of budgetary control.
13. Define budgetary control. Explain the merits of budgetary control.
14. Explain the advantages and limitations of budgetary control.
15. Explain the different types of budgets.
16. Write short notes on the following.
(i) Fixed budget (ii) Flexible budget (iii) Cash budget (iv) Overhead budget (v) Master budget (vi) Budget manual
17. Joce Ltd. manufactures two type of products namely X and Y and sells them in Mumbai and B...alore markets. The following information are related to the year ending 31st March 2007

Market	*Product*	*Budgeted Sales*	*Actual Sales*
Mumbai	X	5000 Units @ Rs. 14	4700 Units @ Rs. 14
	Y	4000 Units @ Rs. 20	3500 Units @ Rs. 20
Bangalore	X	3000 Units @ Rs. 14	3600 Units @ Rs. 14
	Y	2000 Units @ Rs. 20	2300 Units @ Rs. 20

Market Report revealed that product X is popular as it is under priced. If the price is reduced by Re. 1, it will get more sales. On the other hand, Product B is over priced and it is predicted that more sales is possible if the selling price is reduced to Rs. 18. The management has agreed to give effect to the above price change.

On the above basis, the following estimates have been done by the Sales Manager.

Product	*% increase in sales over current budget*	
	Mumbai	**Bangalore**
X	30%	20%
Y	10%	25%

In addition to this, the following additional sales above the estimated sales are possible, with an intensive advertisement.

Product	*Mumbai*	*Bangalore*
X	400 units	300 units
Y	500 units	200 units

Prepare a Sales Budget. (**Ans :** *Rs. 232,000; 232,100; 2,77,450*)

18. The following information are related to a company for 6 months ending 31st March 2007. The units sold for different months are as follows.

October 2006	10,000
November	14,000
December	15,000
January 2007	12,000
February	17,000
March	19,000
April	13,000

Finished units equal to half the sales for the next months will be in stock at the end of each month including September 2006. Budgeted production for the year ending 31st March 2007 is 190,000 units. Material and labour cost per unit are Rs. 20 and Rs. 10 respectively. Total factory overhead absorbed is Rs.640,000.

Prepare Production Budget for each month and summarised Production Cost Budget for six months ending 31st March 2007. *(Ans : 34,20,263)*

19. Prepare a Production Budget for each month and Production Cost Budget for one year from the following information.

The budgeted sales in units are as follows.

	Product P (Units)	*Product Q (Units)*
January	4,000	2,000
February	3,200	1,600
March	5,600	2,400
April	6,400	3,600
May	5,200	2,800
June	4,800	3,000
July	6,000	2,800

The details of expenses are as follows:

	Product P Rs.	*Product Q Rs.*
Direct Material per unit	20	15
Direct Wages per unit	11	9
Total Factory overhead	6,00,000	4,00,000
Total Selling & Distribution overhead	3,00,000	1,40,000
Selling price per unit	65	50

It is assumed that (i) there is no work-in-progress at the end of any month (ii) forecasted units equal to one fourth of sales for the following month will be kept in stock. *(Ans: Rs.29,36,700; Rs.13,17,600)*

20. Prepare Raw Material Purchase Budget from the following.

Particulars	*Materials (Units)*					
	A	*B*	*C*	*D*	*E*	*F*
Estimated Stock on 1st March 2007	11,000	20,000	30,000	13,000	34,000	24,000
Estimated Stock on 1st March	15,000	22,000	30,000	13,000	34,000	24,000
Estimated Consumption	1,70,000	1,20,000	1,40,000	1,30,000	1,39,000	1,50,000
Standard Price per unit (Rs.)	4	6	8	5	3	2

(**Ans:** *Rs.6,96,000; 7,32,000; 1,13,600; 6,80,000; 3,84,000; 3,10,000)*

21. Prepare a Cash Budget for 4 months ending 31st March 2007 from the following particulars.

Months	*Sales Rs.*	*Purchase Rs.*	*Wages Rs.*	*Manufacturing Expenses Rs.*	*Administrative Expenses Rs.*	*Salary Expenses Rs.*
Sep. 2006	1,77,000	79,000	36,000	10,000	20,000	19,000
Oct. 2006	1,40,000	80,000	39,000	17,000	21,600	25,800
Nov. 2006	1,95,000	90,000	17,000	21,000	19,000	24,000
Dec. 2006	2,00,000	1,10,000	21,000	24,000	17,500	21,000
Jan. 2007	1,32,000	72,000	20,000	22,000	17,000	18,000
Feb. 2007	2,10,000	1,20,000	42,000	27,000	24,000	27,700
Mar. 2007	2,30,000	1,35,000	36,000	29,000	26,000	29,000

Additional Information:

1. Balance of Cash in hand on 1st December 2006 Rs. 100,000.
2. Wages are paid in the 1st of next month.
3. Tax amounted to Rs. 34,000, payable in the month of March 2007.
4. A dividend of Rs. 40,000 payable in the month of January.
5. Furniture worth Rs. 27,000 to be purchased in the month of February 2007.
6. A machine worth Rs. 70,000 purchased in the month of September and the payment is to be made in instalment basis @ Rs. 7,000 per month.
7. The Creditors are allowing a credit period of 2 months.
8. Lag in payments of Manufacturing and Selling expenses are two months.
9. The customers are allowed a credit period of 1 month.
10. Lag in payment of Administration expenses is 1/2 month.

(**Ans :** *Cl. Cash balances: Rs. 1,29,950; 109,700; 12,200, 2,200)*

22. Prepare a Cash budget from the following data for 3 months ending 31st March 2007.

Months	*Sales Rs.*	*Purchases Rs.*	*Wages Rs.*	*Other Expenses Rs.*
Nov. 2006	5,50,000	2,90,000	1,50,000	30,000
Dec. 2006	6,00,000	3,10,000	1,40,000	45,000
Jan. 2007	4,80,000	2,89,000	95,000	31,000
Feb. 2007	5,90,000	3,40,000	1,10,000	43,000
Mar. 2007	6,30,000	3,40,00	1,45,000	47,000

Additional information:

1. Corporate tax due for 31st March 2007 is Rs. 40,000.
2. Interest to be received for investment @ Rs. 35,000 monthly.
3. Dividend of Rs. 75,000 to be paid during March 2007.
4. 60% of the sales amount realised in the month, Discount allowed @4%. The balance amount realised equally in two subsequent months.
5. Lag in payment of purchase is 2 months.
6. 40% of the wages remains arrear and will be paid in the following months.
7. Other expenses are paid in the following months.
8. Cash in hand on 1st January 2007 is Rs. 90,000. **(Ans:** *Rs:233,880; 369,720; 412,600)*

23. The information regarding the expenses of a company at 70% capacity are stated as follows.

Particulars	*Rs.*
Fixed expenses:	
Salaries	2,40,000
Rent	80,000
Administrative expenses	96,000
Depreciation	64,000
Variable expenses:	
Material	3,20,000
Labour	1,60,000
Others	80,000
Semi-variable expenses:	
Indirect Labour	88,000
Repairs & Maintenance	72,000
Electricity	48,000

The estimated sales at various levels of capacity are,

Rs. 12,50,000 at 50% capacity, Rs. 14,70,000 at 70% capacity.

Rs. 16,80,000 at 80% capacity, Rs. 18,90,000 at 90% capacity.

The fixed expense will remain same till 100% capacity. Semi-variable expenses remain constant till 70% capacity. It will increase by 20% between 70% to 80% capacity and further increase by 15% when the capacity increases above 80%. Prepare a Flexible budget and calculate the profit at various level of capacities (i.e 50%,70%, 80% and 90%). **(Ans :** *Profit Rs. 1,62,000; 2,30,000; 3,10,400; 4,09,200)*

24. The following information are related to the budgeted production of 20,000 units of a product by G.Ltd. The actual production during the period is 15,000 units. Calculate the budgeted cost per unit.

Particulars	*Rs.*
Direct Material	1,65,000
Direct Labour	1,33,000
Direct Expenses	55,000
Factory Overhead (70% fixed)	2,70,000
Administration Overhead (80% fixed)	3,10,000
Selling Overhead (60% fixed)	1,40,000

(Ans : *Cost per unit Rs. 71.53; Rs.62.85)*

25. The details of overhead of a company at 70% capacity are stated as follows.

Particulars	*Rs.*
Fixed overheads	
Salary	1,12,000
Depreciation	44,000
Insurance	23,000
Rent	27,000
Variable overheads	
Indirect material	77,000
Indirect wages	35,000
Indirect expenses	21,000
Semi-variable overheads	
Electricity (60% fixed; 40% variable)	28,000
Supervisors Salary (70% fixed; 30% variable)	49,000
Repairs & Maintenance (80% fixed; 20% variable)	21,000
Total overheads	**4,37,000**

Estimated direct labour hours are 70,000 at 70% capacity.

Prepare a Manufacturing Overhead Budget and find out manufacturing overhead rate at 60%, 70% and 80% capacities. (**Ans:** *Rs.6.90; Rs.6.24;Rs.5.75)*

26. Prepare a Cash Budget by Adjusted Profit & Loss Account method from the following.

Balance Sheet as on 31st March 2006

Particulars	*Rs.*	*Particulars*	*Rs.*
Share Capital	13,00,000	Premises	9,00,000
Profit & Loss A/c	1,70,000	Plant & Machinery	7,30,000
General Reserve	90,000	Debtors	71,000
Debentures	2,40,000	Cash	50,000
Creditors	50,000	Bills Receivable	25,000
Bills Payable	20,000	Prepaid rent	12,000
Interest outstanding	11,000		
	18,81,000		18,81,000

Projected Trading and Profit & Loss Account as on 31st March 2007

Particulars	*Rs.*	*Particulars*	*Rs.*
To Opening Stock	93,000	By Sales	7,00,000
To Purchase	2,90,000	By Closing Stock	1,50,000
To Wages	80,000		
To Gross Profit c/d	5,10,000		
	9,73,000		9,73,000
To Salary	130,000	By Gross Profit b/d	5,10,000

To Electricity		39,000	By Commission received	40,000
To Telephone		22,000		
To Administrative expenses		35,000		
To Rent	40,000			
Less : Prepaid Current year	9,000			
	31,000			
Add : Prepaid last year	12,000	30,000		
Interest	60,000			
Less : Outstanding Current year	11,000			
	49,000			
Add : Outstanding Current year	5,000	44,000		
Depreciation: Premises		37,000		
Plant & Machinery		30,000		
Net Profit c/d		1,83,000		
		5,50,000		5,50,000
To Dividend paid		95,000	By Balance of Profit last year	1,70,000
To General Reserve		45,000		
To Balance of Profit to be transferred to Balance Sheet		2,13,000	By Net Profit b/d	1,83,000
		3,53,000		**3,53,000**

Closing balances estimated: Debenture Rs.3,50,000; Bills Receivable Rs. 37,000; Bills Payable Rs. 27,000; Debtors Rs. 51,000; Creditors Rs. 62,000; Machinery Rs. 650,000; Premises Rs. 10,00,000, Share Capital Rs.14,00,000.

(Ans: *Rs.2,20,000)*

27. Prepare a Cash Budget by Balance Sheet method from the following.

Balance Sheet as on 31st March 2006

Liabilities	*Rs.*	*Assets*	*Rs.*
Share Capital	10,00,000	Land & Building	6,50,000
Profit & Loss A/c	1,10,000	Plant & Machinery	5,40,000
General Revenue	59,000	Stock	60,000
Debenture	2,00,000	Debtors	44,000
Creditors	42,000	Cash	99,000
Interest outstanding	9,000	Bills Receivable	20,000
		Commission outstanding	7,000
	14,20,000		**14,20,000**

Adjustments:

(i) Balances as on 31st March 2007 - Profit & Loss A/c Rs. 90,000; General Reserve Rs. 77,000; Debenture Rs.1,50,000; Stock Rs.84,000; Debtors Rs. 57,000; Creditors Rs. 45,000; Bills Receivable Rs.14,000; Bills Payable Rs. 15,000; Outstanding Salary Rs. 17,000.

(ii) Plant to be purchased on 1st July 2006 for Rs. 67,000.

(iii) Depreciation for Fixed Assets @ 10% p.a.

(**Ans:** Cash at the end Rs. 106,025)

28. T Ltd. provides the following information as on 31st March 2006.

		Rs.
Sales		7,70,000
Direct Material cost		1,40,000
Direct Wages 60% of the cost of material		
Direct Expenses		30,000
Factory Overheads:		
Work Manager's salary	Rs. 10,000 per month	
Supervisor's salary	Rs. 7,500 per month	
Foreman salary	Rs. 5,000 per month	
Light & Power	Rs. 27,000	
Depreciation on Plant & Machinery	Rs. 33,000	

Consumable stores 1% on sales

Repairs & Maintenance 2% of Plant & Machinery

(Value of Plant & Machinery Rs. 5,00,000)

Administration overhead Rs.76,000 per year;

Selling and Distribution overhead Rs. 46,000.

Prepare a Master Budget (**Ans:** *Estimated Net Profit Rs. 46,300*)

29. The information regarding the expenses of a company at 60% capacity are given below.

Particulars	*Rs.*
Fixed expenses:	
Salaries	2,40,000
Rent	50,000
Administration expense	1,50,000
Depreciation	49,000
Variable expenses:	
Material	1,20,000
Labour	90,000
Others	60,000
Semi-variable expenses:	
Indirect Labour	96,000
Repairs & Maintenance	67,000
Electricity	39,000

The estimated sales at various levels of capacity are,

Rs. 11,10,000 at 60% capacity, Rs. 12,00,000 at 70% capacity.

Rs. 13,00,000 at 80% capacity, Rs. 13,90,000 at 90% capacity.

The fixed expense will remain same till 100% capacity. Semi-variable expenses remain constant till 60% capacity. It will increase by 10% between 65% to 75% capacity and further increase by 20% when the capacity increases above 65%. Prepare a Flexible budget and calculate the profit at various level of capacities (i.e 60%,70%, 80% and 90%).

(Ans: Profit Rs.1,49,000; Rs.1,73,800; Rs.1,88,400; Rs.2,33,400)

❑ ❑ ❑

10

CAPITAL BUDGETING

Capital Budgeting is concerned with decision making with respect to capital expenditure. Capital is a crucial and important factor in an organisation. It is raised through Own Fund and Borrowed Fund. For the Borrowed Fund fixed interest should be paid every year. For the Own Fund, fair return in the form of share of Profit or Dividend should be given. The owners expect a reasonable return for their Capital and for their efforts. Hence, the utilisation of the funds is very important factor for a concern. The utilisation may be mostly with respect to the investments in Fixed Assets and to some extent investment in the securities of other companies. These investments are called Capital Expenditure. There is a need to assess the benefits to be derived in future through such kind of investments (Capital Expenditure). This is because it involves huge amount and normally represents more than 90% of the total Capital Employed (Equity and Debt) and leaving mostly less than 10% for Working Capital. Moreover, there is also a compulsion to invest in huge amount to carry on the Operating Activities of the company. The huge amount invested is giving the benefits for longer period in future. Also once investment is done, then there is no possibility of changing it for a short period. Hence, investment decision assumes importance with respect to the selection of various alternatives available. Capital Budgeting provides different techniques for taking correct and best decision about the Capital Expenditure.

Meaning and Definitions

Capital Budgeting means the method of taking decision for Capital Expenditure. There may be alternative proposals for investment. The best proposal should be selected. The best proposal is one which gives comparatively high return on the investment. The meaning of Capital Budgeting is well known by the analysis of the following definitions.

(i) According to **Richard and Greenlaw** Capital Budgeting means acquiring inputs with long - run returns.

(ii) **Charles T. Horngreen** defined as Capital Budgeting is long term planning for making and financing proposed capital outlays.

(iii) **Philippatus** defined as, "Capital Budgeting is concerned with the allocation of the firms scarce financial resources among the available market opportunities. The consideration of investment opportunities involves the comparison of the expected future streams of earnings from a project with the immediate and subsequent streams of earnings from a project, with the immediate and subsequent streams of expenditure for it."

(iv) According to **Lynch**, "Capital Budgeting consists in planning development of available capital for the purpose of maximising the long term profitability of the concern".

It is clear from the definitions that the Capital Budgeting is an important factor which helps for taking investment decisions. It is concerned with the Capital Expenditure in profitable venture. It is based on the concept that the scarce resources should be properly utilised so that maximum return can be generated. The resources of a concern is raised through loan as well as from the contribution of the owners(Debt and Capital). Hence, there is a need for meeting the cost of the Loan and to give fair return on Capital.

Objectives of Capital Budgeting

The following are the objectives of capital budgeting.

1. To find out the profitable Capital Expenditure.
2. To find out whether replacement of certain Fixed Assets gives high return or not.
3. To decide whether certain project can be selected or not.
4. To help the management to assess the quantum and source of finance for Capital Expenditure.
5. To evaluate the merits of one proposal with other Capital Expenditure proposals.

Importance of Capital Budgeting

The importance of Capital Budgeting are stated as follows.

1. Large Investments: Capital Expenditure involves huge amount. The selection of best investment proposals is a complicated task which can be easily solved through the techniques of Capital Budgeting.

2. Long-term commitment of Funds: The Funds once invested in Fixed Assets or in any other proposals will give benefit for a long period of time say, 10 to 15 years. Hence, Capital Budgeting is a significant factor.

3. Irreversible nature of Capital Investment: Once investment is done in a project or in Fixed Assets, it is not possible to withdraw or change from that. If it is to be changed then it would incur heavy loss for the company. So the investment should be carefully done through Capital Budgeting techniques.

4. Difficulties in making Investment decisions: Investment decision are very complicated since there exists too many alternative proposals. Hence, decision should be taken very carefully. Only source for such kind of decision making is Capital Budgeting.

5. Long-term effect on Profitability: The Capital Expenditure will have a long-term effect on Profitability. Correct Capital Expenditure done with the help of Capital Budgeting will give very good benefits for the company in long term.

6. National Importance: Correct investment decision taken through Capital Budgeting techniques will give more return for the company. It helps for expansion of the business and thereby provide more employment and more tax to Government. Moreover, public are benefited through quality products at reasonable prices.

Kinds of Capital Expenditure Proposals for Capital Budgeting

The types of capital expenditure proposals available for capital budgeting are

1. Independent proposals
2. Mutually exclusive proposals
3. Capital Retaining

1. Independent Proposal: Independent proposal means that there exists no alternative proposals to choose the best one. There may be the only one available proposal or a proposal which is highly preferred by the Company. Capital Budgeting technique should be applied to decide whether the proposal is to be accepted or not. Hence, there is no comparison of cost and revenues of different proposals in this type of proposals.

2. Mutually Exclusive Proposals: If there exists more than one proposal available for which decision regarding selection is to be made, then these proposals are called Mutually Exclusive Proposal. Selection of one proposal automatically eliminates the selection of other proposals. For example, there are three machines namely A, B and C are available in the market, for a company to select one machine. If machine B is selected on the basis of the Capital Budgeting technique then the selection of machines A and C are automatically eliminated.

3. Capital Rationing: If a company is interested in the investment of more than one profitable proposals and the fund is not sufficient for investing in all the proposals, the available fund may be apportioned for investment in various proposals. This is called Capital Rationing. The proposition of investments in various proposals depends upon the relative merits of each proposals.

Process of Capital Budgeting

Capital budgeting process is a complicated and difficult one. It involves different steps to be followed with utmost care. The process of Capital Budgeting is outlined as follows.

1. Identification: The first step in the process of Capital Budgeting is identification of the project proposals. The manager in the organisation should identify different proposals within the objectives and strategies of the Company. The proposals should be submitted to the Budget Expenditure Planning Committee.

2. Screening: The Budget Expenditure Committee will screen the proposals to find out whether the proposals are as per the strategies and objectives of the Company. The proposals which are not within the strategies and objectives of the Company would be rejected immediately.

3. Evaluation: The projects which are selected are evaluated on the basis of cost and future benefits. The projects which give highest return will be selected. In the process of evaluation, the capacity of the Company to invest in the proposals should be kept in mind.

4. Priorities: The projects which gives highest return would be selected. Then the other projects which are also good should be ranked according to their benefits, so that next priority should be given to them.

5. Final approval: The projects which have highest priority should be given final approval. The Budget Expenditure Planning Committee would give final approval to respective Managers to implement the projects.

6. Implementation: After getting the final approval from the Budget Expenditure Planning Committee the proposals should be implemented by the respective Managers who applied for the projects. It is concerned with payment of cash and execution of documents. It may be related to purchase of a Machine or starting of a new Contract Work.

7. Performance Review: Performance review is an important factor after the implementation. It should be known that whether the project is giving expected return or not. If there is any failure within the guaranteed period, proper steps should be taken for replacement of the project.

Capital Budgeting Appraisal Methods

Capital Budgeting is based on the investment of the Capital in a Profitable venture. The investment may be in Projects or in Machines. There are different Projects or Machines to choose for a correct investment. The Project or Machine which gives comparatively maximum return (Profit) should be considered as good project. In addition to the maximum return the number of years required for the recoupment of the investment should also be considered. Since there are different projects, there is a need for the Company to assess the merits of each projects before selecting the best one. The methods adopted by the Company (before selecting a project for the investment of Capital) to assess the merits of all the projects are called Capital Budgeting appraisal methods. The following are the important Capital Budgeting appraisal methods.

1. Payback Period method
2. Accounting Rate of Return method
3. Discounted Cash Flow method
4. Profitability Index method or Excess Present Value method

I. Payback Period method

In this method the investment which can be recouped in a shortest period is considered to be the best project. Payback period is the period in which the investment is recouped, or able to be taken back by the Company. Payback Period is otherwise called as Pay - out method or Pay - off method. Suppose, the initial investment required for a project is Rs.1,00,000 which gives an annual return of Rs.25,000 for a period 9 years, then the company can be able to take back the investment by a period of 4 years (1,00,000/25,000). This 4 years period is called Payback Period. The proposal which has the lowest Payback period is considered as a good proposal.

$$\text{Payback Period} = \frac{\text{Investment}}{\text{Annual Return}}$$

Objectives of Payback Period method

The following are the important objectives of Payback Period method.

(i) The important objective of this method is to take decisions regarding acceptance or rejection of investment proposals. If the Payback Period of a proposal is greater than the standard expected Payback Period of the company, the proposal is rejected. The proposal which gives the lowest Payback Period than the standard expected Payback Period can be accepted.

(ii) Another objective is to trace out various financial proposals available for investment. These proposals are analysed to select the best one so that the company can benefit maximum from the investment.

Merits of Payback Period method

The important merits of Payback Period method are stated as follows.

(i) It helps for selecting the best investment proposal.

(ii) This method is easy to calculate.

(iii) It aims for recouping the initial investment in short period of time.

(iv) It helps for knowing various available proposals.

Demerits of Payback Period method

The important demerits of Payback Period method are as follows.

(i) This method will not consider the total return from the investment from various proposals.

(ii) It takes into consideration of the short-term benefits only.

(iii) The proposals which give highest rate of return in the long-term is not considered.

(iv) The proposals which has the lowest pay back period may not sometimes give normal return in the long-term.

Suitability of Payback Period method

Payback Period method is suitable for concerns which want to get back their investment in short period of time. If the long-term outlook is not good for an industry in which the concern represents, then it is better to invest in proposals which will give early return on the fund invested. Moreover, the concerns which are suffering from liquidity crisis also want to get back their investment in short period of time.

Illustration: 1

Calculate the Payback Period for the three proposals from the following.

	Proposal A	*Proposal B*	*Proposal C*
Investment (Rs.)	1,50,000	2,00,000	1,20,000
Annual Return (Rs.)	30,000	60,000	27,000
Period of Return (Years)	10	11	12

Solution :

Calculation of Payback Periods

$$\text{Payback Period} = \frac{\text{Investment}}{\text{Annual Return}}$$

$$\text{Proposal A} = \frac{1{,}50{,}000}{30{,}000} = 5 \text{ years}$$

$$\text{Proposal B} = \frac{2{,}00{,}000}{60{,}000} = 3.33 \text{ years}$$

$$\text{Proposal C} = \frac{1{,}20{,}000}{27{,}000} = 4.44 \text{ years}$$

Project B is considered to be the best project since it requires lowest Payback Period than other projects.

Calculation of Payback Period for the Uneven Annual Return

The formula of Payback Period may not be applied when the annual return is not a constant value. When the annual return is fluctuating every year, it is called uneven return. Example, return for 5 years for a project may be Rs.20,000; Rs.42,000; Rs.35,000; Rs.24,000 and Rs.39,000. In the uneven annual return condition, the Payback Period is assessed through Cumulative Annual Return. Suppose the investment requirement is Rs. 3,00,000 and the return for 5 years are Rs.52,000; s.74,000; Rs.80,000; Rs.1,10,000 and Rs.70,000, then the Cumulative Annual Return are Rs.52,000; Rs.1,26,000; Rs.2,06,000; Rs.3,16,000 and Rs.3,86,00. The amount recovered till the 3rd year is Rs.2,06,000. Hence, the balance amount to be recovered in the fourth year is (3,00,000-2,06,000) Rs.94,000. the period required in the fourth year is calculated as 94,000/1,10,000 = 0.85 year. The total Payback Period is 3.85 years.

Illustration: 2

Calculate the Payback Periods for Project X and Project Y from the following. The initial investment required for Projects X and Y are Rs.2,00,000 and Rs.1,50,000 respectively. The annual return for these projects for 6 years are stated as follows.

Year	*Project X* Rs.	*Project Y* Rs.
2002	20,000	15,000
2003	45,000	42,000
2004	44,000	73,000

2005	65,000	40,000
2006	40,000	34,000
2007	23,000	29,000

Solution :

Calculation of Cumulative Annual Return

Year	*Project A*		*Project B*	
	Annual Return Rs.	*Cumulative Return Rs.*	*Annual Return Rs.*	*Cumulative Return Rs.*
2002	20,000	20,000	15,000	15,000
2003	45,000	65,000	42,000	57,000
2004	44,000	1,09,000	73,000	1,30,000
2005	65,000	1,74,000	40,000	1,70,000
2006	40,000	2,14,000	34,000	2,04,000
2007	23,000	2,37,000	29,000	2,33,000

Payback Period for Project A

In the 4th year end asset realised = Rs.1,74,000

Balance amount required in 5th year = 2,00,000 – 1,74,000 = Rs.26,000

The period required in 5th year = $\frac{26,000}{40,000} = 0.65$ years

Total payback Period = 4.65 years

Payback Period for Project B

In the 3rd year end amount realised = Rs.1,30,000

Balance amount required in 4th year = Rs.1,50,000 - 1,30,000 = Rs.20,000

The period required in the 4th year = $\frac{20,000}{40,000} = 0.5$ years

Hence, Payback Period = 3.5 years

Since Project Y has lowest Payback Period, it is considered to be the best project.

Illustration: 3

The cost and benefits related to three different machines for a manufacturing Company are stated as follows.

	Machine I	*Machine II*	*Machine III*
Cost (Rs.)	1,50,000	1,00,000	2,00,000
Estimated savings in wages (Rs.)	40,000	30,000	55,000
Estimated savings in scrap (Rs.)	20,000	10,000	30,000
Additional cost of supervision (Rs.)	12,000	8,000	15,000
Additional cost of maintenance (Rs.)	10,000	7,000	9,000
Estimated life (years)	6	5	7

Assume that there is no Tax. The savings and additional costs are related to one year. Calculate the Payback Period and find out which machine is more suitable.

Solution :

Calculation of Payback Period

Particulars	*Machine I* Rs.	*Machine II* Rs.	*Machine III* Rs.
Estimated Savings			
Wages	40,000	30,000	55,000
Scrap	20,000	10,000	30,000
Total Savings	60,000	40,000	85,000
Estimated Additional Cost			
Supervision	12,000	8,000	15,000
Maintenance	10,000	7,000	9,000
Total Cost	22,000	15,000	24,000
Net Cash Inflow	38,000	25,000	61,000
Cost of Machine	1,50,000	1,00,000	2,00,000
	Years	Years	Years
Payback Period	$\frac{1,50,000}{38,000}$	$\frac{1,00,000}{25,000}$	$\frac{2,00,000}{61,000}$
	= 3.95 years	**= 4 years**	**= 3.28 years**

Since Machine III has the lowest Payback Period, it is considered as the best machine.

Illustration: 4

A manufacturing company wants to purchase a new machine. The cost and benefits of three available machines are stated as follows.

	Machine X Rs.	*Machine Y* Rs.	*Machine Z* Rs.
Cost of the machines	5,00,000	6,50,000	4,00,000
Scrap value	60,000	70,000	50,000
Expected Sales	6,50,000	7,80,000	4,40,000
Expected Cost of Production			
Direct material	60,000	74,000	54,000
Direct expenses	25,000	27,000	33,000
Factory overhead	52,000	64,000	27,000
Administration overhead	37,000	86,000	43,000
Selling and distribution overhead	31,000	40,000	27,000

Corporate tax is 40% and the cost of Capital is 10% per annum. The revenue and expenses are related to each year of the economical life of the machines.

Economic life of the machines are 8 years, 10 years and 7 years respectively for machines X, Y and Z respectively.

Calculate Net Cash Inflow, Payback Period and find out which machine is suitable for investment.

Solution:

Calculation of net Cash Inflow

Particulars	*Machine X* *Rs.*	*Machine Y* *Rs.*	*Machine Z* *Rs.*
Sales	**6,50,000**	**7,80,000**	**4,40,000**
Cost of Production			
Direct material	60,000	74,000	54,000
Direct wages	75,000	69,000	46,000
Direct expenses	25,000	27,000	33,000
Factory overhead	52,000	64,000	27,000
Administration overhead	37,000	86,000	43,000
Selling & Distribution overhead	31,000	40,000	27,000
Total cost	**2,80,000**	**3,60,000**	**2,30,000**
Profit before Depreciation and Interest	3,70,000	4,20,000	2,10,000
Depreciation	55,000	58,000	50,000
Interest (Cost of Capital)	50,000	65,000	40,000
Total	1,05,000	1,23,000	90,000
Profit after Depreciation and Interest	2,65,000	2,97,000	1,20,000
Less : Tax	1,06,000	1,18,800	48,000
Profit after tax	1,59,000	1,78,200	72,000
Add : Depreciation	55,000	58,000	50,000
Net Cash Inflow	**2,14,000**	**2,36,200**	**1,22,000**
Cost of the Machines	5,00,000	6,50,000	4,00,000
Payback Period	$\frac{5,00,000}{2,14,000}$	$\frac{6,50,000}{2,36,000}$	$\frac{4,00,000}{1,22,000}$
	= 2.336 yrs	**= 2.752 yrs**	**= 3.279 yrs**

Workings :

i Cost of Capital (Interest) is 10% of the value of each machine.

ii. Depreciation for Machine X $= \frac{5,00,000 \quad 60,000}{8} =$ Rs.55,000

Depreciation for Machine Y $= \frac{6,50,000 \quad 70,000}{10} =$ Rs.58,000

Depreciation for Machine Z $= \frac{4,00,000 \quad 50,000}{7} =$ Rs.50,000

As far as Net Cash Inflow is concerned Machine Y should be preferred. On the basis of Payback Period Machine X can be preferred. Since there is very marginal difference in the Payback Period between Machine X and Machine Y (ie, 0.4 year) Machine Y is most suitable for purchase.

II. Accounting Rate of Return Method

This method is based on the return and investment in a proposal. It is calculated by dividing the return by investment. This value is multiplied with 100 to know the percentage of return on investment. The project which gives comparatively the highest rate of return would be preferred for investment. The rate of return on investment is calculated either by taking into account of the expected average return (Average Profit) or expected total return (Total Profit). It may either be based on the net investment or average investment. Hence, the rate of return method can be classified as follows.

1. Return based on Average Profit
2. Return based on Total Profit

1. Return based on Average Profit

The return based on average profit can be calculated as follows.

a. Based on Net Investment

$$\text{Rate of return} = \frac{\text{Average Profit}}{\text{Net Investment}} \times 100$$

$$\text{Average Profit} = \frac{\text{Total Profit (after depreciation and tax)}}{\text{Number of years of return}}$$

$$\text{Net Investment} = \text{Actual Investment} - \text{Scrap value}$$

b. Based on Average Investment

$$\text{Rate of return} = \frac{\text{Average Profit}}{\text{Average Investment}} \times 100$$

$$\text{Average Investment} = \frac{\text{Net Investment}}{2} \times 100$$

2. Return based on Total Profit

The return based on Total Profit can be calculated as follows.

a. Based on Net Investment

$$\text{Rate of return} = \frac{\text{Total Profit}}{\text{Net Investment}} \times 100$$

b. Based on Average Investment

$$\text{Rate of return} = \frac{\text{Total Profit}}{\text{Average Investment}} \times 100$$

Advantages of Rate of Return Method

The advantages of Rate of Return method are stated as follows.

(i) It is simple to calculate and easy to understand

(ii) It satisfies the interest of the owners since, they are much interested in return on investment.

(iii) It is easy to compare the return for the different projects.

Disadvantages of Rate of Return Method

The disadvantages of Rate of Return method are stated as follows.

(i) It ignores the time value of money.

(ii) The cash flow for different periods are not taken into account in this method.

(iii) It favours the project which gives high rate of return even though the return are realised in longer period. Hence, it ignores the time factor with respect to the inflows from investment.

Illustration: 5

Calculate the Average Rate of Return on Investment based on Average Profit, from the following.

Cost of Investment of the project is	Rs.12,00,000
Estimated Scrap value	Rs. 50,000

Expected Profit after Tax and Depreciation for the five years are Rs.2,50,000; Rs.2,20,000; Rs.200,000; Rs.2,30,000 and Rs.2,40,000.

Solution:

Average Profit $= \dfrac{2,50,000 + 2,20,000 + 2,00,000 + 2,30,000 + 2,40,000}{5}$

$=$ Rs. 2,28,000

Net Investment $=$ Actual investment – Scrap value

$= 12,00,000 - 50,000 =$ Rs.11,50,000

Average Investment $= \dfrac{\text{Net Investment}}{2} = \dfrac{11,50,000}{2} =$ Rs. 5,75,000

Rate of return based on Net Investment

$$= \frac{\text{Average Profit}}{\text{Net Investment}} \times 100 = \frac{2,28,000}{11,50,000} \times 100 = 19.83\%$$

Rate of return based on Average Investment

$$= \frac{\text{Average Profit}}{\text{Investment}} \times 100 = \frac{2,28,000}{5,75,000} \times 100 = 39.65\%$$

Illustration: 6

The investment required for a project is Rs.20,00,000 and the estimated scrap value is Rs.1,00,000. The project has a life of 7 years and the return for the years after adjusting depreciation and tax are Rs.5,00,000; Rs.4,50,000, Rs.5,10,000, Rs.4,90,000; Rs.4,70,000; Rs.5,40,000 and Rs.5,20,000.

Calculate the Average Return on Investment based on the Total Profit.

Solution :

Total Profit $= 5,00,000 + 4,50,000 + 5,10,000 + 4,90,000 + 4,70,000 + 5,40,000 + 5,20,000 =$ Rs.34,80,000

Net Investment $=$ Actual Investment – Scrap value

$= 20,00,000 - 1,00,000 =$ Rs.19,00,000

Average Investment $= \dfrac{\text{Net Investment}}{2} = \dfrac{19,00,000}{2} =$ Rs. 9,50,000

Rate of Return based on Net Investment

$$= \frac{\text{Total Profit}}{\text{Net Investment}} \times 100 = \frac{34,80,000}{19,00,000} \times 100 = 183.16\%$$

Rate of return based on Average Investment

$$= \frac{\text{Total Profit}}{\text{Net Investment}} \times 100 = \frac{34,80,000}{9,50,000} \times 100 = 366.32\%$$

Illustration: 7

WD Ltd. provided the following information related to two projects namely X and Y

	Project X	*Project Y*
Investments required (Rs.)	5,00,000	4,00,000
Expected life	5 years	7 years
Salvage value (Rs.)	50,000	30,000

The expected Annual Return after Depreciation and Tax are stated as follows.

	Years (Rs)						
	1	*2*	*3*	*4*	*5*	*6*	*7*
Project X:	1,00,000	1,30,000	1,20,000	1,40,000	1,10,000	–	–
Project Y:	1,25,000	1,10,000	1,00,000	1,30,000	1,00,000	1,15,000	1,25,000

Calculate the Average Rate of Return and find out which project is to be accepted if the expected rate of return is 30%.

Solution:

Statement of Average Rate of Return

Particulars	*Project X Rs.*	*Project Y Rs.*
Investment	5,00,000	4,00,000
Salvage value	50,000	30,000
Net investment	4,50,000	3,70,000
Total Profit	6,00,000	8,05,000
Average Profit	1,20,000	1,15,000
Rate of return on Investment	$\frac{1,20,000}{4,50,000} \times 100$ = 26.67%	$\frac{1,15,000}{3,70,000} \times 100$ = 31%

Project Y should be accepted.

Illustration: 8

M Ltd has to choose any of the two machines available in the market. The cost price of machine T is Rs.10,00,000 and of Machine C is s.12,00,000. The scrap value of these two machines are Rs.70,000 and Rs.50,000 respectively. The life of the machines are 10 years. The return for these years after depreciation and before tax are stated as follows.

Years	*Machine T Rs.*	*Machine C Rs.*
1	2,70,000	3,00,000
2	4,80,000	4,10,000
3	4,00,000	4,20,000
4	5,70,000	5,00,000
5	6,20,000	6,00,000
Total	23,40,000	22,30,000

The rate of tax is 40%.

Find out which machine is more profitable according to average rate of return method.

Solution :

Statement of Average Rate of Return

	Machine T	*Machine C*
Total Profit before Tax (Rs.)	23,40,000	22,30,000
Less : Tax @ 40% (Rs.)	9,36,000	8,92,000
Total Profit after Tax	14,04,000	13,38,000
Average Profit (Rs)	2,80,800	2,67,600
Add : Average Depreciation	93,000	1,15,000
	3,73,800	3,82,600
Investment (Rs)	10,00,000	12,00,000
Less : Scrap value (Rs)	70,000	50,000
Net Investment (Rs)	9,30,000	11,50,000
Average Rate of Return	40.19%	33.27%

Note : (i) Depreciation T = 9,30,000/10; C = 11,50,000/10

(ii) Average Profit T = 14,04,000/5; C = 13,38,000/5

Since Machine T gives high average rate of return, it should be preferred.

(iii) Average Rate of Return : T = (373,800 × 100)/930,000; C = (382,600 × 100)/1150,000

III. Discounted Cash Flow Methods

Discounted Cash Flow methods are modern methods of Capital Budgeting (Capital Expenditure decision-making). These methods are based on the present value of the returns which are received in subsequent future periods. It is based on the concept that the rupee received today has more value than the rupee received in future. The Discounted Cash Flow methods are of two types. They are (1) Net Present Value method and (2) Internal Rate of Return method.

1. Net Present Value method: Net Present Value method is a modern method of Capital Budgeting. It is a method of assessing the worth of the return from a Capital Expenditure on the basis of present value of money. The present value of the return expected to be received in subsequent years are assessed on the basis of the expected rate of return. The expected rate of return varies from Companies to Companies on the basis of the investment policies and nature of the investment. Net Present Value method is based on the concept that the money received today is having more worth than the money received in future.

Procedures in the assessment of the Net Present Value method

The following are the procedures is the assessment of Net Present value of the inflow of cash from Capital Expenditure.

1. The first step is the determination of the expected rate of return. It varies from Company to Company. It depends upon the investment policies and nature of the proposals. It is the rate mostly the proprietor expects to receive from the capital employed. The rate is otherwise called as Cost of Capital.
2. Then the total cost of the project should be assessed. If the full amount is to be paid in the initial period itself then, the Net Present Value of the outflow is same as the cost of the proposal. If

the amount is to be paid in subsequent years or any additional expenditure is required for maintenance even after the full payment is done in the initial period, then the Present Value of such outflow should be separately calculated on the basis of expected rate of return (Cost of Capital). The Present Value of the outflow is calculated by multiplying the value of outflow with the Present Value factor (Discount factor). From this the Present Value of the Total Cash Outflow should be calculated.

3. Next step is the assessment of the expected life and the returns for those years for the different proposals for which assessment is to be done.
4. After the assessment of the expected cash inflow for different periods the Present Value of the return for different periods should be calculated on the basis of the expected rate of return (or Cost of Capital). The Present Value of the cash inflow is calculated by multiplying the value of inflow with the Present Value factor (Discount factor). From this Present Value of the Total Cash Inflow should be calculated.
5. Then the Net Present Value of the cash inflow should be calculated. It is the difference between the Present Value of Total Cash Inflow and Present Value of the Total Cash Outflow.
6. On the basis of the Net Present Value of the inflow the decision regarding the acceptance or rejection of a project should be taken. If the Net Present Value is positive or zero then the project can be accepted or it can be rejected if the Net Present Value is showing negative values. If two or more projects are to be compared, the project which gives comparatively high Net Present Value of Cash Inflow should be preferred and other projects should be given priority on the basis of the comparative high Present Value of the Cash Inflow.

Calculation of Present Value Factor (Discount Factor)

The Present Value Factor or Discount Factor means the Present Value of Re.1 received in future years. It can be calculated through the following formulae.

$$PV = \frac{1}{(1+r)^n}$$

[PV = Present Value

r = Rate of interest or Discount rate

n = Number of years]

The Present Value of the Total Cash Inflow received for all the years can be calculated as follows.

$$\text{Total Present Value of Cash Inflow} = \frac{A_1}{(1+r)} + \frac{A_2}{(1+r)^2} + \frac{A_3}{(1+r)^3} + \dots \frac{A_n}{(1+r)^n}$$

A = Expected Annual Cash Inflow for different periods.

The Present Value Factor (Discount Factor) is available in Tabulated Form as Index in the textbooks of Management Accounting and Financial Management.

Advantages of Net Present Value Method

The following are the advantages of Net Present Value method.

(i) It is based on time value of money.

(ii) This method helps to assess the Net Present Value of Cash Inflow for all the periods of the life of the project.

(iii) It helps to make a comparative assessment of different projects.

Disadvantages of Net Present Value method

The following are the disadvantages of Net Present Value method .

(i) It is not easy to calculate.

(ii) It will not study the total number of years required to recoup the Capital Expenditure.

(iii) It is difficult to determine the expected rate of return.

Illustration: 9

G Ltd. wants to buy a machine. The Company has two alternative machines to choose. The cost of each machine is Rs.2,00,000. The cash inflow for these two machines for the first five years are as follows.

Year	*Machine I* *Rs.*	*Machine II* *Rs.*
2003	35,000	30,000
2004	44,000	20,000
2005	45,000	29,000
2006	20,000	51,000
2007	20,000	44,000

The expected return on capital is 12% p.a. The Discount Factors for the first five year @ 12% interest is stated as follows.

Year:	*1*	*2*	*3*	*4*	*5*
Discount Factor:	0.893	0.797	0.712	0.636	0.567

Find out which machine is more profitable according to the Discounted Cash Flow method.

Solution:

Calculation of Discounted Cash Inflow

Year	*Discount Factor*	*Machine I* Cash Inflow Rs.	*Machine I* Discounted Cash Inflow Rs.	*Machine II* Cash Inflow Rs.	*Machine II* Discounted Cash Inflow Rs.
2003	0.893	35,000	31,255	30,000	26,790
2004	0.797	44,000	35,068	20,000	15,940
2005	0.712	45,000	32,040	29,000	20,648
2006	0.636	20,000	12,720	51,000	32,436
2007	0.567	20,000	11,340	44,000	24,948
Total		**1,64,000**	**1,22,423**	**1,74,000**	**1,20,762**

Machine I gives highest Discounted Cash Inflow compared to Machine II though Machine II gives highest Cash Inflow. Hence, Machine I should be preferred.

Illustration: 10

W.D. Ltd has to decide whether to invest in a project costing Rs.15,00,00. The project is expected to yield for 7 years as follows.

Year:	*1*	*2*	*3*	*4*	*5*	*6*	*7*
Cash inflow: (Rs.)	2,00,000	4,00,000	3,50,000	4,20,000	3,90,000	3,50,000	3,70,000

The Present Value factor for 7 years @ 14% interest are stated as follows.

Year:	*1*	2	3	4	5	6	7
Discount Factors	0.877	.769	.675	.592	.519	.456	.399

Find out whether it is advisable to invest in the project.

Solution:

Calculation of Net Present Value

Year	*Present Value Factors*	*Cash Inflow* (Rs.)	*Present Value* (Rs.)
1	0.877	2,00,000	1,75,400
2	0.769	4,00,000	3,07,600
3	0.675	3,50,000	2,36,250
4	0.592	4,20,000	2,48,640
5	0.519	3,90,000	2,02,410
6	0.456	3,50,000	1,59,600
7	0.399	3,70,000	1,47,630
Total		**24,80,000**	**14,77,530**

It is not advisable to invest in the project, though it gives reasonable Cash Inflow. The Net Present Value is below the total investment.

Illustration: 11

A Company has to select one of the proposals, each costing Rs.2,50,000. Find out the best project from the Cash Inflow of these projects which are stated as follows.

Years	*Project I* Rs.	*Project II* Rs.
1	90,000	1,00,000
2	1,00,000	90,000
3	70,000	50,000
4	60,000	70,000
5	80,000	90,000

Project I requires an additional investment of Rs.30,000 and II requires Rs.24,000 at the end of 1st year. The cost capital is 10%. The Discount Factors are stated as follows.

Year:	1	2	3	4	5
Discount Factors:	0.909	0.827	0.751	0.683	0.621

Solution:

Calculation of Net Present Value

Year	Discount Factor	Project I Cash Inflow Rs.	Project I Present Value Rs.	Project II Cash Inflow Rs.	Project II Present Value Rs.
1	0.909	90,000	81,810	1,00,000	90,900
2	0.827	1,00,000	82,700	90,000	74,430
3	0.751	70,000	52,570	50,000	37,550
4	0.683	60,000	40,980	70,000	47,810
5	0.621	80,000	49,680	90,000	55,890
Total		**4,00,000**	**3,07,740**	**4,00,000**	**3,06,580**

	Project I Rs.	Project II Rs.
Present Value of Total Inflow	3,07,740	3,06,580
Cash Outflow	2,50,000	2,50,000
Present Value of Additional Cash Outflow	[30,000 × .909]	[24,000 × .909]
	27,270	21,816
Total Cash Outflow	2,77,270	2,71,816
Net Cash Inflow	**30,470**	**34,764**

Project II can be preferred.

Illustration: 12

X Ltd has to choose one machine from among the two popular machines available in the market. The cost price of the machines are Rs.10,00,000 each and the scrap value are Rs.50,000 and Rs.30,000 respectively for the two machines. The Net Cash Inflow for the five year of the life of the machines are stated as follows.

Year	Machine A Rs.	Machine B Rs.
2003	3,50,000	3,00,000
2004	2,90,000	4,10,000
2005	3,10,000	3,90,000
2006	4,20,000	3,50,000
2007	4,50,000	4,00,000

The expected return on investment for the company is 12% and the risk premium rates are 5% and 4% respectively for Machine A and Machine B.

The discount factors are stated as follows.

Year:	*1*	*2*	*3*	*4*	*5*
Discount Factor 12%	0.893	0.797	0.712	0.636	0.567
Discount Factor 16%	0.862	0.743	0.641	0.552	0.476
Discount Factor 17%	0.855	0.731	0.624	0.534	0.456

Find out which machine should be selected by the company.

Solution:

Calculation of Net Present Value

	Machine I			*Machine II*		
Year	*Discount Factor 17%*	*Net Cash Inflow* Rs.	*Present value of Cash Inflow* Rs.	*Discount Factor 16%*	*Net Cash Inflow* Rs.	*Present Value of Cash Inflow* Rs.
2003	0.855	3,50,000	2,99,250	0.862	3,00,000	2,58,600
2004	0.731	2,90,000	2,11,990	0.743	4,10,000	3,04,630
2005	0.624	3,10,000	1,93,440	0.641	3,90,000	2,49,990
2006	0.534	4,20,000	2,24,280	0.552	3,50,000	1,93,200
2007	0.456	4,50,000	2,05,200	0.476	4,00,000	1,90,400
2007	0.456	50,000	22,800	0.476	30,000	14,280
Total			**11,56,960**			**12,11,100**

Net Present Value of return from Machine A = 11,56,960 – 10,00,000

= Rs. 1,56,960

Net Present Value of return from Machine B = 12,11,100 – 10,00,000

= Rs. 2,11,100

Machine B should be preferred

Illustration: 13

W. Doyle & Co. Ltd has to choose any one of the proposals namely X and Y. The cost and revenue aspects of the two project proposals are stated as follows.

Cost of Project X	Rs. 20,00,000
Cost of Project Y	Rs. 17,00,000

Cash inflow associated with profitability factor for 5 years of the life of the project are stated as follows.

Year	*Project X* Rs.	*Probability*	*Project Y* Rs.	*Probability*
2003	7,50,000	.3	6,00,000	.1
2004	8,00,000	.1	7,00,000	.1
2005	6,70,000	.2	6,00,000	.2

2006		5,00,000	1	5,00,000	2
2007		6,90,000	3	5,50,000	4

The cost of capital is assumed to be 12% per annum. The Discount Factors are stated as follows.

Year:	1	2	3	4	5
Discount Factors:	0.893	0.797	0.712	0.636	0.567

Find out the project which gives more return.

Solution:

Calculation of Net Present Value

Year	Project X					Project Y				
	P.V. Factor	*Cash Inflow Rs.*	*Profit-ability*	*Monetary Value Rs.*	*Present Value Rs.*	*P.V. Factor*	*Cash Inflow Rs.*	*Profit-ability*	*Monetary Value Rs.*	*Present Value Rs.*
2003	0.893	7,50,000	0.3	2,25,000	2,00,925	0.893	6,00,000	0.1	60,000	53,580
2004	0.797	8,00,000	0.1	80,000	63,760	0.797	7,00,000	0.1	70,000	55,790
2005	0.712	6,70,000	0.2	1,34,000	95,408	0.712	6,00,000	0.2	1,20,000	85,440
2006	0.636	5,00,000	0.1	50,000	31,800	0.636	5,00,000	0.2	1,00,000	63,600
2007	0.567	6,90,000	0.3	2,07,000	1,17,369	0.567	5,50,000	0.4	2,20,000	1,24,740
					5,09,262					3,83,150
Initial Investment Rs.					5,00,000					3,50,000
Net present value Rs.					**9,262**					**33,150**

Project Y is preferred since it gives the highest Net Present Value.

Illustration: 14

Calculate Net Present Value from the following Cash Inflow and Cash Outflow of a project.

Year	*Out flow Rs.*	*Inflow Rs.*
0	12,00,000	–
1	1,00,000	–
2		3,90,000
3	50,000	4,50,000
4		4,70,000
5		3,10,000
6		3,70,000
7		4,00,000

The scrap value for the machine is Rs.1,10,000. The Discount Factors at 10% rate of return per annum are stated as follows.

Year:	1	2	3	4	5	6	7
Discount Factors:	0.909	.827	.751	.683	.621	.564	.514

Solution:

Calculation of Net Cash Inflow

Year	*P.V. Factor*	*Outflow*		*Inflow*	
		Actual Rs.	*Present Value Rs.*	*Actual Rs.*	*Present Value Rs.*
0	1.00	12,00,000	12,00,000	–	
1	0.909	1,00,000	90,900	–	
2	0.827			3,90,000	3,22,530
3	0.751	50,000	37,550	4,50,000	3,37,950
4	0.683	–	–	4,70,000	3,21,010
5	0.621	–	–	3,10,000	1,92,510
6	0.564	–	–	3,70,000	2,08,680
7	0.514	–	–	4,00,000	2,05,600
7	0.514	–	–	1,10,000	56,540
	Total		**13,28,450**		**16,44,820**

Net Cash Inflow = 16,44,820 – 13,28,450 = Rs.3,16,370

Illustration: 15

Calculate Net Present Value from the following and advise the management whether the project can be accepted.

Cost of the project	Rs.27,00,000
Life of the project	12 years
Scrap value	Rs.3,00,000
Annual return after tax without adjusting Depreciation	Rs.3,50,000
The Present Value of 1 rupee received annually for 12 years @ 10% p.a. is	Rs.6.814
Present value of 1 rupee received at the end of 12 years @ 10% p.a.	Rs.0.319
Depreciation is to be charged on straight line basis	

Solution:

Calculation of Annual Cash Inflow

Particulars	*Rs.*
Annual return after Tax	3,50,000
Add : Depreciation $\frac{27,00,000 \quad 3,00,000}{12}$	2,00,000
Annual Cash Inflow	5,50,000

Calculation of Present Value of Cash Inflow

Year	P.V. Factor	Cash Inflow Rs.	Present Value Rs.
1-12	6.814	5,50,000	37,47,700
12	0.319	3,00,000	95,700
Total Present Value of Cash Inflow			38,43,400
Cost of the Project			27,00,000
Net Present Value			**11,43,400**

Illustration: 16

X Ltd. wants to replace a machine bought during 2000 for Rs.50,000. The cost of the new machine is Rs.90,000. If the machine is sold for (i) Rs.20,000 (ii) Rs.30,000 (iii) Rs.50,000 (iv). Rs.65,000 (v) Rs.15,000. Calculate the net cash outflows.

Assume that the present book value of the machine is Rs.20,000, Income Tax @ 40% and Capital Gain Tax @ 25%.

Solution:

Calculation of Net Cash Outflow

	Particulars	Rs.
(i)	Price of the Machine	90,000
	Less : Sale of Old Machine	20,000
	Net Cash Outflow	**70,000**
(ii)	Price of the Machine	90,000
	Less : Sale of Old Machine	30,000
	Profit Rs.10,000	60,000
	Add : Income Tax on Profit (10,000 × 40/100)	4,000
	Net Cash Outflow	**64,000**
(iii)	Price of the Machine	90,000
	Less : Sale of Old Machine	50,000
	Profit Rs.30,000	40,000
	Add : Income Tax on Profit (30,000 × 40/100)	12,000
	Net Cash Outflow	**52,000**
(iv)	Price of the Machine	90,000
	Less : Sale of Old Machine	65,000
	Profit	25,000
	Add : Income Tax on Profit (30,000 × 40/100)	12,000
	Add : Capital Gain Tax (15,000 × 25/100)	3,750
	Net Cash Outflow	**40,750**
(v)	Price of the Machine	90,000
	Less : Sale of Old Machine	15,000
	Loss	75,000
	Less : Savings in Tax Liability due to loss on sale of the Machine (5000 × 40/100)	2,000
	Net Cash Outflow	**73,000**

Illustration: 17

Calculate the net cash required for replacing a machine on 1st April 2007 from the following.

	Rs.
Cost of the New Machine	3,00,000
Cost of the Old Machine bought on 1st April 2002 with a life of 8 years	2,00,000
Sale of old Machine on 31st March 2007	1,00,000
Additional Working Capital required	20,000
Installation charges for the New Machine	30,000

Depreciation is charged on the basis of straight line method. Income Tax is 50% and Capital Gain Tax is 25%.

Solution:

Calculation of the requirement of cash for replacement of the Machine

Particulars	*Rs.*
Cost of the New Machine	3,00,000
Add : Installation charges	30,000
Additional Working Capital	20,000
Additional Tax Liability:	
Income Tax (25,000 × 50/100)	12,500
Capital Gain Tax	–
	3,62,500
Less : Amount reduced on sale of the Old Machine	1,00,000
Net Cash Outflow	**2,62,500**

Note:

Depreciation for the Old Machine per year = 2,00,000/8 = Rs.25,000

Book value of the Old Machine = 2,00,000 – (25,000 × 5) = Rs.75,000

Profit on Sale = 1,00,000 – 75,000 = Rs.25,000 (to be Taxed)

Illustration: 18

A manufacturing company has the option of investing in two plants, namely Plant I and Plant II. The expected life of these two plants is 9 years each and there is no salvage value for these plants at the end of the life of these plants.

The annual instalments to be paid and the annual costs connected with these plants are stated as follows.

	Plant I *Rs.*	*Plant II* *Rs.*
Annual instalments	10,45,000	12,50,000
Direct Labour cost per annum		
Normal hours	1,85,000	75,000

Overtime	1,65,000	–
Maintenance cost	50,000	60,000
Overhead	1,20,000	70,000

Cost of Capital is 12% per annum.

Solution:

Calculation of present savings in cost of Plant II

Particulars	*Rs.*
Savings in Labour cost: Normal (1,85,000 – 75,000)	1,10,000
Overtime	1,65,000
Savings of Maintenance cost (50,000 – 60,000)	(10,000)
Savings in Overhead (1,20,000 – 70,000)	50,000
	3,15,000
Less : Additional instalment (12,50,000 – 10,45,000)	2,05,000
Present Savings in Cost of Plant II	**1,10,000**

Alternatively,

Savings Cost = Cost for Plant I – Cost for Plant II

= (10,45,000 + 1,85,000 + 1,65,000 + 50,000 + 1,20,000)

- (12,50,00 + 75,000 + 60,000 + 70,000)

Present Savings in Cost of Plant II = Rs.1,10,000

Hence, Plant II can be preferred.

Illustration: 19

K Ltd. provided the details about the Cash Inflows from two proposals as follows.

Year	*Proposal I Rs.*	*Proposal II Rs.*
1	60,000	1,10,000
2	50,000	95,000
3	1,80,000	60,000
4	40,000	1,00,000
5	90,000	55,000

The cost of the proposal is Rs.2,50,000 each and the additional cost is Rs.30,000 for Project I at the end of first year and Rs.24,000 for project II at the end of second year.

The expected return on investment is 10% p.a. The Discount Factors for 10% interest are stated as follows.

Year:	*1*	*2*	*3*	*4*	*5*
Discount Factors:	0.909	.827	.751	.683	.621

Calculate the Discounted Cash Flow for the two proposals. Also find out which project is profitable according to the Payback period method.

Solution:

Calculation of Cash Inflow

Year	Discount Factor	*Proposal I*		*Proposal II*	
		Cash Inflow Rs.	*Discounted Cash Inflow* Rs.	*Cash Inflow* Rs.	*Discounted Cash Inflow* Rs.
1	0.909	60,000	54,540	1,10,000	99,990
2	0.827	50,000	41,350	95,000	78,565
3	0.751	1,80,000	1,35,180	60,000	45,060
4	0.683	40,000	27,320	1,00,000	68,300
5	0.621	90,000	55,890	55,000	34,155
Total		**4,20,000**	**3,14,280**	**4,20,000**	**3,26,070**

Cash Outflow for **Proposal I** = 2,50,000 + (30,000 × 0.909) = 2,50,000 + 27,270 = **Rs.2,77,270**

Cash Outflow for **Proposal II** = 2,50,000 + (24,000 × 0.827) = 2,50,000 + 19,848 = **Rs.2,69,848**

Net Cash Inflow for Proposal I = 3,14,280 - 2,77,270 = **Rs.37,010**

Net Cash Inflow for Proposal II = 3,26,070 - 2,69,848 = **Rs.56,222**

Calculation of Payback Period

Year	*Proposal I*		*Proposal II*	
	Inflows Rs.	*Cummulative Inflows (Rs.)*	*Inflows* Rs.	*Cummulative Inflows (Rs.)*
1	60,000	60,000	1,10,000	1,10,000
2	50,000	1,10,000	95,000	2,05,000
3	1,80,000	2,90,000	60,000	2,65,000
4	40,000	3,30,000	1,00,000	3,65,000
5	90,000	4,20,000	55,000	4,20,000
Total	**4,20,000**		**4,20,000**	

$$\text{Payback period for Proposal I} = 2 \text{ years} + \frac{2,80,000 \quad 1,10,000}{1,80,000}$$

$$= 2 + 0.93 = 2.944 \text{ years}$$

$$\text{Payback period for Proposal II} = 3 \text{ years} + \frac{2,74,000 \quad 2,65,000}{1,00,000}$$

$$= 3 + 0.09 = 3.09 \text{ years}$$

As per the Net Present Value method, Proposal II can be preferred and as per Payback Period method, Proposal I can be preferred.

2. Internal Rate of Return method

It is one of the important modern methods of Capital Budgeting. This method is also called as Trial and Error method, or Yield method. This is one of the methods related to Discounted Cash Flow. The speciality of this method is that the expected rate of return is determined (Discount factor or Present Value factor) on the basis of Cash Inflows for different periods. In Net Present Value method, the Present Value is calculated by applying the Present Value factor based on the expected rate of return. In Internal Rate of Return method, the expected Rate of Return (which is called Internal Rate of Return) is determined on the basis of Trial and Error through various Present Value factors. Internal Rate of Return is a rate at which the Net Present Value of total Cash Outflow is equal to the Present Value of the total Cash Inflow. This concept is represented as

$$\frac{\text{Cash Inflows}}{\text{Cash Outflows}} = 1$$

i.e., Cash Outflow = Cash Inflow

i.e. Net Present Value of total Cash Outflow = Net Present Value of total Cash Inflow.

It may be represented as

$$C = \frac{A}{1+r}$$

i.e., $$C = \frac{A_1}{(1+r)} + \frac{A_2}{(1+r)^2} + \frac{A_3}{(1+r)^3} + ... + \frac{A_n}{(1+r)^n}$$

[where C = Cash Outflow for different periods; A = Annual Cash Inflow; r = Rate of interest (Cost of capital); n = Number of years]

In Internal Rate of Return method C, A and n are known factors. Hence, r (Discount rate or Internal Rate of Return) should be calculated.

Procedures in the assessment of Internal Rate of Return

The procedures of assessment of Internal Rate of Return are as follows.

1. Calculation of Approximate Present Value factor and Discount Rate

The approximate value of Present Value factor and Discount Rate are calculated as follows.

(i) If the Annual Return are equal then the Present Value factor is Calculated as,

$$\frac{\text{Cash Outflow}}{\text{Annual Cash Inflow}}$$

This value shall be traced out in Present Value of Annuity Table corresponding to the total life of the project. The approximated two or three rates of interest should be identified for calculation For example, if the total cost of the project is Rs.5,00,000, and Annual return for 7 years is @ Rs.1,20,000.

$$\text{The Present Value factor} = \frac{5,00,000}{1,20,000} = 4.1667$$

According to the Present Value of Annuity Table for 7 years, the factor 4.1667 is approximately in Discount rates 14%, 16% and 17%.

(ii) If the Annual Return are not equal, then the Average Annual Return should be calculated so that the Cash Outflow can be divided with it. It may be calculated as follows.

$$\text{Approximate Present Value factor} = \frac{\text{Cash Outflow}}{\text{Average Annual Cash Inflow}}$$

$$\text{Average Annual Cash Inflow} = \frac{\text{Total Cash Inflow for different periods}}{\text{Life of the Project in years}}$$

For example, if the Cash Outflow for a Project is Rs.10,00,000 and Annual Cash Inflows for 5 years are Rs.3,40,000, Rs.4,00,000, Rs.4,40,000; Rs.4,10,000 and Rs.4,30,000, the approximate Present Value factor and Discount Rate are assessed as follows.

$$\text{Average Annual Cash Inflow} = \frac{3{,}40{,}000 + 4{,}00{,}000 + 4{,}40{,}000 + 4{,}10{,}000 + 4{,}30{,}000}{5}$$

$$= \text{Rs. } 4{,}04{,}000$$

$$\text{Approximate Present Value factor} = \frac{10{,}00{,}000}{4{,}04{,}000} = 2.4752$$

The reference to Present Value of Annuity Table shows that the factor 2.4752 for 5 years is approximately in the Discount Rates 28%, 29% and 30%.

2. Calculation of exact Internal Rate of Return

After the determination for the approximated two or three Discount Rates, the Present Value of the Total Cash Inflow for various periods should be calculated by applying the respective Discount Rates. From this two of the Present Value of the Total Cash Inflows which are near to the Total Cash Outflow should be identified for calculating the correct Internal Rate of Return. (If only two Discount Rates are applied, then that two values should be taken for further calculation.) The Internal Rate of Return is calculated as follows.

$$= \text{Estimated Discount Rate} + \frac{\text{Present value of total Cash Inflow} \quad \text{Cash Outflow}}{\text{Difference in the Present value of total Cash Inflow}} \times \text{Difference in Rates}$$

For example, if the Present Value of total Cash Inflow for discount rates 10% and 12% are Rs.5,75,000 and Rs.5,35,000 respectively; and the Cash Outflow is Rs.5,00,000 then, the Internal Rate of Return is calculated as follows.

$$\text{IRR} = 10\% + \frac{5{,}75{,}000 \quad 5{,}00{,}000}{5{,}75{,}000 \quad 5{,}35{,}00} \times (12 - 10)$$

$$\text{IRR} = 10\% + \frac{75{,}000}{40{,}000} \times 2 = 10\% + 1.75\% = 11.75\%$$

Advantages of Internal Rate of Return method

The advantages of Internal Rate of Return method are stated as follows.

(i) This method takes into account of the time value of money.

(ii) The problem of determination of the Discount rate (Cost of Capital) does not arise in this method.

(iii) This method takes into account of the returns for the entire life of a project.

(iv) It is easy to compare and decide which project is more economical.

Disadvantages of Internal Rate of Return method

The disadvantages of Internal Rate of Return method are stated as follows.

(i) It is difficult to calculate the Internal Rate of Return.

(ii) It won't take into account of the years required for recouping the capital expenditure. Sometimes the Internal Rate of Return method favours a project which comparatively requires a longer period for recouping the capital expenditure.

(iii) The assessment of expected Annual Return is a complicated task.

Illustration: 20

Calculate the approximate Internal Rate of Return if the cost of investment is Rs.30,00,000, and estimated Annual Cash flows for the life of 10 years is Rs.4,00,000.

Solution:

$$\text{Present Value Factor} = \frac{\text{Initial Outlay}}{\text{Annual Cash Inflow}}$$

$$= \frac{30,00,000}{4,00,000} = 7.5$$

According to the Annuity Table, for the Present Value factor of 7.5, for 10 years is 6% approximately. [The value factor for 10 years @ 5% is 7.7217 and for 6% is 7.3601].

Illustration: 21

Calculate Internal Rate of Return for Joyce & Co. Ltd. from the following.

Cost of the investment	Rs. 27,00,000
Life of the project	5 years

Estimated net Annual Cash flows are as follows:

	Rs.		*Rs.*
2003	6,50,000	2006	7,50,000
2004	6,00,000	2007	5,50,000
2005	7,00,000		

Solution:

Calculation of Internal Rate of Return

Year	*Annual Cash Inflow Rs.*	*PVF at 6%*	*Present Value Rs.*	*PVF at 7%*	*Present Value Rs.*	*PVF at 8%*	*Present Value Rs.*
2003	6,50,000	0.943	6,12,950	0.935	6,07,750	0.926	6,01,900
2004	6,00,000	0.890	5,34,000	0.873	5,23,800	0.857	5,14,200
2005	7,00,000	0.840	5,88,000	0.816	5,71,200	0.794	5,55,800
2006	7,50,000	0.792	5,94,000	0.763	5,72,250	0.735	5,51,250
2007	5,50,000	0.747	4,10,850	0.713	3,92,150	0.681	3,74,550
Total	32,50,000		27,39,800		26,67,150		25,97,700
Less Cash Outlay			27,00,000		27,00,000		27,00,000
NPV			39,800		−32850		−1,02,300

According to the Annuity Table IRR is between 6% and 7%.

$$\text{IRR} = \text{Estimated Discount Rate} + \frac{\text{Present value of total Cash Inflow} \quad \text{Cash Outflow}}{\text{Difference in the Present value of total Cash Inflow}} \times \text{Difference in Rates}$$

$$\text{IRR} = 6\% + \frac{39,800}{39,800 + 32,850} \times 1$$

$$= 6\% + 0.55\% = 6.55\%$$

[**Note :** Rate of Interest to be assumed is known through the following calculations.

$$\text{Total Cash Inflow} = \text{Rs.}32{,}50{,}000$$

$$\text{Average Annual Cash Inflow} = \frac{32{,}50{,}000}{5} = 6{,}50{,}000$$

$$\text{Present Value factor} = \frac{\text{Initial Investment}}{\text{Annual Cash Inflow}} = \frac{27{,}00{,}000}{6{,}50{,}000} = 4.154$$

Reference of Annuity Table shows that 4.154 PVF is around 6%, 7% and 8%]

Illustration: 22

W. Doyle & Co. provided the following information about the Cash Outflow and Inflow related to a project.

Cost of the project	Rs.7,00,000
Life of the project	5 years

The Annual Cash Inflow are stated as follows.

Years	*Rs.*
1	2,30,000
2	2,10,000
3	2,50,000
4	2,20,000
5	2,00,000

PV factor for 16%, 17% and 18% return are as follows.

Year	*PV Factors*		
	16%	17%	18%
1	0.862	0.855	0.848
2	0.743	0.731	0.718
3	0.641	0.624	0.609
4	0.552	0.534	0.516
5	0.476	0.456	0.437

Calculate Internal Rate of Return.

Solution :

Calculation of Internal Rate of Return

Year	*Annual Cash Inflow Rs.*	*PVF at 16%*	*Present Value Rs.*	*PVF at 17%*	*Present Value Rs.*	*PVF at 18%*	*Present Value Rs.*
1	2,30,000	0.862	1,98,260	0.855	1,96,650	0.848	1,95,040
2	2,10,000	0.743	1,56,030	0.731	1,53,510	0.719	1,50,780
3	2,50,000	0.641	1,60,250	0.624	1,56,000	0.609	1,52,250

4	2,20,000	0.552	1,21,440	0.534	1,17,480	0.516	1,13,520
5	2,00,000	0.476	95,200	0.456	91,200	0.437	87,400
Total	11,10,000		7,31,180		7,14,840		6,98,990
Cash Outflow			7,00,000		7,00,000		7,00,000
NPV			31,180		14,840		–1010

Hence the IRR is in between 17% and 18%

$$\text{IRR} = \text{Estimated Discount Rate} + \frac{\text{Present value of total Cash Inflow} \quad \text{Cash Outflow}}{\text{Difference in the Present value of total Cash Inflow}} \times \text{Difference in Rates}$$

$$\text{IRR} = 17\% + \frac{14{,}840}{7{,}14{,}840 \quad 6{,}98{,}990} \times 1$$

$$= 17\% + \frac{14{,}840}{15{,}850} = 17\% + 0.94\% = 17.94\%$$

Illustration: 23

M.W.D. Ltd provides the particulars related to Cash Outflow and Inflow for two projects as follows.

	Project M *Rs.*	*Project N* *Rs.*
Estimated Cash outflow	11,00,000	11,00,000
Estimated Cash inflow		
2001	4,00,000	3,50,000
2002	3,00,000	3,40,000
2003	4,20,000	3,30,000
2004	3,70,000	2,30,000
2005	4,10,000	2,90,000
2006	–	3,10,000
2007	–	3,90,000

Present Value factor for different rates of interest are stated as follows.

Year ending	*17%*	*19%*	*21%*	*23%*	*25%*	*27%*
1	0.855	0.840	0.826	0.813	0.800	0.781
2	0.731	0.706	0.683	0.661	0.640	0.610
3	0.624	0.593	0.564	0.537	0.512	0.477
4	0.534	0.499	0.467	0.437	0.410	0.392
5	0.456	0.419	0.385	0.345	0.328	0.291
6	0.390	0.352	0.319	0.289	0.262	0.238
7	0.333	0.296	0.263	0.234	0.210	0.188

Calculate IRR and suggest which project gives maximum return.

Solution :

Calculation of Internal Rate of Return for Proj[illegible]

Year	Cash Inflow Rs.	PVF at 19%	Present Value Rs.	PVF at 21%	Present Value Rs.	PVF at 23%	Present Value Rs.	PVF at 25%	Present Value Rs.
2001	4,00,000	0.840	3,36,000	0.826	3,30,400	0.813	3,25,200	0.800	3,20,000
2002	3,00,000	0.706	2,11,800	0.683	2,04,900	0.661	1,98,300	0.640	1,92,000
2003	4,20,000	0.593	2,49,060	0.564	2,36,880	0.537	2,25,540	0.512	2,15,040
2004	3,70,000	0.499	1,84,630	0.467	1,72,790	0.437	1,61,690	0.410	1,51,700
2005	4,10,000	0.419	1,71,790	0.385	1,57,850	0.345	1,41,450	0.328	1,34,480
Total	19,00,000		11,53,280		11,02,820		10,52,180		10,13,220
Cash Outflow			11,00,000		11,00,000		11,00,000		11,00,000
Net Cash Inflow			53,280		2,820		–47,820		–86,780

The IRR is in between 21% and 23%.

$$\text{IRR} = \text{Estimated Discount Rate} + \frac{\text{Present value of total Cash Inflow} \quad \text{Cash Outflow}}{\text{Difference in the Present value of total Cash Inflow}} \times \text{Difference in Rates}$$

$$\text{IRR} = 21\% + \frac{2,820}{11,02,820 \quad 10,52,180} \times 2$$

$$= 21\% + \frac{5,640}{50,640} = 21\% + 0.11\% = 21.11\%$$

Calculation of IRR for Project N

Year	Cash Inflow Rs.	PVF 21%	Present Value Rs.	PVF 23%	Present Value Rs.	PVF 25%	Present Value Rs.	PVF 27%	Present Value Rs.
2001	3,50,000	0.826	2,89,100	0.813	2,84,550	0.800	2,80,000	0.781	2,73,350
2002	3,40,000	0.683	2,32,220	0.661	2,24,740	0.640	2,17,600	0.610	2,07,400
2003	3,30,000	0.564	1,86,120	0.537	1,77,210	0.512	1,68,960	0.477	1,57,410
2004	2,30,000	0.467	1,07,410	0.437	1,00,510	0.410	94,300	0.392	90,160
2005	2,90,000	0.385	1,11,650	0.345	1,00,050	0.328	95,120	0.291	84,390
2006	3,10,000	0.319	98,890	0.289	89,590	0.262	81,220	0.238	73,780
2007	3,90,000	0.263	1,02,570	0.234	91,260	0.210	81,900	0.188	73,320
Total	22,40,000		11,27,960		10,67,910		10,19,100		9,59,810
Cash Outflow			11,00,000		11,00,000		11.00,000		11,00,000

The IRR is in between 21% and 23%.

$$\text{IRR} = \text{Estimated Discount Rate} + \frac{\text{Present value of total Cash Inflow} \quad \text{Cash Outflow}}{\text{Difference in the Present value of total Cash Inflow}} \times \text{Difference in Rates}$$

$$= 21\% + \frac{11,27,960 \quad 11,00,000}{11,27,960 \quad 10,67,910} \times 2$$

$$= 21\% + \frac{55,920}{60,050} = 21\% + 0.93\% = 21.93\%$$

Since project N gives highest IRR, it should be preferred.

[**Note:** (i) Approximate IRR for project M.

$$\frac{\text{Investment}}{\text{Average Return}} = \frac{11,00,000}{19,00,000/5} = 2.895$$ which lies approximately between 19% to 25% in the Annuity Table.

(ii) Approximate IRR for project N

$$\frac{\text{Investment}}{\text{Average Return}} = \frac{11,00,000}{22,40,000/7} = 3.438$$ which lies approximately between 19% to 25% in the Annuity Table]

Illustration : 24

MW Ltd has to decide whether a project costing Rs.7,00,000 has to be selected or not. The project is expected to give Annual return for 10 years on the following basis.

Year	*Rs.*	*Year*	*Rs.*
1	1,00,000	6	1,80,000
2	1,90,000	7	1,30,000
3	1,20,000	8	1,40,000
4	1,40,000	9	1,25,000
5	1,10,000	10	1,75,000

The Cost of Capital estimated is 12%. Calculate (a) Payback period (b) Net Present value on the basis of 12% rate of interest and (c) Internal Rate of Return, so that the company can decide whether the project can be selected or not.

The Discounting factors for 12% and 17% are stated as follows.

Year	*12%*	*17%*
1	0.893	0.855
2	0.797	0.731
3	0.712	0.624
4	0.636	0.534
5	0.57	0.456
6	0.507	0.39
7	0.453	0.333
8	0.404	0.285
9	0.361	0.243
10	0.322	0.208

Solution:

a. Calculation of Payback Period

Year	*Cash Inflow Rs.*	*Cumulative Cash Inflow Rs.*
1	1,00,000	1,00,000
2	1,90,000	2,90,000
3	1,20,000	4,10,000
4	1,40,000	5,50,000
5	1,10,000	6,60,000
6	1,80,000	8,40,000
7	1,30,000	9,70,000
8	1,40,000	11,10,000
9	1,25,000	12,35,000
10	1,75,000	14,10,000

$$\text{Payback period} = 5 + \frac{40,000}{1,80,000} = 5.22 \text{ years}$$

b. Calculation of Net Present Value

Year	*Net Cash Inflow Rs.*	*P.V. Factor 12%*	*Present Value Rs.*
1	1,00,000	0.893	89,300
2	1,90,000	0.797	1,51,430
3	1,20,000	0.712	85,440
4	1,40,000	0.636	89,040
5	1,10,000	0.567	62,370
6	1,80,000	0.507	91,260
7	1,30,000	0.453	58,890
8	1,40,000	0.404	56,560
9	1,25,000	0.361	45,125
10	1,75,000	0.322	56,350
Total Inflow			7,85,765
Cash of Investment			7,00,000
Net Present Value			85,765

c. Calculation of Internal Rate of Return

Year	*Net Cash Inflow Rs.*	*P.V. Factor 17%*	*Present Value Rs.*
1	1,00,000	0.855	85,500
2	1,90,000	0.731	1,38,890
3	1,20,000	0.624	74,880
4	1,40,000	0.534	74,760

5	1,10,000	0.456	50,160
6	1,80,000	0.39	70,200
7	1,30,000	0.333	43,290
8	1,40,000	0.285	39,900
9	1,25,000	0.243	30,375
10	1,75,000	0.208	36,400
Total Inflow			6,44,355
Cost of Investment			7,00,000
Net Present Value			–55,643

The Net Present Value at 17% Discount Factor gives negative value of Rs.55,645 and positive value of Rs.85,765 at 12% Discount Factor. Hence, the IRR would be in between 12% and 17%. It can be calculated as

$$\text{IRR} = \text{Estimated Discount Rate} + \frac{\text{Present value of total Cash Inflow} \quad \text{Cash Outflow}}{\text{Difference in the Present value of total Cash Inflow}} \times \text{Difference in Rates}$$

$$= 12\% + \frac{85{,}765}{85{,}765 + 55{,}645} \times 5$$

$$= 12\% + 3.03\% = 15.03\%$$

IV. Profitability Index Method

This method is based on the Discounted Cash Flow method. The Present Value of Cash Inflow and Outflow are applied in this method. Profitability index is the ratio between the Present Value of Cash inflow and the Present Value of Cash outflow. It may be represented as,

$$\text{Profitability Index} = \frac{\text{Present Value of Cash Inflows}}{\text{Present Value of Cash Outflows}}$$

$$\text{Net Profitability Index} = \frac{\text{Net Present Value of Cash Inflows}}{\text{Initial Cash Outflow}}$$

[Net Present Value of Cash inflow is the difference between Present Value of Cash inflow and Present Value of Cash outflow].

If the Profitability Index is greater than one, the project is considered for acceptance and otherwise it would be rejected. In the case of Net Profitability Index, if the value is positive then the project may be accepted, and if it is negative, the project should be rejected. Net Profitability Index is also calculated by deducting the Profitability Index with one. On the basis of Profitability Index, the decision regarding acceptance or rejection of a project can be taken. Two or more projects may also be ranked in this method.

Advantages of Profitability Index method

The advantages of Profitability Index method are as follows.

(i) It is easy to take a decision regarding acceptance or rejection of a project through this method.

(ii) It is easy to compare different project proposals.

(iii) It takes into account of the present value of money.

Disadvantages of Profitability Index method

The disadvantage of Profitability Index method are as follows.

(i) It is difficult to calculate Profitability Index.

(ii) It won't take into account of the period of recoup of the Capital Expenditure.

(iii) It is difficult to assess the discount rate for calculating the Present Value of Cash flows.

Illustration: 25

Calculate the Profitability Index on the basis of 12% Discount factor, from the following.

Cost of the Project	Rs. 9,00,000
Estimated Cash Inflow	Rs.
2003	3,00,000
2004	2,50,000
2005	2,40,000
2006	2,70,000
2007	2,90,000

Year:	1	2	3	4	5
PV Factor:	0.893	0.797	0.712	0.636	0.567

Solution :

Calculation of Profitability Index

Year	*Net Cash Inflow Rs.*	*P.V. Factor*	*Present Value Rs.*
2003	3,00,000	0.893	2,67,900
2004	2,50,000	0.797	1,99,250
2005	2,40,000	0.712	1,70,880
2006	2,70,000	0.636	1,71,720
2007	2,90,000	0.567	1,64,430
Total Present Value of Cash Inflow			9,74,180
Initial Investment			9,00,000
Net Present Value			**74,180**

$$\text{Profitability Index (gross)} = \frac{\text{Present Value of Cash Inflows}}{\text{Present Value of Cash Outflows}}$$

$$= \frac{9,74,180}{9,00,000} = 1.082$$

$$\text{Net Profitability Index} = \frac{\text{Net Present Value of Cash Inflows}}{\text{Present Value of Cash Outflows}}$$

$$= \frac{74,180}{9,00,000} = 0.082$$

The project can be accepted since the Gross Profitability Index is greater than one. As far as Net Profitability Index also, it can be accepted since it gives a positive value.

Illustration: 26

G.T. Ltd has two options in the purchase of a machine. The cost of each machine is Rs.21,00,000. The expected returns from the machines after tax are stated as follows.

Year	Cash Inflow	
	Machine I Rs.	*Machine II* Rs.
1	7,00,000	4,50,000
2	7,50,000	5,50,000
3	7,80,000	6,00,000
4	5,30,000	8,90,000
5	4,40,000	8,10,000

The expected Annual return is @ 12% p.a.The Discount Factors at 12% p.a. are as follows.

Year:	*1*	2	3	4	5
Discount Factors:	0.893	0.797	0.712	0.636	0.567

Find out which machine gives more return according to Profitability Index method.

Solution:

Calculation of Profitability Index

Year	*Discount Factor 12%*	*Machine I*		*Machine II*	
		Cash Inflow Rs.	*Present Value* Rs.	*Cash Inflow* Rs.	*Present Value* Rs.
1	0.893	7,00,000	6,25,100	4,50,000	4,01,850
2	0.797	7,50,000	5,97,750	5,50,000	4,38,350
3	0.712	7,80,000	5,55,360	6,00,000	4,27,200
4	0.636	5,30,000	3,37,080	8,90,000	5,66,040
5	0.567	4,40,000	2,49,480	8,10,000	4,59,270
Total		32,00,000	23,64,770	33,00,000	22,92,710
Initial Investment			21,00,000		21,00,000
Net present value			**2,64,770**		**1,92,710**

$$\text{Profitability Index} = \frac{\text{Present Value of Cash Inflow}}{\text{Present Value of Cash Outflow}}$$

$$\text{Machine I} = \frac{23,64,770}{21,00,000}\ 1.126$$

$$\text{Machine II} = \frac{22,92,710}{21,00,000} = 1.092$$

Machine I should be preferred since it gives highest Profitability Index than Machine II, though the total Cash Inflow is high for Machine II.

Illustration: 27

Calculate Profitability Index (Excess Present Value Index) from the following information related to the Cash inflow and outflow.

Years	*Cash Outflow* *Rs.*	*Cash Inflow* *Rs.*
0	11,00,000	–
1	50,000	3,10,000
2	–	3,50,000
3	50,000	3,00,000
4	–	3,70,000
5	–	3,00,000

The Cost of Capital is 15% and the Discount Factors at 15% rate are stated as follows.

Year:	*1*	2	*3*	4	*5*
Discount Factor:	0.870	0.756	0.658	0.572	0.497

Cash outflow for the 1st year end and 3rd year end are due to maintenance of the Plant.

Solution:

Calculation of Profitability Index

Year	*Discount Factor at 15%*	*Cash Outflow Rs.*	*Present Value Rs.*	*Cash Inflow Rs.*	*Present Value Rs.*
0	1	11,00,000	11,00,000	–	–
1	0.870	50,000	43,500	3,10,000	2,69,700
2	0.756	–	–	3,50,000	2,64,600
3	0.658	50,000	32,900	3,00,000	1,97,400
4	0.572	–	–	3,70,000	2,11,640
5	0.497	–	–	3,00,000	1,49,100
Total			11,76,400		10,92,440
Less Present Value of Cash Outflow					11,76,400
Net Present Value of Cash Inflow					**–83,960**

$$\text{Profitability Index} = \frac{\text{Present Value of Cash Inflow}}{\text{Present Value of Cash Outflow}}$$

$$\text{Profitability Index} = \frac{10,92,440}{11,76,400} = 0.929$$

It is not advisable to invest in the project.

Miscellaneous Illustrations

Illustration: 28

Calculate (i) Payback period (ii) Net Present Value and (iii) Profitability Index for two projects namely, X and Y from the following.

Years	*Project X* *Rs.*	*Project Y* *Rs.*
0	–3,00,000	–4,00,000
1	90,000	70,000
2	80,000	50,000
3	85,000	1,50,000
4	1,00,000	2,00,000
5	95,000	1,30,000

The Cost of Capital is 12%. The Discount Factors for 12% rate of interest are as follows.

Year:	*1*	*2*	*3*	*4*	*5*
Discount Factor:	0.893	0.797	0.712	0.636	0.567

Solution:

(i) Calculation of Profitability Index

Year	*Project X*		*Project Y*	
	Cash Inflow *Rs.*	*Cumulative C.I* *Rs.*	*Cash Inflow* *Rs.*	*Cumulative C.I* *Rs.*
1	90,000	90,000	70,000	70,000
2	80,000	1,70,000	50,000	1,20,000
3	85,000	2,55,000	1,50,000	2,70,000
4	1,00,000	3,55,000	2,00,000	4,70,000
5	95,000	4,50,000	1,30,000	6,00,000
Total	4,50,000			6,00,000

$$\text{Payback period for X} = 3 + \frac{45,000}{1,00,000} = 3 + 0.45 = 3.45 \text{ years}$$

$$\text{Payback period for Y} = 3 + \frac{1,30,000}{2,00,000} = 3 + 0.65 = 3.65 \text{ years}$$

[For Project X Rs.2,55,000 is recovered in 3 years and the balance of Rs.45,000 is recovered in the fourth year out of the profit of Rs.1,00,000. Like that, Payback period of Project Y should be calculated].

(ii) Calculation of Net Present Value

Year	*Discount Factor at 12%*	*Project X*		*Project Y*	
		Cash Outflow Rs.	*Present Value Rs.*	*Cash Inflow Rs.*	*Present Value Rs.*
1	0.893	90,000	80,370	70,000	62,510
2	0.797	80,000	63,760	50,000	39,850
3	0.712	85,000	60,520	1,50,000	1,06,800
4	0.636	1,00,000	63,600	2,00,000	1,27,200
5	0.567	95,000	53,865	1,30,000	73,710
Total	4,50,000	3,22,115	6,00,000	4,10,070	
Cash Outflow			3,00,000		4,00,000
Net present value			**22,115**		**10,070**

(iii) Calculation of Profitability Index

$$\text{Profitability Index} = \frac{\text{Present Value of Cash Inflow}}{\text{Present Value of Cash Outflow}}$$

$$\text{Profitability Index for Project X} = \frac{3,22,115}{3,00,000} = 1.074$$

$$\text{Profitability Index for Project Y} = \frac{4,10,070}{4,00,000} = 1.025$$

Conclusion: Project X can be preferred since the Payback period is low, Net Present Value is high and Profitability Index is high compared to the Project Y.

Illustration: 29

The initial investment required for a project is Rs.5,00,000. The project is expected to give annual return after depreciation and before tax @ 40% as follows.

Year:	*1*	*2*	*3*	*4*	*5*
Return (Rs.):	2,40,000	2,10,000	2,00,000	1,80,000	2,50,000

Analyse the return from the project on the basis of (i) Payback period method (ii) Rate of return on Original Investment (iii) Rate of return on Average Investment (iv) Discounted Cash Flow method (v) Profitability Index method (Excess Present Value Index).

The depreciation is charged @ 10% on cost of investment. Cost of Capital is 10%.

The Discount factors for 10% rate of interest are stated as follows.

Year:	*1*	*2*	*3*	*4*	*5*
Discount Factors:	0.909	0.827	0.751	0.683	0.621

Solution :

Calculation of Payback Period

Year	*Profit Before Tax Rs.*	*Tax @ 40% Rs.*	*Profit After Tax Rs.*	*Depreciation Rs.*	*Cash Inflow Rs.*	*Cumulative Cash Inflow Rs.*
1	2,40,000	96,000	1,44,000	50,000	1,94,000	1,94,000
2	2,10,000	84,000	1,26,000	50,000	1,76,000	3,70,000
3	2,00,000	80,000	1,20,000	50,000	1,70,000	5,40,000
4	1,80,000	72,000	1,08,000	50,000	1,58,000	6,98,000
5	2,50,000	1,00,000	1,50,000	50,000	2,00,000	8,98,000
Total	10,80,000	4,32,000	6,48,000	2,50,000	8,98,000	–

(i) Payback Period

$$= 2 + \frac{1,30,000}{1,70,000} = 2 + 0.765 = 2.765 \text{ years}$$

(ii) Rate of Return on Original Investment

$$= \frac{\text{Average Annual Return}}{\text{Original Investment}} \times 100 = \frac{1,29,600}{5,00,000} \times 100 = 25.92\%$$

[Average return = 6,48,000/5 = Rs.1,29,600]

(iii) Rate of Return on Average Investment

$$= \frac{\text{Average Annual Return}}{\text{Original Investment}} \times 100 = \frac{1,29,600}{5,00,000} \times 100 = 51.84\%$$

(iv) Calculation of Net Present Value

Year	*PV Factor @ 10%*	*Net Cash Inflow Rs.*	*Present Value Rs.*
1	0.909	1,94,000	1,76,346
2	0.827	1,76,000	1,45,552
3	0.751	1,70,000	1,27,670
4	0.683	1,58,000	1,07,914
5	0.621	2,00,000	1,24,200
Total			6,81,682
Initial Investment			5,00,000
Net Present Value			1,81,682

(v) Calculation of Profitability Index (Excess Present Value Index)

$$\text{Profitability Index} = \frac{\text{Total Present Value of Cash Inflows}}{\text{Total Present Value of Cash Outflow}}$$

$$= \frac{6,81,682}{5,00,000} = 1.363$$

EXERCISE

THEORY

I. Choose the correct answer for the following

1. Decision making with respect to Capital Expenditure is known as
(i) Capital Budgeting (ii) Control (iii) Organising (iv) Controlling
2. Selection of one proposal will automatically eliminates the selection of other proposals in case of
(i) Independent proposal (ii) Capital rationing (iii) Mutually exclusive proposals (iv) Project proposal
3. Allocation of Capital for various proposals on the basis of fund available is known as
(i) Capital expenditure (ii) Capital rationing (iii) Project proposal (iv) Independent proposal
4. The method of Capital Budgeting based on the shortest period of recoup of Capital Expenditure is called
(i) Capital rationing (ii) Accounting rate of return (iii) Discounted cash flow (iv) Payback period
5. The ratio between the Average Profit and Net Investment is called
(i) Rate of return (ii) Capital (iii) Profit (iv) Assets
6. The method of Capital Budgeting based on the principle "a rupee received today has more value than a rupee received in future, is called
(i) Rate of return (ii) Discounted Cash Flow (iii) Payback period (iv) Expenditure method
7. The Present Value of the returns expected to be received in subsequent years are assessed through
(i) Payback period method (ii) Rate of return method (iii) Capital rationing method (iv) Net Present Value method
8. Expected rate of return (Discount rate) is determined in
(i) Net Present Value method (ii) Internal Rate of Return method (iii) Rate of return method (iv) Profitability Index method
9. The ratio between the Present Value of Cash Inflow and Present Value of Cash Outflow is called
(i) Profitability Index (ii) Price Index (iii) Wage Index (iv) Expenses Index
10. Internal Rate of Return method is based on the concept that the Present Value of cash outflow and Present Value of cash inflow are
(i) Addition (ii) Multiplication (iii) Equal (iv) Not equal

[**Ans :** 1 (i) 2. (iii) 3. (ii) 4. (iv) 5. (i) 6. (ii) 7. (iv) 8. (ii) 9 (i) 10. (iii)].

II. Answer the following questions

1. Define Capital Budgeting. State the objectives of Capital Budgeting.
2. What is Capital Budgeting? Explain the importance of Capital Budgeting.
3. Define Capital Budgeting. Explain the different kinds of Capital Expenditure proposals for Capital Budgeting.
4. What is Capital Budgeting? Explain the process of Capital Budgeting.
5. Give a brief outline of different Capital Budgeting appraisal methods.
6. Explain the procedures of assessing the Payback period.
7. What is Payback period method? State the merits and demerits of Payback period method.
8. State the procedures and objectives of Payback period method.
9. Explain the different types of Rate of Return method.
10. Give a brief outline of Discounted Cash Flow methods.
11. What is Net Present Value method? State the procedures of Net Present Value method.
12. Define Net Present Value method. Explain the merits and demerits of Net Present Value method.
13. Explain the concept of Internal Rate of Return method.
14. What is IRR? Explain the procedures of assessing the Internal Rate of Return.
15. Define Internal Rate of Return method. Explain the merits and demerits of Internal Rate of Return method.
16. What is Profitability Index method? State the merits and demerits of Profitability Index method.
17. Write short notes of the following
(i) Capital Budgeting (ii) Independent proposal (iii) Mutually exclusive Projects (iv) Capital rationing (v) Payback

period (vi) Discounted cash flow method (vii) Present Value method (viii) Rate of return method (ix) Internal Rate of Return method (x) Profitability Index method

III. Solve the following problems

1. Calculate the Payback Period for the three proposals from the following.

	Proposal X	*Proposal Y*	*Proposal Z*
Investment (Rs.)	5,50,000	4,00,000	5,00,000
Annual Return (Rs.)	90,000	70,000	77,000
Period of Return (Years)	10	11	12

(Ans : 6.11; 5.71; 6.49)

2. Calculate the Payback Periods for Project K and Project T from the following. The initial investment required for Projects K and T are Rs.14,00,000 and Rs.10,00,000 respectively. The annual return for these projects for 6 years are stated as follows.

Year	*Project K Rs.*	*Project T Rs.*
2002	3,20,000	2,50,000
2003	3,40,000	2,90,000
2004	4,00,000	3,00,000
2005	3,00,000	2,50,000
2006	3,70,000	3,10,000
2007	3,90,000	2,90,000

(Ans : 4.33; 3.64)

3. The cost and benefits related to three different machines for a manufacturing Company are stated as follows.

	Machine I	*Machine II*	*Machine III*
Cost (Rs.)	4,00,000	3,00,000	2,00,000
Estimated savings in wages (Rs.)	1,00,000	70,000	50,000
Estimated savings in scrap (Rs.)	50,000	40,000	35,000
Additional cost of supervision (Rs.)	37,000	17,000	20,000
Additional cost of maintenance (Rs.)	30,000	22,000	10,000
Estimated life (years)	5	6	7

Assume that there is no Tax. The savings and additional costs are related to one year. Calculate the Payback Period and find out which machine is more suitable.

(Ans : 4.8; 4.2; 3.6)

4. A manufacturing company wants to purchase a new machine. The cost and benefits of three available machines are stated as follows.

	Machine G Rs.	*Machine T Rs.*	*Machine C Rs.*
Cost of the machines	20,00,000	15,00,000	12,00,000
Scrap value	1,60,000	1,00,000	80,000
Expected Sales	27,50,000	20,50,000	16,50,000

Expected Cost of Production			
Direct material	9,60,000	5,40,000	3,51,000
Direct expenses	95,000	1,00,000	74,000
Factory overhead	3,57,000	2,67,000	1,97,000
Administration overhead	3,17,000	2,95,000	2,23,000
Selling and distribution overhead	91,000	1,10,000	1,27,000

Corporate tax is 50% and the cost of Capital is 12% per annum. The revenue and expenses are related to each year of the economical life of the machines.

Economic life of the machines are 8 years, 10 years and 7 years respectively for machines G, T and C respectively.

Calculate Net Cash Inflow, Payback Period and find out which machine is suitable for investment.

(Ans : 7.08; 6.96; 5.39)

5. Calculate the Average Rate of Return on Investment based on Average Profit, from the following.

Cost of Investment of the project is	Rs. 30,00,000
Estimated Scrap value	Rs. 1,00,000

Expected Profit after Tax and Depreciation for the five years are Rs.5,50,000; Rs.7,70,000; Rs.6,90,000; Rs.6,00,000 and Rs.5,90,000.

(Ans : 22.07%; 44.14%)

6. The investment required for a project is Rs.35,00,000 and the estimated scrap value is Rs.3,00,000. The project has a life of 7 years and the return for the years after adjusting depreciation and tax are Rs.7,00,000; Rs.7,50,000, Rs.8,30,000, Rs.7,90,000; Rs.8,10,000; Rs.7,70,000 and Rs.8,50,000.

Calculate the Average Return on Investment based on the Total Profit.

(Ans : 314.29%; 157.14%)

7. WD Ltd provided the following information related to two projects namely X and Y

	Project X	*Project Y*
Investments required (Rs.)	17,00,000	21,00,000
Expected life	6 years	7 years
Salvage value (Rs.)	1,40,000	1,70,000

The expected Profit after tax including depreciation are stated as follows.

	Years (Rs)						
	1	*2*	*3*	*4*	*5*	*6*	*7*
Project X:	3,50,000	4,10,000	3,70,000	3,60,000	3,30,000	4,40,000	–
Project Y:	1,25,000	4,70,000	5,00,000	4,20,000	4,90,000	4,80,000	4,60,000

Calculate the Average Rate of Return and find out which project is to be accepted if the expected rate of return is 22%.

(Ans : Project X; 24.15%; 21.8%)

8. T Ltd has to choose anyone of the two machine available in the market. The cost price of Machine K is Rs.27,00,000 and of Machine C is Rs.24,00,000. The scrap value of these two machines are Rs.1,50,000 and Rs.1,40,000

respectively. The life of the machines are 10 years. The return for these years after depreciation and before tax are stated as follows.

Years	*Machine K* *Rs.*	*Machine C* *Rs.*
1	7,90,000	6,50,000
2	7,50,000	6,20,000
3	6,00,000	6,10,000
4	8,10,000	5,90,000
5	8,40,000	6,40,000
Total	37,90,000	31,10,000

The rate of Tax is 50%.

Find out which machine is more profitable according to average rate of return method.

(Ans : Machine C; 33.46%; 34.53%)

9. K Ltd wants to buy a machine. The company has two alternative machines to choose. The cost of each machine is Rs.11,00,000. The cash inflow for these two machines for the first five years are as follows.

Year	*Machine A* *Rs.*	*Machine B* *Rs.*
2003	2,10,000	3,00,000
2004	3,25,000	3,50,000
2005	3,15,000	3,60,000
2006	3,30,000	2,00,000
2007	3,20,000	2,90,000

The expected return on capital is 12% p.a. The Discount Factors for the first five year @ 10% interest is stated as follows.

Year:	*1*	*2*	*3*	*4*	*5*
Discount Factor:	0.909	0.827	0.751	0.683	0.621

Find out which machine is more profitable according to the Discounted Cash Flow method.

(Ans : Machine B; Rs.11,20,340; Rs.11,49,200)

10. W.D. Ltd has to decide whether to invest in a project costing Rs.22,00,00. The project is expected to yield for 7 years as follows.

Year:	*1*	*2*	*3*	*4*	*5*	*6*	*7*
Cash inflow: (Rs.)	5,00,000	4,90,000	5,40,000	5,10,000	5,50,000	4,60,000	6,00,000

The Present Value factor for 7 years @ 14% interest are stated as follows.

Year:	*1*	*2*	*3*	*4*	*5*	*6*	*7*
Discount Factor	0.877	.769	.675	.592	.519	.456	.399

Find out whether it is advisable to invest in the project.

(Ans : Yes; Rs.22,16,340))

11. A Company has to select one of the proposals, each costing Rs.7,50,000. The Cash Inflowfrom these projects are stated as follows.

Years	*Project G* *Rs.*	*Project R* *Rs.*
1	3,20,000	3,50,000
2	3,40,000	2,90,000
3	2,90,000	3,70,000
4	2,60,000	3,10,000
5	3,90,000	3,00,000

Project G requires an additional investment of Rs.70,000 and R requires Rs.50,000 at the end of 1st year. The cost capital is 15%. The Discount Factors are stated as follows.

Year:	*1*	2	3	4	5
Discount Factor:	0.870	0.756	0.658	0.572	0.497

Find out the best proposal

(**Ans :** Proposal R; Rs.257,910; Rs.300120)

12. H Ltd has to choose one machine from among the two popular machines available in the market. The cost price of the machines are Rs.19,00,000 each and the scrap value are Rs.70,000 and Rs.50,000 respectively for the two machines. The Net Cash Inflow for the five years of the life of the machines are stated as follows.

Year	*Machine X* *Rs.*	*Machine Y* *Rs.*
2003	7,40,000	6,00,000
2004	7,00,000	6,90,000
2005	6,90,000	7,20,000
2006	6,50,000	7,40,000
2007	7,40,000	7,70,000

The expected return on investment for the company is 12% and the risk premium rates are 5% and 4% respectively for Machine X and Machine Y.

The discount factors are stated as follows.

Year:	*1*	2	3	4	5
Discount Factor 12%	0.893	0.797	0.712	0.636	0.567
Discount Factor 16%	0.862	0.743	0.641	0.552	0.476
Discount Factor 17%	0.855	0.731	0.624	0.534	0.456

Find out which machine should be selected by the company.

(**Ans :** Project X, Rs.391, 420; Rs.390, 190)

13. WD Ltd has to choose any one of the proposals namely A and B. The cost and revenue aspects of the two project proposals are stated as follows.

Cost of Project A	Rs. 4,00,000
Cost of Project B	Rs. 4,50,000

Cash inflow associated with profitability factor for 5 years of the life of the project are stated as follows.

Year	*Project A Rs.*	*Probability*	*Project B Rs.*	*Probability*
2003	8,10,000	.2	7,00,000	.2
2004	8,30,000	.1	8,90,000	.2
2005	7,60,000	.3	8,00,000	.1
2006	7,00,000	.2	7,20,000	.2
2007	8,00,000	.2	7,90,000	.3

The cost of capital is assumed to be 17% per annum. The Discount Factors are stated as follows.

Year:	*1*	2	*3*	*4*	*5*
Discount Factor:	0.855	0.731	0.624	0.534	0.456

Find out the project which gives more return.

(**Ans :** Project A; Rs.89,175; Rs.34,706)

14. Calculate Net Present Value from the following Cash Inflow and Cash Outflow of a project.

Year	*Out flow Rs.*	*Inflow Rs.*
0	10,00,000	–
1	1,50,000	
2	–	2,90,000
3	50,000	3,90,000
4		4,10,000
5		3,70,000
6		2,90,000
7		4,20,000

The scrap value for the machine is Rs.90,000. The Discount Factors at 10% rate of return per annum are stated as follows.

Year:	*1*	*2*	*3*	*4*	*5*	*6*	*7*
Discount Factors:	0.909	.827	.751	.683	.621	.564	.514

(**Ans :** Rs.1,48,060)

15. Calculate Net Present Value from the following and advise the management whether the project can be accepted.

Cost of the project	Rs.40,00,000
Life of the project	10 years
Scrap value	Rs.5,00,000
Annual return after tax without adjusting Depreciation	Rs.5,50,000
The Present Value of 1 rupee received annually for 10 year @ 10% p.a. is	Rs.6.1446
Present value of 1 rupee received at the end of 10 years @ 10% p.a.	Rs.0.38554
Depreciation is to be charged on straight line basis	

(**Ans :** Rs.17,23,500)

16. N Ltd. wants to replace a machinery bought during 2000 for Rs.5,00,000. The cost of the new machine is Rs.7,00,000. If the machine is sold for (i) Rs.2,00,000 (ii) Rs.2,50,000 (iii) Rs.5,00,000 (iv) Rs.6,00,000 (v) Rs.2,00,000, calculate the net cash outflows.

    Assume that the present book value of the machine is Rs.2,50,000, Income Tax @ 50% and Capital Gain Tax @ 30%.

    (**Ans :** Rs.8,00,000; Rs,7,25,000; Rs.6,25000; Rs.5,55,000; Rs.7,85,000)

17. Calculate the net cash required for replacing a machine on 1st April 2007 from the following.

	Rs.
Cost of the New Machine	21,00,000
Cost of the Old Machine bought on 1st April 2002 with a life of 10 years	5,00,000
Sale of old Machine on 31st March 2007	3,00,000
Additional Working Capital required	90,000
Installation charges for the New Machine	1,00,000

Depreciation is charged on the basis of straight line method. Income Tax is 40% and Capital Gain Tax is 20%.

(**Ans :** Rs.20,10,000)

18. A manufacturing company has the option of investing in two plants, namely Plant A and Plant B. The expected life of these two plants is 10 years each and there is no salvage value for these plants at the end of the life of these plants.

    The annual instalments to be paid and the annual costs connected with these plants are stated as follows.

	Plant A *Rs.*	*Plant B* *Rs.*
Annual instalments	7,50,000	9,10,000
Direct Labour cost per annum		
Normal hours	90,000	1,00,000
Overtime	50,000	–
Maintenance cost	60,000	70,000
Overhead	1,40,000	1,10,000

Cost of Capital is 10% per annum.

(**Ans :** Plant A; Savings in Cost Rs.1,00,000)

19. R Ltd. provided the details about the Cash Inflows from two proposals as follows.

Year	*Proposal X* *Rs.*	*Proposal Y* *Rs.*
1	2,00,000	2,70,000
2	1,95,000	2,30,000
3	2,10,000	2,00,000
4	2,25,000	1,40,000
5	1,70,000	1,60,000

The cost of the proposal is Rs.4,50,000 each and the additional cost is Rs.70,000 for Project X at the end of first year and Rs.55,000 for project Y at the end of second year.

The expected return on investment is 12% p.a. The Discount Factors for 12% interest are stated as follows.

Year:	*1*	2	3	4	5
Discount Factors:	0.893	0.797	0.712	0.636	0.567

Calculate the Discounted Cash Flow for the two proposals. Also find out which project is profitable according to the Payback period method.

(**Ans :** Rs.2,10,515; Rs.2,52,745; Payback period 2.6 and 2.025; Project Y)

20. Calculate the approximate Internal Rate of Return if the cost of investment is Rs.50,00,000, and estimated Annual Cash flows for the life of 10 years is Rs.7,00,000.

(**Ans :** 7%)

21. Calculate Internal Rate of Return for W. Doyle & Co. Ltd from the following.

Cost of the investment	Rs. 32,00,000
Life of the project	5 years

Estimated net Annual Cash flows are as follows

	Rs.		*Rs.*
2003	9,00,000	2006	7,90,000
2004	8,70,000	2007	9,10,000
2005	8,10,000		

(**Ans :** 10.62%; Rs.50,580; Rs.30,400)

22. Joyce & Co.Ltd provided the following information about the Cash Outflow and Inflow related to a project.

Cost of the project	Rs.37,00,000
Life of the project	5 years

The Annual Cash Inflow are stated as follows.

Years	*Rs.*
1	12,40,000
2	10,50,000
3	9,90,000
4	13,00,000
5	12,60,000

PV factor for 16%, 17% and 18% return are as follows.

Year	*PV Factor*		
	16%	17%	18%
1	0.862	0.855	0.848
2	0.743	0.731	0.718
3	0.641	0.624	0.609
4	0.552	0.534	0.516
5	0.476	0.456	0.437

Calculate Internal Rate of Return.

(**Ans :** 17.18%; Rs.100980; Rs.70,250)

23. M.W Ltd provides the particulars related to Cash Outflow and Inflow for two projects as follows.

	Project M *Rs.*	*Project N* *Rs.*
Estimated Cash outflow	19,00,000	15,00,000
Estimated Cash inflow		
2001	5,00,000	6,70,000
2002	7,00,000	4,50,000
2003	6,80,000	3,90,000
2004	7,20,000	4,40,000
2005	6,50,000	5,10,000
2006	–	3,40,000
2007	–	4,50,000

Present Value factor for different rates of interest are stated as follows.

Year ending	*17%*	*19%*	*21%*	*23%*	*25%*	*27%*
1	0.855	0.840	0.826	0.813	0.800	0.781
2	0.731	0.706	0.683	0.661	0.640	0.610
3	0.624	0.593	0.564	0.537	0.512	0.477
4	0.534	0.499	0.467	0.437	0.410	0.393
5	0.456	0.419	0.385	0.345	0.328	0.291
6	0.390	0.352	0.319	0.289	0.262	0.238
7	0.333	0.296	0.263	0.234	0.210	0.188

Calculate IRR and suggest which project gives maximum return.

(**Ans :** 20.2%; Rs.1,44,400; Rs.1,26,750; 26.28%; Rs.2,97,900; Rs.29,350)

24. KMWD Ltd has to decide whether a project costing Rs.4,50,000 has to be selected or not. The project is expected to give Annual return for 10 years on the following basis.

Year	*Rs*	*Year*	*Rs.*
1	1,10,000	6	75,000
2	70,000	7	1,20,000
3	90,000	8	67,000
4	1,00,000	9	82,000
5	60,000	10	90,000

The Cost of Capital estimated is 12%. Calculate (a) Payback period (b) Net Present value on the basis of 12% rate of interest and (c) Internal Rate of Return, so that the company can decide whether the project can be selected or not.

The Discounting factors for 12% and 17% are stated as follows.

Year	*12%*	*17%*
1	0.893	0.855
2	0.797	0.731
3	0.712	0.624
4	0.636	0.534
5	0.567	0.456
6	0.507	0.390
7	0.453	0.333
8	0.404	0.285
9	0.361	0.243
10	0.322	0.208

(**Ans :** 5.4 years; Rs.43,755; Rs.14.58; Rs.40,909)

25. Calculate the Profitability Index on the basis of 10% Discount factor, from the following.

Cost of the Project	Rs. 31,00,000
Estimated Cash Inflow	Rs.
2003	9,00,000
2004	8,70,000
2005	7,90,000
2006	9,20,000
2007	8,50,000

Year	*1*	*2*	*3*	*4*	*5*
PV Factor:	0.909	.827	.751	.683	.621

(**Ans :** 1.06)

26. G.R. Ltd has two options in the purchase of a machine. The cost of each machine is Rs. 30,00,000. The expected returns from the machines after tax are stated as follows.

Year	Cash Inflow	
	Machine A Rs.	*Machine B* Rs.
1	9,90,000	8,40,000
2	8,80,000	9,30,000
3	9,20,000	9,00,000
4	9,00,000	9,50,000
5	8,70,000	9,40,000

The expected Annual return is @ 10% p.a. The Discount Factors at 10% p.a. are as follows.

Year:	*1*	*2*	*3*	*4*	*5*
Discount Factors:	0.909	.827	.751	.683	.621

Find out which machine gives more return according to Profitability Index method.

(Ans: 1.16; 1.15)

27. Calculate Profitability Index (Excess Present Value Index) from the following information related to the Cash inflow and outflow.

Years	*Cash Outflow* Rs.	*Cash Inflow* Rs.
0	12,00,000	
1	1,20,000	4,40,000
2	-	4,75,000
3	70,000	4,00,000
4	-	4,60,000
5	-	4,10,000

The Cost of Capital is 12% and the Discount Factors at 12% rate are stated as follows.

Year:	*1*	*2*	*3*	*4*	*5*
Discount Factors:	0.893	0.797	0.712	0.636	0.567

Cash outflow for the 1st year end and 3rd year end are due to maintenance of the Plant.

(Ans: 1.17; Rs. 13,57,000; Rs. 15,81,325)

Calculate (i) Payback period (ii) Net Present Value and (iii) Profitability Index for two projects namely, P and Q from the following.

Years	*Project P* Rs.	*Project Q* Rs.
0	-5,00,000	-7,00,000
1	1,50,000	2,40,000
2	2,00,000	2,20,000

3	1,75,000	2,00,000
4	1,40,000	2,30,000
5	1,70,000	2,50,000

The Cost of Capital is 15%. The Discount Factors for 15% rate of interest are as follows.

Year:	*1*	*2*	*3*	*4*	*5*
Discount Factor:	0.870	0.756	0.658	0.572	0.497

(**Ans :** 2.8 years; Rs.61,420; 1.12; 3.17 years; Rs.62,350; 1.09)

29. The initial investment required for a project is Rs.10,00,000. The project is expected to give annual return after depreciation and before tax @ 50% as follows.

Year:	*1*	*2*	*3*	*4*	*5*
Return (Rs.):	5,50,000	4,80,000	5,00,000	6,00,000	5,30,000

Analyse the return from the project on the basis of (i) Payback period method (ii) Rate of return on Original Investment (iii) Rate of return on Average Investment (iv) Discounted Cash Flow method (v) Profitability Index method (Excess Present Value Index).

The depreciation is charged @ 12% on cost of investment. Cost of Capital is 12%.

The Discount factors for 12% rate of interest are stated as follows.

Year:	*1*	*2*	*3*	*4*	*5*
Discount Factors:	0.893	0.797	0.712	0.636	0.567

(**Ans :** 2.66 years; 26.6%, 53.2% Rs.3,88,510; 1.39)

□□□

11

INFLATION ACCOUNTING (PRICE LEVEL ACCOUNTING)

Inflation Accounting is otherwise called as Price Level Accounting. It is based on the principle that the prices of products at different periods are at different levels. The different price levels at different periods have an impact on the price of the products at different periods. For example the machine brought for Rs.5,00,000 in 2000 may have replacement cost of Rs.12,00,000 during 2007. But in the Financial Accounting the replacement value is not considered for calculation. All the values are recorded as per the historical cost of the various items. Hence, the data of Financial Accounting related to the occurrence in the past may not exhibit a fair value for the current year. The data presented in the Balance Sheet may not therefore, exhibit the current status of various items. The data related to the past years concerned with the Capital Expenditure are available mostly in the Balance Sheet. The Balance Sheet will not exhibit a true and fair view of the state of affair due to the price level changes. Hence, there is a need for adjusting the past values according to the current price level. The process of converting the past capital expenditure or receipts according to the current year price level is known as Inflation Accounting.

Meaning of Inflation Accounting

The accounting system adopted for converting the past financial expenditure and receipts according to the Current Price level is called Inflation Accounting. The conversion of the past financial expenditure and receipts can be done by comparing the Current Price Index with the General Price Index of the years in which the expenditure or receipts took place.

Methods of Accounting for Price Level Change

The following are the important methods of accounting for price level change:

1. Current Purchasing Power Method (CPP Method)
2. Current Cost Accounting Method (CCA Method).

1. Current Purchasing Power Method

In this method, the increase or decrease of price level in a period should be adjusted with the items in the Profit and Loss account and Balance Sheet. Hence, the method is based on the General Price Index. According to the Price Index the items should be adjusted to know the real values. For example, if the General Price Index is 250 and the monetary value of Plant and Machinery is Rs.5,00,000 then the value according to the General Price Index is 5,00,000 × 250/100 = Rs.7,50,000. Like this, all the items in the Final Accounts should be calculated to know the real picture of the financial Statements.

Procedures for Inflation Accounting Under Current Purchasing Power Method

The following are the procedures for inflation accounting under current purchasing power method.

(i) Calculation of Conversion Factor

The Conversion Factor is calculated as follows.

$$\text{Conversion Factor} = \frac{\text{Current Price Index}}{\text{Previous Price Index}}$$

(ii) Calculation of converted value

The converted value is calculated as follows

$$\text{Converted value} = \text{Historical Value x Conversion Factor}$$

$$\text{or} = \text{Historical Value} \times \frac{\text{Current Price Index}}{\text{Previous Price Index}}$$

Illustration: 1

Calculate the Converted Value for the year 2007 from the following.

Purchase of Land during 1999 is Rs.5,00,000

The Price Index during 1999 is 200 and the Price Index during 2007 is 450.

Solution :

$$\text{Conversion Factor} = \frac{\text{Current Price Index}}{\text{Previous Price Index}}$$

$$= \frac{450}{200} = 2.25$$

$$\text{Converted Value} = \text{Historical Cost} \times \text{Conversion Factor}$$

$$= 5{,}00{,}000 \times 2.25 = \text{Rs.}11{,}25{,}000$$

Illustration: 2

Calculate the Profit or Loss on sale of a Plant on the basis of Converted Value from the following.

Cost of the Plant is Rs.7,0,000 which was purchased during 2000 when the Price Index is 240, the Plant is sold for Rs.6,50,000 during 2007 when the price index is 450.

Solution :

$$\text{Converted Value of the cost of Plant} = \frac{450}{240} \times 7{,}00{,}000 = \text{Rs. } 13{,}12{,}500$$

$$\text{Sale of Plant} = \text{Rs. } 6{,}50{,}000$$

$$\text{Loss on sale} = 13{,}12{,}500 - 6{,}50{,}000 = \text{Rs. } 6{,}62{,}500$$

Illustration: 3

Calculate the monetary loss or gain on the basis of current purchasing power method from the following

	Rs.	Price Index
Opening balance of Cash (1st March 2007)	42,000	100
Purchase of Raw Material by Cash (5th March 2007)	30,000	110
Cash Sales (14th March 2000)	1,10,000	120

Collection from Debtors (1st April 2007)	40,000	140
Credit Purchase (15th April 2007)	50,000	150
Payment to Creditors (20th April 2007)	25,000	180
Payment of Wages (21st April 2007)	32,000	190
Bills Payable honoured (15th May 2007)	22,000	220
Bills Receivable honoured (20th May 2007)	24,000	230
Closing Balance of Cash (31st May 2007)	1,07,000	250

Solution:

Calculation of Monetary Gain / Loss

Particulars	*Historical Value Rs.*	*Price Index*	*Conversion*	*Converted Value Rs.*
Opening balance of Cash	42,000	100	250/100	1,05,000
Add :				
Cash sales	1,10,000	120	250/120	2,29,167
Collection from Debtors	40,000	140	250/140	71,428
Bills Receivable Honoured	24,000	230	250/230	26,087
	2,16,000			431,682
Less : Payments				
Purchase	30,000	110	250/110	68,182
Creditors	25,000	180	250/180	34,722
Wages	32,000	190	250/190	42,105
Bills Payable honoured	22,000	220	250/220	25,000
	1,09,000			1,70,009
Closing balance of Cash	1,07,000	250		261,673
Monetary Gain	154,673			
	261,673			261,673

Illustration: 4

G Ltd provided the following Final Accounts as on 31st March 2007 as follows.

Profit and Loss Account as on 31st March 2007

Particulars	*Rs.*	*Rs.*
Sales		17,00,000
Cost of Goods Sold :		
Opening Stock	1,10,000	
Purchase	12,00,000	
	13,10,000	
Less : Closing Stock	1,70,000	11,40,000
Gross Profit	560,000	

Less : Operating Expenses	90,000	
Depreciation	50,000	
Interest	60,000	2,00,000
Net Profit		3,60,000

Balance Sheet as on 31st March 2007

Particulars	*Rs.*	*Particulars*	*Rs.*
Share Capital	10,00,000	Fixed Assets	14,50,000
Reserves and Surplus	2,00,000	Stock	1,70,000
Debenture	3,00,000	Debtors	40,000
Loan	2,00,000	Cash	90,000
Sundry Creditors	50,000		
	17,50,000		17,50,000

Adjustments :

(i) General Price Index for 1st April 2006 is 200 and of 31st March 2007 is 400. Average Price Index is 300.

(ii) FIFO method of issue of material is adopted.

(iii) Debtors are distributed evenly throughout the year.

(iv) Creditors remained constant throughout the year.

Prepare the Final Accounts after adjusting the price level changes according to CPP method.

Solution :

Profit and Loss Account as on 31st March 2007

Particulars	*Historical Value Rs.*	*Conversion*	*Converted Value Rs.*
Sales	17,00,000	400/300	22,66,667
Less :			
Cost of Goods Sold			
Opening Stock	1,10,000	400/200	2,20,000
Purchase	12,00,000	400/300	16,00,000
	13,10,000		18,20,000
Less : Closing Stock	1,70,000	400/300	2,26,667
Cost of Goods Sold	11,40,000		15,93,333
Gross Profit	5,60,000		6,73,334
Operating Expenses	90,000	400/300	1,20,000
Depreciation	50,000	400/200	1,00,000
Interest	60,000	400/400	60,000
	2,00,000		2,80,000
Net Profit	3,60,000		3,93,334

Balance Sheet as on 31st March 2007

Particulars	Historical Value Rs.	Conversion	Converted Value Rs.
Liabilities :			
Share Capital	10,00,000	400/200	20,00,000
Reserve and Surplus	2,00,000		7,20,000
Debenture	3,00,000	400/400	3,00,000
Loan	2,00,000	400/400	2,00,000
Sundry Creditors	50,000	400/400	50,000
	17,50,000		32,70,000
Assets :			
Fixed Assets	14,50,000	400/200	29,00,000
Stock	1,70,000	400/300	2,26,667
Debtors	40,000	400/300	53,333
Cash	90,000	400/400	90,000
	17,50,000		32,70,000

Illustration: 5

Calculate the Cost of sales and Closing inventory on the basis of Current Purchasing price method through FIFO and LIFO of pricing of inventory from the following.

	Rs.
Stock (Inventory) as on 31st March 2006	74,000
Stock as on 31st March 2007	1,20,000
Purchase of material	4,50,000

General price index for 2006 and 2007 are 370 and 450 respectively and the average for the year is 410.

Solution :

Cost of Sales and Closing Inventory (FIFO Method)

Particulars	Historical Value Rs.	Conversion	Converted Value Rs.
Inventory as on 31st March 2006	74,000	450/370	90,000
Add : Purchases	4,50,000	450/410	4,93,902
	5,24,000		5,83,902
Less : Inventory as on 31st March 2007	1,20,000	450/410	1,31,707
Cost of Goods Sold	4,04,000		4,52,195

Cost of Sales and Closing Inventory (LIFO Method)

Particulars	*Historical Value Rs.*	*Conversion*	*Converted Value Rs.*
Inventory as on 31st March 2006	74,000	450/370	90,000
Add : Purchases	4,50,000	450/410	4,93,902
	5,24,000		5,83,902
Less : Inventory as on 31st March 2007			
From Opening Inventory	74,000	450/370	90,000
From Current Purchase	46,000	450/410	50,488
Value of Closing Inventory	1,20,000		1,40,488
Cost of Goods Sold	4,04,000		4,43,414

2. Current Cost Accounting Method

Current Cost Accounting Method was introduced during 1975 by the British Government through a Committee known as Sandilands Committee, headed by Francis C.P. Sandilands. The committee suggested that the Current Purchasing Power method can be replaced with Current Cost Accounting method. In this method, the values of Cost of Goods sold, Inventory, Fixed Assets, Depreciation and Working Capital are properly ascertained to exhibit in a fair manner as per the Current Price Level. The application of this method is well presented through the following Illustrations.

Illustration: 6

W.D. Ltd purchased a Machine for Rs.34,00,000 on 1st April 2003. Depreciation of the Machine is provided @ 10% on straight line basis. The price of the Machine as on 31st March 2007 is Rs.50,00,000.

Calculate the treatment of the Machine in the Balance Sheet.

Solution :

Calculation of Cost of the Machine

Particulars	*Historical Cost Rs.*	*Current Cost Rs.*
Cost of the machine as on 1st April 2003	34,00,000	50,00,000
Less : Depreciation for 5 years	17,00,000	25,00,000
	17,00,000	25,00,000

Illustration: 7

KM Ltd., purchased a Machine on 1st April 2002 for Rs.20,00,000. The estimated life of the Machine is 10 years. If the replacement cost of the Machine on 1st April 2006 is Rs.30,00,000 and on 1st April 2007 is Rs.33,00,000, calculate the amount of Depreciation Adjustment.

Solution :

Depreciation on the basis of

Current Cost Accounting method $= \dfrac{30,00,000 + 33,00,000}{2 \times 10}$

$= \text{Rs.}3,15,000$

Depreciation on the basis of

Historical Cost Method $= \frac{20,00,000}{10}$

= Rs.2,00,000

Depreciation Adjustment

= 3,15,000 – 2,00,000 = Rs.1,15,000

Illustration: 8

Calculate the Backlog depreciation from the following.

Purchase of Machine on 1st April 2002 for	Rs. 12,00,000
Replacement cost of the Machine on 1st April 2006	Rs. 22,00,000
Replacement cost of the Machine as on 1st April 2007	Rs. 25,00,000
Life of the Machine is 10 years	

Solution :

Replacement cost of the Machine as on 1st April 2006	Rs.22,00,000
Expired life as on 1st April 2006	5 years
Depreciation under Current Cost Accounting (CCA) method =	$\frac{22,00,000}{10} \times 5$ = Rs. 11,00,000
Replacement cost of the machine as on 1st April 2007	Rs.25,00,000
Expired life as on 1st April 2007	6 years
Depreciation under Current Cost Account (CCA) method	$= \frac{25,00,000}{10} \times 6$ = Rs. 15,00,000

Difference in depreciation	= 15,00,000 – 11,00,000 = Rs.4,00,000
Backlog depreciation	= Difference in depreciation – Depreciation chargeable in Current Year
	= 4,00,000 – 2,35,00 = Rs.1,65,000
[Depreciation for Current year	$= \frac{22,00,000 + 25,00,000}{2 \times 10}$ = Rs.2,35,000]

Illustration: 9

Calculate Current Cost of Sales Adjustment from the following.

	Historical cost (Rs)	*Index Number*
Opening Stock	50,000	100
Purchase	6,50,000	120
	7,00,000	(Average)
Less : Closing Stock	90,000	140
Cost of Sales	6,10,000	

Solution :

Calculation of Cost of Sales Adjustment (COSA)

Particulars	*Historical Value Rs.*	*Conversion*	*Converted Value Rs.*
Opening Stock	50,000	140/100	70,000
Add : Purchase	6,50,000	140/120	7,58,333
	7,00,000		8,28,333
Less : Closing Stock	90,000	140/120	1,05,000
Cost of Sales	6,10,000		7,23,333
COSA	1,13,333		
	7,23,333		7,23,333

Illustration: 10

Calculate Monetary Working Capital Adjustment (MWCA) from the following

	1st April 2006 Rs.	*1st April 2007 Rs.*
Sundry Debtors (Rs)	2,40,000	3,50,000
Sundry Creditors (Rs)	90,000	1,00,000
Index Number	100	140
Average Index Number		120

Solution :

Calculation of Working Capital adjustment (MWCA)

Particulars	*Historical Value Rs.*	*Conversion*	*Converted Value Rs.*
Closing Working Capital (3,50,000 – 1,00,000)	2,50,000	120/140	2,14,286
Opening Working Capital (2,40,000 – 90,000)	1,50,000	120/100	1,80,000
Increase in Working Capital	1,00,000		34,286
Monetary Working Capital Adjustment			65,714
	1,00,000		1,00,000

Illustration: 11

Calculate the Gearing Adjustment Required under CCA method, from the following.

	1st April 2006 Rs.	*1st April 2007 Rs.*
Share Capital	5,00,000	6,00,000
Reserve and Surplus	70,000	90,000
Debenture	2,00,000	2,50,000
Bank overdraft	50,000	70,000

Loan	1,40,000	1,70,000
Cash	1,00,000	1,20,000
COSA	60,000	
MWCA	50,000	
Depreciation	10,000	
Total	1,20,000	

Solution :

Calculation of Net Borrowings

	1st April 2006 Rs.	*1st April 2007 Rs.*
Debenture	2,00,000	2,50,000
Loan	1,40,000	1,70,000
Bank Overdraft	50,000	70,000
Total Borrowings	3,90,000	4,90,000
Less : Cash	1,00,000	1,20,000
Net Borrowings	2,90,000	3,70,000
Shareholder fund		
Share Capital	5,00,000	6,00,000
Reserve and surplus	70,000	90,000
	5,70,000	6,90,000

Average Net Borrowings = (2,90,000 + 3,70,000) / 2 = Rs.3,30,000

Average Shareholders Fund = (5,70,000 + 6,90,000)/2 = Rs.6,30,000

Total Adjustment = 60,000 + 50,000 + 10,000 = Rs.1,20,000

$$\text{Gearing Adjustment} = \frac{3,30,000 \times 1,20,000}{3,30,000 + 6,30,000} = \text{Rs. } 41,250$$

Illustration: 12

The Final Accounts of K Ltd. as on 31st March 2007 are stated as follows.

Profit and Loss Account as on 31st March 2007

Particulars	*Rs.*	*Particulars*	*Rs.*
To Opening Stock	1,15,000	By Sales	21,00,000
To Purchase	11,85,000	By Other Income	50,000
	13,00,000		
Less : Closing Stock	1,50,000		
Cost of Sale	11,50,000		
To Operating Expenses	2,00,000		
To Depreciation	2,50,000		
To Interest	80,000		
To Net Profit	4,70,000		

	Rs.		Rs.
	21,50,000		21,50,000
To Provision for Tax	1,20,000	**By Net Profit**	4,70,000
To Dividend	50,000		
To General Reserve	50,000		
To Balance	2,50,000		
	4,70,000		4,70,000

Balance Sheets

Liabilities	*2006 Rs.*	*2007 Rs.*	*Assets*	*2006 Rs.*	*2007 Rs.*
Share Capital	15,00,000	15,00,000	Fixed Assets	22,45,000	23,15,000
Reserves and Surplus	2,50,000	2,85,000	**Less :** Depreciation	30,000	95,000
Debenture	3,50,000	4,15,000		22,15,000	22,20,000
Loan	2,85,000	2,50,000	Stock	1,15,000	1,50,000
Sundry Creditors	65,000	40,000	Debtors	45,000	30,000
			Cash	75,000	90,000
	24,50,000	24,90,000		24,50,000	24,90,000

General Price Indices are 100, 120 and 130 for opening, average and closing.

The value of Fixed Assets are Rs.30,00,000 and Rs.32,00,000 for 1st April 2006 and 31st March 2007 respectively with an average life of 10 years.

Prepare the Final Accounts on the basis of Current Cost Accounts (CCA) method.

Solution :

Current Cost Profit and Loss Account as on 31 March 2007

Particulars	*Rs.*	*Rs.*
Sales		21,00,000
Profit before Interest and Tax		5,60,000
Less : Current cost Adjustment		
COSA	34,520	
MWCA	51,720	
Depreciation	60,000	1,32,160
Current Cost Operating Profit		4,27,840
Less : Interest		80,000
		3,37,840
Add : Gearing Adjustment		19,615
Current Cost Profit before Tax		3,57,455
Less : Tax		1,20,000
Less : Dividend		50,000
		1,87,455

Current Cost Balance Sheet as on 31st March 2007

Particulars		*Rs.*	*Particulars*		*Rs.*
Share Capital		15,00,000	Fixed Assets	23,15,000	
Reserve and Surplus	2,85,000		**Less :** Depreciation	60,000	
Less : Adjustment	35,000	2,50,000		22,55,000	
			Less : Back Log	70,000	21,85,000
Debentures		4,15,000	Stock		1,50,000
Loan		2,50,000	Debtors		30,000
Sundry Creditors		40,000	Cash		90,000
		24,55,000			24,55,000

Workings :

a. Cost of Sales Adjust (COSA)

$$= (1{,}50{,}000 - 1{,}15{,}000) - 120$$

$$= 35{,}000 - (120 \times 4) = \text{Rs.}34{,}520$$

b. Depreciation Adjustment

$$= \frac{\text{Opening Value} + \text{Closing Value}}{2 \times \text{Life of the Assets}} - \text{Current year depreciation}$$

$$= \frac{30{,}00{,}000 \times 3{,}20{,}000}{2 \times 10} = 2{,}50{,}000$$

$$= \text{Rs.}60{,}000$$

c. Backlog Depreciation

Particulars	*Opening*	*Closing*
Value of Fixed Assets (Rs)	30,00,000	32,00,000
Expected life (years)	3	4
Depreciation (30,00,000 × 3)/10; (32,00,000 × 4)/10	9,00,000	12,80,000
Difference in Depreciation (12,80,000 – 9,00,000)	3,80,00	
Less Chargeable for the year	3,10,000	
Backlog Depreciation (Rs.)	70,000	

d. Monetary Working Capital Adjustment (MWCA)

$$= (2{,}30{,}000 - 1{,}70{,}000) - 120\left[\frac{2{,}30{,}000}{130} - \frac{1{,}70{,}000}{100}\right]$$

$$= 60{,}000 - (120 \times 69) = \text{Rs.}51{,}720$$

[Opening Working Capital = 2,35,000 – 65,000 = Rs.1,70,000

Closing Working Capital = 2,70,000 – 40,000 = Rs.2,30,000]

e. Calculation of Gearing Adjustment

Total Net Borrowings = (3,50,000 + 2,85,000 – 75,000) + (4,15,000 + 2,50,000 – 90,000)
= Rs.11,35,000

Average Net Borrowings = 11,35,000/2 = Rs.5,67,500

Total Shareholders Fund = (15,00,000 + 2,50,000) + (15,00,000 + 2,85,000)

= Rs.35,35,000

Average Shareholder Fund = 35,35,000/2 = Rs.17,67,500

Total of Current Cost Adjustment = COSA + Depreciation Adjustment

= 34,520 + 60,000 = Rs.94,520

$$\textbf{Gearing Adjustment} = \frac{5,67,500}{5,67,500 + 17,67,500} \times 94,520$$

= Rs.22,972

Merits of Inflation Accounting

The merits of Inflation Accounting are stated as follows

(i) It helps to know the correct value of Balance Sheet items.

(ii) It facilitates for the capital expenditure decision making.

(iii) It is useful for the planning and control of cost.

(iv) The real value of the opening and closing inventory can be calculated.

(v) It helps to know the real financial conditions of a business.

Demerits of Inflation Accounting

The demerits of Inflation Accounting are stated as follows.

(i) The price level always changes. Hence, final position according to the price level may change from the already calculated values.

(ii) General Price Index for different products will be at different rates.

(iii) It facilitates manipulating the values of fixed assets safely to owners and creditors.

(iv) This system may not be suitable for different places since the price level varies from place to place.

(v) The real profit as per the exact current prices could not be ascertained.

EXERCISE

THEORY

I. Answer the following questions.

1. Define Inflation Accounting. State the merits and demerits of Inflation Accounting.
2. Explain the needs for the Price Level Accounting. Write a suitable example.
3. What is Inflation Accounting? Explain the different types of Inflation Accounting.
4. State the procedure in the calculation of cost of sales adjustment.
5. Define Inflation Accounting. State the procedure in the calculation of Backlog Depreciation.

II. Solve the following problems.

1. Calculate the Converted Value for the year 2007 from the following.

   Purchase of Plant during 1998 is Rs.12,00,000

   The Price Index during 1998 is 150 and the Price Index during 2007 is 350. **(Ans :** *28,00,000)*

2. Calculate the Profit or Loss on sale of a Land on the basis of Converted Value from the following.

   Cost of the Land is Rs.15,00,000 which was purchased during 1999 when the Price Index is 200, the Plant is sold for Rs.9,00,000 during 2007 when the price index is 350. **(Ans :** *17,25,000)*

3. Calculate the monetary loss or gain on the basis of current purchasing power method from the following

	Rs.	Price Index
Opening balance of Cash (1st March 2007)	74,000	100
Purchase of Raw Material by Cash (5th March 2007)	3,26,000	120
Cash Sales (14th March 2000)	5,00,000	130
Collection from Debtors (1st April 2007)	2,50,000	150
Credit Purchase (15th April 2007)	1,50,000	170
Payment to Creditors (20th April 2007)	90,000	190
Payment of Wages (21st April 2007)	50,000	200
Bills Payable honoured (15th May 2007)	40,000	240
Bills Receivable honoured (20th May 2007)	30,000	250
Closing Balance of Cash (31st May 2007)	3,48,000	270

(Ans : *3,98,767)*

4. K Ltd., provided the following Final Accounts as on 31st March 2007 as follows.

Profit and Loss Account as on 31st March 2007

Particulars	*Rs.*	*Rs.*
Sales		22,00,000
Cost of Goods Sold :		
Opening Stock	90,000	
Purchase	13,50,000	
	14,40,000	
Less : Closing Stock	1,50,000	15,90,000
Gross Profit		6,10,000
Less : Operating Expenses	1,90,000	
Depreciation	70,000	
Interest	50,000	3,10,000
Net Profit		3,00,000

Balance Sheet as on 31st March 2007

Particulars	*Rs.*	*Particulars*	*Rs.*
Share Capital	15,00,000	Fixed Assets	23,20,000
Reserves and Surplus	3,20,000	Stock	1,50,000
Debenture	5,00,000	Debtors	75,000
Loan	3,00,000	Cash	1,55,000
Sundry Creditors	70,000		
	27,00,000		27,00,000

Adjustments :

(i) General Price Index for 1st April 2006 is 300 and of 31st March 2007 is 600. Average Price Index is 400.

(ii) FIFO method of issue of material is adopted.

(iii) Debtors are distributed evenly throughout the year.

(iv) Creditors remained constant throughout the year.

Prepare the Final Accounts after adjusting the price level changes according to CPP method.

(**Ans :** N.P. Rs.11,30,000; N/S Total Rs.51,32,500)

5. Calculate the Cost of sales and Closing inventory on the basis of Current Purchasing price method through FIFO and LIFO of pricing of inventory from the following.

	Rs.
Stock (Inventory) as on 31st March 2006	1,30,000
Stock as on 31st March 2007	2,40,000
Purchase of material	7,00,000

General price index for 2006 and 2007 are 370 and 450 respectively and the average for the year is 400.

(**Ans :** 6,75,858)

6. W.Doyle Ltd., purchased a Land for Rs.25,00,000 on 1st April 2003. Depreciation of the Machine is provided @ 10% on straight line basis. The price is the Machine as 31st March 2007 is Rs.40,00,000. Calculate the treatment of the Machine in the Balance Sheet.

(**Ans :** 2,50,000; 20,00,000)

7. MW Ltd., purchased a Machine on 1st April 2002 for Rs.15,00,000. The estimated life of the Machine is 10 years. If the replacement cost of the Machine on 1st April 2006 is Rs.24,00,000 and on 1st April 2007 is Rs.27,00,000, calculate the amount of Depreciation Adjustment.

(**Ans :** 1,05,000)

8. Calculate the Backlog depreciation from the following

Purchase of Plant on 1st April 2001 for	Rs. 10,00,000
Replacement cost of the Plant on 1st April 2006	Rs. 20,00,000
Replacement cost of the Plant as on 1st April 2007	Rs. 23,00,000
Life of the Plant is 10 years	

(**Ans :** 1,65,000)

9. Calculate Current Cost of Sales Adjustment from the following

	Historical cost (Rs)	*Index Number*
Opening Stock	2,50,000	100
Purchase	12,00,000	130
	14,50,000	(Average)
Less : Closing Stock	3,00,000	150
Cost of Sales	11,50,000	

(**Ans :** 4,38,461)

10. Calculate Monetary Working Capital Adjustment (MWCA) from the following

	1st April 2006 Rs.	*1st April 2007 Rs.*
Sundry Debtors (Rs)	1,00,000	2,40,000
Sundry Creditors (Rs)	50,000	70,000
Index Number	100	150
Average Index Number		130

(**Ans :** 37,667)

11. Calculate the Gearing Adjustment required under CCA method, from the following.

	1st April 2006 Rs.	*1st April 2007 Rs.*
Share Capital	11,00,000	12,00,000
Reserve and Surplus	1,50,000	1,70,000
Debenture	3,00,000	4,00,000
Bank overdraft	30,000	40,000
Loan	2,00,000	3,00,000
Cash	1,40,000	1,50,000
COSA	70,000	
MWCA	60,000	
Depreciation	40,000	
Total	1,70,000	

(**Ans :** 47,600)

12. The Final Accounts of K Ltd. as on 31st March 2007 are stated as follows.

Profit and Loss Account as on 31st March 2007

Particulars	*Rs.*	*Particulars*	*Rs.*
To Opening Stock	90,000	By Sales	18,50,000
To Purchase	13,00,000	By Other Income	1,00,000
	13,90,000		
Less : Closing Stock	1,90,000		
Cost of Sale	12,00,000		
To Operating Expenses	1,50,000		
To Depreciation	1,10,000		
To Interest	70,000		
To Net Profit	3,20,000		
	18,50,000		18,50,000
To Provision for Tax	1,00,000	**By Net Profit**	3,20,000
To Dividend	60,000		
To General Reserve	40,000		
To Balance	1,20,000		
	3,20,000		3,20,000

Balance Sheets

Liabilities	2006 Rs.	2007 Rs.	Assets	2006 Rs.	2007 Rs.
Share Capital	20,00,000	20,00,000	Fixed Assets	27,00,000	28,10,000
Reserves and Surplus	1,75,000	2,50,000	**Less :** Depreciation	1,65,000	1,90,000
Debenture	3,00,000	4,50,000		25,35,000	26,20,000
Loan	2,00,000	1,00,000	Stock	1,25,000	75,000
Sundry Creditors	50,000	70,000	Debtors	75,000	50,000
			Cash	90,000	1,25,000
	27,25,000	28,70,000		27,25,000	28,70,000

General Price Indices are 100, 130 and 140 for opening, average and closing.

The value of Fixed Assets are Rs. 33,00,000 and Rs. 35,00,000 for 1st April 2006 and 31st March 2007 respectively with an average life of 10 years.

Prepare the Final Accounts on the basis of Current Cost Accounts (CCA) method.

❑ ❑ ❑

12

MANAGEMENT AUDIT

Management audit means the activity of examining whether the management policies and plans are properly carried on effectively or not. The management lays down policies and plans to be executed in an organisation. The policies and plans are related to the production, financial, personal and marketing activities. If the policies are properly executed the company can achieve the overall objectives. Hence, the management appoints separate persons to conduct the management audit. The management may also assign the work of management audit to some responsible persons in an organisation, who is also assigned with some other work.

Meaning and Definitions of Management Audit

Management audit is concerned with the appraisal of the various managerial functions and policies performed in an organisation. It also concerned with whether the activities are carried in accordance with the predetermined policies and programmes. The meaning of Management Audit is well known through the following definitions.

1. According to **William P. Leonard**, Management Audit means, "A comprehensive and constructive examination of an organisational structure of a company, institution or branch of Government, or of any component thereof, such as a division or department, and its use of human and physical facilities".
2. **Leslie R. Howard** defines, "Management Audit is an investigation of business from the highest level downward in order to ascertain whether sound management prevails throughout, thus facilitating the most effective relationship with the outside world and the most efficient organisation and smooth running internally".
3. **Taylor and Perry** defines, "Management Auditing is a method to evaluate the efficiency of management at all levels throughout the organisation, or more specifically, it comprises the investigation of a business by an independent body from the highest executive level downwards, in order to ascertain whether sound management prevails throughout, and to report as to its efficiency or otherwise with recommendation to ensure its effectiveness where such is not the case".

It is clear from the definitions that Management Audit means the investigation in the management area to know whether it functions according to the set standard of policies and programs. It evaluates the efficiency of management at all levels of the organisation. It is also concerned with whether the management is maintaining good relationship to the external environment or not. It examines whether the physical and human environment factors are effectively utilised or not.

Objectives of Management Audit

The following are the important objectives of Management Audit:

1. To find out whether the management is functioning according to the rules, regulations and policies.
2. To examine the performance of the management activities.
3. It examines the performance of the management with respect to the external environment.
4. It helps in identifying the defects in the managerial functioning.
5. It helps to identify the defects in the management structure.
6. The authority and responsibility relationship is studied through Management Audit. The defects in the relationship can be identified.
7. It examines whether there is proper division of work in an organisation.
8. It helps to find out whether suitable persons are appointed in different jobs.
9. It suggests whether there is any need for giving managerial training.
10. It gives suggestions for the effective performance of managerial functions.

Scope of Management Audit

The following are the scope of Management Audit:

1. It is possible to measure whether the present organisational structure is enough or there is any need for the change in the organisational structure as per the present day requirements.
2. There is scope of comparison of the performance of the company with other companies in the industry. Hence, the condition of the company with respect to other companies can be known. If the performance of the company is low when compared to other companies then it is possible for the management to take necessary steps to improve the performance.
3. Management Audit analyses the present rate of return of the company and suggests about the optimum return on capital employed for the company.
4. It establishes and defines the relationship between the owner and the business; and the general public and the business.
5. Management Audit is also concerned with the financial planning and control in a business and it provides valuable information in this regard.
6. It also provides valuable information for the effective performance of production department and marketing department.
7. The report submitted by the Management Auditor contains the defects and efficiency in the performance of various management activities. It also gives suggestions for further improvement in the functioning of management. This information will help the Board of Directors to take suitable planning and policy-making.

Procedures in the Conduct of Management Audit

Management Audit is concerned with the examination of the functioning of the managerial activities. It identifies the defects in the performance and also suggests methods for improvement of the performance of the managerial activities. In the process of Management Audit the following procedures should be followed for an effective performance of the audit.

1. The personnels required for management audit should be decided in advance.
2. The authority, nature of work and area of operation of the Management Auditor should be decided. The Management Auditor should get clear instruction from the management about the nature of the work.
3. Management Auditor should get the complete details about the employees in the organisation. In addition to the organisational structure, responsibilities and division of work of all the employees should be known.
4. The policies, programmes and plan of all the work of the concern should be known by the Management Auditor.
5. After collecting all the information, Management Auditor should examine the work performed by the employees.
6. He should examine whether the responsibility centres are well defined. If the responsibility centres are well defined, he can get information about the work executed, from the manager or head in charge of the respective responsibility centres.
7. Management Auditor should examine the statutory audit report and find out whether there is any remark made in the report.
8. He should get the report of the Internal Audit and Cost Audit, if the concern is maintaining Internal and Cost audit.
9. He has the right to enquire with any employees in the organisation with respect to the execution of managerial activities.
10. It is the duty of the Management Auditor to give a report to the management about the management audit conducted by him. In the report, the deviations if any, from the standard work expected and the actual work performed should be clearly mentioned. If he wants to make any suggestions for the improvement of the system, it should also be clearly mentioned in the report.

Management Audit, Cost Audit and Internal Audit

Management Audit is an audit concerned with the managerial performance. It examines whether the management is functioning is accordance to the policies and programmes already laid down. It gives a report about the defaults in the performance and deviations from the standard performance with actual performances.

Cost Audit is entirely different from the Management Audit since in Cost Audit the examination about the standard cost and actual cost is conducted. It is concerned with the identification and reporting about the variances in standard cost for different activities and actual cost. It helps the management to know whether actual cost is exceeding the standard cost so that corrective actions can be taken. It also helps the management to modify the standard cost in various activities according to the present need.

Internal Audit is also different from the Management Audit. In Internal Audit verification and examination about the financial transactions are carried on. It examines whether, the entries are correctly recorded in accordance to the vouchers. It also examines the various systems of financial accounting. The Internal Audit report contains details about the areas where mistakes are committed in the process of recording financial transactions.

Needs or Advantages of Management Audit

Management Audit helps to identify the defects in an organisation and facilitates effective performance of management functions. The following are the advantages of Management Audit:

1. It improves the overall efficiency of management.
2. It provides information for managerial planning, control and decision making.
3. Management Audit facilitates the proper division of work.
4. It helps proper placement of workers in different jobs.
5. It facilitates for the balanced allotment of work.
6. It often reviews the managerial functions so that corrective steps can be taken immediately.
7. It helps in establishing the policies of a concern.
8. It suggests to the management about the need for the change if any, in the present rules and regulations.
9. It helps in establishing proper authority and responsibility relationships.
10. Management Audit facilitates the determination of proper organisational structure for a company.

Demerits of Management Audit

The following are the demerits of Management Audit:

1. It is expensive and hence, only large scale business units can adopt this system.
2. It is based on personal judgments. If the person in charge of the Management Audit is not efficient, then it will affect the smooth functioning of the organisation.
3. There is a possibility of showing personal bias, in the system of Management Audit. If the management Auditor is biased against any employee he will not identify the non performance of such employees.
4. It will interrupt the work of the employees in the organisation and affect the smooth functioning of the organisation.
5. There is a possibility of opposition from the employees for the adoption of Management Audit in a concern. The employees may feel that their weaknesses may be exposed to high officials.
6. If the policies and plans are often changed according to the report of the Management Audit, the overall performance may be very slow. This is because of the fact that the employees need more time to adjust to the new policies and programs.

EXERCISE

1. Define Management Audit. Explain the objectives of Management Audit.
2. Evaluate the merits and demerits of Management Audit.
3. What is Management Audit? Differentiate Management Audit with Internal Audit and Cost Audit.
4. Define Management Audit. What are the scopes of Management Audit?
5. What is Management Audit? Explain the procedures in the conduct of Management Audit.
6. Define Management Audit. State the uses of Management Audit.
7. Write short notes on the following:
   (i) Management Audit
   (ii) Cost Audit
   (iii) Internal Audit
   (iv) Any three merits of Management Audit
   (v) Any three demerits of Management Audit
   (vi) Any three objectives of Management Audit
   (vii) Any three scopes of Management Audit.

❑ ❑ ❑

13

RESPONSIBILITY ACCOUNTING

Responsibility Accounting is an important concept in Management Accounting. Management Accounting is concerned with provision of information to management. Responsibility Accounting is a kind of information provided to management. Other information are related to full cost information and differential cost information to management. Though the quantum of information provided in Responsibility Accounting is comparatively lower than other types of information, it is considered to be the most important one. This is because it directs the entire persons in the organisation to work more efficiently. This accounting fixes responsibility for all the employees so that their performance is measured on the basis of the responsibility. Hence, the management can able to identify those who are performing very effectively and those who are not performing effectively. Responsibility Accounting helps to know the reasons for effective and not effective performances. It helps the management to take the appropriate actions based on this.

Meaning and Definition of Responsibility Accounting

Responsibility Accounting means the accounting of the execution of responsibilities assigned to employees in an organisation. All employees in the organisation are responsible for some activity. It is to be known whether the employees are executing the responsibility in an efficient manner. If they are not executing the responsibility in an efficient manner, the reasons should also be intimated to the management for corrective action. The process of Responsibility Accounting may be stated in a chart as follows:

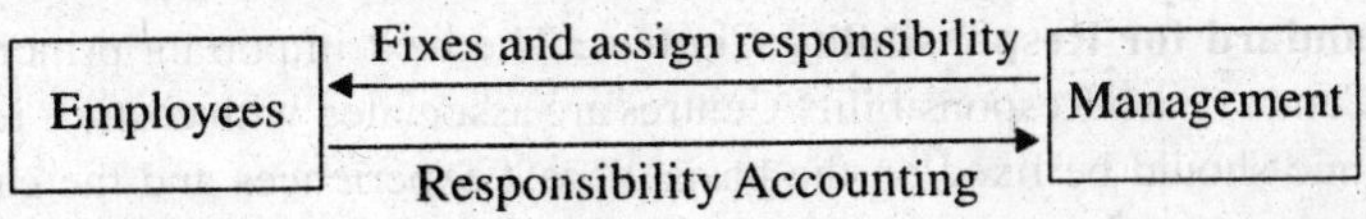

The chart clearly exhibits that the management fixes and assigns responsibilities to employees (individual or team of employees). The employees in turn report to the management about the accomplishment of the responsibilities which is called Responsibility Accounting. The meaning of Responsibility Accounting is further known very clearly by analysing important definitions in this respect. The important definitions of responsibility accounting are stated as follows:

1. **Institute of Cost and Works Accountants of India** defines, "Responsibility Accounting is a system of Management Accounting under which accountability is established according to the responsibility delegated to various levels of management and management information and reporting system instituted to give adequate feedback in term of the delegated responsibility.

Under the system division or units of an organisation under a specified authority in a person are developed as responsibility centres and evaluated individually for their performance".

2. **Eric Kohier** defines Responsibility Accounting as, "a method of accounting in which costs are identified with persons answered to be capable of controlling them, rather than with products or functions. It differs from activity accounting, in that it does not in itself requires an organisational grouping by activities and sub-activities or provide a systematic criterion of system design".
3. **David Fanning** defines Responsibility Accounting as "a system or mechanism for controlling the wider freedom of action that executives - decision centre manager in other words - are given by senior management and for holding those executives responsible for the consequences of their decisions".
4. **Charles T. Horngreen** defines, "Responsibility Accounting is a system of accounting that recognises various responsibility centres throughout the organisation and reflects the plan and actions of each of these centres by assigning particular resources and costs to the one having the pertinent responsibility. It is also called Profitability Accounting and Activity Accounting.

It is clear from the definitions that Responsibility Accounting is concerned with establishment of responsibility centres and employees are put in charge of it so that they are accountable for the accomplishment of the responsibility. It is further clear that costs and revenues are linked with the responsibility centres (employees) so that the utilisation of costs and generation of revenues are measured on the basis of the expected or standard costs and revenues. The most important objective of Responsibility Accounting is reporting to the management about the execution of the responsibilities.

Principles and Techniques of Responsibility Accounting

The important principles involved in Responsibility Accounting are stated as follows:

1. Establishment of Responsibility Centres: The first step in the Responsibility Accounting is fixing of responsibility centres. It is concerned with division of the activities in an organisation in small groups. Each group should be assigned with clear responsibility. These groups with responsibility to accomplish certain task is called Responsibility Centres. The head in charge of the centre may be managers or supervisors. The Responsibility Centres may be related to cost or revenue. Hence, it may be Cost Centre, Revenue Centres, Profitability Centres and Investment Centres. The managers in charge of these responsibility centres should take into account of the limit of the cost to be incurred, minimum amount of revenue to be generated, normal profit to be earned and the reasonable return on investment.

2. Fixing the Standard for Responsibility Centres: The next important principle is fixing standard for the Responsibility Centre. Each Responsibility Centres are associated with costs or revenues. The standard for each cost and revenue should be fixed on the basis of past experiences and the capacity and efficiency of the employees. The maximum variations to be allowed in cost and revenue should be well defined. Normally, maximum limit for cost and the minimum limit for revenue should be determined.

3. Concept of Flexible Budgeting: Responsible Accounting is based on Flexible Budgeting. The budgets should be prepared for different levels of activities. Correction in the budget should be carried in the budget once prepared in the system of Flexible Budgeting.

4. Performance Reporting: The important principle of Responsibility Accounting is performance reporting. The actual performance by all the responsibility centres should be reported to the management often. The report may be for a period of number of days, week or month etc. The frequency of reports depends upon the nature and requirement of management. On the basis of the performance report, the management can take necessary action. It can identify the areas where performance is far below the standard, for immediate action. This kind of action is known as Management by Exception (MBE). The actions of the management will rectify the defects in the system of management and improve the overall efficiency in the system.

Responsibility Centres

Responsibility Centres mean small divisions of overall activities of a concern, and assigning responsibility to each division. The division or segments with certain responsibility is called Responsibility Centres. The centres are provided with suitable employees. On the basis of the nature of work the number of employees may be placed in the centres and one manager or team leader would be selected as head of the centre. He has been assigned with some task or work to be completed. He is responsible for the performance of work more efficiently.

Types of Responsibility Centres

The Responsibility Centres are classified on the basis of the work as Cost Centres, Revenue Centres, Profit Centres and Investment Centres.

1. Cost Centres: Some Responsibility Centres are associated with costs. It may be cost of product, cost of different processes, cost of a department etc. These centres are asked to accomplish the work within specified standard cost. Hence, the leader or manager of such centres should see that the actual cost should not exceed beyond the standard cost. It depends upon the efficiency in managing the affairs of the centres.

2. Revenue Centres: Revenue Centres are those centres associated with revenues of a concern. The Responsibility Centre associated with revenue is mostly related with sales. Sales is the important revenue of a concern. Other revenues may be like rent receivable, interest receivable etc., and the centres associated with these revenues have less responsibility. This is due to the fact that the revenue may be received without any difficulty. But some steps shall be taken if there is any delay in such kind of receipt. But the Responsibility Centre with sales as revenue should take maximum effort to achieve the standard or target fixed. The number of Revenue Centres depends upon the types of products, area of sales, number of salesmen etc.

3. Profit Centre: Profit Centre is a centre associated with profit. The profit is the difference between revenue and cost. Hence, profit centre should see that target profit is achieved or not. The centre should take effort to reduce the cost and to increase the revenue in order to achieve the goal of maximisation of profit. There may be different profit centres on the basis of different products, activities and area. The management can take appropriate steps for improving the efficiency of all the Profit Centres, through analysing the responsibility report.

4. Investment Centre: Investment Centre is a centre which is responsible for the utilisation of fund in a concern. The funds should be effectively utilised to achieve the objective of maximum profit and fair return on investment (capital employed). It is concerned with the investment in fixed assets and shares of other companies; debt-equity ratio and current ratio. If these factors are effectively administered, then the overall performance and efficiency of the company will be improved. Investment Centre may also be divided into different segments.

Responsibility Centres and Cost Centres

Responsibility centre is a broad term which accommodates all the cost and revenue factors. Cost centre is a centre which considers cost only at different stages of production or activities. In cost centre also responsibility is fixed by the management. All the centres for different activities are also fixed with some task and work and these centres are responsible to accomplish the task and work. Hence, Responsibility

Centre is a concept applied in all the centres of a concern. Even all the cost centres are not dependent to each other.

Advantage or Uses of Responsibility Accounting

The advantages of Responsibility Accounting are stated as follows:

1. Fixation of standard in Work: Responsibility Accounting helps for fixation of standard in work. The responsibility accounting of previous period helps for fixation of standard of work.

2. Delegation of Authority: It helps in proper delegation of authority. The type of authority to be delegated is also known through Responsibility Accounting.

3. Evaluation of Performance: Responsibility Accounting helps for measuring the performance of all the employees particularly, the heads so that proper reward can be given for high performance. It helps in taking managerial decisions, planning and control.

4. Corrective Action: It facilitates for corrective action if the performance is below the standard level. Since Responsibility Accounting is to be done within few days, week or a month the corrective action can be taken often, that too with a short period of time.

5. Motivation: Responsibility Accounting motivates all the employees. Since everyone has to accomplish their task and to report to management they are automatically motivated to perform effectively.

6. Develop high morale and efficiency: Performance Accounting creates a competitive spirit among the employees which in turn creates high efficiency and high morale. Without high morale high performance is not possible. In this way overall efficiency and morale of the company will improve.

7. Management by Objectives: The concept of Management by Objectives can be adopted in an effective manner through Responsibility Accounting. Responsibility Accounting helps for identifying the efficient and inefficient departments which is most required for the principle of Management by Objectives.

Limitations of Responsibility Accounting

Inspite of the fact that Responsibility Accounting has numerous advantages, it has few limitations. But the limitations are not significant when compared to the advantages. The important limitation is personal bias. The manager may show favours to some employees and report some employees as low performers, though they performed well. It is possible to assign low work to some of the employees and high work to others. These limitations can be eradicated by the top level management.

Transfer Prices

Transfer price is a price at which the cost of one responsibility centre is transferred to another responsibility centre. It is otherwise called as intra-company transfer price. For a centre which transfers the work, partly finished goods or incomplete service to another responsibility centre is considered as a source of revenue. The responsibility centre which receives the work, considers the transfer price as cost. These centres have to incur additional cost on the work before transferring to another responsibility centre. The different profit centres have to ascertain their respective profits for Responsibility Accounting. Each centre will try to reduce the cost including the transfer price. Hence, correct valuation is a crucial factor both for the transferer and transferee responsibility centres. There are different methods for ascertain of transfer prices, which are stated as follows.

1. Cost price
2. Cost plus normal mark up
3. Shared profit on the basis of cost
4. Incremental cost
5. Market price
6. Negotiated price
7. Dual or two-way price
8. Standard price.

1. Cost Price: In this method, the goods and services partly or fully produced by a centre is transferred to another Responsibility Centre on cost price. The cost incurred by the transferring centre is considered as transfer price.

2. Cost plus Normal mark up: In this method, the transfer price is calculated by adding a normal profit with the cost. It helps the transferring centre to meet contingencies of rise in cost of production in future. It also induces the receiving centre to be more efficient, economical and responsible.

3. Shared Profit Relative to Cost: This method is concerned with the share of profit for all the profit centres. There is no transfer price charged for intra company transfers. The total profit of the company is shared to all the profit centres on the basis of the cost incurred in the respective centres. For example, if the profit of company is Rs.5,00,000 cost is Rs.3,00,000 and the cost incurred in a Profit Centre X is Rs.60,000, then the profit transferred to the Profit Centre X = 5,00,000 x (60,000 / 3,00,000) = Rs.1,00,000.

4. Incremental Cost: According to this method an additional cost is added with the cost actually incurred by the transferring centre. This additional cost may be either based on fixed cost incurred or opportunity cost. Opportunity cost means the amount of profit of the transferring company which is sacrificied by transferring the goods or services to other centres, instead of selling to outsiders.

5. Market Price: According to this method the transfer price is calculated on the basis of market price. A reasonable market price should be found for this purpose by eliminating all the fluctuations in the market conditions.

6. Negotiated Price: In this method, transfer price is determined on the basis of negotiation between the transferring centre and the receiving centre.

7. Dual or Two-way Price: In this method there will be two transfer prices. The transferring centre will record the transfer price as per its cost and revenue expected. The receiving centre (purchasing centre) will calculate the transfer price according to their assessment. Hence, the total profit ascertained by the all the profit centres will be different from the total profit of the company. This method helps in effective management of different profit centres.

8. Standard Price: According to this method, the transfer price is decided on the basis of predetermined standard price for each type of work in a concern. The standard price should be reasonably fixed on the basis of previous experiences.

Selection of a Suitable Method of Transfer Price

The selection of a suitable transfer price depends upon the nature of the product, preferences of the employees and the efficiency of the employees. The management should adopt a suitable method in consultation with the functional managers and representatives of the employees.

EXERCISE

I. Answer the following questions.

1. Define Responsibility Accounting. State the principles of Responsibility Accounting.
2. Define Responsibility Centres. Explain the different types of Responsibility Centres.
3. What is Responsibility Accounting? State the advantages of Responsibility Accounting.
4. What is transfer price? State the different types of transfer price.
5. Write short notes on the following:
   (i) Responsibility Accounting (ii) Transfer Price (iii) Profit Centre (iv) Cost Centre (v) Investment Centre (vi) Revenue Centre (vii) Negotiated Transfer Price (viii) Dual Transfer Price (ix) Responsibility centre and cost centre (x) Flexible Budgeting.

❑ ❑ ❑

14

REPORTING TO MANAGEMENT AND MANAGEMENT INFORMATION SYSTEM

Reporting is an important devise to inform about the various activities carried on in an enterprise. It contains details about the operating and financial performance of the enterprise. Operating performance is related to the profit earned by the company and the rate of return on investment. Financial performance is about the efficiency in the utilisation of finance by the enterprise. In this way, it communicates crucial information to responsible employees in an organisation who are interested in the information, in order to formulate good policies and corrective actions. Apart from this, management report provides valuable information to the owners, banks and financial institutions. The content of reports differs according to the need of the party interested in the reports.

Meaning and Definitions

Report means a statement of facts. It contains information which is useful for some references and understanding. A Report is an instrument which communicates information from one person to another. A report may be oral, written or graphic. Management report is a statement containing information required for management. The word report is derived from the Latin word 'portare' which means carrying. Hence, report is a document which carries information. The dictionary meaning of the word report is 'to convey' or 'to transmit'.

The meaning of report is well clear by analysing the definitions of report. The important definitions of report are stated as follows:

1. According to **Johnson and Savage**, "A good business report is a communication that contains technical information, organised and presented in clear, correct and coherent language."
2. **G.R. Terry** defines report as, "a written statement based on a collection of facts, events and opinions and usually expresses a summarised and interpretative value of this information. It may deal with past accomplishments, present conditions or portable future developments."

It is clear from the definitions that report means a process of communication to the management with information. The information is about facts, events and opinions. It should be expressed in a clear and correct manner so that it should clearly communicate the matter. The person interested in the report must able to get a clear idea without any strain.

Objectives of Reporting

The objectives of reporting are stated as follows:

1. The important objective of report is to explain about the performance of a business to the management and owners.
2. To make judgments on the various activities of an organisation.
3. To compare the operational and financial performances of companies from one period to another.
4. To identify defects in the functioning of an organisation.
5. To take corrective actions in all activities of an organisation in order to have good performance.
6. To formulate policies for various activities in an organisation.

Requirements or Principles of a Good Report

The requirements of a good report are stated as follows:

1. Form and Content: There should be a good form in the preparation of the report. It should be prepared in a clear manner so that it should convey the correct meaning. Proper introduction, findings and suggestion should be clearly explained. The date should also be mentioned in the report. The content of the report should be clear and in logical order. There should not be any mistakes in the content of the report.

2. Relevancy: The report should be relevant to the responsible persons. Only relevant information should be mentioned in the report. For example, a report related to the marketing should not be sent to the production manager; or the matter concerned with marketing should not be included in the report of the production manager.

3. Promptness: Promptness means submission of report in proper time without any delay. There should be delay in the action process based on the report if the report is delayed. Hence, promptness is an important principle in the preparation of report.

4. Simplicity: The report should be prepared in simple sentences only, so that the reader can understand the content of the report. The statistical information in the form of data and figures should also be presented in simple format.

5. Accuracy: There should be accuracy in the information of the report. It should exhibit only factual information. There should not be any manipulation of data either in statements or in data and figures.

6. Consistency: The report should be consistent with respect to the general principles of accounting and the policies of the company.

7. Cost Factor: There should be a reasonable and affordable cost in the preparation of reports. It should not exceed the benefits desired from it.

8. Controllability: The report should clearly mention the variances of the actual result with standard one. The degree of control exercised for controlling the unfavorable variances should also be mentioned. If there is any defect or inefficiency in the control it should also be mentioned in the report.

9. Comparability: The information provided in the report should be capable of being compared with previous periods and with other concerns. Only then, it is possible for the company to take effective steps for improving the efficiency and performance.

10. Frequency: The frequency of the report may be daily, weekly, a few days or monthly. The frequency depends upon the nature of the information and the requirement for managerial decision making.

Methods of Reporting

The important methods of reporting are stated as follows:

1. Written Reporting: Presentation of the report in written statements is called Written Reporting. It may contain data, graph and diagram in addition to the statements.

2. Graphic Reporting: Presentation of the report in the form of graph only is known as Graphical Reporting. In graphical reporting explanations about the graph may also be given. The advantage of graphic reporting is that it explains the facts in a simple manner for easy understanding.

3. Oral Reporting: The report presented orally to the responsible persons is called Oral Reporting. It may be presented directly or in a meeting or conference. The disadvantage of oral reporting is that there is no evidence to substantiate in case of disputes in future.

Kinds or Types of Reports

The reports may be classified as follows:

1. On the basis of objective or purpose
   - (i) Internal report (ii) External report
2. On the basis of function
   - (i) Operating report (ii) Financial report
3. On the basis of nature
   - (i) Enterprise report (ii) Investigative report
   - (iii) Control report
4. On the basis of period
   - (i) Routine report (ii) Special report
5. On the basis of contents
   - (i) Production report (ii) Sales report
   - iii. Cost report

1. On the Basis of Objectives or Purpose

i. Internal Report: The reports meant for different levels of management are known as internal report. The person responsible for the preparation of the report should look into the needs for the manager to whom he is reporting. With respect to internal report, there may be some confidential matters or it may serve no purpose to the outsiders.

ii. External Report: The report prepared for the outside parties is called external report. The outside parties of the company may be shareholders, partners, proprietors, financial institution, creditors, customers and Government. It should be in proper form so that it should give a good image about the company. There should not be any manipulation and only factual information should be presented in the external report. Examples of external reports are Profit and Loss Account, Balance Sheet, Cash Flow statement, Statement of changes in Working Capital etc.

2. On the Basis of Function

i. Operating Report: Operating report is concerned with the operating activities of a concern. It is related with the cost of production, other operating expenses like administrative and selling expenses, and operating income. The actual performances and the variations if any, from the standard operating activities are presented in operating report.

ii. Financial Report: The report concerned with the financial performance is called financial reports. It contains information about the source of finance, application of finance, rate of return, cost of capital and financial ratios. It is related with the effective utilisation of finance. It also reports the variations from the standard with respect to various financial activities.

3. On the Basis of Nature

i. Enterprise Report: The report which highlights the overall performance of a company is called enterprise report. This is like the external report. Enterprises reports are in the form of Profit & Loss account, Balance Sheet, Chairman's report and Auditor's report. These reports explain the financial conditions of a concern. Enterprise reports are useful to the owners, creditors, financial institutions, consumers and Government.

ii. Investigative Report: The report prepared for a special occasion, in order to investigate certain problems and incidents is called investigative report. To explore the real causes related to misappropriation, frauds, inefficiency in any area of the management, the investigation team may be appointed. The report prepared by the team is called investigation report.

iii. Control Report: Control report is related to the steps taken by various responsibility centers about the control measures to prevent the adverse deviation of the actual performance with the standard performance. Control report facilitates for speed implementation and action for the adverse deviations, so as to improve the efficiency in the performance of various managerial activities.

4. On the Basis of Period

i. Routine Report: A report prepared about the day to day activities of a concern is called routine report. These reports are prepared on daily, weekly or monthly basis. The nature and content of the report are related to same aspect for different periods. The improvement in performance over a period can be known through this report. These reports are related to purchase, inventory level, sales, payment of expenses etc.

ii. Special Report: The report prepared for a special situation is called a special report. If the management needs some information related to the misappropriation or frauds it may call for a special investigation and the report prepared for this purpose is called special report. For the expansion of the business also special report may be prepared.

5. On the Basis of Contents

i. Production Report: The report related to the production is called production report. It explains the quantity and value of actual production and deviations of it from the standard quantity and value.

ii. Sales Report: The report related to the sales is called sales report. It explains the quantity and value of sales in a period at different places. It also explains the deviation and reason for it, from the standard level.

iii. Cost Report: This report is related to the cost information. It is concerned with the cost of different activities and different elements like material, wages and overheads. It also reports the variations from the standard.

Reporting Needs of Different Management Levels

Reporting is an important device which supplies valuable information to all levels of management. The need of reports for different levels of management are stated as follows.

1. Reports for Top Management Level: Top level management represents Board of Directors. They are responsible for formation of policies and programmes of a company. The frequency of report required for top level management is low ie., once in 3 months, half yearly or yearly. The type of reports required are Profit and Loss Account, Cost of production, Trend in sales, Fund Flow statement, Cash Flow statement, Statement of working capital etc. The reports related to sales, cost of purchases, collection period for credit sales, payment period for credit purchases should be given often. On the basis of the report the top level management would take necessary policies.

2. Reports for Middle Management Level: Middle level management is represented with functional managers like, production manager, marketing manager, purchase manager, personal manager and finance manager. The reports required for them are submitted by their subordinates in the low level management. The frequency of reports for middle management is more and mostly daily, weekly or monthly reports are required for them. The reason for short period report is that the correction in the operating activities and financial activities should be done immediately.

3. Reports for Low Management Level: Low level management represents foremen and supervisors. They have to prepare report to middle level management. Hence they are receiving the reports from their subordinates. The frequency of the reports required for low level management is very high. Mostly daily reports are required. The reports are like utilisation of labour, performance of workers, inventory utilisation etc.

Advantages of Reporting

The advantages of Reporting are stated as follows.

1. Reporting highlights the weakness in the system of performance.
2. It helps in taking necessary corrective actions immediately.
3. It facilitates in the proper division of work and placement of employees in an organisation.
4. It helps the Board of Directors to frame new policies and to change the existing policies and programmes.
5. It facilitates for taking necessary action against non performers in an organisation and giving incentives and promotion to high performers.
6. Report helps the owners to know whether the capital is properly utilised or not.
7. It provides information to financial institutions about the financial status of the company.

Demerits of Reporting

The demerits of Reporting are stated as follows.

1. Reporting is a costly and time consuming affair.
2. If the report is not accurate, then the action taken on the basis of report may affect the normal functioning of a concern.
3. There is possibility of showing bias in the preparation of reports.
4. The normal work will be affected if the reports are prepared often.
5. It is an additional work for the managers and supervisors.

Management Information System (MIS)

Management information system means the system of providing management information to the right person at the right time. The importance of management is increasing day by day due to high competition and technology. It requires the management to maintain a lot of information to face the competition as well as to adopt the latest technology. The information is mostly required for the effective functioning of an organisation. The data related to the performance of the company from the inception period should be maintained to measure the performance and to take appropriate steps to improve the performance and efficiency. In addition to this, data related to other concerns in the industry and the policies of the Government should also be maintained in a company. At present, management information system is controlled by separate persons and designated as a Responsibility Centre for efficient performance. The person in charge of the information system should have a thorough idea about the computer system.

Types of Management Information System

The Management Information system is classified as:

(1) Management Operating System and (2) Management Reporting System.

1. Management Operating System: Management operating system is a system which meets the information needs of the employees in an organisation. It provides the relevant data required for all the functional managers (production, personnel, finance, marketing etc). In this respect, it is required to maintain the data in separate files as hard copies and soft copies. All activities are recorded and stored at one place. Hence, it is possible to access the information at any time so that comparison of data can be done to measure the status and performance in the respective responsibility centre.

2. Management Reporting System: Another aspect, apart from the management operating system is known as management reporting system. Management reporting system is a process of analysing the data (information) in a systematic manner through classification so as to make a clear cut report out of it. If the whole information is provided as it is, it is very difficult to get an idea out of it. Moreover, it may have a lot of pages and the top level management may not able to study all of it due to the time factor. Hence, a clear cut report needs to be prepared as per the requirement of the top level management for framing new polices or to modify the existing policies.

Process of Management Information System or Installation of Management Information System

Process of management information system may also be called as elements of management information system. It starts with the input of information and ends with output of the information. In between there is a need for processing the information. The process of management information system are outlined as follows.

1. Determination of the Need of Information: The first step is the assessment of the information needs of an organisation. It depends upon the nature of business, size of the business, character of the industry etc. The quantum and types of information required from the external environment like Government, financial institution, consumers and general public should also be assessed.

2. Determination of the Source of Information: Then the various sources from where information to be collected should be determined. The sources which are internal to the company as well as external to the company should be decided for the effective management information system.

3. Collection of the Information: The information should be collected from the internal and external sources which are already identified. In the process of collection of data, only accurate information should be collected. The data should be collected within the specified time and from the right sources.

4. Processing of Information: The information collected should be processed to identify the relevant and accurate information. Irrelevant information should be eliminated. When the information is processed it should be properly classified, codified and tabulated as per the need.

5. Preparation of Statements and Reports: The processed data should be properly analysed and prepared in report form for easy understanding by the people who are in need of it. Mostly the reports are needed for top level management for policy making.

EXERCISE

I. Choose the correct answer for the following

1. An instrument which communicates information from one person to another is called —
(i) Report (ii) Balance sheet(iii) Facts (iv) Management
2. Submission of reports in proper time without any delay is known as —
(i) Relevancy (ii) Simplicity (iii) Promptness (iv) Accuracy
3. Report presented without any documents in hard copy or soft copy is called —
(i) Written report (ii) Oral report (iii) Graphic report (iv) Accurate report
4. Report prepared for the shareholders and general public is known as —
(i) Internal report (ii) Control report (iii) Routine report (iv) External report
5. The reports meant for different levels of management is called —
(i) External report (ii) Operating report (iii) Internal report (iv) Financial report
6. The report prepared for the day-to-day activities is called —
(i) Internal report (ii) Routine report (iii) Control report (iv) Special report
7. The report prepared by the foreman and supervisors are to meet the request of —
(i) Board of Directors (ii) Lower level management (iii) Owners (iv) Middle level management
8. One of the drawbacks of report is —
(i) Timely action (ii) Performance evaluation (iii) Personnel bias (iv) Planning and control
9. One of the merits of report is —
(i) Personal bias (ii) Time consuming (iii) Costly affair (iv) Performance evaluation
10. The system of providing information to right persons at right time is known as —
(i) Operation (ii) Management information system (iii) Control (iv) Planning

[**Ans:** 1. (i) 2. (iii) 3. (ii) 4. (iv) 5. (iii) 6. (ii) 7. (iv) 8. (iii) 9. (iv) 10. (ii)]

II. Answer the following questions:

1. Define report. State the objectives of report.
2. What is report? Explain the merits and demerits of report.
3. Define report. What are the principles of reporting?
4. Give an outline of different types of reports.
5. Define report. Explain the reporting needs at different management levels.
6. Explain the process of installation of Management Information System.
7. What is Management Information System? State the procedures in the MIS.
8. Define Management Information System. Distinguish between management operating system and management reporting system.
9. Write short notes for the following:
(i) Report (ii) Reporting, (ii) Oral report, (iv) Written report, (v) Graphic report, (vi) Internal report, (vii) External report, (viii) Operating report, (ix) Financial report (ix) Routine report
10. Write short notes for the following :
(i) Special Report, (ii) Production Report, (iii) Sales Report, (iv) Management Information System (v) Management operating system (vi) Management reporting system

❑ ❑ ❑